The Journals and Miscellaneous Notebooks

of

RALPH WALDO EMERSON

The Journals and Miscellaneous Notebooks

of

RALPH WALDO EMERSON

VOLUME X

1847–1848

EDITED BY

MERTON M. SEALTS, JR.

THE BELKNAP PRESS

OF HARVARD UNIVERSITY PRESS

Cambridge, Massachusetts

1973

CENTER FOR EDITIONS OF
AMERICAN AUTHORS
AN APPROVED TEXT
MODERN LANGUAGE
ASSOCIATION OF AMERICA

Library of Congress Catalog Card Number: 60–11554
SBN 674–48473–8

Typography by Burton J Jones
Printed in the U.S.A. by the Harvard University Printing Office
Bound by Stanhope Bindery, Inc., Boston, Massachusetts

Preface

The editors and volume editor wish to thank a number of institutions and persons for help of various kinds.

The Ralph Waldo Emerson Memorial Association has continued to provide regular grants-in-aid which have been indispensable to the progress of the edition. Cora Kaplan and Frances T. Webb transcribed the manuscript journals and wrote the preliminary descriptive notes for volume X. The Research Committee of the Graduate School, The University of Wisconsin-Madison, provided photocopies of the manuscript journals for editorial use and underwrote research leaves for Mr. Sealts, the editor of this volume, and annual stipends for his project assistants: Susan Stanford Friedman (1966–1969), Barry Gaines (1969–1970), Duane MacMillan (1970–1971), and Mary Stevens (1971–1973). There was no other subvention for volume X. Ruth Mackenzie Sealts, in addition to typing notes, collaborated with Mr. Sealts in both collation and proofreading of texts.

For other assistance and courtesies we thank Miss Carolyn Jakeman, Professor William H. Bond, and the staff of Houghton Library; Mr. Theodore G. Alevizos and the staff of Widener Library; the staffs of the Bibliothèque Nationale, Boston Athenaeum, the University of Wisconsin-Madison Department of English and Memorial Library, and the State Historical Society of Wisconsin; Mr. Jacob Blanck; Professors Hélène M. Cassidy, Emmett L. Bennett, Paul C. Plass, and Lorin Uffenbeck; Mrs. Richard G. Bennett and M. Georges Lubin.

Unless otherwise noted, translations of classical quotations are from the Loeb Classical Library and are reprinted by permission of Harvard University Press and the Loeb Classical Library.

All the editors named on the edition title page have responsibilities of various kinds for the edition as a whole. The Chief Editor has the primary responsibility for the edition, and for certification of individual volumes.

W. H. G.

Contents

FOREWORD TO VOLUME X

The Journals: 1847–1848 ix
Chronology xxvi
Symbols and Abbreviations xxvii

PART ONE

THE TEXTS OF THE JOURNALS

AB 3
CD 58
GH 124
Sea-Notes 200
London 208
LM 288

PART TWO

THE TEXTS OF THE MISCELLANEOUS NOTEBOOKS

JK 365
Pocket Diary 1 405
England and Paris 407
Pocket Diary 3 446
Xenien 458
Platoniana 468
Warren Lot 489
ED 494

Textual Notes 571
Index 573

Illustrations

Following page 226

Plate I   *Journal CD, page 4*

Plate II   *Notebook England and Paris, page 41*

Plate III   *Journal London, page 57*

Plate IV   *Notebook ED, page 206*

Foreword to Volume X

THE JOURNALS FROM 1847 TO 1848

The principal event in Emerson's life during the period covered by this volume was the visit to Europe that began in October of 1847 and concluded in July of 1848. His friend Alexander Ireland, then editing a newspaper in Manchester, England, had sent him a note in November of 1846, delivered by William Lloyd Garrison, suggesting a British lecture tour; in the following February Ireland renewed the invitation. At first reluctant, Emerson gradually came to think more favorably of the proposal, discouraged as he was by the current national issues of slavery and the outbreak of war with Mexico in 1846 and plagued by the old question of his own proper role in the "Lilliput" of contemporary American society. In a journal entry made late in March of 1847 he lamented that he lacked "the stimulus of a stated task" — more pungently, "a whip for the top." "A Scholar," he wrote, "is a candle which the love & desire of men will light. Let it not lie in a dark box. But here am I with so much all ready to be revealed to me as to others if only I could be set aglow. I have wished for a professorship. Much as I hate the church, I have wished the pulpit." What should he be doing? In "this emergency," as he called it, one of his friends had advised "Europe, and especially England," but he was not yet persuaded. "If I followed my own advices, — if I were master of a liberty to do so — I should sooner go toward Canada. I should withdraw myself for a time from all domestic & accustomed relations & command an absolute leisure with books — for a time."

Emerson's prevailing discomfort and indecision are reflected in other journal entries of early 1847. His purchase from his neighbor Cyrus Warren of three acres of land adjoining his own property came to seem a mistake. "In an evil hour I pulled down my fence and added Warren's piece to mine," he wrote. "No land is bad, but land is worse. If a man own land, the land owns him." As for the accustomed tasks of his study, he appeared to be living on accumulated literary capital rather than producing significant new work. Since publishing his first volume of poems in 1846 he had written little. His staple lectures were those in the series on "Representative Men" that he had first given in Boston during the winter of 1845–1846 and was still repeating; his one publishing venture in 1847 was a new edition of the essays he had first printed in 1841; several of his current notebooks he devoted to a laborious compiling or indexing of passages from earlier journals. ("Among the seven ages of human life," he wrote in the spring of 1847, "the period of indexes should not be forgotten.") On the more positive side are scattered entries extolling the value of change and transition. Finally, toward the end of July, Emerson at last decided to sail for Liverpool in time for the fall lecture season in England. Once again, as he had done repeatedly in earlier times of stress, he thus determined on travel — despite his ingrained reservations about the virtues of mere change of place — as an antidote to lowered vitality and spiritual depression. From early August until his actual departure in October there is a new element in the journals, ranging from lists of chores to be done before sailing and addresses of correspondents abroad to notes on the French and their language. An excursion to France being part of his plan from the outset, Emerson now prepared himself by taking a French-language newspaper and going to Boston for lessons in French conversation.

If one of the reasons for traveling abroad was simply to withdraw temporarily "from all domestic & accustomed relations," another was certainly to attain a new perspective on the total American scene. "We go to Europe to see aristocratic society with as few abatements as possible," runs another journal entry. "We go to be Americanized, to import what we can. This country has its proper glory, though now shrouded & unknown. We will let it shine." But a season of lecturing to strange English audiences was obviously not going to provide that "absolute leisure with books" Emerson had associated with his desired withdrawal from accustomed routine.

Throughout his stay abroad, as the journals and letters reveal, there was a constant tension between the demands of his lecturing and the need both to absorb new experience and to commit his responses to some written form. Though he affirmed while abroad that he had put down in the journal "all that seems really important" about his trip, it became clear in later years, as he began assembling materials for the book he was to call *English Traits* (1856), that his letters to family and friends were almost equally important as records of his experience. Relevant too are the lectures composed in England and France, some of them based on the earlier journals of 1847 and the reading and thinking embodied in them, and also the lectures on England and the English delivered during the season of 1847–1848 as the first fruits of his travels.

Some of Emerson's reading in the months before his departure for England may well have been done with the object of writing or revising lectures for future use abroad. He envisioned a new series of six lectures on "Mind & manners in the XIX Century" (*JMN*, IX, 403, 443), but after his decision to make the trip there were other obligations that continually interrupted the "great pleasure" of preparing lectures for England, as he complained in a letter to his brother William written late in September. Besides "reprinting & correcting & motting" his first series of *Essays*, published in October, he was obliged to contribute to the inaugural issue of the new *Massachusetts Quarterly Review*, which had been projected at a meeting in his home during the previous April. As a result, he had begun "too late" to work on his lecture manuscripts, and was now "sadly fretted with miscellaneous parts." This difficulty may have led Emerson to fall back once more on the "Representative Men" series; some of his reading earlier in 1847 appears to suggest that he had enrichment of these lectures in mind. Besides dipping into various dialogues of Plato in Thomas Taylor's translation he consulted August Boeckh's *The Public Economy of Athens* for information on the daily life of the Greeks, making extracts both in the journals and in a loose sheaf of notes headed "Platoniana." He examined Swedenborg's *Economy of the Animal Kingdom*, *Principia*, and *Angelic Wisdom* and made further extracts; he copied observations on the character of Napoleon from Madame de Staël's *Dix Années d'Exil*; and he turned not only to Goethe's *Werke* but also to the *Sprüche in Reim und Prosa* and a new translation of the *Autobiography*.

In these months Emerson was also reading the popular poetry and mythology of a number of diverse peoples. From the Harvard College Library in January of 1847 he borrowed the *Popular Ballads and Songs* compiled by the Scottish anthologist Robert Jamieson, two other collections: *Ancient Scottish Poems* and *Lays of the Minnesingers*, and a volume of Chalmers's *Works of the English Poets*; in July he withdrew Atkinson's translation of *The Sháh Námeh* of Firdausi, Chodzko's *Specimens of the Popular Poetry of Persia*, and Bishop Percy's version of Paul Henri Mallet's *Northern Antiquities: or, A Description of the Manners, Customs, Religion and Laws of the Ancient Danes*. He read the *Divan* of Hafiz in his own copy of the German translation by Joseph von Hammer, whose *Geschichte der schönen redekünste Persiens* was also in his library, and turned favorite passages from both works into English. In the journals of 1847 he copied verses from Jamieson, made notes on Persian mythology from von Hammer and the *Sháh Námeh*, and took long extracts from Chodzko about the exploits of Kurroglou, the popular Persian hero; some of the material from Persian literature went into lectures on Hafiz and Persian poetry, subsequently revised in England as "The Superlative in Manners and Literature." There are still other extracts from Robert Southey's *Chronicle of the Cid*, whose Spanish hero and his horse Bavieca reminded Emerson not only of Kurroglou and his steed Kyrat but also of Rustem and Rakush and of Alexander and Bucephalus. Passages from *Northern Antiquities* and *The Younger Edda* show an interest in Scandinavian myth and legend that anticipates the early chapters of *English Traits*; reading the *Edda* in 1847 and later the *Heimskringla*, a history of Norse kings that he brought back from England in 1848, led Emerson in a journal passage to class them with such other "primitive histories" as the Pentateuch and the *Vishńu Puráńa*.

There is no special pattern of interest suggested by other books mentioned in the journals of 1847, Emerson's citations ranging from Rousseau's *Confessions* and *The Writings of Hugh Swinton Legaré* to William Hazlitt's *Conversations of James Northcote* and Ellery Channing's *Conversations at Rome*. For shipboard reading on his way to England in October he carried the manuscript diary of his great-grandfather Joseph Emerson of Malden, from which he copied amusing extracts in the journal, and more recent works such as Fanny Kemble Butler's *A Year of Consolation* and the second volume of Ruskin's *Modern Painters*, both named in a letter to his wife; in addition, the ship's library provided novels by Dickens, Dumas, Lever, and Marryat. When Emerson reached Liverpool there was some initial confusion: Alexander Ireland was unable to meet him as intended, and a letter from Carlyle "addressed to 'R.W.E — on the instant when he lands in England'" was not put into his hands until a couple of days later. But soon Ireland had arranged a base of operations for Emerson in Manchester, and there was time to take a train for London to visit the Carlyles before his lecturing began on November 2. Meanwhile he planned to ship home "the old carpet bag & some books"; now, with a full schedule of lectures and travel ahead, together with unexpectedly heavy social engagements and a proliferating British correspondence, there would be few hours left for reading during the busy months in prospect.

Emerson's first lectures in November, scheduled concurrently in Manchester and Liverpool, required him to shuttle back and forth by rail between the two cities; although he settled in lodgings at Manchester he maintained a furnished parlor and bedroom in Liverpool as well. For both the Manchester Athenaeum and the Liverpool Mechanics' Institution he read six lectures from the series on "Representative Men": "Uses of Great Men," "Swedenborg," "Montaigne," "Shakspeare," "Napoleon," and "Goethe." Reviews and comment in the local press were mixed; Emerson himself cautiously described his reception as "rather dubious." His remarks on Swedenborg and the Swedenborgians offended members of the New Jerusalem Church; his religious liberalism troubled orthodox believers, with the result that in several other cities efforts were made to cancel his scheduled appearances or at least persuade him to tone down what he might say, but Emerson and his sponsors were unmoved. Meanwhile, he had undertaken an independent lecture series for the Manchester Mechanics' Institution, giving "Eloquence," "Domestic Life," and two newly composed lectures: one on "Books or a Course of Reading," previously outlined in his journals, and the other on "The

Superlative in Manners and Literature," a possible component of the projected series on "Mind and Manners." In addition, he spoke at a soirée of the Manchester Athenaeum on November 18 and lectured on "Reading" at a new branch of the Roscoe Club in Liverpool on December 4.

What did trouble Emerson in the press coverage of his appearances was that the provincial newspapers, as he put it, "report my lectures and London papers reprint so fully, that they are no longer repeatable." His alternatives, he felt, were either to "dive deeper into the bag & bring up older ones, or write new ones, or cease to read." Evidently Emerson had brought with him not only a supply of finished manuscripts but materials for completing others, as he had done in Manchester. At Sheffield in January of 1848 he "made shift with some old papers & some pages suggested lately" to "muster a discourse on 'Science'"; for Edinburgh, where he was unwilling to go without a wholly new lecture, he composed the discussion of "Natural Aristocracy" he had projected as part of the "Mind and Manners" series. He was admittedly surprised, however, when local committees repeatedly called for such "musty old lectures" (his own phrase) as "Domestic Life," "Eloquence," "Napoleon," and "Shakspeare." "We have heard of these; advertised these," they told him; "there can be no other."

Emerson's first impression of England and the English had been influenced by the sheer size and wealth of the public buildings in Liverpool and the "complete incuriosity & stony neglect each of every other" that he saw in her people, whose appearance and constitution seemed utterly distinct from the American model. But as the excellent British railways carried him among the various manufacturing cities of the Midlands he began to record different impressions in the journal, storing up material for what would become the chapters on "Land" and "Race" in *English Traits*. He noted the advantages of what he called the best working climate in the world, offset only by the darkness and dirt of the omnipresent coal-smoke. To that climate, the density of population, the presence of an aristocracy or model class, a generous diet, and a naturally robust constitution he traced the peculiarities of English manners that he observed and described. It became his custom to stay overnight in private homes rather than at inns or hotels as in America. The rapid pace of his tours offered some difficulty, and his sleep was troubled by dreams of "gas light, heaps of faces, & darkness." But what reconciled him to "the clatter & routine," as he told his wife, was the opportunity to "see men & things in each town in a close and domestic way." His acquaintance in the provinces was chiefly with the middle class — "the merchants the manufacturers the scholars the thinkers" — rather than the aristocracy or the workingmen. Instead of the differences between Englishmen and Americans that had struck him at first he now saw everywhere counterparts of men well known to him at home. He was particularly interested in individuals like the saddler who entertained him at Bridlington, an ardent friend of both the local Mechanics' Institute and the Temperance Society; elsewhere he was the guest of municipal mayors, as at Leeds and Worcester, or wealthy mill owners, as at Newcastle. In every city he found the same profuse kindness, and his acknowledged admiration and love of the English rose day by day. "If I stay here long," he wrote in the journal, "I shall lose all my patriotism, & think that England has absorbed all excellences."

When Emerson reached Scotland in February the countryside had an iron-gray look; the land seemed cold and poor and the people "plainer drest, plainer mannered, than the English," but again his hosts proved generous in their hospitality. He stayed at Edinburgh with Dr. Samuel Brown, with whom he had been in correspondence. Through Brown, a scientist and friend of both Carlyle and Margaret Fuller, he met the principal literary figures of the city, including Jeffrey and Wilson ("Christopher North"); he sat for a portrait to the artist David Scott. At Catherine Crowe's he spent an evening with the shy Thomas De Quincey, who invited him to dinner and even attended one of his lectures. Despite the now-familiar opposition from conservative religious leaders and circulation of a pamphlet attacking Emerson's alleged pantheism, there was no interruption of his scheduled engagements in Scotland. His correspondence and journals say less about the Scottish tour itself than about the people he met. A long letter to his wife recounts his social engagements in Edinburgh; in the journal he recorded De Quincey's talk, listed the principal Scottish periodicals and their editors, and noted the "wonderful crop of mediocre and super-mediocre poets" lying "3, 6, or 10 deep" in Scotland "instead of single as in America."

Leaving Scotland late in February, Emerson traveled to the English Lake district for a visit with Harriet Martineau, whom he had entertained in America, and a renewal of acquaintance with Wordsworth. After stopping briefly in Manchester he reached London on March 2, subsequently taking lodgings at the house of his British publisher John Chapman, where he remained throughout his stay in the city. There would be no more lecturing until after his trip to France in May; instead, the attractions of London itself were now the focus of Emerson's interest, as the journals attest. Looking back in later years on all that he saw and did during the ensuing weeks, he drew up the following survey for the chapter of *English Traits* headed "Personal":

> My visit fell in the fortunate days when Mr. Bancroft was the American Minister in London, and at his house, or through his good offices, I had easy access to excellent persons and to privileged places. At the house of Mr. Carlyle, I met persons eminent in society and in letters. The privileges of the Athenæum and of the Reform Clubs were hospitably opened to me, and I found much advantage in the circles of the "Geologic," the "Antiquarian" and the "Royal" Societies. Every day in London gave me new opportunities of meeting men and women who gave splendor to society. I saw Rogers, Hallam, Macaulay, Milnes, Milman, Barry Cornwall, Dickens, Thackeray, Tennyson, Leigh Hunt, D'Israeli, Helps, Wilkinson, Bailey, Kenyon and Forster: the younger poets, Clough, Arnold and Patmore; and among the men of science, Robert Brown, Owen, Sedgwick, Faraday, Buckland, Lyell, De la Beche, Hooker, Carpenter, Babbage and Edward Forbes. It was my privilege also to converse with Miss Baillie, with Lady Morgan, with Mrs. Jameson and Mrs. Somerville. A finer hospitality made many private houses not less known and dear. . . . Among the privileges of London, I recall with pleasure two or three signal days, one at Kew, where Sir William Hooker showed me all the riches of the vast botanic garden; one at the Museum, where Sir Charles Fellowes explained in detail the history of his Ionic trophy-monument; and still another, on which Mr. Owen accompanied my countryman Mr. H[illard]. and myself through the Hunterian Museum.

Unmentioned in *English Traits*, however, was Emerson's inveterate need to reserve time to himself for thinking and writing. In a letter sent to his friend Ireland shortly after his arrival in the metropolis he reported that though he was "beginning to see London shows," he still valued his mornings as "too precious to go abroad in," being prone to lengthen them to three o'clock. Occupied with his "old tools of book & pen," he was not only maintaining "an English journal which grows a little day by day," as he told his wife in April, but had also "got a new chapter quite forward." This work, which he thought of as "a kind of 'Natural History of Intellect,'" he described to Margaret Fuller in another letter from London as a "Book of Metaphysics" which he might print at home in case he failed to make it ready for lectures in England. The busy mornings spent at his desk, the many visits to points of interest in and near London, and the mixed pleasures of the London social season led Emerson to fill his manuscripts with his own first-hand observations rather than lustres drawn from his reading. Though he does mention the collected works of his late friend John Sterling, which had been sent to him at Manchester, and quotes some shrewd observations on England and the English made some three centuries earlier by a visiting Italian, newly printed in 1847 for the Camden Society, there is relatively little discussion of current books in any of the journals that Emerson kept while abroad.

What Emerson did take care to read "every day," beginning shortly after his arrival in England, was "the Times Newspaper," which he characterized in a letter to his brother William as "a pretty fair transcript of England, & a chief product of modern civilization." He saved clippings from its columns, recorded anecdotes about the paper and its staff in his journals, and visited the *Times* office in London, taking notes on its circulation and its principal writers and managers; much of this material is used in the chapter of *English Traits* on "The Times." After the excitement of "the new French Revolution" of 1848 he speculated that this newspaper might come to replace all other reading for the modern Englishman: in a journal entry he observed that with the *Times* giving its readers "as much as they can read" for a mere five pence a day, the London book trade seemed "reduced to nothing." When he went to France in May he found two hundred newspapers in circulation, most of them new since the Revolution, but none was dominant like the *Times*; "to keep au courant," he was told, one must read a dozen of them daily. Although his own coverage of the French press is not tallied in the journals, he did list the names of eight French publications and their editors and copied extracts from another, *L'Assemblée Nationale*, whose general tone he characterized as "high shop."

Going to France brought a welcome change for Emerson. By the spring of 1848 he was tiring of the life he had been leading in England, though he took a wry amusement from the unaccustomed experience of being lionized there. "You must not think that any change has come over me, & that my awkward & porcupine manners are ameliorated by English air," he had written to his wife; "but these civilities are all offered to that deceiving Writer, who, it seems, has really beguiled many young people here, as he did at home, into some better hope than he could realize for them." In the journal is a revealing passage concerning "Guy," a semiautobiographical persona, whose secret was "to conceal from all mankind that he was a bore." It was wonderful, Emerson remarks, how Guy managed to make even clever people believe that he was witty and agreeable. But if Emerson thus disparaged his own social success in England he also took a measured view of his hosts as well. To Margaret Fuller, on the eve of his departure for France, he wrote that he was leaving "with an increased respect for the Englishman. His stuff or substance seems to be the best of the world. I forgive him all his pride. My respect is the more generous that I have no sympathy with him, only an admiration."

Emerson reached Paris just when an abortive uprising against the new provisional government was brewing; Tennyson, who had tried to persuade him to go to Italy instead, "affected to think" he would never come back alive. He visited several of the radical clubs in Paris and listened to their revolutionary leaders; on May 15 he watched a march on the National Assembly. He also went to the Louvre, saw three performances by the great Rachel, attended lectures at the Sorbonne by Leverrier and Michelet, and heard an address on Poland by Lamartine. There were fewer beggars on the streets, he thought, than in either Manchester or London. Moving about with a group of his English friends, including Monckton Milnes and Arthur Hugh Clough, he learned more concerning the life of the Parisian cafés than that of French society, which he entered only through an invitation from Alexis de Tocqueville and his English wife, arranged for him by Milnes, and a meeting with the Comtesse d'Agoult, who had published an article on his writings in 1846. The city itself he admired, in spite of the physical ravages left by the Revolution; French architecture he thought "far more original, spirited, national" than that of England. All in all, his month in Paris greatly raised his previously low estimate of the French, which is frequently voiced in the earlier journals. "All winter I have been admiring the English and disparaging the French," he acknowledged to his wife. "Now in these weeks I have been correcting my prejudice & the French rise many entire degrees."

Before leaving London Emerson had agreed, with some misgivings, to offer a course of lectures there on his return from France; his stay in Paris had been marred, he complained to Margaret Fuller, by the necessity of preparing material for this engagement. Appearing before the Literary and Scientific Institution, beginning on June 6, he spoke on "The Mind and Manners of the Nineteenth Century" —the topic he had been developing since early in 1847; his six component lectures were "Powers and Laws of Thought," "Relation of Intellect to Natural Science," "Tendencies and Duties of Men of Thought," "Politics and Socialism," "Poetry and Eloquence," and the discourse on "Natural Aristocracy" he had written at Manchester and introduced at Edinburgh. Some of the newer material had been drafted only under last-minute pressure. To his wife he wrote that he had been right in his unwillingness to undertake the series, "for I spoil my work by giving it this too rapid casting," but the wishes of his friends had prevailed. The audience for the opening lectures was smaller than expected, he reported; moreover, the financial yield for the series, which had been estimated at two hundred pounds, amounted at its conclusion to but eighty. Needing additional funds for his steamer passage home, Emerson consented to give a seventh lecture under the same sponsorship for ten guineas, speaking on "The Superlative in Manners and Literature," and to offer a more popular course at Exeter Hall, reading "Napoleon," "Domestic Life," and "Shakspeare" for another thirty-five guineas.

The final days of Emerson's stay in England brought more invitations than he could possibly accept. Chapman gave him a fare-well party on July 1. Having spent two nights at Oxford at the end of March, he now paid a one-day visit to Cambridge on July 6, and on the following day went with Carlyle to Stonehenge and Win-chester. Their old friendship, begun with a brief meeting at Craigen-puttock in 1833, had prospered better through correspondence over the intervening years than it did during Emerson's second visit abroad. On their reunion in October of 1847 they had differed sharply about Carlyle's estimate of Cromwell; by the following April, as journal entries suggest, Emerson was tiring of Carlyle's characteristic sneering and scoffing, his cunning denials of "his own acts & purposes," and his reactionary opinions generally. The excursion to Stonehenge, memorialized in a chapter of *English Traits*, seems to have effected a kind of reconciliation. Carlyle's farewell gift was a copy of Wood's *Athenae Oxonienses*; Emerson also carried home two other books that his friend had particularly recommended, Bede's *Ecclesiastical History of England* and Lowth's *Life of William of Wykeham*, but five other works on a much-copied list of desirable titles suggested by Carlyle are not recorded among his purchases. He had bought Laing's translation of the *Heimskringla*, the *Mégha Dúta* of Kali-dasa, Wordsworth's *Guide to the Lakes*, Dr. William Jacobson's translation of Aeschylus, and John Stuart Mill's *Political Economy*. In addition he had the *Essays and Tales* of John Sterling and un-bound sheets of Dr. John Carlyle's translation of Dante's *Inferno*, which after prolonged negotiations in Boston and New York he subsequently managed to place with an American publisher.

After his return to Concord, Emerson made good use of Wood, Laing, and other works of reference in preparing lectures for the coming winter season; as he put it to Dr. Carlyle in December of 1848, he had been reading "up & down in English history & topo-graphy" in order to "verify & fix such memoranda as I brought home from my journeying last winter." Together with the drafting of new lectures, which were given in 1848–1849 under such titles as "England," "London," "England and the English," and "Why England is England," he seems to have made further revisions in the old series published in 1850 as *Representative Men*. As early as November of 1848 he borrowed additional works on Plato's philo-

sophy by Schleiermacher, Ast, and Sewell, copying extracts in Platoniana that in several instances bear on the published version, and
on December 4 he spoke on Plato at the Freeman Place Chapel in
Boston. It is worth noting that Emerson had omitted his lecture on
Plato from the course on "Representative Men" as he gave it in
Manchester and Liverpool, though when he had first presented the
series in America "Plato" came between "Uses of Great Men" and
"Swedenborg" as it does in the published version of 1850; he read it
in England only once, for a group of his Lancashire friends at a
farewell dinner in January at Manchester. Perhaps he had not been
satisfied with the manuscript as it stood when he left for England;
perhaps he even anticipated the indifference toward Plato and Platonism that he noted in the journals during his travels and deplored
in *English Traits* as a weakness both of university training and of
contemporary English literature and culture.

Clearly Emerson returned to America in far better spirits than
when he had left home some nine months before. The change of
scene, the new acquaintance, the generous reception abroad had been
exhilarating, although throughout his travels he had missed his
family and been made uneasy by reports of illness and an accumulation of unpaid bills at home. The journal entries made in September
and early October of 1848 are a coda that brings a sense of completion to his account of the European sojourn. In one of the rare
passages that appears to reflect something of his own domestic relations he tallied the mixed rewards of family life, calling marriage a
"Pandora-box" that yields, "amidst dyspepsia, nervousness, screams,
Christianity, 'help,' poverty, & all kinds of music, some deep & serious
benefits & some great joys. We find sometimes a delight in the beauty
& the happiness of our children that makes the heart too big for the
body." With the poet Ellery Channing he took long walks over the
autumnal countryside, feeling a new identification with growing things
in gardens and orchards and wood-lots as well as with such "old
benefactors" among his Concord neighbors as Captain Abel Moore,
the skilled farmer whose success as a horticulturist he had envied,
then slipping out of life after attaining ripeness "like a huge melon
or pumpkin in the sun." As Emerson recorded the mellowness of the
landscape his thoughts were no longer on Lilliputian wars and

politics, as they had been before the European trip, or even on Paris and London; in his own mood of ripeness he sought to capture on paper the evanescent natural beauty that lay everywhere around him. "Shakspeare saw no better heaven or earth," he affirmed in late September after one of these excursions in Concord, but "seized the dull ugly England, ugly to this, & made it amiable & enviable to all reading men."

Thus Emerson's travels had given him the enlarged perspective to see again the "proper glory" of his own country as he acknowledged the bounty of nature and reflected on "the birth, death, & fate of men." Though the trip had done little to improve his immediate financial situation he was "not without hope," as he told his brother William, "to make the whole Excursion pay itself" in the future. He had the new lectures written abroad, some of which might fit into the projected "Book of Metaphysics"; in his journals and notebooks he had stored up materials for other lectures that could well grow into another book on his travels; he was soon to print *Representative Men*. Meanwhile, it was good to be back. As he had written Elizabeth Hoar shortly before leaving London, his pleasure was in his work, which could be done better at home than abroad, for he got "many more good hours in a Concord week than in a London one." In his study, his *atelier*, he had gradually gathered "a little sufficiency of tools & conveniences," and "missed its apparatus continually in England; the rich Athenæum (Club) Library, yes, & the dismaying Library of the British Museum could not vie with mine in convenience." If his "journeying" had broadened his horizons and furnished him new materials, as surely it had done in good measure, his prolonged absence from Concord made him want that *atelier* the more.

Volume X consists of six regular journals and eight miscellaneous notebooks. The journals cover the period from February of 1847 to October of 1848; the first of the journals, AB, immediately follows Journal O, printed in volume IX. Journal GH and the brief Journal Sea-Notes contain overlapping entries that describe Emerson's voyage to England in October of 1847; there is also minor overlapping between Journal GH and the two journals that

Emerson posted concurrently during the first six months of 1848, London and LM. The eight notebooks cover a longer period than the journals: some of the earlier entries in Notebooks JK and Platoniana apparently date from the early and middle 1840's; the later entries in Notebooks Xenien and ED ("England") belong to 1852 and 1853. Even so, the notebooks are all related in some way to Emerson's activities of 1847 and 1848. Thus Notebook JK was brought together and bound in 1847; Pocket Diaries 1 and 3 and Notebooks England and Paris and the homemade Xenien were variously used in connection with the trip abroad in 1847–1848, with a number of their entries overlapping; additions to Platoniana were made late in 1848; and in Notebook Warren Lot, dated 1849, are recorded plantings on land Emerson had bought two years before, as mentioned in Journals AB and CD. Jottings in two of the notebooks, England and Paris and Xenien, were expanded in both Journal London and Journal LM, which in turn were drawn upon for Emerson's lectures on England and the English in 1848 and 1849, for the retrospective Notebook ED, begun in 1852, and ultimately for *English Traits*, published in 1856. Three of the accompanying plates — II, III, and IV — illustrate the relation between an initial entry in Notebook England and Paris and its later reworking in Journal London and Notebook ED.

Editorial technique. The editorial process follows that described in volume I and the slight modifications introduced in subsequent volumes of the edition. In volume X there is relatively little of the difficulty with erased pencil writing that confronted the editors of volumes VII, VIII, and IX. The principal editorial problem here has been to trace the complex interrelationships among the notebooks and journals concerned with Emerson's trip abroad, to show the parallels between certain entries and passages in letters to friends and relatives at home, and to determine the use of notebook and journal passages in his published works. It has not been possible to establish the sequence of all the overlapping entries, or to pursue in detail the relation between the journals and unpublished lectures. Some of the journal material, for example, evidently found its way into *English Traits* by way of lectures on England delivered in 1848 and 1849, some through reworking under topical headings in Note-book ED in 1852 and 1853, and some through a still undetermined combination of routes. Although the genesis of *English Traits* can thus be traced in broad outline, details of the story will be filled in only after the lecture manuscripts have been analyzed — a project beyond the scope of this volume. Meanwhile, use marks in the journals and notebooks comprising volume X have been carefully described, transcriptions and expansions of passages within the volume have been recorded, and uses in *English Traits* and other published works have been noted where possible, often with help from the locations sup-plied by Edward W. Emerson in the manuscripts.

In the manuscripts, Emerson's topical headings are sometimes underlined, sometimes set off by a rule or by enclosing or partly enclosing straight or wavy lines; unless he seems to have intended something more than marking to identify the matter as a heading, the various forms are interpreted by setting the heading in italics. Whenever one of Emerson's hyphens coincides with the compositor's end-of-line hyphenation, two hyphens have been set, one at the end of the line and one at the beginning of the following line. When the text is quoted in the notes, no silent emendations are made; hence there are occasional variations between notes and text.

Numbering of "Fragments on Nature and Life" and "Frag-ments on the Poet and the Poetic Life" follows that assigned by Edward Emerson or by George S. Hubbell, *A Concordance to the Poems of Ralph Waldo Emerson.*

In accordance with the policies of the Center for Editions of American Authors, a list of silent emendations has been prepared; copies are to be deposited in the Rush Rhees Library of the University of Rochester, the Library of Congress, Houghton Library, Hunt-ington Library, and Newberry Library. The following statement describes the silent or mostly silent emendations. These range from numerous — as with punctuation of items in a series, supplying periods at the ends of sentences if the next sentence begins with a capital, or expansion of contractions — to occasional, as with supplying quotation marks, dashes, or parentheses missing from intended pairs.

Emendation of prose. A period is silently added to any declar-ative sentence lacking terminal punctuation but followed in the same paragraph by a sentence beginning with a capital letter. If a declarative sentence lacking a period is followed by a sentence beginning with a small letter, either a bracketed semicolon is supplied, or a bracketed period is supplied and the small letter is silently capitalized. In the second instance the reader will automatically know that the capital was originally a small letter. If a direct question lacking terminal punctuation is followed by a sentence in the same paragraph beginning with a capital the question mark is silently added. Punctuation of items in a series, since Emerson habitually set them off, is silently inserted. Small letters at the beginning of unquestionable paragraphs or of sentences which follow a sentence ending with a period are silently capitalized. Where indispensable for clarity a silent period is added to an abbreviation. Quotation marks, dashes, and parentheses missing from intended pairs have been silently supplied; so have quotation marks at the beginning of each of a series of quotations. Apostrophes have been silently inserted or normalized in possessives and contractions. Superscripts have been lowered and double or triple underscorings have been interpreted by small or large capitals. Common Emersonian contractions like y^t for *that*, y^e for *the*, *wh* for *which*, *wd* and *shd* for *would* and *should*, and *bo't* for *bought*, are silently expanded. His dates have been regularly normalized by the silent insertion of commas and periods.

Emendation of poetry. On the whole, Emerson's poetry has been left as it stands in the manuscripts; apostrophes and some commas, periods, and question marks have been supplied, in accordance with the rules for emending prose, but only where Emerson's intention was unmistakable.

Certain materials are omitted, either silently or with descriptive annotation; these will not be reported in the list of emendations. Omitted silently are slips of the pen, false starts at words, careless repetitions of a single word, and Emerson's occasional carets under insertions (assimilated into the editor's insertion marks). Underscoring to indicate intended revisions is not reproduced. Omitted, but usually with descriptive annotation, are practice penmanship, isolated words or letters, and miscellaneous markings.

CHRONOLOGY 1847–1848

1847: January, Emerson lectures at Pawtucket, Woburn, New Bedford, Taunton, Malden, Exeter (N.H.), Wayland, Watertown, and Natick; January 6, he buys three acres of land from Cyrus Warren, taking possession on April 1; February 10–24, he lectures at Boston, Concord (N.H.), Salem, and Concord (Mass.); February 28, he answers a letter from Alexander Ireland of Manchester pursuing Ireland's earlier suggestion of a lecture tour in England; March 2 and 30, he lectures at Lincoln and Wayland; April 14, a group meets at Emerson's house to discuss the projected *Massachusetts Quarterly Review*; May, Emerson gives seven lectures at Nantucket; July 31, he writes to Alexander Ireland and James William Hudson of Leeds agreeing to lecture in England during the autumn and winter; August, in the expectation of visiting France, he begins lessons in French conversation with Dr. Emile Arnoult of Boston; October 5–22, he sails from Boston to Liverpool aboard the packet *Washington Irving*, Captain Caldwell, leaving Henry Thoreau as caretaker of the house in Concord; October 25–29, he is in London to renew acquaintance with Thomas and Jane Carlyle; November 2–30, he lectures alternately at Manchester and Liverpool; November 18, he speaks at the soirée of the Manchester Athenaeum; December 1–30, he lectures at Preston, Rochdale, Nottingham, Derby, Chesterfield, Birmingham, Huddersfield, Leicester, and Worcester.

1848: January 3–21, Emerson lectures at Leeds, Bradford, Halifax, Ripon, Sheffield, York, Beverley, Bridlington, and Driffield; January 27, he attends the Free Trade banquet in Manchester; February 7–26, he lectures at Halifax, Barnard Castle, Newcastle, Edinburgh, Glasgow, Dundee, Perth, and Paisley; February 27–29, he visits Harriet Martineau at Ambleside and renews acquaintance with William Wordsworth; March 2, he returns to London, where on March 3 he takes lodging with John Chapman, his British publisher; March 7, he attends a Chartist meeting in National Hall, Holborn; March 12, he visits Hampton Court; March 14, George Bancroft gives a dinner in Emerson's honor, introducing him to London society; March 30–April 1, he visits Oxford at the invitation of Arthur Hugh Clough; April 5, he tours the botanic gardens at

Kew with Sir William Jackson Hooker; April 15, he visits the British Museum with the Bancrofts under the guidance of Sir Charles Fellows; April 25, he meets Charles Dickens at a dinner given by John Forster; May 5, he meets Alfred Tennyson at a dinner given by Coventry Patmore; May 6, he leaves London for Paris, via Folkestone and Boulogne; May 15, he witnesses an unsuccessful attempt to overthrow the French government; May 25, he meets Alexis de Tocqueville; June 2, he leaves Paris for London, via Amiens, Boulogne, and Folkestone; June 6–17, he delivers six lectures before the Literary and Scientific Institution on "The Mind and Manners of the Nineteenth Century"; June 23–30, he gives three lectures at Exeter Hall under auspices of the Metropolitan Early Closing Association; June 26, he gives an additional lecture before the Literary and Scientific Institution; June 29, he visits the Hunterian Museum under the guidance of Richard Owen; July 4, he visits Stoke Poges, Eton, and Windsor; July 6, he visits Cambridge; July 7–9, he goes with Carlyle to Salisbury, Stonehenge, Bishop's Waltham, and Winchester; July 11, he leaves London for Coventry, Stratford-on-Avon, and Liverpool; July 15, he sails from Liverpool on the steamer *Europa*, Captain Lott, reaching Halifax on July 25 and Boston on July 27; November 22 and 28, he lectures at Lowell; December, he lectures in Boston, Concord (Mass.), Providence, Newport, Newburyport, Lowell, Waltham, and New Bedford, introducing material on England and London.

SYMBOLS AND ABBREVIATIONS

⟨ ⟩   Cancellation
↑ ↓   Insertion or addition
/ /   Variant
‖ ... ‖   Unrecovered matter, normally unannotated. Three dots, one to five words; four dots, six to fifteen words; five dots, sixteen to thirty words. Matter lost by accidental mutilation but recovered conjecturally is inserted between the parallels.

xxvii

⟨‖ ... ‖⟩ Unrecovered canceled matter

‖msm‖ Manuscript mutilated

[ ] Editorial insertion

[...] Editorial omission

⟦ ⟧ Emerson's square brackets

⌐ ¬ Marginal matter inserted in text

[ ] Page numbers of original manuscript

ⁿ See Textual Notes

-- Two hyphens are set when the compositor's end-of-line hyphen coincides with Emerson's.

ᐱ Emerson's symbol for intended insertion

[R.W.E.] Editorial substitution for Emerson's symbol of original authorship. See volume I, plate VII.

* Emerson's note

epw Erased pencil writing

☞

☜ Hands pointing

✍

ABBREVIATIONS AND SHORT TITLES IN FOOTNOTES

CEC *The Correspondence of Emerson and Carlyle.* Edited by Joseph Slater. New York: Columbia University Press, 1964.

E t E Kenneth W. Cameron. *Emerson the Essayist.* Raleigh, N.C.: The Thistle Press, 1945. 2 vols.

J *Journals of Ralph Waldo Emerson.* Edited by Edward Waldo Emerson and Waldo Emerson Forbes. Boston and New York: Houghton Mifflin Co., 1909–1919. 10 vols.

JMN *The Journals and Miscellaneous Notebooks of Ralph Waldo Emerson.* William H. Gilman, Chief Editor; Alfred R. Ferguson, Senior Editor; Harrison Hayford, Ralph H. Orth, J. E. Parsons, A. W. Plumstead, Editors (Volume I edited by William H. Gilman, Alfred R. Ferguson, George P. Clark, and Merrell R. Davis; volumes II–VI, William H. Gilman, Alfred R. Ferguson, Merrell R. Davis, Merton M. Sealts, Jr., Harrison Hayford, General Editors). Cambridge: Harvard University Press, 1960–

L *The Letters of Ralph Waldo Emerson.* Edited by Ralph L. Rusk. New York: Columbia University Press, 1939. 6 vols.

Lectures *The Early Lectures of Ralph Waldo Emerson.* Volume I, 1833–1836, edited by Stephen E. Whicher and Robert E. Spiller; volume II, 1836–1838, edited by Stephen E. Whicher, Robert E.

Spiller, and Wallace E. Williams; volume III, 1838–1842, edited by Robert E. Spiller and Wallace E. Williams. Cambridge: Harvard University Press, 1959–1972.

Life   Ralph L. Rusk. *The Life of Ralph Waldo Emerson.* New York: Charles Scribner's Sons, 1949.

W   *The Complete Works of Ralph Waldo Emerson.* With a Biographical Introduction and Notes, by Edward Waldo Emerson. Centenary Edition. Boston and New York: Houghton Mifflin Co., 1903–1904. 12 vols. I — *Nature Addresses and Lectures*; II — *Essays, First Series*; III — *Essays, Second Series*; IV — *Representative Men*; V — *English Traits*; VI — *Conduct of Life*; VII — *Society and Solitude*; VIII — *Letters and Social Aims*; IX — *Poems*; X — *Lectures and Biographical Sketches*; XI — *Miscellanies*; XII — *Natural History of Intellect.*

YES   *Young Emerson Speaks.* Edited by Arthur C. McGiffert, Jr. Boston: Houghton Mifflin Co., 1938.

PART ONE

The Journals

AB

1847

Journal AB, a regular journal consisting mainly of undated entries, bears the date *"Feb. 1847"* on the flyleaf. It follows Journal O, 1846–1847, printed in *JMN*, IX, 355–470. The first entry to be dated is that of March 3, 1847, on page [37]; the last is that of April 15, 1847, on page [126].

Journal AB is written in a hard-cover copybook. The cover, 16 x 20.2 cm, is of brown marbled paper over boards; the spine is brown, with two horizontal gold lines, an ink inscription ("AB"), and mending at both top and bottom. The front cover is inscribed, in ink, "AB / 1847"; the back cover, also in ink, "AB". The pages, faintly ruled, are 15.6 x 19.8 cm. Including flyleaves (i–ii, 133–134), there are 136 pages, all numbered in ink except those partly torn out (97, 98), unnumbered (i, ii, 6, 14, 37, 38, 45, 47, 51, 59, 85, 131, 132), or numbered in pencil only (29, 44, 46, 94, 99); page 78 is numbered in pencil and again in ink. Nine pages are blank (ii, 14, 36, 59, 85, 100, 131, 132, 133). A portion of the leaf bearing pages 97 and 98 is torn out; Emerson indexed page 97 under both Metamorphosis and Woman, page 98 under both Morals and Persistency. An irregularly cut piece of cardboard, 4 x 13.6 cm, inscribed in ink "Concord[']s Enchanted Places" and intended as a place marker, now laid in between pages 34 and 35, probably belongs between pages 44 and 45; it seems to refer to a passage on page 45. A printed article, "Joseph Tuckerman" by Rev. Charles F. Barnard, is laid in between pages 44 and 45.

[front cover]   AB

1847

[front cover verso]   [Index material omitted]

Caput est artis decere.[1]

[i]   R.W.Emerson.
                                                     Feb. 1847

AB

[ii] [blank]
[1] Transition
Mediation
Equation
Centrality   80
Epiphany

— What is the oldest thing? a dimple or whirlpool in water. That is
Genesis, Exodus, & all.

Indirection   O 10,
Boulder   12
Transit   104
Croisement   107
Currency   112
Whip   61, 123
Paint
Reading   2

     (7 Fancy)[2]

---

[1] Cicero, *De Oratore*, I.xxix.132: "the chief thing in art is to observe good
taste."
    [2] "(7 Fancy)" is in pencil; see p. [7] below. The other page references on

[2]³   *Lecture on Reading*

The boy that reads Homer in American farmhouse   N 108

The Muse's Commandment   N 110

Theophrastus's saying   N 113

Paracelsus   N 129, 130, 131, 133

Bible ⟨10⟩N 10

New Bible   N 18

Of lending books   N 17

Use of books   N 17

Scribacious Cornelius Agrippa, Burton, &c   N 126 ⁴

Flattering   art of language & letters   N 94

Garrulity is our religion & philosophy   N 95

Merit of ↑a↓ tragedy Empirical   N 80

———

Books are written by the successful class   J 14 ⁵

———

Proclus &c   R 65

———

Reading Timaeus   J 96

———

---

p. [1] are also to Journal AB, with a single exception: for "O 10" (i.e., Journal O, p. [10]), see *JMN*, IX, 361. The foregoing items, all but one in ink and entered on the first page of the journal to be numbered by Emerson, may well be more than routine index headings. Their common theme is "Transition" or "Genesis"; several of the passages cited in individual listings have significant autobiographical implications. A partially corresponding list occurs on p. [65] below under the caption *"Topics"* — presumably drawn up with a possible lecture or lecture series in view; compare the outline headed *"Lecture on Reading"* on p. [2] below.

³ On this and succeeding pages throughout Journal AB a number of letters within individual words have been rewritten in pencil for clarity — probably by Edward Emerson. Here, for example, the "k" in "lending books", the word "pit", and the "G" in "G. Waldo" are so rewritten.

⁴ "Scribacious . . . N 126" is struck through in ink with a diagonal use mark; the passage cited, in *JMN*, VIII, 301, is used in "Books," *W*, VII, 211–212. For the eleven preceding references to Journal N, see *JMN*, VIII, 292–294 (N 108, 110, 113); 302–304 (N 129, 130, 131, 133); 252 (N 10); 255 (N 18); and 254 (N 17).

⁵ "Books . . . J 14" is struck through in ink with a diagonal use mark. The passage cited, in *JMN*, VIII, 152, is used in "Books," *W*, VII, 195; see also Notebook JK, p. [25], in the present volume. For the three preceding references to Journal N, see *JMN*, VIII, 286 (N 94, N 95) and 280 (N 80).

Shelley   J 96

——

Novels   J 132   V 46, 65, R 112,
Bettine   J 139
Cheap literature makes a pit audience   Z 80
Confucius   J 52 [6]
List of Books furnished to G[iles]. Waldo. ↑Li. 108↓
The Roxborough Club from Dibdin   J̄K̄ [7]

[3]   List of Books, continued.   AB 35

Translations
We are a little civil to books.   O 299
But where is great design in mod. Eng. poetry?   O 327 [8]

Division
    Bibles
    1 Fable, as Edda, Homer, ↑Prometheus↓ Vishnu Purana

    2. Desatir, Bhagavat, [9]

[4]   Ancora imparo [10]
Scholar perpetual

[6] Emerson's citation may be in error; the passage cited, in *JMN*, VIII, 163–164, concerns not Confucius but Emerson's son Waldo, who had died two days before the entry was written. Here as in Journal J, on the front cover verso, he may have intended to cite p. 52 of "Hea Lun" in the "Memoirs of Confucius" printed in *The Chinese Classical Work Commonly Called The Four Books*, trans. Rev. David Collie ([Malacca], 1828); see *JMN*, VIII, 146. For the nine preceding references to Journals R, J, V, and Z, see *JMN*, VIII, 378–379, 178, and 191 (R 65, J 96, J 132); *JMN*, IX, 117–118 and 126 (V 46, V 65); *JMN*, VIII, 402, 194, and 343 (R 112, J 139, Z 80).

[7] "The Roxborough . . . JK" is struck through in ink with a diagonal use mark; there is nothing corresponding to this entry in Notebook JK as now constituted. Emerson may have had in mind a story he credits to the bibliographer Thomas Frognall Dibdin in "Books," *W*, VII, 209–210: an account of the sale in 1812 of the library of the Duke of Roxburghe.

[8] For these two references to Journal O, see *JMN*, IX, 438, 449.

[9] Emerson expanded this uncompleted list in "Books," *W*, VII, 217–218.

[10] See "Michel Angelo Buonaroti," *Lectures*, I, 103: one of the artist's last draw-

Vice of men is setting up for themselves too early. I can't go into the quarrel or into the tavern, &c. because ⟨I am 44 years old⟩ ↑I am old;↓ or into the abolition meeting at Faneuil Hall & attempt to speak, it won't do for me to fail!

But I look at wise men, & see that I am very young. I look over those stars yonder & into the myriads of the aspirant & ardent souls, & I see I am a stranger & a youth, & have yet my spurs to win. Too ridiculous are these airs of age.

Ancora imparo. I carry my satchel still.

————

A scholar brooks no interruptions. He must post his books every day. For want of posting the books at Greenwich, the star was lost — by Adams & England.[11]

[5] Legare's Writings.[12]
Some important references to ⟨(Hermann's)⟩ [13] "Manual of the Political Antiquities of Greece historically considered". From the German of Charles Frederick Hermann. Oxford, 1836. [Published by D. A.] *Talboys.*

————

ings was "a sketch . . . of an old man with a long beard in a go-cart and an hourglass before him and the motto 'ancora inparo' [*sic*], I still learn."

[11] Johann Gottfried Galle, working from calculations of Urban Jean Joseph Leverrier, discovered the planet Neptune on September 23, 1846; John Couch Adams of Cambridge University was its independent discoverer. In 1912 Edward C. Pickering, director of the Harvard Observatory, in answering a query about the present passage from Edward Emerson, noted that the discovery "was claimed by Adams' friends for him. I do not know of any evidence that the failure to find this object in England was due to 'For want of posting the books at Greenwich'. . . ." See Bessie Z. Jones, "Diary of the Two Bonds: 1846–1849: First Directors of the Harvard College Observatory," *Harvard Library Bulletin*, XV (October 1967), 384, n. 44.

[12] Emerson's notes on pp. [5] and [6] refer to Legaré's "Constitutional History of Greece," in *The Writings of Hugh Swinton Legaré*, ed. Mary Swinton Legaré, 2 vols. (Charleston, S.C., 1845–1846), I, 367–442. The article reviews translations of two German works: William Wachsmuth, *The Historical Antiquities of the Greeks* (Oxford, 1837), and Charles Frederick Hermann, *A Manual of the Political Antiquities of Greece* (Oxford, 1836); Emerson cites the latter work below. Emerson was reading Legaré in February, 1847 (*L*, III, 373; *JMN*, IX, 390).

[13] "Hermann's" was first enclosed in penciled parentheses and then canceled in ink. Similar instances occur on succeeding pages.

"[August] Bockh's Public Economy of Athens" also in English translation Legare prefers to Muller's Dorians[.] [14]

In Jefferson's Works Vol 4, p. 286 "the important letter to Kercheval which reveals Jefferson's whole system." [15]

"Party," the mystery of *constructive majorities*, "the art of thinking for the people" [Legaré, I, 387]

[6] Individuality the characteristic of modern society. [Legaré, I, 420]

The ancients thought the citizen existed for the government[.] [Legaré, I, 420]

"The evils of popular government appear greater than they really are, said Machiavel.
There is compensation for them in the spirit & energy it awakens" [16] *Legare* [I, 421]

Vitality & vigor in repub. govt resists corruption for a time [Legaré, I, 421]
in the ancient world, citizenship was an affair of race: Spatium est urbis et orbis idem [17] [Legaré, I, 423]

[7] Apples of gold in silver salvers set.[18] We used to think that

---

[14] *Writings of Hugh Swinton Legaré*, 1845–1846, I, 367–368. The translations cited are August Boeckh, *The Public Economy of Athens, with a Dissertation on the Silver Mines of Laurion*, 2 vols. (London, 1828), which Emerson borrowed from the Harvard College Library on March 30, 1847, and Karl Otfried Mueller, *History and Antiquities of the Doric Race*, trans. Henry Tufnell and George Cornewall Lewis, 2 vols. (Oxford, 1830), vol. I of which he had borrowed from the Boston Athenaeum December 23, 1831–January 3, 1832.

[15] Quoted from *Writings of Hugh Swinton Legaré*, 1845–1846, I, 347, note. Legaré is documenting, as "substantially stated" by Thomas Jefferson in the letter cited, the observation that when in the United States "we came to write our constitution, we had nothing to do, and did nothing, but transcribe magna charta, with the petition of right, and bill of rights."

[16] " 'The evils . . . awakens' " is struck through in ink with a vertical use mark.

[17] See "Boston," *W*, XII, 188: "It was said of Rome in its proudest days . . . , — 'the extent of the city and of the world is the same' (*spatium et urbis et orbis idem*)." The Latin phrase occurs also in Journal London, p. [i], in the present volume.

[18] A metrical rendering of Prov. 25:11: "like apples of gold in pictures of silver."

great thoughts ensured musical expression, but these Thirlwalls & Grotes write Greek history in dullest prose.

Montaigne is one who shows the differences between quiddity & ⟨accident,⟩ quality, entity & accident, without a professor's gown, on the saddle, & not in a square cap, and thenceforth we forswear grammar[.] [19]

We wanted to show Prometheus a working plan or recipe by which he could make a *fancy* in his mannikin. [20]

[8] Caput est artis decere [21]

[9]   ↑See C̄D̄ 65↓

What I want is a Dictionary, & not a library.
Bana means *Sermons*
Vishnu means *entrance* & *pervading*
Saadi means *felicity*
Buddha means *He who knows* [22]

[⟨9⟩10] The mechanic advantage which all men give themselves is of great value, as e.g. the sublime tool which the astronomer uses in the base of the Earth's orbit: but scholars use no mechanics as they might. If you meet the intelligent often & easily with express design to communicate mutually your results, each becomes by that act more master of his results; he can certainly explain them better after than before the meeting.

[11] All conversation is a series of intoxications[;] the talkers re-

---

[19] This paragraph, written in pencil and struck through in pencil with a vertical use mark, is used in "Montaigne," *W*, IV, 166.

[20] This sentence is in pencil. See p. [1] above.

[21] See the front cover verso above.

[22] For earlier journal entries concerning Buddha, Bana, and Vishnu, see *JMN*, IX, 293, 305. "What . . . *Sermons*" and "Bana . . . *knows*" are struck through in ink with diagonal use marks. All four definitions are incorporated in the entry headed "Dictionary" in Journal CD, p. [65] below, indicated by Emerson's cross-reference at the top of p. [9]. (Hereafter, Emerson's cross-references to other journals and notebooks in this volume are not annotated.)

cover themselves at intervals, see how pleasant the gas was, inhale it again, and disport themselves gladly. If they kept cool, there would be no joy.

> 'Tis merry in hall
> When beards wag all [23]
> [Shakespeare, *II Henry IV*, V, iii, 37]

Go on & justify the ways   Show the basis of science
The river makes its shores. Set down nothing but what will help somebody. The avatars [24]

Wine is properly drunk as a salutation; it is a liquid compliment.

[12] *Shakspeare*   Boulders
In the Lecture on Shakspeare, the origin Grotius has given to the Lord's Prayer is to be remembered. Proverbs are boulders & get the roundness of boulders.[25]
↑See p 80 | Eng. liturgy↓

Every time we say a ⟨⟨thing⟩⟩ ↑fact↓ in conversation we get a certain mechanical advantage in detaching it well & deliverly.
I value the mechanics of conversation. It is pulley & lever & screw. To fairly disengage the mass & send it jingling down[,] a good boulder —— [26]
↑Our pavingstones have been formed by the attrition of a thousand years[.]↓

↑See p 10↓

[13] *Affirmative*
Set down nothing but what will help somebody[.] [27]

---

[23] The couplet is in pencil and struck through in pencil with three diagonal use marks.
[24] "Go on . . . avatars" is in pencil. With "justify the ways", cf. Milton, *Paradise Lost*, I, 26. For "The river makes its shores.", see *JMN*, IX, 363, 364.
[25] This entry, struck through in ink with a vertical use mark, is used in "Shakspeare," *W*, IV, 200.
[26] This paragraph, incorporating phrases from p. [10] above, is used in "Clubs," *W*, VII, 228.
[27] See p. [11] above.

[14] [blank]

    [15] Saadi's five classes of men that may travel, are, the rich ↑merchant↓; the learned; the beautiful; the singer; and the mechanic; because these are ⟨always⟩ everywhere sure of good reception.

The rich, he says, is everywhere expected, & at home; whilst the poor man is an alien in his own house, — not being able even there to command the comforts of life.[28]

And see this terrible Atlantic stretching its stormy chaos from pole to pole terrible by its storms, by its cold, by its ice-bergs, by its Gulf stream ⟨—⟩ the ⟨⟨awful⟩⟩ desert in which no caravan loiters, but all hurry as thro' the valley of the Shadow of Death ⟨see this ⟨is bridged⟩⟩ as unpassable to the poor Indian through all [16] ages as the finer ocean that separates him from the moon; let him stand on the shore & ↑idly↓ entreat the birds or the wind to transport him across the roaring waste. Yet see, a man arrives at the margin with 120 dollars in his pocket, and the rude sea ⟨also⟩ grows civil, and is bridged at once for the long thre⟨t⟩e thousand miles to England, with a carpeted floor & a painted & enamelled walls & roof[,] with ↑books &↓ gay company & feasting & music & wine[.] [29]
      ↑"See what money will buy"
              O. p. 41.↓ [30]
↑All he looked on was his own[.]↓ [31]

    [17] ↑In a cellar↓ even[n] punk & old fish will for a short time yield a dismal light.

    [18] Jamie heard as he went a bark like a knell. ——————
As he approached the house he heard again the bark of the dog he had once already ⟨he⟩remarked; it was hoarse & determined

---

    [28] See Ch. III, Tale XXVIII, in Sa'adi, *The Gûlistân; or, Rose Garden*, trans. Francis Gladwin (London, 1808), pp. 151–153, 151, in Emerson's library. "The rich . . . at home;" is used in "Wealth," *W*, VI, 95,
    [29] For "the valley . . . of Death", see Ps. 23:4. "and the rude . . . wine", struck through in pencil with a vertical use mark, is used in "Wealth," *W*, VI, 95.
    [30] See *JMN*, IX, 372.
    [31] Evidently a reminiscence of Waldo; see *JMN*, VIII, 163–164.

as the voice of a man; & he soon saw this mastiff wh⟨o⟩ich with an air of some captain of the watch went directly to a spot where he could best command the entrance of the yard, & there seated himself with a gruff resolution as if he would say — Now d⟨—⟩↑am↓n you! But the dream is irrevocable.

[19] ↑Well-born? or able?↓

The chief good of life seems, this morning, — to be born with a cheerful happy temper, & well adjusted to the tone of the human race: for such a man feels himself in the harmony of things, & conscious of an infinite strength. He need not do any thing. But if he is not well mixed & averaged, then he needs to achieve something, build a rail road, make a fortune, write an Iliad, as a compensation to himself for his abnormal position, & as we pinch ourselves to know that we are awake[.] [32]

↑See Temperament; below, p. 95↓

"He who wears a shoe, — 'tis the same as if the earth were covered with leather[.]"   And he who carpets a ship carpets the Atlantic.[33]

[20]   ↑Character↓

Lycurgus is not jelly, nor volatile salt, that must not be exposed to the open air. There is something in him which he cannot be laughed out of, nor argued out of, nor can he be terrified, nor bought off.

⟨(You cannot)⟩ In good society a fish is left to be a fish, and an opossum an opossum with all their elements & belongings, and not masqueraded into mannikins, as the circus riders do with dogs & horses & apes.

[21] *Arboretum*   should contain
          Sandal tree   Flowers
          Banian   Haemony

[32] "as we . . . awake" is struck through in ink with four vertical use marks.

[33] For " 'He who . . . leather' ", see *JMN*, VIII, 356 and 489, quoting *The Hĕĕtōpădēs of Vĕĕshnŏō-Sărmā, in a Series of Connected Fables, Interspersed with Moral, Prudential, and Political Maxims . . .* , trans. Charles Wilkins (Bath, 1787), p. 61, altered. " 'He who . . . Atlantic." is used in "Wealth," *W*, VI, 95.

Upas   Moly [34]
Magnolia

↑Continued p 38↓ [35]

[22]   Badge

A smooth hat and polished boots are badges as universally worn ↑by the young men↓ as the signs of guilds & classes in mediaeval Europe or in India, and yet we fancy we have no superstitions.

French cantine-women[:] red trowsers, short blue frock, & glazed hat [36]

[23] *Temperance*

In the Ballad of Lady Jane in Jamieson's Ballads. Vol II p 78 I find this verse;

> "O she has served the lang tables
> Wi' the white bread & the wine;
> But ay she drank the wan water,
> To keep her colour fine." [37]

"Charles XII late king of Sweden did not know what that was that others called fear; nor what that spurious valour & daring that is excited by inebriating draughts, for he never tasted any liquid but pure water. Of him we may say, that he led a life more remote from death, &, in fact, lived more than other men"

Swedenborg: E.A.K. Vol 1
p 192 [38]

Demosthenes drank fair water.

[24] Health, south wind, ↑books↓, old trees, a boat, a friend.

---

[34] "Flowers", "Haemony", and "Moly" appear to be additions, being in a darker ink.

[35] This addition is in pencil.

[36] "French . . . hat" is in pencil.

[37] Robert Jamieson, ed., *Popular Ballads and Songs*, 2 vols. (Edinburgh, 1806), borrowed from the Harvard College Library on January 14, 1847.

[38] Emanuel Swedenborg, *The Economy of the Animal Kingdom, Considered Anatomically, Physically, and Philosophically*, trans. Augustus Clissold, 2 vols. (London, 1845–1846), in Emerson's library. The quotation, struck through in pencil with a vertical use mark, is used in "Courage," *W*, VII, 267.

[25] ↑Mesmerism↓   ↑See O 346↓ [39]

I thought again of the avarice with which my man looks at the Insurance Office & would so fain be admitted to hear the gossip that goes forward there. For an hour to be invisible there & hear the best informed men retail their information he would pay great prices. But every company dissolves at his approach.[40] He so eager — & they so coy. A covey of birds do not rise more promptly from the ground when he comes near, than merchants, brokers, lawyers, disperse before him. ⟨Well⟩ He went into the tavern, he looked into the window of the grocery shop with the same covetous ears. They were so communicative, — they laughed aloud, — they whispered, they proclaimed ⟨aloud⟩ [41] their sentiment: — he opened the door — & the conversation received about that time a check, — & one after another went home. Boys & girls who had so much to say provoked scarcely less [26] curiosity, & were equally inaccessible to the un-magnetic man.

↑See again p 86↓
↑And R 105↓ [42]

[27] ⟨The ra⟩ Great men are much when you consider that the race goes, with us, on their credit. The knowledge that here & there in Boston is a man who has perception enough of relations of matter to have invented the magnetic telegraph & the use of sulphuric ether, raises the credit of all the similar organizations in caps & hats & hoods which throng that city.[43]

All the rest *when their wires are continued & not cut,* can do as much & as signal things, and in different parts of nature. What is a man but a centre for nature, made & meant to preside & to run out his ⟨subtle⟩ ↑fine↓ threads of relation through & through every thing subtle ⟨&⟩or solid, — material, ⟨&⟩or moral; and each according to his

---

[39] *JMN,* IX, 458.

[40] With this sentence, cf. "Considerations by the Way," *W,* VI, 269.

[41] The cancellation is in pencil.

[42] "See . . . 86" is in pencil. For Journal R, p. [105], see *JMN,* VIII, 398–399.

[43] Emerson's reference is to his brother-in-law, Dr. Charles T. Jackson; see *JMN,* IX, 172. This paragraph, struck through in ink with a wavy vertical use mark, is used in "Uses of Great Men," *W,* IV, 4.

quality to bring ⟨it⟩ ↑a↓ new part of nature into use by interpretation. ⟨The success of⟩ Justice has been done to [28] steam & to coal gas & to iodine, ↑to pears↓ & to iron for roads, ↑to loadstone,↓ & to ↑some↓ other things.⁴⁴ Now let the men, these arch-machines[,] be tenderly treated, & care taken that the wires are not cut, & communication will pass to all the other provinces, & chaos be reduced to order presently. Our hope is in the men.

See how much has been made of cotton, — one plant of 50 000 plants that make the flora of the globe. Every other one will have its turn.

‖epw‖   ↑J. Oswald Murray
                    Paris
                    [17] Rue de Beaux Arts↓ ⁴⁵

[29]⁴⁶ What is society? what has it? I answered The best of it is ↑(↓to speak mystically↑)↓ legs & feet. A man, a woman, a boy reared in it shall carry in his eye the expression of legs & feet, i.e. of centrality, of substantialness; & unless you have the same centrality shall throw you into the feeling that you are a stranger[.]

Greek architecture is geometry. Its temples are diagrams in marble & not appeals to the imagination like the Gothic. ↑powers of the square & cube↓

How can ↑we↓ hear children ask for a story or men for a novel or the theatre & not realize the necessity of the imagination in Education. We must have symbols.

———

[30] Now we feel out of doors as we do in a parlour with a high

———

⁴⁴ "What is a man . . . other things." is used in "Uses of Great Men," *W*, IV, 9.
⁴⁵ The addition is set off by a curved line, in ink. Emerson sat for a crayon portrait by Murray while in Paris during May of 1848. Following Murray's name are nine lines of erased penciled writing, in prose, of which the following words have been recovered: "The", "the", "in a Man . . . of a fish" [space]; "Plato thot a s . . . like a . . . to the . . . but was lifted on legs & feet by way of convenience to keep it out of the mud." See the following paragraph, on p. [29], which appears to incorporate part of the canceled phrasing.
⁴⁶ Pp. [29] and [30] are in pencil.

ceiling that we are little, but when our imaginations are addressed, & we are cultured, we shall not.

||epw|| [47]

In seeing them I do not see any escape yet from marriages & magistrates, said Alcott[.]

Whilst there are no capacious rooms & no statues & pictures a man is not yet properly dressed. It is as if he should come with only his shirt on[.]

[31] Swendenborg calls crabs, dogs, bees, birds, &c. which find their way living magnets[.]

[32] Willie resisted the cherrybirds ⟨with⟩ ↑by↓ swinging scraps of tin suspended from the boughs of his cherry trees, with red rags & with stones. But one day going to the woods he noticed loud chatter & whistling of birds. As he approached the thicket, one or two birds rose, & seeing him, began to say as intelligibly as birds could, "Aha! Aha Willie!" Immediately, as if understanding their note, the whole flock rose & with a note that seemed almost to laugh, cried, "Aha, ⟨a⟩Aha, Willie!" Willie was so struck with this strange familiarity that he himself exclaimed

> Well away sing, it one thing shows me
> Ah Willie! camest thou here?
> Every bird in Concord knows me
> How they scorn me far or near! [48]

[33] ↑Morals↓

There came a man to us with great doctrines of faith & self denial. He performed on one occasion a generous bold action, & never another: and, after gradually losing his faith, he went away

---

[47] Of three lines of prose only the last three words have been recovered: "Latin or jingle"; cf. the last sentence on p. [47] below.

[48] Except for part of the initial "H" and the concluding exclamation point, the fourth line of the quatrain is in pencil.

a much less man than he came. I have seen another person in whom faith has been long on the decline. And one who steadily increases. The moral must be the measure of health. If your eye is on the eternal, your intellect will steadily grow, & all your estimates, conclusions & actions will ⟨be full⟩ have a genius & beauty which no learning or combined advantages of other men can rival. The moment of your loss of faith & acceptance of the lucrative standard will be marked in the ⟨loss⟩ pause, the solstice of genius, & the sequent retrogression. And the inevitable loss of attraction to other minds.

[34] The vulgar are sensible of the change in you, & of your descent, though they clap you on your back, & congratulate you on your increased common sense.[49]

[35]   List of Books
                         ─────────────
───

Conversations of James Northcote by W. Hazlitt.[50]

───

The Prose or Younger Edda commonly ascribed to Snorri Sturluson translated from the Old Norse by G. W. Dasent, London. W. Pickering.
        1842 [51]

───

Von Hammer [52]

Heimskringla [53]

---

[49] "The moral . . . sense.", struck through in ink with a vertical use mark on p. [33] and with two vertical use marks on p. [34], is used in "Worship," W, VI, 218.

[50] William Hazlitt, *Conversations of James Northcote, Esq., R.A.* (London, 1830).

[51] Published in Stockholm and London; in Emerson's library.

[52] Emerson's library includes two volumes by Baron Joseph von Hammer-Purgstall (1774–1856), the Austrian Oriental scholar: (1) his translation of Hafiz, *Der Diwan von Mohammed Schemsed-din Hafis*, 2 vols. (Stuttgart and Tübingen, 1812–1813), and (2) his *Geschichte der schönen redekünste Persiens, mit einer Blüthenlese aus zweyhundert persischen Dichtern* (Wien, 1818).

[53] *The Heimskringla; or, Chronicle of the Kings of Norway*, trans. from the Icelandic of Snorro Sturleson by Samuel Laing, 3 vols. (London, 1844). Emerson bought this work in England: see Journal London, p. [207] below.

Life of Wm. of Wykeham, by Lowth [54]

[36] [blank]
[37] March 3.

At Lincoln, last night, read a lecture in the schoolhouse. The architect had a brighter thought than ordinary there. He had felicitously placed the door at the right of the desk, so that when the orator is just making a point and just ready to drive the last nail, the door opens at his side & Mr Hagar & Deacon Sanborn & Captain Peck come in, & ↑amiably↓ divide with him the attention of the company. Luckily the sleighbells, as they drove up to the door, were a premonitory symptom, & I was able to rein in my genius a little, whilst these late arrivers were bundling out & stamping their feet before they ⟨riveted on themselves⟩ ↑usurped↓ the attention of the house.

[38] *Greenhouse*

Put Dittany in your greenhouse[;] asphodel, lotus, nepenthe; moly,
        poppy, rue, selfheal
        ⟨moly,⟩ haemony,
        euphrasy,   acanthus.

He hoed the desart — his potatoes were poled — his asparagus grew to trees — his melons & gourds ran for miles, & had roots like oak-trees.[55]

[39]   *Orchard*
———

        Baldwin's fruit in the even years

———

        Curculio first appears, say, 20 May.

In the Arboretum at Chatsworth [56] is the Amherstia Nobilis, to procure which the Duke sent a special agent to India ⟨to procure⟩.

---

[54] Robert Lowth, *The Life of William of Wykeham, Bishop of Winchester* . . . (London, 1758).
[55] See *JMN*, VIII, 190; "Concord Walks," *W*, XII, 174.
[56] The mansion of the dukes of Devonshire, in Derbyshire, England.

and pinus Douglassii
and pinus Nobilis

My Warren field measures   363 ft. from the road to the brook,
along my old fence,
   〈Fr〉Along the road the line is   293 ft and contains 2¼ acres,
      feet.[57]

            For Hedge〈'〉s, Rhamnus Catharticus & 2 000 plants
            to 1 000 feet.

[40]   Orchard, Land, &c
H.D.T[horeau]. finds my boundary of woodlot on Walden Pond
to measure 130 rods.

      Memorandum
26 April 1847. I set out by the hands of John Hosmer & John
Garrison & Anthony Colombe in the Warren-lot 24 apple trees〈,〉
and 40 pear trees; and six apple trees in the east side of the heater
piece.   = 70 trees.[58]

      ↑*Pears*

            3 to J Moore
            1 to Frank Brown
            〈2〉3 to S Ripley
            2 to J. Hosmer
            4 to J. M. Cheney
            5 to W. Munroe

[57] Emerson had bought nearly three acres of land from Cyrus Warren on January
6, 1847; he took possession on April 1 (*L*, III, 371, n. 9). Cf. *JMN*, VIII, 545,
and Journal CD, p. [74] below.
   [58] In December of 1838 Emerson had bought the lot of land he called "the
heater piece" because its triangular shape resembled that of a "heater" for a flatiron.
With this memorandum, cf. *JMN*, VIII, 545, an entry in Notebook Trees[A:II]:
"1847, April 26 J. Hosmer set out for me 24 appletrees in the Warren lot   6 apples
trees in the east side of the heater piece, and 40 pears in Warren lot"; the present
entry suggests that Hosmer had the assistance of Garrison and Colombe, both local
laborers.

3 to B Frost
2 to J. S. Keyes
40 set out

11

remaining in Nursery↓ [59]

[41] Alcott wishes to call together the Club of Notables again. But the old objection recurs: Better let your tongue lie still till it forgets its office, than undertake for God before he calls you. Thence comes Charlatanism[,] Unitarianism. "If the other train do not arrive," said Mr Superintendent of the ⟨s⟩Single-track Rail Road, "⟨r⟩do not move until your wheels rust off." And many a life was saved by his tyrannical caution.

We lie for the right.

[42]   ↑*On the Beauties of Concealment.*↓

I have a question to propose to the company. Whether it is worth any man's while to relax any private rule. If he has drank water, why should he not drink wine?[n] If he finds it best to add mortgages & securities to the good strength of love; to pray and also keep his powder dry; ⟨to⟩prayer, but also manure[.]

What is the harm of a little indulgence, so it be decent — that is — secret?

Why nothing; an imbecility is the only consequence. And that does not signify, does it? To remain a boy, an old boy at 50 years. He covered up all his particular frauds, but ⟨his sharp face he did not.⟩ they made his face sharp. He concealed as well as he could all his effeminate & cowardly habits, but [43] they made him cowering, & threw him on the Whig side, & he looked irritable & shy, & on his guard in public.

The aspect of that man is repulsive. I do not wish to have anything to do with him.

This other youth looks humble & manly. I choose him.

[59] The list headed "Pears" is in pencil. The persons named as recipients of pear trees are Concord neighbors of Emerson; John Moore, J. M. Cheney, and William Munroe are also mentioned in Notebook Trees[A:II]; see *JMN*, VIII, 536, 537.

Look at this woman[.] ⟨a⟩Thereⁿ is no beauty, nor longer any youth; there are no brilliant sayings; no ⟨spec⟩ distinguished power to serve you. Yet she seems wholesome. Her whole air & impression are respectable, and all see her gladly.

I suppose all these are the secret biographies.[60]

Babyish people

[44] On the Power of Insanities, or the blinding of men by their talents. The ⟨Boston⟩ New York men dwell in delusions: the poor countryman having no system of carpets, carriages, dinners, wine, & dancing, in his head to confuse him, is able to look straight at you without refraction or prismatic glories; and he sees whether you look straight also, or whether your head is addled by all this mixture of wines.[61]   ↑See p 77↓

[45] [62] Concord had certain roads & waste places which were much valued for their beauty but which were difficult to find. There was one which whoso entered could not forget, — but he had more than common luck if he ever found it again, let him search for it with his best diligence. ↑Run boy from the swamp beside the lake to the big hemlock where a chestnut has been chopped down ↑at↓ twelve feet high from the ground then leave the high wood road & take the ox path to the right; — pass one ⟨tur⟩right hand turn, & take the second, & run down a valley with long prairie hay covering it close; an old felled pine-tree lies along the valley, follow it down till the birds do not retreat before you; then t⟨h⟩ill the ⟨m⟩faint daymoon rides nearer; then till the valley is a ravine with the hills of Nobscot seen at the bottom of it across the Bay↓ [63]

---

[60] "The aspect . . . biographies.", struck through in ink with a series of three vertical use marks, is used in "Behavior," W, VI, 184–185.

[61] This paragraph, struck through in pencil with a vertical use mark, is used in "The Superlative," W, X, 169.

[62] Laid in between pp. [44] and [45] is an offprint of a two-column essay by Rev. Charles F. Barnard on Joseph Tuckerman (1778–1840), who had been a Unitarian "minister at large" among "the poor and the neglected classes" of Boston.

[63] The place marker described in the bibliographical headnote to Journal AB, reading "Concord[']s Enchanted Places", probably refers to this passage. In J, VII, 249–250, n. 1, Edward Emerson wrote: "In this route given to the boy, though fancifully treated, can be traced a walk to which Mr. Emerson once took his

[46] I value morals because it gives me something to do today. It enhances all my property. The foreign has lost its charm. The beauty of my youth has come back. I woke up ↑⟨the⟩one↓ [64] morning & find the ice in my pond promised to be a revenue. It was as if somebody had proposed to buy the air that blew over my field. Well, it should have taught me that my richest revenues were in fasting & abstaining, in enduring & waiting, in bearing insult & rendering good service. Can you go to Boston in the cars tomorrow & come back at night safe & not degraded?

Purpose[,] tendency I have learned to value & nothing else. Have you made the life of man clearer of any snag or sawyer? [47] Is Marriage righted? this despicable conservatism defied? Is your love, your freedom, the love & the freedom of all souls? & not a screened corner of self indulgence? Are you clear with your expen⟨s⟩diture? Do you pay for the Church? for the state, and its wars, & slaves?

They who are in Boston ⟨a⟩up to their breasts or up to their chins, it does not signify that with their heads still aloft over the stream they cry aloud that it is dirty, & that they prefer the land.

The basis of reformers & poets is mercantile. ⟨wh⟩What signifies then a little Latin or jingle? [65]

[48] I think the whole use in literature is the moral. Men may well come together to confirm their confidence in goodness. A.B.A[lcott]. well said that the club might well meet if it would have the effect to send them all home dispirited.

Morals differ from intellectuals in being instantly intelligible to all men.

   "Farewell, Thomas, I wend my way
   I may no longer stand with thee

---

children from the southern bank of Walden, beside the swamp by the railroad into which the pond drains under the glacial moraine, and thence down the little brook, named by Mr. Channing the Sanguinetto, to its outlet into that enlargement of the river under the cliffs, called Fairhaven Bay."

[64] Emerson wrote "the" in ink; "one" is written over "the" in pencil — possibly by Edward Emerson.

[65] An earlier version of this entry was written in pencil on p. [30] and erased.

Give me some token, my lady gay,
That I may say I spake with thee

To harp & carp,* ⟨Thomas,⟩ where so ever ye gone,   * talk
Thomás, take th⟨|| . . . ||⟩ou these with thee.↑" — ↓

"Harping", he said, $\frac{\text{"ken}}{\text{kepe}}$ I none,

For tongue is chief of minstrelsy."↑ — ↓

↑ — "↓If thou will $\frac{\text{spell,}}{\text{spae}}$ or talés tell,

Thomas, thou shàlt make never lye;
Wheresoever thou go to frith or fell
I pray thee speak never no ill of me." [66]

[49] [67]   Eloquence
And let it be well considered in Eloquence that what we praise
& allow is only relatively good, & that perhaps a person is there
present who, if he would, could ⟨make all th⟩ unsettle all that we
have just now agreed on. We have fallen into a poor beggarly way
of living, & our orators are of the same poverty & deal in rags & cold.
The imagination, the great awakening power, the morals, the great
creator of genius & men, are not addressed. But though the orators &
poets are of this jejune rule of three faction, the capacities remain.
The child asks you for a story! & is ⟨inparadised as soon as you give
him⟩ ↑thankful for↓ the poorest. It is not poor to him but a symbol
all radiant with meaning. The man asks you for a novel? that is,
asks you for leave to be a poet, & to paint things as they ought to be
for a few hours.

[50]   ↑Eloquence↓

The youth asks for a poem[.]

The stupidest wish to go to the theatre[.]

---

[66] Thomas of Erceldoune ("Thomas the Rhymer"), "True Thomas, and the
Queen of Elfland: The Second Fytte," in Robert Jamieson, ed., *Popular Ballads and
Songs*, 1806, II, 27. These verses, found also in Scott's *Ministrelsy of the Scottish
Border*, "were favorites with Mr. Emerson" (*J*, VII, 251, n. 1).
   [67] This page is in pencil.

We must have idolatries, mythologies, some swing & verge for the eternal & creative power lying coiled & cramped here driving us to insanity of crime if it do not find vent.[68]

Examples of sarcasm are Brougham on the Bishops   see *W* p. 45 and O'Connell on D'Israeli; O, p. 98 [69]

———

Wait till the noisy speaker has done, & then leave him out in your reply. Laws of the world in this also   J 79 [70]

———

    Debate not quite useless.   J 111 [71]

Eloquence is to stablish those moods. America has no masculine genius: Or it is the country of Emancipation & Genius. Poverty is the devil or the ⟨Angels⟩ seraphim as we look. These cars, then go back or forward with equal celerity, are built so.[72]

Representativeness of good speakers. O 91.[73]

    [51] "Plum cake ate itself & did not live a minute," says Edie[.] [74]

What shall I say of a costly skill in Eloquence⟨.⟩ we have not seen? a Master who should play on an assembly as a Musician on a Piano: who seeing the temper of the people furious, should soften & compose them; seeing them dull, should know how to inflame them; seeing them reckless & animalized, should call out the imagination & the Intellect; and so should bring them at will into that key which

---

[68] "The youth . . . vent." is in pencil. "We haven fallen . . . vent.", struck through in pencil on pp. [49] and [50] with single vertical use marks, is used in "Books," *W*, VII, 212–213.

[69] See *JMN*, IX, 201 (Brougham) and 387 (O'Connell).

[70] "J 79" is set off by diagonal lines in ink. See *JMN*, VIII, 170–171.

[71] See *JMN*, VIII, 184.

[72] "Eloquence . . . so." is in pencil. In the final sentence, "then" is circled in pencil.

[73] See *JMN*, IX, 385.

[74] Emerson's daughter Edith, born in 1841.

he desired. Show him his audience, he carries their hearts in his mouth, & they shall carry & execute that verdict he pronounces.[75]

[52]   Life, Biography, might say

Young man never finds that thing which he has to say quite appropriate   ↑J 31↓ [76]

———

All sensible men selfish and like to play Providence & judge of law and fact

———

of the courages ↑p. 101↓ [77]

Will.   Freedom
All sensible men are selfish & like to play Providence, & judge of law & fact.

[53]   *Opportunity*
What need have I, said the poet, to cross the sill of my door? The Genius whispers me by night & I report it to the young men at morn: I ride in them who hear me: I traverse sea & land in those missionaries. The Engineer in the locomotive is waiting for me: the steamboat at the wharf is hissing, & the wheels already whirling to go.
                    See also end of the Lecture on Eloquence [78]

What need has he[,] the man of thought[,] to meddle with politics? If he thinks it a⟨n⟩t midnight before morning 'tis on its way to all mankind.[79]

---

[75] "What shall . . . pronounces.", in pencil and struck through in pencil with a vertical use mark, is used in "Eloquence," *W*, VII, 65.

[76] See *JMN*, VIII, 157–158.

[77] "Life . . . p. 101" is in pencil. With "All sensible . . . fact", cf. *JMN*, IX, 379, 383.

[78] Emerson had read his lecture on "Eloquence" in Cambridge, Mass., on December 16, 1846.

[79] "What need have . . . Eloquence", struck through in pencil with one vertical and one curved diagonal use mark, and "What need has . . . mankind.", struck through in pencil with a vertical use mark, are used in "The Scholar," *W*, X, 269–270.

[54] *Swedenborg* [80]

"If the mind be well-connected with the organs of the senses, or, in other words, if man be truly rational," — says Swedenborg in the first sentence of the *"Principia"*.[81]   ↑|See above p 27↓

"that first of mortals who is said to have been in a state of perfect integrity,   i.e.   who was formed according to all the art image & connexion of the world, before the existence of vice"   *Principia* [I,] p. 34

"the conti/n/g/uity being then complete all the mundane system must have been familiar to him after a little contemplation & custom." [Cf. *ibid*., I,] p. 40

Before the *wires were cut* every thing that transpired was immediately apparent to him at the centre through his sensations[.] [82]

[55]   Swedenborg
    See the *Moral Suites* p. 44 *"Principia."*

"He found," says ⟨Clissold⟩ ↑Wilkinson↓, "that nature is no other than philosophy & theology embodied in mechanics: or, more reverently speaking, she is the mechanism or means of which truth & good are the end."

                         Econ. An. Kingd.
————————   Introd. Essay [vol. II,] p lxxvii [83]

---

[80] In a letter of March 25, 1847, to Samuel Gray Ward, Emerson remarked that he had been reading "little but Swedenborg" — probably to revise his lecture on Swedenborg "in preparation for England," as Rusk conjectures (*L*, III, 387).

[81] Emanuel Swedenborg, *The Principia; or, The First Principles of Natural Things, Being New Attempts Toward a Philosophical Explanation of the Elementary World*, trans, Augustus Clissold, 2 vols. (London, 1845–1846), I, i; in Emerson's library.

[82] For the italicized phrase, see p. [27] above.

[83] Emanuel Swedenborg, *The Economy of the Animal Kingdom*, trans. Augustus Clissold, 1845–1846; both the Preface and the Introductory Essay by the Editor are bound at the end of the second volume. Emerson's substitution of "Wilkinson" for "Clissold" apparently reflects a statement in the Preface, II, vii–viii, that "Mr. Wilkinson . . . is responsible for the . . . Introductory Remarks." James John Garth Wilkinson had translated *The Animal Kingdom* by Swedenborg, 2 vols. (London, 1843–1844), also in Emerson's library.

Nature

↑Truth stranger than fiction↓ [84]

↑"Almost↓ as ⁿ large a demand ⟨is⟩upon our faith is made by nature as by miracles themselves." Swedenborg E[conomy]. A[nimal]. K[ing-dom] Vol. 1, p 188

"Indeed" he proceeds "it seems as if when proceeding ⟨through⟩ from first principles through her several subordinations there were no state thro' which she did not pass, or, as if her path lay thro' all things[.]" [85]

[56]   Swedenborg
See "Econ. An. K." p. 7 & 8 for S's reasons for using the observations of other men, & not his own.
     Same thing in Econ A.K. Vol II p 207

Arterial blood is courage & life &c[—] an important passage
                                   Econ. A K
                                   Vol I p[p.] 191–2

———

Passage concerning Hans Sloane & the bird ⟨is⟩I find in "Angelic Wisdom concerning the Divine Love & the Divine Wisdom" p 163.[86]
—But it does not seem to me the same passage which I read as quoted in N[ew]. J[erusalem]. Magazine.—

———

[57] The one-legged race of trees [87]

[84] Inserted in pencil. Cf. Byron, *Don Juan*, XIV, ci; see *JMN*, VI, 191.

[85] " 'Almost . . . things' ", struck through in ink with a vertical use mark, is used in "Swedenborg," *W*, IV, 112–113; another version of " 'Almost . . . them-selves.' " is used in "Demonology," *W*, X, 12.

[86] Emanuel Swedenborg, *Angelic Wisdom Concerning the Divine Love and the Divine Wisdom* (Boston, 1847), pp. 179–180; in Emerson's library. Swedenborg, in paragraph 344, reports that he had "heard two presidents of the English Royal Society, Sir Hans Sloane and Martin Folkes, conversing together in the spiritual world." By the appearance of "a beautiful bird" that represented "an affection of some angel," Swedenborg explains, "Sir Hans Sloane was convinced that . . . plants and animals . . . are produced solely by what flows into the natural world out of the spiritual world."

[87] The hyphen in "one-legged" is added in pencil.

[58] Every science serves an apprenticeship to some elder art before it sets up for itself. Chemistry served the[88] apothecary & physician, then the cook, ⟨then⟩ manufacturer &c until now it is itself a science. Astronomy served navigation, surveying, and fortune-telling[.][89]

[59] [blank]
[60]   ↑Scholar↓
The Scholar's courage may be measured by his power to give an opinion of Aristotle, Bacon, Jordano Bruno, Swedenborg, Fourier. If he has nothing to say to these systems let him not pretend to skill in reading.

[61]   Scholar
[c. March 25, 1847.][90] We must have society, provocation, a whip for the top. A Scholar is a candle which the love & desire of men will light. Let it not lie in a dark box.[91] But here am I with so much all ready to be revealed to me as to others if only I could be set aglow. I have wished for a professorship. Much as I hate the church, I have wished the pulpit that I might have the stimulus of a ⟨task⟩ stated task. N. P. Rogers spoke more truly than he knew, perchance, when he recommended an Abolition-Campaign to me. I doubt not, a course of mobs would do me ⟨a world of⟩ ↑much↓ good.[92] A snowflake will go through a pine board, if projected with force enough. I have almost come to depend on conversation for my pro-

[88] Following "the" is what is possibly a Greek "φ" but is probably a false start, enclosed in penciled parentheses for tentative cancellation.
[89] The hyphen is added in pencil.
[90] There are close correspondences in phrasing between the entry which follows and passages of Emerson's letter of this date to Samuel Gray Ward (L, III, 387–388).
[91] "We must . . . box." is struck through in pencil with one vertical and one diagonal use mark. "A Scholar . . . light." is used in "Society and Solitude," W, VII, 11.
[92] Cf. Journal AZ, p. [155]: "A course of mobs was recommended to me by N. P. Rogers to correct my quaintness and transcendentalism." Rogers (1794–1846) was an Abolition journalist; A Collection from the Newspaper Writings of Nathaniel Peabody Rogers (Concord, N.H., 1847) is in Emerson's library. "I doubt . . . good.", struck through in pencil with a vertical use mark, is used in "Power," W, VI, 78.

lific hours. I who converse with so few & those of no adventure, connexion, or wide information [62].ⁿ — A man must be connected. [of Continuity see O, 202] [93] He must be clothed with society, or we shall feel a certain bareness & poverty, as of a displaced[,] disfurnished person. — He is to be drest in arts, picture-galleries, sculpture, architecture, institutions, as well as in body garments.[94] Pericles, Plato, Caesar, Shakspeare, will not appoint us an interview in a hovel. ↑—↓ ↑—↓ [95] My friends would yield more to a new companion. In this emergency, one advises Europe, & especially England. If I followed my own advices, — ⟨I should⟩if I were master of a liberty to do so — I should sooner go toward Canada. I should withdraw myself for a time from all domestic & accustomed relations & command an absolute leisure with books — for a time.

I think I have material enough to serve my countrymen with thought & music, if only it were not scraps. But men do not want handfuls of gold dust, but ingots. ↑See p. 123↓ [96]

[63] The name of Washington ↑City↓ in the newspapers is every day of blacker shade. All the news from that quarter being of a sadder type, more malignant. It seems to be ⟨a⟩ settled that no act of honor or benevolence or justice is to be expected from the American Government, but only this, that they will be as wicked as they dare. No man now can have any sort of success in politics without a streak of infamy crossing his name.

Things have another order in these men's eyes. ⟨Solid⟩ ↑Heavy↓ is ⟨light⟩ ↑hollow↓ & good is evil. A western man in Congress the other day spoke of the opponents of the Texan & Mexican plunder as "Every light character in the house," & our good friend in State street speaks of "the solid portion of the community" [64]ⁿ meaning, or course, the sharpers. I feel, meantime, that those who succeed in life, in civilized society, are beasts of prey. It has always been so.

[93] *JMN*, IX, 414.
[94] "He must . . . garments.", struck through in pencil with a vertical use mark, is used in "Society and Solitude," *W*, VII, 10.
[95] Following "hovel." Emerson inserted a pair of dashes in ink, at least one of which was evidently intended to close up space and so to cancel the paragraph-beginning, at "My", that originally followed.
[96] The insertion is set off by a diagonal line in ink following "ingots."

The Demostheneses, the Phocions, the Aristideses, the Washingtons even, must bear that deduction that they were not pure souls, or they would not have been fishers & gunners. They had large infusions of virtue, & hence their calamities & the mischievous dignity they have lent to the rogues that belong in those piratical employments.

↑See "Talleyrand" in V↓ [97]

[65]   *Topics* [98]
On the Solstice of Genius
On the function of the devil's attorney.
On the progressive value of money. ↑See p. 15, &↓ ↑O. 10,↓ [99]
On the difference of power in men to make transits. ↑See p 104↓ [100]
On stimulation, or a whip for the top. p 61, 62, ↑123↓
On opportunity. 53,
On paint.   ↑Great is paint.↓
Why have the minority no influence? ↑p. 122,↓

[66] We are necessary partialists; such halves; men of war are birds of prey; & success is an infamy. Yet we that are in the Academy, are impatient of that, & of each other, & see no spheral men[.]

We live in Lilliput. The Americans are free willers, fussy, self asserting, buzzing all round creation. But the Asiatics believe it is writ on the iron leaf & will not turn on their heel to save them from famine, plague, or sword. That is great, gives a great air to the people[.] [101]

We live in Lilliput. Men are unfit to live, from their obvious inequality to their own necessities, or they suffer from politics or

---

[97] See *JMN*, IX, 176–178.
[98] Cf. the preliminary listing on p. [1] above.
[99] See *JMN*, IX, 361.
[100] The addition is in pencil.
[101] Parts of this and the following paragraph are written in ink over some eight lines of almost wholly erased pencil writing; a few recovered words match the phrasing of this paragraph.

from sickness, & they would gladly know that they were to be dismissed from the duties of life.

[67] Now let these people know that when they die they are not dismissed. ⟨When they die they catch a Tartar⟩ They shall not wish for death out of pusillanimity: but the weight of the Universe is pressed down on the shoulders of each slave to hold him to his task: the only path of escape is Virtue. Cause & Effect are the gamesters who win and it will beget a resignation to Fate that even the Americans will be exalted.[102]

↑Printed↓

[68] ‖epw‖ [103]

———

Transit   to make perfect transits [104]

———

[69] Blame yourself. You do not obey your genius; how should they obey it? You have Intellect & ⟨employ it⟩ use it for a puppet show. Can they use it as an oracle?
He is only in fun!
Duties of the intellect   majestic duties
The Conscience of the Intellect
                    ↑See R 68   J 95↓ [105]
        ↑We do not absorb thoughts or adequately receive them
                                                    W 120↓
                    ↑U 109↓ [106]

[70] The question recurs whether we should descend into the ring. My own very small experience instructs me that the people are

[102] "Men are . . . exalted.", struck through in ink with vertical use marks on pp. [66] and [67], is used in "Worship," W, VI, 239–240. An earlier version of this material was first written in pencil on pp. [66] and [67] and then erased.
[103] Apparently a continuation of the matter written in pencil on p. [67]. Of four lines of prose, only part of the final line has been recovered: "& fixed except in . . . Cause."
[104] This entry and the enclosing rules are in pencil.
[105] See JMN, VIII, 379, 177.
[106] See JMN, IX, 239, 62.

to be taken in very small doses. Vestry meetings & primary assemblies do not edify me. And I caution philosophers & scholars to use lenses & media.

[71] Articulateness, finished extremities, complete development, is Man.
A snake is ⟨his⟩ Man's spine, make the head a new spine only for a new evolution and open every vertebra into ribs and each extremity as ⟨arm or leg⟩ shoulder or thigh into a new spine for new evolution of extremities & we have Man[.] [107]

[72]   *Club*   Café Procope
Theology, Medicine, Law, Politics, Trade have their meetings & assembly rooms. Literature has none. See how magnificently the Merchants meet in State street. Every Bank & Insurance office is a Palace, & Literature has not a poor café, not a corner even of Mrs Haven's shop [108] ↑in which↓ ⟨in.⟩ By a little alliance with some of the rising parties of the time, as the Socialists, & the Abolitionists, and the Artists, we might accumulate a sufficient patronage to establish a good room in Boston. ↑As Ellery Channing says there is not a chair in all Boston where I can sit down.↓ [109]

[73] Alcott said, The rest of the man will follow his head. His head is not his contemporary, but his ancestor & predecessor. Let him be a Cause.

[74] Here, said the foreigner, your astronomy is an espionage. I dare not go out of doors & see the moon or stars, but they seem to ask me how many lines or pages are finished since I saw them last. Not so as I told you was it in Mull. [110]   ↑printed↓   ↑See GH 66↓

---

[107] This paragraph is in pencil. The theme is elaborated in "Swedenborg," *W*, IV, 107.
[108] The Boston *Almanac* for 1848 lists M. F. Haven, 38 Cambridge Street, a dressmaker.
[109] This sentence, struck through in ink with four vertical use marks, is used in "Clubs," *W*, VII, 244.
[110] This paragraph, struck through in ink with a diagonal use mark, is used in "Works and Days," *W*, VII, 181. See also Notebook JK, p. [42] below.

> Forever where the trees grow biggest
> Huntsmen find the easiest way [111]

[75] I hate vulnerable people[.]

To the lonely his loneliness ⟨give⟩ yield[.] [112]

[76]   Ancients & Moderns
The ancients brought the fire, the moderns collect ⟨the⟩ coal⟨s⟩.

[77] It becomes those who want animal spirits ⟨never to⟩to take the low tone; never to take the initiative. Such are chameleons, &, in the presence of the wise, they are transparent & serene; in the presence of the worldly, they are turbid & weak.

Superlative

———

Let others grumble that they see no faeries nor muses, I rejoice that my eyes see the ⟨erect eternal⟩ ↑real↓ world always ⟨the same⟩ ↑stable↓ & erect, without blur or halo.[113] ↑See p 44↓

———

When my man loses a tooth, he thinks the universal thaw & dissolution of things is now at hand.
(Choate's stupendous peculiarity) [114]

———

[111] These two lines of verse, struck through in ink with a diagonal use mark, are used in "Quatrains," *W*, IX, 291.

[112] Emerson both canceled "give" and also wrote "yield" in pencil.

[113] This sentence, struck through in pencil with a vertical use mark, is used in "The Superlative," *W*, X, 166. See also *JMN*, IX, 24; Notebook JK, p. [17] below.

[114] "When my . . . peculiarity)", struck through in pencil with a vertical use mark, is used in "The Superlative," *W*, X, 164. In his index for Journal AB Emerson cited this page under Osman — i.e., "my man." No source for the name Osman is known. Emerson uses it to designate the ideal man and, more often, the ideal poet. As indicated by identifications in Index Minor[A], p. [162], Jones Very was sometimes a model for this figure. Contexts suggest that Osman is at times autobiographical: in Journal O, Emerson indexed p. [199] (printed in *JMN*, IX, 413–414) under both Autobiography and Osman, though Osman is not mentioned on the page. See *JMN*, VIII, 4, n. 4.

See Hafiz's superlative.

———

See O 323, 364

———

Superlative of contraries ⟨3⟩O 323 [115] ↑CD 62↓ ˙

[78]   Horoscope

They have given each but one chance, and that is in his brain.

⟨L⟩ ↑When↓ he comes forth from his mother's womb, the gate of gifts closes behind him.

Let him value his hands & feet[,] he has but one pair.[116]

[79] ↑Police↓

Nature has taken good care of us. She knew what rowdies & tigers she was making & she created a police first in the Conscience, then in the ⟨fea⟩preaching propensity, which she gave indifferently to the worst and to the decent; & lastly in the terror of gossip with which she cowed the boldest heart. ↑God has delegated himself to a thousand deputies↓[.] [117]

The virtue of Democrats is to rail against England, the Lowell companies, & Mr Webster's pension.

[80]   Scholar

Centrality Centrality. "Your reading is ⟨impertinent.⟩ ↑irrelevant.↓" Yes, for you, but not for me. It makes no difference what I read. If it is irrelevant, I read it deeper. I read it until it is pertinent to

---

[115] For the passages in Journal O, see *JMN*, IX, 448, 466, 448.

[116] P. [78] was first written in pencil, then rewritten in ink. "When . . . pair.", struck through in ink with a diagonal use mark, is used in "Fate," *W*, VI, 10–11. The first sentence — "a quotation from one of the Oriental writers," as Edward Emerson noted (*W*, VI, 340) — is also adapted in the quatrain "Horoscope," *W*, IX, 294.

[117] "& she created . . . deputies", struck through in ink with a diagonal use mark, is used in "Worship," *W*, VI, 222–223. There is also a wavy vertical use mark through "& she . . . propensity," and a short diagonal use mark through "which she . . . deputies".

me & mine, to nature & to the hour that now passes. A good scholar will find Aristophanes & Hafiz & Rabelais full of American history.[118]

I believe in Omnipresence & find footsteps in Grammar rules, in oyster shops, in church liturgies, ⟨as⟩ in mathematics, ⟨as readily as⟩ ↑and↓ in solitudes & ↑in↓ galaxies. I am shamed out of my declamations against churches by the wonderful beauty of the English liturgy, an anthology of the piety of ages & nations[.] [119]

[81] *Courage*

I have written in different places of the courage pertinent to Scholars. The Greeks seem to have had a fine audacity as in Aristophanes. I remember the saying of Brumoy (?) that the Greeks believed that the gods understood fun as well or better than men, & therefore the comic writers did not hesitate to joke the gods also pretty hardly.

Courage

Here is a man who loves fight. "Stranger, will you liquor?" "No." "Then perhaps you will fight." ⟨But⟩Our Kentuckian cannot see a⟨nother⟩ man of good figure but he thinks he should like to break his back over an iron banister, or give him a fall that would finish him. But the other man ⟨tho⟩cannot see the sun or stars without the wish to wrestle with them, & here is Descartes, Kepler, ↑Newton,↓ Swedenborg, Laplace, ↑Schelling,↓ who wish to wrestle with the problem of Genesis & [82] [120] occupy themselves with constructing Cosmogonies. ⟨It is plain that this⟩ Nature is saturated with deity, ⟨that⟩ the particle is saturated with the elixir of the Universe. Little

---

[118] There is a wavy pencil line in the right margin beside this paragraph — possibly a use mark.

[119] This sentence, struck through in ink with a vertical use mark and four shorter vertical use marks, is used in "Shakspeare," *W*, IV, 200.

[120] In the manuscript, "A man . . . long again." stands at the top of the page, set off above and below with ink lines. When Emerson expanded the comments on "Courage" that begin on p. [81] he followed "A man . . . long again." with "occupy themselves . . . their brain." and wrote above the new material: *"see last page"* — i.e., p. [81] — and the index heading *"Cosmogonies"*. The entry "Here is . . . their brain." beginning on p. [81] has been printed as an unbroken unit, with "A man . . . long again." following it.

men just born, Copernicise. They cannot radiate as suns or revolve as planets, and so they do it in effigy, by building the orrery in their brain.[121]

A man complained that in his way home to dinner he had every day to pass through that long field of his neighbor's. I advised him to buy it, & it would never seem long again.

[83]   *Compensation*

———

"Equation of quantity & quality in the fluids."
Swedenborg   E.A.K. Vol I p 189 [122]

———

↑See-saw, W 122.↓ [123]

———

If capital punishment is abolished, private vengeance comes in. If Eng[land]., France, America are forbidden war with each other, they spend their ferocity on Sikhs, Algerines, & Mexicans & so find a vent for their piratical population. You shall not as feudal lords kill the ⟨ch⟩ serfs, but now as capitalists you shall in all love & peace eat them up as before.[124]

———

We devour Mexico as the stomach arsenic, but it brings us down at last.[125]

———

"What living creature slays or is slain? What living creature(s)

---

[121] "Newton" and "Schelling" are inserted in pencil.
[122] Emanuel Swedenborg, *The Economy of the Animal Kingdom*, trans. Augustus Clissold, 1845–1846.
[123] See *JMN*, IX, 240–241.
[124] See *JMN*, IX, 424–425.
[125] Cf. *JMN*, IX, 430–431.

preserves or is preserved? Each is his own destroyer or preserver as he follows evil or good." Vishnu Purana p 135 [126]

———

[84]   *Compensation*
Every intellectual advantage bought at the expense of manhood. Lumpers better than grocers. In the fine clerical water party the skipper of the boat the only man.[127]

[85] [blank]
[86] ↑*Mesmerism*↓   ↑(See also *supra* p. 25, & ↑O 346↓ [128])↓
We want society on our own terms. Each man has facts ↑that↓ I want, &, though I talk with him, I cannot get at them for want of the clue. He does not know what to do with his facts; I know. If I could draw them from him, it must be with his ↑keys,↓ arrangements & reserves. Here is all Boston, — all railroads, all manufactures, & trade, in the head of this well-informed merchant at my side: What would not I give for a peep at his rows & rows of facts! Here is Agassiz with his theory of anatomy & nature: I am in his chamber & I do not know what question to put. Here is ⟨Dr⟩Charles T. Jackson whom I have known so long, who knows so much, & I have never been able to get anything truly valuable from him. [87] Here is all Fourier in Brisbane's head; all languages in Kraitsir's; all Swedenborg in Reed's; ↑all the Revolution in old Adams's head; all modern Europe & America in J.Q.A.'s,↓ [129] and I cannot appropriate any fragment of all their experience. I would fain see their picture-books as they exist. Now if I could ⟨turn⟩ ↑cast↓ a spell on this man at my side & ⟨v⟩see his pictures without his intervention or organs, and,

[126] *The Vishńu Puráńa, A System of Hindu Mythology and Tradition,* trans. H. H. Wilson (London, 1840); cf. *JMN,* IX, 319. The passage is versified in *JMN,* IX, 354, and "Brahma," ll. 1–2, *W,* IX, 195.
[127] For these three sentences, see *JMN,* IX, 282.
[128] *JMN,* IX, 458.
[129] Emerson's references are to Albert Brisbane (1809–1890), the American advocate of Fourierism; Charles Kraitsir (1804–1860) of Boston, said to be "the best teacher of languages in existence" (*L,* III, 373); Sampson Reed, the "Swedenborgian druggist" of Boston mentioned frequently in earlier journals; and John Adams and John Quincy Adams, former American Presidents.

having learned that lesson, turn the spell on another, lift up the cover of another hive & see the cells & suck the honey, & then another, & so without limit, — they were not the poorer, & I were ⟨wi⟩rich[n] indeed. So I think this mesmerism, whereof the fable adheres so pertinaciously to all minds, will one day realize itself. It is for this news, these facts, that I go to Boston, and visit A. & [88] B. & C. Boston were ten times Boston if I could learn what ↑I↓ go thither for.[130]

The ring of Gyges prefigures this — society on our own terms.

But Osman answered & said, I do not know whether I have the curiosity you describe. I do not want the particulars which the merchant values, or the lawyer, or the artist, but only the inevitable result which he communicates to me in his manner & conduct & in the tone & purpose of his ⟨sp⟩ discourse.

Speech is to conceal [131]

Then again said Guy, If he could inspect these experiences, what would it signify? [132] ⟨If he⟩ He can, if he wishes, as things are. He can devote himself to brokerage & stocks until he sympathizes practically [89] with the merchant. Then he will have that clue he wants. He can study Humboldt until he can talk with Humboldt. He can read Bettine until he can predict her speech. If he could arrive at their pictures by the short cut you imagine, he must still be imprisoned in their minds by his dedication to their experience, & lose so much career of his own, or so much sympathy with still higher souls than theirs.

[90]   Aristocracy

Democracy & even philanthropy ⟨have⟩ are great cloaks for spite. The only relief that I know against the invidiousness of superior position is that you exert your faculty; for, whilst each does that, he

---

[130] The inserted "I" is in pencil.

[131] Cf. Charles Maxime Catherinet de Villemarest, *Life of Prince Talleyrand*, 4 vols. (London, 1834–1836), I, 53, as paraphrased in *JMN*, IX, 176.

[132] Guy, like Osman, may be a semi-autobiographical persona, as the subject of the poem "Guy" appears to be. See *W*, IX, 33–34; *JMN*, VII, 333–334, 525.

excludes hard thoughts from the spectator. All right activity is
amiable.[133]

[91] One lesson Osman learned, — to accept the event as an intention. If he ⟨were⟩ called on a friend, & the ⟨friend were⟩ servant told
him the party ⟨were⟩was not at home, he never called again, accept-
ing that intimation as final, and equal⟨ly⟩ to him the decree of the
event or the will of the friend[.] [134]

[92]   Selfexistence   & self⟨support⟩help
⟨Every⟩ Want a partridge, catch a partridge. If the troops want a fort,
the captain says, Build one, then. Before the sun can react on planets,
it first makes them; according to the theories. When the planet ⟨is thus
self made,⟩ ↑has made itself↓ it has to get its own living.[135] The stone
is to have aeons to decompose its surface & the lichens work[;] then
the ↑fire-ages, water ages,↓ moss-ages, & then ⟨pines⟩ferns & pines,
then the trilobite[.]
Every river make[s] its own shores.[136]
The world was all thought once; & matter is its shore & sediment;
as the whole of the animal body, — bones, nails, hair, horns, — was
once in the blood, & before that, in the Spirit.   The body of
man is "a self-moving travelling carriage" & must be carefully driven
lest it upset. The world is full of young rowdies yet so excellent
[93] a regulator is put into the machine[,] in the police (described
p. 79 ↑introduce that clause on *Conscience*↓)[,] [137] that anarchies &
reigns of terror seldom happen. The watch-watch at Waltham [138]
and the gasometer are copies after nature.

---

[133] "Aristocracy . . . amiable.", struck through in pencil with a vertical use
mark, is used in "Aristocracy," *W*, X, 47.
    [134] These two sentences are struck through in ink with a diagonal use mark.
    [135] "If the troops . . . own living." is used in "Fate," *W*, VI, 38. See *JMN*,
IX, 363, for notes anticipating the present passage.
    [136] See p. [11] above.
    [137] The insertion is in pencil. "Nature," Emerson had written on p. [79] above,
"knew what rowdies & tigers she was making & she created a police first in the
Conscience. . . ."
    [138] See *JMN*, IV, 21; *L*, I, 426.

[94] Man is a manufacturer. He makes sense out of nonsense, wealth out of rags. There must be chiffoniers[.]
Discontinuity is a vexation[;] discontinuity of thought or other material. Sleezy material; spite, apathy, bad blood, novels, is only dispersed matter. Call the chiffoniers!

The rowdies ⟨to⟩sent ⁿ to Mexico will cover you with glory! Tuttle found a use for our moth and Chandler liked the worst best.[139]

Nonsense is only sense deranged, chaos is paradise dislocated, poverty is wealth decomposed; spite, apathy, bad blood, frivolity is only dispersed matter & light.

[95]   ↑See p 19 *supra* and O p. 159↓ [140]
Temperament is fortune, & we must say ⟨s⟩it so often. In a thousand cups of life only one is ⟨a fine⟩ the right mixture, — ⟨a⟩the fine adjustment to the existing elements[.]

When that happens, when the well mixed man is born, with eyes not too dull nor too good, with fire enough & alloy enough, capable of impressions from all things, & not too susceptible; ——— then no gift need be bestowed on him, he brings with him fortune, followers, love, power; men will need him, & he is rich & eminent by nature. That man cannot be too late, or too early. Let him not hurry nor hesitate. Though millions are there already, his seat waits for him; though ⁿ millions be there, they only multiply his servants & agents. It never troubles the orator what multitudes come to hear him though benches crack & galleries bend.[141] ↑See, too, p 53↓

[96]   *A national man*
Pericles, ↑Caesar,↓ Luther, Dr Johnson, Mirabeau, Goethe, Webster
   A large well-built brain with a great trunk below to supply it,

---

[139] Tuttle is probably Emerson's neighbor, Augustus Tuttle, who lived on the Concord-Boston turnpike. Daniel Chandler, superintendent from 1835 to 1839 of the Boston Asylum and Farm School for Indigent Boys, told Emerson that "he did not wish any good boys. The worse boys were, the better scholars & men they would make" (*JMN*, VIII, 186).

[140] *JMN*, IX, 402.

[141] "*Temperament* . . . power;" and "men will . . . bend." are used in "Aristocracy," *W*, X, 43–44, 45, respectively.

as if a fine alembic were fed with liquor for its distillations from broad full vats in the vaults of the laboratory.[142]

But the men we see are above or below the population, & life, if there were only one life, would not be a blessing. In the whole they must be fit, or they would not exist, & in their next births we shall like them better. ↑they are unrelated, lonely, helpless↓ [143]

[97] [144] || ... ||
[98] [145] || ... ||
By always intending my mind, ||said|| ⁿ Newton[.] [146]

Persistent man works after Nature whose productions are secular & cumulative[.]

Therein is the grandeur of British intellect[.]
A man must do the work with that faculty he has now. — But that faculty is the accumulation of past days. No rival can rival backwards. What you have learned & done is safe & fruitful. Work & learn in evil days, in insulted days, in days of debt & depression [99] & calamity. — Fight best in the shade of the cloud of arrows.[147]

Lafayette's voice after 25 years silence

The concealment of learning & the concealment of charity is the aim & the persistence of noble souls. Rely on God to the last! What is stronger than fire? said the Koran, Σ 43

---

[142] "A large . . . laboratory." is used in "Aristocracy," *W*, X, 43.

[143] "they are . . . helpless" is in pencil.

[144] Most of the upper half of the leaf bearing pages [97] and [98] has been torn out, with the loss of approximately ten or eleven lines on each. Only portions of three initial letters remain on the stub of the upper part of p. [97]; the lower part is blank. Emerson indexed the page under both Metamorphosis and Woman.

[145] "By always . . . & cumulative" is in pencil. On the stub of the upper part of the page is visible a part of one word: "ted". Emerson indexed p. [98] under both Morals and Persistency.

[146] Used in "Power," *W*, VI, 75; see *JMN*, IX, 335.

[147] "Therein . . . arrows" is written in ink over the same words in pencil. "A man . . . depression" is struck through in ink on p. [98] with three vertical use marks.

Persistency   N. 88   Progress   N 11
If there were constancy great men would dwindle   N 8, 88 [148]

Time respects only what he has himself made[.] [149]

[100] [blank]
[101] Courage
     I am not afraid of accident as long as I am in my place.[150] These
dangers are not for me[.]

⟦The human hand is the medal[.]⟧

I see that you are not assured of protection as long as I refer to
opinion.

Only the religious can expect the succour of religion[.]

Is there only one kind of courage? No, but as many kinds as men.
     W 43   O 193 [151]

Scholar's courage should be as terrible as the Cid's.

Scholar's courage should grow out of his conversation with [102] [152]
spiritual nature, not out of temperament & brawn, like Johnson's
knocking down Osborne.[153]
Fine audacity of the Greeks; *supra* p 81.
     No weakness, Danton. No imbecilities of men[,] of cigars &
wine! Let the scholar measure his valour by his power to cope with

----

[148] See *JMN*, VIII, 283 (N 88), 252 (N 11), 251 (N 8).

[149] "Lafayette's . . . made" is in pencil. For "Time . . . made", see *JMN*,
VIII, 307.

[150] This sentence, struck through in ink with a vertical use mark, is used in "Worship," *W*, VI, 232.

[151] See *JMN*, IX, 199–200, 411.

[152] "*Courage*" is centered at the top of the page as an index heading.

[153] On Johnson and Thomas Osborne, see James Boswell, *The Life of Samuel
Johnson*, ed. George Birbeck Hill, revised and enlarged by L. F. Powell, 6 vols.
(Oxford, 1934–1950), I, 154, 375 n. 1, 534; III, 344. "Scholar's courage should be
. . . Osborne." is used in "Greatness," *W*, VIII, 311–312.

intellectual giants. Others can count votes, & calculate stocks. Can he weigh Plato? judge of the probabilities of Laplace's hypothesis? give me a considered opinion on the modern cosmogonies; & know Newton & Humboldt; criticize Swedenborg; dispose of Fourier?

Courage of insight, courage of the chart, courage of having done it before.[154]

I see the same courage in Æschylus's poetry as in Nelson's fight.

[103]   *Courage*

Can the scholar disentangle the thread of truth through all the confused appearances of the Free Trade facts? —

Every man has his own courage, & is betrayed because he seeks in himself the courage of other persons.[155]

When I read Proclus, I am astonished at the vigor & breadth of his performance. Here is no epileptic modern muse with short breath & short flight, but Atlantic strength everywhere equal to itself, & dares great attempts because of the life with which it is filled.[156]

———

↑But whence is Boldness   K 122   D 72 [157]

———

Thomas Taylor.   V 2,3,4,5,[158]

———

See also the verse from Goethe on ⟨L⟩Energy on the inside of the cover of book K↓ [159]

———

[154] See p. [60] above. "Let the scholar . . . Courage of insight," is used in "Greatness," *W*, VIII, 311; "courage of having done it before" is used in "Culture," *W*, VI, 139.
[155] See *JMN*, IX, 112, and Notebook JK, p. [103] below; cf. "Courage," *W*, VII, 270.
[156] For "When I . . . filled.", see *JMN*, VIII, 243.
[157] See *JMN*, VIII, 243, VII, 51–52.
[158] See *JMN*, IX, 95–97.
[159] *JMN*, VIII, 199.

[104]   Transit

Some men cannot possibly make the metonomy or transit so far as to illustrate their experience by any circumstance but the historical one that befel them. If they ↑would↓ describe an insult, my life on it, ↑it↓ is the very insult they suffered;[160] if they speak of an accident or a wound to which human life is liable, & he the speaker was once hurt by a pitchfork or a peat-knife, he is sure to speak of a wound by pitchfork or a peat-knife.

It is like Dr Chauncy's torpidity in prayer who at Thursday Lecture prayed that the death of the little boy who was just drowned in Frog Pond might be made salutary to all[.] [161]

↑Genius takes three steps or four. G 109 J 70↓ [162]

Mem. see in Second Series Essays that the transit is fairly described & also that the value of a trope is the hint it affords of trope or ⟨m⟩transmigration to the mind of the reader himself[.] [163]

[105]   La Nature aime les Croisements [164]

We ↑seem to↓ approach an analysis of Burke's wonderful powers by observing the employment of his early years. To a man quite ignorant of mechanic arts, a penknife, a thimble, a pin, seems to be made with inexplicable ingenuity. But, on visiting the shop where it is made, & seeing the successive parts of the work, in how simple a manner it is put together, the fabric loses part of its value, the composition is so easy. Something like this disappointment is felt by those who trace that complex product eloquence to its elements. We listen with joy to Burke explaining to [the] House of Commons on the rise of an unexpected debate all the intricacy of the Revenue

[160] "Some men . . . suffered" is struck through in ink with a vertical use mark.

[161] This paragraph, struck through in ink with a vertical use mark, is used in "Eloquence," *W*, VIII, 127. Rev. Charles Chauncy (1705–1787) is remembered as an enemy of the religious emotionalism of the Great Awakening.

[162] See *JMN*, VIII, 49, 167.

[163] See "The Poet," *W*, III, 30: "If the imagination intoxicates the poet, it is not inactive in other men. The metamorphosis excites in the beholder an emotion of joy. . . . This is the effect on us of tropes, fables, oracles, and all poetic forms."

[164] See *JMN*, IX, 50, 296, 300, and "Inspiration," *W*, VIII, 289.

Laws or the constitution of a commission or reviewing the details of legislation for years. — In the midst of accurate details, he surprises us with some deep philosophic remark [106]¹⁶⁵ which besides its own splendour astonishes by contrast with the habits of so practical a man of business[.]

But when we explore his youth & find him ⟨the⟩ for years the author of the Annual Register & ⟨for this⟩in the service of that work spent his days in the gallery of the House of C. & that in those same years he also wrote a philosophical Treatise on Taste & the Sources of the Sublime & Beautiful, we cease to wonder at the minuteness of his official knowledge or of the loftiness of his speculation[.]

Croisements
Mixtures
Alternation

[107]   Croisement
Nature loves crosses, as inoculations of barbarous races prove: and marriage is crossing.
Where two shadows cross, the darkness thickens: where two lights cross, the light glows.
Milton, Bacon, Gray, are crosses of the Greek & Saxon geniuses.

———
↑Croisement, O 25↓ ¹⁶⁶

[108] *Journal*
'Tis purposed to establish a new Quarterly Journal.¹⁶⁷ Well, 'tis always a favorable time, & now is.

The essential ground of a new book is that there be a new spirit; that the authors really have a new idea, a higher life, see the direction of a more comprehensive tendency than others are aware of and this with that fulness or steadiness of perception as to falter never in

¹⁶⁵ "Croisement" is centered at the top of the page as an index heading.
¹⁶⁶ See *JMN*, IX, 366.
¹⁶⁷ *The Massachusetts Quarterly Review* (1847–1850), founded at the particular urging of Theodore Parker and Samuel Gridley Howe, with Parker as editor.

affirming it, but take the victorious tone, as did the Edinburgh Review, the London Times, & the Boston Chronotype.[168]

↑See Delf's opinion. K 13↓ [169]

─────

↑Dial should be the Bible of the Americans

─────   R 56, 47↓ [170]

↑Vice of journals that they contain the second best.↓

[109]   ↑Journal   see p 126↓
    I think at this moment any Journal would be incomplete that did not admit the Zoroastrian element[.]

Ward, Lowell, Story, Hill, James, Talbot
Newcomb, J. P. Robinson, B. P. Hunt,

─────

C. T. Jackson, Pierce, Mitchell,

─────

Wilkinson, Margaret Fuller,

─────

(Isaac Brayton, Ravenna, Ohio) [171]

Ozanam auctore, G. P. Bradford.[172]

───

[168] This paragraph is used in "The Preacher," *W*, X, 233. For the "victorious tone" of the *Daily Chronotype*, see *JMN*, IX, 371.

[169] See *JMN*, VIII, 203, concerning Thomas Delf and *The Dial*. Delf was a young Englishman employed by the publishers Wiley and Putnam in New York when Emerson met him there in 1842 (*JMN*, VIII, 202).

[170] See *JMN*, VIII, 375, 370. Emerson's cross-references make it apparent that this statement is by Thomas Delf, who also complained that *The Dial* "has not piety."

[171] Evidently a list of potential contributors to the proposed *Review*, including Emerson's friend Samuel Gray Ward, James Russell Lowell, the jurist Joseph Story or his son the lawyer-artist William Wetmore Story, Emerson's classmate John Boynton Hill, the senior Henry James, Emerson's friend Charles King Newcomb, the lawyer John Paul Robinson of Lowell, Emerson's former pupil Benjamin Peter Hunt, Emerson's brother-in-law Dr. C. T. Jackson, possibly Professor John Pierce of the Divinity School in Cambridge, possibly William Mitchell of Nantucket (see Journal CD, p. [12] below), and the English Swedenborgian James John Garth Wilkinson. Talbot and Brayton are unidentified.

[172] Antoine Frédéric Ozanam, *Dante et la philosophie catholique* (1839), which

Articles on the State by C[harles]. Sumner
↑&↓ on Disunion by W[endell]. Phillips.
in the same number.
Alcott's subjects

———

Travelling

———

Daniel Webster

———

Harvard University

———

The New Testament

———

Plato

———

Pythagoras

———

Fourier

———

↑The↓ Demoniacal

———

A list of books
[———
Osman

———

Vita Nuova
Vita Nuovissima [173]
Saadi apud Goethe
Hafiz

———

Emerson borrowed from the Harvard College Library on March 30, 1847. In a letter
to James Elliot Cabot, April 21, 1848, Emerson was to suggest that Bradford "could
write something valuable on Dante, perhaps an abstract of the Ozanams . . ." (*L*,
IV, 60).
[173] Cf. *JMN*, VIII, 369, on Margaret Fuller: "whilst Dante's 'Nuova Vita' is
almost unique in the literature of sentiment, I have called the imperfect record she
gave me of two of her days, 'Nuovissima Vita.' "

Rabelais's Muses

———

Bacon

———

English Dictionaries.]

[110] An autobiography should be a book of answers from one individual to the main questions of the time. Shall he be a scholar? the infirmities & ridiculousness of the scholar being clearly seen. Shall he fight? Shall he seek to be rich? Shall he go for the ascetic or the ⟨popular⟩conventional life? he being aware of the double consciousness. — Shall he value mathematics? Read Dante? or not? Aristophanes? Plato? Cosmogonies, & scholar's courage. What shall he say of Poetry? What of Astronomy? What of Religion?

Then let us hear his conclusions respecting government & politics. Does he pay taxes⟨?⟩ and record his title deeds? ⟨som⟩ Does Goethe's Autobiography answer these questions? So of love, of marriage, so of playing providence. It should be a true Conversation's Lexicon for earnest men.[174] Saadi's Gulistan is not far from this. It should confirm the reader in his best [111] sentiment. It should go for imagination & taste. It should aspire & worship.

↑Every man prefers something[,] calling it Art or Music or something else, perhaps a misnomer.↓

It should contemplate a just metaphysics and should do justice to the coordinate powers of man[.] Imagination, Understanding, Will, Sensation, Science.

Novels, Poetry, Mythology   ⟨A⟩must be well allowed for an imaginative being. You do us great wrong, Henry T[horeau].[,] in railing at the novel reading. The novel is that allowance & frolic their imagination gets. Everything else pins it down. And I see traces of Byron & D'Israeli & Walter Scott & George Sand in the deportment of these stately young clerks in the streets & hotels. Their education is neglected but the ballroom & the circulating

[174] *Brockhaus' Konversations-Lexikon* was an encyclopedia begun in 1796 by the German firm of F. A. Brockhaus.

library, the fishing excursion & Trenton Falls make such amends as
they can.[175]

[112]   Autobiography
In this circle of topics will come *Education* & what we have to say of
guns as liberalizers & dancers, & chess, & dancing & dress & languages.* For if the man is not a profound man[,] a quarry, but is
rather ⟨winged⟩ legged & winged & intended for locomotion he must
be furnished with all that breeding which gives currency as sedulously
as with that which gives worth.

Travelling is as fit for some men as it is pernicious for others.[176]
↑Nature has given us in a shell the architecture applied to locomotion[.]↓

[113]

                    Day! hast thou two faces
                    One which partly I detect
                    Shown to the prosperous & strong
                    A nob a picture in a carved frame
                    And one by humble laborers seen
                    Chill, & wet, unlighted, mean,
                    Making one place two places
                    And let us pray life be not long [177]

[114] Pythagoras cured distempers with music.[178] ⟨&⟩If people
are grieved we go over the sorrow in words & the more cunning the

* See Y. p. 102,.[179]

---

[175] "It should contemplate . . . can.", struck through in ink with a vertical use
mark, is used in "Books," *W*, VII, 212, 213.
[176] "& chess . . . others." is struck through in ink with a vertical use mark; "but
is . . . others." is struck through in pencil with a vertical use mark. "In this circle
. . . languages." and "For if . . . for others." are used in "Culture," *W*, VI, 142,
and 146, respectively.
[177] The verse, struck through in ink with a vertical use mark, is an early version
of "The Chartist's Complaint," *W*, IX, 232.
[178] Cf. *Iamblichus' Life of Pythagoras*, trans. Thomas Taylor (London, 1818),
pp. 43–44 and 80, and *JMN*, IX, 108.
[179] *JMN*, IX, 294; cf. *JMN*, IX, 48, and Notebook JK, p. [17] below: "a gun
is a liberalizer."

repetition of it in words the better consoled they are; or we lend them a book:— cure with music still. Administer literature, as "Suspiria de Profundis". ↑or Milton↓

> "Harping, said he, ken I none,
>   For tongue is chief of minstrelsy" [180]

[115] My first distribution of mankind is into the class of benefactors & malefactors. The second class is by far the largest as is obvious by this that a person seldom falls sick without inspiring the hope in the bystanders that he will die. Valuable lives are few. ↑'Tis a case for a gun.↓ [181]

[116] [182]   Sciolists & society starve the imagination[.]
       Teach the feeding of the Imagination[.]
       The strict omnipresence, idle complaining, of the grasping of men who quote Xn[Christian] texts. They are as good as they can be. Inevitable impediments[:] frost, rain, hunger, children, & fifteen dependents. People are a great deal better than they seem to be.
       American fuss against Asiatic Fate [183]

       Optimism. A hard row, debt, fever, bad wife, are symptoms only of the ever ever convalescent constitution. Alfieri shaved one side of his head. Your Genius looks out for the essentials, & secures the solitude your infirmity requires[.]
       We hate the bran bread, but he takes away all other. Spartans in our own despite[.]

       Teach the indigence of ⟨cockneys⟩ the upper circles[.]

    ———

       Teach the sovereignty of the moral[.]

[117]   ↑Longevity.   Boulders↓
       How glad were Orchards if we could make the world wheels turn a little faster or what were the same thing if life were longer.[184]

---

[180] See p. [48] above.
[181] "My first . . . gun.", struck through in ink with a vertical use mark, is used in "Considerations by the Way," *W*, VI, 248.
[182] This page is in pencil.
[183] Cf. p. [66] above.
[184] This sentence is in pencil.

Orchards should not be squares or quincunxes, but fruit-woods.

↑Longevity↓

The fable of the Wandering Jew is agreeable to men because they want more time & land to execute their thoughts in:—but a higher poetic use must be made of that fable. Take me as I am with my experience & transfer me to a new planet, & let me digest for its inhabitants what I could of the wisdom of this. After I have found my depth there, & assimilated what I could of the new experience, transfer me to a new scene. In each transfer I shall have acquired a new mastery of the old thoughts in which I was too much immersed, by seeing them at a distance.[185]

[118] Our system is artificial. We are born into government, trade, & cities. We drive wooden piles & lay stonework on them & build an e⟨l⟩ternal city on punk[.]

———

Take hay & egg shells, & lay granite on that, then build up ⟨up⟩[.]

[119] How delicious & how rare is literary society!

It is certain that if for education inducation were possible, and one man could actually impart his talent instead of its performances[,] a mountain of guineas would be readily paid for tuition fees.

[120] 5 April. The best feat of Genius is to make an audience of the mediocre & the dull. They also feel addressed; they are for once fairly blended with the intelligent.[186] The same things interest them which interest the wise; the iron boundary lines fade away, and the stupid & mean have become interesting also. Dr J. J.[187] said, the whole art of medicine lay in removing & withholding the cause of irritation[.]

———   ↑See *CD* 84↓

[185] This paragraph is used in "Immortality," *W*, VIII, 339.

[186] These two sentences are used in "Aristocracy," *W*, X, 53.

[187] Presumably Dr. James Jackson, a Boston physician and Harvard professor.

Fancy-prices must be paid for position in society. It is as when a man has the misfortune to be in love[.]

↑☞↓ 188

[121] Boston respectable by its Academy, its Warren Club of 25 members, and its Natural History society. The Academy offers to print gratuitously with plates any original matter falling within its scope that is sent to it.[189]

———

Greatness

||epw|| [190]   ↑Pr[inted]. Aristocracy↓

To the grand interests a superficial success is of no account. It prospers as well in mistake as in luck, in obstruction & nonsense as well as among the Angels. It reckons fortunes mere paint. Difficulty is its delight; perplexity its noon-day.[191]

[122] Why have the minority no influence? If Lycurgus were in the cars Boutwell would not dare that morning to offer resolutions of homage to Zachary Taylor.[192]

Is it not better not to mix or meddle at all, than to do so ineffectually? Better mind your lamp & pen as man of letters, interfering not with politics, but knowing & naming them justly, than to inculpate yourself in the federal crime without power to redress ⟨it⟩ the state, & to debilitate yourself ⟨for⟩ by the miscellany & distraction for your ⟨ex⟩proper[n] task.

---

[188] The hand points to the entry headed "Greatness" on p. [121].

[189] The American Academy of Arts and Sciences was incorporated at Boston in 1780; the Boston Society of Natural History was organized in 1830.

[190] The paragraph which follows is written in ink over some six lines of prose, none of which has been recovered.

[191] This paragraph is used in "Aristocracy," W, X, 59. "Pr. Aristocracy" is in pencil.

[192] General Zachary Taylor's defeat of Santa Anna at Buena Vista in February of 1847 not only ended the war in northern Mexico but made him a potential candidate for the presidency in 1848 in the eyes of politicians of both parties, though he was both a Southerner and a slaveholder. George S. Boutwell (1818–1905) was then a Democratic leader in the lower house of the Massachusetts legislature; his opposition to slavery led to his election as a "Free-Soil" governor in 1851–1852. Emerson evidently regarded his "homage" to Taylor as a victory of politics over principle.

Our people have no proper expectations ⟨r⟩in regard to literary men:
They expect a practical reformer[.]
Gustavus was justly censured for not distinguishing between a car-
abine & a general[.] [193]

[123]   Whip
A whip for our top! A cold sluggish blood thinks it has not quite
facts enough to the purpose in hand and must decline ⟨the⟩ its turn
in the conversation. But they who speak have no more; — have less;
the best success of the day is without any new facts.
Heat, heat, is all. Heat puts you in rapport with magazines & worlds
of facts.[194]

My stories did not make them laugh, my facts did not quite fit
the case, my arguments did not hit the white. Is it so? then warm
yourself, old fellow, with ⟨w⟩hot[n] mincepie and half a pint of port
wine, & they will fit like a glove, & hit like a bullet.

                                    ↑See above p 62
                                        and   p 86↓
↑Young man never finds that thing which he has to say quite
appropriate.   J 31↓ [195]

                    ———
                    over
[124] Look at literary New England, one would think it was a
national fast. All are sick with debility and want of object; so that
the literary population wears a starved, puny, & piteous aspect.

Transcendentalism says, The Man is all. The world can be
reeled off any stick indifferently.[196] Franklin says, The tools; riches,
old age, land, health; the tools. But experience says, The Man and
the tools. We must have the best of both.
↑See p 129↓ [197]

[193] This sentence, struck through in pencil with two vertical use marks, is used in
"Aristocracy," W, X, 57.
[194] For "A whip . . . top!", see p. [61] above. "A cold . . . new facts." is
used in "Society and Solitude," W, VII, 12.
[195] See JMN, VIII, 157–158; p. [52] above.
[196] Cf. JMN, VIII, 447, n. 19.
[197] "Transcendentalism . . . p 129" is in pencil.

[125] ⟨Th⟩A master *and* tools, — is the lesson I read in every shop and farm and library. There must be both. The populace of science & of the streets insist on the value of tools. — Who could not do it that had them? — The man of genius insists on the commanding genius who is not nice in pencils,[198] who can do every thing with nothing: — but the wise man sees that we cannot spare any advantages,[199] and that the tools are effigies & statues of men also; their wit, their genius perpetuated; and he that uses them becomes a great society of men as wise as himself[.]

What a tool is money in a skilful hand. What a nuisance in a fool's.

↑Tools were all strokes of genius   R 169↓ [200]

[126]   *1847*   ↑Club↓   ↑AB 48↓
15 April. Yesterday Theodore Parker, W. H. Channing, Charles Sumner, Alcott, Thoreau, Elliot Cabot, Dwight, Stone, Weiss, J. F. Clarke, Stetson, & Mr Arrington of Texas spent the day with me & discussed the project of the journal.[201] G. P. Bradford & I made fourteen.

[127] Success also the sentiment of man requires. Virtue should take the world with it[.]

[128] ↑*Dyspathy.*↓ ↑We are hard to please.↓
It costs me many shrinkings & starts, the remembrance of the virtues of those whom I cannot respect. Lumps of iniquity become missionaries of charity to the starving & house⟨ss⟩less; the heady & sentimental become religiously interested in freedom & quietism, and how

---

[198] See *JMN*, VI, 126 (" 'No great painter ever nice in pencils.' Reynolds").
[199] "we cannot . . . advantages" is used in "Perpetual Forces," *W*, X, 69.
[200] See *JMN*, VIII, 439.
[201] The group included Emerson's friends James Elliot Cabot, John Sullivan Dwight, Rev. Thomas Treadwell Stone of Andover, Maine, Rev. John Weiss, Rev. James Freeman Clarke, and Rev. Caleb Stetson. Alfred W. Arrington, an ex-preacher, lawyer, and politician, published *The Desperadoes of the South West* in 1847. According to Emerson, "the plan of the meeting proceeded first from Mr Alcott" (*L*, III, 392).

can we reject their eager offering; yet we cannot overcome our aversation.

Reality

   The way to make our rhetoric & our rites ⟨sublime⟩ & badges sublime, is to make them real. Our flag is not good because it does not represent the population of the U.S. but the Baltimore Caucus. Not union & sentiment, but selfishness & cunning. If we never put on the liberty cap until we were freemen by love & self-denial, the liberty cap would mean something.

[129]   *Freedom*   ↑Frey↓
The proudest speech that free-will ever made is in Hafiz' Divan.
             Vol II p 386
 ⟨Wo to⟩It stands written on the Gate of Heaven,
 Wo to him who suffers himself to be betrayed by Fate! [202]

        ↑*Transcribed in* EO *p. 177*↓
I have heard that they seem fools who allow themselves easily to be engaged & compromised in undertakings, but that at last it appears quite otherwise, & to the gods otherwise from the first. I affix a like sense to this text of Hafiz; for he who loves is not betrayed, but makes an ass of Fate.

↑One more good fable I have concerning Freedom in the Edda that the god Freye has a sword so good that it will itself strow a field with carnage whenever the owner ordered it.↓ ↑But Freye could slay Bela with a blow of his fist had he had a mind to it. ↑Yet the dwarves killed him.↓↓ [203]

---

[202] Emerson's English version of two lines from *Der Diwan von Mohammed Schemsed-din Hafis*, trans. Joseph von Hammer, 1812–1813. The lines are used in "Fate," *W*, VI, 29. Cf. also "Persian Poetry," *W*, VIII, 245.
 [203] *The Prose or Younger Edda Commonly Ascribed to Snorri Sturluson*, trans. George Webbe Dasent, 1842, pp. 42, 47. "One more . . . ordered it." is added at the bottom of p. [129]; "but Freye . . . killed him." is added at the bottom of the facing page, [128], set off by an ink line. "I have heard . . . ordered it." is struck through in ink with a diagonal use mark.

[130] ⟨Philan⟩Hari ⁿ was[204]

_____

as tall as a giraffe

_____

as spiteful as a philanthropist

_____

as hardy as grass

_____

out in the morning ↑at work↓ before the whippoorwill had done singing. —

_____

⟨a boa is a python⟩

_____

as close as a box turtle

_____

as smart as a steel-trap

_____

Bread at discretion

_____

he grows like corn

_____

as dirty as a clam

_____

as dark as a pocket

_____

as black as an ant

_____

as economical as ants

_____

money as plenty as rain

_____

↑as convenient as money↓
↑as gray as a goat↓ [205]
↑as nervous as a squirrel↓

[204] Emerson had been reading of Hari in the _Vishṅu Puráṅa_; see _JMN_, IX, 322.
[205] For "as economical as ants" and "money as plently as rain", see _JMN_, IX, 334. "as gray as a goat" is added in pencil.

[131]–[133] [blank]
[134] [epw] [Index material omitted] [206]
[inside back cover] [Index material omitted]

[206] The erased pencil writing is Emerson's initial page-by-page listing of index material, subsequently rewritten in ink on the inside back cover in alphabetical order; the omitted index material on p. [134] consists of three additions to the alphabetical listing.

CD

1847

Journal CD is a regular journal consisting, like AB, largely of un-dated entries. The first entry to be dated by Emerson is that of May 23, 1847, on page [1]; the last is that of July 31, 1847, on page [142]. Not all dated entries are in sequence: see pages [107] (dated July 10), [126] (July 25), [138] (July 18 and 15), and [145] (July 25). Among the entries left undated, Emerson's scattered extracts from Alexander Chodzko, *Specimens of the Popular Poetry of Persia*, must have been made subsequent to July 26, 1847, when he borrowed the book from the Harvard College Library.

Journal CD is written in a copybook bound in green marbled boards and with a green leather spine; the cover measures 17.4 x 20.4 cm. The spine has five horizontal gold lines, the inscription "CD" in ink, and remnants of a paper label or reinforce-ment. The cover is inscribed in ink: "CD / 1847"; the back cover is inscribed in ink: "CD". The pages, faintly ruled, measure 17 x 19.7 cm. Including flyleaves (i–ii, 151–152), there are 156 pages, all numbered in ink except 11 numbered in pencil (36, 37, 46, 59, 60, 62, 83–86, 148) and 13 unnumbered (i, ii, 2, 10, 11, 13, 15, 17, 47, 97, 149, 151, 152); pages 26, 58, and 126 are numbered in pencil and again in ink. Emerson omitted numbers 56 and 57, going from 55 to 58; he numbered two successive pages as 115 (here, 115_1 and 115_2) but compensated by omitting 117, going from 116 to 118. Two pages (133 and 149) are blank. Of three loose leaves laid into the journal, the first, inserted between pages 22 and 23, and here designated 22_a–22_b, is irregularly torn at the top and right edges, measuring 12.8 x 16.5 cm on its widest and longest axes. Laid in between the back flyleaf and the inside back cover are the leaves designated 152_a–152_b, of faintly ruled blue paper 20 x 25.5 cm, and 152_c–152_d, of yellowed paper 21.6 x 26 cm, now twice folded.

[front cover]
                              ___
                              CD

                             1847

[front cover verso] [Index material omitted]

[i]   R. W. Emerson
                                              1847
                              ___
                              CD
                              ___

Θεου θελοντος και επι ριπον αν πλεοις [1]

[ii]

    20 cents   drachma
    3 1/3 cents   1 obolus [2]

[1] 1847
May 23. Boeckh estimates the Attic drachma ⟨as⟩ of silver as nearly
equal to 9 3/4 pence of English coinage; then, the mina, to £4, 1s.
3d.; and the talent to £243. 15s.[3]
        8 chalci made   1 obolus

---

[1] Correctly, θεοῦ θέλοντος, κἂν ἐπὶ ῥιπὸς πλέοις. In Notebook Morals, p. [162],
Emerson entered both the Greek phrasing and a verse translation: " 'Were it the
will of Heaven, an osier bough / Were vessel safe enough the seas to plow.' Quoted
doubtfully from Pindar[:] See *Plutarch's Morals* [. . . *Translated from the Greek,
by Several Hands*, 5th ed., 5 vols. (London, 1718), in Emerson's library] ('Why the
Pythian Priestess ceases her oracles in verse?') Vol III p. 123"; see also *JMN*, VI,
388. This proverbial expression is now attributed to Euripides, *Thyestes*, Fragment
401: see *Euripidis Tragoediae*, ed. August Nauck, 3 vols. (Leipzig, 1869–1901),
III, 318.
        [2] "20 . . . obolus" is written in pencil, diagonally.
        [3] August Boeckh, *The Public Economy of Athens*, trans. George Cornewall
Lewis, 2nd ed., revised (London, 1842), p. 16. Emerson borrowed this book from
the Harvard College Library on March 30, 1847 — probably after finding it cited
by Legaré; see Journal AB, p. [5] above.

6 oboli made   1 drachma
100 drachmas   1 mina
60 minas   1 talent

4 (or 3/⟨or 4⟩) cotylas made 1 choenix
48   choenices   1 medimnus =

(1 1/2 bushel
English) [4]

drachma   20 cents nearly
obolus   3 1/3 cents

[2] The area of Attica & the two small Islands Salamis & Helena contains about 874 square miles[.]

Boeck[h] estimates the population of Attica at the time of the Peloponnesian War
as   90 000 citizens
     45 000 resident aliens
     365,000 slaves

Athens contained above 10 000 houses[.] [5]

[3] Henry Truman Safford born at Royalton, Vt Jan 6, 1836. In ⟨1845⟩ 1846 was examined for 3 hours by Rev H W Adams of Concord N.H. & Rev C N Smith of Randolph Vt. and at last was bidden[:]

"Multiply in your head 365 365 365 365 365 365 by 365 365 365 365 365 365!" eighteen figures by eighteen. "He flew round the room like a top pulled his pantaloons over the top of his boots, bit his hand rolled his eyes in their sockets sometimes smiling & talking & then seeming to be in agony until in not more than one minute, he said, 133,491,850,208,566 925 016,658,299,941,583,225. The boy's father Rev C. N. Smith & myself had each a pencil & slate to take down the answer, & he gave it us in periods of three figures each as fast as it was possible for us to write them. And what was still more wonderful he began to multiply at the left

---

[4] August Boeckh, *The Public Economy of Athens*, 1842, pp. 15, 91, 60.
[5] August Boeckh, *The Public Economy of Athens*, 1842, pp. 31, 36, 39.

hand & to bring out the answer from left to right giving first 123, 491 &c. Here confounded above measure I gave up the examination. The boy looked pale & said he was tired. He said, it was the largest sum he ever did." [6]

[4] May 24. The days come & go like muffled & veiled figures sent from a distant friendly party, but they say nothing, & if we do not use the gifts they bring, they carry them as silently away. [7]

Safford

"He has found a new rule to calculate eclipses. He told me it would shorten the work ↑nearly↓ one third. When finding this rule for two or three days, he seemed to be in a sort of trance. One morning very early he came rushing down stairs, not stopping to dress him, poured on to his slate a stream of figures, & soon cried out in the wildness of his joy, ⟨")↑'O,↓ ⁿ father, I have got it! I have got it! it comes, it comes.'"

[5] Mr Knowall the American has no concentration: he sees the artists of fame[,] the Raffaelles ↑&↓ Cellinis ⟨& Angelos⟩ with despair. He is up to Nature & the First Cause in his consciousness; but that wondrous power to collect & swing his whole vital energy into the act, and leave the product there for the despair of posterity, he cannot approach[.]

Safford

"In the spring of 1845 Henry began to be much engaged with the idea of calculating an almanac — Every old almanac in the house was treasured up in his little chest, — and sun's declination⟨s⟩ rising & setting, moon southings, risings & settings, seemed to occupy all his thoughts.

[6] Emerson's quotations here and below from Rev. H. W. Adams's report of Truman Henry Safford (1836–1901), evidently drawn from contemporary newspaper accounts, reflect the wide publicity given the young mathematician. In 1846 the entire Safford family had come from Royalton, Vermont, to Cambridge in order to enter the boy at Harvard. After graduating there in 1854, as Emerson noted on p. [6] below, he served on the Observatory staff until 1866.
[7] "The days . . . away." is used in "Works and Days," *W*, VII, 168; cf. "Days," *W*, IX, 228. See Plate I.

"His almanac was put to press in the autumn of 1845, & was cast when Henry was 9 years & six months old. 'the most accurate of any of the common almanacs of N. England' "

[6] Eighteen or twenty centuries of European & Asiatic men have been trained to check their actions by regard for a Judgment Day. Now it begins to look to the knowing ones as if life were more correctly an affair for Punch.

Safford
"His infant mind drinks in knowledge as the sponge does water. Chemistry botany philosophy geography & history are his sport."
H. W. Adams

↑———— Trumannus Henricus Safford graduated at Harvard College, 1854.↓

[7] On the seashore at Nantucket I saw the play of the Atlantic with the coast. Here was wealth[:] every wave reached a quarter of a mile along shore as it broke. There are no rich men, I said to compare with these. Every wave is a fortune. One thinks of Etzlers and great projectors who will yet turn this immense waste strength to account and save the limbs of human slaves.[8] Ah what freedom & grace & beauty with all this might. The wind blew back the foam from the top of each billow as it rolled in, like the hair of a woman in the wind. The freedom makes the observer feel as a slave. Our expression is so slender, thin, & cramp; can we not learn here a generous eloquence? [8] This was the lesson our starving poverty wanted. This was the disciplinary Pythagorean music which should be medicine.[9]

Then the seeing so excellent a spectacle is a certificate that all imaginable good shall yet be realized. We should not have dared to believe that this existed: Well what does not the actual beholding of a hero or of a finished woman certify?

[8] Emerson delivered seven lectures at Nantucket in 1847, beginning on May 4. John Augustus Etzler, *The Paradise within the Reach of all Men, without Labour, by Powers of Nature and Machinery* (London, 1842), proposed harnessing the winds and the tides.
[9] See Journal AB, p. [114] above.

↑"Il faudrait pour bien faire que tout le monde fût million↑n↓aire."
[Augustin Eugène] Scribe
Le Mariage d'Argent↓ [I, iv, 99] [10]

[9] [11] Nation of Nantucket makes its own war & peace. Place of winds bleak shelterless & when it blows a large part of the island is suspended in the air & comes into your face & eyes as if it was glad to see you. The moon comes here as if it was at home, but there is no shade. A strong national feeling. Very sensitive to every thing that dishonours the island because it hurts the value of stock till the company are poorer[.]

50 persons own 5/7 of all the property in the island. Calashes.[12] At the fire they pilfered freely as if after a man was burnt out his things belonged to the fire & every body might have them[.]

Before the Athenaeum is a huge jawbone of a sperm whale & at the corners of streets I noticed (Chester street) the posts were of the same material. They say here that a northeaster never dies in debt to a southwester [10] but pays all back with interest[.]

↑Capt↓ Isaac Hussey who goes out soon in the "Planter"[13] had his boat stove in by a whale[;] he instantly swum to the whale & planted his lance in his side ↑& killed him↓ before he got into another boat. The same man being dragged under water by the [n] coil of his line got his knife out of his pocket & cut the line & released himself. Capt Brayton[14] was also dragged down but the whale stopped after a short distance & he came up[.]

I saw Captain Pollard[.] [15]

The captains remember the quarter deck in their houses.

[10] See vol. III of Scribe's *Oeuvres choisies*, 5 vols. (Paris, 1845), in Emerson's library.

[11] Pp. [9] through [12] are in pencil.

[12] "An old-fashioned light hood for women, made usually of silk, wadded. It was distended by hoops of light cane, so that it could be pulled forward over the face like a chaise-top, or pushed back" (*J*, VII, 272, n. 1).

[13] The *Planter* sailed July 4, 1847, under the command of Isaac B. Hussey (1807–1852), returning to Nantucket on December 7, 1851.

[14] Both David Brayton (b. 1788) and Isaac Brayton (b. 1801) were Nantucket whaling captains.

[15] Captain George Pollard, Jr. (1791–1870), was one of five survivors of the whaler *Essex*, stove in by a whale on November 20, 1820. See *L*, III, 398–399, for a brief reference to the sinking.

Fifty five months are some voyages[.]

9500 people	80 ships
New Bedford	300 ships

I saw Capt Isaac Hussey in the steamboat & asked him about that penknife. He said no he felt in his pocket for his knife but had none there[;] then he managed to let down his trowsers & get the line off from his leg & rose. At last he saw [11] light overhead & instantly felt safe. When he ⟨ca⟩ broke water his men were a quarter of a mile off looking out for him[.] They soon discovered him & picked him up[.]

Capt Brooks [16] told me that the last whale he killed was 72 feet long, 52 feet in girth & he got 200 bbls of oil from him.

The young man sacrificed by lot in the boats of the ship Essex was named Coffin, nephew of Capt Pollard & a schoolmate of Edw. Gardner[.] [17]

"Grass widows" they call the wives of these people absent from home 4 or 5 years[.]

Walter Folger has made a reflecting telescope and a clock which is now in his house & which measures hours, days, years, & *centuries*. In Wm Mitchell's ⟨house I⟩ observatory I saw a nebula in Casseopeia the double star at the Pole, the double star Zeta Ursi[.] [18]

———

At Nantucket every blade of grass describes a circle on the sand[.]

———

[12]   Community

At Brook Farm one man ploughed all day, & one looked out of the window all day & drew his picture, and both received the same wages.

[16] Probably Captain William Brooks, Jr. (1794–1848), who had last sailed from Nantucket in 1833.

[17] Owen Coffin (1802–1821), shot and eaten by the survivors in his boat, his uncle among them.

[18] Both Walter Folger (1765–1849), inventor of "Folger's astronomic clock," and William Mitchell (1791–1869), amateur astronomer, were residents of Nantucket.

M[ary] M[oody] E[merson]. went out to ride horseback in her shroud[.] [19]

Miss Pratt & the dead earl

Bloodroyal never pays[.]

"How lucky that that man died last night. I can put you right into his bed."

[13]   "For, when sad thoughts perplex the mind of man,
            There is a plummet in the heart that weighs
            And pulls us living to the dust we came from."
                                Beaumont & Fletcher
                                Laws of Candy. [IV, i, 41–43]

        Go out into Nature and plant trees
        That when the southwind blows
        You shall not be warm in your own limbs
        but in ten thousand limbs & ten million leaves
        Of your blossoming trees of orchard & forest

Why should all this power be wasted? Why should you not mix with nature & the day? That is to be rich, to be related, and so to make the sun & the air & sea toil for you[.] [20]

[14] Solomon had 3 things; 1, the Ring by which he commanded spirits, 2 the Glass in which he saw the secrets of his enemies & of all things figured, 3 the Eastwind for his horse. Asaph was his vizier. Simorg king of birds[,] ↑the allwise bird,↓ was his counsellor[,] who lived ever since the beginning of the world; & now lives on ↑the highest summit of↓ Kaf. No fowler has taken him, & none now living has seen him. All the beasts laden with presents appeared before the throne of Solomon. Behind them all ⟨appeared⟩ came the ant⟨s⟩ with a blade of grass. Solomon did not scorn the gift. Asaph lost the seal of Solomon, which one of the Dews found, &, governing in the name of Solomon, by help of it, deceived the people. On the ⟨nam⟩ seal was the name of God engraven before which hell

---

[19] Cf. "Mary Moody Emerson," *W*, X, 428.
[20] "Go . . . for you" is in pencil.

trembled. |"In the palace which S. ordered to be built against the
arrival of the Q. of Sheba the floor or pavement was of transparent
glass laid over running water in which fish were swimming."

ap Moore

———

Karun the immeasureably rich maker of gold with all his treasures is
buried in the sea called by his name not far from the pyramids[.] [21]

———

[15] Conversations of James Northcote by W. Hazlitt   Lond. 1830

In Northcote are praised Vanbrugh's comedy of the "Provoked
Husband" and "The Journey to London" which some one called
the best play in the language.[22]
Sir R[ichard]. Phillips came up to Coleridge & offered him nine
guineas a sheet for his conversation.[23]

———

Solomon
↑"When↓ Solomon travelled he had a carpet of green silk on which
his throne was placed of a prodigious length [—] length & breadth
sufficient for all his forces to stand upon[,] the men placing themselves on
the right hand & the spirits on his left. And when all were in order the

---

[21] "Solomon had . . . pyramids", in pencil and struck through in pencil with a
vertical use mark, is used in "Persian Poetry," *W*, VIII, 240, 241, 241–242. For
" 'In the palace . . . swimming.' " see *The Poetical Works of Thomas Moore,
Collected by Himself*, 10 vols. (London, 1840–1841), IV, 84, n.; Moore's note, on
a passage of *Lalla Rookh* recounting the Queen of Sheba's visit to King Solomon,
in turn cites Ch. 27 of *The Koran; Commonly Called the Alcoran of Mohammed*,
trans. George Sale. In "Persian Poetry," *W*, VIII, 241, Emerson observes that "the
annals of . . . Karun (the Persian Crœsus)" are written in the *Sháh Námeh* of
Firdausi.
[22] "Richards (the scene painter)" told Northcote that "the players thought the
Provoked Husband the best acting play on the stage" ("Conversation the Fourteenth,"
p. 201), and also that he himself considered *The Journey to London* "the best play
in the language" ("Conversation the Nineteenth," pp. 276–277). *The Provoked
Husband* was Northcote's own "Grosvenor-Square of art" ("Conversation the
Twentieth," p. 298).
[23] William Hazlitt, *Conversations of James Northcote*, 1830, p. 76. "Conversations of . . . conversation." is in pencil; "Sir R. Phillips . . . conversation." is
rewritten in ink over the original pencil, omitting quotation marks enclosing "nine
. . . conversation."

⟨East⟩ Wind at his command took up the carpet & transported it with all that were upon it wherever he pleased[,] the army of birds at the same time flying over their heads & forming a kind of canopy to shade them from the sun" *Sale's Koran Vol II p 214* [24]

[16]   Reading
He only can read Plato who loves the smell of woolen cloth.[25]

———

Great is the power of Compound Interest, which, in eleven years, doubles the principal. For not only is twice one cent two cents, but twice one planet is two planets.

———

[17] [26]   Hafiz   Vol 1, 285 [27]

Who gave thy cheek the mixed tint
Of tulip & rose
Is also in state to give
Patience & rest to me poor
Who taught cruelty
To thy dark hair
Is also in state to give
The right against myself
I gave up hope of Ferhad
⟨F⟩Once for all on the day
When I learned he had given
His heart to Schirin
Surely I have no treasure
Yet am I richly satisfied

[24] *The Koran; Commonly Called the Alcoran of Mohammed*, trans. George Sale; edition unidentified; Emerson is quoting Sale's note to Ch. 27. The quotation, written in pencil and struck through in pencil with a vertical use mark, is used in "Persian Poetry," *W*, VIII, 240–241.
[25] This sentence, struck through in ink with a diagonal use mark, is used in "Success," *W*, VII, 297. Edward Emerson's note to the passage cited calls it "a bit of autobiography."
[26] Pp. [17] and [18] are in pencil.
[27] Emerson is putting into English the German text of *Der Diwan von Mohammed Schemsed-din Hafis*, trans. Joseph von Hammer, 1812–1813.

God has given that to the Shah
And this to the beggar
The bride of the world is truly
Outwardly richly dressed
Who enjoys her must give
His soul for a dowry.
At the cedar's foot by the brook
[18]   Lift I freer my hands
When now the blowing of the East
Gives tidings of May   &c&c

――――

The place on which the sole
Of thy foot falls
⟨Is the a⟩ Will be the ⟨asylum⟩ ⟨resort⟩ goal
Of all reasonable men

――――

As moths to the light
So all these flock to thee

[19] "Mythology 'the luxury of belief'"
Norse
Hindoo
Persian
Greek
Jewish

[20] When I see my friend after a long time, my first question is, Has any thing become clear to you?

Loose the knot of the heart, says Hafiz. At the Opera I think I see the fine gates open which are at all times closed, and that to-morrow I shall find free & varied expression. But tomorrow I am mute as yesterday. Expression is all we want: ⟨We⟩Not knowledge, but vent: we know enough; but have not leaves & lungs enough for a healthy perspiration & growth. Hafiz has: Hafiz's good things, like those of all good poets, are the cheap blessings of water, air, & fire. The observations, analogies, & felicities which arise so profusely [21] in writing a letter to a friend. An air of ⟨poverty⟩ sterility, poor, thin, arid, reluctant vegetation belongs to the wise & the unwise whom I know. If they have fine traits, admirable properties, they have a palsied side. But ⟨a⟩ ↑an utterance↓ whole, generous, sustained, equal, graduated-at-will, ⟨utterancy,⟩ such as Montaigne, such as Beaumont & Fletcher so easily & habitually attain, I miss in myself most of all, but also in my contemporaries.[28] A palace style of manners & conversation, to which every morrow is a new day, which exists ⟨f⟩extempore and is equal to the needs of life, ↑at once↓ tender & bold, & [22] with great arteries like Cleopatra & Corinne, would be satisfying, and we should be willing to die when our time came, having had our swing & gratification. But my fine souls are cautious & canny, & wish to unite Corinth with Connecticutt. ⟨As⟩I see no easy help for it. Our virtues too are in conspiracy against grandeur, and are narrowing. Benvenuto Cellini. — He[n] had concentration and the right rage.

⟨This is⟩ The[n] true nobility⟨,⟩ ↑has floodgates, — ↓ an equal inlet & outgo[.]
⟨floodgates, floodgates.⟩

[22ₐ][29] Bonaparte
———

Vertu dignité de l'ame, religion, enthousiasme, voila quels sont a ses yeux *les eternels ennemis du continent.*
pour me servir de son expression favorite[30]
            De Stael sur Bonaparte
Les Anglois l'irritent surtout parce qu'ils ont trouvé le moyen d'avoir ↑du↓ succès avec de l'honnêteté
il faut faire quelque chose de nouveau tous les trois mois pour captiver l'imagination de la nation francoise. Avec elle quiconque n'avance pas est perdu.

———
[28] "Loose the knot . . . contemporaries." is used in "Persian Poetry," *W*, VIII, 247.
   [29] Emerson used the loose leaf bearing pp. [22ₐ] and [22ᵦ] for extracts copied somewhat inaccurately from a book he withdrew from the Boston Athenaeum July 7–August 12, 1845: *Dix Années d'Exil,* vol. XV of Mme de Staël, *Oeuvres complètes,* 17 vols. (Paris, 1820–1821), pp. 14 ("Vertu . . . favorite", "Les Anglois . . . l'honnêteté"), 15, and 23.
   [30] For "Vertu . . . favorite" see *JMN*, VI, 358. "Vertu . . . *continent.*" is struck through in ink with a diagonal use mark.

[22ᵦ] Son grand talent est d'effrayer les foibles, et de tirer parti des hommes immoraux.[31]

[23] Thus the name of Sappho inspires; the expressive person; not that Casella or Corinne or Simonides has better thoughts than ⟨I⟩ ↑we↓, but that what we all have, ⟨is not⟩ ↑shall not be↓ pent & ⟨con-⟩ smouldered & noxious in ⟨one person⟩ ↑the possessor↓, but ⟨is⟩ ↑shall↓ pass⟨es⟩ over into new forms.

"Keep the body open," is the hygeian precept, and the reaction of free circulations on growth & life⟨,⟩. — ⟨t⟩The fact that the river makes its own shores, ↑—↓ is true⟨st⟩ ↑for↓ ⁿ the artist.[32]

Large utterance! [33] The pears are suffering ⟨to⟩ ↑from↓ *frozen sap*↑-↓ *blight*↑,↓ the sap being checked in its fullest flow, & not being able to form ⟨f⟩leaves & fruit, which is ↑the↓ [24] perspiration & utterance of the tree, becomes thick, unctuous & poisonous to the tree.

The jockey looks at the chest of the horse, the physician looks at the breast of the babe, to see if there is room enough for the free play of the lungs. —

Arteries, perspiration. ⟨There is⟩ Shakspeare sweats like a hay-maker, — all pores.

Kvasir, in the Norse legend, was a man so wise "that none asked him any ⟨question⟩thing⟨s⟩ that he knew not how to answer;" but the dwarves made away with him, & told the Asa "that he had choked in his wisdom, none there being wise enough to ask him enough about learning." [34]

---

[31] An English version of "Les Anglois . . . l'honnêteté" is used in "Truth," *W*, V, 119. For "il faut . . . perdu." and "Son grand . . . immoraux.", see *JMN*, VI, 357–358.

[32] In this and the preceding paragraph "is not", "one person", and "es" are canceled in pencil; "st" is canceled in both pencil and ink; "the possessor", "shall", and "for" are inserted in pencil. For "the river . . . shores," see Journal AB, pp. [11], [93] above. "Thus the name . . . artist." is used in "Persian Poetry," *W*, VIII, 247–248.

[33] See *JMN*, VII, 185: "The large utterance of the early gods.", from Keats, *Hyperion*, I, 51. Emerson also uses the quotation in *Memoirs of Margaret Fuller Ossoli*, 2 vols. (Boston, 1852), I, 275.

[34] *The Prose or Younger Edda Commonly Ascribed to Snorri Sturluson*, trans. George Webbe Dasent, 1842, p. 91. The Asa, or Aesir, were twelve gods and twenty-four goddesses who made their home in Asgard, where slain heroes also dwelt.

[25] Has the Creator put some valve between the hand & the brain of wisest men? [35]

The life of the Arabian a perpetual superlative. Khoja Yakub brings Kurroglou[36] the miniature of the handsome Ayvaz. K orders Khoja Y. to be instantly chained by neck & legs[:] "If the youth justify thy praises I will gild thy head with a shower of gold; if not, I will tear the root of thy existence from the soil of life. xx I go alone to fetch my future son; I must either die, or return with him." [pp. 43-45]
        He asks the shepherd for a slice of bread ———
S. "I have, but no son of man will eat it"
K. "If it be but a trifle softer than stone, give it me."
S. "It is ⟨baked⟩ ↑made↓ of barley & millet, I have baked it for my dogs, it[n] will break thy teeth."

———

K. broke & minced it all into a tub of milk until ⟨he could ↑⟨leave⟩↓ stick⟩ the spoon ↑stood↓ in⟨to⟩ it motionless in a vertical position — then ↑he twisted aside his long mustachios↓, he opened a mouth similar to the entrance of some cavern, & thrusting his hands under the tub he devoured its contents to the very bottom. The shepherd said, ↑"⟨He is the ghost of the Wilderness, he is a famine.↑"↓ [pp. 46-48]

———

"I can /grind/chew/ steel /in my teeth/to atoms/, & then spit it towards heaven. O why do we not fight today?"[37] ↑See p 27 over leaf↓

[26] "Napoleon, who lived wholly in the ideal, ⟨coul⟩yet could not consciously comprehend it. He denies all the ideal throughout, denies to it all reality, whilst he eagerly strives to realize it. ⟨To

———

[35] This sentence is in pencil.
[36] For the extracts that follow, see Alexander Chodzko, *Specimens of the Popular Poetry of Persia, as Found in the Adventures and Improvisations of Kurroglou* (London, 1842), pp. 43-48. Emerson borrowed the book from the Harvard College Library on July 26, 1847.
[37] Cf. Alexander Chodzko, *Specimens of the Popular Poetry of Persia*, 1842, pp. 32, 83.

s)Such an inner perpetual contradiction, however, can his clearer incorruptibler Understanding not endure, and it is of the highest importance ⟨once⟩when he, as if necessitated, expresses himself ⟨on that head⟩ ↑thereupon↓ quite originally & agreeably."

"He considers the Idea a spiritual being which certainly has no reality, but, when it departs, leaves behind a residuum (caput mortuum) to which we cannot deny altogether reality. If this also seem to us ↑too↓ stark & material, he also elsewhere speaks ⟨as if⟩quite otherwise, when he entertains [27] his friends with the incessant sequel of his life & striving, — with belief & confidence. Then confesses he gladly that life produces ↑the↓ living, that an essential fruiting works actively on all times. He likes to see that he has given to the affairs of the world a ⟨new⟩fresh impulse & a new direction."

Goethe, Sprüche. p. 204,[38]

↑Arabian Superlative↓ [39]
If Kurroglou but so much as slap a groom, he knocks four teeth down his throat which the groom swallows. [p. 313]

"if thou shouldst reveal it — tho' thou wert seated in the seventh heaven I would throw a noose & drag thee down, or if thou shouldst turn jinn, & hide thyself in the depths of the earth, I would pull thee up with tongs to the surface." [Cf. p. 105]

"I am the true Azrail. I drag the corpses on the sand. I shall sow barley where you stand now" [pp. 38, 138]

"my soul, my grandson, my parrot of Paradise." [pp. 59, 61]

[28] Our guide boards ↑(say from Boston)↓ should be wooden statues such as make the figure heads of ships extending one arm with ⟨a⟩ ↑an air of↓ smiling hospitable recommendation ⟨To Linco⟩ with a scroll in the hand "To ⟨Lincoln⟩ ↑Cambridge↓"; and ⟨a⟩the

---

[38] Johann Wolfgang von Goethe, *Sprüche in Reim und Prosa* (no imprint; vol. III of *Sämmtliche Werke*), p. 205; Emerson's page reference, if it is to this edition, is in error. The volume is in his library.

[39] Under this heading Emerson is continuing from p. [25] his extracts from Alexander Chodzko, *Specimens of the Popular Poetry of Persia*, 1842.

other arm with the eyebrow nearest it raised a little, "To ⟨Carlisle⟩ ↑Hull↓?"

bother
"Whippoorwill hollooing all night." [40]

———

Yesterday 5 June. Saw Hedge sail in the Washington Irving, the mariners sung their cheeriest song in heaving the anchor & hoisting the sail. It was the opera by daylight[.] [41]

Manners. The boy thinks the rich have no appetite. ↑They eat as if they ate for courtesy.↓ If, afterwards, he one day discovers his aristocrat eating a little fiercely—
↑See O. 6,[42] and AB↓

[29] [43]   ↑See p 36 & 43.↓
Anthropomorphism. drive the thoughts into heaps. organizing power, Genius constructive, known by form. formless American mind.
Genius magnetizes, inundates armies, a whole generation with his own purpose which is irresistibly executed. They say, there is in America no thought, no delineated form, no ⟨r⟩Reading. But who ever saw metaphysics passing into history? Who ever stood so high & so near as to detect the transition, which yet no one doubts?

[30] What beauty in the mythology of Arabia; the Anka or Simorg, the Kaf mountain, the fountain Chiser, the tree of Paradise, Tuba; the mirror of Jamschid, the seal of Solomon, the treasure of Karun, the horse of Solomon[—] that is, the East Wind↑, his bird language, Kaf the mountain ridge which begirt the world↓[.] [44]

----

[40] Cf. p. [62] below, on the nightingales.
[41] "bother . . . daylight" is in pencil. On June 2, 1847, Emerson had addressed a letter of introduction to Thomas Carlyle for his old friend Frederic Henry Hedge (1805–1890) of Bangor, Maine (L, III, 399).
[42] See JMN, IX, 359.
[43] The writing on this page appears to be a recopying in ink over essentially the same matter in pencil, now partially erased; the cross-reference originally read "See p 36".
[44] The passage reflects Emerson's current reading in von Hammer's translation of Der Diwan von Mohammed Schemsed-din Hafis, 1812–1813, and Geschichte der

Well is it less in Greece or much more in the fine picture gallery
which has become an alphabet of the world's poetry & conversation[?]

Is it less in India with its colossal & profuse growth, like a giant
jungle in which elephants & tigers pass[?]
the adventures of Hari, the Metamorphosis, the Fate,

or less in the Danish & Scaldic[—] Thor, Freya, Loki, Asgard, Igdra-
sil & Balder, where ↑Sea↓, Fire, Old Age, and Thought are the mead,
the Eater, the wrestler & the runner? Valhalla thatched with shields
for shingles[.]

[31]⁴⁵ Zal son of Sam was born with white hair; was exposed
on Kaf; was taken by the Simorg, & cherished for several years by
that respectable griffin: taught the language of the country, & some
accomplishments, as there were no schools — Sam came, & the Simorg
gave him up, & gave him a feather of his own wing, bidding him put
it in the fire when his aid should be wanted[.]
It was burned when Rudebeh his wife was about ↑to↓ bring forth
Rustem. Rustem looked a year old when newborn, & required milk
of ten nurses[.] ⁴⁶

Afrasiyab was ↑as↓ strong as an elephant, his shadow extended
miles, his heart bounteous as the ocean, & his hands like the clouds
when rain falls to gladden the thirsty Earth. ↑The crocodile has in
the rolling stream no safety.↓

Yet he was but an insect in the grasp of Rustem who seized him by

---

schönen redekünste Persiens, 1818. The insertion is added in pencil. "the mirror
. . . world" is struck through in pencil with a vertical use mark; cf. "Persian
Poetry," W, VIII, 242.
    ⁴⁵ This page is in pencil.
    ⁴⁶ See The Sháh Námeh of the Persian Poet Firdausi, trans. and abridged by
James Atkinson (London, 1892), pp. 49–52, 64–65. Emerson borrowed the 1832
edition of this translation from the Harvard College Library on September 2, 1846,
and again on July 26, 1847. "Zal son . . . be wanted" is struck through in pencil
with a vertical use mark.

the girdle & dragged him from his horse. Rustem was so moved with anger at the arrogance of the K[ing] of Mazenderan that every hair on his body started up like a spear[.] The gripe of his hand cracked the sinews of an enemy[.] [47]

[32] Festus & Shelley have both this merit of timeliness; that is the only account we can give of their imposing on such good heads. ⟨But⟩Yet Bailey is a brilliant young man who has got his head brimful of Faust, and then ⟨writes⟩pours away a gallon of ink. But no secondary inspiration as on Milton, ⟨Sh⟩on Shakspear, or on Goethe, is permitted; only an inspiration direct from the almighty. [48]

In the palace of Kaus built by demons & Alborz, gold & silver & precious stones were used so lavishly & the brilliancy produced by them combined effected so great, that night & day appeared the same. [49]

[33] To a right aristocracy, to Hercules, Theseus, Odin, the Cid, and Napoleon; to Sir Robert Walpole, to Fox, Chatham, Webster, to the men, that is, who ↑are↓ incomparably superior to the populace in ways agreeable to the populace, showing them the way they should go, doing for them what they wish done, & cannot do; ↑—↓ of course, every thing will be permitted & pardoned, gaming, drinking, adultery, fighting — these are the heads of party who can do no wrong, — every thing short of incest & beastliness will pass. But if the cambric handkerchief gent⟨ry⟩leman who serves the people in no wise, & adorns them not, is not even not afraid of them, — if such a one go about to set ill examples & corrupt them, [34] who shall blame them if they shoot him in the back, or burn his barns, ↑or↓ insult his children? Who shall blame them? Not I. ⟨They⟩ ↑He↓ eat↑s↓ ⟨his⟩ ↑their↓

---

[47] "Afrasiyab . . . enemy", struck through in pencil with a wavy vertical use mark, is used in "Persian Poetry," *W*, VIII, 242. See *The Shâh Nâmeh* of Firdausi, trans. James Atkinson, 1892, pp. 73–74, 88, 90, 109.

[48] The English poet Philip James Bailey (1816–1902) published *Festus, A Poem*, based on the story of Faust, in 1839. Emerson had read it in December of that year; see *JMN*, VII, 325.

[49] "In the . . . same.", rewritten in ink over the same words in pencil, is used in "Persian Poetry," *W*, VIII, 242. For the building of the palaces of Kaus, see *The Shâh Nâmeh* of Firdausi, trans. James Atkinson, 1892, p. 117.

bread. ⟨They⟩ ↑He↓ⁿ do↑es↓ not scorn to live by ⟨his⟩ ↑their↓ labor, and, after breakfast, ⟨they⟩ ↑he↓ cannot remember that these are human beings.⁵⁰

[35] Every thing teaches transition, transference, metamorphosis: therein is human power, in transference, not in creation; & therein is human destiny[,] not in longevity but in removal. We dive & reappear in new places[.]

↑See what I have written of Rotation   O 149 and of not getting out of nature until you are clean   O 40⁵¹

Transition in Art   O 116↓⁵²

                                                    ↑printed↓
The savages in the islands delight in playing with the surf & coming in on the top of a wave, then swimming out & repeating the delicious manoeuvre for hours. Well, human life is made up of such transits as this.⁵³ The first glance the man gives at any thing, the angle at which he sees any object, contains all his future, but he loves to vary the applications indefinitely[.] ⁵⁴

[36]⁵⁵   ↑See p 29↓

Nationality is babyishness for the most part[.] ⁵⁶

World is a temptation, and worst, a dissipation[.]

---

⁵⁰ "To a right . . . beings.", struck through in pencil with vertical use marks on pp. [33] and [34], is used in "Aristocracy," W, X, 51–52.

⁵¹ See JMN, IX, 400, 371.

⁵² See JMN, IX, 392.

⁵³ These two sentences, struck through in ink with four vertical and two diagonal use marks, are used in "Works and Days," W, VII, 181; "printed" is set off above by a curved line in ink.

⁵⁴ This sentence is marked in the left margin by an ink line, possibly a use mark.

⁵⁵ On this page, "See . . . years." is in pencil.

⁵⁶ This sentence is struck through in pencil with a diagonal use mark.

American mind a wilderness of capabilities[57]

↑Is↓ ⟨T⟩the air of America ⟨seems to be⟩ loaded with imbecility, irresolution, dispersion↑?↓[58]

Climate. Give me a climate where people think well, & construct well; I will spend six months there, & you may have all the rest of my years.

Luther's drunken peasant. You get a judge—he will have a bias: the lawyers know that some cases fare ill with him. His law is piracy as Story's in Maine land cases. Yet in hundreds of cases where that whimsy does not warp him he does substantial justice.[59]

———

"Whites have no rights."[60]

———

Rotation is our remedy for loaded individuals.

[37] Eloquence, True Thomas, Pied Piper, Le Menetrier de Meudon

His music had the power to make the drunken sober & the sober drunk[.][61]

Eloquence

————————

       "Harping, quoth he, ken I none.
       For tongue is chief of minstrelsy."[62]

————————

[57] "American . . . capabilities" is struck through in pencil with a vertical use mark.

[58] This sentence is struck through in pencil with a vertical use mark.

[59] "Luther's . . . justice." is rewritten in ink over substantially the same matter in pencil, now partially erased. On the character of Judge Joseph Story as it appeared to a resident of Maine, see *JMN*, IX, 458.

[60] See *JMN*, VII, 416.

[61] "Le Ménétrier de Meudon," in Pierre Jean de Béranger, *Chansons: Nouvelles et dernières* (Paris, 1833), pp. 187–191, concerns a fiddler "who could even make the mourners in a funeral dance" (*J*, VII, 298). "Eloquence . . . drunk" is in pencil. Cf. "Eloquence," *W*, VII, 65.

[62] See Journal AB, pp. [48], [114] above.

[38] [63] Scholar wishes that every book & chart & plate belonging to him should draw interest every moment by circulation.

———

Expression

>"No man is the lord of any thing
>Till he communicates his part to others
>Nor doth he of himself know them for aught
>Till he behold them formed in the applause
>Where they're extended; where like an arch
>   reverberates
>The voice again, or like a gate of steel
>Fronting the sun, receives & renders back
>The figure & its heat."
>[Shakespeare,] ↑Troilus & Cressida↓ [III, iii, 116–123]

[39] Wh⟨at⟩y should men complain of stupid people as if a man's debt to his inferiors was not at least equal to that to his superiors? [n] If men were his equals, the waters would not move; but the difference of level which makes Niagara a cataract, makes eloquence, indignation, & poetry in him who finds there is much to communicate. ↑See also O, p. 72↓ [64]

In Carlyle as in Byron, one is more struck with the rhetoric than ↑with↓ the matter. He has manly superiority rather than intellectuality, & so makes good hard hits all the time. There is more character than intellect in every sentence. Herein strongly resembling Samuel Johnson.

[40] A woman is as much withered & injured in the saloon in full dress[,] ⟨in⟩ starved for thought & sentiment, as in the kitchen. In labours of house & in poverty I feel sometimes as if the handiness & deft apparatus for household toil were only a garb under which the softest Cleopatra walked concealed.

---

[63] Underlying the writing on this page is a series of large capital letters in pencil: D, A, B, O, E, E, E.

[64] "Wh⟨at⟩y should . . . communicate." is used in "Greatness," *W*, VIII, 320. For Journal O, p. [72], see *JMN*, IX, 379.

[41] How is it that the sword runs away with all the fame from the spade & the wheel?ⁿ From the most accumulated Civilization we are always running back at once to any drum & fife. There is skepticism for you.⁶⁵

And they only in trade & in law-courts & in saloons ⟨prosper who⟩ and in orchard & farm, too, prosper ↑who↓ engineer in the sword & cannon style. But I prefer the manners of pears to those ↑of most↓ men & women.

Courage forever, & this is the proof.

_____

My only secret was that all men were my masters.⁶⁶ I never saw one who was not my superior, & I would so gladly have been his apprentice if his ⟨secr⟩craft had been communicable[.]

[42] Alas for America as I must so often say, the ungirt, the diffuse, the profuse, procumbent, one wide ↑ground↓ juniper, out of which no cedar, no oak will rear up a mast to the clouds! it all runs to leaves, to suckers, to tendrils, to miscellany. The air is loaded with poppy, with imbecility, with dispersion, & sloth.
Eager, solicitous, hungry, rabid, busy-bod⟨ied⟩y America attempting many things, vain, ambitious to feel thy own existence, & convince others of thy talent, by attempting & hastily accomplishing much; yes, catch thy breath & correct thyself and failing here, prosper out there; ⟨this⟩ speed & fever are never greatness; but reliance & serenity & waiting & ⟨negligency are better signs of late but large fruit.⟩,⁶⁷ ↑perseverance, heed of the work & negligence of the effect↓[.]

_____

Great country, diminutive minds,

_____

See the Oak-Hall story. Σ p 6⁶⁸

⁶⁵ This paragraph, struck through in pencil with a vertical use mark, is used in "Aristocracy," *W*, X, 37, 38.
⁶⁶ Cf. "Greatness," *W*, VIII, 313.
⁶⁷ "are better . . . fruit.)" is enclosed in penciled brackets and canceled in pencil; "⟨negligency . . . fruit.)" is canceled in ink.
⁶⁸ "One of our compatriots being in South America, was asked by a native, what

[43] America is formless, has no terrible & no beautiful condensation. Genius always anthropomorphist, runs every idea into a fable, constructs, finishes, as the plastic Italian cannot build a post or a pumphandle but it terminates in a human head.

[44] How attractive is land, orchard, hillside, garden, in this fine June! Man feels the blood of thousands in his body and his heart pumps the sap of all this forest of vegetation through his arteries. Here is work for him & a most willing workman. He displaces the birch & chestnut, larch & alder, & will set oak & beech to cover the land with leafy colonnades. Then it occurs what a fugitive summer flower papilionaceous is he, whisking about amidst these longevities. Gladly he could spread himself abroad among them; love the tall trees as if he were their father; borrow by his love the manners of his trees, and with nature's patience watch the giants from the youth to ⟨ag⟩the age of golden fruit or gnarled timber, nor think it long.

[45] It seems often as if rejection[,] sturdy rejection[,] were for us; choose well your part, stand fast by your task, and let all else go to ruin if it will. Then instantly the malicious world changes itself into one wide snare or temptation, — escape it who can. With brow bent, with firm intent, I ⟨walk⟩ ↑go↓ musing in the garden walk. I stoop to pull up a bidens that is choking the corn, and ⟨ne⟩find there are two; close behind it is a third, & I reach out my arm to a fourth; behind that, there are four thousand & one. I am heated & untuned, and by & by wake up from my idiot dream of chickweed & ⟨bidens⟩ ↑redroot↓, to find ↑that↓ I with my adamantine purposes, am a chickweed & pipergrass myself.[69]

↑I remember the retired grocer at Medford who went down daily to the corner to see the Gentlemen go to Boston. "There, Mr

---

was his country? 'The United States.—' 'Is not that somewhere near Oak-Hall?' ⟨‖ ... ‖⟩ inquired the native." Oak Hall was a clothing store in Boston noted for its advertising; see *JMN*, VII, 9.

[69] This paragraph, struck through in ink with a vertical use mark, is used in "Wealth," *W*, VI, 115.

Ward's gone, Mr Sargent, & Mr Brooks. I'll stay till Mr Furness
goes by, & then go home."↓

[46]⁷⁰   ↑*See p. 146*   infra↓

↑To↓ every ⁿ ⟨thing⟩ creature ⟨God commanded⟩
⟨Should go by⟩ ↑Adam gave↓ its name
Every one should ⟨hang out⟩ ↑disclose↓ its ⟨banner⟩
        ↑feature↓
And cognizance
⟨Not a bug creeps⟩ ↑Moth & bug & worm & snail↓
⟨Not a worm hides⟩ ↑Mite & fly & creeping atomy↓
But is ⟨required⟩ ↑challenged to proclaim↓
⟨To make proclamation of itself⟩ ↑⟨Its lineage⟩↓ ↑to
        proclaim↓ ⁷¹
⟨And to have⟩ ↑Its↓ ↑function ⟨&⟩↓ its ↑lineage &↓ name
        ⟨& aims⟩
↑These are↓ publicly ⁿ enrolled
Not a plant obscure
But once a year its flower blooms
And tells the Universe
Its family & ⟨line⟩ ↑fame↓
Not ⟨a⟩ fly nor aphis ↑bites the leaf↓
⟨⟨But⟩Bites the leaf⟩
But comes a day
When its egg or ⟨ravage⟩ ↑fretted path↓ ⟨shows⟩ ↑betray⟨s⟩↓
The ⟨small⟩ ↑petty↓ ⟨conspirator⟩ ↑thief↓
And his small murder plot
Many things the garden shows
And pleased I wander
From ⟨pear to pear⟩ ↑tree to tree↓
Watching the pear flowers
Infested quince & plum

---

⁷⁰ This page is in pencil.
    ⁷¹ Emerson may have intended "to proclaim" to follow "its lineage & name"
n the following line, though he did not so indicate in the manuscript. "To Every
. . . proclaim", struck through in pencil with a diagonal use mark, is rewritten on
p. [146].

[47] [72]   And I could walk thus
Till the slowripening tree had reached
Its fruiting time nor think it long
The good husband
Allows no life in the garden
Than he wots of
Wastes no globule of sap
⟨And makes⟩
Waters his trees with wine [73]

Where is Skrymir Giant Skrymir
⟨To⟩ ↑Come↓ transplant the woods for me
⟨Bid him⟩ Scoop [n] up ⟨that⟩ ↑yonder↓ aged beech
That century pine and oaks that grew
↑Oaks that grew↓ in [n] the Dark ages
⟨And⟩ Bring [n] them heedful⟨ly⟩ & set them ⟨out⟩ ↑straight↓
In ⟨soft &⟩ sifted soil before my house
⟨Then let him⟩ ↑Now↓ turn the river on their roots
So that their topmost bough shall never droop
⟨Th⟩His tall erected plume nor a leaf wilt.

[48]   ↑*Printed in "Power."*↓

In history the great moment is when the savage is just ceasing
to be a savage with all his Pelasgic strength directed on his opening
sense of beauty; [n] you have Pericles & Phidias, not yet having passed
over into the Parisian civility. Every thing good in nature & the
world is in that moment of transition, the foam hangs but a moment
on the wave; the sun himself does not pause on the meridian;
literature becomes criticism, nervousness, & a gnawing when the first
musical triumphant strain has waked the echoes[.] [74]

Civilization is symbolized (how wittily) by a cake, in ⟨‖ ... ‖⟩ ↑the
hierological↓ cipher of the Egyptians. —

---

[72] This page is in pencil.
    [73] Emerson was thinking of his neighbor Abel Moore: see pp. [80] and [94]
below.
    [74] "In history . . . echoes", struck through in ink with four vertical use marks
and one diagonal use mark, is used in "Power," W, VI, 70–71.

[49]   *Worship of the Dollar.*

I may well ask when men wanted their bard & prophet as now? They have a Quixote gallery of old romances & mythologies, Norse, Greek, Persian, Jewish, & Indian, but nothing that will fit them, and they go without music or symbol to their day labor.

Channing proposed that there should be a ⟨large⟩ ↑magnified↓ Dollar, say as big as a barrel head, made of silver or gold, in each village & Col. Shattuck or other priest appointed to take care of it & not let it be stolen; [75] then we should be provided with a local deity, & could bring it baked beans or other offerings & rites, as pleased us.

But what have we to do with elucidating Shakspeare & reading that which ends with the reading? Let life be a [50] ⟨solemn⟩ stately self-respecting march, & not a mendicant tricked out in foreign patch-work[.]

Literature should be the counterpart of nature & equally rich. I find her not in our books. I know nature, & figure her to myself as exuberant, ⟨fer⟩tranquil, magnificent in her fertility, — coherent, so that every thing is an omen of every other. She is not proud of the sea or of the stars, of space or time; for ⟨every weed & grass shares the⟩ all her kinds share the attributes of the selectest extremes. But in literature her geniality is gone[—]her teats are cut off, as the Amazons of old[.]

[51]   Rocking stones

It is said that when manners are licentious, a revolution is always near: ⟨‖ ... ‖⟩the virtue of woman being the main girth or bandage of society; because a man will not lay up an estate for ⟨his⟩ children any longer than whilst he believes them to be his own. I think, however, that it is very difficult to debauch society. This chastity which people think so lightly lost, is not so. 'Tis like the eye which people ⟨t⟩fancy is the most delicate organ, but the oculist tells you it is a very tough & robust organ, & will bear any injury; so the poise of virtue is admirably secured. Unchastity ↑with women↓ is an acute disease, not a habit; the party soon gets through it. Men are always being instructed more & more in the chastity of women.

---

[75] Colonel David Shattuck (1790–1867) was president of the Concord Bank.

[52] "In March many weathers" said the proverb; and in life, many. If any thing were but true two days. But now we go forth austere & dedicated, believing in the iron links of Destiny irreversible & will not turn on our heel to save life, and we become strong with the same magnetism[.]

Well if it could last.

But tomorrow we are spiritualists, beleive in power of the will. We are ⟨an⟩the angel Gabriel & the Archangel Michael, the ring on our finger is the seal of Solomon, our sword or spade or pencil ↑or↓ pen is to open the secret caverns of the Universe. Who but we? and where is the bondman of the Parcae? Well, next day, we whistle & are speculative, & have a profusion [53] of common sense, ⟨& think there is much to be said on both sides,⟩ and think that the army is, ⟨the⟩after all, the gate to fame & poetry & "all that"; and that one story is good till another is told; and also that ⟨wine & beef have the best effect on the individual mind.⟩ ↑English scholars have been eaters & drinkers↓[.]

We go by Captain M[oore].'s farm, and say, Selfishness plants ↑best,↓ & prunes best; Selfishness makes the best citizen & the best state. The good & the true make us puke. Resistance is good, and obedience is good, but who under Heaven knows how to mix the two? Our approval of one or another is all retrospective. No man ever said "I will do well" & then did well. Instinct, yes; but that is to be [54] born not won[.]

Then we look over into George Minott's field & resolve to plough & hoe by old Cause & Effect henceforward. Life is a puzzle & a whirl & the cards beat the best players.[76]

---

[76] " 'In March . . . state", struck through in ink with a series of three vertical use marks on p. [52] (" 'In March . . . proverb"; "But now . . . the will"; "the ring . . . Solomon") and three on p. [53] ("of common . . . sides,)"; "the army . . . all that' "; "Selfishness plants . . . state"), is used in "Montaigne," *W*, IV, 175–176. Both Abel Moore (1777–1848) and George Minott (d. 1861) were neighbors of Emerson at Concord; "Captain Moore was sheriff and jailor" of Middlesex County "and, after the easy-going fashion of those days, employed the prisoners on his farm, an arrangement beneficial and not disagreeable to them" (*J*, VII, 297, n. 1). With "the cards . . . players.", cf. *JMN*, VI, 94, IX, 89, and "Nominalist and Realist," *W*, III, 241.

Dr Van Mons at Louvain in Belgium had in his nurseries in 1823 no less than 2000 seedlings of merit (Beurre Diel, ↑&↓c) "From among the 80 000 seedlings raised by himself" &c. Inventor of the pear. Some of Roman pears were called *proud*, would not keep; & Pliny says, "All pears are but a heavy meat unless they are well boiled or baked"[.]

"tree must be in a state of variation." "older the tree, nearer will seedlings raised from it approach a wild state, without, however, ever being able to return to that state."
[55] Van Mons.

"Sow, resow, sow again, sow perpetually, in short do nothing but sow." [77]

Kurroglou [78]

"Serdar, hear me, I am wont to sing some verses in the heat of ⟨the⟩ battle. A song has just come into my mind. Listen to it first & we shall fight afterwards." [p. 38]

"The peasant looked at him (Kurroglou) & saw a head like ⟨a⟩the cupola of a church, mustachios extending up beyond the ears, & a beard that reached down to the waist, & the height nearly equal to that of a minaret." p 237

"Whenever he heard a woman's voice he used to lose his senses." p 316

"in answer he shouted so loud that it seemed that a gun was fired from the well." p 316

His bill of fare. Prepare for me every day, for *breakfast*, 22½ lb of the best meat, lb 15 of the whitest bread, lb 15 of brandy, & lb 15 of wine.
for supper lb 22½ of rice amber-scented for *pillaw* over the rice put a whole baked unweaned lamb, &c————&c [p]p [317–]318
he possessed such an extraordinary strength in his hand that he could

[77] Andrew Jackson Downing, *The Fruits and Fruit Trees of America* (New York, 1846), pp. 5–7, 317; in Emerson's library. Jean Baptiste van Mons (1765–1842) was a Belgian horticulturalist. " 'Sow . . . sow.' " is used in "Instinct and Inspiration," *W*, XII, 76.
[78] As on pp. [25] and [27] above, Emerson is quoting from Alexander Chodzko, *Specimens of the Popular Poetry of Persia*, 1842.

squeeze a piece of money between his fingers so as to obliterate the ciphers coined on it. [p. 68]

[58] [79] The verse which enumerates the signs of the Zodiack is a good example of the mnemonics of music or rhyme[.]
The Ram, the Bull, the heavenly Twins &c [80]

Song to his horse. "I shall kiss all over thy dear little head, my darling Kyrat. If a man were to buy thee at the price of his soul he would have thee at a low price. I give him every evening 40 measures of barley. I have furnished his curry comb with two little bells that he may not find his time too tedious in the stable. Trappings of velvet upon thy back will be cheap to me. Thy silver shoes with their nails of gold are cheap to me." [pp. 253–]254 [81]

[59] [82] Socrates (in Gorgias) "I myself heard Pericles when he gave us his advice concerning the middle wall." Taylor Vol. IV. p 366 [83]

[Ibid.,] p 386 "For I know how to procure one witness of what I say, namely, him with whom I discourse, but I bid farewell to the multitude."

———

Socrates was celebrated for his exact domestic economy which Boeckh thinks consisted in keeping his family at work. "His income,

[79] Emerson numbered the verso of p. [55] as "58", thus omitting pp. [56] and [57]. "*Kurroglou*" is written in ink at the top of the page as an index heading to the entry concerning Kurroglou's song to his horse.
[80] "The verse . . . &c" is in pencil. See Isaac Watts, *Works . . .* , ed. D. Jennings and P. Doddridge, 6 vols. (London, 1753), IV, 706–707:
"The *Ram*, the *Bull*, the heavenly *Twins*,
And near the *Crab* the *Lion* shines,
    The *Virgin* and the *Scales*,
The *Scorpion*, *Archer* and *Sea-Goat*,
The man that holds the *Water-pot*,
    And *Fish* with glittering tales."
Emerson also alludes to the verse in "Poetry and Imagination," *W*, VIII, 46, and quotes it in Journal CO, p. [172], reading "glittering scales" rather than "glittering tales". Journal CO will be published in a later volume.
[81] Alexander Chodzko, *Specimens of the Popular Poetry of Persia*, 1842.
[82] This page is in pencil.
[83] *The Works of Plato*, trans. Floyer Sydenham and Thomas Taylor, 5 vols. (London, 1804). This edition is in Emerson's library.

according to Xenophon from his property might amount to 24 drachmas, together with some additional contributions of his friends, his necessary expenses were exceedingly small, & no one could live as he did. He lived in the strictest sense upon bread & water, except when he was entertained by his friends; and may have been much rejoiced at barley being sold at the low price of a quarter obolus the choenix. He wore no undergarment & his upper garment was ⟨so⟩ slight, the same for summer & winter. He generally went barefooted, & his dress shoes which he sometimes wore, [60] probably lasted him his whole life. A walk before his house served him for opson for meals, in short no slave lived so poorly as he did" Boeckh p. 110 [i.e., pp. 111–112] [84]

"The most moderate person required every day for opson 1 obolus[;] for a choenix of corn, 1 quarter obolus[;] & for clothes & shoes 15 drachmas in a year. A family of four adults must therefore at the lowest ⟨rates⟩ have required 360 drachmas for the specified necessaries."

Boekh p. 109-

Socrates could be goaded to seriousness & then it was as if the sea & sky spoke. He it was who in Gorgias (Taylor [*The Works of Plato . . .* , 1804,] Vol. IV. p 458) expressed the hope of mankind[:]

"I think there will be hereafter worthy & good men who will be endued with the virtue of administering justly things committed to their trust."

↑See infra p 127 of this ms.↓

[61] Anthropomorphism

"Of Ymir's flesh
Was Earth y shapen
But of his sweat seas
rocks of his bones
trees of his hair
but of his skull heaven

---

[84] Cf. August Boeckh, *The Public Economy of Athens*, 1842; see *JMN*, IX, 412. Both this and the following extract from Boeckh, also somewhat condensed, are in pencil.

> But of his brows
> Made the blithe powers
> Midgard for men's sons
>
> But of his brain
> Were hard of mood
> The clouds all y-shapen."
>
> Gylfi's mocking.
Younger Edda [85]
>
> p 9.

Edda = Grandmother

↑Snorro Sturleson an Icelander born 1179

Soemund born 1057↓ [86]

[62] Criticism should not be querulous & wasting, all knife & root puller, but guiding, instructive, inspiring, a south wind, not an east wind[.]

Contrarious temperament with chills, Muff, & buffalo when the mercury reaches 90 degrees, and a fan at Zero and parasol. On going to bed wants strong coffee as a soporific and when we must write at night sup on baked beans, lettuce, and popp⟨ies⟩y-juice. He dislikes to hear nightingales hallooing all night but finds something soft & lulling in the voice of a pig[.] [87]

[63] "This religious coat," says Hafiz ↑to his mistress,↓ "puts me into no small confusion; make thou me a monk with thy irresistible glan⟨ce⟩ces." Unlike his commentator, I should read— Not the dervish, not the monk, but I, in spite of all my love of pleasure, have at heart the true spirit which makes the ascetic & the saint: and

---

[85] *The Prose or Younger Edda Commonly Ascribed to Snorri Sturluson*, trans. George Webbe Dasent, 1842.

[86] The insertion is written in the upper right corner of the page and set off by a long diagonal line in ink.

[87] Cf. p. [28] above, on the whippoorwill. This paragraph is struck through in pencil with a diagonal use mark.

not their mummeries, certainly, but, what is strange to say, thy glances only can impart to me the fire & virtue needful to such selfdenial.[88]

By help of tea   tea was renounced.[89]

Ah if a lobster could taste himself or a terrapin or an oyster[!]

[64] What do we know of Albert the Great, ↑⟨D⟩the "Wonderful Doctor"↓, ↑AD↓ 1195–1280, of Saint Buonaventura, 1221–1274, the "Seraphic Doctor," of Thomas Aquinas, 1224–1274, the "Angelic Doctor," of Roger Bacon, 1214–1294, who knew powder, steamboats, rail-road cars, telescopes,[—] what know we of all these books which made the sufficient culture of their age⟨s⟩ & the following ones? ⁿ Well Dante (born 1265) absorbed it & he survives for us.[90]
                    ↑printed or its result in "Quotation
                              & Originality"↓

[65]   *Dictionary*
Rome   means force   Ῥώμη
Goethe   = the fine Goth
Buddha   = He who knows
Vishnu   = pervading or entrance.
Bana   = sermons
Odin   = movement
Hafiz   "signifies one gifted with so good a memory that he knows
             the whole Koran by heart." *Von Hammer* [91]
Saadi   = felicity
Natura   = (to be born) Becoming or Transition

---

[88] *Der Diwan von Mohammed Schemsed-din Hafis*, trans. Joseph von Hammer, 1812–1813, II, 294; the translator's commentary on the stanza Emerson has put into English reads: "Meine Kutte setzt mich in grosse Verlegenheit, weil ich nichts weniger als den wahren Geist des Mönchthums besitze. Nur deine Blicke können mir Muth und Kraft zur nöthigen Selbstverleugnung einflössen." "Not the dervish . . . selfdenial." is used in "Persian Poetry," *W*, VIII, 248.

[89] See *JMN*, VII, 358.

[90] This and the previous sentence, struck through in ink with a curved diagonal use mark, are used in "Quotation and Originality," *W*, VIII, 181.

[91] *Der Diwan von Mohammed Schemsed-din Hafis*, trans. Joseph von Hammer, 1812–1813, I, ix.

Edda   = Grandmother [92]
Cochituate = "Pure Water in plenty at a moderate price." *Quincy* [93]
↑Michel Angelo
Raffaelle Sanzio↓

↑Copied in *RT* 37↓ [94]

[66]   *Orientalist*
      Joseph Von Hammer, ↑born 1774,↓ ⟨wrote⟩published in ⟨1818⟩
1818.   History of Persian Belles Lettres.
1813.   Divan of Hafiz
1823.   Motenebbi, from the Arabic
1825.   the Baki, from the Turkish [95]

      Debistan   from the Hindoo [96]

↑Orientalism is Fatalism, resignation: Occidentalism is Freedom
& Will.
      We occidentals are educated to wish to be first. W. 76 [97]
      Teaching that shows the omnipotence of the will spiritual.
                                             D 271↓ [98]

[92] See the briefer listing in Journal AB, p. [9] above, and, for "Edda", p. [61]
above.
      [93] Josiah Quincy, Jr., mayor of Boston from 1845 to 1849, was instrumental in
bringing a supply of water to the city from Long Pond in the town of Natick, Massachusetts. The pond was renamed "Cochituate" at his suggestion.
      [94] "Dictionary . . . Sanzio" is struck through in pencil with three diagonal
use marks; other pencil lines run from "Vishnu" down to and around "Raffaelle Sanzio" and then to the right margin; "Copied . . . 37" is in pencil.
      [95] Baron Joseph von Hammer-Purgstall (1774-1856), to whose translations "we
owe our best knowledge of the Persians," Emerson was to write in "Persian Poetry,"
W, VIII, 237. In addition to the first two books listed, both of which Emerson owned,
the reference is to *Motenebbi der grösste Arabische Dichter* (Vienna, 1824), which
translates the *Divan* of al-Mutanabbi (915?-965), and *Baki's, des grössten Turkischen
Lyrikers, Divan* (Vienna, 1825).
      [96] *The Dabistán, or School of Manners*, translated from the original Persian,
with notes and illustrations, by David Shea . . . and Anthony Troyer . . . , 3 vols.
(London, 1843).
      [97] See *JMN*, IX, 218-219.
      [98] See *JMN*, VII, 183.

[67] *Orientalist*

Says Goethe (*Works*. VI. 241 [99]) "The English translator of the Cloud-Messenger, Megadhuta, is likewise worthy of all honor, since the first acquaintance with such a work always makes an epoch in our life."

[68] *Expression.* I have not yet, I believe, collected, and I suppose cannot yet collect into propositions what I think on this oft repeated word. But I think it plain; that there are great expressors with little ⟨subject matter;⟩ stuff; as Byron: that expression, again, is tantamount to life.

Shakspeare is nothing but a wonderful expressor. We cannot find that any thing in his age was more worth expression than any thing in ours; nor give any account of his existence, but only the fact that there was a wonderful symbolizer & expressor who has no rival [69] in all ages, in his way, & who has thrown an accidental lustre over his time & subject[.] ↑See of him above p. 24↓ [100]

↑See also particularly a passage in O, 23.↓ [101]

---

[70] The problem of the poet is to do the impossible in this wise[,] namely to unite the wildest freedom with the hardest precision; he is to give the pleasure of colour, and is not less the most powerful of sculptors. Music seems to you sufficient, or the subtile & delicate scent of lavender; but Dante was free imagination, all wings, yet he wrote like Euclid.

↑Transcribed in PY 194↓ [102]

[71] In the garden a most important treatment is a good neglect. It

---

[99] *Werke*, 55 vols. (Stuttgart and Tübingen, 1828–1833), VI, 242; Emerson's page reference, if it is to this edition, is in error.

[100] The insertion is in pencil.

[101] See *JMN*, IX, 366.

[102] "The problem . . . Euclid.", struck through in ink with a curved diagonal use mark, is used in "Poetry and Imagination," *W*, VIII, 72. The addition refers to Notebook PY (Theory of Poetry).

must be a capital care that will make tomato or apple or pear thrive like a lucky neglect. ↑Put a good fence round it & then let it alone a good deal. Fence it well, & let it alone well.↓

In George Sand's books, of course, the deduction is to be made of the cockney civilization. There is genius, yes, but also the fifteen thousand francs. The genius draws Porpora; the franc draws the underground plot of Zdenko and the caves of castles & the law of Vehm.[103] One must not look for music & emancipation in a [72] book, unless of one of those stalwart harpers who go by only once in 500 years.

Continued from p 25 [104]

There was a ravine at the foot of one of the sides of the mountain twelve yards broad. Kurroglou sat before it three days & then encouraged his horse with a song; "On! on! my soul, Kyrat, carry me to Chamly Bill. Alas my horse let me not look upon thy shame. I will have thee wrapped in velvet trappings. I will shoe thy fore & thy hind legs with pure gold. O my Kyrat, my chosen one of 500 horses &c ↑thou shalt have a bath in a river of red wine.↓"

Reyhan Arab meantime with his band watched him from below with a telescope — "Kurroglou ↑with Ayvaz in the saddle↓ continued to walk Kyrat until the foam appeared in his nostrils. At last he selected a spot [73] [105] where he had room enough for starting & then giving his horse the whip pushed him forward. The brave Kyrat sprang forward & stood on the very brink of the precipice; the whole of his four legs were gathered together like the leaves of a rosebud: he

[103] Porpora and Zdenko are characters in George Sand's *Consuelo* (1842); the former is drawn from Nicolo Porpora (d. 1767), an Italian composer studied by the novelist's grandmother. For "the underground plot . . . castles", see *La Comtesse de Rudolstadt* (1843), Ch. 23 and 27, in which a kind of occult tribunal, the francs-juges (equivalent to the German Wehme, or Sainte Wehme), acts in opposition to aristocratic tyranny.

[104] As on pp. [25], [27], [55], and [58] above, Emerson's quotations are from Alexander Chodzko, *Specimens of the Popular Poetry of Persia*, 1842.

[105] On this page in the manuscript the remainder of the extracts from Chodzko follows "The Archangel . . . shirt.", which stands at the top of the page; a horizontal line in ink separates the entries.

struggled awhile then gave a spring & leaped to the other side of the ravine nay he cleared two yards farther than were necessary." ⟨p 81⟩

"As for Kurroglou even his cap did not move on his head nor did he even look behind as if any thing extraordinary had happened. He then rode quietly away with Ayvaz." [pp. 78–81]

"Without Kyrat life & the world is but a sin to me" [p. 165]. "He has cleared a broad river   I have recognized his foot marks. Oh I shall kiss every one of his hoofs, I shall kiss each of his burning eyes." [p. 175]

This horse can run in one day from Ardebil to Kashan 350/m. What cares he for the Sultan who is mounted on this horse! [p. 175]

The Archangel Gabriel in pantaloons & ruffled shirt.[106]

---

[74] In an evil hour I pulled down my fence & added Warren's piece to mine.[107] No land is bad, but land is worse. If a man own land, the land owns him. Now let him leave home, if he dare. Every tree and graft, every hill of melons, every row of corn, every hedge- -shrub, all he has done and all he means to do, stand in his way like ⟨creditors &⟩ duns when he so much as turns his back on his house. Then the devotion to these vines & trees & cornhills I find narrowing & poisonous. I delight in long free walks. These free my brain & serve my body. Long marches [75] would be no hardship to me. My ⟨fra⟩ frame is ⟨a⟩ fit for them. I think I compose easily so. But these stoopings & scrapings & fingerings in a few square yards of garden are dispiriting[,] drivelling, and I seem to have eaten lotus, ↑to be↓ ⟨w⟩robbed of all energy, & ↑I↓ have a sort of catalepsy, or unwillingness to move, & have grown peevish & poorspirited.

↑The garden is like those machineries which we read of every month in the newspapers which catch a man's coatskirt or his hand & draw in his arm, his leg, & his whole body to irresistible death.[108] ⟨‖ ... ‖⟩ See p↓

---

[106] Cf. *JMN*, IX, 430: "Archangels in satinette & gambroon."

[107] On Emerson's purchase of the Warren lot, see Journal AB, p. [39] above.

[108] These two paragraphs, struck through in ink with vertical use marks on pp. [74] and [75], are used in "Wealth," *W*, VI, 115–116.

[76] Everything hastens to its Judgment Day. The merriest poem[,] the sweetest music rushes to its critic. From Calvinism we shall not get away. See how sedulously we plant a pair of eyes in every window to overlook our own goings & comings. And I know my Parcae through all the old hats, ⟨&⟩ pea jackets, and blue farmer's frocks which they wear on every road I walk in.

[77] The parents wished the girl to stay from home; the girl insisted on living at home. The girl was right, though the parents were poor. Work grows like grass everywhere; and labor is capital. Wherever created, it is exchangeable for every coin of the globe.

↑See JK 95↓ [109]

[78] Garrison accepts in his speech, all the logic & routine of tradition, and condescends to prove his heresy by text & sectarian machinery with a whole new calendar of saints. What a loss of juice & animal spirits & elemental force! [110]

↑I cannot live as you do. It is only by a most exact husbandry of my resources that I ⟨succeed in being⟩am any body.↓

↑See O 115↓

↑W 31↓ [111]

[79] ⟨It costs⟩
What a spendthrift you are, o beautiful Corinne! What needless webs you weave, what busy arts you ply. It costs you no exertion to paint the image of yourself that lies on my retina. Yet how splendid that benefit! and all your industry adds so little and puts in peril so much. A post even can be a post, and that is much. What that is not a post, can seem so? And every one can do his best thing easiest.[112]

---

[109] The insertion is written in pencil. Emerson is expanding notes on "L[ouisa]. A[lcott]." and on the subject of work that he had entered in Notebook Trees[A] [Sequence I]; see *JMN*, VIII, 523. With "Work grows like grass everywhere", cf. "Duty grows everywhere, like children, like grass" in "Character," *W*, X, 111.

[110] This entry is expanded from a note on Garrison made in Notebook Trees[A] [Sequence I]; see *JMN*, VIII, 523.

[111] *JMN*, IX, 391–392, 194–195.

[112] "⟨It costs⟩ . . . easiest." is expanded from an entry in Notebook Trees[A] [Sequence I] about Margaret Fuller; see *JMN*, VIII, 524. "It costs you . . .

[80]　　　　Garden

Do you not understand values said Sylvan. I economize every drop of sap in my trees as if it were wine.[113] A few years ago these trees were whipsticks. Now every one of them is worth a hundred dollars. Look at their form. ⟨‖ ... ‖⟩Not a branch nor a twig is to spare. They look as if they were arms & hands & fingers holding out to you the fruit of the Hesperides.

Montaigne took much pains to be made a citizen of Rome. I should greatly prefer to ⟨be ma⟩have the freedom presented me of a peach-orchard or of some old plantations of apples & pears ↑that I know↓ than of any city[.] [114]

[81] ↑June 22↓

An orientalist recommended to me who was a Hercules among the bugs and curculios, a Persian experiment of setting a lamp under the plum tree in a whitewashed tub with a little water in it, by night. But the curculio showed no taste for so elegant a death. A few flies & harmless beetles perished, & one genuine Yankee spider instantly wove his threads across the tub, thinking that there was likely to be a crowd & he might as well set up his booth & win something for himself. ↑At night in the garden all bugdom & flydom is abroad. —

This year is like Africa or New Holland[,] all surprising forms & masks of creeping, flying, & loathsomeness↓[.]

[82][115] 27 June

A. thought G. & his company ⟨the sport of some great instinct⟩ a symptom of some new & finer class.

Irresistibility of the American; no conscience; his motto like

---

benefit!", struck through in ink with three vertical use marks, is used in "Uses of Great Men," *W*, IV, 6.

[113] See p. [47] above. "Sylvan" is evidently Captain Abel Moore, Emerson's neighbor; cf. p. [94] below.

[114] "Do you . . . city" is struck through in pencil with a vertical use mark; "Do you . . . Hesperides." is used in "Country Life," *W*, XII, 145.

[115] The entries on this page through "last of it" are rewritten in ink over what appears to be substantially the same matter in pencil, now partially erased.

nature's is, 'our country right or wrong.' He builds shingle palaces
↑and shingle cities↓; yes, but in any altered mood perhaps this afternoon he will build stone ones, with equal celerity. ⟨Great race i⟩
Tall,ⁿ restless Kentucky strength; great race, but tho' an admirable
fruit, you shall not find one good sound well-developed apple on the
tree. ↑Nature herself was in a hurry with these hasters & never
finished one.↓

Happy blending of advantages in the climate. ↑We get in
summer↓ the splendor of the Equator & a touch of Syria, with
enormous natural productiveness; goes into the genius, as well as
into the cucumbers, whilst the poor polar man only gets the last of
it[.]

↑Our Superstitions. R. 137↓ [116]

[83] [117]

Art. The sands of the granite get wind of the power to please
which belongs to all the elements & begin to coquette with men &
angels. ↑This is seen in dreams.↓

Nature in this climate ardent; rushing up after a shower into a
mass of vegetation.

Mythology
We do not understand in old biblical history the idol business;
but we have a plenty of sub-gods ourselves. Who is not an idolater?
I remember being at a loss to know why those Israelites should have
such a passion for the idols.

Art's office is to furnish us with an ideal circumstance so that our flour
barrel & milk pan[,] bureau & wash stand shall begin to be symbols[.]

[116] See *JMN*, VIII, 419–420.
[117] The original writing on this page was in pencil. "Art . . . for the idols."
is rewritten in ink over what appears to be substantially the same matter in pencil,
except that "I remember . . . idols." is added. "Art's . . . symbols" remains in
pencil.

[84] A[lcott] says Why is an arbour ornamental & intellect is not surely so regarded? I reply, Because an arbour remains an arbour; but ↑the man of↓ intellect is willofthewisp & fantastical [—] a bird, a bat. It ⟨w⟩should have reverence enow if it remained itself.[118]

The solitude. All intellectual men are believers in an aristocracy, that is, a hierarchy. But I think them honest; because it is the prerogative of genius to melt every many ranked society into one company, merging distinction in their sincere curiosity & admiration.[119]   See AB 120

The solitude. Dreadful to sit on the dais, happy to sit near the salt. Happy who is never seen except rightly seen! Happy whose dress no man ever could remember to describe.

Ah[—] who has society! people to talk to? people who stimulate? Boston has 120 000 and I cannot now find one: and elsewhere in the world I dare not tell you how poor I am, how few they are.[120]

[85] [121] ⟨Of the strange⟩ Skepticism of the Intellect. It will not speak to the Intellectual on the platform of Ethics. And that out of a true integrity. It has strange Experience. It knows that it is a debtor to sin & degradation[.]

Certainly certainly let it do homage in silence to the soul. But in speech I think it should bravely, as it certainly will with the Intellectual, own the actual[.]

That is sublime — to abandon onesself against all experience to the Absolute & Good[.]

> But God will keep his promise yet
> Trees & clouds ⟨no liars are⟩ ↑are prophets sure↓

---

[118] This paragraph is in pencil.

[119] "The solitude . . . admiration." is rewritten in ink over what appears to be substantially the same matter in pencil.

[120] "The solitude . . . they are." was originally written in pencil; "Dreadful . . . they are." is rewritten in ink over what appears to be substantially the same matter.

[121] This page is in pencil.

And new & finer forms of life
⟨Cometh surely to the pure⟩
↑Day by day approach the pure.↓

[86] [122] Loci   Chaucer's Blood of gentilesse like fire
Rabelais' Muses
Luther's puddings [123]
        & Latiners that God wondereth at us
Dibdin's Booksale
Ivo Bishop of Chartres [124]
Kurroglou & his improvisation
Chaucer's Friendship in Roman de la Rose
Pascal's Integrity

[87] *Temperance.* The worst of brandy is that it makes a craving.

The Age
    Age of Humboldt, Van Mons, Goethe, Rothschild, Brunel, Hudson, Charles T. Jackson, Paxton, [125]

[88] It needs a great apparatus to give the scholar play. It is not a hand loom or a spinning wheel, but wheels that roll like the solar system.
I think you must give him an academy with models, better than any that is known, gardens, towns, astronomy, courts & kings, a freedom of the city, — a ticket that admits to all parts of the house.

The mysterious laws of Poetry, the natural history of a poem are not known, no practical rules, no working-plan was ever given.

[122] This page is in pencil.
[123] See *JMN*, VI, 349, quoting *Colloquia Mensalia: or, Dr. Martin Luther's Divine Discourses at his Table*, 1652; *JMN*, IX, 245; *L*, III, 412–413.
[124] For "Dibdin's Booksale", see Journal AB, p. [2] above, and "Books," *W*, VII, 209–210. For "Ivo . . . Chartres", see *JMN*, IX, 60.
[125] Of those not previously mentioned, Emerson has in mind the banking family of Rothschild; the engineer Sir Marc Isambard Brunel, who constructed the Thames Tunnel; George Hudson, the English "Railway King"; and the architect and horticulturalist Sir Joseph Paxton, who designed the conservatory and gardens at Chatsworth: see Journal AB, p. [39] above.

It is miraculous at all points. The slate given, a little more or a good deal more or less performance seems indifferent. There is much difference in the stops, but the running time ⟨can⟩need be but little encreased to add great results.

As we say, one master could so easily be conceived as [89] writing all the books of the world. They are all alike.[126]

Here is the separation by Nature of men to the⟨ir⟩ literary office, — ⟨& then⟩separation as by brazen walls, — & then no power to do that ⟨f⟩which they were separated for. They must not do much, nor forbear much: they must not eat or drink or fast or sleep or wake. If they make a hit, that is bad too, for then they go to copy themselves & are spoiled.

[90] Railroads are to civilization what mathematics were to the mind. Their immense promise made the whole world nervous with hope & fear, & they leave society as they found it.[127] The man gets out of the railroad car at the end of 500 miles in every respect the same as he got in. But a book or a friend opens a secret door at his side ↑that ↑may↓ lead⟨s⟩ to Parnassus.↓

Railroad whistle like the whir of a gigantic musqitoe close to your ear at night / And sometimes like an Aeolian harp[128]

[91]   Affirmative in trees

My trees send out a moderate shoot in the first summer heat and then stop. They look all summer as if they would presently burst the bud again, & grow; but they do not. ⟨R⟩The fine tree continues to grow. — Well, there is the same thing in the men. The commonest remark, if the man could only extend it a little, would make him a genius; but he ⟨ends⟩ ↑rests↓ in leaves without new shoots all his days.

[92] The tadpoles shed their tails as they grow older: Men shed

---

[126] With "As we say . . . alike.", cf. JMN, IX, 42, 58. "The mysterious . . . conceived as" is struck through in pencil with a vertical use mark; "The mysterious . . . alike." is used in "Instinct and Inspiration," W, XII, 72.

[127] Cf. JMN, IX, 448: "Mathematics leave the mind where they found it."

[128] "Railroad whistle . . . harp" is in pencil.

their heads. They become *shouldery* or *necky*, stiff-necked, long-legged. Ages of arms, & thighs, & reins; but the age of the Brain waits until that of soldiers, hunters, husbandmen, & brokers, is past.

↑Capt Moore
& the barometer↓ [129]

History.
It is not determined of man whether he came up or down; Cherubim or Chimpanzee.[130]

Crocker fancied the Western RailRoad was a mistake: it should have gone through Fitchburg.[131]   Yes, you can go by a screwing[,] twisting ro⟨ad⟩ute from New York, but the main road is through Boston!

[93] With that contentment which belongs to the man who has found out what is the matter with him, and who seems already to amend.
The garden's the matter

Tools.   Cotton-Age
Tools. The ship Skidbladnir made by dwarves & given to Freyr was so great that all the asa with their wargear might find room on board; and as soon as the sail is set, she has a fair wind w↑h↓ither she shall go, & when the voyage is over, Freyr can fold her together like a cloth & keep her in his bag.[132]

We make dahlias to order, & horses & swine. Owen & Fourier say we shall make men yet of the right sort[.]

He likes the garden because it minds him so well. ↑See GH 27↓

[129] "Capt . . . barometer" is in pencil. On Abel Moore, Emerson's neighbor, see pp. [53] above and [94] below.
[130] Cf. *JMN*, VIII, 362.
[131] Alvah Crocker was president of the Fitchburg Railroad; cf. *JMN*, IX, 133, 428.
[132] *The Prose or Younger Edda Commonly Ascribed to Snorri Sturluson*, trans. George Webbe Dasent, 1842, p. 50.

[94] My young friend believed his calling to be musical, yet without jewsharp, catgut, or rosin. Yes, but there must be demonstration. Look over the fence yonder into Captain Abel's land. There's a musician for you, who knows how to make men dance for him in all weathers, & all sorts of men, paddies, felons, farmers, carpenters, painters, yes, and trees, & grapes & ice & stone, hot days, cold days. Beat that, Menetrier de Meudon! if you can! Knows how to make men ⟨dance⟩ saw, dig, mow, & lay stone wall, and how to make trees bear fruit God never gave them, and grapes from France & Spain yield pounds of clusters at his door. He saves every drop of sap as if it were his own blood. His trees are full of brandy. You would think he watered them with wine.[133] See his cows, see his swine, see his horses [95] and he[,] the musician that plays the jig which they all must dance[,] biped & quadruped & centipede[,] is the plainest[,] stupidest looking harlequin in a coat of no colours. But his are the woods & the waters[,] the hills & meadows[.]

With a stroke of his ⟨fiddle⟩ ↑instrument↓ he danced a thousand tons of gravel ⟨from⟩ from yonder blowing sandheap on to ⟨yonder⟩ ↑the↓ bog meadow ↑beneath us↓ where now the English grass is waving ↑over countless acres.↓ With another he terraced the sand hill, and covered it with peaches & grapes; with ⁿ another he sends his lowing cattle every spring up to Peterboro to the mountain pastures[.]

The farmer ⟨does not thin⟩ when thinning ⟨out⟩ his ⟨musk⟩melon↑s↓ ⟨vines⟩, takes advice of the bug, & ⟨saves⟩ ↑spares↓ those sweet ⟨ones⟩ ↑vines↓ which the bug has nearly eaten, & throws away the ⟨thrifty⟩ ↑fair↓ ones that are not gnawed. ↑Let the tree instruct you how to prune it. Too old a farmer to take a large apple.↓

[96] ⟨The⟩It would be easy to go round the world on our railroads in the shortest intervals, if only we could keep up the running time. It is the stops which consume the day.

---

[133] See the references to Captain Abel Moore in *JMN*, VIII, 239; pp. [53], [80], [92] above; and the verse on p. [47]: "Wastes no globule of sap . . . Waters his trees with wine." "Look over . . . with wine." is used in "Country Life," *W*, XII, 145.

⟨Yankee Speculators⟩

Nesmith of Lowell[,] a little gnarled man as A[bel].A[dams]. says[,] projected the City of Lawrence, persuaded Sam[ue]l Lawrence to work with him and he interested Abbott Lawrence. The two received, I think, $30 000 each for their services.

The Ogdensburgh speculators of Boston sent up Billy Kendrick to bond the land at O. of the farmers. And he went talking & gossiping about, with his "trees to sell," and actually bonded 900 acres. [⟨Kendrick was to have 1/16 of the shares.⟩] He had a Judge Hall of the place behind him to execute the papers. A man named Bigelow at Brighton who first came there from Vermont [a] barefoot, seventeen years old boy, to help a man drive his sheep down; and he thought he would stay there a little while, "his father wouldn't find no fault;" then he drove a butcher's cart; now he was one of these Ogdensburg speculators[.]

[97] An American in this ardent climate gets up early some morning & buys a river; & advertises for 12 or 1500 Irishmen; digs a new channel for it, brings it to his mills, and has a ↑head of↓ 24 feet of water: then, to give him an appetite for his breakfast, he raises a house; then carves out within doors ⟨half⟩a quarter township into streets & building lots, ⟨school⟩ tavern, school, & methodist meeting house — sends up an engineer into New Hampshire, to see where his water comes from &, after advising with him sends a trusty man of business to buy of all the farmers such mill privileges ⟨to⟩as will serve him among their waste hill & pasture lots [98] [134] and comes home with great glee announcing that he is now owner of the great Lake Winnipiseosce, as reservoir for his Lowell mills at Midsummer.

↑Nantucket Bangor Lawrence↓

They are an ardent race and are as fully possessed with that hatred of labor, which is the principle of progress in the human race, as any other people. They must & will have the enjoyment without

---

[134] On this page of the manuscript the continuation of the passage on the American entrepreneur follows "The one event . . . my gate", which stands at the top of the page; a horizontal line in ink separates the entries.

the sweat. So they buy slaves where the women will permit it; where they will not, they make the wind, the tide, the waterfall, the steam, the cloud, the lightning, do the work, by every art & device their cunningest brain can achieve.

The one event which never loses its romance is the alighting of superior persons at my gate[.]

---

[99] ↑Come see what weeds grow behind this fence!↓

My pear. This noble tree had every property ⟨th⟩which should belong to a plant. It was hardy and almost immortal. It accepted every species of nourishment & could live almost on none. It was free from every species of blight. Grubs, worms, flies, bugs, all attacked it. It yielded them all a share of its generous juices, but when they left their eggs on its broad leaves, it thickened the fiber & suffered them to dry up, & ⟨bu⟩shook off the vermin. ↑It grows like the ash Yggdrasil.↓ [135]

⟨Edw⟩The country gentleman delights in raising living monuments to Van Mons[,] the inventor of pears.

[100] I observe false instincts or the want of true ones. I think I never mistake my relation to any person. I discover very quickly whether we have any thing for each other, and ropes could not hold me after my welcome is out. But people come to me and fancy that they are the people; and I have nothing for them in my heart but waiting — waiting — till they be gone. One would think that the affinities would pronounce themselves with a surer reciprocity. ↑See *RS.* 100↓ [136]

One other thing is to be remarked concerning the law of affinity. ⟨There are people⟩ Every constitution has its natural enemies & poisons, which are to be avoided as ivy & dogwood are by those whom those plants injure. There are those who, disputing, will make [101] you dispute; and nervous and hysterical and animalized, will produce a like series of symptoms in you; though no other persons

---

[135] "It grows . . . Yggdrasil." is used in "Country Life," *W*, XII, 146.

[136] Journal RS will be printed in a later volume.

⟨ever⟩ produce the like phenomena in you, & though you are conscious that they do not properly belong to you, but are a sort of
extension of the diseases of the other party into you. I have heard
that some men sympathize with their wives in pregnancy, as, for
example in the nauseas with which women are affected, a ridiculous &
incredible circumstance, but it, no doubt, grew out of this observation.
⟨It is said to be a⟩ ⟨which⟩ Liebig has discovered ↑a↓ law of bodies↓ [137]
— "the contagious influence of chemical action." It is thus; "A body
in the act of combination or decomposition enables another body with
which [102] it may be in contact to enter into the same state." [138]

"A substance which would not of itself yield to a particular chemical
attraction, will nevertheless do so if placed in contact with some other
body which is in the act of yielding to the same force."

"He who betaketh himself to a good tree hath good shade: for the Cid
knew how to make a good Knight as a good groom knows how to make a
good horse." Cid. p. 230 [139]

Easy to live with heroes [140]

[103] Rich & Poor
The demands of the day are often more than enough for the day;
as, when I receive letters in the morning mail which occupy ↑all↓
the hours & leave no time for the proper studies of that day. Then
we eat our cherries & have planted no corn for the coming year.
He is the rich man who on every day more than answers the
demands of the day.

————

There is a contest between the demands of the poor & the
demands of the rich: the demands of the rich are they not legitimate also? Thus I have never seen a man truly rich[,] ↑that is↓ with

[137] "ever", "It is said to be a", and "which" are canceled in pencil; "a law of
bodies", originally written between "to be a" and "which", is circled in pencil for
insertion after "discovered".
[138] Justus Liebig, *Chemistry in Its Application to Agriculture and Physiology*,
ed. Lyon Playfair, 2nd edition (London, 1842), p. 262. "Liebig . . . same state."
is used in "Powers and Laws of Thought," *W*, XII, 23.
[139] Robert Southey, *Chronicle of the Cid, from the Spanish* (Lowell, Mass.,
1846); in Emerson's library.
[140] These five words are in pencil.

an adequate command ⟨that is⟩ of nature. But men are stimulated incessantly from the ideal to acquire the command over nature. It is the interest of the universe of men that there should be dukes of Devonshire, Croesuses, Karuns, & King⟨s⟩ Solomon↑s↓.

[104] I find the farming poisonous —   See p. 74

Yet cattle, horses, & carts, are good toys for boys[.]

Fine hair must be paid for, whether it grow on one's own head or on some other.

————

Among the seven ages of human life the period of indexes should not be forgotten.

————

[105] Gardens, trees in clumps, a bath in the brook, the pond paved with coloured pebbles, an arboretum, fireworks over water.

[106] Yes, Dumas has doubtless journeymen. In Paris they can be procured, and why not ↑the have journeymen↓ as well as Thorwaldsen or Upjohn? [141] How much better, really better would he not write for having the less vigorous but yet original vein of another man put entirely under his command, with that man's honest experience & imagery.

[107] 10 July
     Ellery Channing has written a lively book on Rome which certifies that he has been there. He has the reputation of being a man of genius and this is some guarantee of it.[n] ⟨yet⟩ He has approached sometimes the lightness & pungency of his talk, but not often. He has used his own eyes and many things are brought to notice here

————

[141] Alexandre Dumas (1802–1870), the French novelist and playwright, reportedly employed a staff of assistants. Bertel Thorwaldsen (1768–1844) was a Danish sculptor; Richard Upjohn (1802–1878), an English-born American architect. "Dumas has doubtless journeymen." is used in "Power," *W*, VI, 58.

that had ↑not↓ been reported, as the fountains, the gardens, lively
⟨& accurate⟩ charcoal sketches of the cafe, the trattoria, and the bacon
dealer's shop, the vettura & postillion, the agriculture in the Campagna. It was a lucky thought to introduce Montaigne in Rome, and
the tribute to Raffaelle ⟨in the⟩ over his tomb in the Pantheon, & to
Michel Angelo, are warm & discerning. A very catholic spirit[.] [142]

[108] Kurroglou [143]
Hussein Khan approached at the head of 1500 horse. "My madmen,
my souls!" cried Kurroglou to his band, "fear nothing: with the
help of God & the heavenly mediation of the pure essence of Ali's
soul, I shall disperse them in an hour." p[p. 37–]38

Kurr-oglou   Son of a blind man [144]   [p. 26]
"I ⟨have⟩ sought thee in heaven I have found thee on earth," says
K. to Ayvaz; "the arched line of thy eyebrows has been sketched by
the pen of the Almighty." [p. 77]

When he comes home angry ⟨angry men⟩his madcaps disperse[:]
"Every one of them like a rat hid himself in some hole or other."
[p. 167]

"Each arrow that he shot from the bow went bleating through the air
like a calf that seeks the cow its mother." [145] [Cf. p. 203]

"The son of the European minister standing in the door of his tent saw a
woman pass on horseback that way accompanied by a man who sat, himself
like a mountain upon another mountain — his horse." p 142

[109] T. sometimes appears only as a gen d'arme[,] good to knock

---

[142] Emerson's reference is to William Ellery Channing, *Conversations at Rome:
Between an Artist, a Catholic, and a Critic* (Boston, 1847); a copy is in his library.
This paragraph is struck through in ink with two wavy diagonal use marks —
("Ellery . . . Campagna") and one diagonal use mark ("It was . . . spirit").
[143] The quotations which follow are from Alexander Chodzko, *Specimens of the
Popular Poetry of Persia*, 1842.
[144] "Hussein . . . man" is struck through in pencil with a wavy vertical use
mark.
[145] "When he . . . mother.'" is struck through in pencil with a diagonal use
mark.

down a cockney with, but without that power to cheer & establish, which makes the value of a friend[.] [146]

Goethe in this 3d vol. autobiography, which I read now in new translation,[147] seems to know altogether too much about himself[.]

Luther, according to Mr Blecker, advises ↑in one of his letters,↓ a young scholar who cannot get rid of his doubts & spiritual fears, to get drunk.
There is also a wellknown proverb of his remaining, which kicks the pail over. ↑which see in *TU* p. 76↓ [148]

[110] "[The Prose or] Younger Edda commonly ascribed to Snorri Sturluson" Translated from the old Norse by Geo. Webbe Dasent B.A. Stockholm & London 1842 [149]

"Under the root (of ⟨the⟩ ⟨as⟩Yggdrasil's ash) that trendeth to the Hrimthursar there is Mimir's spring where knowledge & wit are hidden; and he that hath the spring hight Mimir, he is full of wisdom, for that he drinks of the spring from the horn Gioll. Thither came Allfadir & begged a drink of the spring, but he got it not before he left his eye in pledge." [150]

"Well know I, Odin,
Where thou thine eye hast hid,
'Tis in the mere
Mimir spring:
Mead drinks Mimir
Every morning
From Valfadir's pledge.

p 17   Are ye wise yet or what?"

[111] p 20

"Yggdrasil's ash
beareth hardships

---

[146] Emerson indexed p. [109] under Thoreau.

[147] Probably that by Charles A. Dana: vol. III in *The Auto-Biography of Goethe. Truth and Poetry; from My Life*, ed. Parke Godwin, 4 vols. (New York, 1846–1847).

[148] "Luther's famed verse is 'Wer nicht liebt Wein, Weib, und Gesang, / Der bleibt ein Narr, sein leben lang.'" "Luther . . . drunk.", struck through in ink with a vertical use mark, is used in "Montaigne," *W*, IV, 153.

[149] This reference is set off by a curved ink line at the left and below.

[150] This paragraph is used in "Culture," *W*, VI, 137–138.

More than men wot of
The hart bites above
but at the side it rots
Nithhavgg scores it beneath"

"More worms are lying
Under Yggdrasil's ash
Than every silly ape thinks of;

Goinn & Moinn,
Grabakr & Grafiav⟨i⟩lluthr,
Ofnir & svafnir,
Methinks must for aye gnaw
The boughs of the tree." [p. 20]

                                        Woman
                        Weirds all
                        Methink Frigg knoweth
                        Though she telleth them never [151]
                                        p 24

"The Gods have erected a bridge from earth to heaven which is called Bifrost or Rainbow" [p. 13]

[112]   *Edda*
    I also find it significant, what is said of Thor's house, ↑(Bil-skirnir)↓ that "it has five hundred & forty floors." [152]   See p. 25.

    See p[p.] 30[-31; abridged:]

"Heimdallr the white As is warder of the gods and sitteth at heaven's end to keep the bridge against the Hillogres; he needeth less sleep than a bird; he seeth day & night alike a hundred miles from him; he heareth be it grass that groweth on earth, or wool on sheep & all things louder than these; he hath the horn Gioll, and its blast is heard in all worlds."

"Hel has power over nine worlds and shares those abodes with the men that are sent to her & these are they who die of sickness or eld.
Her domains are great, & her yard-walls of strange height, & her grates [113] huge. Elindnor hight her hall, hunger her dish, starving her knife, Ganglati her thrall, Ganglot her maid (they can scarce creep for sloth) a

---

[151] These three lines are used in "Woman," *W*, XII, 406.
[152] The saying is used in "Culture," *W*, VI, 137.

beetling cliff is the threshold of her entry, care her bed, burning bale the hanging of her hall; she is half blue & half the hue of flesh —"
p. 33 [adapted]

The fetter for Fenris wolf ↑See GH. p 6↓ was made of six things, footfall of cat, beard of woman, root of stone, sinew of bear, breath of fish, & spittle of bird. —— ↑How↓ the fetter was smithied[:] smooth & soft as a silken string. The Asa coaxed him to put on his foot the limp silken band and Tyr put his hand in the wolf's mouth for a pledge.[153]

[114]   *Poet*
Significant again that "Balder the good dreamed dreams great & perilous for his life: but he told ↑the↓ Asa the dreams."
                    [*The Prose or Younger Edda*, 1842,] p. 69
So the whole fable, 'that Frigg took an oath of fire & water, iron & all ores, stones, earth, trees, sicknesses, beasts, birds, venoms, & worms, that they would spare Balder'[.]

The mistletoe was too young to crave an oath of. A blind man shot him to death with that, "and that is the greatest mishap that has befallen gods & men."   [*Ibid.*, pp. 69–71]

[115₁][154] Conversation that would really interest me would be those old conundrums which at Symposia the seven or seventy Wise Masters were wont to crack — What is intellect? What is time? What are the runners and what the goals?
But now there is no possibility of treating them well. Conversation on intellect & scholars becomes pathology. What a society it needs! I think you could not find a club at once acute & liberal enough in the world. Bring the best wits together and they are so impatient of each other, so worldly, or so babyish, there is so much more than their wit, so many follies & gluttonies & partialities, so much age & sleep & care that you have no academy. The questions that I incessantly ask

---

[153] *The Prose or Younger Edda Commonly Ascribed to Snorri Sturluson,* trans. George Webbe Dasent, 1842, pp. 35–36.
[154] Emerson numbered both p. [115] and its verso as "115".

myself [155] [1152] as, What is our mythology? (which were a sort of test object for the power of our lenses) never come[n] into my mind when I meet with clergymen; & what Academy has propounded this for a prize?

But of what use to bring the men together, when they will torment & tyrannize over each other, & play the merchant & the ⟨fop⟩ statesman. Conversation ↑in society↓ is always on a platform so low as to exclude the Saint & the Poet after they have made a few trials.[156] Ah we must have some gift of transcending time also, as we do space, & collecting our club from a wider brotherhood. Crier[,] call Pythagoras, Plato, Socrates, Aristotle, Proclus, Plotinus, Spinoza, Confucius & Menu, ↑Kepler, Friar Bacon↓

[116]   ⟨Our people you say are un⟩
Gardening, A[lcott]. thought today, was a good refuge for reformers, Abolitionists, &c. that they might ⟨give⟩ acquire that realism which we so approve in merchants and in Napoleon. ↑Yes;↓ gardening[n] and architecture would certainly be affirmative wholly, & so remedy this "unlimited contradicting" & chiding which is "a flat affair."

↑*Insufficient Forces*↓ [157]
We have experience, reading, relatedness enough, o yes, & every other weapon, if only we had constitution enough. But, as the doctor said in my boyhood, — "You have no *stamina*."

[118] [158] It is not to be disguised, we may phrase it ⟨a⟩how we will, but there are few men. Most of these ↑we see↓ are masks & counterfeits. These are not men, but hungers, thirsts, fevers, desires, and, especially, certain fruits or earthly productions animated &

[155] "Conversation . . . myself" is struck through in pencil with a diagonal use mark. In "Clubs," *W*, VII, 235, is a reference to the conundrums described in the opening sentence of the passage.

[156] "Conversation . . . Poet", struck through in ink with four diagonal use marks, is used in "Clubs," *W*, VII, 230.

[157] Both heading and rules are insertions.

[158] Emerson so numbered the verso of p. [116], omitting "117", and thus compensated for duplicating "115".

anthropomorphized: As if a gardener were a pear-tree raised to the highest power, that it might preside over the race of Pears.

The Deity wants his earth gardened, so in addition to frost & heat & wet, which do not work fast enough[,] he perfects the disintegrating ⟨tool⟩ ↑pick or spade↓ to the uttermost, & sends the ears of corn & the potato vines *in human shape*, [119] & they cultivate these, break up the rock, the bog, & the sand⟨b⟩hill, & terrace & ditch & dress & adorn them[.]

Always where there is metal there is mould said Alcott[.] [159]

Fine tools, we say, — the railroad & telegraph, — only without sufficient use when ended.

C. Stow wanted his bog-meadow brought into grass. He offered Antony Colombe, Sol. Wetherbee, & whosoever else, seed & manure, ↑& team,↓ & ⟨the half or⟩ the whole crop; which they accepted, & went to work, & reduced the tough roots, the tussucks of grass, the uneven surface & gave the whole field a good rotting & breaking & sunning, and [120] [160] now Stow finds no longer any difficulty in getting good English grass from the smooth & friable land. What Stow does with his field, what the Creator does with the planet, the Yanke⟨s⟩es are now doing with America. It will be friable, arable, habitable, to men & angels yet.[161]

"A spirit haunts the last year's bowers" [162]
Ah 'tis a mocking fiend, he hides under the grapevines of this year also, and he will touch you with rheumatism & your heart with apathy, if you put so much as your hand to the plants.

---

[159] This sentence is in pencil.
[160] On this page of the manuscript the continuation of the passage on Stow's bog-meadow, headed "from p 119", follows " 'A spirit . . . plants.", which stands at the top of the page; a horizontal line in ink separates the entries.
[161] Cyrus Stow (1789–1876) was the town clerk of Concord, 1840–1848; Colombe did occasional work for Emerson also.
[162] An echo of Tennyson's "Song," lines 1–2: "A Spirit haunts the year's last hours / Dwelling amid these yellowing bowers."

[121] Garden

The genius of scholarship & of gardening are incompatible. One is concentrative[,] electrical in sparks & shocks, the other is diffuse strength. So that each disqualifies its votary from the other duties.[163]

refinous & vitreous

——— electricity.

[122]   ↑See Introd. of Lecture on the *Skeptic*.↓
          Tools.   Mechanic Powers.

Shall a man see wheels every day of his life on every cart, car, & loom, and not learn the value of manners as ⟨a⟩ ↑wheels or↓ currency to himself? Shall he ⟨see the⟩ in his garden cut down the spindling shoots of his pear tree ↑or pinch off the redundant buds of his grape-vine↓ to give robustness to the stock, & not ⟨reject⟩ learn the value of rejection in his own spiritual economy?

Shall he see that all his gardening is a selection, and then a new, and then a newer selection, and not apply that ⟨to his⟩ lesson to his life?

Or shall he see in chemistry that law of superinducing & contagion [mentioned above p. ↑100,↓] and not see that Plato Platonizes & Napoleon Napoleonizes men; that a merchant sets every body on edge for [123] stocks; Spurzheim fills America with plaster-skulls,[164] & Agassiz makes anatomists where he goes?

"Corpora non agunt nisi soluta." [165]

[124]   *Freedom*

"There is but one & only liberator in this life from the demons that invade us; and[n] that is Endeavour, earnest entire consentaneous Endeavour. Partial activity sets free but some part of us, nor is the freedom it gives but partial, even in those parts. The fountains of life must be stirred & sent bounding throughout our system, or else we ebb so soon into the Stygian pool of Necessity to drink of its infatuating bowl, & seal our doom

---

[163] This and the preceding sentence, struck through in ink with a vertical use mark, are used in "Wealth," *W*, VI, 116.

[164] Johann Kasper Spurzheim (1776–1832) was the cofounder of phrenology.

[165] "They do not exert themselves unless unfettered" (Ed.), or "Bodies only act when freed" (*J*, VII, 307, n. 1). See "The Fortune of the Republic," *W*, XI, 533.

of servitude. Once bondsmen of choice, but ⟨new⟩ servants of consent no
more" A. B. Alcott

"The liberation of the will from the d⟨a⟩emon world is the end & aim of
this mundane state." A B A

[125]   Pathology
Plato says, instead of medicine we have cookery, instead of legislation we have the adulatory art: ⟨th⟩so I find the Hotel poetry
offered in these days instead of that of mountains, and what is called
possession by the Muses has at moments, a strange resemblance to
dragons.[166]

[126] ↑July 25↓
    Of Alcott it is plain to see that he never loses sight of the order
of things & thoughts before him. The thought he would record is
something, but the place, the page, the book, in which it is to be
written are something also, not less than the proposition, so that
usually in the attention to the marshalling, the thing marshalled
dwindles & disappears.
    One thing more. I used to tell him, that he had no senses. And
it is true that they are with him merely vehicular, and do not constitute a pleasure & a temptation of themselves. We had a good proof
of it this morning. He wanted to know "why the boys waded into
the water after pond lilies?" — Why, because they will sell in town
for a cent apiece & every man & child likes to ⟨have one⟩ ↑carry one
to church↓ for a cologne bottle. "What," said he, "have they a per-
fume? I did not know it." ↑/ See also the account of Chaucer's
Canon   D 194↓[167]

[127] Plato.   Socrates.
In Gorgias. ↑(Taylor Vol. IV. p 397)↓

Callicles. "Tell me, Socrates, whether we must say that you are now in

[166] Cf. *Gorgias,* in *The Works of Plato,* trans. Floyer Sydenham and Thomas
Taylor, 1804, IV, 374. This paragraph is used in "Plato; or, the Philosopher," *W,*
IV, 59.
    [167] See *JMN,* VII, 133.

earnest or in jest? For, if you are in earnest and these things which you say are true, is not our human life subverted, & are not all our actions, as it seems, contrary to what they ought to be?"

———

↑See also the diatribe against philosophers (in Gorgias, [*ibid.*, p]p. 400–1)↓

[128] Soc. "One wise man is better than ten thousand who are unwise, according to your assertion &c"

Gorgias [*ibid.*,] p 406

"The true coin for which all else ought to be changeable is a right understanding of what is good." [168]

in Phaedrus

[129] *Astronomy*   *Cambridge Telescope*
For Wm Mitchell's Account of the Cambridge Telescope, see Σ, p. 67 — where the printed columns are pasted on the page.[169]

[130] The distinction between speculative & practical, seems to me much as if we should have champions appointed to tilt for the superiority respectively of each of the Four Elements — except insofar as it ⟨describ⟩ covers the difference between seeming & reality. In this ⟨dream⟩world of dreamers, it makes small difference whether the men devote themselves to nouns or to laying stone walls, but whether they do it honestly or for show. In the neighborhood of the new railroad the other day, in Westminster, I found two poor English or Irishmen playing chequers on a little board where the spots were marked with ink, & the *men* were beans & coffee berries. They played on, game after game, one sure of beating, the other indignant at defeat, and I left [131] them playing. Why not? & what difference? all the world is playing backgammon, some with beans & coffee, & some with Texas & Mexico[,] with states & nations.

[168] Heinrich Ritter, *The History of Ancient Philosophy*, 4 vols. (Oxford, 1838–1846), II, 412; see *JMN*, IX, 393.
[169] P. [67] of Notebook Σ is covered with Mitchell's three-column newspaper description of "The Great Telescope at Cambridge," which had an "object-glass" of 15 inches and an overall length of about 24 feet. The description is in the form of a letter to the editor of the *Nantucket Enquirer*, dated "7th mo 19th, 1847."

Eyes outrun the feet, & go where the feet & hands can never follow. So Plato the practicalists[.] [170]

Plato challenges study[.] [171]

[132] Compensation
In the Essay should have been adduced the fable of Faust as the contribution of Christian mythology to the dogma; and Balder's blessing by Frigga from all harms but the mistletoe; and the eye ⟨pl⟩ left in pledge by the Allfadir when he drank of Mimir's spring; The wolf Fenris is not chained except at the expense of the hand of Tyr; [172]

[133] [blank]
[134] Platforms many. Thor's house has five hundred & forty floors. Every man has no less.[173]

To live without duties is obscene[.] [174]

[135] Beattie is an example of successful poetic expression. What can be finer than

> "See in the rear of the ⟨su⟩warm summer shower
> The visionary boy for shelter fly." [175]

[136] Dr P. at S. reduced Unitarianism to a thin cold affair. There is one anecdote of him which I do not find in any of the Eulogies.[176] One Sunday, ⟨he baptized a child⟩ a man & his wife brought their child to be baptized. It happened that the sexton had neglected to

---

[170] "Eyes . . . practicalists" is rewritten in ink over substantially the same writing in pencil, with "practicalists" replacing "practicals".

[171] These three words are in pencil.

[172] See Emerson's notes on the *Younger Edda*, pp. [110], [113]–[114] above. His reference is to "Compensation," in *Essays* (1841).

[173] See p. [112] above.

[174] This sentence is used in "Aristocracy," *W*, X, 52.

[175] James Beattie, "The Minstrel; or, The Progress of Genius," I, xxx, 1–2; see *The Minstrel . . . and Other Poems* (New York, 1821), in Emerson's library.

[176] The entry to this point is struck through with a diagonal line in ink, possibly a use mark.

put water in the font, & Dr P. ⟨went through⟩ though a little em-
barrassed went through the usual motions, just as if there was water,
and went on with the rite to the end. The parents, however, discovered the omission, and there was much gossip & regret in the
following week, &, next Sunday, ⟨the⟩ to prevent scandal, water was
put into the font & Dr P went through with the sacrament once more
with real water, & baptized the child this time to purpose.

> [137] "For in my youth I never did apply
>   Hot & intemperate liquors to my blood"
> [Shakespeare, *As You Like It*, II, iii, 49–50]

W[illiam].E[llery].C[hanning]. describes the effect of sulphuric
ether as a whole railroad train ⟨going⟩ driving all the time thro' his
brain: he is fast arriving at the jumping off place: that which he
has been searching for in all his life, he is now just on the edge of
finding: but, over all this power, on the tip-top, is perched still a
residuum of the old state, the old limitation, & he learns that it can
in no wise be got rid of; so that sulphuric ether "shows him the ring
of necessity." Brandy, opium, nitrous oxide gas, sulphuric ether, hell-
-fire itself, cannot get rid of this limp band, O Asa! [177]

[138] *July 18, 1847.* Thor, too, I think — or Skrymir was it? [n] —
must have taken ether, when he mistook the fierce strokes of Thor's
hammer for the ⟨falling⟩ dropping of acorns, or of leaves from the
trees.[178]

↑*Books*↓

O day of days, when we can read! The reader and the book.
Either without the other is naught.

Thursday 15 July. Alcott, Thoreau & I went to the "island" in
the Walden wood-lot, & cut down & brought home 20 hemlocks for
posts of the arbour. And these have been growing when I was sleeping, fenced, bought, & owned by other men, and now in this new
want of mine for an ornament to my grounds, their care and the long

[177] See p. [113] above: the story of the Fenris wolf, from the *Younger Edda.*
[178] A further reference to the *Younger Edda.*

contribution of [139] the great agents, sun & earth, rain & frost, supply this rich botanic wonder. ↑of our isle↓ [179]

[140]   Cid   ↑Southey's Chronicle↓
Rodrigo Diaz de Bivar, born A.D. 1026,
Ruydiez el Campeador:

my Cid, my Fortunate, he who never was conquered, he of good fortune, my Cid RuyDiez he who in a happy hour first girt on his sword [180]

A rather aristocratic book is the history of the Cid[.]

The horse Bavieca, like Kurroglou's horse ↑Kyrat,↓ is the sub-god in the poem, and then the swords Colada & Tizona like Arthur's Excalibar.
      ↑Rustem had the horse Rakush
      Alexander had   Bucephalus
      Guy of Warwick had
      Cid   Bavieca↓ [181]

[141]   ↑*Power & Circumstance*↓
      In youth we go for freedom, for man; want a fort, build a fort; Θεου θελοντος, και επι ριπον αν πλεοις.[182] ⟨Great⟩ ↑True↓ [n] painter can paint with chalk, charcoal, tar. Qui fait chanter ne se fatigue pas. Instead of an army we send Belisarius. He ⟨is⟩ collects an army where he goes. One lion: a herd of lions were superfluous[.]
Later, we hear of great geniuses, thwarted by unfriendly circumstances; of seeds killed by rain or frost or worms. Of the prodigious change in war by rules & inventions; no valor, not Hector or Achilles

---

[179] The insertion is in pencil. As Emerson reported in a letter to Margaret Fuller, "Alcott (in whom do you know a Palladio was lost?) is building me (with Thoreau) a summerhouse of growing — alarming dimensions — peristyle gables, dormer windows, &c in the midst of my cornfield" (*L*, III, 413). On Thoreau's reaction, see Journal LM, p. [127] below.
[180] Robert Southey, *Chronicle of the Cid*, 1846, pp. 47, 65, 245, 135, and *passim*.
[181] The horses of Alexander, the Cid, Rustem, and Kurroglou are also listed in an undated entry in Notebook T, *JMN*, VI, 374.
[182] See p. [i] above. For "want . . . build a fort.", see Journal AB, p. [92] above.

or Scipio or the Cid, could resist the powers of modern artillery &
fortification. Science & tools have made individualism nothing.
Then we are shown the power of circumstance ($\langle$S$\rangle$see GH 29) and
then the felicity when man & tools meet, as in Bonaparte.

[142] Rich & Poor   "Paix et Peu." *Charron*
    Whilst there are no capacious rooms & no statues & pictures a
man is not yet properly drest. It is as if he should come abroad in
his night gown[.]

[143] 1847
24 July. Peartrees this morning in high prosperity. Hardly a tough,
dry, wormy dwarf in all the garden but is forced to show a bud or a
shoot today. Flemish Beauty meanwhile and the Golden Beurre of
Bilboa and the Green Princes who keep their incognito so well near
the plum trees$\langle,\rangle$ ↑(nos 98, 99,)↓ [183] show a foot & a half of growth
respectively.

1847
31 July.[184] Antonio Dabrado[,] a poor Italian boy who came two
months ago from Barga[,] twenty miles from Leghorn, and now
lives with his master in Bowdoin street no 199, Boston, came here &
sold his images to the children.

[144]   The Divine Man

    Alexander the Great emitted from his skin a sweet odour, and
Henry More believed the same thing of himself, and who does not
remember the southwind days when he was a boy, when his own
hand had a strawberry scent.

[145]   ↑Aristocracy↓ [185]
[July] 25. But the day is darkened when the golden river runs down

---

[183] See Emerson's list of plantings in Notebook Trees[A] [Sequence II], *JMN*,
VIII, 542.
    [184] The entry for this date, written on p. [142], is partly encircled in pencil with
an arrow leading to the penciled word "here" near the center of p. [143].
    [185] "Aristocracy" is in pencil.

into mud, when Genius grows idle & wanton, & reckless of its fine duties of being Saint, Muse, Inspirer, to its humbler & duller fellows, baulks their respect & confounds their understanding by silly extravagances that have to the people all the appearance of guilt.[186] There is no⟨thing that⟩ individual trait that will not with a little selfindulgence grow to a fanaticism, ↑as↓ the artistic or the stoical humour, and then beauty is deformity, and our delightful Image of Grace & Friendship is a mournful Chasm, — as now; henceforth a subject of tedious explanation[.]

[146]¹⁸⁷   To every creature   ↑See p. 46 supra↓
                     Adam gave its name
                     Every one must disclose
                     Its name & feature & cognisance

                     Moth & worm & snail
                     Mite & creeping atomy
                     But is challenged to proclaim
                     Its function lineage & name
                     These are publicly enrolled

[147] ↑One Idea↓   ↑W him.↓
     Sir the history of the grasshopper remains unwritten.[188] A French D'Israeli has written the epic of La Pipée and finds that the historians of France & of Europe have not sufficiently insisted on the influence of *Pipée* (bird-call) & the passion for red-breasts which transform, it seems, the *gamin* of Lorraine into heroes of Europe[.]

                     ↑W him.↓
And, in England, one man thought Music the ruin of England: And Mr Walker thought it the neglect of the cemeteries. And D'Israeli the Baronetage. And Brindley the want of canals. And Chadwick want of aquaducts. Mr Fisher thinks the cause of crime in

---

¹⁸⁶ "But the day . . . extravagances" is used in "Aristocracy," *W*, X, 51.
¹⁸⁷ This page is in pencil.
¹⁸⁸ Cf. *JMN*, VIII, 374: "The history of grasshoppers said the Reformer has never been written."

New England is the church. In England, Reid believed the one thing needful was ventilation (See *LM* 9). ↑Another gentleman believed the corruption of the age was marked by the disuse of the surtout & introduction of the sack, & every button the less marked a dereliction the more↓[.] [189]

[148] *Subjects*
    Ballads
    Fables
    Hafiz
    Reading   ↑AB 2↓
    Garden   ↑CD 116, 44,↓ [190]   Country Life
    Rich & Poor
    The Superlative
    Morals.   ↑Lexington & Nantucket, & Second Church.
    Scholar.   Middlebury Oration.
    Human Life
    Autobiography.   AB 110.
    Conduct of Life.   LM 3↓

[149] [blank]
[150] *Intellect*
    The two inspirations [CD] 5, 22–3, 38
    The transit moment in all things   48
    Dumas has journeymen   106
    Skepticism of intellect   85
    Conundrums of the seven wise masters, ⎤
    What is intellect? &   ⎦   114

    ———

    Garden & scholar   121

    ———

[189] This entry headed *"Whim."* was apparently written after Emerson's visit to England and Scotland, where he heard Carlyle's praise of Chadwick (Journal London, p. [59] below) and encountered the views of Walker, Reid, and the man suspicious of music (Journal LM, p. [9] below). For an earlier reference to James Brindley (1716–1772), an English engineer, see *JMN*, V, 177.
    [190] "CD . . . 44," is in pencil.

Endeavor   124

---

possession of muses is possession by dragons ⎫   125
false health   ⎬
Eyes outrun the feet, & thought outruns   ⎫
the eyes as far, Rest must follow   ⎬   131
the head   ⎭

Expression, large utterance   22, 24, 68 [191]

Science

One by one to every creature.
Adam gave its name;
⟨Every one should disclose⟩ ↑Let each to all unmask↓
    its feature
And cognizance ⟨|| ... ||⟩ proclaim;
↑No↓ moth ⁿ & bug ⟨&⟩ worm & snail
Mite & fly & creeping atomy
⟨But is required⟩ ↑Nor each nor any fail↓
Its lineage to proclaim

[151]   ⟨And have⟩ ↑⟨Be⟩↓ [192] ↑Let↓ its function & its name
↑Be↓ publicly ⁿ enrolled:
Not a plant obscure
But ⟨once a year⟩ ↑on a day↓ [193] its flower↑s↓ ⟨bloom⟩ ↑unfold↓
And tell⟨s⟩ the universe
Its family & fame;
No⟨t⟩ fly nor aphis bites the leaf
But comes a day
When egg or fretted path betray
The petty thief
And his small malfaisance.
Many things the garden shows
And, pleased, I ⟨wander⟩ ↑stray↓

[191] *"Intellect . . . 68"* is written in pencil, evidently in preparation for a lecture or essay.
[192] "And have" is canceled in pencil; "Be" is both inserted and canceled in pencil.
[193] "once a year" is canceled in pencil; "on a day" is inserted in pencil.

From tree to tree
Watching the ⟨pear⟩ ↑pyrus↓ flowers,
Infested quince or plum.
I could walk thus
Till the slow ripening secular tree
Had reached its fruiting time
Nor think it long.[194]
The ⟨good⟩ gardener↑'s love↓
Allows no more life in the garden
Than he wots of
[152] [195]   Wastes no globule of sap,
Waters his trees with wine.[196]

Where is Skrymir? giant Skrymir!
Come, transplant the woods for me,
Scoop up yonder aged beech
⟨That century⟩ ↑Centennial↓ pine, & oaks that grew,
Oaks that grew in the Dark Ages.
Heedful bring them, set them straight,
In sifted soil, before my house.
Now turn the river on their roots,
So the top shall never droop
Its tall erected plume, nor a leaf wilt.[197]

[Index material omitted] [198]

[152ₐ] [199]   From the beginning,
         ⟨Sin⟩ ↑Pride↓ blunders & brags;

[194] "Many things . . . long." is printed as "The Garden" among "Fragments on Nature and Life," XXI, *W*, IX, 343.
[195] Beneath the writing on this page are erased notes in pencil for the alphabetical index on the facing page, the inside back cover.
[196] Concerning "Wastes . . . wine.", see pp. [47], [94] above.
[197] For an earlier draft of the verse, see pp. [46]–[47] above.
[198] There are three items, evidently intended as additions to the alphabetical index on the facing page, the inside back cover.
[199] For a physical description of pp. [152ₐ]–[152ᵦ], see the bibliographical head-note to Journal CD.

True making true winning
Go hidden in rags.

Wit has the creation
Of worlds & their fame,
On one stipulation, —
Renouncing the same.

⟨Choose⟩ ↑Have↓ the strain it discourses,
Or the oatpipe & reed,
Hold the mystical forces,
Or ⟨skies⟩ ↑worlds↓ which they breed.

When gold first encloses
The brows of her son,
The Muse him deposes
From kingdom & throne.

[152_b] [blank]
[152_c] [...] [200]
[152_d] [blank]
[inside back cover] [Index material omitted]

[200] On p. [152_c] is a copy in ink made by Emerson of James Russell Lowell's "Saturday Club. To Charles Eliot Norton Agro Dolce". For a physical description of pp. [152_c]–[152_d], see the bibliographical headnote to Journal CD.

GH

1847–1848

Journal GH is a regular journal begun at the time Emerson had filled Journal CD. The first dated entry, on page [64], is for August 24, 1847, but an entry on page [9] may have been made as early as August 2 or shortly thereafter. Both GH and Journal Sea-Notes (pages 200–207 below) carry entries concerning Emerson's voyage to England, October 5–22, 1847; as his own note on page [i] of GH records, "This manuscript was written in England, from the page 112 to the end." The last dated entry, on page [132], is for December 30, 1847, but additional writing must have been done early in 1848: for example, an entry on page [138] can be dated as on or after January 13.

Journal GH is written in a copybook bound in brown boards with brown leather corners and spine; it has been rebacked in brown leather, on which is mounted a fragment of the original leather bearing part of an ink inscription, upside down: "G[H]". The cover, which measures 17.5 x 20.9 cm, is inscribed "GH / 1847". The pages, very faintly ruled, are 17.5 x 20.2 cm. Including flyleaves (i–ii, 147–148) there are 150 regular pages, all numbered in ink except those unnumbered (i, ii, 2, 3, 83, 145–148) or numbered in pencil only (4, 17, 32, 34, 37, 40, 74, 76, 82, 105, 125); pages 18, 33, 35, and 36 are numbered in pencil and again in ink. Emerson made an error in numbering two consecutive pages as 15 (here, 15_1 and 15_2) but compensated by designating two later pages as 30 and 30½. Three pages (68, 146, 147) are blank. Clippings are mounted on the front cover verso and on pages 40, 49, and 66; at one time there was also a mounting on page 24, as shown by marks on the page. There are eight additional pages written on inserted leaves. Pages 73_a–73_d are on a single leaf of 17 x 21 cm, folded once to make four pages and fastened with sealing wax to page 73; the inscription is Emerson's. Pages 108_a–108_d are on a loose leaf of cream paper, 23 x 18.5 cm, folded once to make four pages, with an embossed shield on page 108_a containing an "N" in script; the inscription on these pages is not Emerson's.

[front cover]   GH
                       1847

[front cover verso] [1] Memoranda

                   X ⟨T. How's State Reports⟩
Paris.   ⟨Harro Harring's books at Munroe's⟩
————   ⟨Boat⟩
Hotel Windsor   ⟨William Lane⟩
   Rue de Rivoli   ⟨Rebecca Black⟩
                      Abel Moore's a/c
                      ⟨S. Foord⟩
⟨C⟩hapman[n] 142 Strand. ⟨Upham⟩
                      ⟨Palmer⟩
T. Delf   17 Warwick st,   ⟨Mr Hale of Rutland⟩
———Golden Square,   ⟨G. S. E , letter⟩
J. W. Hudson   Leeds ⟨C. G. Ripley⟩ [2]

---

[1] The writing on the front cover verso is in pencil; "Memoranda" is partly circled in pencil. At one time fastened to the front cover verso but now separated from it are four advertisements clipped, according to Emerson's notation, from the *Times* of London. The first concerns transportation between London and Paris; the second, steamship transportation to Italy; the third offers literary assistance with "inviolable secrecy" ("By post, care of x.y.z" at a London address) — see Journal London, p. [76] below; the fourth advertises a diamond oil lamp, "the best light in the world."

[2] The entries in the left column to this point concern, respectively, a recommended Parisian hotel; the London addresses of Emerson's English publisher John Chapman and his friend Thomas Delf; and James William Hudson, who arranged Emerson's lecture engagements in Yorkshire. In the right column to this point, "⟨T. How's State Reports⟩" has not been identified. On Emerson's efforts to help Harring, a Danish novelist then living in New York, see his letter to William Emerson, March 7, 1847, *L*, III, 381–383; James Munroe was presumably among the Boston publishers Emerson approached in Harring's behalf. "⟨Boat⟩" probably concerns Emerson's impending voyage to Liverpool on the *Washington Irving*; he requested a reservation on September 18, 1847 (*L*, III, 416). William Lane, an English contributor to *The Dial*, had accompanied Bronson Alcott to America on the latter's return from England in 1842. Emerson had met Mrs. Black in New York in 1842. Sophia Foord was a former teacher of Emerson's daughters Ellen and Edith. "⟨Upham⟩" may be Thomas C. Upham, who had written Emerson on July 25, 1847. "⟨Palmer⟩" is probably Joseph Palmer, from whom Emerson received money on September 3, 1847 (see Notebook England and Paris, p. [71] below). "Hale" has not been identified. "G. S. E" may be George Samuel Emerson, son of Emerson's

⟨Deed Recorded⟩

B W Procter, ↑13↓ Upper Harley st.   ⟨M. M. E. $29.00⟩

Cavendish Square.   ⟨Ice business⟩

Thomas Hogg   56 Stafford st [3]

Espinasse   Mrs Moore's,   19 Athol Place,

⟨lx⟩   ⟨S G W⟩

Wm Staley,   41 Peel Terrace   Carter st, Greenheys [4]

⟨G.⟨B⟩P.B. Savings Bk book to S. R.⟩

⟨T Parker   *Swedenborg*⟩

⟨Edw Bangs   Hafiz⟩

⟨Vattemare⟩

Dr Arnoult

W Ropes [5]

[front cover verso_a] [6]   Errata

---

second cousin George Barrell Emerson. Christopher Gore Ripley was the son of Reverend Samuel Ripley of Waltham; in October of 1847 Emerson paid him $5.00 (see Pocket Diary 1, p. [7] below).

[3] Continuing in the left column are the London addresses of the poets Procter ("Barry Cornwall") and Hogg; Emerson wrote Procter on September 30, 1847, before leaving for England. The deed mentioned in the right column is probably that received from Cyrus Warren for purchase of the "Warren lot" in January of 1847; it is recorded in the Probate Court at East Cambridge, Massachusetts (*L*, III, 371, n. 9). Emerson refers to the deed and to a payment of $29.00 in behalf of Mary Moody Emerson, his aunt, in his letter of February 13, 1847, to his brother William, *L*, III, 371–372; in a subsequent letter of March 7 he mentions ice cutting on Walden Pond, *L*, III, 383.

[4] In the last two lines of the left column are the Manchester addresses of Francis Espinasse and William Staley; Staley showed Emerson about the city during his stay there in November of 1847.

[5] In the last five lines of the right column, "⟨S G W⟩" is Samuel Gray Ward, "G.⟨B⟩P.B." is George Partridge Bradford; "S. R." is probably Samuel Ripley of Waltham; "T Parker" is Theodore Parker. That Emerson had intended to send a copy of Hafiz to Edward Bangs, a young Harvard graduate of Boston, is indicated in his letter to Bangs of November 2, 1847, *L*, III, 429. On Alexandre Vattemare, see Emerson's memorandum of August 24, 1847, p. [64] below. Dr. Emile Arnoult of Boston helped Emerson with French pronunciation before his European trip (*L*, III, 409). The name of William Ropes appears in the charging records of the Boston Athenaeum, 1827–1834 and 1849–1850.

[6] [front cover verso_a] is an insert; at one time it was pasted to the cover.

Eng Edit Poems [7]

p   33 For *The* read *In*

   37 for hovered r. honoured

   62 for mountain r. mounting

   69 for trend*r*ant r. trenchant

   73 for purging r surging

   82 for As read At

   84 for Music read secret

   92 for buried r. honied

   95 for globe r glebe

   99 for world warning r. w. warming

 114 for feet r. sect

 130 insert a line "Till dangerous

 134 insert To & fro

 162 for brass read brags

 174 for shirt read skirt

      for then read thou

 175 *dele* cricket

 193 for then read thou

 199 for pent r bent

   68 for mighty r. nightly

   53 for mouse r. moose

 194 for *is*   r   his

 196 for locks read ⟨‖ msm ‖⟩

⟨right⟩
Pillsbury [8]

[i] [9] [Index material omitted]

[7] On the errors in Emerson's *Poems* (London, 1847), see his memoranda for John Chapman, his London publisher, *JMN*, IX, 468, and his letter of January 31, 1847, to Carlyle, *CEC*, p. 413.

[8] "⟨right⟩" and "Pillsbury" are written upside down. Emerson's reference is presumably to the abolitionist Parker Pillsbury.

[9] Two somewhat similar pencil sketches or diagrams appear below the last entry on the page. In each, two parallel diagonal lines are closed at the right by two oblongs, one higher than the other.

GH

1847

———

↑This manuscript was written in England, from the page 112 to the end.↓

[ii] [10]   *Memoranda for the Voyage*
Books   C T Brooks letter
Germ Dictionary   Mrs Black's
French Dict   James Brown
Hafiz   D Bixby [11]
Map of England

[1] George Crawshay, 46 Westgate st Newcastle on Tyne
Thomas Hornblower Gill, Calthorpe ⟨st⟩Place, Bristol Road,
        Birmingham
William Mathews. Calthorpe st., Edgbaston, Birmingham
James Pope   Frederick st, Newhall Hill, Birmingham
George Appleby, 12 Upper Priory, Birmingham.
Thomas S. Tunaley. Full street. Derby   .
Charles Harding Esq   Bale Hall Tamworth

↑Dr↓ J. A. Carlyle, 19 Hemus Terrace. Chelsea, London
Daniel Jefferson, 5 Kingsgate st. Holborn, London

W. Allen. Shiffnal, Salop
R.W. Birch, Esq. *Wardwell*, Derby
William Enfield Esq, Nottingham
Herbert New, Evesham.
Joseph Biggs, Knighton, Leicester.

[10] This page is in pencil.

[11] Charles Timothy Brooks had sought Emerson's help in placing his translation of Richter's *Titan* with an English publisher, writing him on July 31, August 27, and September 6, 1847; see *L*, III, 411. James Brown is probably the Boston bookseller, partner in Little, Brown & Co., for whom Emerson carried books to England; see Notebook England and Paris, p. [1] below. His friends Rebecca Black and Daniel Bixby, a publisher of Lowell, Massachusetts, may also have asked Emerson for assistance abroad.

Swanwick (   ) ↑Chesterfield↓
H.C. Attenburrow, Nottingham
C.E. Rawlins, Jr. 28 Catherine st. Liverpool
A H Clough. Oriel College, Oxford.
Wm Staley, 41 Peel Terrace, ↑Carter st↓ Greenheys, Manchester
⟨Miss⟩ Geraldine E Jewsbury, Carlton Terrace, Greenheys, Manchester [12]

[2] Alfred Turner Blythe. Chesterfield.
William Allingham, Done⟨g⟩gal, Ireland.
W.B. Scott. Newcastle on Tyne
Henry McCormac, Belfast, Ireland
Charles Wicksteed   5 Kingston Terrace *Leeds*
W.E. Forster, *Rawdon*, near Leeds.
T.B. Blackburne, *Birkenhead*, Liverpool ·
F.T. Elgie, Esq |*Worcester*|.   Maurice Davis. Foregate street.
Rev John Kenrick, 16 Gilligate, *York*.
            Walbran, *Ripon*
W. Harrison   *Ripon*   Mr Williamson
W. Fisher, Jr. Belmont, Hospital Road, Park, *Sheffield*
T.W. Stansfeld. Care of John Swire & Son. Liverpool

[12] The names on p. [1] are those of English correspondents or persons Emerson met in England. Crawshay, Emerson's host in Newcastle, was an iron manufacturer. Gill was a hymn-writer and poet, "a young man of genius . . . who outweighed all Birmingham" for Emerson (*L*, III, 455). Mathews "hospitably entertained" Emerson and promised him letters to Sir Marc Isambard Brunel (*L*, III, 455). Pope was in correspondence with Emerson in December of 1847; see also Journal London, p. [202] below. Appleby wrote to Emerson on October 28, 1847. Tunaley accompanied Emerson on a visit to Keddleston Hall in Derby; see p. [122] below. Harding has not been identified. Dr. Carlyle was Thomas Carlyle's younger brother. Jefferson had written Emerson on April 3, 1846, urging him to come to England (*L*, III, 367n). Emerson met Allen, a friend of Alcott, at Birmingham (*L*, III, 455). Birch, also a friend of Alcott, entertained Emerson at Derby (*L*, III, 451). Enfield was secretary of the Nottingham Mechanics' Institute. New, a friend of Gill from Worcester, had written Emerson in 1846 (*L*, III, 455). Biggs entertained Emerson when he lectured at Leicester in December (*L*, IV, 6–8). Emerson dined with Swanwick at Chesterfield; see p. [129] below. A Miss M. Attenburrow and her mother entertained Emerson at Nottingham (*L*, III, 445); "H.C." may be her father's initials. Rawlins had a part in the initial stages of Emerson's friendship with Clough, a native of Liverpool. Miss Jewsbury, the novelist, was a close friend of Jane Welsh Carlyle.

Rev Mr Shannon. Hull
R.M. Milnes, 26 Pall Mall
David Scott Eastern Dalry Edinburgh
F.T. Palgrave. Exeter College. Oxford
J.A. Froude Exeter College Oxford
Fred. J. Foxton Bwlch Gwyn Rhayaderr Radnorshire
John Forster Lincoln's Inn Fields
Charles Dickens
Tom Taylor
Robert Chambers Edinburgh
Joshua Bates 46 Portland Place London [13]

[3] Seddon & McBride Sculptors Russell st Liverpool
Bust of Mr Bailey
Sara Tagart, 21 Sandon st. Liverpool
⟨W A⟩Thos. Jevons, 9 Park Hill Road, Liverpool
Rev D. Thom, 3 St Marys Place, Edgehill, Liverpool [14]

[13] Blythe, not otherwise identified, addressed a letter to Emerson on December 11, 1847. Allingham, the Irish poet, is mentioned in Journal LM, p. [166] below, as among the persons Emerson saw in Europe. Scott was a poet and painter, brother of David Scott. Emerson had known MacCormac's work as a translator (L, III, 359); the two were in correspondence as late as 1872 (L, VI, 213). Wicksteed, a Unitarian minister, was Emerson's host in Leeds. W. E. Forster, a Quaker and friend of Carlyle, entertained Emerson at Rawdon. Blackburne has not been identified. Elgie was Mayor of Worcester; see p. [143] below. Davis has not been identified; Emerson received a letter from a Maurice Davis in 1873. Kenrick, not otherwise identified, wrote Emerson on January 7, 1848. Walbran, Harrison, and Williamson have not been identified. Mr. Fisher was Emerson's host in Sheffield (L, IV, 4). Stansfeld was a merchant of Leeds en route to America (L, IV, 4-5). Shannon has not been identified. Milnes, introduced to Emerson's works through Carlyle, had written a notice of his early works in the *Westminster Review*, XXXIII (March 1840), 345-372. Scott, the Scottish painter and engraver, painted Emerson during his visit to Edinburgh. Emerson dined with Palgrave and Froude during his visit to Oxford in 1848. Foxton wrote Emerson on March 25 and June 8, 1848, explaining that Emerson's writings had influenced his resignation from the ministry (L, IV, 45). Emerson dined with Dickens at the home of John Forster in London and was with Tom Taylor, the dramatist, in Cambridge (L, IV, 96n). Emerson met Chambers, the Scottish publisher and author of *Vestiges of Creation*, in Edinburgh; see Journal London, p. [33] below. Bates was the American-born partner in Baring Bros. & Co., international bankers.

[14] "Mr Bailey" is probably Philip James Bailey, the author of *Festus*, whom Emerson met at Nottingham; see p. [128] below. Sara Tagart wrote to Emerson in

[4] [15] *Intellect*

Natural History

Vegetable Growth   see next page too

Inspiration

Moral origin

[5]   Edda   ↑Snorri Sturleson ↑AD↓ 1178↓ [16]
Man's history told in other fables or apologues close by him, — as in
his grafted pears & plums. No ⟨nation comes⟩ aboriginal race arrives
at civility. Nature loves crossing of stocks. Pelasgi by the Greeks.[17]
The Asgard of the Edda are the intruding Asiatic tribes, & might
well strike Eylfi as Gods with their better civility.

——

The allegory is easy to see in the transparent first chapters of
the Edda; the Northern Nature; Frost, southwind, the Northern
spring after winter gleam up in the ↑third↓ fable of the Giant Ymir
& the Cow Œdumla.[18]

Thor's 3 precious things; ↑1,↓ his hammer or mace, Miollner, which
he hurls thro' the air at the ⟨m⟩ Giants of the Frost & the Mountains.

————

November of 1847. Thomas Jevons, having heard Emerson lecture, gave him a
pamphlet of his own and poems by his wife; Emerson acknowledged the gifts on
November 20, 1847 (*L*, III, 440). Thom was Emerson's host in Liverpool; see
Journal London, p. [124] below.

[15] This page is in pencil.

[16] This insertion, in ink, is set off by two short lines in ink, one vertical and one
horizontal, to the left of "Snorri".

[17] For "Nature . . . stocks.", see Journal AB, p. [105] above: "La Nature
aime les Croisements". "Man's history . . . Greeks." is used in "Powers and Laws
of Thought," *W*, XII, 25–26.

[18] Paul Henri Mallet, *Northern Antiquities: or, A Description of the Manners,
Customs, Religion and Laws of the Ancient Danes . . . with A Translation of the
Edda*, trans. Bishop Thomas Percy, 2 vols. (London, 1770), II, 18–19. Emerson
borrowed this book from the Harvard College Library on July 26, 1847.

2. his Belt of Prowess, which, when he puts on, he becomes as strong again as he was before.

3. his gauntlets

[6]   Poetry
On the columns of Balder's palaces, in Briedablik, are verses capable of recalling the dead to life.[19]

↑*Selfhelp*↓ [20]
In the Edda, the wolf Fenris made a very sensible remark to the gods who coaxed him to ⟨put⟩ suffer them to put their limp band upon his feet. If ⟨he could⟩ ↑you can↓ not break it, they said, we shall see that you are too feeble to excite alarm, & shall set you at liberty without delay.

"I am very much afraid," replied Fenris, "that if you once tie me so fast that I cannot work my deliverance myself, you will be in no haste to unloose me." [21]

[7] Our chapter on the superlative should be inscribed to the God Brage, "celebrated for his wisdom, eloquence, & majestic air." [22]

Wakes tired [23]

Dr Bragg's pills.[24]

[8] *The culture of the intellect*
Hint of the dialectic   JK ⟨36⟩41
Vegetable principle   K 119, Y 210,[25]   GH 13
The rest of the man will follow his head   AB 73

---

[19] Paul Henri Mallet, *Northern Antiquities*, 1770, II, 66, 70.

[20] "*Selfhelp*" is set off from the preceding entry by a curved line in ink.

[21] Paul Henri Mallet, *Northern Antiquities*, 1770, II, 93. The story of Fenris and the limp band is used in "Wealth," *W*, V, 161, and "Fate," *W*, VI, 20.

[22] Paul Henri Mallet, *Northern Antiquities*, 1770, II, 80. This sentence, struck through in ink with a diagonal use mark, is used in "Cockayne," *W*, V, 147.

[23] "Wakes tired" is in pencil. See *JMN*, VIII, 122–123: "the young American . . . wakes up tired. . . ."

[24] See *JMN*, IX, 194.

[25] See *JMN*, VIII, 242, IX, 335.

Not to speak of the Mount in cold blood. Inspiration.   O 356, 256

Intellect puts an interval   E 340, O 17, G 56,
↑A↓ small ⁿ acceleration in intel. processes makes Paradise   O 11
If the wit of all were exalted, would there be loss? O 359 ²⁶

———

We hive innumerable facts of no visible value   JK. 59

———

Do not give up your thought because you cannot answer an objection
&c   JK 107

———

⟨Worthless wit; we want a new daylight. GH 134⟩

———

The artist must be sacrificed. GH 42.
Solar system in the brain; & good rules, Y 35 ²⁷
Little men copernicise. AB 82

———

Poor trees do not shoot, & poor wits do not, CD 91
Inspiration. *Index* [II] 189   O 178, 247,²⁸   Health. *Index* 155.
Writer. *Index* 421
By always intending my mind. Y 210 ²⁹
All wit knows itself. K 23   but with apology.
Time assists criticism. V 82.³⁰   *Index* 66
Conditions of wit GH 39   Necessity of being what they are.
A man measured by the angle of his vision GH 100 ³¹

[9] Concord River in July 25 and 2 August is decorated with the
nymphaea, the cardinal flower, & the button-bush, asclepias & eupatoriums; especially ⁿ the willow adorns it with a sort of green smoke.

At Cambridge the piccory

---

²⁶ See *JMN*, IX, 460–461, 422–423 (O 356, 256); VII, 466–467 (E 340);
IX, 363 (O 17); VIII, 27–28 (G 56); IX, 361, 464 (O 11, 359).
²⁷ See *JMN*, IX, 268–269.
²⁸ See *JMN*, IX, 407, 419.
²⁹ See *JMN*, IX, 335; Journal AB, p. [98] above.
³⁰ See *JMN*, VIII, 207 (K 23), IX, 136 (V 82).
³¹ See also Journal CD, p. [35] above.

Writer's apparatus should be big as the solarsystem   CD 88
The old paint-pot   O 179
The singing Iopas   W 125 [32]

Worthless wit. we want a new daylight. GH 134
The insanity of Scotland
Luther's finical curled thoughts R 127 [33]
icy light [34]
After all our accumulation of riches, we are as poor in thought. Z 3 [35]
What is the effect of thoughts   GH 91
We must take thought & weather as they come   GH 47
We cannot quite trust men of thought. GH 47
Talents & ideas. O 6 [36]
Moth must fly to the lamp, & we must solve the questions though we die.

[10] To rail at intellect is great nonsense. It is health-giving.
And ⟨tis⟩ rare is the ↑bad↓ example of Bacon, and rare that of Coleridge.
I think a stern treatment of these culprits best. The literary scamp to the lamppost. ↑'Tis like the vicious clergyman, — hanging is too good for him.↓
majestic duties
We do not absorb thoughts, or adequately receive them. W 120 [37]

          "Before the starry threshold of Jove's Court"
                                        [Milton, *Comus*, l. 1]
Rely confidently on an idea. &c. V 37 [38]
No hope so bright but is beginning of its fulfilment. Every thought of genius an emanation.

---

[32] See *JMN*, IX, 407 (O 179), 242 (W 125). On Iopas, see Vergil, *Aeneid*, I, 740 ff.
[33] See *JMN*, VIII, 413.
[34] See *JMN*, IX, 293.
[35] See *JMN*, VI, 288–289.
[36] See *JMN*, IX, 359.
[37] See *JMN*, IX, 239.
[38] See *JMN*, IX, 113.

All knowledge assimilation.[39]

What is life? — What a man is thinking ⟨of⟩ all day.
The double-life   O 325

We are waiting until some tyrannous idea. Y 74 [40]
Moral superiority explains intellectual. GH 118
See *Result. Index* 335

———

A practical man will never do it. Y 264 [41]

———

Charter of wit
Prestige of originality. GH 25

[11]   ↑Aristocracy↓ [42]
    The astronomers are eager to know whether the moon has an atmosphere. Cambridge telescope seems to think it has. I am only concerned that every man have one. I observe however that it takes two to make an atmosphere as well as a bargain. I am acquainted with persons who go attended with this lustrous cloud. It is sufficient that they come, it is not important what they say. They also are respectful.
    ↑From these↓ I ⁿ suffer no intrusion, & human life is at once respectable & excellent. Others I meet who have no deference, and who denude & strip one of all attributes but material values. As much health & muscle as you have, as much land, as much houseroom & dinner, — avails —. Of course a man is a poor bag of bones. There is no gracious interval, not an inch, allowed. Bone ⟨g⟩rubs against bone; Life is thus a Beggar's Bush. My Dr A & W M J [43] are examples of this impoverishing animalism. [12] I meet a Hunger[,]

———

[39] See *JMN*, VII, 430: "All knowledge is assimilation to the object of knowledge."
[40] See *JMN*, IX, 448-449 (O 325), 282 (Y 74).
[41] See *JMN*, IX, 353-354.
[42] In pencil.
[43] Presumably Dr. Arnoult, with whom Emerson was currently perfecting his French pronunciation, and William M. Jackson of Plymouth, a family friend of Lidian Emerson.

a Wolf. Rather let me be alone whilst I live, than meet these lean kine, ⟨w⟩these moons without atmospheres. ↑Man should emancipate man; he does so not by jamming him, but by distancing him. The nearer my friend, the more spacious is our realm, or the more diameter our spheres have.↓ [44]

There came here, the other day, a pleasing child, whose face & form were moulded into serenity & grace. We ought to have sat with her serene & thankfully with no eager demand. But she was ⟨catechised⟩ made to run over all the list of South Shore acquaintance. How is Mrs H's cholera-morbus, & the Captain's rheumatism? When will Miss B. buy her carpets, and are there plums this year in P[lymouth]? When I got into the P. coach in old [13] times a passenger would ask me, "How's fish?"

↑*Travelling*↓

Men run away to other countries, because they are not good in their own; and run back to their own, because they pass for nothing in the ⟨new⟩ ↑foreign↓ places. Achieve a mastery in any place, and it is good in all. [45]

⟨Every⟩ The highest value of natural history & mainly of these new & secular results like the inferences from geology, & the discovery of parallax, & the resolution of Nebulae, is its translation into an universal cipher applicable to Man viewed as Intellect also. All the languages should be studied abreast, says Kraitsir. Learn the laws of music, said Fourier, & I can tell you any secret in any part of the universe, in anatomy, for instance, or in astronomy. Kepler thought as much before[.]

Ah that is what interests me. When I read in a true History what befals in that kingdom where ⟨a day⟩a thousand years is one day, [46] I[n] see that it is true through all the sciences, in the laws of thought as well as of chemistry. [47] No Marsaillaise is sung in that high region.

---

[44] "The astronomers . . . have." is used in "Aristocracy," *W*, X, 55–56.

[45] This paragraph, struck through in ink with a vertical use mark, is used in "Culture," *W*, VI, 145.

[46] Cf. 2 Pet. 3:8.

[47] "Ah that . . . chemistry." is used in "Powers and Laws of Thought," *W*, XII, 4.

[14] The weight that passes over a bridge is spread equally on every square inch.

———

Whip for our top.[48]
The young scholar buys an alarm clock, he invents a clepsydron, he plants a dial in his garden, he reads Greek by candlelight before breakfast. When this fury is first over, he tries travelling with book & pen, & relishes his Greek poet in country barrooms, or in sea-beaches & lighthouses, or in a cabin in the woods[.]
Later, a public occasion, an expecting audience, or the pride of printing a book flagellates[n] the drowsy muse.

[15₁][49] Theatre des Varietés
There are many mansions in my Father's house:[50] Poetry is one, Gardening is one, Chemistry is one, Geology is one, Engineering is one.
They are all ⟨convertible⟩ intertranslateable language; all dialects of the true Sanscrit[:] indeed the Sanscrit answers word for word to each of all the dialects.[n]

↑Ombrelville↓
Jamie[n] lent Jock an umbrella in a shower. Jock ⟨be⟩came ↑to be↓ king, & gave ⟨Jem⟩ ↑Jamie↓ a tract of land for a barony, as long as he should lend him an umbrella in his need. Jamie forthwith set up a silk factory, silk, & horn handles, & built the town of Umbrelbury.[51]

[15₂]   Metamorphosis
The interest of the gardener & the pomologist ⟨is⟩ has the same foundation as that of the poet, ↑namely,↓ in the Metamorphosis: These also behold the miracle, the guided change, the change conspicuous, the guide invisible; a bare stick studs itself over with green

---

[48] See Journal AB, pp. [61] and [123] above.
[49] Emerson numbered two consecutive pages as 15; they are designated here as [15₁] and [15₂].
[50] Cf. John 14:2.
[51] "Ombrelville . . . Umbrelbury." is in pencil.

buds which become again leaves, flowers, & at length, ⟨the most⟩ delicious fruit[.]

[16] Genius. Skidbladnir   the ship of the gods.
    Obey your genius[.]
    ⟨Who⟩ Though dwarfs built Skidbladnir as soon as its sails are unfurled, a favorable gale arises & carries it of itself to whatever place it is destined. It will hold them all with all their wargear on, & when they have no mind to sail, they can fold it up like a cloth in their pocket.[52]

        ↑Cleverness↓   ↑Aristocracy↓ [53]
Hark again! When Thor & his companions arrive at Utgard, Loke asks for a specimen of his talent, *"for nobody is permitted to remain here, unless he understand some art, & excel in it all other men."* [54]

"It is royal work to fulfil royal words." Heimskringla [55]

[17]   [Mallet,] N[orthern]. A[ntiquities]. [II,] p[p. 228–]229

    The whole ocean seemed as one wound
                              King Regner Lodbrog's Ode [56]
"In the shower of arms Rogvaldar fell. I lost my son. The birds of prey bewailed his fall. They lost him that prepared them banquets."
                              King Regner Lodbrog's Ode
                                   [*Ibid.*, II, 230]

    [18] ⟨Compare these my compatriots with the old Persian or Roman⟩
What is Europe but the chance of meeting with such a man as Montaigne?

----

[52] Paul Henri Mallet, *Northern Antiquities*, 1770, II, 116. Cf. Journal CD, p. [93] above.
    [53] "Cleverness" and "Aristocracy" are in pencil.
    [54] Paul Henri Mallet, *Northern Antiquities*, 1770, II, 123. "Hark . . . *men.'* ", struck through in ink with a vertical use mark, is used in "Ability," *W*, V, 89.
        [55] "Hark . . . Heimskringla" is struck through in ink with an additional vertical use mark; cf. "Powers and Laws of Thought," *W*, XII, 9. " 'It is royal . . . words.' " is used in "Truth," *W*, V, 117–118.
        [56] "N. A. . . . . Ode" is in pencil. The quotation is used in "Poetry and Imagination," *W*, VIII, 57.

On the value of a Servant

The engraver must not handle a shovel or lay stone wall

On the importance of circumstance as inferred from the theory of the Egg

Agassiz & the civet [57]

[19] I read the fabulous magnificence of these Karuns & Jamschids & Kai Kans & Feriduns of Persia, all gold and talismans; then I walk by the newsboys with telegraph despatches; by the Post Office; & Redding's shop with English steamer's journals; & pass the Maine Depot; & take my own seat in the Fitchburg cars; & see every man dropped at his estate, as we pass it; & see what tens of thousands of powerful & armed men, science-armed society-armed men sit at large in this ample land of ours obscure from their numbers & the extent of territory[,] and muse on the power which each of these can lay hold of at pleasure. These men who wear no star nor gold laced hat, you cannot tell if they be poor or rich. And I think how far these chains of intercourse & travel go, what levers, what pumps, what [20] searchings are applied to nature for the benefit of the youngest of these exorbitant republicans[,] and I say, What a negrofine royalty is that of Jamschid & Solomon; what a real sovereignty of nature does the Bostonian possess!

Caoutchouc, steam, ether, telegraph, what bells they can ring! [58] Every man who has a hundred dollars to dispose of, a hundred dollars a year over his bread, is rich beyond the dreams of the Caesars.[59]

↑Tools↓

And as all this leaves the man where he was before, the in-

[57] "⟨Compare . . . civet" is in pencil; "What . . . Servant" is struck through in pencil with a diagonal use mark; "What . . . Montaigne?" is written in ink over "⟨Compare . . . Roman⟩" (a conjectural reading), possibly to cancel the earlier writing.

[58] This sentence is in pencil.

[59] "I read . . . of the Caesars.", struck through in ink on pp. [19] and [20] with single vertical use marks, is used in "Editors' Address," W, XI, 383–384 (written for the Massachusetts Quarterly Review, December, 1847).

dividualism, the importance of a man to himself, the fact that his power of self & social entertainment is all, makes quickly these miracles cheap to him; the greater they are the less they really become.

[21]   Value of a servant.
The New Englander is attentive to trifles, values himself on a sort of omniscience, knows when the cars start⟨,⟩ at every depot; feels every waterpipe & furnace-flue in his house; knows where the rafters are in the wall, how can he be absorbed in his thought? how can he be contemplative? He must have a servant, he must call Tom to ask the prices & hours. What day of the month it is, & when the mail closes. Who is Governor of the state, & where is the police office? But Tom does not come at a call. Nothing is so rare in New England as Tom. Bad for the New Englander. His skin is ocular. He is afflicted with the second thought. Not for an instant can he be great & abandoned to a sentiment. Let the countrymen beware of cities. A city is the paradise of trifles. Your hat & your shoes which you knew not of, ⟨have become visible,⟩ ↑stick out,↓ [60] [22] and the current sets so strong that way that the city seems a hotel & a shop, ⟨and⟩ a gigantic clothes-mart & tog-shop, and, if one perchance meet ↑in the street↓ a man of probity & wisdom, an accomplished & domestic soul, we are taken by surprise, and he drives the owls & bats that had infested us, home to their holes again.
                    ↑Aristocracy↓ [61]
What is it that makes the nobleman? loyalty to his thought. That makes the beautiful scorn, the elegant simplicity, the directness, the commanding port, which ⟨Y⟩ all admire, & which men not noble affect. For the thought has no debts, no ↑impair, no↓ low obligations, or relations[;] no hurry or ⟨plot⟩ intrigue or business, no murder, no envy, no crime[.] [62]

[23] "Give me the thought that I may refresh myself," that I may dilate[.] ↑See the same thing once more. p. 43↓

    [60] "Let the . . . stick out," is struck through in ink with two wavy vertical use marks.
    [61] Added in pencil.
    [62] "What is it . . . no crime" is used in "Aristocracy," W, X, 55.

[24] [63] *French Superlative*
The idioms of French speech are false: "One cannot speak ten words in that language without lying." Je suis enchanté, je suis desolé, à ce que vous arrive, some trifle or other.[64]

L'Etat de New York a fait hommage à la chambre, de l'histoire naturelle⟨,⟩ de cet Etat 10 gros volumes in 40, avec planches coloriées,

Tout le monde   Our false compliments are borrowed
                       from the French, but are idioms there.
the fortnight "forevers" of the French, & a constitution granted by the king at ten minutes' notice.

[25] Originality. "That is my rat which you have described to the Academy,[n] how dared you interfere with me?" says Dr M. to Dr H.; and Boston divides itself into factions on Dr J.'s discovery of ether;[65] and London & Paris contest the priority of having found Neptune in the skies. It is not that Dr Jackson or Mr Morton, that Leverrier or Mr Adams will be in the least enlarged or ameliorated by conceding to them the coveted priority,[66] — but there is evidently a feeling of an aweful power in this creative saliency, this saliency of thought, this *habit of saliency*, of not pausing but going on, which is a sort of importation & domestication of the Divine Effort, in a man.[67] The Jockey very properly pays a new price for every roll of the horse on the ground. This is *la vera nobilità↑,↓*[68] for [26] which millions of money were no offset[.]

State of melioration
Originality again
                       I heard old J. K⟨.⟩↑eyes↓[69] say "that it was

[63] To the right of "*Superlative*" is a drop of sealing wax; at one time a clipping may have been affixed to this page.

[64] "The idioms . . . other." is used in "The Superlative," *W*, X, 163–164; " 'One . . . lying.' " is used in "Truth," *W*, V, 118.

[65] Cf. "Powers and Laws of Thought," *W*, XII, 8.

[66] Emerson's brother-in-law, Dr. Charles T. Jackson, and William T. G. Morton both claimed priority as discoverer of ether as an anaesthetic. On Adams and Leverrier, see Journal AB, p. 7 and n. 11.

[67] This sentence is used in "Powers and Laws of Thought," *W*, XII, 59.

[68] The comma is added in pencil.

[69] John Keyes (1787–1844), a lawyer of Concord.

a story (that of importing the stone of the stone chapel) which he had told so often that he now firmly believed it himself:" so is it no doubt with many of my originalities. I have a good many commonplaces which often turn up in my ⟨thinking⟩ writing & talking, which I have used so often that I have the right of the strong hand unto; ↑—↓ [70] but that they are indigenous in my brain, I do not know nor care.

[27] ↑A.B.↓A[lcott]. found, after all his efforts on that most incorrigible of all materials, man, a real comfort in working on that most corrigible & docile of all ⟨materials,⟩ ↑pupils,↓ Nature.

[28]   ↑Superlative in life↓
The diamond & the pearl are proper to the oriental world, and accidental to ours. All or nothing is the genius of Arabian ↑&↓ Persian life. The diver dives a beggar, & rises (a prince) with the price of a kingdom in his hand. This is fitting too, where insecure institutions make every one desirous of property instantly convertible & concealable[.]
        ↑a bag of sequins, a single horse,↓ [71]

"Mamma, they have begun again," said a little girl in the house with the philosophers talking.[72]

Benvenuto Cellini   an exaggerated character and fortune.

        ——

                negative superl[ative]. They call the rainbow a discoloration.[73]

[29]   ↑Egg↓   ↑Circumstance.↓

[70] The dash is inserted in pencil.
        [71] "a bag . . . horse," originally written below the entry which follows (" 'Mamma . . . talking."), is marked for transposition here. "The diamond . . . horse," is used in "The Superlative," W, X, 177.
        [72] The reference is to one of Bronson Alcott's daughters. See J, VI, 371, n. 1, and JMN, VIII, 374.
        [73] "negative . . . discoloration", in pencil, is used in "The Superlative," W, X, 165.

What vast importance the Circumstance acquires in the revelations of modern science. The egg — all we know of its development is, another vesicle, and if science, after 500 years, makes one step more, it is ↑to↓ discover hitherto latent, — another vesicle. In vegetable & animal tissue it is the same thing — ↑the↓ bean & cheese ↑are↓ identical chemically, — and all that the primary power operates is still vesicles, vesicles ad infinitum. Well but the tyrannical *Circumstance*; a vesicle ⟨lodged⟩ in new circumstances, a vesicle lodged, for example, in the womb, suffers instantly modifications which eventuate ⟨in new organs,⟩ in unsheathing ⟨the⟩ miraculous capabilities in the once ⟨monotonous⟩ ↑rigid↓ vesicle, and it becomes an organized human form armed with limbs & senses. Once we thought the ⟨Man⟩ ↑positive power↓ was all, now we learn that ⟨cir⟩ the negative power, namely, the Circumstance is half.[74]

[30]   ↑Detachment↓
‖ ... ‖ Goethe, was, that with all his spiritual perception he never fell into spiritualism — and of the material powers we use that it would teach men by & by that the domestic man the power of self- & social-entertainment were all, since these miracles were so cheap[.] [75]

Circumstance! Yes that is Nature. Nature is what you may do. There's much you may not. The Circumstance, and the life.[76]

[30 ½] [77] The superstitions of our age are,
the fear of Catholicism
the fear of Pauperism
the fear of immigration
the fear of manufacturing interests

----

[74] See p. [18] above: "On the importance of circumstance . . . the Egg". "What vast . . . half.", struck through in ink with two discontinuous vertical use marks, is used in "Fate," *W*, VI, 14–15.
[75] "Detachment . . . cheap" is written in pencil. "Goethe . . . spiritualism —" is used in "Powers and Laws of Thought," *W*, XII, 45.
[76] This paragraph, struck through in ink with one diagonal and one vertical use mark, is used in "Fate," *W*, VI, 14–15.
[77] So numbered by Emerson, possibly to compensate for his numbering two pages as "15".

the fear of radicalism or democracy,
and faith in the steam engine.[78]

Nemesis takes care of all these things, balances fear with fear, eradicates nobles by upstarts, supplants one set of nobodies by new nobodies[.] [79]

⟨It is to⟩ ↑So it↓ be read as a mystical book↑,↓ then it is read safely; if as a literal history, it is naught.[80]

With powers that should have constituted him an equal of Phidias or Plato[,] that he should have been unformed is a calamity to mankind[.] [81]

[31] ‖ epw ‖ I am always reminded, & now again by reading last night in Rousseau's Confessions, that it is not the events in one's life, but in the faculty of selecting & reporting them, that the interest lies. Mrs Marshall over the way if she could write would make as interesting a life as Robinson Crusoe. And this because poetry needs ⟨no⟩ ↑little↓ history. — It is made of one part history & ninety nine parts music; or, shall I say, fact & affection[.]

———

↑"↓If I knew as much as Daniel Webster,↑"↓ is a Yankee proverb.[82]

[78] "faith . . . engine." is used in "Worship," *W*, VI, 208.

[79] "Nemesis . . . nobodies" is in pencil.

[80] "So . . . naught." is in pencil and struck through in pencil with a vertical use mark.

[81] This sentence, in pencil, is struck through in pencil with two vertical use marks. What appears to be a continuation of this entry on p. [31] has also been struck through in pencil with a vertical use mark, erased, and written over in ink by the entry "I am . . . proverb." What has been recovered of the erased pencil writing reads as follows: "& mt danger us in a life so relatively ‖ . . . ‖ these curiosities ‖ . . . ‖ false ‖ . . . ‖ Swedenborg ‖ . . . ‖ professed[?] ‖ . . . ‖ Every ‖ . . . ‖ would him once ‖ . . . ‖ & them ‖ . . . ‖ it ‖ . . . ‖ Shout[?] ‖ . . . ‖ O how ‖ . . . ‖ What ‖ . . . ‖ ⟨health⟩ ‖ . . . ‖ health it costs ‖ . . . ‖ equal to Phidias & Shakspeare & Newton E‖ . . . ‖ has had similar dreams ‖ . . . ‖ them."

[82] The quotation marks are added in pencil. See *JMN*, IX, 29.

The selfpoise of a human being should not be easily disturbed[.]
Elevated by intellectual power to simplicity [83]

[32] A man should make life & nature happier. Otherwise we are bankrupt[.] [84]

The moths fly to the lamp & he must solve these questions tho' he expire[.] [85]

Strange that this monk without domestic experience living in library should write conjugial Love[.] [86]

The selfpoise of a human being should not be easily disturbed[.] [87]

"This machine," said my friend, "must be far from perfect; see how complex it is."

The highest simplicity of structure is the last & requires the most composite.[88]

Association adopts this tool making & would extend this & in-experienced men lend themselves readily to it. The plan is magnificent, but when executed has no attractions for us. We know too well the refractoriness of the material.

[33] || epw || [89]
In England, Landor, De Quincey, Carlyle, three men of original

[83] "The selfpoise . . . simplicity" is written in pencil, possibly as a continuation of the erased pencil writing above.
[84] "A man . . . bankrupt", in pencil and struck through in pencil with vertical use marks, is transcribed on p. [42] below.
[85] This sentence, in pencil and struck through in pencil with a vertical use mark, is incorporated in the entry on p. [42] below. Another version appears on p. [9] above.
[86] This sentence, in pencil, is struck through in pencil with a vertical use mark.
[87] See p. [31] above.
[88] "The" is written immediately below an uncanceled "S" — apparently a false start.
[89] There appear to be ten lines of erased pencil writing, the last three of which are transcribed in ink on p. [49] below: "The universe . . . there." The remainder is unrecovered.

literary genius; but the scholar, the catholic cosmic intellect, Bacon's own son, the Lord Chief Justice on the muses' ⟨b⟩Bench is Wilkinson.[90]

Elevated by intellectual power to simplicity.[91]

The useful the badge of the true. What profits Coleridge or Hume? [92]

The savage amusing himself in coming in on the surf is a true symbol of our human life which is a perpetual series of transits[.] [93]

————

In England the lines of tendency usually meet in an apex, so that a man has executive talent. In America, we are swamped by capabilities which do not reach an apex.[94]

[34] [95] Selfpoise that can easily redress itself
Oxygen & azote have their constant proportions[.] [96]

Education should leave the child obscure in his youth[,] protected so[,] as the green apple in its crude state[.] [97]

Life consists in what a man is thinking of all day[.] [98]

---

[90] James John Garth Wilkinson (1812–1899), the Swedenborgian. Emerson speaks highly of him in a letter of August 29, 1847, about the time of this entry (L, III, 414), and praises his powers in "Literature," W, V, 250.

[91] See p. [31] above.

[92] This and the preceding sentence, in pencil and struck through in pencil with a diagonal use mark, are revised on p. [47] below.

[92] This and the preceding sentence, in pencil and struck through in pencil with See Journal CD, p. [35] above; "Works and Days," W, VII, 181.

[94] This paragraph is struck through in pencil with a diagonal use mark.

[95] This page is in pencil.

[96] This sentence, struck through in pencil with a vertical use mark, is incorporated in the entry under "Selfpoise." on p. [38] below.

[97] This sentence, struck through in pencil with a diagonal use mark, is revised in ink on p. [35].

[98] This sentence is struck through in pencil with a vertical use mark; cf. p. [10] above and "Powers and Laws of Thought," W, XII, 10.

One thing is certain[:] He cannot afford to be a fool.[99]

non agunt nisi soluta [100]

If a man read ⟨what interests him⟩ a book because it interests him and read in all directions for the same reason, his reading is pure, & interests me, but if he read with ↑ulterior↓ objects, if [he] read that he may write, we do not impute it to him for righteousness.[101] In the first case he is like one who takes up only so much land as he uses; in the second he buys land to *speculate* with[.] [102]

[35] "If regret came to me at all it is for the lapse of myself in the oblivions of sleep, & the wastes of immortalities in spending this mortal." A[lcott?].

I should say, wastes of immortalities in *husbanding* the mortal.

———

A man cannot be always staring at burning coals, without the nature of the coal reacting in some way on him.

———

Of Expense.

———

One thing is certain[:] he cannot afford to be a fool.[103]

———

Education should leave the child obscure in his youth, ↑so↓ protected, ⟨so⟩ as the green apple in its crude state.[104]

[36] Metamorphosis　　　↑Trope↓
　　　　　　　　　　　↑Poetry & Criticism↓ [105]
Conversation is not permitted without a trope. Nothing but great

[99] "One thing . . . fool.", struck through in pencil with a vertical use mark, is revised in ink on p. [35].
[100] See Journal CD, p. [123] above.
[101] Cf. Rom. 4:6, 11, 22; James 2:23.
[102] This paragraph is in pencil.
[103] Cf. p. [34] above.
[104] Cf. p. [34] above.
[105] Two of the index headings are added in the upper right corner of this page: "Trope", set off from the other headings by curved lines, and "Poetry & Criticism", the latter in pencil.

weight in things can afford a quite plain speech: it is ever ornamented by inversion & trope[.]

Nobody eats sugar. Every thing must be flavoured & crossed.
We live & work & speak by indirections.
God himself does not speak prose, but communicates with us by
hints, by omens, by inferences, by dark resemblances in ⟨common⟩
objects lying all round us[.] [106]

[37] [107]   Cleverness   Executive talent   practical
The gardener does not want sap or general vegetable productivity,
but plums and quinces[.]

Literary talent in America   a ground juniper

[38]   *Selfpoise.*   ↑Equation↓
I enumerated some of our superstitions above, p 30, but the selfpoise seems our Nemesis & protector. Thus we have been born & bred
in the belief that unless we came again to some good religion soon,
some Calvinism or Behmenism, there would be the universal thaw &
dissolution.

No Isaiah or Jeremy has come; nothing can exceed the anarchy
that has followed in our Skies, the stern old faiths. 'Tis as clear Lynch
law as that which ⟨prevailed⟩ existed in Massachusetts in the revolution, or which prevails now in the prairies & woods of Wisconsin;
and yet we get on. Men are loyal.

Selfpoise, nature has it in all her works, certain proportions in which
oxygen & azote combine. In winter mercury is always at 32 degrees[.] [108]

[39] "land has been ploughed 1000 years; a little sun & rain & it is
green again."

---

[106] "Conversation . . . round us" is used in "Poetry and Imagination," *W*, VIII,
12.

[107] The three index headings at the top of the page are in pencil and separated
by vertical lines, also in pencil. "Literary . . . juniper" is in pencil.

[108] "*Selfpoise.* . . . combine." is a revision of an entry written in pencil on p.
[34] above. "*Selfpoise.* . . . degrees", struck through in ink with a vertical use mark,
is used in "Worship," *W*, VI, 203–204.

See CD 51   ↑AZ 251↓ [109]

I have that faith in the necessity of all gifts that ↑to ⁿ implore
writers to be a little more of this or that↓ were like advising gunpowder to explode gently, or snow to temper its whiteness, ↑or↓
oaktrees to be less profuse in leaves & acorns, or poplars to try the
vinous habit & creep on walls.
They do as they can, or they must instruct you equally by their
failure as by their talent. That is they must teach you that the world
is farmed out to many contractors, and each arranges all things on
his petty task, sacrifices all for that[.]

[40] Aristocracy may study Hamlet[.]

It is the literature & manual of that[.]

Aristocracy is the moral & independent class. Polk & Webster
must have power & must truckle for it.[110] With patrician airs they
can never be gentlemen. We understand very well what they mean
when they say 'Patriotism,' & unless we are very tired we do not
laugh. But an aristocracy is composed of simple & sincere men for
whom nature & ethics are strong enough and who say what they
mean and ⟨walk⟩ ↑go↓ straight to their objects. ⟨The⟩ It is a Realism.[111]
The prerogatives of the Teacher are determined↑,↓ as one of my
friends said↑,↓[112] not by his profession but by the health he restores
to the body & mind of his patient and the faith he ensures by actual
cure.[113]

[41]   Transcendentalism

"With thoughts beyond the reaches of our souls" [Shakespeare, *Hamlet*,
                                                      I, iv, 56]

[42] The artist must be sacrificed. The child had her basket

[109] Journal AZ will be published in a later volume.
[110] Cf. "Aristocracy," *W*, X, 47: "Whoever wants more power than is the
legitimate attraction of his faculty . . . must truckle for it."
[111] "But an aristocracy . . . Realism." is used in "Aristocracy," *W*, X, 41.
[112] The commas after "determined" and "said" are inserted in pencil.
[113] Pasted to the page following this entry is a clipping from an unidentified
London newspaper advertising openings for "none but gentlemen" at a private school.

full of berries, but she looked sadly tired. The s↑c↓holar is pale.
↑Schiller shuns[114] to learn French that he may keep the purity of
his German idiom↓. Herschel must live in the observatory & draw
on his night-cap when the sun rises, & ⟨fu⟩ⁿ defend his eyes for
nocturnal use. Michel Angelo must paint Sistine Chapels, till he can
no longer read except by holding the book over his head. ⟨It⟩ Nature
deals with all her offspring so. See the poor moths & flies, ⟨on the tr⟩
lately so vigorous, now on the wall or the trunk of the tree, exhausted,
dried up, & presently blown away. Men likewise. They must put
their lives into the sting they give. What is a man good for without
enthusiasm? What is enthusiasm but this daring of ruin for its
object? There are thoughts beyond the reaches of our souls; we are
not the less drawn to them. The moth flies into the flame of the
lamp, & Swedenborg must solve the problems though he be crazed
& killed.[115]

[43]   *Continued from p.* ⟨4⟩22, ⟨4⟩23,
     The difference between ⟨men⟩ ↑riches & poverty↓, as I so often
say, is reverence for superiority. It makes not much difference what
kind that is — but health requires the upward eye. He is beautiful
in face, in port, in manners, who is ⟨respectful⟩ loyal to his thought,
absorbed in objects which he thinks superior to himself. Men affect
to be so. The reason why cities affect me so ⟨disagr⟩ degradingly, is
that they seem immen⟨c⟩se coacervations of trifles and, will he or
will he not, the countryman finds it a low distraction, a chop-house,
a barber's shop.[116] Thus cities make pauperism.
A cockney is a bag of bones.[117]

[44] The young people wish to do something, to write a volume
of poems, to make a picture or bust or building that shall succeed, &

---

[114] "shuns" is preceded by a question mark, from which a line in ink runs to
"shuns" as rewritten in the top margin.
[115] For "There are thoughts . . . souls" and "The moth . . . problems", see,
respectively, pp. [41] and [32] above. "The artist . . . give." is used in "Instinct
and Inspiration," *W*, XII, 86; "The artist . . . sacrificed." and "They must put
. . . killed." are used in "Inspiration," *W*, VIII, 275.
[116] "The reason . . . shop." is used in "Culture," *W*, VI, 153.
[117] See p. [11] above: "a man is a poor bag of bones."

this makes them anxious. What difference does it make with them whether they publish or not? How superior to refrain from the demonstration! Music without resin or catgut.[118]

[45] Henry T[horeau]. says that 12 lb of Indian meal, which one can easily carry on his back, will be food for a fortnight. Of course, one need not be in want of a living wherever corn grows, & where it does not, rice is as good.

[46] Our badges are as fixed as nature[;] there is no turban on a man's head in all England or America as there is no rose in the southern hemisphere[,] no heath in the western.

But Englishman has attended to his own affair for seven generations.[119]

H. D. T when you talked of art, blotted a paper with ink, then doubled it over, & safely defied the artist to surpass his effect.

[47] C[harles]K[ing]N[ewcomb] the fathomless skeptic was here 8 August. Thought he defies, he thinks it noxious. It makes us old, harried, anxious. Yes, but it is no more to be declined than hands & feet are. We must accept our functions, as well as our organs. Thought is like the weather, or birth, or death: we must take it as it comes. Then this is work which, like every work, reacts powerfully on the workman. Out of this anxiety flows a celestial serenity.

The useful is the badge of the true. How does Hume or Kant profit us? [120]

———

As to thought & its diseases, like the weather we must take it as it comes[.] ☞ [121]

———

[118] With "Music . . . catgut.", cf. Journal CD, p. [94] above.
[119] This sentence is in pencil.
[120] See p. [33] above.
[121] See above: "Thought is like . . . it comes."

151

⟨Men of thought⟩ There is this vice about men of thought[:] you cannot quite trust them, — not as much as other men of the same natural probity, — without intellect, — as they have a hankering to play Providence, & make a distinction in favor of themselves from the rules they apply to all the human race.[122]

[48]   Laws of the world.
selfpoise of things. see, above, p 36, 38, 32,
                    also CD p. 51
poise that can easily redress itself: as in the certain proportions in which oxygen & azote so easily combine.[123]

"This land was tilled 1000 years; a little sun & rain & 'tis green again." [124]

———

Corpora non agunt nisi soluta.[125]

———

You have seen those rocking stones which are so well poised that they can be moved by a child's hand, & yet the strength of many yoke of oxen could not overset them.[126]

[49] ↑Division of Labor↓
   The universe is also a great factory. One grinds at the wheel, one pumps at the well, one polishes the pin. Every one must work in his office. *My* body is *my* office. I must work there.[127]

———

[122] This sentence, struck through in ink with a vertical use mark, is used in "Powers and Laws of Thought," *W*, XII, 45. Cf. *JMN*, IX, 379, 383: "All sensible men have a hankering to play Providence, or assume to judge of law & fact."
[123] See pp. [34] and [38] above.
[124] See p. [39] above.
[125] See Journal CD, p. [123] above, and p. [34] above.
[126] "You have . . . them." is in pencil. See Journal CD, p. [51] above, for the heading "Rocking stones".
[127] "The universe . . . there." is a transcription of erased penciled writing on p. [33] above. Following this entry are pasted five individual paragraphs clipped from one or more unidentified British newspapers: the first records the running time of a British express train; the second advises sitting down in case a dog attacks; the third reports the stipend of the Archbishop of York; the fourth names the new editor of the *Edinburgh Review*; the fifth compares the proportionate number of soldiers in Austria, Great Britain, and the United States.

[50]   Realism
                            ↑True aristocracy — ↓
The concurrence for the Cambridge Professorships should be
in this wise. Mr Professor of Botany! do you know the cause of the
decay of the Buttonwood all over North America, for 6 or 7 years
past? the Cause & the Cure?

Do you know the cause & cure of the Potato rot?

If you do not, then pray come down from your chair & give it
up to some one who does. ↑Linnaeus was required by the King to
find the cause of the rotting of the ship timber and he found it &
prevented it.↓

                        ⟨pear-blight⟩
                        ⟨rose-bug⟩ ¹²⁸

[51]   Aristocracy
One word more for a real aristocracy, that, namely, in which
each member contributes something real. Every member commits
himself, imparts without reserve the last results of intellect, because
he is to receive an equivalent in virtue, in genius, in talent, from each
other member. None shall join us but on that condition. No idler,
no mocker, no counterfeiter, no critic, ⟨f⟩no frivolous person⟨,⟩ whatever, can remain in this company. I propose this law with confidence,
because I believe every ⟨good man has⟩ substantial man has somewhat
to contribute. My secret of life is this only, that all men are my
masters,¹²⁹ & can teach me that which I would fain know.

                            ↑See p 40
                            ⟨61⟩ 61↓

[52] I talked with Mr W. of A. B. A[lcott]. W. said, he is impracticable. I said, Yes, as our thoughts are. ⟨Our thought is not
quite practicable.⟩

He said, ⟨There is no thought tha⟩ I do not think ⟨that⟩ ¹³⁰ it

---

¹²⁸ "pear-blight" and "rose-bug" were apparently written after "If you . . . .
who does." but canceled in favor of the insertion concerning Linnaeus. The same
anecdote occurs also in "Success," *W*, VII, 284–285, and "Country Life," *W*, XII,
137–138.
¹²⁹ See Journal CD, p. [41] above, and "Greatness," *W*, VIII, 313.
¹³⁰ Canceled in pencil.

will do to say that our thoughts are quite impracticable. I replied, Nor do I think that any man is quite impracticable. Nor do I feel at liberty to decline the thoughts or the men that go by, because they are not quite easy to deal with & conformable to the opinions of the Boston Post.

[53] Hamlet was prophecy.

"Nothing is more indicative of the deepest culture & refinement, than a tender consideration of the Ignorant" said my friend A. — Yes, and[n] what is agreeable in it is the wealth of nature it indicates; enough has he & to spare.[131]

[54] Individualism has never been tried. All history[,] all poetry deal with it only & because now it was in the minds of men to go alone and now before it was tried, now, when a few began to think of the celestial Enterprise, sounds this tin trumpet of a French Phalanstery and the newsboys throw up their caps & cry, Egotism is exploded; now for Communism! But all that is valuable in the Phalanstery comes of individualism. You may settle it in your hearts that when you get a great man, he will be hard to keep step with. Spoons & skimmers may well enough lie together, but vases & statues must ⟨stand ⟨apart⟩alone⟩ ↑have each its own pedestal.↓

[55] Laws of the world
      The fish in the cave is blind; such[n] is the eternal relation between power & use.[132]

[56] Again, that dream of writing in committee returns, the Beaumont & Fletcherism. The Seckle pear is the best in America. But it is small, & the tree is small. So we bud ⟨the root⟩ an apple tree just above the root from this pear, and the bud becomes root, and is assisted at the same time by the more succulent roots of the

---

[131] This paragraph, struck through in ink with one vertical use mark and one diagonal use mark, is used in "Considerations by the Way," W, VI, 260.
[132] This entry, in ink, is written over an earlier entry in pencil that carried a canceled second heading ("Seckle pear") and continued "Life a superficial phenomenon. The fish . . . use."

apple, and a most vigorous seckle pear is the result. Can we not help ourselves as discreetly by the force of two in literature? Certainly it only needs two well-placed & well-tempered⟨,⟩ for cooperation, to get somewhat far transcending any private enterprise in literature[.]

↑See O 258

also 259↓ 133

↑But it requires great generosity & rare devotion to the aim in the parties & not that mean thievish way of looking at every thought as property.↓

[57] Thought is the property of him who can entertain it. Thought is the property of him who can adequately place it. A certain awkwardness usually ⟨at⟩ marks our use of borrowed thoughts. They are too conspicuous, not being well placed.[134]

[58] The fable of Zohak of whom Eblis asked as the reward of his services that he might kiss the ⟨n⟩king's naked shoulder, & from the touch sprang two black serpents, who were fed daily with human victims; it is easy to see how fast a figurative description of luxury becomes a legend. The peasant sees that ⟨12⟩ a pound of meal is a day's food, and costs a penny, — but that the courtier drinks a cup of wine, or ⟨a⟩ eats a fowl, which costs 50 or 100 prices of his day's provisions; nay, which costs the wages of a man for ten days. Of course, ten men must toil all day, that ⟨that⟩ ↑this↓ trifler may dine at ease. When this is much exaggerated, he says, The children of the courtier are ⟨more⟩ corrupted from the mother's womb; if their father ate up ten men, they twenty, & with wrath & contempt beside: [59] Two snakes have sprung from his shoulder who feed on human brains.[135]

[⟨58⟩60] Realism   Idealism
"We have no land to put our words on, yet our words are true", said my Sacs & Ioways: the philosopher may say the same.

---

[133] See *JMN*, IX, 423–424.

[134] "Thought . . . placed.", struck through in pencil with a vertical use mark, is used in "Shakspeare," *W*, IV, 198.

[135] For the fable of Zohak and the serpents, see *The Sháh Námeh* of Firdausi, trans. James Atkinson, 1892, pp. 10–11.

[61]   Aristocracy

⟨Fri⟩ With the first class of men our friendship or good understanding goes quite behind all accidents of estrangement, of condition, of reputation[.]

———

↑"There is not one of them but I can offend any moment;" said Alcott.↓ [136]

[The Northmen are said to have eaten wild grapes until they were drunk in the American woods; and the first settlers of Concord are described as fainting at the smell of sweetfern in the woods on their march to Musketaquid.]

Culture takes all for granted.[137]

[62] Do it: Bridge the gulf well & truly from edge to edge & the dunces will find it out. There is but one verdict needful & that is mine. If I do it, I shall know it.[138]

[63] Every agent is a reagent. What are governments but awkward scaffoldings by which the noble temple of individual genius is reared. In Greece one must see that the facility of intercourse (arising out of peculiar geography) combined with the absence of a massive priesthood, & the ⟨open⟩ discussion of all political business in the open air by all persons, gave that opportunity, that "easy state of transmission," that "state of amelioration" (which the seedling pear of Van Mons requires) ⁿ so essential to the best genius. — If the spark were struck out, it would be fanned to flame.

[64] ↑Mem.↓ M. Alexander Vattemare brings me compliments &c from M. Ravaisson, maitre des requetes &c au ministere de l'instruction publique, ↑—↓ to which address I am to send copies of two books. —

———

[136] See *JMN*, VII, 395, and "Social Aims," *W*, VIII, 89.
[137] This sentence is struck through in ink with two vertical use marks. Cf. "Aristocracy," *W*, X, 56.
[138] "Do it . . . know it." is struck through in ink with a vertical use mark.

24 Augt. [1847] [139]

---

[65] 1847   Boston

"The arrivals at the port of Boston on Saturday last, (21 August), were 141 coastwise & 22 foreign, — total 169; by far the largest number that ever came into this port in one day. In this number are not included a large number of vessels bringing wood, sand, &c. Cape packets & small craft, but such as arrive from a considerable distance & are booked at the Merchants Exchange."

               Boston Daily Advertiser of Tuesday 24 Aug. 1847 [140]

14 Sept. I read in today's "Post", that, according to the new valuation lists, Boston has increased within one year by the amount of 1034 polls, by $7,644,900. real; and by $5,875,900. personal estate.

        ↑See the further statement of difference
        between B. & N.York. *TU* p↓ [101] [141]

[66] Alas that life with him was one long college examination[.]
        ↑See AB 114↓ [142]

[67] *The French Student* [143]
Translate [this town which is so much smaller than New York]
    [bribe]

---

[139] Within this entry, "*Mem.*" and the date are each set off by ink lines. Jean Gaspard Félix Lacher Ravaisson-Mollien (1813–1900) was a French philosopher and archaeologist; Alexandre Vattemare (1796–1864) was a Parisian who promoted international exchange of books. From 1847 to 1851 he arranged gifts from France to American libraries; out of his efforts grew the Boston Public Library, founded in 1848.

[140] "Boston Daily . . . 1847" is set off by wavy ink lines.

[141] Journal TU will be published in a later volume.

[142] "All my life is a sort of College Examination," Emerson wrote to his brother William on September 24, 1847. "I shall never graduate" (*L*, III, 416); cf. also Notebook JK, p. [43] below. Following this entry are pasted three advertisements clipped from an unidentified London newspaper: the first and third concern private lessons in French; the second, a new play, *Diogène*.

[143] In addition to his lessons in French pronunciation from Dr. Arnoult, in preparation for his visit to Paris, Emerson was reading the *Courrier des Etats-Unis*.

↑relief↓

Pronounce [Un chien comme on en a peu

    peser

    O ciel

    tyrannie

    innocence

    jolie

    monsieur

    sēs sept Sages

    comme il faut

    oeufs in composition has the sound of *e* in *de* [144]

    mot

    sens   ↑sang↓

    tous

    budget

[68] [blank]

[69] Frenchman

I find a secondary tone in every thing written in French journals. The national vanity always appears. England is never out of their mind. How different from the tone of the London Times. Miserable vanity of the French; immense arrogancy in the English: The story Dr C[harles].T[homas].J[ackson]. told me of Louis visiting the hospital secretly in the P.M. with carefullest auscultation at each bed that he might ⟨make an ostentatious visit⟩ pronounce on the case of each patient with ostentatious promptitude on the regular visit with his students the next morning, was characteristic.

I find the French always soldiers. There is a military air in their science, in their social manners. Dr A[rnoult]. my teacher seems to have just left the pistol gallery, and the three days of July.[145]

↑English is long staple, Frenchman short staple. French has street courage, good onset, but the government⟨s⟩ & parties are timid. English dreads blood, but being in, goes to the death.↓

---

[144] A series of vertical ink lines appears to the left of the French words and phrases from "relief" to "oeufs . . . *de*".

[145] For "I find a secondary . . . July.", see *JMN*, VI, 355–356.

[70] George Sand, they told me, speaks of "l'inconstance immortelle des Francais." [146]

[71] Positive qualities. In lack of a great man, give us a great deal of a man; not a pinch of gold dust, but ingots.

[72] "Divination was assigned to madness. No one while endued with intellect becomes connected with a divine & true prophecy: this alone takes place when the power of prudence is fostered by sleep or suffers some mutation by disease or a certain enthusiastic energy."

Timaeus, p. 521 — [147]

Intellect detaches
All things grew, every detachment only prepares a new detachment[.]   Individ[ual] under Genera
Intellect sees these[.] [148]

[73] Οι ρεοντες [149]   Transition

Intellect detaches
In the most decided manner
We touch crimes, depths, mischance & are yet safe[.]
Also with heights, virtues, heroes we find an interval[.]

Intellect detaches the person. In any & every low company he is always salvable. He turns his Gyges ring & disappears from them at ⟨plea⟩ ↑will↓. 'Tis a patent of nobility. Ali. Buonaparte[.] [150]

[73ₐ] [151] Intellect contemplates Detachment

---

[146] See *JMN*, VI, 353.
[147] Plato, *The Cratylus, Phaedo, Parmenides, and Timaeus*, trans. Thomas Taylor (London, 1793).
[148] "Intellect detaches . . . these" is in pencil. For development of the theme of detachment, see "Powers and Laws of Thought," *W*, XII, 38ff.
[149] Cf. Plato, *Theaetetus*, 181A (τοὺς ῥέοντας), an allusion to Heraclitus and his followers. The phrase is rendered as "the flowing philosophers" by Thomas Taylor; see *The Works of Plato* . . . , 1804, IV, 56, and *JMN*, IX, 412.
[150] "Intellect detaches . . . Buonaparte" is in pencil.
[151] For a physical description of the leaf bearing pp. [73ₐ]–[73₄], see the bibliographical headnote to Journal GH.

Detachment of all things
All things let go hands

Intell[ect]. shares the detachment it sees
        makes an interval
        detaches the Person & is a patent of nobility

            Advantage
            CKN[ewcomb] good company
            luxury
            emphasis not laid on persons, & facts.

            Disadvantage⟨s⟩
            spoils virtue
                action
                even conversation

But all this detachment is the preparation for Transition, which is
the organic destiny of the mind.
        Life is transitive[.]

[73b] The moment of Transition in history. CD 48
Value of a trope that the hearer is one.[152]
Certainly, the great law of nature will work here; that the more
transit, the more continuity; or, we are immortal by ↑force of↓
transits.
We ask a selfish immortality, Nature replies by steeping us in the
sea which girds the seven worlds, & makes us ⟨citizens⟩ free of them
all[.]

———

at any pitch a higher pitch   O 176[153]

What we call the universe of today is only a symptom or omen ⟨of
that to which⟩

[152] See Journal AB, p. [104] above.
[153] See *JMN*, IX, 405–406.

[73c] I see the law of the world to be transition.

Our power lies in that, ↑CD 48↓ as, when the knees straighten, there is said to be a certain infinite of Power, which is availed of in the Power Press—

transit in rhetoric,
    in nature. natura
    in time
    in ascension of state

Every atom is on its way onward, the universe circulates in thought. Every thought is passagére[?] in

[73d] Power passes from races of men as from pears. JK last page [154]

[74] We go to Europe to see aristocratic society with as few abatements as possible. We go to be Americanized, to import what we can. This country has its proper glory, though now shrouded & unknown. We will let it shine[.]

Patriotism is balderdash. Our side, our state, our town is boyish enough. But it is true that every foot of soil has its proper quality, that the grape on either side of the same fence has its own flavor, and so every acre on the globe, every group of people, every point of climate has its own moral meaning whereof it is the symbol. For such a patriotism let us stand.[155]

"What is a foreign country to those who have science?"

The fever, though it groweth in my body, is my enemy: the febrifuge, though it groweth in the distant forest, is my friend.   (?) [156]

---

[154] See Notebook JK, p. [153] below; JMN, VII, 90.

[155] "We go . . . stand." is in pencil. "We go . . . Americanized" is used in "Culture," W, VI, 147; "Patriotism . . . stand." is used in "Editors' Address," W, XI, 387.

[156] For " 'What is . . . my friend.", see JMN, VIII, 491, 492, where Emerson is quoting and paraphrasing, respectively, The Hĕĕtōpădēs of Vĕĕshnŏŏ-Sărmā . . . , 1787, pp. 79 and 208 ("A distemper, although generated in the body, is malignant; whilst a drug produced in the woods proveth salutary.").

[75] [157] How simple is the problem ⟨of life⟩ which Watts or Hyde or Coombs, these labourers, have to solve, merely to secure a subsistence, and every part of their action in this work, cutting peat, sawing wood, mowing hay, digging potatoes, is comely & solid. Whilst they occupy themselves in this matter /they are/life has/ ⟨s⟩pyramidal, a cubic solidity, the farmer, the merchant makes nature responsible for his ⟨prof⟩ performance[.]

Not so the idealist, as the poet, the saint, the philosopher, they must be to a certain extent farmers & merchants, & they propose to themselves an impossible aim. The farmer has the conquest of nature to the extent of a living; practicable: the poet the conquest of the Universe; impracticable.

Why can we not let the broker, the grocer, the farmer, be themselves, and not addle their brains with sciolism & religion? [n]
But the spiritualist needs ⟨the⟩ ↑a↓ decided bias to the life of contemplation. Else what prices he pays! poor withered Ishmaelite, Jew in his Ghetto, disfranchised, odd one; what [n] succors, what indemnities, what angels from the celestial side must come in to make him square!

[76] What a misfortune is a swedenborg church. It requires for the profitable reading of Swedenborg almost an equal understanding to his own.

————

For just writing a noble fraternity based on ⟨the⟩ magnanimity. Not with our mean thievish way of regarding thought as property & fearing rivals. [158]

The paving stones in our street are boulders rounded by the attrition of a thousand years. [159]

---

[157] Except for the pagination, this page is in pencil. Before "Why can we" is an uncanceled capital "T", apparently the false start of a paragraph.
[158] "What a . . . rivals." is in pencil.
[159] This sentence is written in ink over the same words in pencil.

[77] Are we fit for society? That is an experiment. It by no means follows that we are not, because society is a bore, & we are voted bores also, and our habits are unsocial in the extreme. No, for we remember the few happy hours of life when we encountered the noble & the wise, we seemed then for the first time in our atmosphere, and then first society seemed to exist. That was society & not the saloon of Mount Vernon or of Broadway.

But here is the use of good society — that it is so easy with the great to be great; so easy to come up to the existing standard, be it never so high; men are so provocative; it is so easy to the lover to shoot the gulf & swim to his love, through waves so grim before; it is so hard to mesmerise ourselves, to whip our own top,[160] ↑Sympathetic force of energy & toil   V 56, Y 195,↓[161] ↑We are so relative, made of hooks & eyes,↓[162]

[78] How often I have to remember the art of the surgeon, which, in replacing the broken bone, limits itself to relieving the dislocation, relieving the parts from their false position, putting them free, then they fly into place by the action of their own muscles.[163]

On this art of nature all our arts rely. This is that tree which grows when we are sleeping: Ygdrasil; ↑CD 110↓

The vegetable principle pervading human nature   Y 210   K 119
World is saturated with deity or law.   Y 167
The current knows the way. O 202 [164]

———

As a man's life comes into union with nature, his thoughts run parallel with the creative law.   K 55 [165]

[160] "Are we . . . top," struck through in ink with two vertical use marks, is used in "Society and Solitude," W, VII, 11.
[161] See JMN, IX, 122, 330.
[162] See JMN, IX, 324, and "Worship," W, VI, 202.
[163] "How often . . . muscles." is struck through in ink with a vertical use mark.
[164] See JMN, IX, 335 (Y 210); VIII, 242 (K 119); IX, 319 (Y 167); IX, 414 (O 202).
[165] The leaf bearing pp. [55]-[56] is torn out of Journal K (JMN, VIII, 220n).

So little affinity between the writer & the works[,] the wind must have writ them[.]   J 130 [166]

[79] The history of genius, the history of success, will then be the history of adjustment of these two states, will & no will,
   state of saliency   (See p 25)
   cause & effect *and* miracle
eager acceptance of the inevitable
   entering into the game & heightening the fun
   outshooting God in his own bow

We wish to get the highest skill of finish, an engraver's educated finger, determination to an aim, — ↑&↓ then — to let in mania, ether, to take off the individual's interference & let him fly as with thunderbolt[.]

Yet "Nature is made better by no mean, but nature makes that mean[.]"
Pericles never ascended the Bema without prayer that he might use no unfit word[.] [167]

[80] The secret of life is to preach, you think.

2 Morals to science [168]
 ⟨1. Transference of trust ⟨to social⟩ that nature inspires to social arrangements⟩ [169]

1 Grandeur of the mind in nature
  Unity of plan
  a plan successively realized & the new types were in view at first
  Its laws apprehensible & Cuvier & Agassiz "restore"

---

[166] See *JMN*, VIII, 190. This entry is struck through in pencil with a diagonal use mark.
 [167] Plutarch, Life of Pericles, VIII.4.
 [168] This heading and the succeeding entries on p. [80] are in pencil.
 [169] "⟨1. Transference . . . arrangements⟩" is partly enclosed from the left by a curved line in pencil; it is also canceled in pencil with two diagonal lines. See *JMN*, IX, 271.

2   Identity of Nature's mind & man's
        fish in cave [170]
        hens
    Man too a part of nature & inundated with her mind.
    Vegetable principle pervading nature.[171]

    Is the solar system good art & architecture? The same achieve-
    ment is in my brain, if I can be kept from interference. Hence the
    great arts.

3   Transference of trust &c. *Supra*

    [81] Hafiz characterised by a perfect intellectual emancipation
    which also he provokes in the reader. Nothing stops him. He makes
    the daregod & daredevil experiment. He is not to be scared by a
    name, or a religion. He fears nothing.[172] He sees too far; he sees
    ⟨ever⟩ throughout; such ⁿ is the only man I wish to see and to be.
    The scholar's courage is as distinct as the soldier's and the states-
    man's — and a man who has it not cannot write for me.

[82][173]   Reading
    The culture of the Imagination[:] how imperiously demanded[,]
    how doggedly denied. Theatre, novels,ⁿ poems,
                    Novels   J 132 [174]
    There are books which move the sea & the land, & which are the
    realiti⟨s⟩es of which you have heard in the fables of Cornelius Agrippa
    & Michael Scott[.] [175]

    Sweetness of reading | Montaigne, Froissart, Chaucer

    Ancient | The three Banquets [176]

---

[170] See p. [55] above.
[171] See p. [78] above.
[172] "Hafiz . . . nothing." is used in "Persian Poetry," *W*, VIII, 249.
[173] This page is in pencil.
[174] See *JMN*, VIII, 191–192.
[175] This sentence is used in "Books," *W*, VII, 200.
[176] Cf. "Books," *W*, VII, 200: "An inestimable trilogy of ancient social pictures

Oriental reading |

Grand reading, | Plato   Synesius   Dante N[uova].V[ita].
              Timaeus weather   Cudworth   Stanley
              river of sleep [177]

All-reading | acc[ording to]. Mme de Stael's rule   Rabelais
                      Diderot   Marguerite Aretin

English reading | ⟨J⟩Clarendon, Bacon, Milton   Johnson
                                    Northcote   Gibbon [178]
                 Milton has been discovered several times
                 Milton   apple

Manuals | Bacon's Essays

[83] [179]   Ben Jonson ˣ   Ford ˣ
              ˣ Beaumont & Fletcher

Favorites
              Sully   Burton
              Walpole   White's Selborne | Bartram's Travels
              Evelyn
              Walton   Aubrey

                           French Gai Science, Fabliaux, [180]
                                ↑U 83↓ [181]

Of Translation |

---

are the three Banquets respectively of Plato, Xenophon, and Plutarch." See also *JMN*,
VIII, 313, and "Clubs," *W*, VII, 248.
  [177] For "Timaeus weather" and "river of sleep", see *JMN*, IX, 236 and 292,
respectively.
  [178] "Gibbon" is circled in pencil. On reading Gibbon, see "Books," *W*, VII, 205.
  [179] This page is in pencil.
  [180] Cf. "Books," *W*, VII, 220.
  [181] See *JMN*, IX, 51.

    Mitchell [182]
Importers] Cousin, De Stael, Southey,

Go to mountains & you may find you had better have stayed at home. You cannot find your mountain. Yet from your lowland window there still is the carbuncle visible again.[183] Mountains are haunted. But they would be dull spirits indeed who could not run away from a pair of climbing sweltering cockneys.

⟨drastic⟩ tonic books | Life of Michel Angelo, Gibbon
                     Goethe   Coleridge

novels | Manzoni

[84]   ↑transferred to Autob[iography].↓
    N[athaniel]. L[angdon]. F[rothingham]. ⟨nearly or quite⟩ twenty years ago, found me in his parlour, & looking at the form of my head, said, "if you are good, it is no thanks to you."[184]

[85] An aristocracy is as if a few inventors, like Fulton, Stephenson, Daguerre, and Charles Jackson, should be able to keep their secrets or impart them only to a few. How would those few ride & tyrannize over society[;] all the rhetoric applied now to the gods would be legitimately applied to them.[185]

[86] 5 Sept.
Channing wished we had a better word than *Nature*, to express this fine picture which the river gave us in our boat yesterday. *Kind* was the old word, which, however, only filled half the range of our fine latin word. But nothing expresses that power which seems to

---

[182] Probably Thomas Mitchell, whose translation of Aristophanes Emerson had borrowed from the Boston Athenaeum in 1836; cf. "Books," *W*, VII, 201.

[183] Edward Emerson, commenting on this passage in *J*, VII, 329, n. 1, wrote that "from the hill-top opposite" Emerson's house, rather than "from his study window," there is a clear view of "Wachusett and Watatic in Massachusetts and Monadnoc and the Peterborough and Temple mountains" in New Hampshire.

[184] This paragraph is struck through in ink with a diagonal use mark.

[185] With this paragraph, cf. "Aristocracy," *W*, X, 40.

work for beauty alone, as C. said, whilst man works only for use.[186] The mikania scandens, the steelblue berries of the cornel, the eupatoriums, enriched now & then by a wellplaced Cardinal ⟨made⟩ ↑adorned↓ the fine shrubbery with what C. called judicious, modest colours, suited to the climate, nothing extravagant. &c.

[87] The English are distinguished by general culture. There is & was no such man, one would say, so equally & harmoniously developed; & hence his easy pride when he finds every other countryman inferior to him as a man. But this same culture ⟨is⟩ necessitates a hopeless limitation. He reads Plato only for Greek, and has not the smallest interest in speculation. It requires a partialist for that.

[88] O suppose nature had made man's body as agreeable to man's palate as plums & peaches so that a hungry man could not help biting his son.[187]

"Give us peace in our boarders." wrote M M E, & when shown the misspelling, said, "it would do as it was."

[89] Ah but a God starts up behind the cotton bales also and behind the counter of the bank.[188]

St George of Cappadocia an Arian [189]
Alfred the truest ↑St.↓ George.
Milton's Age of Ages
Homer, Cameron, ↑of Manchester,[n]↓ called, an extinct world preserved in the Homeric stratum.[190]

---

[186] This and the preceding sentence are used in "Works and Days," *W*, VII, 171–172.

[187] This paragraph is in pencil.

[188] This sentence is struck through in ink with two vertical use marks.

[189] Cf. "Cockayne," *W*, V, 152. In a note on that passage, *W*, V, 355, Edward Emerson states that his father "adopted the account of St. George given by Gibbon"; "the real St. George," he adds, was apparently "another who died two generations earlier."

[190] Emerson met John Cameron, a friend of Carlyle and Milnes, in November of 1847, regarding him as "quite superior" (*L*, III, 438); in January of 1848 he heard Cameron lecture "on Readers & Reading" (*L*, IV, 9).

practical shortsightedness
Abelard & Eloisa

"Not good head, but he shaves well."
Englishman chooses to walk in pouring rain with his closed umbrella
for a cane.[191]

[90] And certainly if an age that is to come would know the
history of this it will seek certainly to know what idea we attached
to the word *Nature*.

Trial of gold pens first pen Nov ⟨8⟩9, 1848
Trial of gold pens ⟨first⟩ ↑second↓ pen Nov 9 1848
Trial of gold pens third pen Nov 9 1848
Trial of gold pens fourth pen Nov 9 1848
Trial of gold pens fifth pen 9 Nov 1848
Trial of gold pens sixth pen 9 Nov 1848
Trial of gold pens seventh pen 9 Nov. 1848
Trial of gold pens eighth pen 9 Nov. 1848
Trial of gold pens ninth pen 9 Nov. 1848
Trial of gold pens tenth pen 9 Nov 1848
↑soft↓ Trial of gold pens eleventh pen 9 Nov. 1848
↑best↓ Trial of gold pens twelfth pen 9 Nov. 1848 [192]

[91] What is the effect of thoughts? Certainly of single thoughts
a limited & often an illusory effect; but of those elemental organic
thoughts which we involuntarily express in the very mould of our
features, in the tendency of our characters, there is no measure known
to us. What differences the men & actions of 1847 from those of
1747?

Concord

12th Palo Alto Pen

[191] This sentence, struck through in ink with a vertical use mark, is used in
"Manners," *W*, V, 105.
[192] There is similar writing, dated "November 1848", on the pages of Emerson's
Account Book 4.

soft & sure but not so current as the eleventh.

11th Palo Alto Pen. Perhaps a little dangerously soft.
Concord, Nov. 1848. R.W. Emerson

Eighth pen Congress pen a good writer but with a little hardness
R W E Concord.

[92]   ↑Horoscope↓   ↑Aristocracy↓ [193]

Not the phrenologist but the philosopher may well say, let me
see his brain & I will tell you if he shall be poet, king, founder of
cities, rich man, ⟨demoniacal — or⟩ magnetic, of a ⟨or whether he⟩
secure hand, of a scientific memory, a right classifier, ⟨a good judge⟩
a just judge; or whether he shall fail in what he attempts. ⟨It is very
⟨certain⟩ obvious to me,⟩ ↑I see well enough,↓ that when I bring one
man into an estate, he sees ↑⟨contemplates⟩↓ vague capabilities, what
others might, could, would, or should do with it; if I bring another
man, he sees what he should do himself: He not only ⟨sees⟩ ↑ap-
preciates↓ the ⟨p⟩water privilege, the land fit for orchard, pasturage,
tillage, & so on, the woodlot, the cranberry⟨-s⟩ meadow, but just as
easily, he foresees all the means, all the steps of the process, and
would [93] lay his hand as readily on one ⟨foot⟩ ↑point↓ as ⟨a⟩on
another in that series which conducts the capability to the utmost
fruit. The indolent poet sees keenly enough the result; the well built
head ⟨do⟩ supplies all the ⟨steps⟩ intermediate steps, one as perfect
as another, in the series. If we could see the man well, we should
foresee his history as accurately as we do now that of a ciderpress or
a washstand or a paintbrush[,] a basket, ⟨a key⟩ a pump, a corkscrew
or a steelpen when I see these tools in a magazine of arts. They are
already on their way respectively to apples, to ⟨water⟩ ↑dressing-
room↓, to paint, to the cellar, to the well, to corks, to an inkstand;
and the man's associations & [94] [194] fortunes, his love & hatred, his
residence & rank, the books he will buy and the roads he will traverse,

[193] "Aristocracy" is in pencil.
[194] "Horoscope" is written as an index heading above "fortunes, his love" at the
top of this page.

are foreordained in the result & in the completeness of the details in his brain.[195]

People think it fortune, that makes one rich & another poor. Is it? Yes, but the fortune was earlier in the balance ↑or↓ adjustment between devotion to the present ⟨hour⟩ ↑good↓ & a forecast of the good of tomorrow. G. lives for the moment, praises himself for it, & despises E., that he does not. G., of course, is poor, & E., since he is providing, is provided. The odd circumstance is, that G. thinks it a superiority in himself, this improvidence which ought to be rewarded with E.'s property.[196]

[95] All biography auto-biography [197]

I notice that the biography of each noted individual is really at last communicated by himself. The lively traits of criticism on his works are all confessions made by him from time to time among his friends & remembered & printed.

Present & Future

Do not imagine that I should work for the future, if my services were accepted or acceptable in the present. Immortality, as you call it, is my *pis aller*.

[96] We want poetry[;] we do not want slops. Th⟨y⟩e children want to eat & to run. Avoid, therefore, dysentery & lameness.[198]

[97] Remarkable trait in the American Character is the union not very infrequent of Yankee cleverness with spiritualism. Thus my Wall street ↑cotton-↓broker, Thomas Truesdale; and William Green of Boonton, N.J., iron manufacturer; and Rebecca Black, living by slop work from the tailors; and Sampson Reed, druggist; & Her-

---

[195] "Not the phrenologist . . . brain.", struck through in ink with discontinuous vertical use marks on pp. [92], [93], and [94], is used in "Aristocracy," W, X, 44–45.
[196] "People think . . . property." is struck through in ink with a vertical use mark. "People think . . . tomorrow." is used in "Aristocracy," W, X, 45–46; "G. lives . . . property." is used in "Wealth," W, VI, 124.
[197] "All . . . auto-biography" is used in "Theodore Parker," W, XI, 285.
[198] This paragraph is struck through in ink with two diagonal use marks.

mann, toy seller; and Edward Stabler * druggist in Alexandria —
were all prospering people who knew how to trade & how to pray.[199]
W. G.'s wagon always met T T & R B ⟨W⟩at the ferry when they
went moved by the spirit to visit him, though he had no notice of
their coming.

↑The Quakers blend the same traits↓[.]

[98]   ↑Printed↓

When people tell me they do not like poetry, and bring me Shelley
or Hemans, to show that it is not likeable, I am entirely of their
mind. But this only proves that they do not like slops. But I bring
them Homer, and they like that, & the Cid, and that goes well; and
I read them ↑Lear & Macbeth,↓ Robin Hood's ballads, or Lady Jane,
or Fair Annie, or the Hardyknute, or Chevy Chase, or the Cronach's
cried or Bennachie, and they like that well enough. For this poetry
instead of being daubs of colour, and mere mouthing, is out of the
deep breast of man.[200]

The Americans, ⟨Mr⟩Dr Harris ↑the Librarian,↓ [201] tells me↑,↓
are every day inquiring more after the history of families↑,↓ and we
want the English county histories here for that end.

* the friend of Mary Rotch
† E. 338 [202]

[199] Emerson had met Thomas Truesdale, William Green, and Rebecca Black
while lecturing in New York in 1842; see *JMN*, VIII, 202. Sampson Reed, a Boston
Swedenborgian, and Edward Stabler of Alexandria, Virginia, Emerson had long considered among his spiritual benefactors. Hermann has not been identified.

[200] "When people . . . man.", struck through in ink with a curved diagonal
use mark and a wavy diagonal use mark, is used in "Poetry and Imagination," *W*,
VIII, 25. Emerson's references to the ballads of Robin Hood, "Lady Jane," "Fair
Annie," and "Chevy Chase" reflect his reading in such collections as Robert Jamieson's
Popular Ballads and Songs, 1806. "Hardyknute," written by Lady Elizabeth Wardlaw (1677–1727), was circulated as a purported fragment of an ancient ballad.
Emerson's "Cronach" is evidently "coronach," defined by Sir Walter Scott as "the
lamentation for a deceased warrior, sung by the aged of the clan"; see *Minstrelsy
of the Scottish Border*, 5th ed., 3 vols. (Edinburgh, 1812), III, 307, n. "Bennachie"
may be an error for "Banachie," the highest class of old Celtic noblemen.

[201] Thaddeus William Harris (1795–1856), librarian at Harvard from 1831
until his death.

[202] See *JMN*, VII, 465.

[99] [203] The Present
The present moment is a boat in which I ⟨fearlessly⟩ embark without
fear; boat & pilot at once.

———

The present & the future. see above, p 95

———

———

Modern times.

———

The modern architecture is ship-building; & the modern art is music;
and the new power, steam.

Hallam's History of
Literature [vol.] 2. [p.]40 [204]

[100] A man ⟨measures himself⟩ ↑is measured↓ by the angle at which
he looks at objects.[205] I am ↑reckoned↓ a better man than Mr
O'Shaughnessy, because I am found to see things at a larger angle than
he; that is, not to be quite so much ↑of↓ a trifler or a fly, as he. Well;
here is Alcott looks at every thing in larger angles than any other,
and, by good right, should be the greatest man. But here comes in
another trait: it is found though ↑the lines of↓ his angles are of so
generous ↑contents,↓ the apex of the angle is not quite defined; which
"takes from the pith of nature the noblest attribute." [206] This he
does not understand, & puts ⟨in⟩ another construction on it, "that
mankind are best served indirectly, the divine spark loving to in-
sinuate itself thro' mediators to the minds of the multitude; [101]
he feels that he has the freest access to the minds of the ⟨mu⟩people
thro' the peoples' teachers." &c. &c.

[102] One might expect a great immorality from the new arts, such

[203] On this page, slightly to the left of center, are two concentric circles drawn
in pencil with the aid of a compass, their center falling between "new power" and
"Hallam's".
[204] Henry Hallam, *Introduction to the Literature of Europe in the Fifteenth,
Sixteenth, and Seventeenth Centuries*, 4 vols. (Paris, 1839), is in Emerson's library.
[205] Cf. p. [8] above. The sentence is used in "Powers and Laws of Thought,"
W, XII, 10.
[206] Cf. *Hamlet*, I, iv, 20–22; see *JMN*, VII, 136.

as daguerre, telegraph, & railroad, on the ground that all that frees talent without increasing self-command, is noxious — a Gyges-ring, as young travellers are licentious who are faultless at home, but, as these arts are for all, the morals of society remain unaltered.

⟨T⟩A tool is that which is used purely for my benefit, without any regard to its own. But all love is of that nature that it instantly respects the instrument also, &, though it be a ship ⟨a⟩or a wheel or bootjack, raises it instantly into personality & seeks to give it an interest of its own & to ⟨respect⟩treat it as if it had.

[103] The beginning of wealth is in wealth of nature in the man. Sickness is poorspirited, & cannot serve any one, because it must husband its resources to live. It does not ask a question, or hazard a look at other people. But health or fulness answers its own needs & has to spare, & runs over, & inundates the neighborhoods & creeks of other men's necessities[.]

Is it not a little pathetic to find genius too resting at last so much on money? It should be one of many means, & it continues from year to year the main resort. Well what is money, then, but the token of material power; & should not Genius possess all manner of root & relation to the globe[?]

———

Money

The diamond ring tells stories, says the ⟨f⟩French novel, "but pistoles have no names." ↑A Spanish dollar speaks all languages.↓

[104] Good writing is a kind of skating which carries off the performer where he would not go↑,↓ [207] & is only right admirable when to all its beauty & speed a subserviency to the will like that of walking is added.[208]

---

[207] The comma is added in pencil.
[208] This sentence is used in "Veracity," W, VIII, 31.

↑PANTHEISM↓

"Most men are pantheists at heart, say what they may of their theism. No other path is indeed open for them to the One; intellectually at least. Man delights in freedom, even to license, & claims infinite indulgence from the powers seen & unseen, to whom he would in turn give indulgence. In a word, he would conquer & surrender in his own way, being no less open to the power of love than of hate. Swayed by gods & demons, he is never in his freest moments quite himself. His audacity is immense; his impieties are his pieties; he wins & loses, to win & lose. He reveres, dallies with, ⟨&⟩ defies & overcomes every god & demigod of the Pantheon, in quest of his freedom & thus liberates humanity from the demons [105]ⁿ by these twelve labors." *Alcott*

At sea Oct. 13.[209]

In mines & bottomry the last debt is paid first. The Irishman at Liverpool wished Capt. Barstow to carry him to N.Y. & his brother would meet him there on the wharf, & pay him. Does he live in N Y? No, not just in N.Y. but a little out of it, in a place called Illinois. | Cotton pays a fair freight, when it pays a cent a pound to Liverpool. That on board pays a farthing. Yankees up-country have a mill into which they put a stick of wood & it goes through the hopper & comes out a chair.[210] If a man does not like dust, let him go to sea. The sailor says, that all the sailors are runaway boys. The steersman's rule is, it is of no use to carry any more sail than you can steer steady. I detected in our unanimous zeal & interest in the ship's gains every hour that some of our passengers feared to arrive.[211] Oct. 14. The good ship darts thro' the water all night like a fish, quivering with speed. Sliding thro' space, sliding from horizon to horizon. She has passed Cape Sable[;] she has reached the Banks[;] gulls, hag⟨dons⟩lets,ⁿ ducks swim, dive, & hover around; no fishermen; she has passed the Banks, left five sail behind her, far on the edge of the west, ⟨wh⟩ at sundown, who were far east of us at morn,

---

[209] Emerson had sailed from Boston on October 5, 1847, aboard the *Washington Irving*. For other entries concerning the voyage, see Journal Sea-Notes, pp. 200–207 below.

[210] For "Yankees . . . a chair.", see *JMN*, IX, 105.

[211] The entry for October 13 is in pencil. One sentence, "The sailor . . . boys.", struck through in pencil with a vertical use mark, is used in "Voyage to England," *W*, V, 30; cf. Journal Sea-Notes, p. [8] below.

tho' they say at sea a stern chase is a long race. ⟨T⟩And still we fly for life. The ship cost $56 000.00. The shortest sea line from Boston to Liverpool [106]ⁿ is 2850 miles. This the steamer keeps, & saves by keeping her course 150 miles. Captain Caldwell says that he can never go in a shorter line than 3000 & usually much longer than that. The sailor is the practical ropedancer. The ship may weigh with all its freight 1500 tons. Every bound & plunge is taking us out of danger. If sailors were contented, if they had not resolved again & again never to go to sea any more, I should respect them. ↑I can tell you what secrets the sea yielded me.↓ ²¹²

[107] It occurred in the night watches that the true aristocrat is at the head of his own order, & that disloyalty is to mistake other chivalries for his own. Let him stop at the hotel of *his fashion:* &, whatever he does or does not, let him know & befriend his friends.

———

↑The Captain says,↓ "'Tis of no use to carry more sail than you can steer steady." ²¹³

[108] It is not well perhaps that a general should be a carabine, as they said of Gustavus,²¹⁴ yetⁿ perhaps a scholar should carry with him a little trunk of specimens also, and be able to wile his lowest company from their meat & lowness by the new charms of romance & of reason.

———

Coals to a market

Can you not fancy that after all your elections you are still carried in some degree by the genius & habit of your countrymen, of your profession? There is less of this which you have & know & are, where you are going than you left at home. Ah! is it so? Then an idea leads you, & outcalculates your calculations. Well; is there no insurance in that? Can you not say then, By the leave of God we will arrive?

———

²¹² The entry for October 14, written in pencil and struck through in pencil with a series of three vertical use marks, is used in "Voyage to England," *W*, V, 26–27, 28, 31.
²¹³ See p. [105] above.
²¹⁴ See Journal AB, p. [122] above.

[109] [215] Oct. 18. In reading last night this old diary of Joseph Emerson of Malden [216] ending in the year 1726, one easily sees the useful egotism of our old puritan clergy. The minister *experienced* life for his flock. He gave prominence to all his economy & history for the benefit of the parish. All his haps are providences. If he keeps school, marries, begets children, if his house burns, if his children have the measles, if he is thrown from his horse, if he buys a negro,[n] & Dinah misbehaves, if he buys or sells his chaise, all his adventures are fumigated with prayer & praise, he /preaches/improves it/ next Sunday on the new circumstance ⟨or improves⟩ and the willing flock are contented with this consecration of one man's adventures for the benefit of them all, inasmuch as that one is on the right level & therefore a fair representative.

[His cow & horse & pig did duty next sunday in the pulpit[.]] [217]

Another circumstance appears from all the names in the Diary, that the [110] leading families in New England seem chiefly descended from some clergyman of that time, as, Hancock, Lowell, Sewall, Bulkeley, Chauncy, Forbes, Walter, ⟨Upham⟩ Parsons, Greenleaf, Thacher, Oxenbridge, Barnard, Colman, Green, Foxcroft, Tappan[.]

[111] ↑Religion↓
The Catholic religion respects masses of men & ages. If it elects, it is yet by millions, as ⟨the⟩ when it divides the heathen & christian. The Protestant, on the contrary[,] with its hateful "private judg-

---

[215] Laid in between pp. [108] and [109] is a list of readings in the works of Ernst Moritz Arndt, Friedrich von Sallot, Heinrich Steffens, E. T. A. Hoffmann, Freiherr Adolf von Knigge, Friedrich Heinrich Jacobi, Johann Gottfried Seume, and Karl Immermann; for a physical description of the insert, see the bibliographical headnote to Journal GH. Concerning von Knigge, the unidentified author of the list notes: "I remember his novels interested me much when I was a young man; they are out of date now. George Sand makes much of him in the Countess at Rudolstadt. . . ."

[216] Emerson's great-grandfather; see p. [123] below. Emerson may have taken the diary on his voyage in preparation for visiting places associated with his English forebears.

[217] "His cow . . . pulpit" is in pencil.

ment"[,] ⟨p⟩brings parishes, families, & at last individual doctrinaires & schismatics, &, verily, at last, private gentlemen into ⟨no⟩play & notice, which to the gentle musing poet is to the last degree disagreeable. This of course their respective arts & artists must build & paint. The Catholic church is ethnical, & every way superior. ⟨The⟩ It is in harmony with Nature, which loves the race & ruins the individual. The Protestant has his pew, which of course is only the first step to a church for every individual citizen — a church apiece — [.]

[112] Liverpool, 30 Oct. 1847
Everything in England bespeaks an immense population. The buildings are on a scale of size & wealth out of all proportion to ours. The colossal masonry of the docks & of all the public buildings attests the multitudes of men who are to be accommodated by them, & to pay for them. So the manners of the people, the complete incuriosity & stony neglect each of every other↑:—↓ each man ⟨e⟩walks, eats, drinks, shaves, dresses, gesticulates, & in every manner is, acts, & suffers, without the smallest reference to the bystanders, & in his own fashion. It is almost an affront to look a man in the eye before being introduced. In mixed or in select companies, they do not introduce persons to each other so that a presentation is a circumstance as valid as a contract. The Englishman has thus a ↑necessary↓ talent of ⟨leaving⟩ letting alone all that does not belong to him. ⟨Which is⟩They are physiognomically & constitutionally distinct from the Americans. They incline more to be large-bodied men; they are stocky, & especially the women seem to have that defect to their beauty; no tall slender [113] girls of flowing shape, but stunted & stocky. The Englishman speaks with all his body; his elocution is stomachic; the American's is labial. The Englishman is very petulant & precise about his ⟨inn⟩ accommodation at inns & on the road; a quiddle about his toast & his chop, & every species of convenience, & loud & pungent in his expressions of impatience at any neglect. The axes of his eyes are united to his body, & only move with the trunk. His introductions are sacraments.[218]

[218] "Everything [p. [112]] . . . sacraments.", struck through with vertical use marks both in pencil ("Everything . . . contract."; "They are . . . the trunk.")

The English *Oh* much cheaper ⟨‖ ... ‖⟩ than the American *Indeed*, & quite significant. Universal clipping; Dr Cook Taylor who writes for the Athenaeum, I never doubted was Dr *Coutell*.[219] Scotch cadence, "He told me, he would make sh*ooooe*s, and this is a true ve*racio*us account of the thing."

[114] Carlyle has a hairy strength which made his literary vocation a mere chance, and what seems very contemptible to him. I could think only of an enormous trip hammer with an "Aeolian attachment." ⟨C.⟩He said, he had received £800 from his Cromwell in England. i.e. from the first edition.[220]

Rogers[221] told of Talleyrand's visit with the Duchess of Orleans blazing with beauty, & Paméla, afterwards Lady Fitzgerald, who was more attractive by "the sweet seriousness of sixteen." Talleyrand's answer to Mme de Stael who asked which he would save on a plank in shipwreck, Recamier or herself? "Why, you can swim." One who said that if you could only know one English word in coming to England when this princess of Orleans was coming, — they urged "Yes." "No," said the other, "If I knew but one, it would be *no*; because no sometimes means yes, but yes never means no." To a lady who wished to witness a great victory, Lord Wellington said, "⟨M⟩Ah! Madam, a [115] great victory i⟨t⟩s the greatest of

---

and in ink, is used in "Manners," *W*, V, 104–105, 105–106. "They incline . . . & stocky." is used in "Race," *W*, V, 65–66.

[219] The reference is to William Cooke Taylor (1800–1849).

[220] After arriving at Liverpool on October 22 and receiving a delayed letter directed to him there by Thomas Carlyle, Emerson had taken a train for London on October 25, staying with the Carlyles in Chelsea until his return to Liverpool on the 29th. His lecturing began at Manchester on November 2. For Emerson's account of his reunion with the Carlyles, see Notebook ED, pp. [189]–[195] below; the expression "trip hammer with an 'Aeolian attachment' " is used there on p. [193].

[221] Emerson was presented to the poet Samuel Rogers on October 27, 1847, during a visit to the National Gallery in London, by Mrs. George Bancroft, wife of the American minister to Great Britain; he was invited to accompany her to one of Rogers's famous breakfasts on Friday, October 29. For a fuller account of his host's conversation, see *L*, III, 425–426 (a letter to Lidian Emerson completed at Liverpool on November 1) and Notebook ED, pp. [111]–[118] below (a collection of materials concerning Rogers).

tragedies⟨,⟩ except one, a defeat." ²²² To ⟨one⟩ ↑an Englishman↓ who said, "They worship the sun in your country"; the Persian Ambassador replied, "So would you, if you ever saw him."

Sidney Smith said, Macaulay had improved, he has flashes of silence.²²³
Of the giraffe, he said, that he would take cold; & think of having two yards of sore throat!

"The two styles, the Antediluvian & Postdiluvian: men, nowadays, have not time to lounge seventy years over a pamphlet."

––––––

Young ladies made the clergyman 50 pairs of slippers. "How do you take him for a centipede?"

T.C[arlyle] said of Samuel Brown,²²⁴ "that he was that kind of man, that if God Almighty wished to hang a new ⟨planet⟩ ↑constellation↓ in the sky, he would give him an estimate for the same." ²²⁵

↑Mr Upcott ↑who↓ lived in Autograph Cottage had the writing found in Felton's hat and a page of the diary of Princess Charlotte, & the death warrant of Mary Q[ueen]. of Scots.
Hogg wrote "Scott's Novels" on the back of Waverley, &c. W. Scott said "Jamie, do you spell Scots with twa *ts*?"↓

[116]   ↑England↓   ↑Rev. Edw. Irving↓
⟨T.C. &⟩ Edw Irving & T[homas] C[arlyle] kept schools at the

––––––

²²² "Rogers . . . a defeat.' ", struck through in pencil with vertical use marks, is transcribed in Notebook ED, pp. [116]–[117] below.
²²³ See Emerson's letter to his wife, London, March 23 and 24, 1848 (*L*, IV, 43).
²²⁴ Dr. Samuel Brown (1817–1856), a physicist and chemist who had entertained Margaret Fuller and learned of Emerson from her, was Emerson's host during his stay in Edinburgh.
²²⁵ "To ⟨one⟩ an Englishman . . . the same.' " is struck through in pencil with one diagonal use mark. There are additional use marks in pencil through "To ⟨one⟩ an Englishman . . . saw him.' ", which is transcribed in Notebook ED, p. [118] below; "Sidney Smith . . . centipede?' "; and "T. C . . . the same.' "

same time at Kirkcaldy & Dysart respectively, and were in the habit of walking together along the beach.[226]

———

Whately declined cat to his clergy.

———

The only girth or belt that can enable one to face these Patagonians of beef & beer, is an absorbing work of your own. Otherwise with their excessive life they hustle you out of their world.   ↑See p 121↓

———

    ↑These Centaurs are always on horse, ↑and every inn room is lined with pictures of races, &c.↓↓ [227]

———

'Tis a peculiarity ⟨of⟩ that ↑on the railway⟨s⟩,↓ they always ride ⟨backward in⟩ with their back to the engine, ⟨in the trains:⟩ & turn to the left:

Dr B[rown]., I think, must be a Jew: his manners are of Monmouth street.[228]

———

Woman is cheap & vile in England[.]

———

And I begin to understand that this arrogance & contempt of all people around him is brought to the Genius by numerous experiences of disappointments in the promise of characters in a *great population*.

    [117] My little Edie costs me many a penny.[229]

———

[226] This sentence is transcribed in Notebook ED, p. [219] below.

[227] "The only . . . races, &c." is struck through in pencil with a vertical use mark; "Otherwise . . . &c." is struck through in ink with a vertical use mark. "These Centaurs . . . races, &c." is used in "Race," *W*, V, 73.

[228] Monmouth Street, now part of Shaftesbury Avenue in London, was once noted for its numerous old-clothes shops.

[229] See Emerson's letter written at Manchester, December 1, 1847, to Lidian Emerson, which similarly observes that "Woman is cheap & vile in England . . . — Childhood, too, I see oftenest in the state of absolute beggary. My dearest little Edie" — i.e., his daughter Edith — ". . . costs me many a penny, day by day. I cannot go up the street but I shall see some woman in rags with a little creature just

Great population also clips all words.

———

It rains at every tide ↑at Manchester every day, and at Lake Killarney a shower is three weeks↓:ⁿ and Mr P. said, there was about one day in the year that they could do without fire in the parlour.[230]

———

Only three or four percent of this population are idle. Everybody works in England, said Mr Rawlins[.][231]

———

Very small attendance usually in house of lords ↑20 or 30↓. With such an immense stake the nobles are utterly negligent and are quietly at home devoured by ennui.[232]

———

In Manchester they attribute the better ⟨habits of⟩ character of this people for prudence & industry to the universal habit here of dining at 1 o'clock. If they are to go to business again in the P.M., they say, we shall not eat so much.

———

I wish I had remarked who it was they said uttered the quite English sentence "So help me God. I will never listen to evidence again." — In one debate of the house of lords Duke of Wellington had fifty proxies in his pocket.[233]

[118] We are very slow to ⟨admit⟩ believe the moral superiority of

---

of Edie's age & size, but in coarsest ragged clothes, & barefooted, . . . and the far-off Edie wins from me the halfpence for this near one" (L, III, 442).

[230] "It rains . . . parlour.", struck through in ink with a vertical use mark, is used in "Land," W, V, 39–40, where the remark of "Mr P." is attributed to "a gentleman in Liverpool." During one of Emerson's visits to Liverpool he was the guest of a Swiss merchant family, the Paulets (L, III, 443).

[231] "Only three . . . Rawlins" is struck through in pencil with a vertical use mark. Charles E. Rawlins, Jr., was among Emerson's friends in Liverpool.

[232] "Very small . . . ennui.", struck through both in pencil and in ink with single vertical use marks, is used in "Aristocracy," W, V, 183.

[233] "I wish . . . pocket." is struck through in pencil with a curved vertical use mark and in ink with a diagonal use mark. The first sentence is used in "Truth," W, V, 125; the second, in "Aristocracy," W, V, 184.

another; but once admitted that explains all intellectual advantage he has of us.[234]

———

All we ask of any man is that he should thoroughly like his own way of life.[235]

[119] England[:] "Lord Clarendon has pluck like a cock, & will fight till he dies;" "but Peel has that damned smile".[236] Pitt said of Canning "that he had never seen such a prostitute, as that young man of 21." Old Gladstone discovered at 80 that the annuity tables were all loose after 75 or 80 years so he bought annuities & lives now on the receipt of 13 000 pound per annum which cost him but 90 pound[.]

Lord Althorp "Honest"

Eglintoun suspended payment. That gewgaw of a tournament, (when Coeur de Lion appeared under an ⟨am⟩ umbrella,) [237] cost £700,-000.[238]

English must have made up people as I think, must have strong constitutions, & animal spirits. You must have an atmosphere, or you are a Jew among them. Horror of adventurers in Parliament, & elsewhere.[239]

Two styles of dress[:] the tortoise style and the supple or becoming. But the former, wherein the man speaks out of his building[,] suits Eng[lish] manners well.

[120]   ↑England↓

Among the local objects are horses & hounds *clothed all over,* and postillions in livery on every span of horses↑; and mourning coaches covered with nodding plumes; and gigs & carts with little

---

[234] "We are . . . us." is struck through in ink with a vertical use mark.

[235] Below this entry, along the left margin, is a drawing in ink of a woman's bonnet with ribbons and a scalloped edging.

[236] " 'Lord Clarendon . . . smile'." is struck through in ink with two vertical use marks; " 'Lord Clarendon . . . dies;' " is used in "Manners," *W*, V, 102.

[237] "am" is canceled in pencil.

[238] An attempt was made in 1839 to revive the ancient tourney, at Eglinton Castle in Ayrshire.

[239] "Horror . . . elsewhere." is used in "Truth," *W*, V, 122.

horses of the Canadian(?) breed.↓ ↑& dogs, & sedan chairs; & men dressed in shawls.↓

———

⟨But the beggars are fat⟩
↑and turn their horses to the left hand when they meet, and in Manchester lately there is an order for foot passengers to turn to the right, & escutcheons on the walls for one year after death.↓
The English love conventional manners, & do not excuse the want of them. A man not *made up* after their fashion, is like a man not drest, & is not presentable. Their bearing, on being introduced, is cold, even though they wish very much to see you, & mean to make much of you.[240]
Penny postage yields £800 000 revenue over the cost. Postage stamps are a very useful currency in a country where there is no paper money of less amount than £5.

————————

Stealing
Duke of Buckingham in exile for debt, & transferred the furniture, &c. he had bought of tradesmen, to his son, so that the tradesmen could not attach them.
Beaufort an exile

[121]   ↑England↓
The Berserkir in all his hairy might here still. It requires a good constitution to travel in Spain. I say as much of England, simply on account of the ⟨pluck &⟩ brawn of the people. Any other countryman looks ⟨&⟩slight beside them. I know nothing but the most serious business ↑see p 116↓ that could give me any counterweight to these Baresarks, though they were only to order eggs & muffins for their breakfast; "They put the heart into it, man, they put the heart into it."[241]

All life moves here on machinery, 'tis a various mill. The Englishman never touches the ground. The steamer delivers him to the

[240] This sentence is used in "Manners," *W*, V, 106.
[241] "The Berserkir . . . it.' ", struck through in pencil with a vertical use mark and also in ink with a vertical use mark, is used in "Manners," *W*, V, 103–104.

cab; the cab to the railway train; the train to the cab; the cab to the hotel; & so onward.

Most of the differences between American & English, referrible to dense population here, and will certainly be lost as ⟨that country⟩ ↑America↓ fills up.   ↑See p 116↓

[122] [December 4, 1847.] What a misfortune to America that she has not original names on the land but this whitewash of English names. Here every name is history. I was at Rochdale yesterday; I asked, where is the Rock? "That river down there." ↑So at Sheffield, the Sheafe↓. Prestwick[,] Greenwich[,] is the Priest's /vicus/street/, the green vicus, so that all means somewhat. And poor America is born into cast-off clothes, and her alphabet is secondary, & not organic.[242]

Dec. 10. I visited from Derby with Mr R. W. Birch and Mr Thomas Tunal⟨y⟩ey Kedleston Hall, seat of Lord Scarsdale   Curzon[.]
At Derby, *All Saints Church* tower; and bells.
At Nottingham, the Castle & Mortimer's Hole.[243]

Dec. 11. I visited Wo⟨o⟩llaton Hall, seat of Lord Middleton. Willoughby built in Elizabeth's time[.]
In the road between Manchester & Sheffield I passed through ↑a tunnel of↓ 3↑¼↓ miles ⟨of tunnel⟩ ↑to Dunsford Station. One man drives the engine there all day through it.↓
Beautiful desolations are these houses.[244]

----

[242] This paragraph is used in "Aristocracy," *W*, V, 179.

[243] Nathaniel Curzon, 3rd Baron Scarsdale, had "never spent a night in the house," according to Emerson's letter of December 15, 1847, to his wife describing his visits to Derby and Nottingham (*L*, III, 450). Cf. "Aristocracy," *W*, V, 172.

[244] The phrase "beautiful desolations" also occurs in Emerson's letter of December 15, written on paper bearing a cut of Wollaton Hall (*L*, III, 449, n. 267), and later in "Aristocracy," *W*, V, 172. The letter, like the present entry, dates Emerson's visit to the hall as of Saturday, December 11; in Notebook England and Paris, p. [9] below, the fees paid there are entered under December 12.

The Earl of Breadalbane goes out from his house over his own land 100 miles in a straight line to the sea.[245]

———

£80 000 were spent to repair B[isho]p. of Gloucester's palace.
↑Bp of Armagh has near £100 000 a year.↓

[123][246] Joseph Emerson born at Chelmsford 20 April 1700[.]
[His Grandfather was——⟨Mr——————Waldo⟩ ↑Edward Emerson Waldo↓]
His maternal grandfather was Mr
His parents resided at Newbury.
Entered college July 1713 graduated 1717
Oct 1717 kept school at York
1721 Oct. settled at Malden
Dec Married Mary Moody daughter of Sam Moody of York
1722 ⟨Feb⟩Dec. 22 daughter Hannah born
1724 Aug. house burned
Aug 25 son born Joseph

1732 June 15 son Bulkeley born "My Grandmother Emerson was the daughter of Rev. Edward Bulkeley of Concord"
1735 June 23 Son Waldo born

[124] ↑Rev. Joseph Emerson, Malden.↓[247]
The minister notes 1735 Jan 31, "Bought a Shay ⟨a⟩for £27.10s. The Lord grant it may be a comfort & blessing to my family!" In the following March, he has "a safe & comfortable journey" to York. But, in Apr. 24, we find, "Shay overturned with my wife & I in it, yet neither of us much hurt. Blessed be our gracious Preserver. Part of the shay, as it lay upon one side, went over my wife, & yet she was scarcely anything hurt. How wonderful the preservation!" Then again, "*May 5*. Went to the Beach with three of the children. The Beast being frightened (when we were all out of the shay,

---

[245] This sentence is used in "Aristocracy," *W*, V, 182.
[246] This page is in pencil.
[247] This heading is in pencil.

overturned & broke it. I desire (I hope I desire it.) that the Lord would teach me suitably to resent ⟨it⟩this Providence, to make suitable remarks upon it, & to be suitably affected with it."

"Have I done well to get me a shay? Have I not been proud or too fond of this convenience? Do I exercise the faith in the divine care & protection which I ought to do? Should I not be more in my study, & less fond of diversions? Do I not withhold more than is meet from pious & charitable uses?"

[125] Well, on 15 May, we have this, "Shay brought home; mending cost 30 shillings. Favoured in this respect beyond expectation"[.]

"16 May. My wife & I rode together in the Shay to Rumney Marsh. The Beast frighted several times."

And at last we have this record, —

"June 4. Disposed of my shay to the Rev. Mr White." [248]

$$\begin{array}{r} 1735 \\ 1874 \\ \hline 139 \end{array}$$

$$\begin{array}{r} 1848 \\ 176 \\ \hline 2024 \end{array}\,[249]$$

[126] This morning more than ever I believed the world is wise; the world & not the individual. Wordsworth knows very little about his Ode, has as little to do with that, as any reader. If you see the man, you would say, he is not the writer; and would warmly advise him to read that poem.[250] In Plutarch's "*Placita Philosophorum*," I remember some one found the soul in the air circulating, respired

---

[248] The account of the shay, pp. [124]–[125], is used in "Ezra Ripley, D.D.," *W*, X, 384–385, where Emerson notes that the diary of Joseph Emerson was "written in the blank leaves of the almanac for the year 1735."

[249] The computations on this page are in pencil.

[250] "Ode: Intimations of Immortality. . . ." This entry may have been made on or after February 27, 1848, when Emerson renewed his acquaintance with Wordsworth at Ambleside: see Notebook ED, p. [245] below.

& expired by all alike.[251] Yes, Wisdom is in the air, & good health gets it all.

———

Ellen Tucker's poetry was very sweet, & on the way to all high merits & yet as easy as breathing to her who wrote.

———

[127]   Rich & Poor
The insurance of the first class carriages in the railway is the Parliamentary carriage which goes with them; and the telegraph ⟨wires⟩lines which convey the messages of Rothschild & Lloyd, would be surely cut if it were not known that tidings also of interest to the million were vibrating ⟨invisibly⟩ along the ↑same↓ wires.[252]

———

Bulkeley	Moody
Bulkeley	↑W↓ Emerson
↑J↓ Emerson	↑W↓ Emerson
↑W↓ Emerson	↑RW↓ Emerson
↑W↓ Emerson	⟨Emerson⟩
R W E	

[128] Mr ⟨Tyass⟩ (?) ↑Twiss?↓ [253] reporter to the Times newspaper, in some place where reporters were forbidden went in with his hands in his coat pocket & with pencil in one hand & book in the other, made his report so.
Twiss is the condenser of the reports of Parliamentary debates.
↑Sterling Barnes   Alsiger↓ [254]

---

[251] See "Of Those Sentiments Concerning Nature with which Philosophers Were Delighted," in *Plutarch's Morals . . . Translated from the Greek, by Several Hands,* 1718, III, 138–139: "*Anaximenes* . . . pronounceth, That Air is the Principle of all Beings; from it all receive their Original, and into it all return; he affirms, That our Soul is nothing but Air. . . ." *De Placitis Philosophorum,* formerly included in editions of Plutarch, is now attributed to Aëtius.

[252] "invisibly" is canceled in pencil; "same" is inserted in pencil; the writing following "wires" on p. [127] is in pencil.

[253] The cancellation of "Tyass" and the inserted "Twiss?" are both in pencil.

[254] Emerson is referring to the reporter Horace Twiss (1787–1849); Edward Sterling (1773–1847), the father of Carlyle's friend John Sterling, a writer of

13 Dec. At Newstead Abbey — Col. Wildman [255]
Gypsies. Boswell is the king in England, another in Scotland.
King ⟨is⟩ [256] baptised; & buried in churchyard.

Lady Hope did not know her servant's husband in professional
costume.[257]
↑I met↓ Philip Bailey, & Henry Sutton, at Joseph Neuberg's, Nottingham.[258]

William Enfield
H.C.   Attenburrow.
Mrs Catharine Turner. Lenten Field   Nottingham

George Hyde Esq, Joseph Lupton,   Carbutt, Esq, Mayor, *Leeds*
Rev Charles Wicksteed   Potter at Bridlington
Rev. Mr Shannon, Hull [259]

[129] The English will not break up, or arrive at any strange

powerful editorials for the *Times* of London; Thomas Barnes (1785–1841), its
editor from 1817 until his death; and Thomas M. Alsager (d. 1846), another staff
member, whose name Emerson has mispelled. "Mr . . . Alsiger" is struck through
in pencil with two contiguous diagonal use marks; "Mr . . . so." is struck through
in ink with a diagonal use mark. The entry is used in "The Times," *W*, V, 266,
266–267.
    [255] Emerson's letter of December 15, 1847, to his wife mentions his visit to
"Newstead Abbey now inhabited by Colonel Wildman . . . who bought it of Lord
Byron" (*L*, III, 450).
    [256] The cancellation is in pencil.
    [257] Emerson does not record a meeting with Lady Hope, the granddaughter of
Sir Walter Scott, though in April of 1848 he saw her husband at Lady Palmerston's
(*L*, IV, 47; Notebook ED, p. [149] below).
    [258] Henry Sutton had quoted Emerson on the title page of his *Evangel of Love*
(1847). Joseph Neuberg, a German-born merchant and president of the Literary
Department of the Nottingham Mechanics' Institute, was Emerson's host when he
lectured in Nottingham in December, 1847; Emerson later introduced him to Carlyle.
To Lidian Emerson on December 16, 1847, Emerson wrote candid impressions of
both Bailey and Sutton (*L*, III, 451).
    [259] Mrs. Catherine Turner, a cousin of Harriet Martineau, was Emerson's hostess
in Nottingham (*L*, III, 440–441); Hyde, Lupton, Carbutt, and Wicksteed were
his hosts during his several visits to Leeds in January of 1848 (Journal London, pp.
[6]–[7] below); Potter, a sadler, entertained Emerson at Bridlington on January 20
and on the next day accompanied him to Flamborough Head (p. [140] below).

revolution, for they have as much energy as they ever had. They are not suffering a history but enacting it.[260]

These made up people I see everywhere, but as soon as I come upon an intellectual person, I ⟨forget⟩fancy a resemblance to the Americans. But truly intellectualists are of no country.

23 Dec. Dined at Mr Swanwick's, Chesterfield, with George Stephenson↑, inventor of the railroad car.↓ [261]
    ¼ lb. coke will carry 1 ton 1 mile.

24 [December.] Met T.H. Gill at Mr Mathews' Birmingham. Mosley writes the articles in the Times on the bishops. Alsiger wrote the city articles↑, Furo & Sampson.↓
    Jones Lloyd the banker writes on trade.[262]
No dissenter rides in his coach for three generations; ⟨it⟩he infallibly falls into the establishment[.]

———

The English phrase "you know" is particularly inapplicable in the ears of the traveller.

———

Liverpool has come to be the commercial capital[.]
Poole's Welsh scenery at Norton Lees. No more was attempted than was done.[263]

[130]

———

    The English have sunk all their capital in rail roads; and the age has sunk its capital in railroads.

———

[260] "The English . . . it.", struck through in pencil with a vertical use mark, is used in "Manners," *W*, V, 106.
    [261] Writing to Lidian Emerson on December 25, 1847, Emerson described Stephenson as "one of the most remarkable men I have seen in England" (*L*, III, 455).
    [262] Of the names not previously mentioned, "Mosley" is presumably Rev. Thomas Mozley (1806–1893); "Jones Lloyd" is Samuel Jones Loyd, later Baron Overstone (1796–1883). Furo and Sampson have not been identified.
    [263] Possibly a reference to the English painter Paul Falconer Poole (1807–1879); there is nothing in Emerson's letters to throw light on the passage.

A painter here called himself "an educated brush"[.]

———

In Leicester, the conversion of the letter H remarkable. An Act of Parliament is a Hact.

———

Lizzie & Carrie Biggs [264]

———

"The bishops show such a nasty temper". "He never uses those nasty phrases, 'Blood of Christ,' 'Atoning Covenant,' " &c. ↑"I had one or two nasty tumbles in riding."↓

———

At Preston, I saw sedan chairs carried about the streets, and at Birmingham a kind of cab drawn by a man. At Birmingham a milk--cart, or something like it, drawn by two dogs. At Leicester (Leir--castra) the river "Leir," now "Soar"; a Roman pavement; part of the "temple of Janus"; a stockinger at work at his frames; and the remains of the old castle of John of Gaunt. [265]

[131]   ↑England — it is the Times Newspaper↓
The Times newspaper suddenly changed its tone on free trade one morning, about a week before the secret was out that Peel would adopt it, and began its article "The League is a great fact." Peel gave it the information; for the support of the Times was wanted, & that paper would appreciate the importance to its interests of the early intelligence, mortifying all the other prints which fancied themselves the ministerial organs.[266]

[264] Elizabeth and Caroline, the daughters of Joseph Biggs of Knighton, near Leicester, England. On January 24, 1848, Emerson wrote to Elizabeth, the younger daughter (L, IV, 6–8).
[265] "Leicester . . . Soar' " is used in "Aristocracy," W, V, 179. Emerson was at Preston on December 1 and 15, 1847; at Birmingham on December 16 and 23; and at Leicester on December 20 and 21.
[266] "England — it . . . organs." is struck through in pencil with a vertical use mark; cf. "The Times," W, V, 264: "It adopted the League against the Corn Laws, and, when Cobden had begun to despair, it announced his triumph." In a letter to his brother William on December 26, 1847, Emerson wrote: "I read every day the Times Newspaper, which is a pretty fair transcript of England, & a chief product of modern civilization. Every anecdote relating to this journal interests me, &, first & last, I hear a great many" (L, III, 458).

"Times" ⟨n⟩has no fixed rates for advertisement, but sets its own price.

Knight paid £500 for ↑filling↓ one side one day, with advertisement of his books.

Its arrogance is calculated too. Who would care for it, if it opined so & so, or ventured to predict, &c; No, *it is so*, and *so it shall be.*

Among the advertisements is that ⟨of⟩ ↑concerning↓ Lord William Paget; a reward offered to any one who will put him in a county gaol. He having been convicted of obtaining money under fraudulent pretences, — son of Marquis of Anglesea.[267]

[132] The one rule to give to the traveller in England is, Do not sneak about diffidently but make up your mind & carry your points. The one thing the English value is pluck. The merchants have it, the bishops have it, the women have it, the newspapers have it, and the "Times" is the "pluckiest" thing in England.[268]

↑In Worcester, 27 or 30 000.↓

30 December. I went over Worcester Cathedral, part of which ⟨was⟩has stood 900 years (?). I saw the tomb of King John; | of Prince Arthur son of Henry VII, and especially, & with most delight, some old tombs of crusaders with their mailed legs crossed in marble, and the countenances handsome & refined as the English gentleman of today, & with that uncorrupt youth in the face of manhood, which I often see here.[269] From the tower I had the fine picture of the Severn for many a mile⟨,⟩ & the Malvern Hills.

But the reason why any town in England does not grow, is, that it is a Cathedral town. If Birmingham had been a cathedral town, they say it would have been no larger than Worcester[.]

---

[267] " 'Times' ⟨n⟩has . . . Anglesea." is struck through in pencil with a wavy vertical use mark; "Its arrogance . . . gaol." is struck through in ink with a vertical use mark. This material is used in "The Times," *W*, V, 269–270.

[268] This paragraph, struck through in pencil with a vertical use mark, is used in "Manners," *W*, V, 102.

[269] "I went . . . here." is used in "Race," *W*, V, 66.

[133]   English Aristocracy

Homage to the Aristocracy universal in England. Why need they stir? they know well that every body works for them. The hardest radical instantly takes off his cap & changes his tone to a lord,[270] and, as Lafayette would find every door ↑in every town↓ in America open to him, so do these men in England[.]

"He looks as if he had got all the choice parts of the turtle." Your horses are fond of walking up the hills, "Yes, & they are fond of galloping too, the rogues."

It is curious to see the overflowings of aristocratical manners & culture in the inferior classes, especially in the coachmen, who see & hear so much from their superiors. My omnibus driver from Worcester with his quotations from Shakspeare & his praise of his horses, & his condescending humour & his account of the visit of his relations to him with a little boy were deferring of Dickens or Ellery Channing.

[134] ⟨Men⟩ ↑Writers↓ drop crotchets, are ingenious & worthless; but ⟨a man⟩ the mind should be a second daylight to see things well, — Reason coming with the sun in her hand.

In England is the best working climate, one would say, in the world. It is never hot or cold. The only drawback on this advantage that I know is the darkness. It strains my eyes. ↑Night & day are too nearly of one color.↓ The coalsmoke makes some of the manufacturing towns, like Sheffield, Leeds, Bradford, very dirty. There the sheep are black (from smoke), & the trees black, & the human spittle black.[271]   ↑See p. 139↓

[135]   English idioms, phrases, &c
"I went with my sister to buy pots," i.e. crockery.   Nottingham
↑Are you poorly this morning?↓
"He is poorly." the common phrase for sickness.

---

[270] "Homage . . . lord," is used in "Aristocracy," W, V, 183–184.
[271] "In England . . . black.", struck through in ink with a vertical use mark, is used in "Land," W, V, 38–39.

"Aye" for Yes
"A very nice town is Nottingham"
"You know you know you know you know"
lēver for lĕver
"Have you not hurt your shinbone?, nor your toes?"
They call a leg of man or woman, a leg.
I am almost starved (with cold)
In Yorkshire (& in Derbyshire)   foot is fut   and public is pūblic

                                 Sūgar is sugar   up   is ūp

                                 fūlly is fully

                                 būtcher   butcher

In Beverley, I noticed a sign "James Grove, Fire Extinguisher" which means a sweep.[272] Elsewhere, I observe "the Whitster's Arms."

"There is a nasty twist about the head" (of Wyatt's horse of D. of Wellington) [273]
"By train" i.e. by railway
"benighted."
"Oh!" for *indeed*!
"just so," "pre[c]isely so," "exactly so."
I dĕrsāy —   I dare say
I beg your pardon,   *for* I did not hear you.

[136] [January 28, 1848.] English leave & French leave certainly differ inasmuch as the retiring Englishman shakes hands with all the company however large. And last night at the Free Trade Banquet, in the Manchester Free Trade Hall,[274] an old gentleman rose to go, & began to bid so many affectionate goodnights, that I feared he was to go the round of these thousands with his grip; but, at last, a bright thought occurred to him, he cried "Goodnight All," & let go hands.

[272] Emerson lectured in Beverley on January 19, 1848.
[273] An equestrian statue at Aldershot by Matthew Cotes Wyatt.
[274] Emerson "heard Cobden, Bright, Peyronnet Thompson, Gibson (V. President of the Board of Trade) & other eminent men of that party," according to a letter to his brother William also written on January 28 (*L*, IV, 12).

York Minster
Westminster Abbey
House of Commons
British Museum
Times Newspaper
Punch
Oxford Quadrangles
Kew Gardens, and ⟨R⟩Hampton Court, ↑& Richmond↓
London Clubhouses

[137] I trace then the peculiarities of English manners to their
working climate; their dense population; the presence of an aristocracy or model class ⟨of⟩for manners & speech; their diet generous &
orderly taken; and their force of constitution. ⟨They have real independence in⟩ Their ⁿ manners betray real independence, and they
are studiously inoffensive. They are castles compared with our men;
the porter, the drayman, above all the coachman & guard, — what
substantial, respectable old grandfatherly figures they are, & with
the manners & speech appertaining. An American feels like some
invalid in their company.[275]

At York. I saw the skull of a Roman centurion[.]
I saw the tree planted by Geo Fox; I saw the prison, the pews in
which the prisoners are locked up; the scales with which they can
weigh their own food[.]
casts of felons' ⟨fel⟩faces & skulls
a boy sentenced seven years for stealing boots [276]

[138] In ↑the↓ minster I heard "God Save the King," of Handel,
played by Dr Camidge on the grand organ. It was very great. I
thought I had never heard anything so sublime. The music was
made for the minster, & the minster for the music.
In the choir was service of evening prayer read & chanted. It was
strange to hear the whole history of the betrothal of Rebekah &

---

[275] "They are castles . . . company." is used in "Race," W, V, 65.
[276] Emerson passed through York on January 8, 1848; on January 13 he returned in time for sightseeing before his lecture of that evening.

Isaac in the morning of the world read with all this circumstantiality in York minster, 13 Jan. 1848, to the decorous English audience just fresh from the Times Newspaper & their wine, and they listening with all the devotion of national pride. That was binding old & new to some purpose. The reverence for the Scriptures is a powerful element of civilization, for thus has the history of the world been preserved, & is preserved. Every day a chapter of Genesis and a leader in the Times.[277]

[139] England a working climate, yes, and the profusion of working materials, — water, stone, coal, & iron, every thing but wood.[278]

↑p 134↓

The architects of York minster are not known; yet what brains were those! It is beautiful beyond belief.
It is lighted with gas; but cold as a vault.

In Bridlington, I was received one evening at the house of Mr Potter, sadler, with a very cordial hospitality. And the next day he accompanied me to Flamborough Head, to show me the cave, the "Danes' Dyke," the castle, the Light House, &c.[279] All the objects interested me, but my conductor more. He had waited ⟨me⟩on me in the morning at my hotel with his ⟨wa⟩apron tucked up under his coat, & very likely it was on still, under his surtout; but he told so well the story of his life, and that he saves 200 pounds every year, [140] and means by & by to devote himself principally to the care of the Mechanics' Institute & of the Temperance Society, of both of which he is the ardent friend;
He is sent however by these institutions to wait on Yarborough Graeme, Esq., on Sir   Prickett, & other gentlemen of the county families, & is always kindly received by these gentlemen.

----

[277] "In the minster . . . Times.", struck through in ink with a diagonal use mark, is used in "Religion," W, V, 218–219.
[278] "England . . . wood.", struck though in pencil with a vertical use mark, is used in "Land," W, V, 38–39.
[279] On January 20 and 21, 1848.

I see here continually the counterparts of faces, complexions, & manners ↑well↓ known to me at home, & have ⟨often⟩ ↑sometimes↓ [280] a sure key to the new man I talk with, through my experience of his antipode in America.

↑See *LM* 14,↓ [281]

[141] I saw a young man yesterday whose body is in greatest part covered over with a hard scale like that of the armadillo. He was naked, or nearly so, and I had the nearest view of him, though I declined touching him. There are a great many talents in a drop of blood, and a little suppression or retardation would ⟨bring out⟩ unchain & let out what horns & fangs, what manes & hoofs, what fins & flippers, what feathers & coats of mail which are now subdued and refined into ⟨white⟩ ↑smooth↓ & shapely limbs, into soft white skin, into the simple erect royal form of man.

My ⟨n⟩Nights repeat my day, & I dream of gas light, heaps of faces, & darkness.

[142] It was at Bridlington (pronounced Burlington) that one of the company asked me, if there were *many* rattlesnakes in the city of New York? and another whether the Americans liked to call their country *New England*?

[143] "How many hours the sun mt. be above the horizon I cannot say, he is so rarely to be seen in winter, & never but at midday."
"Ital. Relation" [282]
p 12

"the kingdom of Scotland is very rainy."　　　　　Ib[id]. [p. 14]

"The Eng. are great lovers of themselves & of everything belonging to them: they think that there are no other men than themselves, & no other world but England: & whenever they see a handsome foreigner, they say that he looks like an Englishman, & it is a great pity he shd not

[280] "often" is circled in pencil, evidently for possible cancellation; "sometimes" is inserted in pencil without the lining out of "often".
[281] See also Notebook England and Paris, p. [54] below.
[282] *A Relation, or Rather a True Account, of the Island of England . . . about the Year 1500.* Translated from the Italian by Charlotte Augusta Sneyd (London, 1847).

be an Englishman: & when ⟨ever⟩ ⟨on⟩they partake of ⟨|| ... ||⟩any delicacy with a foreigner, they ask him whether such a thing is made in ⟨their⟩ ↑this↓ [283] country. They take great pleasure in having a quantity of excellent victuals, & also in remaining a long time at table, [being very sparing of wine when they drink it at their own expense.]" [*Ibid.*,] p 21 * [284]

"And they think that no greater honour can be conferred or received than to invite others to eat with them or to be invited themselves, & they wd sooner give five or six ducats to provide an emtertainment for a person than a groat to assist him in any distress." [285] [*Ibid.*,] p[p. 21–]22

[144] "They all from time unmemorial wear very fine clothes, and are extremely polite in their language, wh. although it is as well as the Flemish derived from the German, has lost its natural harshness, & is pleasing enough as they pronounce it." &c. [*Ibid.*,] p 22

"They have a very high reputation in arms, and from the great fear the French entertain of them, one must believe it to be justly acquired. But I have it on the best information, that when the war is raging most furiously, they will seek for good eating, & all their other comforts, without thinking of what harm might befal them." [286] [*Ibid.*,] p 23
    "They have an antipathy to foreigners, & imagine that they never come into their island but to [145] make themselves masters of it, & to usurp their goods: neither have they any sincere & solid friendships among themselves — I have ⟨no⟩ never noticed any one, either at court or among the lower orders, to be in love; — very [287] jealous, — though any thing may be compensated in the end by the power of money."
                          [*Ibid.*,] p[p. 23–]24

* I remember the sensation at Mr Mayor ↑Elgie's↓ table, at W[orces-ter]. when our host announced that the port we were now to draw was from the D↑uke↓ of Buckingham's cellar.

    [283] "their" is enclosed in penciled parentheses for possible cancellation, then canceled in pencil; "his" is inserted in pencil.
    [284] Emerson's footnote is added on the facing page, [142]. " 'The Eng. . . . expense.]' " is struck through in ink with a diagonal use mark; " 'The Eng. . . . country.", struck through in ink with a second diagonal use mark, is used in "Cockayne," W, V, 145.
    [285] " 'And . . . distress.' ", struck through in ink with a wavy vertical use mark and in pencil with another vertical use mark, is used in "Manners," W, V, 113.
    [286] "But I . . . them.' ", struck through in ink with three vertical use marks, is used in "Truth," W, V, 124.
    [287] Between "love;" and " — very" is an ink line, perhaps intended to close the space Emerson had left between successive lines of his quotation.

the riches of England are greater than those of any other country in Europe.

[*Ibid.*, p. 28]

From
"A Relation or rather a true account of the island of England. &c about the year 1500." Translated from the Italian, by ⟨Augusta⟩ Charlotte Augusta Sneyd

printed for the Camden Society

Lond. 1847

[146]–[147] [blank]
[148] [Index material omitted] [288]
[inside back cover] [Index material omitted]

[288] There are (1) erased penciled notes for Emerson's alphabetical index, in ink, on the facing page (inside back cover) and (2) one entry in ink for insertion in the alphabetical listing on the facing page.

Sea-Notes

Oct. 1847

Journal Sea-Notes, dated "Oct. 1847", includes nine dated entries — October 14, 16, 17, 18, 19, 20 (two), 21, and 22 — covering incidents of Emerson's second voyage to England, which began at Boston on October 5 and ended at Liverpool on October 22; there are other entries concerning the voyage in Journal GH, which covers a longer time-span. Sea-Notes may be the "rough & blotted scrap journal" Emerson mentioned in his letter to Lidian Emerson begun at sea on October 21, 1847 (*L*, III, 421).

Journal Sea-Notes is written in ink on four unbound sheets of unruled blue paper, measuring 20.3 x 25.7 cm, folded once to make a booklet of unnumbered pages; a pin through the center fold holds the leaves together. The entire booklet has been folded lengthwise, perhaps for carrying in a pocket. Pages 3–4 and 5–6 have been partly torn out, leaving only a portion of the inscription visible — chiefly on pages 3–4.

[front cover]   Sea-Notes.

Oct. 1847

Letters by Geo H. Pollock   Care of Brown, Shipley, & Co.
Liverpool [1]

[front cover verso] In the distribution of lots the merchant seems to me often enviable. His social position is so good. He mixes with people on a ground so free from all hypocrisy. He has no part to play, but stands on the strength of things. ⟨His⟩ He acquires facility,

[1] "Letters by . . . Liverpool" is written in pencil beneath "Oct. 1847". Pollock, a young Boston merchant who sailed to Liverpool with Emerson, carried one or more letters for Emerson when he returned to Boston on November 4 (*L*, III, 427).

knowledge of things, knowledge of modes, knowledge of men; knows that which all men gladly hear[.] [2]

[1] As we see the human body or one of its limbs undraped, so here ⟨the⟩Nature shows us a limb of our planet in undress, & we see the nakedness of the sea-line. It is a sublime curve, certainly, yet begets in the spectator an uncomfortable feeling. To nature as to man, he says, Still be drest! still hide a poverty even so grand under the ornamented details of a broken ⟨surface of⟩ landscape. [3]

You shall put no more dependance on a dead-reckoning than on a dream [when there are clouds & currents.]

[2] It is greatly to the credit of the German nation that a book of the range & pretension to ⟨learning⟩ science, sense, & information of the Encyclopaedia should be called Conversation's Lexicon. [4] There is a wide difference between the ⟨sterile⟩ taciturnity of savages, taciturn because thoughtless, or the gossip of shops or the yarns of the forecastle, and the magazine of classified & sifted experience & induction which purports to be ↑only↓ the reported ⟨conversation⟩tabletalk of well informed circles of European men. [5]

[3] [6] The ship is ranked 750 ‖msm‖
now perhaps, all told, ‖msm‖
mast from the upper ‖msm‖
or button at its top ‖msm‖
Its bowsprit & gi‖msm‖
proudest place ‖msm‖

[2] "In the . . . good." and "He mixes . . . hear" are struck through in ink with discontinuous vertical use marks. Cf. Journal LM, p. [16] below.

[3] "Still be drest!" echoes the song in Ben Jonson, *Epicœne*, I, i: "Still to be neat, still to be dress'd. . . ." "As we . . . landscape.", struck through in ink with a vertical use mark, is transcribed in Journal LM, p. [8] below.

[4] See Journal AB, p. [111] above.

[5] This paragraph is struck through in pencil with a vertical use mark.

[6] Part of the leaf bearing pp. [3] and [4] has been torn out. On this page, a curved use mark in ink extends through "The ship . . . proudest place" to the torn edge of the leaf; cf. "Voyage to England," *W*, V, 28.

seems to be ||msm||
smelling ||msm||
daring be||msm||
the stem. — ||msm||
from stem ||msm||
—— ||msm||
In the E||msm||
certain ||msm||
them g||msm||
motio||msm||
Wheth||msm||
done||msm||
dee||msm||
so tha||msm||
are ke||msm||
They see ||msm||
a youn||msm||
very a||msm||
unavail||msm||

[4]⁷ ||msm||E with "his hurrying & im
                       ||msm||what would R B say & [to?]
                       ||msm||who keeps his kites on
                       ||msm|| studding sails alow
                       ||msm||straight steering
                       ||msm||ses a rod of
                       ||msm||ant watchful.
                       ||msm|| watch on watch
                       ||msm||ee the ship
                       ||msm|| took off

                            ||msm||sail in
                            ||msm||cifer matches

⁷ With the fragments of writing on this page, cf. (1) "Voyage to England,"
W, V, 27, and (2) Journal LM, p. [72] below: "The Americans would sail in a
steamboat built of lucifer matches, if it would go faster."

‖msm‖ by young
‖msm‖ Scott
‖msm‖ in Flod-

[5]–[6] [8] [7] men's necessities. The sick are selfish & those not called sick are yet too puny to make any inquiries about the steerage, or to help amuse the children; they must husband their resources; yet are not vicious, only poor.

————

Sparrows & a pigeon-woodpecker alighted on the ship & kept about it whilst we loitered at 40 or 50 miles from land. A hawk came hunting the sparrows. A whale passed us deliberately showing all his length. Schools of mackerel make the water rough; blackfish roll over & over, — their long fins horn-like revolving like the spokes of a wheel, ⟨m⟩these peculiar institutions of the deep. Mully meanwhile lows & talks of land in her ⟨‖ . . . ‖⟩stall amidships. The children are frolicking in the cabin & their voices every morning like birds about your windows.[9] 'Tis strange too what ⟨sea-gods⟩ ↑men↓ we bring out here among the sea-gods; namely Dickens, Dumas, Lever, Marryatt[.] [10]

Neither is the sea so black as he is painted but, when it runs highest, breaks behind us into the most delicious & I may say joyful green that ⟨can⟩ fancy can like, and would say the terrible plain around you covers heaven also[.] [11]

————

There is at least this pleasure in hurrying over these abysses that whatever dangers we are [8] running into, we are ⟨at⟩certainly run-

[8] The leaf bearing pp. [5] and [6] has been torn out, leaving a stub of from .2 to 1.4 cm in width. Only isolated fragments of single letters, inscribed in ink, are visible on both recto and verso.

[9] "Sparrows & . . . windows." is struck through in ink with a wavy vertical use mark. There is similar phrasing in Emerson's letter of October 21, 1847, to Lidian Emerson (L, III, 420).

[10] In "Voyage to England," W, V, 31, Emerson wrote: "We found on board the usual cabin library; Basil Hall, Dumas, Dickens, Bulwer, Balzac and Sand were our sea-gods." His letter of October 21, 1847, employs phrasing similar to that of the present passage (L, III, 421).

[11] "Neither . . . also" is struck through in ink with a curved diagonal use mark.

ning out of the risks of hundreds of miles every day which have their own ⟨squalls &⟩ⁿ chances of ↑squall,↓ collision, sea-stroke, piracy; cold, thunder, & the rest.[12]

————

In 1844, Dec. 12 the Captain tells me he was shipwrecked in the Dorchester, the sea having swept his masts & drowned the mate & the carpenter. The Rochester, Capt. Britton, took him off the wreck with 65 souls after drifting ⟨a⟩ ↑2 or 3↓ day↑s↓ ⟨or two⟩[.]
The little runaway ↑Walters who came out in Ocean Monarch↓ on board has got rigged out in a Guernsey frock & a belt with a sailor's knife, &, when asked, how he likes the sea, "O first rate," he replies. The mate says, ask all the sailors how they came to sea? and you will find they are all runaway boys. Jack has the hardest life, with tremendous risks, incessant abuse, and the worst pay. It is little better with the mate & not as much better as you might expect, with the Captain. Say $100. a month is reckoned high pay[.][13]

[9] ⟨l⟩Lettuce, apple, or melon, in season — so long it is good. So is it with every work of man[:] epic poem, hymn, architecture, ship, naval skill, commerce, law, & whatever else. When their hour is past do not try to move the hand back on the dial & do them again but try that undone something which is in season now, celery, ice, or cucumbers. As long as the faith is settled, the architecture was, & abbeys were built. Now, vacillating faith, & motley architecture.[14]

[10] ↑14 Oct. Thursday, 47.48 N. Lat.
46.30 W Long.↓
↑For↓ greatⁿ power, great body also. You must draw on the extremes. Before concentration, there must be sleep.

---

[12] "There is . . . rest.", struck through in ink on pp. [7] and [8] with single vertical use marks, is used in "Voyage to England," *W*, V, 27.

[13] "The little . . . pay", struck through in ink with a vertical use mark, is used in "Voyage to England," *W*, V, 30–31. A version of the remark about sailors as runaway boys occurs in Journal GH, p. [105] above; the story of Walters is told also in Emerson's letter of October 21, 1847, to Lidian Emerson (*L*, III, 421).

[14] "⟨l⟩Lettuce . . . architecture." is rewritten in ink over substantially the same matter in pencil. The passage as first drafted in pencil began "Peas, and apple, or a melon . . . "; in the third sentence "celery" was "celery or lettuce".

Who can doubt the fate of races, who sees the position of Eng[lish]., French, & Germans, planting themselves thus on S. America, & monopolizing the commerce of the country. But America is the commercial nation, with what resources, & powers, & space, & taste, & head, & all but heart! [15]

16 Oct. at noon, the ship has made 1617 miles. From 9 Oct. at noon, to 16 Oct. at noon, one week, the ship has made 1467 miles.[16] And now at night she seems to hear the steamer behind her which left port today at 2, and she is flying before this grey southwind at eleven & a half knots every hour. The sea shines tonight not only in its wake but far around wherever a wave breaks with phosphoric light. I found I could see the hour 9¾ on my watch by this light. Near [11] the equator the mate tells me he can read print by it. He describes the phosphoric animalcules when taken up there, in a pail, to be shaped like a Carolina potato.[17]

17 Oct. Sunday; 1848 miles from Boston
18 [October.] Monday noon. Reckoned distance from Boston ⟨‖ ... ‖⟩-2024 miles[.] [18]
19 Oct. Tuesday. The Providence of the Master extends thro' all the ship, & he has one remedy for all ails. If a child cries, the Captain says, "Steward, give that child something to eat." If the cow lows, "Steward, give that cow something to eat & stop that noise." The nine children in the cabin who make our "interesting company," as the owners phrased it, come every day to our table after dinner to the Captain for plums. I reckon these noisy little sailors so full of play & without a suspicion of danger, our insurers. The steerage too is "interesting" as well [as] the cabin[.] [19]

---

[15] "Who . . . heart!" is struck through in ink with a vertical use mark.
   [16] The paragraph to this point is transcribed from an entry in pencil at the top of p. [12] that had been written over by "The ship . . . miles."
   [17] "And now . . . potato." is struck through in ink on pp. [10] and [11] with vertical use marks; "From 9 . . . potato." is used in "Voyage to England," *W, V,* 28.
   [18] The figure "2024" is taken from a penciled notation at the top of p. [12] that has been written over by "245 miles:".
   [19] "The nine . . . cabin" is struck through in ink with a vertical use mark.

↑Ships' names. John Gilpin, Fortune, Seahorse, Sandfly↓

[12] The ship has made at noon today, 245 miles: making the entire distance from Boston, 2269 miles.[20]

———

20 October, Wednesday. As we near the land, its genius is felt. This is ⟨surely⟩inevitably the English side; as that we left, the American. In every man's thought arises now a new system, English sentiments, English loves & fears, English history, & social modes[.]

I cannot look on a little voyaging without owing a debt to it. Yes, George, you had better go to Europe. In a ship's cabin you shall intimately see representatives of several classes of society in a manner not to be found with equal convenience at home. A species of instructive travellers' conversation goes on which makes the man of the world, and every now & then a memorable fact is turned up which you have long had a vacant niche for, & now seize with the joy of a collector.[21]

[inside back cover] 20 October. Our distance at noon from Boston is 2470 miles, having made 201 miles since yesterday noon. We are now 104 miles from Cape Clear, which we may come up with, with a good wind by midnight.

21 October. Thursday. Last night at half past one o'clock I heard the watch cry out, "Light ahead!" and the Captain reply, "Where away?" "Right ahead, sir." And, this morning, when I opened the bullseye of my stateroom, I saw the coast of Cork, at the distance of a few miles.

---

[20] "245 miles:" is written over "245" in pencil and, above it, "2024" — a notation used in the entry for October 18 on p. [11]. "2269" is taken from a penciled notation circled in the right margin. Also underlying this sentence is the original draft, in pencil, of what are now the opening sentences of the entry for October 16 on p. [10].

[21] "20 October, Wednesday . . . of a collector" is struck through in ink with a vertical use mark. "As we . . . modes" is used in "Voyage to England," W, V, 33; "I cannot . . . collector" is used in "Voyage to England," W, V, 31-32.

At noon 1⟨34⟩76 miles from yesterday; 234 now remain to reach Liverpool. Instead of bubbles to measure our progress by, we have at last Kinsale, Cork, Ardmore, & Waterford[.]

[back cover] Ireland looks like a country as well-cultivated & plentiful as Brookline & Brighton. I see towers, towns, and grain-fields, & fishermen, but no curse.

22 October. This morning finds us off Holyhead, and the mountainous coast of Wales ⟨in full view⟩. At 10 o'clock, we take in a pilot under the ⟨mountains⟩ ↑heights↓ of Pemmanmaur, but the weather is too thick to show us Snowdon.[22] The fortune of the ship has continued unbroken to this last hour. Captain C. promised to reach Tuskar Light by 9' o'clock, and at 9, we were abreast of it. It is 90 miles from Tuskar to Holyhead, and this morning at 7 we were at Holyhead. ⟨We were long⟩The pilot was long in coming down to us or we should have saved one tide and reached Liverpool this P.M. by 4 in what is called 15 days[.]

[22] "At noon [inside back cover] . . . Snowdon." is used in Emerson's letter of October 21, 1847, to Lidian Emerson (L, III, 421–422). "At noon . . . curse.", struck through in ink on the inside back cover and back cover with single vertical use marks, is used in "Voyage to England," W, V, 33.

London

1847–1848

Journal London is a regular journal kept during Emerson's second visit to England and France. Although he may have bought and titled the copybook containing it late in 1847, as dates on the front cover and front cover verso suggest, most of the entries were evidently made in 1848 after he had filled Journal GH. Entries on pages [3]–[5] refer to his visits to Halifax, Leeds, and Bradford, where he was lecturing in January of 1848; the first dated entries, on pages [26] and [34], are for "February '48" and "15 Feb." respectively. The latest dated entry, on page [128], is for May 3, but on page [176] is a reference to shipboard conversation during his return voyage to America, July 15–27, 1848. Other material from Emerson's subsequent reading was added to the original journal entries as late as 1852: for example, quotations on pages [49], [101], and [171] from Bristed's *Five Years in an English University*, which he borrowed from the Boston Athenaeum in July and August of that year. A reference on page [132] to events of May 22, 1848, also appears to be a retrospective addition.

Journal London is written in a copybook bound in boards; both the cover, which measures 11.5 x 18.9 cm, and the spine are orange. On the front cover, inscribed in ink, is "LONDON / 1847-8." The pages, faintly ruled in light blue, measure 11.5 x 18.9 cm. Including flyleaves (i–ii, 209–210), there are 212 pages, all numbered in ink with the exception of i–ii, 4, 6, 8, 10, 20, 22, 24, 35, 39, 47, 64, 67, 71, 81, 83, 85, 87, 89, 91, 93, 105, 117, 119, 127, 134, 156, 167–168, 171–173, 177, 180–181, 185, 191, 193, 195, 199–201, 205, 208–210, all unnumbered, and 9, 30–31, 34, 36, 38, 40, 42, 44, 46, 48–50, 66, 68–70, 74, 82, 84, 86, 88, 90, 92, 94, 96, 99, 111, 120–124, 128, 130–131, 135–139, 179, which are numbered in pencil, with corrections in numbering on pages 106–108. There are 13 blank pages: 20, 64, 66, 168, 181, 185, 190, 192–195, 197, and 199; pages 200–201 are also blank except for mounted clippings. There are other clippings mounted on the front cover verso and on pages 14, 60, 136, 152, 164, 200, and 201. A note by Edward Emerson is fastened to page 38. Laid in are (1) a page from a London bookseller's catalogue, between pages 172 and 173; (2) an irregularly shaped penciled slip, approximately 1.5 x 10.5 cm, between pages 196 and 197; (3) an article on "British Royalty" by Donald G. Mitchell, also between pages 196 and 197; and (4) three leaves of blue laid paper, between page 210 and the inside back cover, folded to make 12 pages, each 11.3 x 17.5 cm; on pages 1–10 of these leaves, inscribed in ink by an unidentified hand, is an index to Journal London.

[front cover]

─────────

LONDON

─────────

1847–8.

[front cover verso] [1]   *R. W. Emerson.*

1847–1848

Toto divisos orbe Britannos.[2]

────

Ich dien [3]

────

[Index material omitted]
Brut says, "In short, God has not made since Adam was, the man more perfect than Arthur, *praeteritis melior, majorque futuris.*" [4]

"Quid vult, valde vult." [5]

[i] There are 500 British Islands, in the home seas.

────

London

"Spatium est urbis et orbis idem." [6]

──────────────────────────

"L'angleterre est un vaisseau. Notre île en a la forme; la proue tournée au nord, elle est comme à l'ancre au milieu des mers, surveillant le con-

---

[1] On this page "1/6" — evidently the price of the copybook — is in pencil in the upper left corner. The notation is probably that of an English stationer.

[2] Virgil, *Eclogues*, I, 66, quoted in full in Notebook ED, front cover verso below: "Et penitus toto diviso orbe Brittanos" ("And the Britons wholly sundered from all the world"). Cf. "Land," *W*, V, 41.

[3] The motto of the Prince of Wales.

[4] "Better than past men, and greater than men to come" (Ed.). For "Brut . . . *futuris.*'", see Sharon Turner, *The History of the Anglo-Saxons*, 3 vols. (London, 1823), I, 271, notes 11 and 23, quoting, respectively, a Welsh manuscript and the *Antiocheis* of Joseph of Exeter.

[5] Probably an allusion to Cicero, *Letters to Atticus*, XIV, i, 2: "quicquid volt, valde volt" — "whatever he wants, he wants it badly." See "Result," *W*, V, 305: "*Quid vult valde vult.* What they do they do with a will."

[6] See Journal AB, p. [6] above.

tinent. Sans [ii] cesse, elle tire de ses flancs d'autres vaisseaux faits à son image, et qui vont ↑la↓ representer sur toutes les côtes du monde. Mais c'est à bord du grand navire qu'est notre ouvrage à tous. Le ro⟨y⟩i, les lords, les communes sont au pavillion, au gouvernail, et à la boussole; nous [1] autres nous devons tous avoir la main aux cordages, monter aux mâts, tendre les voiles, et charger les canons. Nous sommes tous de l'équipage, et nul n'est inutile dans la manoeuvre de notre glorieux navire.

Mais, mon garcon, cria le gros Beckford, que diable peut faire le [2] poète dans la manoeuvre?
Il dit, Le poète cherche aux étoiles quelle route nous montre le doig⟨ht⟩t du Seigneur."   *A. De Vigny.*[7]

These seakings may take to their floating castles, once again, & swear anew never to sleep under a smoky roof, nor to own a yard of land.[8]

[3] In Halifax, Mr Crossley employs in his carpet mills 1500 operatives.[9] Beautiful tapestry, carpets at 7/6 per yard: saw the pattern sent to the Queen. Vista made by the looms resembled a church aisle. Mr Acroyd's stuff mills employ 5 or 6 000 operatives. In one hall I saw 800 looms. In many, they were making ponchos. Here was a school spaciously built & well furnished for the children. In England, the manufacturers are not joint stock companies but individuals.

The Piece-Hall in H. was built in better times [4] & held 20 000 children & teachers on a festival a few years ago, in its quadrangle.[10]

Remains of the old gibbet. By the local law, theft to the amount of 13½ d. was death by the gibbet, till the law was abrogated 160 years since. As we were returning down "Gibbet Lane," a respectable old

[7] Alfred de Vigny, *Stello* (1831), Ch. 17; see 3rd ed. (Paris, 1882), pp. 73–74.

[8] This paragraph, struck through with two vertical use marks, one in ink and one in pencil, is transcribed in Notebook ED, p. [53] below, and used in "Character," *W*, V, 141.

[9] Emerson was at Halifax, England, on January 5, 1848, as the guest of James Stansfeld, returning on February 7.

[10] The Manufacturers Piece-Hall in Halifax was first opened for the sale of goods on January 2, 1779.

lady accosted Mr Stansfeld to pray him to get the name altered, as she owns a house here, which she cannot ⟨let⟩rent, as tenants do not wish to live in Gibbet Lane.

[5] The parish church 600 years old.
Near Leeds & Bradford, I observed the sheep were black, & fancied they were black sheep; no, they were begrimed by the smoke. So all the trees are begrimed. The human expectoration is black here.[11] The hopelessness of keeping clothes white, leads to a rather dowdy style of dress, I was told, among the ladies; and yet they sometimes indemnify themselves; & Leeds in the ballroom, I was assured, ⟨was⟩is a very different creature from Leeds in Briggate.

Mr Marshall's mill covers two acres of ground. The [6] former owner James Marshall presided in this immense hall at a dinner given to O'Connell; and the Chartists having threatened an attack, Mr M. had a waterpipe under his chair which was supplied by a steam engine, & which he was ready to direct on the mob, if they had ventured to disturb him.[12]

I spent one night here [Leeds] with Rev. Mr Wicksteed; one night with Mr Carbutt the Mayor; of whom Mrs Carbutt told me some excellent anecdotes.
[7] One night with George Hyde, Esq. & one with Joseph Lupton, Esq.[13]

Every where anecdotes of the "London Times," which, it seems, is perfecting its printing machinery, & will drive the "Morning Chronicle" & the "Daily News," out of circulation. Its own circulation estimated at 30 000. Its readers are disappointed if there is not a great public event in each day's paper; & so wide & high is its correspondence, that it can almost satisfy that demand. Mr Mosely named as the writer of these papers on the Bishops; Mr Bailey, as

---

[11] Cf. Journal GH, p. [134] above.
[12] The flax mill, at Leeds, was owned by James Garth Marshall (1802–1873), Member of Parliament. A version of the anecdote concerning its former owner is used in "Resources," W, VIII, 148.
[13] This entry may have been made on or after January 14, 1848; Emerson lectured in Leeds on January 3, 6, 10, and 14.

a young Cambridge man who wrote & offered a paper to the Morning Chronicle, & was refused, [8] sent it to the "Times" & received ten guineas, & request for more communications; & is a regular contributor. Mr Jones Lloyd writes often on financial matters. Old Walter wrote on Poor Laws[.] [14]

"The grand feature which recommends *the Times* is its independence. X X X Let us not know, when we take it up, what our paper is going to say. And this can be asserted only of the Times."
London Critic [15]

[9] "The English (in the street,) ↑always↓ walk straight before them like mad dogs," says the French Editor of *"La Patrie"*.

"i⟨t⟩ls s'amusaient tristement selon la coutume de leur pays." *Froissart*

Englishman has hard eyes. He is great by the back of the head. [16]

[10] In the new Parl[iament]. House, great poverty of ornament, the ball & crown repeated tediously all over the grand gate, near the Abbey, & *Vivat Regina*, written incessantly all over the casements of the windows in H[ouse] of Lords. But Barry built the Reform Club House. [17] The Parliament Houses, up to March 1848,

[14] On "Mosely" (Mozley?) and "Lloyd" (Loyd), see Journal GH, pp. [128] and [129] above. "Bailey", who has not been otherwise identified, may be the "Mr Bailey" who entertained Emerson in London on April 27, 1848 (Pocket Diary 3, p. [70] below; cf. p. [208] below). "Old Walter" is John Walter (1776–1847), the former editor. "Every where . . . Laws", struck through in ink and in pencil with vertical use marks on pp. [7] and [8], is used in "The Times," *W*, V, 264, 266.
    [15] " 'The grand . . . *Critic*", struck through in pencil with a vertical use mark, is used in "The Times," *W*, V, 261.
    [16] Theodore-Casimir Delamarre edited *La Patrie* from 1844 until his death in 1867. With " 'i⟨t⟩ls . . . pays.' ", cf. William Hazlitt, "Merry England," in *Sketches and Essays* (London, 1839), p. 47: " 'They (the English), says Froissart, 'amused themselves sadly after the fashion of their country' — *ils se rejouissoient tristement selon la coutume de leur pays.*" All three entries on p. [9], struck through in pencil with a vertical use mark, are transcribed in Notebook ED, p. [5] below; " 'The English . . . *Froissart*", also struck through in ink with a vertical use mark, is used in "Character," *W*, V, 128.
    [17] Sir Charles Barry (1795–1860), who designed and built the Houses of Parliament, 1840–1860, had in 1837 built the Reform Club House, noted for its imposing architecture.

have cost £945000 in thirteen years. Houses of Parilement↓ a magnificent document of Eng. power & of their intention to make it last.
The Irish harp & shamrock are carved with the rose & thistle over
all the house. The houses cover eight acres, & are built of Bolsover
stone. Fault, that there is no single view commanding great lines,
only, when it is finished, the speaker of the H. of Commons will be
able with a telescope to see the Lord Chancellor ↑in the Lords!↓ But
mankind can so rarely build a house covering 8 acres, that 'tis pity
to deprive them of the ⟨pleasure⟩joy of seeing a mass & grand &
lofty lines[.] [18]

[11] In H. of Commons, when a man makes his first speech, there
is a cry of "New member, New member," & he is sure of attention.
Afterwards, he must get it if he can. In a body of 648 members every
man is sure to have some who understand his views on whatever
topic. Facts they will hear, and any measure proposed they will entertain, but no speculation, & no oratory. A sneer is the habitual expression of that body. Therefore Cobbett's maiden speech, "I have
heard a great deal of nonsense, since⟨,⟩ I have been sitting here," was
quite in their vein, & secured [12] their ear.
If a member rise a second time in the same debate, they cry, "Spoke."
If they do not like his speech, they cry "Divide." [19]

Stand at the door of the House of Commons, & see the members go
in & out, & you will say these men are all men of humanity, of good
sense, [20]

[13] ↑Universities   *RS* 244

Power of the Religious sentiment   *RS* 270↓ [21]

---

[18] This entry, in pencil, is struck through in pencil with a vertical use mark.
Cf. p. [110] below.
[19] This entry is struck through in pencil with curved vertical use marks on pp.
[11] and [12]. "A sneer . . . body." is used in "Aristocracy," *W*, V, 62.
[20] This entry, evidently uncompleted, is struck through in pencil with a curved
vertical use mark.
[21] "Universities" is struck through in pencil with a curved vertical use mark.
Journal RS will be published in a later volume.

[14] An English lady, on the Rhine, hearing something said to ⟨the⟩her party, respecting foreigners, exclaimed, "No, we are not foreigners; 'tis you that are foreigners; we are English." [22]

[15] To use the shopkeepers' word, England has "a good *stand*." It is just in the middle of the world, so that every manufacturer knows that he can sell all he can possibly produce.[23]

The commercial relations of the world are so intimately drawn to London, that it seems as if every dollar in the world contributed to strengthen the English government.[24]

[16] Mr F↑oster↓. said, he had repeatedly ridden all the way from London to Leeds in the first class carriages ⟨&⟩with the same persons, & no word exchanged. The clubhouses were established to cultivate social habits, & it is rare that more than two eat together, & oftenest you eat alone.[25]

Milnes was called by Sidney Smith "the cool of the evening"; and some stories are told of his easy effrontery. Carlyle at the first meeting of the London Library proposed to sacrifice Milnes as a sort of acceptable Iphigenia. Milnes has evidently the largest range of affinity & acquaintance of any man in society, as he is on the best terms with all men from [17] ⟨The English are the best dressed people in the world⟩ dukes & archbishops down to Chartists.[26] When

[22] The entry on this page, struck through in ink with five curved vertical use marks and in pencil with one vertical use mark, is used in "Cockayne," *W*, V, 149. Pasted below the entry is a cartoon clipped from an unidentified newspaper or periodical. Emerson has labeled its three figures as "D[uke]. of Wellington", "L[or]d. Brougham", and "Lord John Russell".

[23] This paragraph, struck through in ink and in pencil with two curved vertical use marks, is used in "Land," *W*, V, 40, 41.

[24] See *JMN*, VIII, 277. This paragraph, struck through in ink with a wavy vertical use mark and in pencil with a vertical use mark, is transcribed in Notebook ED, p. [10] below, and used in "Wealth," *W*, V, 92.

[25] The insertion "oster" is in pencil. These two sentences, struck through in both pencil and ink with single vertical use marks, are transcribed in Notebook ED, p. [6] below, where the comment is attributed to "W. E. Forster of Rawdon", and used in "Character," *W*, V, 129, as the remark of "a Yorkshire mill-owner."

[26] "Milnes was . . . men" is rewritten in ink over substantially the same matter in pencil; with "Milnes has . . . Chartists.", cf. p. [84] below. "⟨The English . . .

he breakfasted ⟨with⟩ somewhere with the Abp. of Canterbury, his friend said, "Now I beg you, Milnes, don't slap him on the back & call him *Canterbury*, before breakfast is over." His good humour is infinite, & 'tis the common charge made on him, that he wishes to play the part of Lamartine in England. He makes very bad speeches of exquisite infelicity, & joins in the laugh against himself. He is very liberal of his money, & sincerely kind & useful to young people of merit.[27]

[18] The English have no curiosity about any foreign country.[28] The Scotchman ⟨ha⟩is as curious as an American.
The English good sense is equally seen in the wit of Punch, as in the London Times. Some of his caricatures are equal to the best pamphlets.[29]
The English have stamina, can take the initiative in all companies. The foreigner is on the defensive & takes the low tone.[30]

[19]   ↑ Idĕrsāy↓
They require character in public men. The want of it makes the Irish members contemptible. One hundred twenty seven all voting like sheep, never proposing anything, but all but four voting the Income Tax[.][31]

"If Louis Philippe had had the pluck of a louse," ———— [32]

---

world)", which stands at the top of p. [16], was apparently canceled to allow room for continuing from p. [15] the entry on Milnes that Emerson rewrote and expanded.
    [27] The paragraph concerning Milnes, struck through in pencil with single curved vertical use marks on pp. [16] and [17], is transcribed in Notebook ED, pp. [142]-[143] below. Cf. Emerson's letter to his wife, London, March 23 and 24, 1848 (*L*, IV, 42); p. [84] below.
    [28] This sentence, struck through in pencil with a vertical use mark, is used in "Cockayne," *W*, V, 144-145.
    [29] This and the preceding sentence, struck through in pencil with a vertical use mark, are used in "The Times," *W*, V, 271.
    [30] "The English have stamina . . . tone.", in pencil, is struck through in pencil with a vertical use mark.
    [31] "Idĕrsāy", Emerson's humorous transcription of "I dare say" (see Journal GH, p. [135] above), is added in pencil. This entry, struck through in pencil with a vertical use mark, is transcribed in Notebook ED, p. [120] below.
    [32] Cf. Journal CO, p. [117]: ". . . we New-England idealists . . . might have

Richard Owen's vinous face is a powerful weapon; he has an air of virility that penetrates his audience — a surgical smile. But there was no need that he who thinks lightly of the accumulation of facts should run counter to his own genius & attack the transmutationists, for, it is they who obey the idea which makes him great.[33]

[20] [blank]
[21] I hear it said, that the sense which the manufacturers have of their duties to the operatives, & the exertions they have made in establishing schools & Mechanics' Institutions for them, is recent, & is, in great part, owing to Carlyle. At Huddersfield, I was told that they have over-educated the men in the working class, so as to leave them dissatisfied with their sweethearts & wives; and the good Schwanns & Kehls there, were now busy in educating the women up to them.

Mr Kehl thought that my Lecture on Napoleon was not true for the operatives who heard it at H. but was true only for the [22] commercial classes, and for the Americans, no doubt; that the aim of these operatives was to get 20 shillings a week, and to marry; then, they joined the "Mechanics' Institute," hear lectures, visit the news-room, & desire no more. I thought it despair.[34]

At Rawdon, I inquired, how much the men earned who were breaking stone in the road; & was told Twenty pence; but they can only have work three days in the week, unless they are married; then they have it four days.[35]

_____

taken Boston long ago, 'had we had the pluck of a louse,' to use the more energetic than elegant expression of my travelling friend." (the "friend" is not identified). Journal CO will be published in a later volume.

[33] The entry concerning Owen, struck through in pencil with a vertical use mark, is transcribed in Notebook ED, p. [120] below; it also appears in Journal LM, p. [72 1/2] below.

[34] "I hear . . . despair." is struck through in pencil with single vertical use marks on pp. [21] and [22]. Emerson had been in Huddersfield on December 17 and 18, 1847. Writing to Elizabeth Hoar on December 28, he mentioned "a sort of people" in England "whom we hardly have the like of in New England, — great manufacturers who exercise a paternal patronage & providence over their district. Such are the Brights at Rochdale . . . and the Schwanns at Huddersfield; — best of their sort" (L, III, 460).

[35] This sentence is struck through in pencil with a vertical use mark.

The chartists, if you treat them civilly, & show any goodwill to their cause, suspect you, think you are going to *do* them.[36]

[23] At Manchester, William Staley showed me over the whole warehouse of Messrs Watts, in which 150 persons are employed in selling all manner of "dry goods." The arrangement was excellent. On the upper floor, I found ribbons, & was told their stock of this kind was never less in value then £ ⟨6⟩20,000.

2   hero, interior, year
1   vary Mary
3   glory story tory
4   sure puritan curious Europe
    shirt   shar [37]

At the opera, only, is enthusiasm permitted.[38]

[24] A London dwellinghouse is perforated with systems of pipes for water fresh & hot & waste, for gas, for heat, for sound, [the servants in the kitchen are at a vast distance from the 3d story parlo⟨ur⟩r & must be informed through pipes of the wants of the parlo⟨ur⟩r after the bell is rung;] for bells; and lastly, for light, by means of glass doors, & floors, & sky lights. Over the chamber in which I breakfasted this morning is a glass floor ⟨an⟩1¼ inch thick, over that another ↑chamber↓ before you come to the skylight.

[25] [39] infe↑tee↓rior   superior   *f*ere *p*ere
year   yer
sure   ssher, injurious   *shar*
person   p͞err - son
Derby & Perth
glory, story, &c

---

[36] This entry is struck through in pencil with a vertical use mark. See Journal LM, p. [24] below.
   [37] "2 hero . . . shar" is in pencil.
   [38] This sentence, struck through in ink with a vertical use mark, appears also in Journal LM, p. [94] below, Notebook ED, p. [67] below, and "Manners," *W*, V, 112.
   [39] This page is in pencil; the additions are in ink. In the fourteenth line, "is almost" is circled in pencil.

signified	signifyd	(Scotch)
trait	tray	
engine	ingin	
fury	fure - y	
interesting	interrr esting	
interference	interf - ĕrence	
Europe	Yer - up	
more is almost	mar	
gore quite	gar	
curious curate	kyer-ious &c	
shirt	↑sheert↓	
↑steward	steeryerd	
	[a monosyllable]↓	

[26]   ↑(February '48)↓

Glasgow the rapidest growth in Britain after Liverpool ⟨adds 1000 souls a month to the population⟩. As soon as you cross the border at Berwick & enter Scotland, the face of things changes, the grass is less green. The country has an iron gray look. It is cold & poor; the railways are ill served: no well trained porters; you must carry ⟨off⟩ your own luggage[:] the⟨y⟩ ticket master weighs your sovereign; it is a rare piece & finds it light. You can pay in ⟨pen⟩ copper now for what always cost silver in Eng[lan]d. Nobody rides in first class carriages: and the manners become gross & swainish in some observed particulars.[40]

[27] The Scotch speech has a most unnecessary super⟨ficial⟩fluous energy of elocution & of rolling the r[:]
           seed pearl purrrrl
Great talkers, very fond of argument, but aimless & insane.

Scotch are plainer drest, plainer mannered, than the English, not so clean; & many of them look drunk when they are sober.
Americans undersized men

[40] This entry, in pencil and struck through in pencil with a vertical use mark, is used in "Race," W, V, 53. Emerson entered Scotland on February 11, 1848, and first lectured at Glasgow on February 14.

Scotch are intelligent reading & writing people but Edinburgh is still but a provincial city & the tone of society is incurably provincial.

> Had Cain been Scot God had reversed his doom
> Instead of roving made him stay at home [41]

[28] The English clergy are all ⟨reckoned as⟩ identified with the aristocracy. They say here, that, if you talk with an English clergyman, you are sure to find him wellbred, informed, candid; he entertains your thought or your project with entire sympathy: But two of them together are ⟨invariably⟩ inaccessible to your thought; and whenever it comes to action, the clergyman ⟨always⟩ ↑invariably↓ acts with his church.[42]

In Westmoreland, Mr Greg said, the parishioner told the new curate — "I hope thou beest not as great a blackguard as that other chap"; and the parish found another "not up to sample"[.] [43]

[29] ⟨I⟩An Englishman discovers a dissenter or a churchman by his manners.[44]

St George of Cappadocia an Arian.[45]

[30] [46] At Newcastle saw at Mr Crawshay's ironworks the Nasmith hammerund which will strike with a weight of 6 tons, yet so manageable that Nasmith will put his hand under it ⟨and⟩ if one of his own men directs the stroke. Crawshay put his ↑new↓ hat under & received a slight damage.

[41] Quoted inexactly from John Cleveland, "The Rebel Scot," ll. 63–64; the two lines are sometimes anthologized separately under the title "On Scotland." "The Scotch speech . . . home" is in pencil; "The Scotch . . . provincial." is struck through in pencil with a vertical use mark.

[42] This paragraph, struck through in ink and in pencil with two vertical use marks, is used in "Religion," W, V, 223.

[43] This paragraph is in pencil. William Rathbone Greg, the essayist, was living near Ambleside, where Emerson arrived on February 27, 1848, for a visit with Harriet Martineau.

[44] This sentence, struck through in ink and in pencil with vertical use marks, is transcribed in Notebook ED, p. [68] below.

[45] This entry is struck through in ink and in pencil with vertical use marks. See Journal GH, p. [89] above; cf. "Cockayne," W, V, 152.

[46] This page is in pencil.

Then an old hat was exploded.

Telegraphed a message to Edin. At Edinburgh saw Wilson. Lord
Jeffrey told me in his ⟨first⟩ visit to Boston, he saw Edward Everett
then a boy, & E. E. accompanied him to the Cambridge Library, &c.[47]

[31] De Quincey at Mrs Crowe's, very fine face.[48] He had walked
10 miles ↑in the rain — ↓ but was so drest that 10 miles could not
spoil him. He had walked home in the rain lately from Mrs C's
dinner, he told us, because he could not find money to ride; as ↑of↓
two street girls ↑one↓ had taken his 8 shillings out of his pocket, &
the other his umbrella. He can now write one article ↑in↓ every
number of the N[orth]. Brit[ish]. Review. The Quarterlies pay 16
guineas a sheet. Tait vulgarizes him. Hanna is Editor of the N[orth]
B[ritish]. De Q. has never seen Landor but grieves over the loss of
a finely bound copy of Hellenics sent him by L.[49] He has also lost
5 manuscript books of Wordsworth's Excursion (continued),[n] loses
every thing. Such gentleness & simplicity [32] perfect. Takes Dr
B[rown] into the ⟨street⟩ middle of the street to tell him where his
lodgings are. Yet does not owe more than 100 ⟨d⟩pound. Estimates
"Paradise Regained" very highly, thinks the author always knows.
Thinks the guest has duties. Turnbull said he would go to hell for
Sir William Hamilton.[50] Wilson said, I know but I will not tell
De Quincey's age, for it is my own. We were at Oxford together,
but not acquainted. Game cocks. In ⟨Wales⟩ ↑Wales↓ a theatre fracas
in which W. was ignominiously mauled made their acquaintance.
[Indians live by the leg not by the arm] D[aniel].W[ebster]. the

[47] At Newcastle on February 11, 1848, having been misinformed by Crawshay
about which train he should take for Edinburgh, Emerson telegraphed ahead to
ask that his lecture audience of that same evening be held for his late arrival (L, IV,
18). On February 12, in Edinburgh, he was presented to John Wilson ("Christopher
North"), and on the next day to Lord Jeffrey.

[48] In Edinburgh on Sunday, February 13, 1848, Emerson dined at the home
of the novelist Catherine Stevens Crowe (1800?-1876) with Thomas De Quincey,
David Scott, and his host in the city, Dr. Samuel Brown; in a letter to his wife,
February 21-22, he gives a parallel account of the occasion (L, IV, 19-20).

[49] The Hellenics of Walter Savage Landor, Enlarged and Completed (London,
1847).

[50] Probably William Barclay David Donald Turnbull (1811-1863), an archi-
vist and antiquary; Sir William Hamilton (1788-1856) was professor of logic and
metaphysics at Edinburgh.

biggest hat in America. DeQ said Wordsworth appropriated **what**
another said so entirely as to be angry if the originator claimed any
part of it. "Mine". "Yours!" "Yes." "No it is mine"[.] [51]

[33] [52] Thousand millions are the ocean in which panics are the local
storms of English money. Mr Dunlop & S B. [53]
R[obert].Chambers prints 70 000 copies of his Miscellany or Journal
& sends 50 000 to England. He showed me the house where Scott
was born & that where Beatoun was murdered[.] [54]

Insertion of a death in Times 9/6 no. "but I paid 7/6." "Let us see
your receipt;" O then [it] is "deeply regretted." [55]

Cobden was the better leader for that which he did not see; like a
horse with blinders[.] [56]
David Scott repeated a line from Festus[,] "Friendship passes like a
ship at sea"[;] De Q said, "he could not bear the ship repetition."

Dined with De Q at Lass-Wade. He lives with his 3 daughters
Marg[are]t, Florence, &   [.] [57]

---

[51] The entire entry concerning De Quincey is in pencil. "De Quincey at . . .
pocket,", "De Q. has . . . acquaintance.", and "Wordsworth . . . mine", struck
through in pencil with vertical use marks, are transcribed in Notebook ED, pp. [167]–
[171] below; the anecdote concerning Wordsworth is used in "Quotation and
Originality," *W*, VIII, 192.

[52] This page is in pencil.

[53] "Thousand millions . . . S B" is struck through in pencil with a vertical use
mark. "Mr Dunlop" was "a travelled, well informed Scotch laird . . . of Broch-
loch" who had been in America; Rusk identifies him as John Dunlap (*L*, IV, 20).
"S B" is Emerson's host in Edinburgh, Samuel Brown.

[54] Emerson dined with Robert Chambers, his brother William, and Emerson's
London publisher John Chapman in Edinburgh on February 15, 1848 (*L*, IV, 21).
David Beaton or Bethune (1494–1546), Scottish Roman Catholic prelate and statesman, was murdered in revenge for the death of George Wishart, burned at the stake
as a heretic.

[55] This entry is struck through in pencil with a vertical use mark.

[56] This entry is struck through in pencil with a vertical use mark.

[57] "David Scott . . . Florence, &", struck through in pencil with a vertical use
mark, is transcribed in Notebook ED, pp. [172]–[173] below, where Emerson corrects the quotation; see Philip James Bailey, *Festus* (Boston, 1849), p. 366. Emerson

[34] [58] Glasgow. 15 Feb. 320 000 people. Students in scarlet cloaks. Americans here & a consul. Dr Hudson tells me some strange stories about the Foundation at Eton, & that the subscription made previous to entering, declares that the signer is a beggar, yet is signed by noblemen. It confounds my understanding. Glasgow adds 1000 a month to its population. At G. I spoke in a cavern called City hall, to 2 or 3 000 persons[.] [59]

In Liverpool the population swarms into holes which the police cannot keep shut. In Dublin they live in holes in the ground. & Lord /Coburn/Cockburn/ said put a molasses hogshead or a puncheon of sugar in London streets & it would instantly be inhabited[.] [60]

In the salt market &c I saw many women standing about barefooted on 16 Feb[.] [61]

[35] [62] H.C. vowed to adhere to B. ↑Dr Brown↓ when all means failed them to pursue an experiment & they had nothing to pawn, C. came triumphantly with the article wanted from the druggist. "How did you get it?" "I sold two old pair of breeches." [63]

⟨R⟩ W[illiam] C[hambers] at Edin[burgh]. speaking of Am. copy-

---

dined at Lass-Wade on Saturday, February 19, 1848 (*L*, IV, 22); during the previous week David Scott had begun the portrait of Emerson that now hangs in the Concord Free Public Library.

[58] This page is in pencil.

[59] Within the entry of February 15 to this point, "Dr Hudson" is James William Hudson of Leeds; on p. [196] below is a query concerning "those alleged abuses of the charity foundations at Eton." "Glasgow adds . . . population." is struck through in pencil with a vertical use mark; a similar statement is canceled on p. [26] above. With "At G. . . . persons", cf. *L*, IV, 20.

[60] "In Liverpool . . . inhabited" is struck through in pencil with a vertical use mark. Emerson is quoting Henry Thomas Cockburn, a judge of the Court of Sessions in Edinburgh and hence referred to locally as a lord; a letter mentioning Cockburn refers to him as "lord Coburn" (*L*, IV, 22).

[61] This sentence is struck through in pencil with a vertical use mark. Cf. *L*, IV, 22: "I saw next day the Saut Market and O plenty of women (fishwives & others) & children, *barefooted*, barelegged, on this cold 18th of February in the streets."

[62] This page is in pencil.

[63] "H.C." is probably "Craig, Dr B's Siamese twin, his shadow," as Emerson described him in a letter, "the sharer of all his chemistry or alchemy; working with him now for many years without any reward" (*L*, IV, 18). "H.C. . . . breeches.'" is struck through in pencil with a vertical use mark.

right, said, As long as you do not grant copyright, we shall instruct you.[64]

[36] S[amuel]B[rown] told me the story of Mrs MacBold for D[e Quincey] had replied to the remark that his enemy had removed to another part of the city. Ah if the one of the Furies should arrive in Edin[burgh] it would make little difference at what hotel she put up.[65]

[37] [66] De q. said that Bl[ac]k[wood's Magazine]. paid him 12 guineas the sheet. To others, 10. To Wilson 20. The Quarterlies pay 16, i.e. a guinea a page. Hanna edits N B.
                    Landreth, Mc'phail.
Ferrier son in law of Wilson helps on Blackwood in which Ayton, Smith, Moir (Δ), & others write. Blk. once reached 8000 copies. Theod. Martyn is Le bon Gualtier[.] [67]
⟨A⟩In seeing old castles & cathedrals I sometimes say, as today at Dundee church tower, (which is 800 years old) this was built by another & a better race than any that now look on it.[68] And, at other times, I say, if idealists will work as well as these men wrought, we shall see a new world apace.

[38] Two gentlemen shot two dogs of Wilson's that had belonged to his wife. They came & made their apology. But Wilson carried it

---

[64] The Edinburgh firm of W. & R. Chambers published many inexpensive educational works. This sentence, struck through in pencil with a vertical use mark, is used in "Land," *W*, V, 36.

[65] This entry, in pencil, is struck through in pencil with a vertical use mark. The story is expanded in Notebook ED, p. [176] below.

[66] This page is in pencil.

[67] William Hanna edited the *North British Review*; P. Landreth edited *Macphail's Edinburgh Ecclesiastical Journal and Literary Review*; James Frederick Ferrier, William Edmondstoune Aytoun, William Henry Smith, and David Macbeth Moir (known as "Δ") were associated with *Blackwood's Edinburgh Magazine*; Theodore Martin collaborated with Aytoun in *The Bon Gaultier Ballads* (1845). "De q. said . . . page." is struck through in pencil with a diagonal use mark and "Blk. . . . copies" is struck through in pencil with a horizontal use mark (possibly a cancellation); cf. Notebook ED, p. [172] below.

[68] This sentence, struck through in pencil with a vertical use mark, is used in "Religion," *W*, V, 215.

to the law. Their friend came to Wilson & hoped he would have the magnanimity to forgive them. Magnanimity[,] Sir, ↑was there ever any so enormous as mine?↓ those two men stood where you now stand, & I did not pitch them out of the window.[69]

Heard Wilson lecture. And thought of our dear fat S[tetson]. & then of the Washingtonians. But really it was S without the wit[:] per*fervid*um, yes, but heavy. A speaking ox. No spark. When eligible for this chair he feared much the gamecocks would be brought against him.[70]

[39] [...]
[40] [71] Tholuck said to Chalmers, that he was astonished that none of the theologians here had had the candour to read Strauss. Sir, said C. I will read it on your recommendation; but is it a big book? for I am old.[72]

I find here a wonderful crop of mediocre and super-mediocre poets, they lie 3, 6, or 10 deep, instead of single as in America.

But, as at home, the merchants seem to me a greatly superior class to the clerisy. & they have a right to a great contempt of these.

[69] Pasted to the bottom of p. [38] is a slip of paper with Edward Emerson's comment in ink, evidently concerning this anecdote: "RWE's *story* told at John Brown Meeting taken up by State St—"; on the verso is written "December, 1856." According to *J*, VII, 396, n. 1, Emerson used the story in an unsuccessful attempt to quiet a mob that broke up a meeting of the Massachusetts Anti-Slavery Society in 1861.

[70] "Two gentlemen . . . him." is in pencil; the insertion "was there . . . mine?" is written in pencil on p. [39] (which is unnumbered by Emerson), with penciled lines leading to the entry on p. [38]. The writing on both pages is struck through in pencil with single vertical use marks; in Notebook ED, pp. [272]–[274] below, Emerson transcribed this material with some rearrangement and expansion, drawing also on the account of Wilson in a letter to his wife that makes a similar comparison of Wilson with Rev. Caleb Stetson (*L*, IV, 21). According to the letter, Emerson heard Wilson lecture at the University of Edinburgh on Tuesday, February 15, 1848, but Notebook ED, p. [272] below, gives the date as "the next day" after he met Wilson, to whom he had been presented on the 12th (*L*, IV, 19; p. [30] above). Wilson's appointment as Professor of Moral Philosophy was made in 1820.

[71] This page is in pencil.

[72] "Friedrich August Gottreu Tholuck, Professor of Theology at Halle, who had written an answer to Strauss's *Life of Jesus*. Rev. Thomas Chalmers, Professor at the University of St. Andrews and Edinburgh" (*J*, VII, 396, n. 2).

[41] H[arriet]. M[artineau]. said that W[illiam]. W[ordsworth]. in his early housekeeping at the cottage was accustomed to offer his friends bread & plainest fare, but if they wanted anything more, they must pay ↑him↓ for their board. I heard the story with admiration, as evincing English pluck more than any thing I know.[73]

H.M. said in her trance that there was no ultimate atom, only forces; and this, she learned, was the stupendous discovery of Faraday.[74]

[42] P. T. visited H[arriet]. M[artineau]. at N[orwich?] with R[ichard] C↑obden↓ and on departing came back to say that R.C. said, that 'twas a sad business this agitation, for his own little boy thought him, when he went home, a gentleman who visited his mother.[75]
Sir Charles Fellows showed me a watch that belonged to Milton, his name being engraved on the face of it. He told me that on one occasion he showed this to Wordsworth who took it on one hand & then drew out his own & held it up with the other before the company — but no one made the expected remark.[76]

[43] Duke of Cleaveland's land extends from
(the point where we first entered it, coming from Darlington, toward Barnard Castle,) 23 miles to High Force, where the Tees falls 212 feet.
    After passing Raby Castle, we met the Duke returning from hunting with his hounds, the horses & dogs very much blown & spent.

[73] Emerson visited Harriet Martineau at Ambleside on February 27–29, 1848, seeing Wordsworth himself on the 28th. These two sentences, struck through in pencil with a vertical use mark, are transcribed in Notebook ED, p. [250] below.
    [74] This sentence is in pencil. Mounted on the front cover verso of Journal LM is a newspaper clipping concerning Faraday's scientific work; Miss Martineau's "trance" presumably means what Emerson elsewhere called her "cloud of mesmerism" (L, IV, 31).
    [75] The insertion "obden" is in pencil; in "R.C. said . . . agitation," the periods and commas are added in pencil; after "thot" (here printed as "thought") is noted in pencil: "(thought".
    [76] "Sir Charles . . . remark.", struck through in pencil with a vertical use mark, is transcribed in Notebook ED, p. [253] below, where Emerson notes that the incident took place at the house of Sir Charles — i.e., on Thursday, April 11, 1848: see Pocket Diary 3, p. [66] below.

The huntsman, as he passed us, told ⟨the⟩our coach man that they had had a desperate run of 2 hours 25 minutes, without check. ⟨With⟩ ↑Beside↓ him, rode the whipper-in, and, a little behind, the Duke & a gentleman, in red hunting coats.[77]

[44] [78] English are trained to the highest inoffensiveness[.] ⟨They⟩ The Americans are sun[-]dried[,] the English are baked in the oven. The upper classes have only birth, say people here, & not thoughts; yes, but they have manners, & 'tis wonderful how much talent runs into manners. Nowhere & never so much as in England. And when they go into America & find that this gift has lost its power, the gold has become dry leaves, no wonder they are impatient to get away[.]

Every man in the carriage is a possible lord.

Yet they look alike & every man I meet in London I think I know[.]

English have hard eyes[.] [79]

[45] The Englishman is not trained to neglect the eyes of his neighbours. He is really occupied with his own affair, & does not think of them. In the first class carriage a clergyman takes his ↑stout↓ shoes out of his carpet bag & puts them on instead of thin ones on approaching the station. Every man in the street or in the house consults only his convenience in this polished country as a pioneer in Wisconsin: and as the Englishman has been doing this for seven generations, it is now in the blood.[80]

---

[77] The parentheses and the commas after "it" and "Darlington" are in pencil. The hyphen in "whipper-in" and the commas in "and, a . . . behind," are added in pencil. The incident described took place on February 9, 1848; there is a parallel account in Emerson's letter of the following day to his wife (L, IV, 15–16). "Duke of . . . feet." is used in "Aristocracy," W, V, 182.

[78] This page is in pencil.

[79] With "Yet they . . . know", cf. Journal GH, p. [140] above, and Notebook England and Paris, p. [54] below; for "English have hard eyes", see p. [9] above. "English are . . . inoffensiveness", "The upper . . . eyes", and "Every man . . . eyes" are struck through in pencil with discontinuous vertical use marks; cf. Notebook ED, pp. [5] and [67] below.

[80] This paragraph, struck through in pencil with a vertical use mark, is used in "Manners," W, V, 105.

May 24 The days come to us like muffled & veiled figures sent from a distant friendly party, but they say nothing, & if we do not use the gifts they bring, they carry them as silently away.

Safford

"He has found a new rule to calculate eclipses He told me it would shorten the work nearly two thirds When finding this rule for two or three days, he seemed to be in a sort of trance. One morning very early he came rushing down stairs, not stopping to dress him, poured on to his slate a stream of figures, & soon cried out in the wildness of his joy; O father, I have got it! I have got it! it comes, it comes."

It is droll to hear this talker talking against talkers, and this writer writing against writing.

Had such a person as Cromwell [could] come now it would be of no use, he could not get the ear of the House of Commons. You might as well go into Chelsea Graveyard yonder, & say, Shoulder Arms! and expect the old dead churchwardens to rise.

In architecture he thought it would be right now for an architect to consult only what was necessary, & to attempt no kind of ornament, Say, I can build you a coffin for such dead persons as you are, & for such dead purposes as you have, but no ornament.

He prefers Cambridge to Oxford. But Oxford & Cambridge Education indurates them, as the Styx hardened Achilles so that now they say we are proof we have gone thro' all the degrees, & are case hardened against all the veracities of the universe nor man nor God can penetrate us.

Plate III   *Journal London, page 57*   *Text, pages 232–233*
On Carlyle's talk, incorporating item 3 of Plate II

206

Yet he liked to hear him.

He prefers Cambridge to Oxford.
But Oxford & Cambridge education
indurates the young men, as the
Styx hardened Achilles, so that,
when they come forth of them,
they say; Now. we are proof, we
have gone through all the degrees,
& are case-hardened against all
the veracities of the Universe,
nor man nor God can penetrate
us.'

His jeers & scoffs are thrown
in every direction. He breaks every
sentence with a scoffing laugh,
"windbag", "monkey", "donkey", "bladder",
and, let him describe whom
he will, it is always "poor fellow!"

Plate IV   Notebook ED, page 206   Text, page 545
A retrospective version of material shown in Plates II and III

An Englishman always conceals his name. At the hotel, if they ask his name at the book office, he stoops & gives it in a low voice. If he gives you his private address on his card it is like an avowal of friendship; and Q took B into the middle of the street before he named his lodgings.[81]

[46] [82] Wordsworth said Ed[inburgh] Review wrote what would tell & what would sell[;] he thought Cobden had weakly described the French. His wish was father &c.[83] ↑He↓ thought the elder Tennyson, at first, the best poet[.]
[C said they looked alike, & some one came in & saw this brother lying on the sofa, & said, "Ah Alfred I am glad to see you," and he said, "I am not Alfred but Septimus, ↑I am↓ the most morbid of all the Tennysons."] Wordsworth thought the Ed. Review had changed its whole tone of literary criticism from the time when a letter was written to the Editor by Coleridge. After that, it had greatly more breadth. Mrs W. had had the Editor's answer.
⟨W⟩ In speaking of I know not what style, he said, that, "to be sure, it was the manner, — but then the matter always comes out of [47] the manner." He thought Rio Janeiro the best place for the capital of the world[.] [84]

⟨W⟩⟨Jane C goes up & down⟩ ↑Jane Carlyle said to me "I go up & down↓ like an ichneumon eating crocodile's eggs"[.]

[48] Old Walter died 1847
     Dr Stoddart afterwards Sir John
Thomas Barnes   died 1841
Edw Sterling from 1830 to 1840 [85]

──────

[81] "Q" is De Quincey: see p. [32] above. "An Englishman . . . lodgings.", struck through in pencil with a curved vertical use mark, is used in "Manners," *W*, V, 106.
 [82] Pp. [46] and [47] are in pencil.
 [83] Cf. Shakespeare, *II Henry IV*, IV, v, 93.
 [84] "Wordsworth said . . . world", struck through on pp. [46] and [47] with single vertical use marks, is transcribed in Notebook ED, pp. [246]–[247], [277] below.
 [85] All four men were associated with the *Times* of London. "Old Walter", men-

Present writers according to London Critic
Delaine
Mowbray Morris
    Tyas   now, 70 aetat.
    Macdonald
    Dr Richardson
    Thornton
    Bailey
    Meagher, Paris Correspondent
    Fillmore, Berlin d[itt]o
    Robt Lowe.   Australian
    Ward
    Oxenford
    Saml. Philips
    Henry Reeve
    Rev. Thomas Mozley of Guildford St.[86]

[49] The "Times" prints 35 000 copies daily. The circulation has increased by 8 000 copies since February. Their old press has

---

tioned on p. [8] above, was John Walter (1776–1847), second son of its founder and his successor as manager; he was followed in turn by his own son John in 1847. Sir John Stoddart (1773–1856), after writing for the paper from 1812 to 1816, founded the *New Times* in 1817. Barnes (1785–1841) edited the *Times* from 1817 until 1841, being given full control of its policies in 1819; Sterling (1773–1847) wrote for it from 1812 to 1840, first in a series of letters signed "Vetus."

[86] John Thadeus Delane (1817–1879), who joined the *Times* in 1840, served as its editor from 1841 to 1877; Mowbray Morris (1819–1874) was its manager from 1847 to 1873. John Tyas was a veteran reporter; John Cameron MacDonald, also a reporter, later became chief engineer and successor to Morris as manager. John Richardson, a writer trained in the law who took orders in the Church of England, published his *Recollections* in 1856; Emerson apparently confused him with Sir John Richardson, M.D. (1787–1865), scientist and explorer. Thomas Thornton was a Parliamentary reporter; on "Bailey," see pp. [7]–[8] above. The three foreign correspondents were J. B. O'Meagher, Lewis Filmore, and Robert Lowe (later Viscount Sherbrooke). "Ward" may be Robert Plumer Ward, novelist and politician, or William George Ward, a theological pamphleteer. John Oxenford contributed art and dramatic criticism to the *Times*; Samuel Philips was an art critic and book reviewer. Henry Reeve, after writing for the paper from 1840 to 1855, principally on foreign affairs, resigned on becoming editor of the *Edinburgh Review*. Rev. Thomas Mozley was a highly paid leader-writer, serving from 1843 until 1886.

printed 5 or 6 000 sheets an hour. Their new machine, which I saw, is to print from 10 to 12 000 copies per hour.[87]

↑"Among these *penny-a-liners* are, to my own personal knowledge, Fellows & Professors of Colleges, eminent clergymen, rising barristers, noblemen's sons, & even ladies of good family."
                                    Bristed.↓ [88]

[50] [89] Times.   "has ears everywhere"
Rev Arthur Moseley.
"Our reporter was accommodated with a seat in the train with Louis Philippe to London" March 4,
Sterling, Bacon, & Barnes [90]
No principle has that paper, say all.

"Our Reporter" means that any person who finds himself on the spot where anything noteworthy falls out, writes a letter describing it to the Times, &, if it is printed receives 3 guineas.

Times is now in its palmiest state[.]

⟨After⟩ You must buy the newspaper in the first ⟨hour⟩ ↑time↓ when it passes. They are all snapped up in a few hours & you can never recover it.

---

[87] This paragraph is used in "The Times," W, V, 265, where the information is attributed to "Mr. Morris" of the *Times*. What appear to be rough notes for this entry occur in Notebook England and Paris, p. [41] below.

[88] Charles Astor Bristed, *Five Years in an English University*, 2 vols. (New York, 1852), II, 143–144, note. This entry was added in 1852. Emerson borrowed vol. II of Bristed from the Boston Athenaeum on July 8, 1852, and vol. I on July 17, returning both on August 1.

[89] This page is in pencil; "Sterling . . . Barnes" is written over a line of erased pencil writing: "In ‖ . . . ‖ writes dramatic criticism".

[90] Emerson's reference to "Rev Arthur Moseley" may be an error for Rev. Thomas Mozley, who like Edward Sterling and Thomas Barnes was associated with the *Times*; see notes 85 and 86 above. Francis Bacon, after serving as theater critic and Parliamentary reporter, was assistant editor of the paper from 1835 until his death in 1839. The *Times* for March 4, 1848, p. 8, observed that "Our own reporter was also accommodated with a seat in the train" — not to London with Louis Philippe, as Emerson has it, but from London to Newhaven after the King's arrival there from France.

Mrs. B was [n] ruined in buying newspapers[.]

The Times advertises a child's caul for sale. Horace Twiss makes the parliamentary digest for £700 a year[.]

Walter has sold out his property to Loyd[.] [91]

[51] It is remarkable here that no one inquires who wrote this or that paragraph in The Times. The best-informed men, who might easily know, read & admire without asking.

Was never such arrogancy on the face of the earth as the tone of this paper. Every slip of an Oxonian or Cantabridgian who writes his first leader assumes that *we* subdued the world before we sat down to write this particular Times. But the habit of brag runs through all classes from the Times, ⟨Carlyle,⟩ Wordsworth, Carlyle, Macaulay, down to the boys at Eton[.] [92]

"Taking their pleasure sadly, after the manner of their nation," said Froissart.[93]

[52] Carlyle's realism is thorough. He is impatient of a literary trifler & if Guizot is to make Essays after being a tool he thinks it nothing. Actors & actresses all mad monkeys. He saw Rachel in an impossible attitude & learned it was the lead in her dress & he despises her ever since. This English parliament with its babble he denounces. They gather up six millions of money every year to give to the poor, & yet the people starve. He thinks if they would give it to him to provide the poor with labor & with authority to make them work or shoot them & he to be hanged if he did not do it, he could find them in plenty of Indian meal. These idle nobles at Tattersall's [94] there is no work or word of serious [53] purpose in them, and they have this great lying Church, & life is a humbug[.]

[91] The entries on p. [50] are struck through in pencil with a succession of vertical use marks. "Times. 'has . . . everywhere'", "Times is . . . palmiest state", and "You must . . . it." are used in "The Times," *W*, V, 263–264.

[92] "It is . . . Eton" is struck through in pencil with two vertical use marks. "Was never . . . Eton" is transcribed in Notebook ED, p. [75] below. "Was never . . . Times." is used in "The Times," *W*, V, 269; "But the . . . Eton" is used in "Cockayne," *W*, V, 150.

[93] See p. [9] above, where the remark is given in French.

[94] A London horse auction mart; see *JMN*, VII, 442.

Of course, this French Revolution is the best thing he has ever seen & the teaching this great swindler Louis Philippe that there is a God's justice in the Universe after all, ⟨a⟩is a great satisfaction.[95] "No man speaks truth to me".

"Yes, they come to hear me and they read what I write, but not one of them has the smallest intention of doing these things." [96]

He values Peel as having shown more valor as a statesman than any other of these men. Wellington he esteems real & honest; he will not have to do with any falsehood.[97]

[54] Chalmers he valued as a naif honest eloquent man, who, in these very days believed in Christianity, and though he himself, when he heard him, had long discovered that it would not hold water, yet he liked to hear him.[98]
Tennyson dined out every day for months; then Aubrey de Vere[,] a charitable gentleman, 30 miles from Limerick, on a beautiful estate, came up & carried him off. Tennyson surrendered on terms; — that he should not hear anything of Irish distress; that he should not be obliged to come down to breakfast; & that he should smoke in the house. So poor [55] Tennyson, who had been in the worst way, but had not force enough to choose wh⟨ich⟩ere to go & so sat still, was now disposed of.
Since the new French Revolution, C has taken in the Times newspaper, the first time he has ever had a daily paper.[99]

[95] "Carlyle's realism . . . satisfaction.", struck through in pencil with vertical use marks on pp. [52] and [53], is transcribed in Notebook ED, pp. [199]–[200] below.
[96] " 'No man . . . things.' " is written in ink over erased pencil writing; at least the first sentences of both entries are identical. The passage, struck through in pencil with a vertical use mark, is transcribed in Notebook ED, p. [207] below.
[97] "He values . . . falsehood.", struck through in pencil with a vertical use mark, is transcribed in Notebook ED, p. [202] below. Carlyle's remark about Wellington is noticed also in a letter Emerson wrote to his wife dated by Rusk about March 15, 1848 (L, IV, 40).
[98] Thomas Chalmers (1780–1847), a Scottish theologian, was noted for his preaching. "Chalmers . . . him.", struck through in pencil with a vertical use mark, is transcribed in Notebook ED, pp. [205]–[206] below.
[99] "Tennyson dined . . . paper." is struck through in pencil with single vertical use marks on pp. [54] and [55]. "Tennyson dined . . . disposed of." is transcribed

"If he should go into Parliament, the thing he should do would be to get those reporters thrust out, and so put an end at once to all manner of mischievous speaking 'to Bunkum,' and windbags. In the Long Parliament, the only great parliament, they sat secret & silent ↑grave↓ as an Oecumenical Council, and I know not what they would have done to any body that had got in there & attempted to tell out of doors what they did." [100]

He finds nothing so depressing to him as the sight of a great mob. He saw one once[,] three or four miles of human beings & fancied [56] that the earth was some great cheese, and these were mites. [101]

He reads Louis Blanc. He can't get any true light on Cobden's Free Trade. He does not believe with Cobden. Every labourer a monopolist. The navigation laws of this country made its commerce. St John was insulted by the Dutch & came home, & got the law passed that foreign vessels should pay high fees, & it cut the throat of the Dutch & made the Eng. trade. [102]

C. says, that a man deposited £100 in a sealed box in the Dublin Bank & then advertised to all somnambulists, mesmerisers, & others that he whoever could tell him the number of his note should have the money. He let it lie there six months, the newspapers now & then stimulating the attention of the adepts, but none ever could tell him; & he said, now let me never be bothered more with this proven lie. [103]

[57] It is droll to hear this talker talking against talkers, and this writer writing against writing. [104]

⟨That⟩If such a person as O[liver] Cromwell should come now it would be of no use[,] he could not get the ear of the House of

---

in Notebook ED, p. [185] below. The reference to Carlyle and the *Times* is paralleled in a letter to his wife that Emerson wrote on March 8 and 10, 1848 (*L*, IV, 34).

[100] " 'If he . . . did.' ", struck through in pencil with a vertical use mark, is transcribed in Notebook ED, pp. [203]–[204] below.

[101] "He finds . . . mites.", struck through in pencil with single vertical use marks on pp. [55] and [56], is transcribed in Notebook ED, p. [225] below.

[102] "He reads . . . trade.", struck through in pencil with a vertical use mark, is transcribed in Notebook ED, p. [203] below.

[103] "C. says . . . lie.", struck through in pencil with a vertical use mark, is transcribed in Notebook ED, p. [12] below.

[104] "It is . . . writing.", struck through in pencil with a vertical use mark, is transcribed in Notebook ED, p. [225] below.

Commons. You might as well go into Chelsea Graveyard yonder, & say, Shoulder Arms! and expect the old dead churchwardens to arise.[105]

In architecture he thought it would be right now for an architect to consult only what was necessary, & to attempt no kind of ornament, & say, I can build you a coffin for such dead persons as you are, & for such dead purposes as you have, but no ornament.[106]

He prefers Cambridge to Oxford. But Oxford & Cambridge education indurates them, as the Styx hardened Achilles so that now they say we are proof[;] we have gone thro' all the degrees, & are case hardened against all the veracities of the universe, nor man nor God can penetrate us.[107]

[58] "The idea of a pigheaded soldier who will obey orders, & fire on his own father, at the command of his officer, — is a great comfort to the aristocratic mind," said C.

C. called Lady [Duff] G[ordon]. a female Brummel, & said, Brummel was a sort of inverse Saint Peter, who could tread the waters of humbug without sinking.[108]

Wicksteed told me of an American who enlarged, to Carlyle[,] on free institutions, sure of his sympathy; ⟨who⟩ ↑and C.↓ replied, "that he preferred a tranquil large-minded White Russian to any other kind of man": for C., it seems, had lately seen [59] Nicholas. And I repeatedly found that Nicholas was one of his few living heroes. For in the ignominy of Europe when all thrones fell like

---

[105] "If such . . . arise.", struck through in pencil with a vertical use mark, is transcribed in Notebook ED, pp. [205]–[206] below.

[106] "In architecture . . . ornament.", struck through in pencil with a vertical use mark, is transcribed in Notebook ED, p. [205] below.

[107] "He prefers . . . us.", struck through in pencil with a vertical use mark, is transcribed in Notebook ED, p. [206] below. For an earlier note, apparently the basis of the present passage, see Notebook England and Paris, p. [41] below. Plates II, III, and IV reproduce the three versions of Carlyle's comment on the universities.

[108] Emerson had met Lady Duff-Gordon when he visited Cambridge on July 6, 1848; this sentence concerning her is expanded from an entry in Notebook England and Paris, p. [44] below, made during his subsequent visit to Stonehenge with Carlyle. " 'The idea . . . sinking.", struck through in pencil with a diagonal use mark, is transcribed in Notebook ED, p. [208] below.

card houses & no man was found with conscience enough to fire a gun for his crown, but every one "ran away in a coucou through the Barriere de Passy," one man remained who believed he was put there by God Almighty to govern his empire, & by the help of God had resolved to stand there.

Chadwick is the other hero, Chadwick who proposes to provide every house with pure water, sixty gallons to every head, at a penny a week; and Carlyle thinks, that the only religious act which a man nowadays can securely perform, is, to wash himself well.[109]

[60] In England, Plato is read as a Greek book, & nowise from sympathy.[110]
In England, spirit of system. An Englishman is àplomb.[111]

H.D.T[horeau]. thought ⟨a⟩ what we reckon a good Englishman is in this country a stage-proprietor[.] [112]

[61] It is very plain from the security of their manners that these people have sat here a thousand years & will continue to sit.

Let who will fail, England will not. She could not now build the old castles & abbeys, but the Nineteenth loves club-houses, railways, & docks & mills, & builds them fast enough.[113]

[62] The Englishman is cheerful, and his voice is.[114]

---

[109] "Wicksteed . . . well." is struck through in pencil with single vertical use marks on pp. [58] and [59]. "Wicksteed . . . of man' " and "Nicholas was . . . well." are transcribed in Notebook ED, pp. [224], [201]–[202] below.

[110] Contrast *JMN*, IX, 248; cf. also Journal GH, p. [87] above. This sentence, struck through in pencil with a vertical use mark, is transcribed in Notebook ED, p. [59] below.

[111] "An . . . àplomb." is in pencil. On English àplomb, see "Manners," *W*, V, 104. Pasted below this entry is a clipping from an unidentified German-language newspaper. The single complete sentence concerns the association of religion with politics by the English aristocracy.

[112] This sentence is struck through in pencil with a vertical use mark. Cf. Notebook ED, p. [7] below.

[113] "It is . . . enough.", struck through in pencil with two vertical use marks, is used in "Manners," *W*, V, 106.

[114] This sentence, struck through in pencil with a vertical use mark, is used in "Character," *W*, V, 128.

Everywhere I observe an exact economy & nothing of that uncalculated headlong expenditure which families use in America. If
they cannot pay, they do not buy. For they have no presumption of
better fortunes, next year, as our people have.[115] J[ane]. C[arlyle].
said, that the rich people whom she knew had occasion for all the
shillings they could find. ↑The spending is, for a great part, in
servants. Thirty five servants in Lord A.'s house[.]↓ [116]
↑When   sing before Duke of Wellington &
other grandees, a cord is stretched between the singer & the company.↓ [117]

[63] The people have wide range, but no ascending range in their
speculation. An American like a German has many platforms of
thought. But an Englishman requires to be humoured or treated
with tenderness as an invalid, if you wish him to climb.[118]

[64] [blank]
[65] In Ireland, Mr G. said, his father found that all the policies of
life assurance on three lives included the king's as one. The reason
was, that it would be known when the king died, but of no person in
Ireland could it be known.[119]
Mr G. said that he would leave his children either a necessity of
labour or a great fortune. An inheritance of 500 a year, is sure to
make fainéants.[120]

[115] "Everywhere . . . have.", struck through in pencil with a vertical use mark,
is transcribed in Notebook ED, p. [9] below.
[116] "J. C. . . . house" is struck through in pencil with a vertical use mark. "The
spending . . . servants." is used in "Aristocracy," W, V, 193. "Lord A." may be
Lord Ashburton; cf. p. [100] below.
[117] "When . . . company." is struck through in pencil with a diagonal use mark.
The anecdote as reported in Notebook ED, p. [68] below, is used in "Aristocracy,"
W, V, 194; the present passage, an insertion, may have been written later than the
entry in Notebook ED, which quotes an item dated 1852 as its source.
[118] "The people . . . climb.", struck through in pencil with a diagonal use
mark, is transcribed in Notebook ED, pp. [57]–[58] below.
[119] "In Ireland . . . known." is struck through in pencil with a vertical use
mark.
[120] "Mr G. . . . fainéants." is in pencil.

[66] [blank]

[67] Mr J↑oshua↓ B↑ates↓[,] [121] the best informed man, one would say, hesitates to testify before the H[ouse]. of Commons to the advantage of the proposed abolition of Navigation Laws, because he thinks the English shipowners & shipmasters cannot compete with those of America, here in their own ports.

[68] Mr Van de W. said that Louis Philippe has not now £800 a year.[122]

Louis Philippe could not be received publicly, but he went privately to the Queen, & made her & her company laugh very heartily by his account of his escapade, & the incidents of his disguise, voyage, & landing in England.

On one occasion Thalberg (?) played on the piano at Windsor, & the Queen accompanied him with her voice. On the news of this getting abroad, all England shuddered from sea to sea. It was never repeated.[123]

[69] The penny post pays   revenue to government.[124] It has its good & evil. Since the penny post, say they, we have had to give up reading.

[70] [125]   *plural London*
        Immeasureable London, evidently the capital of the world, where men have lived ever since there were men. Yet it seems deliberately built[.]
an aggregation of capitals

[121] In "Joshua Bates" the first insertion is in pencil and the second in ink; each replaces a period.

[122] Sylvain Van de Weyer, the Belgian Ambassador, was a son-in-law of Joshua Bates who had entertained Louis Philippe and his family on March 1, 1848; Emerson met him at dinner with Bates on Sunday, March 5 (*L*, IV, 34).

[123] "On one . . . repeated.", struck through in pencil and in ink with two vertical use marks, is transcribed in Notebook ED, p. [68] below, and used in "Manners," *W*, V, 112.

[124] See Journal GH, p. [120] above.

[125] This page is in pencil.

London has too many glass doors to afford a riot[.] [126]
There are several little nations here. A German quarter in White-chapel. A French quarter where they still carry on a silk business in Spital fields[.] [127]

In London only could such a place as Kew gardens be overlooked. Wealth of shops bursting into the streets. Piles of plate breast high on Ludgate hill. In ↑a↓ London Dock Mr B said he had seen 19 miles of pipes of wine piled up to the ceiling.[128]

[71] Many of the characterizing features of London are new. Such as gas light, the omnibuses, the steam ferries, the penny post↑, & the building ⟨over⟩ ↑up↓ the West end↓[.] [129]

One goes from show to show, ↑dines out↓, & lives in extremes. Electric sparks 6 ft long, light is polarized, Grisi sings, Rothschild is your banker, Owen & Faraday lecture, Macaulay talks, Soyer cooks[.] [130]

Is then not an economy in coming where thus all the dependence is on the first men of their kind[?] [131]

    I stayed in London till I had become acquainted with all the styles of face in the street & till I had found the suburbs & their

---

[126] "Immeasureable . . . riot" is struck through in pencil with a vertical use mark. Similar phrasing occurs in Emerson's letter to his wife written on March 8, 1848 (*L*, IV, 35).

[127] "There . . . fields" is struck through in pencil with a vertical use mark.

[128] "In London . . . ceiling." is struck through in pencil with a vertical use mark. "Mr B" is probably Joshua Bates.

[129] "Many . . . post" is in ink; the commas and "& . . . end" are added in pencil. "Many . . . end" is struck through in pencil with a vertical use mark.

[130] On April 18, 1848, Emerson attended a performance of Rossini's *Stabat Mater* at Covent Garden; one of the soloists was the Italian soprano Giulia Grisi (1811?–1869). Two days earlier he had met Alexis Benoit Soyer (1809–1858), the "renowned" chef of the Reform Club and author of *The Gastronomic Regenerator*. See *L*, IV, 55–56.

[131] "One goes . . . kind", in pencil, is struck through in pencil with a vertical use mark.

straggling houses on each end of the city. Then I took a cab, left my farewell cards, & came home.[132]

[72] Trades of despair [133]

[73] I find a prose in certain Englishmen which exceeds in woody deadness all possibility of rivalry, & seems today like the gates of Hell, "Leave all hope behind."   ↑See BO 164↓ [134]

It is a nation where mediocrity is entrenched & consolidated, funded & decorated, in an adamantine manner.[135]

Of national brag, ↑see BO 169↓ [136]

[74] [137] incompatibility ⟨of th⟩ in the Italians of dealing with other nations, of treating with them. Conspicuous of [138]

⟨Every man in the carriage a possible lord.⟩ [139]
In the newspapers they set down the number of the cab, ↑2003↓[,] ⟨th⟩ in which M. Guizot drove to his lodgings from the pier at Folkestone.

_____

English women wear their grey hair:[140] in the rain, they tuck up their gown about the waist & expose their skirt:

_____

[132] This paragraph, in pencil, is struck through in pencil with a vertical use mark.

[133] This phrase, in pencil, is used in an enumeration on p. [120] below.

[134] Journal BO will be published in a later volume. The allusion is to Dante, *Inferno*, III, 9.

[135] "I find . . . manner.", struck through in pencil with a curved vertical use mark, and "I find . . . behind.' ", struck through in ink with a vertical use mark, are transcribed in Notebook ED, p. [57] below, and used in "Manners," W, V, 111–112.

[136] Journal BO will be published in a later volume.

[137] On this page, "incompatibility . . . skirt:" is in pencil.

[138] "incompatibility . . . Conspicuous of" is struck through in pencil with a vertical use mark.

[139] See p. [44] above.

[140] "Women in America, at this period, when their hair began to turn grey wore 'frisettes' or 'false fronts,' often of a singular warm chocolate-brown which heightened the unreality" (J, VII, 413, n. 1).

England a little top-heavy still, though she keeps her feet much better since the Cornlaws were thrown overboard[.]

[75] 9 March. I attended a Chartist meeting in National Hall, Holborn. It was called to hear the report of the Deputation who had returned after carrying congratulations to the French Republic. The Marsaillaise was sung by a party of men & women on the platform, & chorused by the whole assembly: then the "Girondins." The leaders appeared to be grave men, intent on keeping a character for order & moral tone in their proceedings, but the great body of the meeting liked best the sentiment, 'Every man a ballot & every man a musket'[.]
Much was whispered of the soldiers,—that "they would catch it," i.e. the contagion of chartism & rebellion.[141]

"cet affreux silence que l'on observe en marchant en ligne,—" was said of English troops.

[76] In the Times, advertisement of literary assistance. Thomas Roscoe sold his name to a book. Thomas Delf sells his book to a name of Mr Cunningham bookseller.[142]

[77] The British Museum holds the relics of ancient art, & the relics of ancient nature, in adjacent chambers. It is alike impossible to reanimate either.
The arrangement of the antique remains is surprisingly imperfect & careless,[143] without order, or skilful disposition, or names or numbers. A warehouse of old marbles. People go to the Elgin

---

[141] "I attended . . . rebellion." is struck through in pencil with a vertical use mark. A similar account of the meeting, held on March 7, 1848, occurs in a letter to his wife that Emerson began on March 8 and concluded on March 10 (*L*, IV, 34–35).
[142] This page is in pencil. The advertisement mentioned is one of three that Emerson clipped from the *Times* and mounted on the front cover verso of Journal GH. Thomas Roscoe (1791–1871) was a prolific author, editor, and translator; Delf, whom Emerson had known in New York, was again in London, being associated for a time with John Chapman, Emerson's English publisher (*L*, IV, 159, n. 119). The particular books Emerson had in mind have not been identified.
[143] The comma is added in pencil.

chamber many times & at last the ⟨w⟩beauty of the whole comes to them at once like music. The figures sit like gods in heaven.

⟨P.C. s⟩ ↑Coventry Patmore's↓ remark was that to come out of the other room to this was from a room full of snobs to a room full of gentlemen[.] [144]

[78] There are 420 000 volumes in the library, as Mr Panizzi assured me, and 50 or 60 000 manuscripts. In the Bodleian library, probably not more than 120,000. books. Five Libraries have the right to a copy of every book that is printed, This, the Bodleian, the Advocates at Edinburgh, the Dublin ↑University|?↓ and ↑Trinity College Cambridge|?↓

The King's Library at Paris is much larger than this ↑1 ⟨o⟩500 ⟨o⟩500 said Colman↓.[145] Here the line of shelves runs twelve miles.

It is impossible to read from the glut of books. I looked at some engravings in the print room with Mr Patmore who is connected with the Library.

[79] It would be a good occupation for a young man in London to make himself master of the antiques in the Museum with the view of explaining them to visitors and advertise himself as Tutor to the British Museum offering his services to those who wished a thorough showing. It would be a very instructive profession to the professor himself for a good while & the road to other employment.[146]

[80] One cannot enough admire the English names. A rich cloak of

---

[144] "⟨P.C. s⟩ . . . gentlemen" is written in pencil. "The British . . . gentlemen" is struck through in pencil with a vertical use mark. Emerson's visit to the British Museum, probably on April 15, 1848 (see p. [108] below), is described in a letter of April 20 to his wife: "The best sights I have seen lately are; the British Museum; whose chambers of Antiquities I visited with the Bancrofts on a private day, under the guidance of Sir Charles Fellows. . . . Then, the King's Library, which afterwards I saw under the guidance of Panizzi, the Librarian, and afterwards of Coventry Patmore, a poet, who is a sub-librarian" (L, IV, 55).

[145] "University|?", "Trinity . . . Cambridge|?", and "1 ⟨o⟩500 ⟨o⟩500 . . . Colman" are inserted in pencil. "Colman" may be Henry Colman, a Unitarian minister studying agriculture in England whose name appears in the Carlyle-Emerson correspondence.

[146] "It would . . . employment." is struck through in pencil with a vertical use mark.

wild poetic legendary melody spread over all the land. With what good taste the aristocracy, too, choose & use their own.

Ah! There is a nation completely appointed, and perhaps conveniently small.

"Barbarous names have much emphasis, great conciseness, & less ambiguity, variety, & multitude.
The Barbarians are stable in their manners, & firmly continue to employ the same words. Hence they are dear to the Gods." Jamblichus [147]

[81] St Paul's is, as I remembered it, a very handsome noble architectural exploit, but singularly unaffecting. When I formerly came to it from the Italian cathedrals, I said, "Well, here is New York." It seems the best of show-buildings, a fine British vaunt, but there is no moral interest attached to it.

[82] R[ichard Monckton]M[ilnes] told of Landor that he threw his ⟨how⟩ cook out of the window, & then exclaimed, "Good God! I never thought of those poor violets!" He said[n] that he had talked with the son ⟨Arnold⟩ & told him he must be on his guard against his father's furious fits. "O no," he replied, "I just keep out of the way when the fit comes, & besides I am getting stronger every day & he is getting weaker"[.]
L thinks that our custom of eating ⟨together⟩ in company is very barbarous, & he eats alone with half closed windows because the light interferes with the taste. A tribe in Crim Tartary he has heard of who eat alone, much superior to the English, of course. L walking in London came to the top of a street [83] full of people & foamed at the mouth with indignation.
Good story of Merriwether's[—] no portrait.[148]

---

[147] Jamblichus, *On the Mysteries of the Egyptians, Chaldeans, and Assyrians*, trans. Thomas Taylor (Chiswick, 1821), p. 298, in Emerson's library; see *JMN*, VIII, 74–75. In the left margin of p. [80], next to "consciseness", "38" is written and circled in pencil. "One cannot . . . their own." and "'Barbarous names . . . Jamblichus", struck through in pencil with vertical use marks, are used in "Aristocracy," *W*, V, 179.
[148] "RM told . . . portrait." is in pencil. "RM told . . . indignation.",

Mr MacGrath, secretary of the Athenaeum, told me that Sir Thomas Lawrence charged him never to put a print in a gilt frame, but a dark print in oak & a light one in maple wood.[149]

T[homas]B[abington]M[acaulay] said that he had arrested ⟨a bill⟩ on its progress to be printed[,] a bill for civilizing & Christianizing the natives of   in Africa appropriating thousand pounds ⟨and⟩ 1. for an expense of for adjusting pipes &c on the ↑paddle↓ wheels of [a] steamboat for squirting hot water, ⟨on the⟩⟨as a means of defence,⟩ on the natives.[150]

Two seasons every night in which the House of C[ommons] was ferocious, at the dinner hour by hunger & at 2 o'clock by sleep[.] [151]

[84] [152] Mr A had made £30 000 in one year by his profession[.] [153]

Milnes has great range, from Archbishop to chartist, fraternizes with all[.] [154]

↑Samuel Rogers.↓
S[amuel]. R[ogers] said on hearing the marriage of ↑the younger↓ Miss ↑⟨Charlotte⟩↓ Cushman with ⟨Lord⟩Mr. Musprat, that he always understood that at the end of the season Miss C↑⟨harlotte⟩↓. was to marry her sister.[155]

---

struck through in pencil with single vertical use marks on pp. [82] and [83], is transcribed in Notebook ED, pp. [147]–[149] below.

[149] Edward Magrath was secretary of the Athenaeum Club from 1824 to 1855. Emerson was elected a member for the duration of his stay in England, as he reported to his wife in a letter of March 23 and 24, 1848 (L, IV, 42).

[150] Emerson dined with Macaulay and others at the Bancrofts' on March 14, 1848 (L, IV, 37); he described Macaulay in a letter as "the king of diners-out" (L, IV, 42).

[151] "TBM . . . sleep", in pencil, is struck through in pencil with a vertical use mark.

[152] Pp. [84]–[86] are in pencil.

[153] On March 23, 1848, Emerson reported to his wife that he had recently met "a certain brilliant Mr Charles Austin . . . who makes or 'has made £30,000 in one year by his profession,' (of law)" (L, IV, 41). Cf. "Eloquence," W, VII, 80.

[154] This sentence, struck through in pencil with two vertical use marks, is transcribed in Notebook ED, p. [141] below; cf. also p. [17] above.

[155] In 1848 the Boston-born Susan Cushman (1822–1859) had married Dr. James

When S[usan]. C[ushman]. asked him whether he should not go to America, he replied that "it had always been his intention to visit America before he died, but now that I have seen *you* I have no longer any desire to do so."[156]

[85] The London tailor tells you that your coat was of a French or American fashion & would be noticed but here is a coat that you may go ↑⟨with⟩↓ into any ⟨other⟩ part of the world with[n] & it will not be noticed.[157]

Chadwick offers to get pure water for every house ⟨at a penny a day⟩ 60 gallons to every head, at a penny a week. And T. C. sees that the only religious act which a man nowadays can securely perform is to wash himself well.[158]

[86] Mr Owen explained the process by which the bird roosts without falling in sleep & that by which the ostrich outspeeds the racer[:] the forepart of the body flying[,] the hind part running[.]

When the wings of the bird are widespread all the air cells are distended[.]

Spallanzani thought birds swallowed pebbles from stupidity[.] [159]

Sheridan Muspratt, of Liverpool; her sister Charlotte (1816–1876), a singer and actress, played male as well as female stage parts.

[156] The inserted heading is set off above by a curved line, in pencil. "S. R . . . so.' " is transcribed in Notebook ED, p. [115] below.

[157] This sentence is struck through in pencil with a vertical use mark. In Notebook England and Paris, p. [20] below, Emerson recorded payment for a frock coat in London on March 12, 1848.

[158] "Chadwick . . . well." is struck through in pencil with a diagonal use mark. See p. [59] above.

[159] Richard Owen (1804–1892), the comparative anatomist and zoologist, had given Emerson a card of admission to his lectures at the Royal College of Surgeons in London and shown him through the Hunterian Museum, as Emerson reported to his wife on March 23, 1848 (L, IV, 41); in Notebook Xenien, below, are a reference to "Owen's Marsupial Carnivora", p. [5], and what may be notes on one of Owen's lectures, pp. [25]–[26]. Lazzaro Spallanzani (1729–1799) was an Italian naturalist. "Mr Owen . . . stupidity", struck through in pencil with a vertical use mark, is transcribed in Notebook ED, p. [121] below.

[87] B[arry].C[ornwall]. said that he knew Wordsworth very well early. He had no personal friend. He was not amiable. He would receive anything but never gave. He would spend well enough, when Lord Lonsdale came to see him. It was Sir James Lowther who was the Sir Giles Overreach, who ruined the elder Wordsworth, who was his steward. The last Lord Lonsdale had given to the Wordsworths (four) 10,000 pounds in consideration of the debts of his father to them.[160]

↑In Aug. 10, 1848. L[or]d. John Russell asks in H[ouse]. of Commons, "What was it that had induced people to lay out capital to the extent of £.300 000 000 on railways in this country within the past few years."↓ [161]

[88] [162] In America we fancy that we live in a new & forming country but that England was finished long ago. But we find London & England in full growth[,] the British Museum not yet arranged[,] the board/s/ing/ only taken down the other day from the monument & fountains of Trafalgar Square[.] [163]

Two poles here gather[:] all the wealth & all the poverty[.]

[89] If I stay here long, I shall lose all my patriotism,[n] & think that England has absorbed all excellences.
⟨I look at⟩ ↑My friend A[lcott]. came↓ here & brought away a couple of mystics & their shelf of books from Ham Common, & fancied that nothing was left in England, & I see that Kew Gardens & so many ↑great↓ men & things are obscure.[164]

---

[160] "B.C. . . . them.", in pencil and struck through in pencil with a vertical use mark, is transcribed in Notebook ED, pp. [252]–[253] below. The paragraph also has its parallel in a letter of April 20, 1848, from Emerson to his wife (L, IV, 57–58).
[161] This sentence, struck through in pencil with a vertical use mark, is used in "Wealth," W, V, 160.
[162] Pp. [88]–[92] are in pencil.
[163] "In America . . . Square" is struck through in pencil with a vertical use mark.
[164] "If I . . . obscure." is struck through in pencil with a vertical use mark. The "mystics" were Charles Lane (1800?–1870) and Henry G. Wright (1814?–1846); see JMN, VIII, 303.

I look at the immense wealth & the solid power concentrated, & am quite faint: then I look in the street at the little girls running barefoot thro' the rain with broom in hand to beg a ↑half↓ penny of the passenger at the crossing & so many Lascars & pitifullest trades & think of Saadi who barefooted saw the man [90] who had no legs, & bemoaned himself no more.[165]

At Oxford, in the Bodleian Library Mr Bandinell showed me the manuscript of Plato of the date, AD 896, brought by Dr Clarke from Egypt, and a complete MS of Virgil of the 9th Century also. Also the first Bible, printed at Mentz 1450(?) and a duplicate of the same which had been deficient in about 20 leaves at the end. But in Venice, he bought a room full of books & Mss for 4000 louis d'ors, ⟨& had⟩ every scrap & fragment, & had the doors locked & sealed by the Consul, & in examining his purchase he found the deficient pages of his Bible perfect & brought them to Oxford & placed them triumphantly in the Volume but will not have [91] it new bound. The oldest building here is 200 years younger than the frail Mss I just now mentioned. No candle or fire is ever lighted in the Bodleian. A catalogue of the Bodleian is the standard catalogue of every library here, and, if the College has the book, they underscore the name of it. But the theory is, that the Bodleian has all books.
I saw a Clarendon's History interleaved with all appertaining scraps, songs, caricatures, portraits on a like plan with Clark's Sartor at home. One chamber is filled with "topography of England" alone. One with Mr Douce's ⟨3⟩20 000 books[.] [166]

[92] In Merton which is the oldest college, I found books still chained to the shelves.[167]

---

[165] See Sa'adi, Ch. 3, Tale XIX, in *The Gulistan or Rose Garden*, trans. Francis Gladwin, 1808, p. 139; *JMN*, IX, 39.
[166] Emerson visited Oxford on March 30–April 1, 1848; see *L*, IV, 47–48. Bulkeley Bandinel, D.D. (1781–1861), was librarian of the Bodleian. Edward Daniel Clarke, LL.D. (1769–1822), traveler, antiquary, mineralogist, wrote *Travels in Various Countries of Europe, Asia, and Africa* (1816–1824). Francis Douce (1757–1834), English antiquary, left his library to the Bodleian. "At Oxford . . . books", struck through in pencil with single vertical use marks on pp. [90] and [91], is used in "Universities," *W*, V, 203–204.
[167] This sentence, struck through in pencil with a vertical use mark, is used in "Universities," *W*, V, 201.

In New College that is Winchester College I found William of Wykeham's motto, "Manners makyth man" on the gates.[168]
The students throughout the University are locked up every night[.]
Dr Daubeny told me that no duel had ever occurred at Oxford.[169]

[93] boating, cricket, archery, riding costumes
There's nothing new or true — and no matter,[n] said the country gentleman[.] [170]

It is usual for every nobleman, or indeed for almost every wealthy student on quitting college, to leave behind him as a memento some article of plate. & the number of such persons who annually leave in the larger colleges cannot be less than ten or fifteen.[171]

——

"*Seven* years residence is the theoretic period for a master's degree. In point of fact, it has long been 3 years residence, & 4 years more of standing. This 3 years is about 21 months in all."
See Huber Vol II. p. 304 [note] [172]

"a knowledge of the classics connected more with an ability to quote passages than aught else" [Huber, II, 304]

[94] [April 1, 1848.] In Sir Thomas Lawrence's (?) collection were the cartoons of Raphael & Michel Angelo, inestimable, but offered to Oxford University for £7000. They collected 3000 &

[168] This sentence is struck through in pencil with a curved vertical use mark.
[169] Charles Giles Daubeny, M.D. (1795–1867), was a professor of chemistry at Oxford. "The students . . . Oxford.", struck through in pencil with a vertical use mark, is used in "Universities," *W*, V, 200.
[170] "boating . . . gentleman" is in pencil. "There's nothing . . . gentleman", struck through in pencil with a vertical use mark, is used in "Montaigne," *W*, IV, 154, where it is attributed to a "languid gentleman at Oxford."
[171] This paragraph, struck through in pencil with a vertical use mark, is used in "Universities," *W*, V, 202.
[172] Victor Aimé Huber, *The English Universities*, trans. Francis W. Newman, 2 vols. in 3 (London, 1843). This and the following quotation are struck through in pencil with a vertical use mark; " '*Seven* years . . . in all.' " is used in "Universities," *W*, V, 204.

among other ⟨fu⟩ friends called on Lord Eldon to subscribe. Instead of £100 he put down his name for £3000 to their great delight. They said they should very easily raise the rest. No, he said, your men have probably contributed all they can spare. I can as well give the rest & he withdrew his cheque for 3 000 & wrote £4 000.

I saw the whole collection this day 1 April in the Randolph Gallery.[173]

[95] At Kew Gardens which enclose in all more than 600 acres Sir William Hooker showed us his new glass Palm house 362 ft. long, 100 wide, by 66 high; which cost £40,000.[174] The whole Garden an admirable work of English power & taste. Good as Oxford or the British Museum. No expense spared. All climates searched. The Echinocactus visnaga which is 1000 years old, cost many hundred pounds to transport it from the mountains in Mexico, to the sea. Here was tea growing, green & black, here was clove, cinnamon, chocolate, lotus, caoutchouc, gutta percha, kava [175]

[96] The English are more abroad than they are at home. The English hold their government responsible for the success of measures. If the measure turns out well for the trade of the island, they sustain ministers; if not, they oust them. Hence, they must have great intellectual ability in the government. For the whole administration is a *tour de force*.

The whole fabric is [97] [176] artificial & can only be maintained by ability of administration.[177]

---

[173] "In Sir . . . Gallery.", in pencil and struck through in pencil with a vertical use mark, is used in "Universities," *W*, V, 202–203, where the anecdote is attributed to "My friend Doctor J." — i.e., William Jacobson, the Regius Professor of Divinity at Oxford, with whom Emerson breakfasted (*L*, IV, 47).

[174] Emerson visited Kew Gardens on April 5, 1848; for the date, see *L*, IV, 50, n. 182. Sir William Jackson Hooker, his host, had been director of the gardens since 1841, introducing such notable improvements as the palm house, completed in 1848. In "Personal," *W*, V, 293, Emerson lists the occasion among "two or three signal days" he had spent in London.

[175] The entry is continued on p. [98].

[176] "*Oxford*" is written in ink as an index heading at the top of this page.

[177] "The English . . . administration." is struck through in pencil with single vertical use marks on pp. [96] and [97]. "The whole fabric . . . administration." is used in "Ability," *W*, V, 93–94.

Jan. 1842	5 & 6 000 *names*
	Members
University College	207
Balliol	257
Merton	124
Exeter	299
Oriel	293
Queens	351
New	157
Lincoln	141
All Souls	98
Magdalen	165
Brazennose	418
Corpus Christi	127
Christ Church	949
Trinity	259
St Johns	218
Jesus	167
Wadhams	217
Pembroke	189
Worcester	231

↑See De Quincey vol V↓ [178]

[98] [179] upas, baobab, orotava, the papaw which makes tough meat tender, the graphtophyllum pictum or caricature-plant on whose leaves were several good Punch portraits ⟨eng⟩visible to me, (lately, there was one so good of Lord Brougham appeared, that all men admired;) the ivory nut; the stretibzja Regina, named for Queen Charlotte, one of the gayest flowers in nature, it looked like a bird, and all but sung; the papyrus; the banian; a whole greenhouse or "stove" full of wonderful orchises, which are the rage of England now,

[178] See Thomas De Quincey, *Works*, 14 vols. (London, 1853–1860), V, 51–52: a discussion of the relations between the several Oxford colleges and the English public schools. The insertion is in pencil; it may have been added as late as 1856, when vol. V of the edition cited was published.

[179] This page continues the entry begun on p. [95].

↑See Account of Kew in Lond[on] Athen[a]eum for July 1850↓ [180]

[99] [181] Sidney Smith said of Whewell, that science was his forte & omniscience was his foible[.] [182]

T[homas]. C[arlyle]. thought the clubs remarkable signs of times. That union was no longer sought, but only the association of men who would not offend one another. There was nothing to do but they could eat better[.]

He was very serious about the bad times. He had seen it coming, but thought ⟨he should be⟩ it would not come in his time. But now it is coming, and the only good he sees in it, is the visible appearance of the gods. He thinks it the only question for wise men, &, instead of art, & fine fancies, & poetry, & such things especially as Tennyson plays with, ↑to address themselves to the problem of society↓[;] he sees this confusion to be the inevitable end of such falsehood & nonsense as they have been[.] [183]

[100] T. C. said, There are about 70,000 of these people who make what is called "Society." ↑Of course, they do not need to make any acquaintance with new people like Americans.↓

It costs £4000 to keep a house of L[or]d. Ashburton's empty. The aristocracy spend most of their money on houses. They might be little providences on earth & they did nothing[.] [184]

Plato was very unsatisfactory reading. Very tedious. The use of intellect not to know that it was there, but to do something with it[.] [185]

---

[180] Emerson is citing an unsigned article, "Kew Gardens," *The Athenæum* (London), No. 1187, July, 1850, 789–790. The addition is in pencil.

[181] This page is in pencil.

[182] William Whewell (1794–1866), philosopher and mathematician, was professor of moral philosophy and master of Trinity College, Cambridge. This sentence is struck through in pencil with a diagonal use mark.

[183] "T. C. . . . . been", struck through in pencil with a vertical use mark, is transcribed and completed in Notebook ED, pp. [208]–[209] below.

[184] "It costs . . . nothing" is in pencil; "Ld." is rewritten in ink. "T. C. said . . . nothing" is struck through in pencil with a vertical use mark; "T. C. said . . . Society.' " is used in "Aristocracy," *W*, V, 198.

[185] "Plato . . . it" is in pencil.

[101] ↑$750. a year at Cambridge is decidedly economical, & $1500 not extravagant[.] Bristed
All necessaries of life cost twice as much as at New Haven.↓ [186]

John will have you in the wrong[.]
    I don't like him. He don't eat supper.
    Yes but he has no appetite[.]
    Well, if he had not stuffed himself so immoderately at dinner, he would have an appetite.
    It is cold. If the snow had fallen two days ago, it would have lasted till now & given you as pretty a winter as we have in America[.]
    Yes but it makes such a deal of dirt when it goes that we don't like it.[187]

↑Expenses of private tuition may be set down at 175. per annum or above $600. for the whole course of 3½ years[.]   Bristed↓ [188]

[102] Oxford, House of Commons, British Museum, York Minster, Times Newspaper, Kew Gardens, Punch, Hyde Park Corner

———

Universities educate *gentlemen.*   RS 244 [189]

———

"The whole expense of ordinary college tuition at Oxford is about sixteen guineas a *year.*"   *Sewell* p 178 [190]

---

[186] Charles Astor Bristed, *Five Years in an English University*, 1852, II, 153. The first of these two sentences, struck through in pencil with a curved vertical use mark, is used in "Universities," *W*, V, 205.
    [187] "John will . . . it." is in pencil.
    [188] Charles Astor Bristed, *Five Years in an English University*, 1852, II, 154. "Expenses . . . years", struck through in pencil with a vertical use mark, is used in "Universities," *W*, V, 205.
    [189] Journal RS will be published in a later volume. This and the following entries on p. [102] must have been written not earlier than the first three months of 1849, when p. [244] of Journal RS was inscribed, and possibly much later; the writing resembles that in Notebook ED, inscribed in 1852–1853. Note the entry on p. [101] above of material from Bristed's *Five Years in an English University*, published in 1852.
    [190] The quoted sentence, struck through in pencil with a vertical use mark, is

University. See *RS* 102 ↑103↓ for Memoranda of Oxford

[103] Sir Thomas (?) Lucy at Charlcote ha⟨d⟩s 7000 acres, and his income is 14 000 pounds sterling, a year. When his second son was born, he was much at a loss how to provide for him. He took the advice of Mr Flower's grandfather, bred the boy for the church, & gave him the living of this parish.[191]

[104] Mr W. said, that the old Walter was printer of The Times, & had arranged the whole materiel of it and he demanded a small share in the proprietary; but was refused. Then he said, Do as you please, gentlemen, and if you will not grant it, why then you may take away the Times from this office whenever you will, and I shall publish the New Times next Monday morning. The proprietors[,] who had already complained that his charges for printing were too high, found that they were in his hands, [105] and gave him whatever he wished.[192]

[10⟨5½⟩6] 10th of April was the day of the Chartist demonstration. 150 000 special constables were sworn. For the first time the aristocracy exerted themselves.[193]

————

40 *per cent* of the English people cannot write their names. One half of one *per cent* of the Massachusetts people cannot, & these are probably Britons born[.] [194]

————

used in "Universities," *W*, V, 204–205, where it is attributed to "Professor Sewel" — possibly James Edward Sewell or William Sewall, both of Oxford; the work cited here has not been identified.

[191] As indicated by entries in Notebook England and Paris, p. [40] below, and Journal LM, p. [75] below, Emerson heard this story from Edward Fordham Flower of Stratford; he used it in "Wealth," *W*, VI, 117–118. Below this entry is a computation, in pencil: 21 × 24 × 16 = 8064.

[192] "Mr W. . . . wished." is used in "The Times," *W*, V, 264–265. "Mr W." is probably John Walter III (1818–1894), who had become sole manager of the *Times* on the death of his father ("the old Walter") in 1847.

[193] This paragraph, struck through in pencil with a vertical use mark, is used in "Aristocracy," *W*, V, 184.

[194] This paragraph is struck through in pencil with a vertical use mark. The same material appears in Journal RS, p. [90]; Journal RS will be published in a later volume.

It is certain that more people speak English correctly, in the United States, than in Britain.

[10⟨5 2/3⟩7] ⟨Mr Dickens said⟩The Government [195] offers free passage to Australia for 25 000 women. In A. are six men to one woman. Miss Coutts has established a school to teach poor girls taken out of the street how to read & write & make a pudding & be a colonist's wife. They do very well so long as they are there but when it comes to embarking for Australia they prefer to go back to the London street, though in these times it would seem as if they must eat the pavement. Such is the absurd love of home of English race, said Dickens[.] [196]

[108] [197] 15 April at the British Museum with the Bancrofts under the guidance of Sir Charles Fellows. [198] Lycian art. The triumphal Temple plagiarism of the Parthenon. Exact truth & fitness of every particular of Greek work. There are ten statues because ten cities sent aid out of 13. Every statue stands on an emblem, as crab, dove, snake, &c which the coins now show to be the *arms* of the ten cities. The gods are at the eastern end.
The friezes describe accurately the siege of the city[.]
The reconstruction of the Temple, like that of the Dinornis[,] the most beautiful work of archaic science. ↑Hist[ory], Geology, Chemistry, & good sense.↓
The temple itself imitates ↑in stone↓ the old carpentry of the country still visible in the huts of the peasantry. And is an ark. The women wear the same ornaments. The boys have the same tuft of hair[.]

---

[195] "The Government" is written over "Mr Dickens said", which is in pencil and partially erased.
[196] "The Government . . . Dickens", in pencil, is transcribed in Notebook ED, p. [223] below. Above the present entry Edward Emerson has noted: "Dickens told this to RWE, see *ED*". Emerson met Dickens at dinner on April 25, 1848, at the home of John Forster (see Pocket Diary 3, p. [70] below) "and liked him very well" (*L*, IV, 66). "Miss Coutts" is the philanthropist Angela Georgina Burdett, who had assumed the surname Coutts on inheriting the fortune of her grandfather Thomas Coutts in 1837.
[197] Pp. [108]–[112] are in pencil.
[198] In "Personal," *W*, V, 293, Emerson lists the occasion among "two or three signal days" he had spent in London.

[109] The inscriptions are calculated for the perspective ⟨so⟩ in the size of the letters, so that when printed of equal size they assume a pyramidal form. The Parthenon is also of a perspective architecture, & has no straight lines. The line of the roof ⟨ri⟩ curves upward a little, being ⟨a curve⟩ an arc of a circle of /eight/seven/ miles. So the Panathenaic frieze is beautiful if lighted from below, as it is on the Parthenon. Otherwise the feet of horses seem finished, & the heads of men bald[.]
The ϕasia [199]

Illustration of Homer & Herodotus
England holds these things for mankind & holds them well. Conservative[,] she is conservator.

[110] The gorse or furze is said never to be quite out of bloom. The girl who did not like her suitor declared she would marry him when the gorse was out of bloom. Every day she took her walk, & every day she brought home a flower.[200]

Houses of Parliament a magnificent document of English power, & of their intention to make it last.
Houses cover eight acres[.]
Built of Bolsover stone and a wonderful sample of the delight the English have in spending money. ↑But there is no single view commanding great lines (only, when it is finished, the speaker of the H[ouse] of C[ommons] will be able with a telescope to see the Lord Chancellor.) But mankind can so rarely build a house covering eight acres, that 'tis pity to deprive them of the joy of seeing a mass, & grand & lofty lines.↓ [201]

[111] Owen said he fell in with a sentinel in crossing the French

---

[199] Emerson followed "The" with what appears to be a Greek phi — possibly as the beginning of a Greek word — but which may be an English G; "asia" is at best a conjectural reading of the next four letters. His intended meaning or reference remains obscure.

[200] This paragraph is struck through in pencil with a vertical use mark.

[201] See p. [10] above. "Houses of . . . lines." is struck through in pencil with a vertical use mark.

frontier who cried out, "Who are you?" Mr Arnott said, he should have replied, "The creature of circumstances." [202]

The admirable working of Demand & supply in keeping things right & in keeping people informed.

L[or]d. John Russell would take the command of the channel fleet[.] [203]

Very evang[elical] lady wanted the comp[an]y to subscribe to send [a] missionary to India. The people believed in devils & worshipped devils. Yes said the Uncle ⟨&⟩ I tell you my dear those are no jokes of devils, those in India; they actually eat or cause to be destroyed one per cent of the population. But, niece, they ⟨have⟩ worship devils too in Europe and news were just brought that this is creeping into [112] England, and, instead of one per cent, they say ⟨these⟩ ↑their↓ devil sends to eternal damnation nineteen out of every twenty. The niece who had expected a contribution to her missionary purse, shut her eyes & her mouth. [204]

⟨April⟩ Decent [n] debility said Sidney Smith of the clergy[.]
'Tis a long step from the cromlechs to York Minster. [205]

Col Thompson's theory of Primogeniture, is, that it is to make one son⟨e⟩ strong enough to force the public to support all the rest. [206]

---

[202] Perhaps an allusion to Napoleon, who called himself "the child of circumstance." See *JMN*, V, 226, IX, 65. Neil Arnott (1788–1874) was a Scottish physician and inventor with whom Emerson dined at the home of John Minter Morgan on May 4, 1848 (*L*, IV, 71; Pocket Diary 3, p. [72] below).

[203] This sentence, struck through in pencil with a vertical use mark, is used in "Manners," *W*, V, 102.

[204] "Very evang . . . mouth." is transcribed in Notebook ED, p. [152] below, where it is identified as "Dr Arnott's Story".

[205] "'Tis . . . Minster.", struck through in pencil with a vertical use mark, is used in "Land," *W*, V, 38.

[206] "Col . . . rest." is struck through in pencil with a vertical use mark. The same passage occurs in "notes on English politics . . . used in lectures" on Emerson's return from England, quoted in *W*, V, 364–365. Emerson heard Thomas Peronnet Thompson, known as the "Father of Free Trade," when he attended the Free Trade banquet at Manchester on January 27, 1848 (*L*, IV, 12).

[113] I have never heard, I believe, but one man in England speak of "Our Saviour."

At the dinner of the Geological Club, I sat between Sir Henry Delabeche & Lord Selkirk. When I remarked, that I understood the accepted view of the creation of races to be, that many individuals appeared simultaneously, & not one pair only, Lord S. ⟨remark⟩replied, that there was no geological fact which is at variance with the Mosaic History.[207]

[114] In London, ⟨you⟩ one sees that nature aims at certain types of face in thousands of individual faces. For, you shall see close approaches to every kind of face you know in America.

[115] Coventry Patmore described Tennyson as spending the evening with a dozen friends as nearly his own equals as any that could be collected, but Tennyson would not say one word, but sat with his pipe silent, and, at last, said, 'I am going to Cheltenham; I have had a glut of men.' When he himself proposed one day to read to Tennyson a poem⟨,⟩ which he had just finished,[208] that Tennyson might tell him of anything which his taste would exclude T replied, "Mr Patmore, you can have no idea how many applications of this sort are made to me." [209]

[116] [210] 25 April. Dined with Mr Forster, Carlyle & Dickens, & young Pringle. Forster called Carlyle's passion Musketworship. Disraeli↓, thought C., betrayed whoredom; & all the house of commons universal incontinence. Chastity was given up in Europe. L. Hunt thought it indifferent. Dickens said 'twas so much the rule that he should be scared if his son were particularly chaste[.] [211]

---

[207] Emerson attended the dinner on April 5, 1848, by invitation of the Club's president, Sir Henry De la Beche (L, IV, 49, 51; Pocket Diary 3, p. [64] below). "I have . . . History." is struck through in pencil with a vertical use mark.

[208] The comma is added in pencil.

[209] "Coventry . . . me.' ", struck through in pencil with a vertical use mark, is transcribed in Notebook ED, pp. [278]–[279] below.

[210] Pp. [116]–[120] are in pencil.

[211] "25 April . . . chaste", struck through in pencil with a vertical use mark, is expanded in Notebook ED, pp. [221], [223] below. In the top margin above "Mr Forster" is a penciled note: "See ED 221–23".

No king in Europe who believed he had any right there except the Czar.[212] O quite ready to go[.]

"Kicking up tranquillity" & "I have the honor to be"

[117] Here was much foothold as is always in England, foothold everywhere[.]

Napier of the Edin[burgh] Review was named Napier McVay but seeing the talent & reputation of the Napiers he thought it would be a good speculation to turn his name upside down so he bought prints & pictures of all the Logorithmic & Naval Napiers & set up for a man of genius & passed for that till this day.[213]

[118] Owen told the story of Buckland's objection to the gigantic Rat who pulled down the trees of the elder world that he would get killed by their fall & when the skull of one was examined it was found *double*, of an immoderate thickness, & also with great fractures healed over.[214]

The Jerboa rat & other animals of that kind in enormous numbers [—] prolific [—] have their function to destroy corrupt animal matter & are like the infusoria in that office[.]

The Bat analogous to the cetacea[:] one mammal adapted to swim & one to fly. Then again to the mole & shrew[,] one moving by displacing air & the other earth. Spallanzani blinded & deafened a bat & strung threads across the room [119] & the bat flew without touching them. ⟨Hybernation is the⟩ Sleep is the hybernation of the day. Hybernation the sleep of the year. Light is not the exciting cause always for some animals wake in dark & sleep in day. ⟨Nor⟩

---

[212] Evidently a remark by Carlyle: see p. [59] above.

[213] The reference is to Macvey Napier (1776–1847), who became editor of the *Edinburgh Review* in 1829. According to the *Dictionary of National Biography*, XIV, 68, he changed his name "in deference to a wish of his grandfather."

[214] "healed over" appears to be rewritten over pencil writing which is unrecovered. William Buckland (1784–1856) was an English geologist.

Light ⟨it⟩ was thought the exciting cause in sleep, & Heat in hybernation. And yet there were animals who sleep during the hottest & driest part of the equatorial year. The hybernation is determined by the season of food. The bat living on insects would die when the insects died but now he sleeps thro' this long fast without respiration[.]

Mr Owen is an excellent lecturer with perfect self command & temperance, master of his wide nomenclature, & stepping securely from stone to stone[.] [215]

[120] Among the trades of despair [216] is the searching the filth of the sewers for rings, shillings, teaspoons, &c which have been washed out of the sinks. ⟨Mr Col⟩ These sewers are so large that you can go underground great distances. Mr Colman saw a man coming out of the ground with a bunch of candles. "Pray Sir Where did you come from?" "O I've been seven miles,"[n] the man replied. They say that Chadwick rode all under London on a little brown pony.

Lud-gate still keeps the hoary memory of Lud's town. Lud[,] son of Beli is represented in the romantic chronicles as the elder brother of Cassivellaunus who fought with Julius Caesar[.]

[121] Dr Carpenter's microscopes magnify 1500 diameters and 225 000 surfaces[.] [217]

Henry de Blois nephew of Henry I was made by him Bishop of Winchester 1128–9, & founded the Hospital of St Cross 1136. Winchester Cathedral is 556 ft long by 290 broad in transept.

[215] The entries on pp. [118] and [119] evidently refer to one of Richard Owen's lectures; cf. Notebook Xenien, p. [67] below. "Owen told . . . stone", struck through in pencil with single vertical use marks on both pages, is transcribed in Notebook ED, pp. [120], [122]–[124] below. On hibernation, cf. "Fate," W, VI, 37.

[216] See p. [72] above.

[217] This sentence is in pencil. William Benjamin Carpenter was Fullerian Professor of Physiology at the Royal Institution. Emerson heard him speak at a meeting of the Geological Society on March 22, 1848; on April 4 he dined with Carpenter and on April 6 heard him lecture (L, IV, 42, 51; Pocket Diary 3, p. [64] below).

The crypt was built in part in the early part of the 4th Century. The first story of the transept by Kenelwalch 1 AD 584/648[;] other parts of the Cathedral by Walkelyn 1079. Then Wykeham

In Winchester, Alfred was crowned & was buried.[218]

[122][219] J Francis came with his triedron & described his life[:] "For three years" he said "I was in a perpetual glow of heavenly gratification[;] my workshop & my bookroom[220] were the same" but he had their crazy punning, "Manual Emanuel." "Intellect," he said, "modifies its bounds, is a modifying instructor." He admired Alcott[:] "The initions flow with him exceedingly. Every inition is a positive law." It was pathetic to see this savage of figures.[221]

Mr B. with his courteous manners & real excellence saw Malibran at the opera in former days. And when the actress was to cross the ruined arch, he rose in his place & assured the actress & the audience, that "the bridge [123][222] is cracked."[223]

Dr Ashburner ⟨informs⟩ ↑tells↓ me, that he suspended a gold ring by a filament of silk & willed it to approach him, & it swung towards him; and this experiment succeeded twice.

Mr Sylvester.[224] Pauperism always accrues in English arrangements. Like sediment from brackish water incrusting the locomotive & choking it. Prisons breed prisons, workhouses workhouses. Army,

---

[218] "Henry de Blois . . . buried." is used in "Stonehenge," *W*, V, 289–290.

[219] This page is in pencil.

[220] Although there is a pencil line through "room" it appears to have been made accidentally rather than to indicate a cancellation.

[221] Presumably the "John Francis" whose London address is listed in Pocket Diary 3, p. [34] below.

[222] This page is in pencil.

[223] This paragraph is used in "Truth," *W*, V, 125, where "Mr B." is identified as "a very worthy man, — a magistrate, I believe he was, in the town of Derby." Maria Felicia Malibran (1808–1836) was a French opera singer.

[224] Probably Charles Sylvester, civil engineer, author of *The Philosophy of Domestic Economy* (Nottingham, 1819). In a letter of May 4 and 5, 1848, to his wife, Emerson mentioned "a Mr Sylvester, an architect . . . who invites me to the Engineers' Society" (*L*, IV, 68); see p. [129] below.

Government, Church all have their pauperism & the means of remedy directly are found to have theirs.

[124] In Westminster Abbey, I was surprised to find the tombs cut & scrawled with penknives, and even in the coronation chair in which ⟨Queen⟩ is contained the royal stone of Scone & in which for hundreds of years the Kings & Queens of England have been crowned, Mr Butter & Mr Light, and Mr Abbott have recorded their humble pretensions to be remembered[:] "I Butter slept[n] in this chair" is explicitly recorded by that gentleman's penknife on the seat.[225]

At Liverpool, ⟨M⟩Rev. David Thom invited me to his house. I fixed an evening, & went.[226] Mr Thom introduced me particularly to all his guests, &, on my return to Manchester, on the following [125][n] day, I received a letter from him, — I think, of three sheets, — describing biographically all of the company, & not only so, but those persons who were invited & failed to come. This was a supererogation of hospitality which I never met elsewhere.

↑Nobility. See Campbell's remark in *BO* 71↓ [227]

[126] I wonder the young people are so eager to see Carlyle. It is like being hot to see the Mathematical or the Greek professor, before you have got your lesson.
They fancy it needs only clean shirt & palaver. If the genius is true, it needs genius[.] [228]

[127] The Englishman is finished like a seashell. After the spines & volutes are all formed, or with the formation, the hard enamel varnishes every part. Pope, Swift, Johnson, Gibbon, Goldsmith, Gray. It seems an indemnity to the Briton for his precocious maturity. He

---

[225] Emerson visited Westminster Abbey on November 28, 1847 (*L*, III, 426). This paragraph, in pencil, is struck through in pencil with a vertical use mark.
[226] On November 30, 1847 (*L*, III, 441).
[227] Journal BO will be published in a later volume.
[228] This paragraph, in pencil and struck through in pencil with a vertical use mark, is transcribed in Notebook ED, p. [228] below.

has no generous daring in this age. The Platonism died in the Elizabethan. He is shut up in French limits[.]
X X X
But Birmingham comes in, & says, 'never mind, I have some patent
lustre that defies criticism.' Moore made his whole fabric of the
lustre: as we cover houses with a shell of inconsumable paint[.] [229]

[128] ↑3 May↓ I heard Alboni sing last night in Cenerentola, &
the Times today calls it the best of her triumphs. I found only the
noble bursts of voice beautiful & the trills & gurgling & other feats
not only not interesting, but, as in all other performers, painful; mere
surgical or, rather, functional acts[.] [230]

An Englishman of fashion is like one of those souvenirs bound in
gold & vellum, enriched with delicate engravings ↑on↓ thick hot-
-pressed vellum paper fit for ladies & princes but nothing in it worth
reading or remembering.[231]

[129] Mr Sylvester told me that Mr Fa⟨e⟩rie could draw a model of
any loom or machine ⟨from⟩ ↑after↓ once seeing it, for Rees' Cyclo-
pedia, and did so in Mr Strutt's mills.[232]

Mr Hallam asked me, at Lord Ashburton's, "whether Swedenborg
were all mad, or partly knave?"
He knew nothing of Thomas Taylor, nor did Milman, nor any
Englishman.[233]

[229] "The Englishman . . . paint", struck through in pencil with two discontinuous vertical use marks, is transcribed in Notebook ED, pp. [58]–[59] below.
[230] This paragraph is in pencil. The Italian diva Marietta Alboni (1823–1894)
sang the title role in Rossini's La Cenerentola at Covent Garden with the Royal
Italian Opera on May 2, 1848, receiving two mid-opera curtain calls.
[231] This sentence, struck through in pencil with a curved vertical use mark, is
transcribed in Notebook ED, p. [69] below.
[232] John Farey (1791–1851) began drawing at the age of fourteen for various
encyclopedias, including that first published in London in 1786 by Abraham Rees:
Cyclopædia; or An Universal Dictionary of Arts and Sciences. Jedediah Strutt
(1726–1797), a partner of Richard Arkwright, built a cotton mill at Nottingham,
England; the Strutt family figures prominently in Sylvester's The Philosophy of
Domestic Economy.
[233] "Mr Hallam . . . Englishman.", struck through in pencil with a vertical

[130] [234] Tennyson no dandy. Plain, quiet, sluggish ⟨stre⟩ sense & strength; refined as all English are. Goodhumoured, totally unaffected, the print of his head in Horne too rounded & handsome[;] an air of general superiority that is very satisfactory[.]

He lives with his college set. Spedding, Brookfield, Hallam, Rice, & the rest[.] [235]

Thought Carlyle wholly mistaken in fancying the Christian religion had lost all vitality. They all feel the caprice & variety of his opinions. It is his brother Tennyson Turner, who wrote the verses which Wordsworth praised. [236]

In C[arlyle] a large caprice

[131] [237] You can't estimate a town by the number of lamps as you approach[.]

I find the French all soldiers, all speakers. The àplomb which these need, every Frenchman has. Every gamin a certain trimness or trigness & a certain fancy cut like a dandy boat at a regatta[.]

A certain ingenuity & verbal clearness of statement they require & that satisfies them that they have a new & lucid & coherent statement

---

use mark, is transcribed in Notebook ED, pp. [59]–[60] below. Emerson was at Lord Ashburton's dinner on March 24, 1848, sitting next to the historian Henry Hallam (Pocket Diary 3, p. [60] below; L, IV, 49); on March 14 he dined with the poet Henry Hart Milman at the Bancrofts' (L, IV, 37, n. 132).

[234] This page is in pencil.

[235] Emerson dined with Tennyson at the home of Coventry Patmore on May 5, 1848 (L, IV, 66; Pocket Diary 3, p. [72] below). His reference is to the frontispiece to vol. II of Richard Henry Horne, A New Spirit of the Age, 2 vols. (London, 1844). Tennyson's "college set" included James Spedding (1808–1881), Rev. William Henry Brookfield (1809–1874), Arthur Hallam (1811–1833), and Stephen Spring Rice (1814–1865); Emerson in making this entry was apparently unaware that Hallam was no longer living.

[236] Charles Tennyson had taken the name Turner in 1830; for Wordsworth's comments, see p. [46] above. "Tennyson no dandy . . . praised.", struck through in pencil with a vertical use mark, is transcribed and expanded in Notebook ED, pp. [178] and [181] below.

[237] This page is in pencil. The entries on pp. [131]–[164] concern Emerson's trip to France, May 7–June 3, 1848.

though it is artificial, & not an idea. Verbally helped & not really. M. Lambert is the servant of his literary theory. But where is the emancipation & joy that comes from new life of an idea?

I find the French intensely masculine. I find them expressive not reticent. Their heads are not so round as the English head[,] said Doherty[.] [238]

[132] From Boulogne to Paris 56 leagues
7½ mortal hours [239]

George Sand describes "l'inconstance immortelle des Français." [240]

↑22↓ May 1848
Citizen Blanqui, a lame man with the face & air of a conspirator; and Barbès (head of the Club de la Revolution,) were the leaders of the émute on the ↑22d May, I think,↓ which I saw.[241]

↑for↓ Details of May, 1848, in Paris, see "Remains of A.H. Clough" pages 100–130

---

[133] [242] 'Tis cĕrtain
       Fete du 21 Mai
Ballon tricolore 500 jolies filles les vivandieres et les cantinieres et

---

[238] Hugh Doherty, an Irish Fourierist, editor of the *London Phalanx*. Emerson had been given a letter of introduction to Doherty in Paris by J. J. G. Wilkinson (*L*, IV, 75).
      [239] "From Boulogne . . . hours" is in pencil.
      [240] See Journal GH, p. [70] above.
      [241] "22" and "22d . . . think," are added in pencil. Louis Auguste Blanqui and Armand Barbès were leaders of the French Revolution of 1848; Emerson visited their respective clubs, Club des Droits de l'homme and Club de la Revolution, while in Paris. This and the following entry, Edward Emerson noted, "were evidently written twenty years later, after Clough's death" in 1861 (*J*, VII, 462). Emerson dined daily with Clough during his stay in Paris; *The Letters and Remains of Arthur Hugh Clough* (London, 1865) is in his library.
      [242] This page is in pencil. When Journal London was microfilmed in 1955, an envelope addressed to Emerson in Concord was laid in between pp. [132] and [133]; it has since been removed.

les petits enfans de chaque sexe vetus comme soldats ou dans rubans
de fete marchant dans le cortege[.]
drum major   vast men with baton & huge cap of fur
sapeurs & pompiers

children on stilts
merrygorounds

[134] [243] In approaching Paris, it seemed a nation of soldiers[.]
The climate seemed altered & 'tis incredible that this Syrian capital[,]
all ↑the people↓ poured into the street[,] should be so near to London.
Barbés' Club
Blanqui's
Palais Royale
Theatre Francais   Rachel
Varietes   Bouffé
Porte St Martin. Le Maitre
Restaurant
Appartement garni
Chapeau Rouge

[135] [244] I was glad to leave my Mss on the table[.] [245]
'Tis certain that they are dreadfully in earnest at these clubs.
La vie à bon marché, is the idea of Paris.
l'inconstance immortelle des Francais.[246]

[136] femme incomprise
homme borné⟨e⟩
homme ⟨reglé⟩ rangé
mauvais sujet [247]
tete montée

[243] This page is in pencil.
[244] This page is in pencil.
[245] Because in Paris "nobody could read English"; see Journal LM, p. [126]
below.
[246] See p. [132] above.
[247] With "homme ⟨reglé⟩ rangé" and "mauvais sujet", cf. JMN, VIII, 27.

IMPERSONALITY OF JOURNALS. There is no other newspaper in the world which wields so great an influence as the London *Times*. It has placed itself at the head of the press in Europe, and speaks with a degree of authority which kings might envy. The individuals concerned in its management are nothing — the paper itself is everything. In its columns, public questions are continually discussed with masterly ability. It may easily be conjectured that no one mind could originate, prepare, and utter from day to day the erudite, far-reaching disquisitions which tell so powerfully upon the opinion of the world; but that is a matter of no consequence. The *Times* speaks, and its word is potential. It is a gigantic impersonality, a disembodied oracle, whose voice penetrates every corner of the civilized world, and moulds the thoughts of a large portion of the human family. Those who are familiar with the way in which machinery is made to operate, know that many pens are regularly employed upon that sheet. Yet nothing is more evident than the fact, that all its articles, from whatever source they come, bear a single impress. The *Times* utters one language. It scorns to tell the public that it disapproves of what itself has said. It never strangles its own offspring. The absence of a "responsible," or the indiscretion of an "assistant," is never proclaimed as the excuse for an acknowledged blunder. Such a practice would soon bring even that great journal into contempt.

Yet the *Times* has a "responsible editor," one who while he scarcely ever writes anything himself, carefully supervises, alters and corrects every editorial, and gives a consistent character to all the utterances of the paper. He never informs the public that nobody writes for his journal except himself, well knowing that nothing else he could say would injure it so much. Several men of learning, talent and experience, are engaged upon a liberal stipend to write regularly for its columns. They furnish articles upon such subjects as may be suggested by their principal, or by their own judgment. They are all carefully read, examined, and usually altered and corrected by the editor. No writer can have any assurance that his production will appear in the shape given it by himself; and none is ever at liberty to claim in any way the authorship of his own articles. It is thus by making the paper great, and those who conduct it nothing, that the *Times* has come to be the most considerable journal in existence. It well knows that the public care less than nothing about the individuals who sit at its desks. All its readers want is an able, intelligent, and comprehensive daily paper, and that it is careful to furnish. The machinery behind the curtain it has the sense and taste to conceal. — *Rochester American*.[248]

[248] This and the foregoing paragraph, clipped from an unidentified newspaper (which is quoting the Rochester *American*) and dated in ink along the top margin "Dec   1848[?]", are mounted on p. [136] immediately following the entries "femme . . . montée". Both the content and phrasing are used in "The Times," *W*, V, 268.

[137] [249] The architecture of Paris ⟨I⟩ compares most favorably with that of London[,] is far more original, spirited, national. Here is a royal Palace. They have spent a great deal of money & they have something to show for it. This Thuilleries, this Louvre, this Hotel de Ville, Palais de ⁿ Justice, & old tower de la Boucherie
Jacques   ↑Efflorescence of France↓ [250]

[138] But especially the grisette institution interests the young stranger[.]
The Journal L'Assemblee Nationale is high shop[.]
     La Vraie Republique[:] G Sand, Leroux, Barbés
Commune de Paris   was Sobrier
                    Dumas
La Presse, Girardin
La Réforme, Ledru Rollin
Journal des Debats   Michel Chevalier
Le Siecle Constitutionelle   Odillon Barrere
National, Marrast

                                        Leon Foucher [251]

Gustave D'Eichthal
Rome 1833 [252]

[139] And A ⁿ represents it as the highest merit of B that he stood Mrs B[.]

[249] This page is in pencil.
[250] Cf. Notebook Xenien, p. [66] below.
[251] "But especially . . . Foucher" is in pencil. "Leon Foucher" is probably Emerson's error for Jean Bernard Léon Foucault (1819–1868), a French physicist in charge of scientific articles for the *Journal des Débats*. Pierre Leroux (1797–1871) and George Sand founded the *Revue Indépendante* in 1841; Alexandre Dumas (1802–1870) was editing *La Liberté* in 1848. "Sobrier" has not been identified; the other editors or contributors named, in addition to Armand Barbès, are Emile de Girardin (1806–1881), Alexandre Auguste Ledru-Rollin (1807–1874), Michel Chevalier (1806–1879), Camille Hyacinthe Odilon Barrot — Emerson's "Odillon Barrere"? — (1791–1873), and Armand Marrast (1801–1852).
[252] As Emerson explains in Notebook ED, p. [110] below, he had met d'Eichthal (1804–1886) in Rome during his first European trip; d'Eichthal was instrumental in putting Emerson in touch with both John Stuart Mill and Carlyle.

'Tis true that a breakfast consists of a certain number of mouth-fuls[—]well in France they count the number of mouthfuls say thirty ⟨two⟩ or sixty and put a price on the mouthfuls[:] three centimes[,] five centimes a spoonful[.] [253]

Torchlight processions have a seek & slay look, dripping burning oil drops, & the bearers now & then smiting the torch on the ground, & then lifting it into the air[.]

[140] In Paris, my furnished lodgings, a very comfortable suite of rooms (15 Rue des Petits Augustins) on the second floor cost me 90 francs a month or 3 francs a day. My breakfast, which is brought to me at my chamber, & consists of bread, butter, one boiled egg, milk & coffee, costs one franc a day; my dinner at the Cafe "Cinq Arcades" in the Palais Royale costs 2 francs 2 sous and a cup of coffee in the evening 10 or 12 sous more[.] Say the expenses of living for a day, at my rate, are 6 francs 15 sous, or seven francs.

[141] In Paris, the number of beggars does not compare with that in London, or in Manchester even.
I looked in all the shopwindows for toys this afternoon, and they are very many & gay; but the only one of all ⟨they re⟩which I really wish to buy is very cheap, yet I cannot b⟨y⟩uy it, namely, their speech. I covet that which the vilest of the people possesses.
French poetry is peu de chose and in their character & performance is always prose, prose ornée, but never poesy.
Madame de Tocqueville, who is English, tells me, that the French is so beautiful a [142] language[,] so neat, concise, & lucid, that she can never bear to speak English.[254] 'Tis a peculiarity of the French that they assimilate all foreign words, & do not suffer them to be pronounced in the foreign manner. *libretto* is livret, *charivari*⟨s⟩ is *sharivari, & so on, so that every blouse in the street speaks like an academician; which is not possible in England. I do not distinguish

---

[253] "And . . . spoonful" is in pencil.
[254] On May 25, 1848, Emerson went to a soirée at the de Tocquevilles' (*L*, **IV**, 78).

between the language of a blouse talking philosophy in a group, & that of Cousin.

I understand↑,↓ from ↑young↓ Murray↑,↓ that Elihu Burritt coming hither with his 50 languages, was sadly mortified to find that he could not understand but one word in any French sentence.[255]

[143] After the pair of noble fountains which play all day, the principal ornament of the Place de la Concorde is the Obelisk brought from Thebes in the Ship Luxor, in   , gift of
    , and with admirable engineering set up here by ↑M.↓ Lebas on a huge pedestal of granite[.] [256]

The Boulevarts have lost their fine trees, which were all cut down for barricades in February. At the end of a year we shall take account, & see if the Revolution was worth the trees.

[144] J'ai promis d'y être mardi le 6 Juin.[257]

  [145] Le Club des Conspirateurs
C'est l'aristocratie de la démocratie.
Le Club des Conspirateurs déclare que la France est une terre de conspiration. Il reconnaît les droits de l'émeute, et un Conspirateur Suprême. La Conspiration est en permanence.
Il sera crée au College de France une Chaire de Conspiration.
On chargera le Citoyen Blanqui de rediger dans le silence du cabinet un manuel de conspiration à l'usage des enfans.

  [146] In the Spanish Gallery in the Louvre, it is easy to see that Velasquez & Spagnoletto were painters who understood their business.

---

[255] "young" and the commas after "understand" and "Murray" are added in pencil. Elihu Burritt (1810–1879), an American linguist and advocate of world peace, organized the Brussels Peace Congress in 1848.
 [256] The obelisk, presented to Louis Philippe by Mohammed Ali, Viceroy of Egypt, was brought to France in 1831 and erected in Paris in 1836 under the direction of J. B. Lebas.
 [257] On that day Emerson was to begin a course of six lectures at the Literary and Scientific Institution, Portman Square, London. Writing to his wife on May 17, he noted that he had just forwarded his program for the course (L, IV, 74).

I fancy them both strong swarthy men who would have made good soldiers or brigands, at a pinch. And, in running along the numberless cartoons of old masters, the eye is satisfied, that the art of expression by drawing & colour has been perfectly attained; that on that side, at least, humanity has obtained a complete transference of its thought into the symbol.

[147] These Spaniards paint with a certain ferocity. Zu↑r↓barra who paints monks, & specially one monk with a skull in his hands, which seems the reflection of his own head, is a master so far.

Zurbarra

[148] It is impossible in a French table d'hote to guess the social rank & the employment of the various guests. The ⟨un⟩military manners universal in young Frenchmen, their stately bow & salutation through their beards, are, like their beards, a screen, which a foreigner cannot penetrate.

[149] At the Club des Femmes, there was among the men some patronage, but no real courtesy. The lady who presided spoke & behaved with the utmost propriety, — a woman of heart & sense, — but the audience of men were perpetually on the look out for some équivoque, into which, of course, each ↑male↓ speaker would be pretty sure to fall; & then the laugh was loud & general.

⟨l⟩Le Club des Clubs was one which consisted of the chiefs of all the Clubs, & to which was accorded a tribune in the Assembly. But they were so dictatorial & indolent [150] that the Chamber at last mustered courage enough to silence them, &, I believe, to turn them out.

The noble buildings of Paris are, the truly palatial Thuilleries; Notre Dame; Le Palais de Justice, & the Chapel la Sainte Chapelle, adjoining it, (built by Louis IX in the 13 Century); the old tower, St Jacques de la Bucherie; l'Hotel de Ville; le Pantheon;

I went to the Pantheon & learned that the tomb of Napoleon was at the Invalides. Rousseau & Voltaire sleep under the Pantheon.

[151] I have seen Rachel in Phedre, in Mithridate, & now last night in Lucrece, (of Ponsard) in which play she took ⟨but⟩two parts[,] that of Lucrece & that of Tullia.²⁵⁸ The best part of her performance is the terror & energy she can throw into passages of defiance or denunciation. Her manners & carriage are throughout pleasing by their highly intellectual cast. And her expression of the character is not lost by ↑your↓ losing some word or look, but is continuous & is sure to be conveyed. She is extremely youthful & innocent in her appearance and when she appeared after the curtain fell to acknowledge the acclamations of the house & the heaps [152] of flowers that were flung to her, ⟨she bowed with a⟩ her smile had a perfect good nature & a kind of universal intelligence.²⁵⁹

[153] ↑May↓

At the Chamber of the National Assembly, by the kindness of Mr Rush, who lent me his diplomatic ticket. Lamartine made his speech on the question of Poland.²⁶⁰ He was quite the best and indeed the only good speaker I heard in the house. He has a fine head, and a free & superior style of delivery, manly & cultivated. But he was quite at his ease, no swords or pikes over his head this time, and really little energy in his discourse. He read many extracts from letters sent him from Italy, and when he was tired, the members cried out, Reposez vous, & the President gave an intermission for half an hour.

[154] The whole house of 900 members obviously listened with great respect & gladly to Lamartine, for they want information, and

²⁵⁸ Emerson saw Rachel in Racine's *Phèdre* on May 9 or 13, 1848; in Racine's *Mithridate* on May 17 or 18; and in *Lucrece* after May 25 and before May 31 (*L*, IV, 73, 75, 77, 79, and notes).
²⁵⁹ Pasted below this entry is a cartoon captioned "Consolation in Distress" showing a gentleman being bitten by a monkey in a cage while an attendant looks on. An advertisement, overleaf, describes the weekly *Puppet-Show*, "A Pungent Penny Pictorial Periodical!"
²⁶⁰ On May 23, 1848, as Emerson reported in a letter to his wife (*L*, IV, 77). Richard Rush (1780–1859) served as American minister to France from 1847 to 1849.

it has been rather parsimoniously given by any whom they could trust. His speech is reckoned wise & moderate. To me it looks as if a wise Frenchman should say to his country, Leave Poland & China & Oregon to themselves. You have more than enough to do, at present, in constructing your own government & dealing with disorder, hunger, & faction in France. — But Lamartine praised the new republic because it had not a moment of Egoism, but had adopted Poland & Italy.

[155] We now dine daily at a table d'hote at No 16 Rue de Notre Dame des Victoires, where 500 French habitués usually dine at 1 franc 60 centimes. Of course it is an excellent place for French grammar. Nouns, verbs, adverbs, & interjections furnished gratuitously.

I am told that there are 12 000 students connected with the University, including all the faculties. 'Tis a noble hospitality, & well calculated also, as it brings so great a population of foreigners to spend their money in France.

[156] ↑Do thy goo queek   lee ↑en Amérique↓
te mash eens↓↑?↓ [261]
Paris has great merits as a city. Its river is made the greatest pleasure to the eye by the quays & bridges: its fountains are noble & copious[,] its gardens or parks far more available to the pleasure of the people than those of London. What a convenience to the senses of men is the Palais Royal: the swarming Boulevards, what an animating ⟨stroll⟩promenade: the furnished lodgings have a seductive independence: the living is cheap & good; then what a luxury is it to have a [157] cheap wine for the national beverage as uniformly supplied as beer in England. The manners of the people & probably their inferiority as individuals make it as easy to live with them as with so many shopkeepers whose feelings & convenience are nowise to be consulted.[262] Meantime they are very civil & goodtempered,

---

[261] "Do thy . . . lee" and "te mash eens" are in pencil; "en Amérique" and the question mark are in ink.

[262] "Paris has . . . consulted." is struck through in pencil with single vertical use marks on pp. [156] and [157].

polite & joyous, and will talk in knots & multitudes in the streets all day for the entertainment of the passenger. Then they open their treasures of art & science so freely to the mere passport of the traveller [158] & to all the world on Sunday. The University, the Louvre, the Hotel de Cluny, the Institute, the Gallery of the Luxembourg, Versailles. Then the Churches are always open, Notre Dame; La Sainte Chapelle, built by St Louis, & gorgeous within; St Sulpice; the Madeleine;

Then there is the Pantheon; and there is the Jardin des Plantes worthy of admiration. Everything odd & rare & rich can be bought in Paris; & by no means the least attractive of its shows is the immense bookstalls in the streets[:] maps, pictures, models, busts, sculptures, & libraries [159] of old books spread abroad on tables or shelves at the side of the road. The manners of the people are full of entertainment so spirited, chatty, & coquettish, as lively as monkeys. And now the whole nation is bearded & in military uniform. I have no doubt also that extremes of vice are found here & that ⟨in general⟩ there is a liberty & means of animal indulgence hardly known by name or even by rumour in other towns. But any extremes are here also exceptional & are visited here by the fatal Nemesis who climbs all walls[,] [160] dives into all cellars [and I notice that every wall in Paris is stigmatized with an advertisement of La Guerison des Maladies secretes] but also the social decorum seems to have here the same rigours as in England with a little variety in the application.

A special advantage which Paris has is in the freedom from aristocratic pride manifest in the tone of society. It is quite easy for any young man of liberal tastes to enter on a good footing the best houses. It is not easy in England. Then ⟨chea⟩the customs are cheap & inexpensive; [161] whilst it is a proverb almost, that, to live in England at all, you must have ⟨a⟩ great fortune; which sounds to me as certain a prediction of revolution as musket shots in the streets.

So that on the whole I am thankful for Paris, as I am for the discovery of Ether & Chloroform; I like to know, that, if I should need an amputation, there is this balm; and if hard should come to hard, & I should be driven to seek some refuge of solitude & independency, why here is Paris.

The cafés are not to be forgotten, filled with newspapers[,] blazing with light, [162] sauntering places, oubliettes or Remember-nothings. One in Paris who would keep himself up with events must read every day about twelve newspapers of the 200 that are printed there.[263] Then in the street the affiches ⟨at⟩ ↑on↓ every spot of dead wall, attract all eyes & make the text of all talk for the gazing group. The Government reserve to ⟨themselves⟩ ↑their own↓ the exclusive use of White Paper. All others are in colours.

[163] After 25 days spent in Paris I took the railroad for Boulogne, stopped at Amiens half an hour, & saw the Cathedral [which has nothing equal to it in Paris in the elaboration of the details of its moulding & sculpture on the exterior, (saw the weeping angel also)]. ⟨a⟩And at Boulogne, (where 6000 English reside for cheapness,) I took the night steamboat for Folkestone.[264] The twentyseven miles of roughest sea between Boulogne & Folkestone made a piteous scene, of course, in the Saloon of the boat, but as that wild strip of sea is from age to age the cheap Standing army of England & worth a million [164] of troops, no Englishman should grudge his qualms.[265]

[165][266] Saw Rowland Hill at Hampstead. He says in 1845 which is the right year of comparison the Post Office yielded 1,600 000 pounds ↑net↓ revenue. In 184⟨8⟩7 1 000 000 only; but the number of postoffices is nearly or quite doubled. He thinks ocean penny postage not quite practicable. The increase of letters is in the short distances & not in the long.

---

[263] See Notebook England and Paris, p. [63] below, and the list on p. [138] above.

[264] Emerson left Paris for London on June 2, 1848.

[265] Pasted below this entry, which expands a note made in Notebook England and Paris, p. [63] below, is an unidentified newspaper clipping of two paragraphs, in German, concerning the public buildings of Paris. Advertisements overleaf indicate that the clipping is from a German-language paper published in New York City.

[266] This page is in pencil.

At Mr Field's Hampstead[.] [267]
Was at Mr Stanfield's, who showed me some of Turner's pictures &
his own. Each of Turner's cost 100 guineas. Went with ↑Mr Field &↓
him to Mr Windus to see his collection of Turners. Which justify
Ruskin's praise. Turner told Stanfield he will not suffer any portrait
to be taken of him, for nobody would ever believe that such an ugly
fellow made such beautiful things.[268]

[166] Paris & London have this difference, that Paris exists for the
foreigner, serves him; — whilst in London is the Londoner, who is
much in the foreigner's way. England has built London for its own
use. France has built Paris for the world.

The French have this wonderful street courage. The least dislike,
the smallest unpopularity, is intolerable to them. But they will take
your fire with indifference. And is this a world to hide virtues in?
There must then be revolutions to bring them out.[269]

[167] In Blanqui's *Club des droits de l'homme*, an orator in
blouse said, "Why should the rich fear that we shall not protect their
property? — We shall guard it with the utmost care, in the belief
that it will soon be our own."   ↑See LM 68
                                                   77↓ [270]

[168] [blank]
[169] With Mr Kenyon & Hillard I joined the Jays in a visit to

---

[267] Rowland Hill, the English postal authority, was a guest with Emerson,
Clarkson Stanfield, the marine painter, and others at a dinner given by Edwin
Wilkins Field of Hampstead, an amateur artist and art patron, on June 25, 1848
(*L*, IV, 93).

[268] On June 26, 1848, Emerson breakfasted with Stanfield and "went with him
to see a famous gallery of Turner's pictures at Tottenham" (*L*, IV, 93); B. G.
Windus of Tottenham owned a hundred or so of Turner's drawings and paintings,
as Emerson notes on p. [178] below. In Notebook ED, p. [130] below, Emerson
states that Windus told him of Turner's remark.

[269] See Journal GH, p. [69] above ("French has street courage"), Shakespeare,
Twelfth Night, I, iii, 140 ("Is it a world to hide virtues in?"), and Notebook
Xenien, p. [4] below, from which these five sentences are transcribed.

[270] The insertion is in pencil. Emerson visited Blanqui's club on Saturday and
Sunday evenings, May 13 and 14, 1848 (*L*, IV, 73).

Stokes Regis[271] where we found Gray's Churchyard then to Eton where we found 6 or 700 boys, the flower of English youth, engaged in cricket on the green, or rowing in the river and remembered Lamb's remark "What pity that these fine boys should be changed into frivolous members of Parliament." Kenyon re⟨mem⟩called verses of his own "O give us back our lofty youth, &c" and the whole place remembered Gray. Kenyon recited a passage addressed to the Duke of Grafton wherein a dirty request was to be couched in beautiful verses. After seeing the chapel we ⟨set⟩went to Windsor castle the Jays having tickets for the admission of the party [170] to the private apartments of her majesty. We saw the fine corridors which are a gallery of sculpture & painting, then the chambers, & dining room & reception rooms of this palace. The Queen's bedroom was not shown us. The green expanse of trim counties which these fine windows command beginning with a mile of garden in front, excellent. Then to the Royal Mews where a hundred horses are kept, looked at these & the carriages. If hard come to hard, the camel has a great deal of hump left to spend from.

↑Mem. Mr Kenyon's opinion about the gem-like character of stained glass windows at St George's Chapel, Windsor. Lady Morgan would have carpets spread, not nailed, & they should seem like jewels trodden in.↓

[171] From Windsor we went to Virginia Water[,] the fine toy-lake & fishing-house of George IV. Important to the show were a couple of red flags hanging from the little frigates afloat. I suppose the three people in the boat were hired at a penny a day to sit there,[272] and all the houses were like Queen Catherine's pasteboard villages, & one feared that the rocks were sugar-candy. There is a made waterfall, and a made ruin, the Persepolis of the woods. This last is constructed of stones brought from the ruins of Carthage.[273]

[271] Emerson's "Stokes Regis" and "Stokes Pogis" (*L*, IV, 97) are of course Stoke Poges, which he visited on July 4, 1848. The party included John Kenyon, English poet and philanthropist; George Stillman Hillard, a Boston lawyer; and Mr. and Mrs. Jay, Americans staying at Fenton's Hotel in London — possibly the William Jays of New York (Notebook England and Paris, p. [78] below; *L*, IV, 95, n. 336).

[272] Cf. "Beauty," *W*, VI, 291.

[273] This account of the visit to Stoke Poges, Eton, Windsor, and Virginia Water

↑"A boy at Eton, in a tutor's house costs his father altogether, including all his personal expenses, clothes, pocket-money, journeys, not less than £200, a year." *Bristed.*

Number of boys about 600.

six years ago   7⟨3⟩7↓ [274]

[172] [275] Renton	Editor	of Spectator
Wilson & Greg		of Economist —
Harvey		of Athenaeum
Lucas		of Tablet
Forster		of Examiner
Dr Empson		of Edinburgh Review
Hanna		of North British
Lockhart		of Quarterly
Landreth		of Macphail's Maga
Ferrier, Ayton, Smith, Moir,		of Blackwood

Theodore Martin is Le Bon
  Gualthier. [276]

[173] [277] ↑Hon.↓ Mrs Norton said, that, Milnes & Disraeli were the two remarkable political failures which she had known.

---

enlarges upon notes made in Notebook England and Paris, p. [44] below, concerning Gray's "For Music" (addressed to the Duke of Grafton) and in Notebook Xenien, p. [3] below, concerning the chapel windows at Windsor. "With Mr Kenyon . . . Carthage.", struck through in pencil with single vertical use marks on pp. [169]–[171], is transcribed in Notebook ED, pp. [132]–[137] below.

[274] Cf. Charles A. Bristed, *Five Years in an English University*, 1852, I, 368, 362.

[275] The first five lines on this page are rewritten in ink over the same matter in pencil; "Edinburgh Review" is written in ink over "Inquirer" in pencil; the other writing is original ink inscription.

[276] Emerson is in error with respect to two of the names: not "Renton" but Robert Stephen Rintoul (1787–1858) was editor of the *Spectator*; not "Harvey" but Thomas Kibble Hervey (1799–1859) was editor of the *Athenæum*. The other editors not previously identified are James Wilson (1805–1860), Frederick Lucas (1812–1855), William Empson (1791–1852), and John Gibson Lockhart (1794–1854).

[277] Between pp. [172] and [173] is inserted a printed leaf bearing pp. 41 and 42 of a catalogue issued by William Brown, Old Street, London; p. 41 carries the running head "English Books". There are marginal lines marking Lot 764: "Hai Ebn Yokdhan, The Improvement of Human Reason exhibited in the Life of," translated by Simon Ockley (1708).

Viscount Melbourne's letter in reply to Lord Brougham's sheets of objections[:] "Dear B. I am sorry you don't like my appointment of N. Pray expedite the matter thro' all the forms as fast as possible. Yours, M." [278]

Duke of Buckingham, when the dog bit him, wished him a young wife & an estate in the country.

The King of Naples said of his troops, No matter how you dressed them, they would all run away.[279]

[174] Topics of conversation in England are Irish affairs; universal suffrage; pauperism; public education; Right & Duty of governments to interfere ↑with↓ increase of population; taxes[.] [280]

[175] The English habit of betting makes them much more accurate than we are in their knowledge of particulars. — "Which is the longest river the Missisippi or the Missouri?" — They are about the same length. "About! that won't do; I've a bet upon it." Captain Lott says, that 'tis difficult to know in America the precise speed of a boat, because the distances are not settled between the cities, and we overrate them. In England, the distance from Boston to New York would be measured to half a foot. He says, that the boat is yet to be built that will go thro' the water 19 miles per hour.[281]

[176] In cabin the conversations about England & America, T. A↑ppleton↓ amused us all by tracing all English performance home to the dear Puritans, & affirming that the Pope also was ↑once↓ in South America, & there met a Yankee, who gave him notions on politics & religion.[282]

[278] "Hon. Mrs Norton . . . Yours, M.' " is expanded here from notes in Notebook England and Paris, p. [41] below. The first sentence, struck through in pencil with a vertical use mark, is transcribed in Notebook ED, p. [150] below.

[279] "Duke of . . . away." is transcribed here from Notebook Xenien, p. [3] below.

[280] "Topics of . . . taxes" is transcribed from Notebook England and Paris, p. [42] below.

[281] Captain E. G. Lott commanded the royal mail steamer *Europa*, on which Emerson left Liverpool on July 15, 1848, arriving in Boston on July 27. This paragraph is expanded from an entry in Notebook England and Paris, p. [61] below.

[282] Among Emerson's fellow passengers on the voyage to Boston was Thomas

[177] M. Lehmann, in Paris, who made a crayon sketch of my head for Madame d'Agout, remarked that in American heads ⟨he⟩ was an approach to the Indian type; & in England, ⟨p⟩or perhaps from David Scott at Edinburgh, I heard a similar observation.[283]

[178] I went with Edwin Field & Mr Stanfield the painter, & his son, to the house of Mr Windus, Tottenham, to see his collection of Turner's pictures & drawings of which ↑altogether↓ he may have a hundred. This gallery was that in which Ruskin had studied. It is quite necessary to see all these pictures to appreciate the genius of Turner through his extravagances.[284] Two days afterwards, Mr Owen carried me to Turner's own house, to see what is there. Mr Owen said, that, in his earlier pictures, he painted conventionally, painted what he knew was there; finished the coat & hat & buttons; in the later he paints only what the eye really sees, & gets [179] the genius of the city or landscape. He was to paint a whaleship, & he came to Owen to see a (mullet)? and studied this with the utmost accuracy. But Owen could not find it in the picture, though he doubted not it was there.[285]

[180] Nobility. In the University the noblemen are exempted from the public exercises for the degree, &c. by which they attain a degree called *honorary*[;] at the same time the fees they have to pay for matriculation, & on all other occasions are much higher. *Huber*[286]

Gold Appleton, the Boston wit, whom he had seen in both London and Paris. This paragraph expands an entry in Notebook England and Paris, p. [60] below.

[283] Emerson is referring to Charles Ernest Rodolphe Henri Lehmann (1814–1882), a painter who had opened his studio in Paris in 1847, and Marie de Flavigny, Comtesse d'Agoult (1805–1876), a French writer known as "Daniel Stern," whom Emerson had seen in Paris (L, IV, 78). Cf. Notebook England and Paris, p. [61] below: "The artists found in my face the Indian type."

[284] See p. [165] above; the visit had taken place on June 26.

[285] Richard Owen, the anatomist, showed Emerson through the Hunterian Museum on June 29, 1848, and then took him to Turner's house; Emerson should have written that these events occurred *three* days after his visit to Mr. Windus. "Owen carried . . . there.", struck through in pencil with single vertical use marks on pp. [178] and [179], is transcribed in Notebook ED, pp. [127]–[128] below.

[286] Cf. Victor Aimé Huber, *The English Universities*, trans. Francis W. Newman, 1843, II, 262. "In the . . . higher.", struck through in pencil with a vertical use mark, is used in "Aristocracy," W, V, 195.

[181] [blank]

[182] Alfieri said, that "Italy & England are the only countries in which it is desireable to live; the former because there nature vindicates her rights & rises triumphant over the evils inflicted by the governments; the latter, because art conquers nature, & transforms a rude ungenial land into a paradise of comfort & laughing abundance." [287]

[183] Gilpin's "Forest Scenery" is a good ex⟨p⟩ample of the sincerity of English culture.[288]

[184] Margaret Fuller writes concerning *J H Green*'s *"Vital Dynamics"*[:]

"What a fuss these English make ⟨c⟩about presenting *thoughts* to an audience! What long preludes of apology & explanation for taking liberty to alter any thing beyond the poorest truisms! The mental condition of New England must be much the best of the two at present.[289]
No audience here would have patience with all these 20 or 30 pages before he can get upon his subject."   *Journal* 18⟨3⟩41

[185] [blank]
     [186] When Cambridge was a barn.

"Monks of Croyland, 1109–1124 under their abbot Goisfred, taught at a farm called Cottenham, near Cambridge, &, afterwards, in a barn, at Cambridge itself."   *Huber. Vol.* I p[p]. [61–]62 [290]

[187] ↑P A Fiorentino writes from London in ⟨Etat⟩[C]ourrier des Etats Unis June 1851[:]

[287] See *JMN*, V, 413. This paragraph, struck through in pencil with two curved vertical use marks, is transcribed in Notebook ED, p. [3] below, and used in "Land," *W*, V, 34.
    [288] William Gilpin, *Remarks on Forest Scenery, and Other Woodland Views (Relative Chiefly to Picturesque Beauty), Illustrated by the Scenes of New-Forest in Hampshire*, 2 vols. (London, 1791). This sentence, struck through in pencil with a curved vertical use mark, is transcribed in Notebook ED, p. [85] below.
    [289] " 'What . . . New England" is struck through in pencil with a vertical use mark. John H. Green had been agent for *The Dial* in London until succeeded by John Chapman in 1844.
    [290] Victor Aimé Huber, *The English Universities*, trans. Francis W. Newman, 1843. "When Cambridge . . . p. 62" is struck through in pencil with a vertical use mark.

"Go to the Crystal Palace on one of the days when it is open to the operatives. Le peuple sage, serieux, calculateur, qui connait le prix du temps, n'est point venu les premiers jours, craignant que l'encombrement des curieux ne ⟨n⟩l'empêchat de tout voir et tout examiner. Mais, rassuré par la suite, il se rend par d'imp⟨|| . . . ||⟩osantes masses, dans ces immenses galeries, avec un ordre et une tenue admirables. Il porte sur chaque objet l'attention la plus minutieuse et la plus soutenue: il observe, il compare, il juge, il questionne, il s'instruit. Son instinct lui inspire d'etonnantes remarques, des réflexions pratiques, de la plus grande just⟨ice⟩esse, et de la plus haute portee"↓ [291]

[188] In Europe, every church is a kind of book or bible, so covered is it with inscriptions & pictures.

[189] "Britain like other countries abounded once in wood. Fitz Stephen a monk of Canterbury in the time of Henry II., tells us that a large forest lay round London, in which were woody groves, in the covers whereof lurked bucks & does, wild boars & bulls. Even so late as Henry VII.'s time, we are informed by Polidore Virgil, that '*Tertia propemodum Angliae pars pecori aut cervis, damis, capreolis, nam et ii quoque in ea parte sunt quae ad septentrionem est cuniculisve nutriendis relicta* est inculta, *quippe passim sunt ejusmodi ferarum vivaria seu roboraria, quae lignis roboreis sunt clausa: unde multa venatio qua⟨e⟩ se nobiles cum primis exercent.*' " [292]

[190] [blank]

[191] Another lesson I learned from England, was, the power of the religious sentiment, the belief in the immortality of the soul, & the rest, — which inspired the Crusades, inspired the religious architecture, — York, Newstead, Westminster, Winchester, Ripon, Beverley, & Dundee, (works to which the key is lost, with the sentiment that created them); & inspired the English Bible, the Chronicle of Richard of Devizes,[293]

[291] Pier Angelo Fiorentino, "Lettres sur l'Exposition VI," London, June 8, 1851, in *Courrier des Etats Unis*, XXVIII (July 2, 1851), p. 1.

[292] "About a third of Anglia is left as uncultivated pasture-land for the sustenance of stags, does, wild goats (for there are both in that part which lies to the north), or rabbits; as one might expect, there are preserves of wild animals here and there, which if enclosed are fenced with oak: whence much hunting, in which the nobles especially busy themselves" (Ed.). For "Britain . . . exercent.' ", see William Gilpin, *Remarks on Forest Scenery*, 3rd ed., 2 vols. (London, 1808), I, 303–304.

[293] This paragraph, struck through in pencil with a diagonal use mark, is used in "Religion," *W*, V, 215–216.

[192]–[195] [blank]

[196]   *Queries*

What is true of those alleged abuses of the charity foundations at Eton?   See above↑,↓ p ↑34↓ [294]

What is the invention which Mr Acroyd of Halifax bought at Lawrence, Mass.?

What is the population of England
    Scotland?
    Ireland?

What are the 6 points of Chartism? [295]

[197] [296] [blank]
    [198] The story which in England they like to tell of the Frenchman & Englishman who quarreled. Both were averse to fight but their friends put them up to it & there was no getting off. It was agreed at last that they should be left alone in the room, and the lights put out. The Englishman fired up chimney & brought down the Frenchman.[297]

[199]–[201] [298] [blank]
[202] J. A. Froude   Bailey
    A. H Clough
    Stanley

---

[294] "34" and the comma after "above" are added in pencil.

[295] In Notebook ED Emerson entered the population figures on p. [i] below and the six points of Chartism on p. [288] below.

[296] Laid in between pp. [196] and [197] is the slip of paper described in the bibliographical headnote to Journal London. Its penciled inscription, "TC to RWE May 1847", may refer to Carlyle's letter of May 18, 1847 (*CEC*, pp. 421–424).

[297] This paragraph, struck through with two vertical use marks, one in pencil and one in ink, is transcribed in Notebook ED, p. [75] below, and used in "Cockayne," *W*, V, 149.

[298] Pasted to pp. [200] and [201] is an article clipped from an unidentified Boston newspaper headed "The British Aristocracy.", credited to the New York *Courier*; laid in between these same pages is a second article clipped from an unidentified newspaper ("||i-We[ekly?]||") headed "British Royalty.", credited to "Ik. Marvel [Donald G. Mitchell] in N.Y. Courier."

W. E. Forster
           Mills
           Staley
           Shuttleworth
E. R. Larken
    H. Sutton
T. H. Gill
W. B. Scott
David Scott
      S. Brown
      J. Sanderson
           Bray
       A Tennyson
      W. Appleby
Matthew Arnold
           Fletcher
  J J G Wilkinson
Arthur Helps
           Pope
           Sylvester
           Greg
           Martineau
           Wordsworth
Owen   Richard
Owen   Robert [299]

[299] "J. A. Froude . . . Sylvester" is in pencil. Froude, Clough, and the historian Arthur Penrhyn Stanley entertained Emerson at Oxford. "Bailey" may be either the author of *Festus* or the writer for the *Times*; the London address of a Mr. and Mrs. Bailey is listed on p. [208] below and in Pocket Diary 3, p. [70] below. "Martineau" may be either Rev. James Martineau of Liverpool, brother of Harriet, whom Emerson had heard preach (*L*, III, 428), or a Richard(?) Martineau of London who had written Emerson on April 11, 1848 (Notebook England and Paris, inside back cover below; *L*, VI, 514). Of others not previously identified, a Mr. Shuttleworth addressed an undated letter to Emerson (*L*, VI, 584); the address of Rev. Edward R. Larken, near Lincoln, is listed on p. [209] below; John Sanderson of Glasgow wrote Emerson on March 1, 1848 (*L*, IV, 64); Charles Bray entertained Emerson and Mary Ann Evans (George Eliot) at Coventry on July 12, 1848 (*L*, IV, 98; *Life*, p. 356); Emerson met Matthew Arnold in London (*Life*, p. 344); Arthur Helps, an English historian, entertained Emerson and Carlyle at Bishop's Waltham on July 8 and 9, 1848 (*L*, IV, 97; "Stonehenge," *W*, V, 286–290).

[203] *Personalities*
C. J. Vaughan is Master of Harrow[.]

[204] [300]
    ────────────────────────────────
          To Bannockburn & Falkirk ✏
    ────────────────────────────────

[Notice. No stranger poor permitted to beg in Clackmannanshire.]
    a signpost near Stirling.
    ──────────────────

Mrs Barr. Midwife
──────────────────

[205] Promised Mr De Quincey
          Dr B[rown].
          D. Scott   Poems & autog[raph] [301]
          Mrs Crowe
Fred[eric]k J. Foxton, Bwlch Gwyn, Rhayader. Radnorshire

Mr E F Flower, Stratford upon Avon

[206] [302] Who invented Electric Telegraph in England? ↑Wheat-stone↓

Is leather tanned seven years
Is paper made of linen only

How many ⟨pro⟩ landlords in Eng[lan]d

[207] *Books*   £
Heimskringla   1 "   6 "   0
Montaigne   13 "

Arnold
Niebuhr: Lectures on Roman History
Maurice

---

[300] This page is in pencil; the first and last lines are in boxes, interpreted here by printed rules.
[301] "Promised Mr . . . Crowe . . . autog" is in pencil.
[302] This page is in pencil.

Thirlwall [303]

___

Carlyle's list

___

Kennett's History of England. 25 S.
Lowth's Life of Wm of Wykeham
Camden's Brittannia, translated by Holland, 7 or 8 s
Britton's Beauties of England & Wales.

Hainault. Abrégé Chronologique de l'histoire de France

___

Bede

___

Collins' Peerage, 1745. or, any time before Egerton Brydges.

12/6 [304]

---

[303] (1) *The Heimskringla*, trans. Samuel Laing, 1844; (2) presumably the *Essais de Montaigne*, 3 vols., that Emerson bequeathed to James Elliot Cabot: see Kenneth W. Cameron, *The Transcendentalists and Minerva*, 3 vols. (Hartford, 1958), III, 862; (3) possibly Thomas Arnold, *History of the Later Roman Commonwealth*, 2 vols. (London, 1845); (4) Barthold Georg Niebuhr, *History of Rome*, trans. Julius Charles Hare, Connop Thirlwall, W. Smith, and L. Schmitz, 3 vols. (London, 1828–1842); (5) possibly John Frederick Denison Maurice, *The Religions of the World* (London, 1847); (6) Connop Thirlwall, *History of Greece*, 8 vols. (London, 1835–1847).

[304] The list is transcribed here from Notebook Xenien, p. [66] below; see also *JMN*, VIII, 564. The books referred to are White Kennet, *A Complete History of England*, 3 vols. (London, 1706–1719); Robert Lowth, *The Life of William of Wykeham, Bishop of Winchester* (London, 1759), which Emerson borrowed from the Harvard College Library on November 8, 1848; William Camden, *Britain, or, a Chorographicall Description of the Most Flourishing Kingdomes, England, Scotland, and Ireland* . . . , trans. Philemon Holland (London, 1637), which Emerson on November 23, 1848, asked the Boston Athenaeum to order for his use; John Britton and Edward Brayley, *The Beauties of England and Wales* . . . , 18 vols. in 25 (London, 1801–1815); Charles Jean François Hénault, *Abrégé Chronologique de l'Histoire de France* . . . , first published in 1744 (the third edition of a continuation to 1830 was published in Paris, 1842); *History of England. Also the Anglo-Saxon Chronicle*, ed. J. A. Giles (London, 1847), in Emerson's library; Arthur Collins, *The Peerage of England* . . . , first published in 1709 (Emerson borrowed vol. I of the 9-volume London, 1812, edition of Collins from the Harvard College Library on November 8, 1848).

[208]³⁰⁵ Feb 7 Mon   Halifax
          8   Barnard Castle
          9   Newcastle
     11 Fri   Edinb[urgh]
     14 Mon   Edinb
     15   Glasgow
     16   Edin
     17   Glasgow
     18 Fri   Edinb
     21 Mon   Dundee
     22   Perth
     23   Dundee
     x
     25   Newcastle

In London
Sir Charles Lyell, 11 Harley street
Dr Carpenter   6 Regents Park Terrace, Gloucester Gate
Thos. F. Gibson, 31 Westbourne Terrace, Hyde Park
Mrs Bailey, 271 Holborn
Mrs Atkinson. 37 Gordon Square³⁰⁶

[209] W. Staley   41 Peel Terrace, Carter st, Greenheys   Manchester
F. Espinasse   19 Athol Place, Higher Broughton, Manchester
Rev. T E Poynting. Parsonage, Monton, near Eccles.
Mr T. B. Blackburne
T. H. Gill. Calthorpe Place, Bristol Road, Edgbaston. Birmingham
William Mathews   Calthorpe st   Edgbaston   Birmingham
William Rathbone

³⁰⁵ The itinerary for February 7–25, 1848, is in pencil; *"In London . . . Gordon Square"* is written in ink over the earlier writing through the entry for February 9.

³⁰⁶ Emerson saw the Lyells at the Bancrofts' and heard Lyell speak at the Geological Society on March 22, 1848 (*L*, IV, 41, 42); on April 3 he dined with Lyell (*L*, IV, 49; Pocket Diary 3, p. [64] below). Concerning Carpenter, see p. 257 above and note 217. Emerson dined with Gibson on April 19 and with the Baileys on April 27 (Pocket Diary 3, pp. [68], [69] below). In a letter to his wife written on March 23 and 24 he reports a call on a Mrs. Atkinson (*L*, IV, 45).

Mr Rawlins   4 Blackburne Terrace   Liverpool
William Allen, Shiffnal, Salop.
Rev Edmund R. Larken, Burton Rectory near Lincoln [307]

[210] [Index material omitted]

May	7 Sun		
	8 Monday	June	10 Sat
	9 T		11 Sun
	10 W		12 Mon
	11 Th		13 Tues
	12 Fri		14 Wed
	13 Sat		15 Thurs
	14 Sun		16 Fri
	15 Mon		17 Sat
	16 T		18 Sun Mr Robinson 9.30
	17 W		19 Mon Mr Rolt & Wilkinson & Duch-
	18 Th		ess of Sutherland
	19 Fr		20 Tues Leigh Hunt
	20 Sat		21 Wed. Mr Tagart 6.30
	21 Sun		22 Thurs. Lord Lovelace 7½ 12
	22 M		o'clock
	23 T		23 Fri Exeter Hall, 8. Chopin 3
	24 W		o'clock
	25 Th		24 Sat
	26 Fr		25 Sun Mr Field
	27 Sat		26 Mon Marylebone at 8
	28 Sun		27 Tues Exeter Hall
	29 Mon		28 Wed. Lord Morpeth 7¾
	30 T		29 Thurs. Mr [Richard] Owen 12
	31 Wed		30 Fri. Exeter Hall 8 [308]

[307] Of the names not previously identified, Poynting had written Emerson in November and December of 1847 (L, VI, 555); Rathbone entertained Emerson at Greenbank on November 25 (L, III, 443; Notebook England and Paris, p. [73] below).

[308] Among the names occurring in entries for June, 1848, "Robinson" is the diarist Henry Crabb Robinson, who had previously taken Emerson to a dinner of the Society of Antiquaries on May 2 (L, IV, 66, n. 236). The Duchess of Suther-

⟨32⟩June 1 Thursday   July   1 Sat London Univ. 3 Mr Chapman
          1 Thursday   2 Sun. Mr Procter
          2 Fri   3 Mon Mr Rolt 7   52 Harley
          3 Sat   4 Tues 9 o'c Mr Kenyon York
          4 Sun   Terrace 40
          5 Mon   5 Wed eve Mr Cooper
          6 Tuesday   6 Thurs Cambridge
          7   7 Fri Salisbury [309]
          8   8 Sat.
          9   9
                                       10
                                       11

[inside back cover] [310] J Mc Ewen Gray   7 George st   Perth
Francis Mac Donald, Holme Place. Glasgow
          ?   Argyle Place   Helensburgh [311]

_____

land, who attended Emerson's Portman Square lectures, invited him to lunch at
Stafford House on June 19 (L, IV, 84, 89–90); he saw Hunt the following evening
(L, IV, 86). Emerson "had a good evening" at Lord Lovelace's dinner (L, IV, 87),
and on the following afternoon attended a musicale by Chopin, with whom he had
dined on June 15 (L, IV, 87, 84). His three Exeter Hall lectures were on "Napoleon"
(June 23), "Domestic Life" (June 27), and "Shakspeare" (June 30); on June 26
he lectured at Portman Square on "The Superlative in Manners and Literature."
Lord Morpeth had attended Emerson's lecture on "Natural Aristocracy" on June 17
and later came to talk with him (L, IV, 86, n. 303; 94). John Rolt, trained in the
law and later a Member of Parliament and Attorney General, corresponded with
Emerson in June of 1848 (L, VI, 570). Rev. Edward Tagart, general secretary of
the British and Foreign Unitarian Association, was a fellow of both the Geological
Society and the Society of Antiquaries and may have met Emerson at one of their
functions; Dickens was among his parishioners.

[309] Emerson's appointments for July included "a sort of farewell party which
Chapman invites my friends to" on the 1st (L, IV, 94); his excursion to Eton and
Windsor with John Kenyon and others on the 4th (see pp. [169]–[171] above);
an evening with Thomas Cooper the Chartist, whom he had met in April at Garth
Wilkinson's (L, IV, 55, n. 197); a single day at Cambridge with Tom Taylor; and
an expedition to Salisbury and on to Stonehenge with Carlyle.

[310] Laid in between p. [210] and the inside back cover is an index to Journal
London, six pages in length, written in an unidentified hand. Emerson himself did
not make his customary index for this journal; his index entries on p. [210] and
below are limited in scope. One line of index material excepted, the writing on the
inside back cover is in pencil.

[311] Emerson evidently failed to note the name here. This address is enclosed in a
rectangular penciled box. Gray, mentioned above, is not otherwise identified; Emer-

Mrs Case   Gower st
Theodore Martin, 24 James st   Buckingham Gate
Mrs Jameson, 18 North Audley st
Mr Taylor   3 Fig tree Court   Inner Temple [312]

[Index material omitted]

---

son provided "two notes of introduction" for MacDonald in April? 1848 (*L*, IV, 64).

[312] In Notebook England and Paris, p. [78] below, Emerson lists "Mr W. A. Case 20 Upper Gower st" and "Mrs Jameson, 30 Eastbourne Terrace Hyde Pk"; he saw "a good deal" of Anna Brownell Murphy Jameson while in London (*L*, IV, 41). Martin and Tom Taylor have been mentioned previously.

LM

1848

Journal LM is a regular journal kept during and after Emerson's second visit to England and France. He bought the copybook containing it in Manchester, England, in January, 1848 (page [i]) and evidently began making entries concurrently with those in Journal London; the first dated entry, on page [28], is for March 14, 1848, and the last, on page [160], is for October 1, 1848.

Journal LM is written in a copybook bound in green marbled boards, with brown leather corners and spine. The cover measures 19.5 x 23.6 cm. The spine is blind stamped with what were originally five pairs of horizontal lines; the pair at the top is now covered by later mending. The spine is inscribed "LM" in ink; the front cover is also inscribed in ink: "LM / 1848". The pages, faintly ruled, measure 19.2 x 22.9 cm; the edges are marbled green. All of the pages are numbered in ink except 20 numbered in pencil (1–2, 5–11, 76, 116, 118, 120, 122–123, 140–143, 150; 166 is renumbered in ink) and 8 unnumbered (i, ii, 35, 69, 117, 168–170). Emerson omitted numbering pages 134–135 but duplicated numbers for 71 and 72, later marking the duplicates as "71½" and "72½". There are six blank pages (ii, 10, 109, 117, 168, 169). Two leaves have been torn out: pages 111–112 (Emerson indexed page 112 under Concord, Economy, and Housekeeping) and pages 163–164 (Emerson indexed page 163 under Illusion and pages 163–164 under Conduct of Life). A clipping about Michael Faraday is mounted inside the front cover. Laid in are two items: (1) between the front cover and page i, a loose leaf in the hand of Edward Emerson tabulating dated entries in LM, with cross-references to Cabot's *Memoir*; (2) between pages 38 and 39, a loose leaf, 18.4 x 11.4 cm, with a drawing of a young girl watering a plant and, overleaf, four lines of verse in Emerson's hand, presumably addressed to his daughter Ellen.

[front cover]   LM
                                1848

[front cover verso] [1] [Index material omitted]

[i] [2] 2 Fenny street: R.W. Emerson
Higher Broughton:
Manchester; Jan. 1848.[3]

[ii] [blank]
[1] ↑*The Battery*.↓
The staple figure in novels is the man of aplomb, who sits among the
young aspirants & desperates, quite sure & compact, &, never sharing
their affections or debilities, hurls his word like a bullet, when
occasion requires; knows his way, & carries his points. They may
scream like cats, he is never engaged or heated. This figure charms
all readers, ⟨and⟩ yet is never imitated in our houses. Napoleon is
the type of this class in modern history; yet we are all drawn in to
the charivari, answer, cavil, recriminate, and run on.[4]————————

[2] History is the group of the types or representative men of any
age at only ⟨such⟩ ↑the↓ distance of convenient vision. We can see
the arrangement of masses, & distinguish the forms of the leaders.
Mythology is the same group at another remove, now at a pictorial
distance; the perspective of history. ⟨t⟩The forms & faces can no
longer be read, but only the direction of the march, & the result;
so that the names of the leaders are now mixed with the ⟨objects⟩

---

[1] Pasted to the upper left corner is a clipping from an unidentified newspaper:
an account of "Professor Michael Faraday's *second* great discovery of the present
Winter" as copied "from the [Boston] Chronotype"; on Harriet Martineau and Faraday, see Journal London, p. [41] above. In addition to index material there is also
a subtraction, in pencil: 1876 — 1848 = 28.
[2] Laid in between the front cover verso and p. [i] is a loose leaf with notes in
the hand of Edward Emerson, listing dated entries within Journal LM and citing
James Elliot Cabot, *A Memoir of Ralph Waldo Emerson*, 2 vols. (Boston, 1887).
[3] For Emerson's account of his "good lodgings" at Manchester, with a Mrs.
Massey, see *L*, III, 431, 437.
[4] The entry on p. [1], struck through in pencil with two wavy diagonal use
marks, is used in "Social Aims," *W*, VIII, 81.

↑ends↓ for which they strove. Distance is essential. Therefore we cannot say what is *our* mythology. We can only see that the industrial, ⟨&⟩ mechanical, the parliamentary, commercial, constitute it, with socialism; and Astor, Watt, Fulton, Arkwright, Peel, Russell, Rothschild, Geo Stephenson, Fourier, are our mythologic names.

[3]⁵   On the Conduct of life.

———

Our high composite structure. *O*   *LM* 129.
The life we seek, expansion; that we have, obstruction. *O* 5
The heights of our life   *LM* 121   163–4,
We must live by system. *LM* 40   *Y* 40
       Mind your oar & not the rudder   *LM* 150
Society starves us. *O* 204
Voting. "How small of all that human hearts endure," &c
Luck. farmer looking on his vines.
Rothschild in Buxton's Life.⁶
The custom of the country does much for us.⁷
Happiness of old age, *O* 12
Many pounds of grit to one of cheese. *O* 10
City & country   *O* 208
Different velocity, *O* 254, 292
Superficiality. *O*. 185
Ascetic of every day. *Index* 206
Longevity   ↑Stability depends on short life, *O* 311↓
Let us worship the immortal gods   *RS* 57, 63
Enlarge not thy destiny   RS 9
All we ask of any man,—that he be thoroughly contented with his own. LM
a successful man   RS 20   LM 58

———

⁵ The entries on this page are written over 18 lines of erased pencil writing, of which no significant words have been recovered.
⁶ For the references to Journals O and Y, see *JMN*, IX, 358 (O 5), 271 (Y 40), 415 (O 204); for " 'How small . . . endure,' &c", see p. [103] below; for "Rothschild . . . Life.", see p. [37] below. In Notebook England and Paris, p. [56] below, under the heading "On the conduct of life" are the same topics listed here in the entries "Voting . . . Life."
⁷ Cf. *JMN*, IX, 296.

Happy is he who finds easily a good hobby. LM 58
Life teaches perspective   W 127 [8]

[4] [9] ↑*Conduct of Life*↓
Proportionate with this importance is our disappointment in the un-
worthiness of these[:] if for enthusiasm[,] sneers; and for grandeur[,]
indulgence[.]
↑The wonder of life is the absence of any appearance of reconciliation
between theory & practice[.] U 115.↓ [10]
But ah[,] wealth will not buy it[.]

⟨Great⟩
Being used to wealth & so not awkward with it but superior to it
↑Let us do something not for cash payment. RS 57↓

[5] Traits. A soul so much more drawn to itself than to others that
it comes through & out of any events or companies the same: like
metals & the nobler chemical compounds whose particles have that
strong affinity for each other that no solvent can be found. [11]

These distinctions are in man, and as flagrant in democracies as in
oligarchies[.] [12]

> Beauty[:] no reasoning[,] no legislating
> is import[ant.] It will not only remain a
> potent but a differencing ⟨pecularity⟩ ↑aris-
> tocratic↓ quality[.]
> and an engineer[:]

---

[8] For the references to Journals O and W, see *JMN*, IX, 361 (O 12, O 10);
416 (O 208); 422 (O 254); 434 (O 292); 408–409 (O 185); 443–444 (O 311);
244 (W 127). Journal RS will be published in a later volume.
 [9] The inserted entries on this page are in ink; the others are in pencil.
 [10] See *JMN*, IX, 65.
 [11] "Traits . . . found." is rewritten in ink over substantially the same matter
in pencil. The entries which follow on p. [5] are in pencil.
 [12] Cf. "Aristocracy," *W*, X, 38. Emerson had planned a lecture on "the Natural
Aristocracy" in December of 1847 and was engaged in writing it at Manchester on
January 26, 1848 (*L*, III, 443, IV, 8).

'tis as certain that he will have the direction
of estates as that there are estates[.] [13]

Nor will it at all be foreign to my purpose if it should appear
that I am describing that which is the theoretic ⟨nobility⟩ ↑peerage↓,
and not ⟨that which is⟩ ↑one↓ recognized & actualized in any kingdom
on earth. It would be ⟨base⟩ ↑ignoble,↓ would it not, ⟨& ignoble⟩ to
draw our sketch from any [6] ⟨institution⟩ ↑body↓ necessarily so
impure as any that can contrive to exist amidst so much vice, injustice,
& imbecility, as we all confess to in our times? [n]
I have no compliments to pay, & no tenderness ⟨to individuals⟩
⟨and really I confess no ⟨other⟩ interest in this topic personal to⟩ to
one or other renowned name, & really therefore no interest for their
sake, but ⟨for mine & yours⟩ ↑is my own & all men's↓[,] none but ↑a
regard↓ for the behoof of the race that there should be model men,
that we should all have true pictures of such, and, if possible, living
standards. I write of a nobility always existing but its members so
scattered, so heedless of badges, so rarely convened, ⟨t⟩so little in
sympathy with any favorite measure that it is not acknowledged in
any newspaper or in any Peerage.[14]

[7] For the particular of Nature's adopting peculiarities I think
it a sublime hint or beckoning from the outward universe to man
⟨h⟩to hive & insert as many virtues & superiorities as he can into this
web which is to be a fossil[.] [15]

Thus it will be seen that one after the other all the material badges
are dropped like so much tattoo or heraldry & those powers only
worn which subjugate nature[.] [16]

[8]   Vent⟨a⟩ilation all
         ⟨M⟩Love of Music the ruin of England
         If the minister will shove me

---

[13] "Beauty . . . estates" is struck through in pencil with a vertical use mark.
[14] "Nor will [p. [5]] . . . Peerage.", in pencil and struck through in pencil
with single vertical use marks on each page, is used in "Aristocracy," W, X, 31, 32.
[15] This paragraph, in pencil, is used in "Aristocracy," W, X, 34.
[16] This sentence, in pencil, is used in "Aristocracy," W, V, 197–198.

Where goes the surplus produce of every age
Large salaries do not enrich [17]

C[harles]N[ewcomb] remarked as W[illiam].E[llery].C[hanning].
had done, the French trait in H[enry].T[horeau]. & in his family.
Here is the precise voyageur of Canada sublimed, or carried up to
the seventh power. In the family the brother & one sister preserved
the French character of face.

———

↑*Sea line.*↓

As we see the human body or one of its limbs undraped, so here
nature shows us a limb of our planet in undress & we see the nakedness of the sea line. 'Tis a sublime curve yet causes an uncomfortable
feeling. To nature as to man we say, Still be drest! Still hide a poverty
even so grand under the ornamented details of a broken landscape.[18]

[9] Every man has his theory, most of them ridiculous. Mr.
Reid is a man who is skilful in the theory of ventilation, only he has
the misfortune to believe that the one thing needful is ventilation. I
came across another who had discovered the key to all the calamities
of England; it was the love of music, which was the ruin of England:[19] and, at last, I was doomed to meet Mr Walker, who told
me he stood for the ⟨D⟩deadman's question, and he had written a
book called "Gatherings from Graveyards." ↑See RS 84↓[20]

———

↑Lazarus the sun↓[21]

[17] "Vent⟨a⟩ilation . . . enrich" is in pencil. Cf. Notebook England and Paris,
p. [43] below; see p. [9] below.
[18] "As we . . . landscape." is transcribed from Journal Sea-Notes, p. [1] above.
[19] The same reference occurs in "Culture," *W*, VI, 132. In Journal BO, p. [87],
to be published in a later volume, Emerson refers to "Mr Phillips in London who
thought the ruin of England lay in Musical Concerts."
[20] See p. [8] above. David Boswell Reid (1805–1863), a Scottish inventor,
published *Illustrations of the Theory and Practice of Ventilation* (1844); George
Alfred Walker (1807–1884), an English medical practitioner and sanitary reformer,
was known as "Graveyard Walker" after publishing *Gatherings from Graveyards*
(1839) and *Graveyards of London* (1841). Reid, Walker, and the man suspicious
of music are mentioned in Journal CD, p. [147] above. Journal RS will be published
in a later volume.
[21] These three words are in pencil. A later entry on p. [158] below identifies
"Lazarus".

In France, they told me, that now, since ⟨th⟩February, Paris was not Paris, nor France France, everything was triste & grim.

All the members of the provisional government had become aged since February, except only Arago.[22]

[10] [blank]

[11] Of Immortality the soul, when well employed, is incurious. It is so well that it is sure it will be well. It asks no questions of the Supreme Power. The son of Antiochus asked his father, "When he would join battle?" "Dost thou fear," replied the king, "that thou only in all the army wilt not hear the trumpet?"[23]

Nobody should speak on this matter polemically. But it is the Gai Science and only to [be] chanted by Troubadours.

[12] In dreams, the ordinary theory is that there is but one person; the mystical theory is that there are two or more[.]

⟨"A child is better unborn than untaught"⟩[24]   Gascoigne

"It was so dry that you might call it wet."[25]

There's a great affinity between wit & oxygen; with the oxygen in these crowded parlours my wit always departs.

T[homas].C[arlyle]. has great vigour of constitution so that he can dispose of poison very well. He is a perfect sot in the strong waters of vituperation & reminds me of the rich swearing of the truckmen which W. described[.][26]

---

[22] François Arago (1786–1853), a scientist, was minister of war and marine in the French provisional government of 1848.

[23] Told of "King *Antigonus*" and his son in Plutarch, "Of Garrulity," *Plutarch's Morals . . . Translated from the Greek, by Several Hands*, 1718, IV, 231. "Of Immortality . . . trumpet?'", struck through in ink with two vertical use marks, is used in "Worship," *W*, VI, 239.

[24] This sentence, apparently canceled by a horizontal line in ink and also struck through in ink with two diagonal use marks, is used in "Culture," *W*, VI, 139.

[25] In "Thoreau," *W*, X, 479, Emerson attributes the saying to Thoreau.

[26] These two sentences are in pencil and struck through in pencil with a vertical use mark. Emerson arrived in London on March 2, 1848; in a letter of March 7 he reported that he had "seen Carlyle one good day" and on March 8 he mentioned having dined with him (*L*, IV, 29, 33). "W." appears also on p. [17] below.

[13] England is the country of the rich. The great Poor Man does not yet appear. Whenever he comes, England will fall like France. It would seem that an organizing talent applied directly to the social problem, to ⟨unite⟩ ↑bring↓, for example, labor to market[,] to bring want and supply face to face, would not be so rare. A man like Hudson, like Trevylian, like Cobden, should know something about it.[27]

Montaigne
In the British Museum, Mr Watts showed me the autograph of Shakspeare found in Florio's translation of Montaigne, & informed me that when they had procured a ⟨new copy⟩ duplicate copy of this Montaigne for the use of the library, it was found that an autograph of Ben Jonson was in the new book.[28]

[14] In London you will see that there must be certain types of face, which nature aims at in ⟨o⟩thousands of individual faces. For you shall see close approaches to every kind of face you know in America.   See *GH* 140,

[15] Every Englishman is a House of Commons. As that expects that every speech will propose a measure, so the man of letters here is never contemplative; a stanza of the song of nature ↑the↓ has no ear for, and he does not value the expansive & curative influence of intellectual action, studious of truth without a particular end.[29]
⟨It w⟩He has hard eyes. England is great by the back of the head.[30]

[16] Grievous amount of dross about men of wit, they are so

[27] As in Journal CD, p. [87] above, Emerson is referring to George Hudson, the "Railway King," a popular English hero in 1848; "Trevylian" is probably Sir Walter Trevelyan, "a baronet noted for his income of £40 000," as Emerson described him after a meeting in Edinburgh (*L*, IV, 21). Emerson heard Richard Cobden speak at Manchester and saw him again in London.
[28] This sentence, struck through in ink with a vertical use mark, is used in "Montaigne," *W*, IV, 163. Thomas Watts (1811–1869) was keeper of books at the British Museum, which Emerson visited during the first week of his stay in London (*L*, IV, 34).
[29] "the man of letters . . . end.", struck through in ink with a vertical use mark, is used in "Literature," *W*, V, 258.
[30] "He . . . head." is transcribed from Journal London, p. [9] above. See also Notebook ED, p. [5] below.

heavy, so dull, so oppressive with their bad jokes, & monstrous conceit, & stupefying individualism. Avoid the great man as one who is privileged to be an unprofitable companion.[31]

As a class the merchants are out of all comparison manlier & more sensible, and even the farmers are more real & agreeable.[32] But this is babyish. I hate that a scholar should be an old goody. If excellence as scholars has cost too much & spoiled them for society, let religion, let their homage to truth & beauty keep them in chambers or caves, that they may not by personal presence deface the fair festival which their reason & imagination have dressed. ↑See CD 115↓

[17] The most agreeable compliment that could be paid W. was to say that you had not observed him, in a house or in a street where you had met him. All he wished of his tailor was to provide just that sober mean of colour & cut which should never fix the eye for one moment. He went to Vienna, to Smyrna, to London. In all the immense variety of costumes ⟨that⟩ he saw in these places,—a mere carnival or kaleidoscope or Monmouth street of clothes,— to his horror he never could discover any man in the street who wore any thing resembling his own dress.—↑Briton requires such a tone of voice as excites no attention in the room.↓[33]

[18] The French Revolution just now has surprised every body, (themselves included,) who took any thought on the matter. ⟨No Thiers⟩ No[n] Guizot, no Thiers, no Barrot, no Times newspaper, no party that could remember & calculate but was baulked & confounded. Only the simple workmen, porters, shoeblacks, & women, and the few statesmen who, like Lamartine, could afford through riches & energy of nature to let themselves go without resistance whither the explosion was hurling them, found themselves suddenly right &

[31] This paragraph is used in "Powers and Laws of Thought," *W*, XII, 7.

[32] Cf. Emerson's praise of the merchant in Journal Sea-Notes, front cover verso above.

[33] "The most . . . room." is struck through in ink with two vertical use marks; there is an additional diagonal use mark through the second and third sentences and there are two additional diagonal use marks through the final sentence. "The most . . . dress." is used in "Society and Solitude," *W*, VII, 4–5; "Briton . . . room." is used in "Manners," *W*, V, 112.

well. One would say as S.W. said of the young collegians who drove a gig down his hill, "if they had known how to drive, they would have broken their necks."   ↑See also, V 116↓ [34]

The French are to a proverb so formidable in explosions that every boy sees the folly of Guizot & his master in bearding that lion. It had been plain to them a great while that just by dodging an explosion you might lead [19] the monster quietly into a cage.
This revolution has a ⟨new⟩feature new to history, that of socialism. The American Revolution was political merely.
⟨The⟩ It is not a good feature, the rhetoric of French politics. The manifestoes read like Buonaparte's proclamations, inflated. It strikes one, too, the identity of the nation through all these changes. I ask myself, what makes it? it is like the identity of an individual.

The king & his party fell for want of a shot, they had not conscience to shoot, so entirely was the heart & pith of monarchy eaten out. [35]

In Germany, said N., the former revolution collapsed for want of an idea. Now, all goes well, for they know what they want[.] [36]

The book trade in London is reduced to nothing since the new French Revolution. For the "Times," for fivepence every day gives them as much as they can read.

[20] It is certain that more people speak English correctly in ⟨America⟩the United States, than in Britain. [37]
"*A good time*" is an Americanism. In England, it is a phrase only applied to a woman after ⟨confinement⟩ childbirth.
"fix" in the sense of *arrange*
interēsting accented on the 3d syllable, & without r̲

---

[34] *JMN*, IX, 153. "S.W." may be Samuel Gray Ward.
[35] This sentence is struck through in ink with a vertical use mark. Louis Philippe (1773–1850), elected "Citizen King" of France following the Revolution of 1830, was himself overthrown by revolution in February of 1848; his premier from 1840 to 1848 was the historian François Pierre Guillaume Guizot (1787–1874).
[36] "Neuberg?" is written in pencil above "the", probably by Edward Emerson.
[37] See Journal London, p. [106] above.

↑*English peculiarities.*↓

the sound of *u.*	curious, curate, Europe, sure, purity,
the sound of *o*	glory, glorious, story, tory; O sometimes be-
	comes A.
	↑*More* befãre, twice two is *far* in England.↓ [38]
the sound of *ou*	pound, down, &c has an element of *a.*
the sound of a	arian, unitarian, various, drama,
the sound of e	inferior superior
the sound of *ea*	year, ear, = yer, ⟨er⟩

The English call the letter Z *zed* and not *zee*[.]
The better is the Englishman I meet, the less difference in speech &
accent I observe, and yet now & then I meet a well marked Englishman like Mr Woodfall.

↑Rare in the sense of *ill roasted* is American↓[.] [39]

[21] Every man's expense & economy must proceed from his character: a lame man must buy crutches & high heels; a blind man
goggles, & so on. So it is very well for Socrates & for Franklin, with
their famous tongues, to dress in woolen & serge, & go barefoot, &
spend nothing; but for a man without a tongue, a conformity in dress
must be bought at any price.

[22] The Chartist orator O'Brien insisting on no-property qualifica-
tion for ballot, urged that every working man does pay a tax, & the
capitalist pays only what he has robbed the working man of, & 'tis
not fair that he should rob him of his ballot also.

The delegate who had carried congratulations to the French Republic, said, that "they had determined not to wait even till they
knew whether it was a boy or a girl." [40]

---

[38] The insertion is written on p. [21] opposite "becomes A." Cf. Journal London,
p. [25] above, on "more" and "gore".
[39] This addition is in pencil.
[40] On March 7, 1848, Emerson "attended a meeting of Chartists assembled to
receive the report of the Deputation they had sent to congratulate the French Re-

I am sorry that all the French can say is ça va.

French woman can do most with a ⟨pocket h⟩handkerchief.

The English live in a system of pauperism where every part of the state gets encrusted with barnacles until the wheels can no longer move, prisons breeding prisons, & workhouse workhouse, & pensioners pensioners.   See Red Book p 123 [41]

[23] I see that the Londoner is also, like me, a stranger in London. I have a great deal to tell him of it, and there is no man who at all masters or much affects this self↑-↓arranging [42] mass.
The Englishman is proud; yes, but he is admirable. He knows all things, has all things, can do all: how can he not be proud?

↑*Why London is London.*↓
Sufficiency of the English people, & reason why London is London, & has all the business & all the money of the world — because men found that this people had a faculty of doing which others had not — interested Carlyle.
Americans, he said, go to France, & herd with their countrymen & are amused, instead of manfully staying in London & confronting Englishmen, who really have much to teach them, & acquiring their culture. C[arlyle]. observed this timidity & constant sense of being disliked, in Coolidge. [43] But everything provincial bores the Englishman. [44]

[24] I find all England resounding with one word, — Humbug. [45]

---

public, & which had returned" (*L*, IV, 34). James O'Brien, later James Bronterre (1805–1864), was an Irish journalist and Chartist.
[41] Here and elsewhere Emerson uses "Red Book" to refer to Journal London.
[42] The hyphen is added in pencil.
[43] Joseph Coolidge (1798–1879), a Boston merchant who in 1839 had visited Carlyle in the company of Charles Sumner (*CEC*, pp. 214, 223).
[44] "Sufficiency . . . culture." is struck through in ink with one vertical and one diagonal use mark. "Sufficiency . . . Englishman." is transcribed in Notebook ED, p. [226] below; "Americans, he . . . culture." is used in "Stonehenge," *W*, V, 275.
[45] This sentence is struck through in ink with a diagonal use mark.

The chartists, if you treat them civilly, & show any goodwill to their cause, suspect you, they think you are going to *do* them.[46]

Stephenson executed the idea of the age in iron. Who will do it in the social problem?
We want a moral engineer[.] [47]

[25] I hear sad stories sometimes as of dukes served by bailiffs with all their plate in pawn, and of great lords living by the showing of their houses, and an old man wheeled in his chair from room to room whilst his chambers are shown to the visiter. And many evils & iniquities, no doubt, arise from law of entail: and yet primogeniture built all these sumptuous Halls & Castles, and if they must fall, I am glad to have come hither before their fall. The D[uke]. of Northumberland is not rich enough to live in Northumberland House. Their many houses eat⟨h⟩ them up. They cannot sell them because they are entailed, & they will not lease them but keep them empty, aired, & the grounds mown & dressed at an expense of £.4000 a year.[48]

[26] It was very plain to me that the men of literary & social note such as Sparks, Newman, B., P., Oxenford, Morell, & many more⟨,⟩ were so only ↑by↓ a sort of beaver activity & not by any superiority of talent to the masses among which their names resounded. They were dull & mediocre men, or even less.[49]

———

I travelled, as I said, for a whip for my top. I had noticed that to every person are usually sent six or seven priests, in the course of their (impressible) life, &, to find one of these, he may well cross to

<hr />

[46] See Journal London, p. [22] above.
[47] This sentence is an expansion of an entry in Notebook England and Paris, p. [50₂] below.
[48] "I hear . . . year.", struck through in pencil with a vertical use mark and in ink with two diagonal use marks, is used in "Aristocracy," *W*, V, 193.
[49] These two sentences are struck through in ink with two vertical use marks. The probable references are to the American historian Jared Sparks, John Henry Newman, George Bancroft, Bryan Waller Procter, John Oxenford, and J. D. Morell, author of *An Historical and Critical View of the Speculative Philosophy of Europe in the Nineteenth Century* (London, 1846). Cf. "Power," *W*, VI, 79-80.

Asia, or the Antarctic Zone. It was to be expected that I might find the seventh ⟨in⟩ of mine in England.⁵⁰

[27] The man of the world, in reply to an indiscreet inquiry, says, 'it is not known.'

Mr Foster told Mr Rogers's story of the Englishman & Frenchman who quarrelled, but were both exceedingly unwilling to fight. At last it was agreed that they should fight in the dark. The English-man, to be safe, fired his pistol up the chimney, — & brought down the Frenchman!

The English practical mind shown in the man who deposited £100 in the Bank against the Mesmerisers,⁵¹ & in the man who wished to buy house, servants, & *wife of the landlord*, at   ,
& in the member who asked of the ↑prime↓ minister a place; "No, 'tis promised." — "But I have ten votes." — "Yes, what can I do?" — "But I have ten votes"; & 'twas granted.

England still a little topheavy, though she keeps her feet much better since the Corn laws were thrown overboard.⁵²

[28] ↑March 14↓
It is a proof of the abundance of literary talent here, that no one knows, or, I think, asks the name of the writers of paragraphs & articles of great ability. — It seems strange that literary power suf-ficient to set up twenty such reputations as Quinet, ↑or↓ Michelet, and a hundred Prescotts & Sparkses, is here wasted in some short-

---

⁵⁰ "I travelled . . . England.", struck through in ink with a vertical use mark, is used in "Culture," *W*, VI, 147; cf. also "Character," *W*, X, 101. Concerning Emerson's "priests", see his list in *JMN*, V, 160, of "the scattered company who have ministered to my highest wants."

⁵¹ For "Mr Rogers's story", see Journal London, p. [198] above; for Carlyle's story of the man who deposited £100, see Journal London, p. [56] above, and cf. Notebook ED, p. [12] below. "Mr Foster . . . Mesmerisers," is struck through in pencil with a vertical use mark and in ink with one vertical and one diagonal use mark. "Mr Foster . . . Frenchman!" is transcribed in Notebook ED, p. [75] below, and used in "Cockayne," *W*, V, 149.

⁵² "England . . . overboard." is a rewriting in ink of an erased pencil entry: "England . . . laws went." See also Journal London, p. [74] above.

-lived paper in the ⟨Literar⟩"Christian Remembrancer" — or ⟨T⟩the "Foreign Quarterly", or even in a few leaders in the "Times" Newspaper. The papers surprise me, for I do not meet anywhere the fine tempered talent that could write them, but only such literary men as I have known before. I read this morn the excellent critique ⟨i⟩on Carlyle's Cromwell in the "Christian Remembrancer" for April, 1846.[53]

[29] A man must be in sympathy with society about him, or else, not wish to be in sympathy with it. If neither of these two, he must be wretched.

Nature
The oceanic working of Nature which accumulates a momentary individual as she forms a momentary wave in a running sea.

Goethe speaks of the seriousness of Nature in the "Collector," &c.
      & Plato in Phaedrus[,] Taylor's Vol. III. p. 336, speaks in like manner.[54]

[30] Great is paint.[55] The man of the world slides easily thro' all towns & knows how to be a distingué in all, with a small capital of stars & scarfs & cockades. He wears a red cap in Paris, a red coat in Rome, and a green turban at Constantinople.

> Rags & curds
> The whole marrow
> Are not worth the devil
> Widemouthed laughing

[53] A review of *Oliver Cromwell's Letters and Speeches; with Elucidations*, by Thomas Carlyle, in the *Christian Remembrancer*, n.s., LII (April 1846), 243–315. This paragraph is struck through in pencil with a wavy diagonal use mark; cf. "Power," *W*, VI, 79–80.
[54] Emerson's references are to (1) "The Collector and His Friends," one of the contributions to the *Propylaeum* included in Goethe's *Essays on Art*, trans. Samuel G. Ward (Boston, 1845), pp. 42–117; and (2) Plato, *The Works* . . . , trans. Floyer Sydenham and Thomas Taylor, 1804. See Notebook Platoniana, p. [23] below.
[55] See *JMN*, IX, 444.

Haggling & gaping
Gaping & buying
Heaps of beasts
Children & ⟨cats⟩ brats
Monkeys & cats[56]

[31] The ⟨E⟩Athenaeum excludes Guizot, when his name is proposed as an honorary member. They would be proud of his name,
but the Englishman is not fickle, he really made up his mind to hate
& to despise Guizot, & the altered position of the man, as an exile
and a guest in the country, make no difference to him, as they would
instantly ↑to↓ an American. The Englishman talks of politics & institutions, but the real thing which he values is his home, & that which
belongs to it, — that general culture & high polish which in his experience no man but the Englishman possesses, & which he naturally
believes have some essential connexion with his throne & laws. That
is what he does not believe resides in America, & therefore his contempt of America [is] only half-concealed. — This English tenacity in
strong contrast with our facility. The facile American sheds his
Puritanism when he leaves Cape Cod, runs into all English & French
vices with great zest & is neither Unitarian, nor Calvinist, nor Catholic
nor stands for any known thought or thing; which is [32] very
distasteful to English honour. It is a bad sign that I have met with
many Americans who flattered themselves that they pass for English.
Levity, levity. I do not wish to be mistaken for an Englishman, more
than I wish Monadnock or Nahant or Nantucket to be mistaken for
Wales or the Isle of Wight.[57]

Appleton spends so much wit, anecdote, good nature, on every
conversation, that it is impossible with the ordinary economies of
nature that he can have any stoves, any winter, any ulterior views.
He is like a broker who ⟨buys⟩ lends such sums that you would infer

[56] "Rags . . . cats" is in pencil.
[57] "The ⟨E⟩Athenaeum . . . Wight." is struck through in pencil with a vertical
use mark on p. [31] and another on p. [32] through "Englishman". On p. [31],
"⟨E⟩Athenaeum . . . belongs to it," is struck through in ink with two diagonal use
marks; "culture . . . throne & laws." is struck through in ink with another diagonal
use mark. "The ⟨E⟩Athenaeum . . . an American." is used in "Truth," *W*, V, 121.

that he was rich; but no, he turns all his capital every day. Or, as E
said, a man with a shirt pin. They said he was a rich man but he had
only [33] a shirt pin.

Concord has a horizon like the sea, has woodlands, and is permeable
as a park.

[34] [March 14, 1848.] "Our rivers have their sources in its domin-
ions"; says the German (East Prussian) placard ⟨in speaking⟩ re-
proachfully of Russian dominion. 14 March

"And other grain," Mr Austin said[,] were words introduced by
Franklin into a provision↑-↓bill in Pennsylvania to cover *gunpowder*.[58]

Mr Hallam asked me at Lord Ashburton's, whether Swedenborg
were all mad, or partly knave? He knew nothing of Thomas Taylor,
neither did Milman, or any Englishman.[59]

[35][60] "I rise in the dignity of conscious virtue," said Roebucke in
his first speech in the H[ouse]. of Commons.[61] "Topic" spoiled a
speech the other day[.]
Another proof of the literary wealth of England is the profound
obscurity of T Taylor. Mr Hallam knew next to nothing of him &
Milman nothing.[62]

English society, of course, requires great vigour of health to shine
in it. As we say, you must be a bruiser for Congress. The novice

[58] The hyphen in "provision-bill" and the underlining of "*gunpowder*" are
added in pencil. For the anecdote, see *The Autobiography of Benjamin Franklin*, ed.
Leonard W. Labaree et al. (New Haven, 1964), p. 189.
[59] "Mr Hallam . . . Englishman." is rewritten in ink over substantially the
same matter in erased pencil writing. Cf. Journal London, p. [129] above; Notebook ED, pp. [59], [60] below.
[60] All the entries on this page are rewritten in ink over substantially the same
matter in erased pencil writing.
[61] Emerson's reference is to John Arthur Roebuck (1801–1879), a radical M.P.
brought up in Canada.
[62] The earlier version in pencil of "Another . . . nothing." was struck through
in pencil with a diagonal use mark, now partly erased. See p. [34] above.

fancies that the gladiators say something better than he; No, but they say it better.

Macaulay has the strength of ten men.

An unitarian will presently be shown as a Dodo, an extinct race.

"This is the most cocktail house of Commons," said

That Macaulay should be voted a *bore* in some high aristocratic companies, is pathetic example of the impossibility of pleasing all.[63]

[36] He who strikes ten blows ⟨on⟩with his hammer, whilst the foreign workman only strikes one, is as really vanquishing that foreigner, as if the blows were aimed at & told on his person.[64]

Yes, manners differ. In the Society Islands, if you do not drink kava, you are no gentleman.

T[homas]. A[ppleton]. said, Women were to humbug men.

[37] Mr Neuberg said that the Rothschilds make great fortunes, but they really do a certain important service to ⟨the world⟩society; they are the cashiers of the world: and it is a public mischief when any calamity befals them. People at Nottingham are carried into crime, because Rothschild does not accept bills at Paris; it[n] is quite obvious to him: he can trace it all the way.[65]↑ — So when a bank discounts freely in any district, immediately an impulse is given to population, & new men are born.

See the account Rothschild gave of himself, in Fowell Buxton's life, p.   especially in regard to Luck↓[.] [66]

[63] A similar observation occurs in Emerson's letter of March 24, 1848, to his wife (*L*, IV, 42–43).
[64] This sentence, struck through in pencil with one wavy diagonal use mark and five additional diagonal use marks, and in ink with a single diagonal use mark, is used in "Worship," *W*, VI, 225.
[65] "it is . . . way." is struck through in pencil with three vertical use marks; the entry to this point is used in "Wealth," *W*, VI, 105.
[66] *Memoirs of Sir Thomas Fowell Buxton*, ed. Charles Buxton (London, 1848), pp. 288–290; in Emerson's library. Rothschild's precept was "never to have anything to do with an unlucky place or an unlucky man" (p. 289). "See . . . Luck" is struck through in pencil with a vertical use mark; see the lecture outline on p. [3] above.

[38] Agassiz made lectures on anatomy popular by the aid of an idea: homology, analogy, did that for him, which all the police of Boston could not have done, in holding the crowd together at the Odeon, when Wyman lectured on the same subject[.] [67]

The three ⟨pillars⟩columns of the Temple of Jupiter Stator at Rome, I have heard, were the despair of architects.

An Englishman believes in England, a Frenchman believes in France, but you do not believe in yourself.

[38ₐ] [...] [68]
[39] ↑The new Religion↓   ↑See p 79↓
Yes, there will be a new church founded on moral science, ↑at↓ first cold & naked, a babe in a manger again, a Copernican theory, the algebra & mathematics of Ethical law, the church of men to come without shawms or psaltery or sackbut, but it will have heaven & earth for its beams & rafters, all geology & physiology, botany, chemistry, astronomy for its symbol & illustration, and it will fast enough gather beauty, ↑music, picture, poetry,↓ [69]
It was necessary that this roaring Babylon should fall flat, before the whisper that commands the world could be heard. It seems to every youth that he is alone, & left to fall abroad with too much liberty, when he is left with only God. He does not yet begin to see & to hear[.]

---

[67] There is a similar reference to Agassiz in "Aristocracy," *W*, X, 53–54. Here Emerson is contrasting the popular appeal of Agassiz with that of Jeffries Wyman (1814–1874), physician, anatomist, and ethnologist, who in 1840 became curator and one of the first lecturers of the Lowell Institute in Boston.

[68] Laid in between pp. [38] and [39] is a loose leaf of 18.4 x 11.4 cm bearing a pencil drawing of a young girl with a pitcher, watering a plant in an urn. In pencil, overleaf, Emerson wrote these lines:
> "O Ellen, may these happy hours be sweet to thee,
> For far from happy am I
> While I roam about in this vast great house
> With no one to look on me"

"Ellen" is presumably Emerson's daughter Ellen Tucker Emerson (1839–1909).

[69] "Yes, there . . . poetry," struck through in pencil with a wavy diagonal use mark, and in ink with a diagonal use mark, is used in "Worship," *W*, VI, 241.

The Eng[lish]. church being undermined by German criticism, had nothing left but tradition, & flung itself in to Roman church; distrusting the laws of the universe. The next step is now the ruin of Christendom.[70]

[40] Wisdom always lays the emphasis of reform in the right place, on tendency, on character, & not on some absurd particular, as on the knife & fork, which is sure to produce dislocation & ridiculous jangle. A monk must live in a monastery; an ascetic in Thebais; he cannot get such puddings as he likes, in Nottingham or Concord. Hence the strength of the argument of the socialist. Perhaps he is right and a thousand cockboats will serve his purpose no better than one⟨,⟩ would; he wants a steamboat to cross this flood.

[41] I had rather have a good symbol of my thought, ↑or↓ a good analogy, than the suffrage of Kant or Plato. If you agree with me, or if Locke, or Montesquieu, or Spinoza agree, I may still be wrong: but if the elm tree thinks the same thing,—if running water, if burning coal, if crystals, acids, & alkalis, say what I say, it must be true.[71]

[42] Every soul is sent into nature accompanied by its assessors or witnesses. They are attached to it by similarities which keep them through all changes in the same stratum or plane, & within the same sphere; as the bodies of one solar system never quit their respective distances, but remain, as the foot of an animal follows its head. To his astonishment the man finds that he can never think alone, his thought is always apprehended by equal intellect; that he can never hide his action, but witnesses, & those his intimate acquaintance, look out of the dark of every cave, in an Asiatic desart, in an Arabian Sahara.[72] ↑The rule of the Lowell Corporations was, that no girl should walk in the streets at night, unless with two companions.↓

[70] These two sentences, struck through in pencil and in ink with two diagonal use marks, are used in "Religion," *W*, V, 228.
[71] "I had . . . true." is used in "Poetry and Imagination," *W*, VIII, 13. Cf. *JMN*, IX, 410.
[72] The paragraph to this point is used in part in "Worship," *W*, VI, 226.

[43] Everything connected with our personality fails. We are always baulked of a complete success. No prosperity is promised to that. We have our amends only in the sure success of that to which we belong: and, to secure our disinterestedness, the assurance of private immortality is taken away. That, that is immortal, but we are not⟨.⟩↑, or only through that.↓ [73]

People interest as long as there is some reserve about them. Only that mind draws me which I cannot read.

"The belief that self consists in that which is not self, & that property consists in that which is not our own, is the double fruit of the tree of Ignorance." [74]

[44] The objection, the ↑loud↓ denial not less proves the reality & conquests of an idea, than the friends & advocates it finds. Thus communism now is eagerly attacked, and all its weak points acutely pointed out by British writers & talkers; which is all so much homage to the Idea, whose first ⟨e⟩inadequate expressions interest them so deeply, & with which they feel their fate to be mingled. If the French should set out to prove that three was four, would British journalism bestir itself to contradict them? The Geologic Society and the Stock Exchange would ⟨not⟩ have no time to share it. ↑See p 50↓

"⟨La⟩Le talent s'abaisse avec le caractère. Tel est l'ent[r]ainement des fausses situations; telle est la pente des erreurs d⟨u⟩e principe; telle est la loi du coeur humain, qui emporte les hommes dans des voies perilleuses, quand leur caractere ne domine pas leur passion ou leur talent."
Lettre à De-Lamartine
L'Assemblée Nationale
23 May 1848

il ne fallait plus compter sur vous [75]

[73] "Everything . . . through that." is used in "Immortality," *W*, VII, 342–343.

[74] Cf. *JMN*, IX, 290, quoting *The Vishńu Puráńa*, trans. H. H. Wilson, 1840, pp. 649–650.

[75] Emerson is quoting an open letter attacking Lamartine published on the front page of *L'Assemblée Nationale* for May 23, 1848, signed by the editors; for " ⟨La⟩ Le talent . . . caractère.", see col. 2, ll. 80–81; for "Tel est . . . talent.", see col. 3, ll. 27–32; for "il ne . . . sur vous", see col. 3, ll. 34–35. The third extract should be read in its context: "La journée du 15 mai n'eût-elle produit d'autre

[45] I was struck at least in one interview lately with the mutual timidity of a couple of eminences (of very diverse sorts), each exaggerating the other, & then it appeared that victory was cheap, & lay there waiting for which one first recovered his reason.

"Le regne des épées ⟨est⟩a passé, le jour où celle de Napoleon a été impuissante pour sa defense et pour la nôtre!

"La force brutale des sabres, de la conquête, est brisée: brisez celle des fusils populaires. Que les fusils, comme les epées, s'abaissent aujourdhui devant les idées. Faites vous Général des idées du siècle. xxxxx Ce qui reste aujourdhui des canons de Bonaparte, c'est la mitraille d'idées qu'ils contenaient aussi. ————— [...] Ses codes etaient à la suite de ses armées, comme les *cotons* suivent les armées de l'Angleterre."

Assemblée Nationale
23 May 1848

Letter to M. de Lamartine [76]

[46] "I am very much obleeged to you, Captain Tuttle, but I've done taking rye," said the good farmer whose ⟨house⟩home had been burned, & whose neighbors brought rye & wheat.

⟨All that is required of the lord is to sit securely⟩ [77]

———

At Oxford you may hold what opinion you please so that you hold your tongue.

———

Good story of the three grey wigs of the savant in or near the British Museum and of Lord Aberdeen

———

In going thro' the street you should be in a state of positive electricity not negative[.] [78]

———

malheur que d'apprendre à la France qu'il ne fallait plus compter sur vous, elle serait à jamais détestable! on voudrait pouvoir l'arracher de l'histoire!"

[76] For " 'Le regne . . . l'Angleterre.' ", see *L'Assemblée Nationale*, May 23, 1848, p. 1, col. 3, ll. 100–103, 106–120. The intervening phrasing omitted by Emerson reads: "Une épée a-t-elle sauvé les Bourbons de la branche aînée le 29 juillet 1830? et les Bourbons de la branche cadette le 24 février 1848?"

[77] "⟨All . . . securely⟩" is struck through in pencil with a vertical line, apparently a use mark, and also lined out in ink, apparently for cancellation.

[78] "At Oxford . . . negative" is in pencil.

Mrs Sophia Bradford said, that her girl put her head out of the window, & said, "You can go out this evening, Mrs B., if you like, for I am not going."

[47] If I should believe the Reviews, and I am always of their opinion, I have never written any thing good. And yet, against all criticism, the books survive until this day.

For the matter of Socialism, there are no oracles. The oracle is dumb. When we would pronounce anything truly of man, we retreat instantly on the individual.

We are authorized to say much on the destinies of one, nothing on those of many. It seems cruel that every man should be in false position, &, that, scholar & saint though he be, he should find himself in this most awkward relation to loaves of bread. And the promise of Socialism is to redress this disturbed balance. But I think it needs that we must have the substance in purity which we will analyze, and not only cling to individuals but to angels. We must consider the condition of a youthful [48] soul sent for its education into this University of Nature, and perhaps it must have this drastic treatment of famine & plenty, insult & rapture, wisdom & tragedy, infernal & supernal society, in order to ⟨apply⟩secure that breadth of culture so ⟨secular an⟩ longlived a destiny needs.

O were there times that deserved any attention! but how can these convulsions ⟨a⟩effect any change of mood in ⟨so⟩ any firm Caesarian scholar? [n] Archimedes buried himself in his geometry, &
                              in his painting, when Marcellus or Demetrius were battering down their walls.[79]

[49] I fancied, when I heard that the times were anxious & political, that there is to be a ↑Chartist↓ revolution on Monday next, and an Irish revolution in the following week, that the right scholar would feel, — now was the hour to test his genius. His kingdom is at once over & under these perturbed regions. Let him produce its Charter now, & try whether it cannot win a hearing, & make felt its infinite

[79] Cf. "Courage," W, VII, 270; "Celebration of Intellect," W, XII, 114.

superiority today, even today. As, in the arts, they make winter oil on the coldest, & spermaceti candles on the hottest day of the year.[80]

T[homas]. C[arlyle]. compared the savans of Somerset House to the boy who asked Confucius how many stars in the sky? Confucious replied[,] He minded things near him: Then said the boy[,] How many hairs in your eyebrows? Confucius did not know & did not care.[81]

[50] One sees readily in the embittered acuteness of the Oxonian reviewer in snuffing heresy from far how hapless an unbeliever he is, & why he inveighs so angrily against that which he vainly resists in his own bosom. ↑See p 44↓

People here expect a revolution. There will be no revolution, none that deserves to be called so. There may be a scramble for money. But as all the people we see want the things we now have, & not better things, it is very certain that they will, under whatever change of forms, keep the old system.
When I see changed men, I shall look for a changed world.
Whoever is skilful in heaping money now, will be skilful in heaping money again. But we want

[51] Power. There must be a relation between power & probity. We have, no doubt, as much power as we can be trusted with. We seem to be on the eve of wonderful additions through alchemy & mesmerism, and yet ⟨it will not be given,⟩ our hands will not be unbound, until our sanity is quite secure. We seem already to have more ↑(power)↓ than we can be trusted with.[82] And this preparation for a

[80] A note by Edward Emerson in the top margin of p. [49] suggests that Emerson wrote the foregoing lines during the first week of April, 1848. At that time the Chartists were planning a march on the Houses of Parliament; as Emerson later remarked in a letter to his wife, on April 20, "the Revolution, fixed for the tenth instant, occupied all men's thought until the Chartist petition was actually carried to the Commons" (L, IV, 54).

[81] This paragraph, in pencil and struck through in pencil with a vertical use mark, is used in "Stonehenge," W, V, 274–275.

[82] The insertion is in pencil. It is possible that Emerson wrote "Power" at the

⟨great &⟩ superior race is a higher omen of revolution than any other I have seen. Except to better men, the ⟨meli⟩ augmented science is a mere chemic experiment of the ⟨best⟩ quickest poison.

What wrong road have we taken that all the improvements of machinery have helped every body but the operative? him they have incurably hurt.

[52]   ↑See U. p. 11↓ [83]
A curious example of the rudeness and inaccuracy of thought is the inability to distinguish between the private & the universal con-sciousness. I never make that blunder when I write, but the critics who read impute their confusion to me.

I know, of course, all the grounds on which any man affirms the immortality of the soul. The barrel of water is equally full in every cellar[;] the difference is in the distribution of pipes & pumps over the house. The spring is common; the difference in the aqu⟨a⟩educt.
                                       ↑See O 151↓ [84]

[53] In the question of socialism, which now proposes the confiscation of France[,] one has only this guidance. You shall not so arrange property as to remove the motive to industry. If you refuse rent & interest, you make all men idle & immoral. As to the poor a vast proportion have made themselves so, and in any new arrangement will only prove a burden on the state. And there is a great multitude also whom the existing system bereaves forever of all culture & of all hope.

The masses — ah if you could read the⟨ir⟩ biographies of those who compose them!   ↑See RS 154↓ [85]

The word *pay* is immoral.[86]

---

top of p. [51] as a continuation of "But we want" on p. [50], although "want" is followed there by a word space and then by four blank lines.

[83] *JMN*, IX, 10.

[84] *JMN*, IX, 400. "I know . . . aqu⟨a⟩educt.", struck through in ink with a vertical use mark, is used in "Instinct and Inspiration," *W*, XII, 66–67.

[85] Journal RS will be published in a later volume.

[86] See *JMN*, VIII, 84.

Now we will work, because we can have it all to our snug selves; tomorrow[n] we will not, because it goes to the community, & we all stand on a pauper's footing.

[54] The wonder of the science of Intellect is that the substance with which we deal is of that transcendant & active nature, that it intoxicates all who approach it. Gloves on the hands, glass guards over the eyes, wire gauze masks over the face, volatile salts in the nostrils, are no defence[n] against this virus, or rather gravitation.

Every thing is mover or moved, & we are admonished of omnipotence when we say, let us have intellect on our own terms.[87]

"Many have inquired into the causes of sleep, but the most determined inquirer could not long keep his eyes open[.]" ↑Johnson↓ [88]

There are many kinds of puffing. I fancy the most effective would be to hush up your fact as a secret. "⟨F⟩Mr Michael is going to sing. You must promise not to tell any body, there would be such a crowd." ↑Then the house will be jammed full.↓

[55] Dr Channing's vice, like that of Morgan, & of all the political mediocrities, is to exaggerate the formalities, the formal action of ecclesiastical, academic, political, & social ⟨meetings⟩ bodies.[89]

> Eton, Hanwell, Penshurst
> trades of despair [90]
> English are not allowed to be slovens but are always kept in

high order & ready for a dress dinner at 6[.]
Dr Arnott's story of the Highlander from Strathspey who when in

---

[87] "The wonder . . . terms." is struck through in pencil with both a vertical use mark and a wavy diagonal use mark. "The wonder . . . gravitation" is used in "Powers and Laws of Thought," *W*, XII, 10–11.

[88] Both "Johnson" and the quotation marks are added in pencil, with the quotation marks then rewritten in ink. Emerson is paraphrasing the third and fourth paragraphs of *The Idler*, No. 32 (November 25, 1758); see *JMN*, VI, 171.

[89] Emerson's reference here is probably to John Minter Morgan, a wealthy social reformer, with whom he had engagements on March 17 and 28, 1848 (Pocket Diary 3, pp. [68], [70] below; *L*, IV, 71).

[90] See Journal London, pp. [72], [120] above.

London at dinner small glasses of whiskey were brought about on ⟨waiter⟩ salvers took one & then six & said to the waiter "Yes I like that whiskey; could you bring me a glass of it," taking these for samples[.] [91]

[56] Guidance and determination to an aim? [n] — Yes, certainly, the book must have these, were the author ten times a poet; but it must not be mechanical, not a placing, but a polarity.

"La question de Dieu manque d'actualité," said the director of a Review to Paul Leroux on his article entitled Dieu. [92]

The twist in London conversation, is, that since you have come to France you have lost all correctness in your French[.]
     If there is one test accepted, it is success, & if there be one successful country in the world, it is England. [93] ↑See p 91↓

[57] As certainly as water falls in rain on the tops of mountains and runs down into valleys, plains, & pits, so does thought fall first on the best minds, & run down from class to class until it reaches the masses, & works [n] revolutions. [94] ↑Intellectuality works down.↓

The most important word the Age has given to the vocabulary, is Blouse.* It has not yet got into the Dictionary, and even in America for a year or two it has been of doubtful sound, whether English blouse, or French blouse. But, at last, the French Revolution has decided forever its euphony. It is not that it was new for the workman ⟨to speak in clubs⟩ to have ideas & speak in clubs, but new in its proportions to find not 500, but 200 000 thinkers & ⟨operat⟩orators in blouse. Guizot thought they were but a handful.

* and Humbug
     [91] "Eton, Hanwell . . . samples" is in pencil.
     [92] This sentence is rewritten in ink over the same words in pencil. Struck through in ink with a vertical use mark, it is used in "Worship," W, VI, 209.
     [93] This sentence, struck through in ink with seven diagonal use marks, is used in "Land," W, V, 35.
     [94] This sentence is used in "The Man of Letters," W, X, 249.

[58] Happy is he who gets early in life (or not too late) a good hobby.[95] What happiness & fortune for Charles Fellows was in that ruin at Xanthus, when a Turk with his staff uncovered the base of a stone, & showed him the ⟨scu⟩ reliefs sculptured on it. That has been his university, has taught him Greek, chemistry, geology, history, art, poetry, & made him acquainted with all men.[96] Owen by his fixed idea penetrates all courts, & sees all distinguished men. Morgan's village is his key to Pope, & prelate, author & foreigner. Dr Tuckerman with his Ministry-at-large. So Perez Blood with his telescope. Sir Joshua Reynolds, (Fox said, ↑see *PY* 183↓) had no pleasure in Richmond; he used to say, the human face was his landscape.[97]

[59] What is vulgar but the laying the emphasis on facts instead of on the quality of the fact? Mr Jones, in despair of getting your attention, tells you that ↑this↓ grandmother died this morning. Mr Giles, when there is a pause in the conversation, volunteers the information that he thinks himself dying in these weeks at the liver. Both fail of eliciting any remark.

Happy is ⟨o⟩he who looks only into his work to know if it will succeed, never into the times or the public opinion; and who writes from the love of imparting certain thoughts & not from the necessity of sale — ↑who writes always to *the unknown friend*.↓[98]

[60] Man runs through a greater range of climates than any other animal. And when good, he is good in the open air, & good in the house; in a club, & tête a tète; good with a horse, and good to walk forty miles.

---

[95] See the lecture outline on p. [3] above.

[96] "Happy . . . men." is used in "Education," *W*, X, 145.

[97] Emerson is referring to Richard Owen, possibly to John Minter Morgan (see p. [55] above), Rev. Joseph Tuckerman of Boston, and Perez Blood of Concord, a farmer "who used his small inheritance of money from his father to buy a telescope and celestial globe" (*J*, VII, 432, n. 3). "Sir Joshua . . . landscape." is used in "Inspiration," *W*, VIII, 290–291.

[98] "Happy . . . thoughts" is struck through in ink with a vertical use mark.

The Reform bill took in new partners, & Chartism again takes in more.[99]

———

[61] 22 April. I spent last evening with Coventry Patmore, the poet. He explained to me his theories of architecture. In the gothic it was a copresence of growth & geometry, of liberty & law,[n] which he illustrated excellently by details of ornament as the ball-flower, & especially the spand⟨al⟩ril[n] and the toothed-flower. Then in York Minster he showed the ascension, the suggestion of infinite ascension by ↑ascending↓ parallel lines, the power of the tower, the truncation, & the manner in which the eye was prepared for the truncation. In the Egyptian the fundamental idea is ⟨these⟩the Base or Basis. A Pyramid is the least possible departure from pure base. The base is immensely superfluous, and their temple, he showed, to be a sort of split base. The pillars ridiculously short. The column of Egyptian arch[itectur]e is a picture of a supporter crushed out by the super-incumbent weight. The Greek, I think, he called competence of support:—the flutes of the Doric column represented the upward principle[;] [62] the metopes the descending, and there was always ⟨a little⟩ample support, & a little to spare, which was indicated by channeling, that it, weakening the column⟨,⟩ just at the point where these ascenders & descenders met, that is, where the strain was: and whenever a little weight is added by the projection of the entablature, a row of flowers is added to show the exuberance of strength.

How many faces in the street still remind us of visages in the forest; they have not quite ↑yet↓ escaped from the lower form.[100]

[63] [101] One power streams into all natures[.]
Mind is vegetable, & grows thought out of thought as joint out of joint in corn[.]

---

[99] This sentence was originally written in pencil, with "bill" capitalized; the pencil writing appears below and to the right of this entry.

[100] "how many . . . form.", in pencil, is used in "Powers and Laws of Thought," *W*, XII, 22.

[101] All the entries on this page are in pencil.

Mind is chemical, & shows all the affinities & repulsions of chemistry, & works by presence[.]

Mind grows, crystallizes,   electricity
This all comes of a higher fact, one substance
        Mind knows the way because it has trode it before
        Knowledge is becoming of that thing
        Somewhere sometime some eternity we have played this game before
        Go thro' British Museum & we are full of occult sympathies
⟨azote⟩ ↑I↓ was azote
It is a little fearful to see with what genius some people take to hunting; what knowledge they still have of the creature they hunt; how lately they were his organic enemy; and the physiognomies in the street have their type in the woods.[102]
As in the British Museum one feels his family ties, so in astronomy not less. Little men Copernicise[.] [103]

[64] [104] Saw Clough, — talked of the inevitable civilization, & how much we owe it; as inevitable as we are[.] The development of inevitable parts. We have got our bread & blood out of it until this hour, & must contrive to get our suction-pump or tap-root still applied to it, nor must we protest in parts but in system.
When we do not know our universal tendency, we must take refuge in our particular talent[.]

Let
I take no interest in mechanical writing, only in a true vegetable action[.]

[65] I suppose you could never prove to the mind of the most in-

---

[102] "Mind grows . . . woods." is struck through in pencil with a vertical use mark. "Go thro' . . . woods." is used in "Powers and Laws of Thought," W, XII, 22.

[103] For "Little men Copernicise", see Journal AB, p. [82] above, and Journal GH, p. [8] above.

[104] This page is in pencil with "Saw . . . system." rewritten in ink over the original pencil writing.

genious ⟨of the⟩ mollus⟨ca⟩k that such a creature as a whale was possible.

[66] When men feel & say, "Those men occupy my place," the revolution is near. But I never feel that any men occupy my place; but that the reason I do not have what I ⟨want⟩ ↑wish↓, is, that I want the faculty which entitles. All spiritual or real power makes its own place.[105] Revolutions of violence then are scrambles merely.

dirty as a clam [106]

---

of great men.

I have never met a person superior to his talent, — one who had money in his pocket & did not use it.[107]

W.E.C[hanning]. said with his seek & slay torch of ↑————↓ that he was a man who lied gravely to himself & then believed it.[108]

[67] The insect that feeds on the apple is born within the apple, the weevil or curculio that eats the plum is hatched at the root of the tree. But the man is less surely directed to his bread. ↑See TU↓ [109]

⟨They⟩
The people invite the philosopher to deliver a "Temperance ⟨Address⟩ Lecture" in the Town Hall; the English gentleman, to teach their children dancing. & the poet to write a Cattleshow Glee for the Choir.[110]

[68] An Orator in the French club declares, that "when the

[105] For " 'Those men occupy my place' " — a remark attributed to Talleyrand — see *JMN*, IX, 109. "But I . . . own place." is used in "Aristocracy," *W*, X, 47.
[106] These four words are in pencil. See Journal AB, p. [130] above.
[107] This sentence is also entered in Index Major, p. [123], under Greatness; Emerson added "unless C[harles] K[ing] N[ewcomb]".
[108] The dash is added in pencil within a previously blank space. Cf. Journal London, p. [139] above: "Torchlight processions have a seek & slay look. . . ."
[109] The insertion is in pencil. Journal TU will be published in a later volume.
[110] "⟨They⟩ . . . Choir." is in pencil.

hour arrives for the Second revolution, and it is not far off, the people (who had been too generous at the first revolution in February,) will show that it can avenge as well as pardon"!

An errand boy in France is commissionaire[.]
a kitchen   is laboratoire[.]
applied to   is consacrée[.] [111]

A taper is not a conflagration[.] [112]

In Blanqui's club, an orator in blouse said "Why should they (the rich) fear that we shall not protect their property? We shall guard it with the utmost care, in the belief that it will soon be our own." [113]

[69] I expected to find the men wearing caps for hats[.]

You would think from the pictures [in shopwindows] & in the Louvre that ladies usually here went naked or sat in pink gauze[.] [114]

The negative superlative goes on increasing & by & by when all France is mad & every man takes the other by the throat, Blanqui will hang himself for joy.

[70] ⟨This was‖ ... ‖⟩ ↑An artist's↓ ⟨that ‖ ... ‖ to profit of ‖ ... ‖ and knowing that his⟩ [115] ticket to society ⟨was⟩ ↑is↓ not transferable, ⟨that⟩ he ha⟨d⟩s not an inch of margin to his own footing on this precipice ↑to spare↓, so that, though he possessed the highest social privileges, he could not add to them, and, (what ⟨was⟩ ↑is↓ worse in his own eyes,) could not impart them.

---

[111] "An errand . . . consacrée" is written in ink over four lines of pencil writing: "gallic cock"; "commissionaire"; "consacrée"; "laboratoire".
[112] These six words are in pencil.
[113] This sentence is struck through in ink with two wavy diagonal use marks with the notation (by Edward Emerson?) "Used in London copy"; see Journal London, p. [167] above.
[114] "I expected . . . gauze" is in pencil.
[115] Emerson canceled nearly two full lines at this point with unusually heavy strokes of the pen; the recovered words are conjectural readings.

An artist spends himself, like the crayon in his hand, till he is all gone.

[71] Another dislocation ↑or↓ discontinuity is the incapableness of the scholar to inform his conversation with his genius, the unmagnetic man.

Not a khan but a man.
Give me a rich mind, which does not bring a set of stories to the new companions whom he joins, &, when they are spent, has no more to say, but warm bounteous discourse. What trial is so severe to men as a sea voyage? ⁿ A college examination is nothing to it.[116] ↑He who has not tired or restrained his shipmates in a month's voyage, has won palms that Cambridge or the Academy or the Congress cannot give.↓

[71½] "In coming to Paris, I only see that you have lost some of your good French, & ⟨commit⟩ make a few more mistakes." [117]

What games sleep plays with us! We wake indignant that we have been so played upon, & should have lent ourselves to such mountains of nonsense. All night I was scarifying with my wrath some conjuring miscreant, but unhappily I had an old age in my toothless gums, I was old as Priam, could not articulate, & the edge of all my taunts & sarcasms, it is to be feared, was quite lost. Yet, spite of my dumb palsy, I defied & roared after him, rattled in my throat, until wifey waked me up. Then I bit my lips. So one day we shall wake up from this longer confusion, & be not less mortified that we had lent ourselves to such rigmarole.

But it is base to forget our resolutions; and the difference between men is, that one is obligable, & one is not.[118]

[72] The Americans would sail in a steamboat built of lucifer matches, if it would go faster.[119]

---

[116] "What trial . . . it.", struck through in ink with three diagonal use marks, is used in "Voyage to England," W, V, 32.

[117] Cf. p. [56] above.

[118] This sentence is struck through in ink with a vertical use mark.

[119] Cf. Journal Sea-Notes, p. [4] above. This sentence is struck through in ink with a wavy diagonal use mark.

[72½] Torchlight processions have a seek-&-slay look, dripping ⟨lig⟩burning oil-drops, & the bearers now & then smiting the torch on the ground, & then lifting it into the air as W. described them[.] [120] Owen's vinous face was a powerful weapon. He has I know not what air of virility that penetrates the audience—a surgical smile. But there was no need that he who thinks lightly of the accumulation of facts, should run counter to his own genius & attack the transmutationists, for it is they who obey the idea which has made him great.[121]

[73] Non, non; qu'elle fasse la queue comme les autres[.]

I find in French pictures a colouring of human flesh, analogous to dead gold in jewellery[.] [122]

Mr Doherty thought this a revolution against humbugs; that the English were not so reasonable as they appear, & the French were more reasonable than they appear. All the clubs are armed,—that is, have depots of arms.[123]

[74] ↑Paris, Rue des Petits Augustins, No 15; May 13, 1848.↓
The one thing odious to me now is joking. What can the brave & strong genius of C. himself avail? [n] [124] What can his praise, what can his blame avail me, when I know that if I fall or if I rise, there still awaits me the inevitable joke⟨,⟩? The day's Englishman must have his joke, as duly as his bread. God grant me the noble companions whom I have left at home who value merriment less, & virtues & powers more. If the English people have owed to their House of Commons this damnable derision, I think they have paid an overprice for their liberties & empire. But when I balance the attractions of good & evil, when I consider what facilities, what talents a little

[120] See Journal London, p. [139] above; cf. "seek & slay torch", p. [66] above.
[121] "Owen's . . . great.", rewritten in ink over substantially the same matter in pencil, occurs also in Journal London, p. [19] above, and Notebook ED, p. [120] below.
[122] This sentence is in pencil.
[123] "Mr Doherty . . . arms." is rewritten in ink over substantially the same matter in pencil.
[124] "Carlyle or Clough?" (J, VII, 459, n. 1).

vice would furnish, then rise before me not these laughers, but the dear & comely forms of [75] honour & genius & piety in my distant home, and they touch me with chaste palms moist & cold, & say to me, You are ours.

"Remember to be sober, & to be disposed to believe, for these are nerves of wisdom." [125]

And Mahomet's retribution of the jokers. Y.[126]

The secret of Guy, the lucky & famous, was, to conceal from all mankind that he was a bore. It was wonderful how often & how long by skilful dispositions & timings he managed to make it believed, by clever people, too, that he was witty & agreeable.

One of the principal discoveries, or, say confirmations, obtained in Europe, was, that bigger incomes do not help any body: the demand keeps perfect pace with the supply. Sir Thomas Lucy's distress when his second son was born, ↑they told me↓[.] [127]
The question of history is, what each generation has done with its surplus produce? One bought crusades, one churches, one villas, one horses, & one railroads.

[76] ↑Paris↓
    Beefsteak in Paris is omnibus-horses[.]
    Palais Royal⟨e⟩[:] on the floor[,] m⟨g⟩agasins of clothes, jewellery, perfumery, hairdressers, &c[;] on the premiere[,] Restaurants[;] on the troisieme[,] Billiards & cards &c[;] on the quatrieme[,]

---

[125] " 'Remember . . . wisdom.' ", previously quoted in *JMN*, VI, 321, and VIII, 28, is from *Iamblichus' Life of Pythagoras*, 1818, p. 261; the sentence is used in "Ethnical Scriptures," *Uncollected Writings*, p. 133, and "Instinct and Inspiration," *W*, XII, 80.
[126] See *JMN*, IX, 288, and "Social Aims," *W*, VIII, 98: "On the day of resurrection, those who have indulged in ridicule" will have "the door of Paradise . . . shut in their faces." From *Practical Philosophy of the Muhammadan People . . . being a translation of The Akhlāk-I-Jalāly . . .* , trans. W. F. Thompson (London, 1839), pp. 193–194.
[127] "One of . . . me" is struck through in ink with a vertical use mark. See Notebook England and Paris, p. [40] below; Journal London, p. [103] above.

lorettes, so that Mr P declares it the complete & true shop for the human body.[128]

In Paris 117 new newspapers have been set on foot since the revolution.

This revolution distinguished from the old by the social problem agitated in every club. Arithmeticians get up & cipher very shrewdly before the masses to show them what is each man's share. The good God, they say, is full of good sense & ⟨this revolution came because of⟩ the extreme inequality of property had got so far as to drive to revolution, & now it will not finish until God's justice is established, nor until the labourer gets his wages, nor until there is no idler left in the land. The idler is a diseased person & is to be treated by the state as a diseased person.

as economical as ants [129]

[77] In coming to the city, & seeing in it no men of information, you remain on the outside.

But all this Paris seems to me a continuation of the theatre, when I come out of the theatre, or of a *limonade gazeuse,* when I come out of the restaurant. This is the famous lotus which the mariners ate & forgot their homes. I pinch myself to remember mine.

I went to hear Michelet lecture on philosophy, but the sublime creed of the Indian Buddhists was not meant for a Frenchman to analyze & crack his joke & make his grimace upon.

But I came out hither to see my contemporaries & I have seen Leverrier today ⟨toss⟩working out algebraic formulas on his blackboard to his class quite heedless of politics & revolutions.[130] I have seen Rachel in Phedre & heard her chant the Marseillaise. I have seen Barbé's role in his *Club de la Revolution,* & Blanqui in his *Club des Droits de l'homme,* and today they are both in the dungeon [78] of Vincennes.

---

[128] "Paris Beefsteak . . . body." is in pencil. "Mr P" is probably Mr. Paulet of Liverpool, whom Emerson saw again in Paris (*L,* IV, 74).

[129] See Journal AB, p. [130] above.

[130] There is a vertical ink line in the left margin opposite "But I . . . revolutions.", possibly a use mark. Emerson visited the Sorbonne, where he heard Leverrier and Michelet, on May 15, 1848, later mentioning both men in a letter to his wife (*L,* IV, 72, n. 263; 73).

Old Revolution said Qu'est ce le tiers etat? Rien: Que doit il etre? Tout. The new Revolution reads *le producteur* for *le tiers etat.*

The French have greatly more influence in Europe than the English. What influence the English have is by brute force of wealth; that of the French, by affinity & talent.[131]

An eminent difference between Paris & London is the economy of water. In Paris the stranger is struck with the beautiful fountains on the Place de la Concorde & gives ⟨th⟩ Paris the preference to London. But this water is not drinkable, & the houses in Paris have no wells or pumps & buy all their water by the bucket from water carriers who bring it from certain springs. In London every house has some kind of water privilege; as that in which I lived, received its water from Hertfordshire by an aquaduct which entered at the top of the house.[132]

[79] ↑The New Religion↓   ↑See p 39↓
You need only your own verdict.[133] What if they say you have thrown away your money, you have given fifty guineas for a greyhound, if you know better, & have your money in your pocket. Let them say it. Or what if they tax you with gambling, or drinking, or riot, when you have all your virtue, health, & serenity, safe about you unspent. Let them say it. For the good Laws know whether it be so or not, & they cannot be made false witnesses[.]
Much of the time every man must have himself to his friend.[134]

Nothing seems to me so excellent as a belief in the laws: it communicates dignity & an asylum in temples thenceforward to the character.
The gods themselves could not help us[.] N 38 [135]

---

[131] "The French . . . talent.", struck through in ink with a vertical use mark, is used in "Truth," *W*, V, 125.

[132] "of the house." runs onto page [79]; it is set off by a continuous line in ink from page to page.

[133] This sentence, struck through in ink with three vertical use marks, is used in "Worship," *W*, VI, 241.

[134] "For the . . . friend.", struck through in ink with two vertical use marks, is used in "Worship," *W*, VI, 241–242.

[135] See *JMN*, VIII, 262.

Wealth seems to me to begin with a good pump.[136]

[80] Ah! if a man could explain his own facts, the little system of laws & companions & assessors or witnesses with which he walks surrounded, from which he cannot escape, the planet each of a choir of satellites. He thinks himself free, does he? he goes, I say, with a guard of policemen in citizens' clothes. — Had I not reason to say the secret of the present hour is as hard to tell as that of the future hour[?][137]

Steep & craggy, said Porphyry, is the path of the gods.[138]

[81] That unhappy man, called, of genius, pays dear for his paltry distinction. His head runs up into a spire, and, instead of being a healthy, merry, round, & ruddy man he is some ↑mad↓ dominie. Nature is regardless of the individual, when she has points to carry, she carries them. If she wants a big thumb, she starves all the joints & bones & muscles of the body to gain material, & finishes by making a monster all thumb.[139]

The writers are bold & democratic. The moment revolution comes, are they Chartists & Montagnards? No, but they talk & sit with the rich, & sympathize with them. Should they go with the Chartist? Alas they cannot: These have such gross & bloody chiefs to mislead them, and are so full of hatred & murder, that the scholar recoils; — and joins the rich. That he should not do. He should accept as necessary the position of [82] armed neutrality abhorring the crimes of the Chartist, yet more abhorring the oppression & hopeless selfishness of the rich, &, still *writing the truth*, say, the time will come when these poor enfans perdus of revolution will have in-

---

[136] This sentence, struck through in ink with two vertical use marks, is used in "Wealth," *W*, VI, 87.

[137] This paragraph is struck through in ink with two vertical use marks, the first extending from "& companions" to "escape,", the second from "He thinks" to "clothes."; cf. "Worship," *W*, VI, 226.

[138] See *JMN*, IX, 426. This sentence, struck through in ink with a vertical use mark, is used in "Culture," *W*, VI, 163.

[139] "That unhappy . . . thumb.", struck through in ink with a vertical use mark, is used in "Culture," *W*, VI, 131.

structed their party, if only by their fate, & wiser counsels will prevail, & the music & the dance of liberty will take me in also. Then I shall not have forefeited my right to speak & act for the Movement party. Shame to the fop of philosophy who suffers a little vulgarity of speech & of character to hide from him the true current of ⟨t⟩Tendency, & who ⟨hides retrea⟩ abandons his true position of being priest & poet of those impious & unpoetic ⟨workmen⟩doers of God's work.[140]

[83]   The Latin *Yes*.
                       ─────────────

I remember when I was at the Latin School I wondered how the Romans managed to do their daily talking without any word for Yes. Whether it was verily so, I have forgotten since to inquire. I was reminded of it lately by observing how much the French use ⟨the word *Si*,⟩ the Italian affirmative Si, which perhaps is a part of Etiam, which, I believe, was one of the Roman *quasi*-affirmatives.

Alcott said to me, "You write on ↑the genius of↓ Plato, o⟨n⟩f Pythagoras, o⟨n⟩f Jesus, o⟨n⟩f Swedenborg, why do you not write of me?"

[84] The real difficulty lies here. The Intellect ⟨is⟩ uses & is not to be used. Uses London[,] uses Paris. I wish all that you can show me, ↑tho' it be the conflagration of Moscow,↓ but I decline taking hold of the rope to draw ⟨an⟩the engine or to hand buckets. And it ⟨is⟩ ↑were↓ a false courtesy to hold out the smallest offers of service[.]

Mr Doherty said, the *dogmes* were *malfaisants*. It needed not to inquire whether men made them or God made them. In either case they had every right to take them away. In the natural world, they had tigers, snakes, wolves, & other *dogmes malfaisants*, which they did not hesitate to put away & kill; & so, in the moral world, they had the like, which, like these beasts, had answered their ⟨pu⟩ use for a time, but were now out of time, unfit, noxious.

─────────────

[140] "The writers . . . work." is used in "Aristocracy," *W*, X, 63–64. "Aristocracy (in substance)" is written in pencil above "bold . . . The", probably by Edward Emerson.

[85] It is doubtful whether London, whether Paris, can answer the questions which now rise in the mind[.]

There are parties which are powerful in the dark, like the legitimists in France; they can pay & work. But the moment they take an avowed public form, they are denounced.

There is a pudency about friendship as about love, and fine souls never lose sight of friendship; it is behind their science, behind their genius, behind their heroic life, ⟨yet they⟩the beatitude to which they exist, yet they never name it. It is for young hot masters who kiss & claw, & curse each other after a fortnight, it is for them to talk of it.[141]

[86] Life is cheap. In this anthill of Paris one can see that multitudes sell their future for one day. What prodigality to turn a little beautiful French Edie into the procession to be consumed in the sun & crowd[.]

I have been exaggerating the English merits all winter, & disparaging the French. Now I am correcting my judgment of both, & the French have risen very fast.
But I see that both nations promise more than they perform. They do not culminate.

———

The English mind trifles.

———

'Tis easy to see that France is much nearer to socialism than England. In the gay & admirable illumination of the Champs Elysées, one could see that it was but a few steps to the Phalanstery.[142]

———

Do not mind trifles,—was the lesson so strenuously inculcated on my childhood. I did not learn it, and now I see, England has not.

[141] "There is . . . it.", struck through in ink with a curved vertical use mark, is used in "Considerations by the Way," *W*, VI, 273.
[142] The entries on p. [86] may have been written on or about May 24, 1848; similar phrasing occurs in Emerson's letter of that date to his wife (*L*, IV, 76).

[87] cela vous gene   ↑3↓ [143]
sans vous deranger
c'est peu de choses
comme ça
par exemple

[88] My good friend G.J↑ewsbury↓. declared that one was perpetually forgetting that you had ever done anything, you are so quiet[.]

I write "Mind & Manners in the XIX Century" [144] and my rede is to make the student independent of the century, to show him that his class offer one immutable front in all times & countries, cannot hear the drums of Paris, cannot read the London journals, they are the Wandering Jew or the Eternal Angel that survives all, & stands in the same fraternal relation to all. The world is always childish, and with each gewgaw of a revolution or new constitution that it finds, thinks it shall never cry any more: but it is always becoming evident that the permanent good is for the soul only & cannot be retained in any society or system. This is like naphtha which must be kept in a close vessel.

[89] In England, every man is a castle. When I get into our first class cars on the Fitchburg Road, & see ⟨all manner of⟩ sweltering men ⟨get in take their seats⟩ in their shirt sleeves [145] take their seats with ⟨well⟩some well drest men & women, & see really the very little difference of level that is between them all, and then imagine the astonishment that would strike the polished inmates of English

---

[143] "3" is in pencil.

[144] The title of Emerson's course of six lectures beginning in London on June 6, 1848. Emerson had returned to London on June 3; on the 8th he reported to his wife that he had been "writing all day . . . & must work all tomorrow" on the component lectures (L, IV, 80), which included "Powers and Laws of Thought," "Relation of Intellect to Natural Science," "Tendencies and Duties of Men of Thought," "Politics and Socialism," "Poetry and Eloquence," and "Natural Aristocracy."

[145] In the margin at this point is a circled question mark in ink, probably to suggest revision. In the words of Edward Emerson (J, VII, 477, n. 1), Emerson was not quite sure "whether he remembered shirt-sleeves in a first-class car at home, for at that time there were also second-class cars with a reduced fare."

first class carriages, if such masters should enter & sit beside them, I see that it is not fit to tell Englishmen that America is like England. No, this is the Paradise of the third class; here every thing is cheap; here every thing is for the poor. England is the Paradise of the first class; it is essentially aristocratic, and the humbler classes have made up their minds to this, & do contentedly enter into the system. In England, every man you meet is some man's son; in America, he may be some man's father.[146] But

[90] The integrity of the thinker is intellectual truth. Truth first. The temptation is great[147] to patronize Providence; the virtue of the intellect is ⟨to⟩ its own; its courage is of its own kind; & at last, it will be justified, though for the time it seem hostile to that which it most reveres.

——   ↑New prudence new charity O 144↓ [148]
The real life of the time is quite independant of accidental systems & establishes itself on much the same terms under all politics & manners.
No history is true but what is always true. G 91 [149]

————————————

Byron

————

"I turned from all she brought to ⟨those⟩ ↑all↓ she could not bring."
[Byron,] Childe Harold['s Pilgrimage];
Canto III. xxx. [270] [150]

————

[91] To accuse all men of *niaiserie*, what is it but to postpone the attack on us for that one moment whilst we strike. The grisette institution particularly interests the young men,[151] but every thing is as broad as it is long & grisettes also. ⟨In⟩ France rejoices in the

[146] The appearance of the writing suggests that some or all of this sentence may be a later addition.
[147] "great" is possibly underlined, although the stroke of the pen is irregular and may well have been accidental.
[148] The insertion is in pencil. See *JMN*, IX, 398.
[149] See *JMN*, VIII, 41.
[150] See *JMN*, V, 347.
[151] See Journal London, p. [138] above.

⟨repetition that⟩ hope of a state of things in which every man will be paid two francs a day for doing what ↑of all things↓ he likes best.

It is true that there are no men in England quite ideal, living in an ideal world, & working on politics & social life only from that.[152] Carlyle is mixed up with the politics of the day, earth⟨y⟩['s] ↑son↓ Antaeus. Milton mixes with politics but from the ideal side. —

↑See p. 56.↓

England is the land of success, because it is the land of common sense, of attention to trifles, with a sufficient reserve of power to classify & subordinate them, & even at last to degrade them.[153]

[92]   *Realism*

Whoever knows what happens in the getting & spending of a loaf of bread & a pint of beer,[154] that⟨, what⟩ ↑⟨there is just so much⟩↓ ↑no wishing will change the somewhat rigorous limits of pints & penny loaves;↓[n] for all that is consumed, so much less remains in the basket & ⟨flask⟩ pot;   but what is gone out of these ⟨basket⟩ is not wasted, but well spent, — if it nourishes his body, — knows all ↑of political economy↓ that all the empires of Europe & Asia can teach him[.] [155]

This is a wisdom which I find every day ⟨|| ... ||⟩helpful in the street when I compare the ⟨supposed freedom⟩ libertinism of France with the staidness of ⟨New E⟩Massachusetts.

"Is not this of mine a tolerable gallery?" said Philip Hone. "Yes" said Leslie, "but who would think of valuing a tolerable egg?" [156]

---

[152] "in England . . . that." is struck through in ink with a vertical use mark.

[153] "England is . . . then." is struck through in ink with a diagonal use mark.

[154] Marked for insertion at this point by asterisks is "that . . . loaves.", written below and circled; Emerson neglected to cancel the original "that" following "beer,".

[155] "Whoever knows . . . him", struck through in ink with two wavy vertical use marks and in pencil with one vertical use mark, is used in "Wealth," *W*, VI, 106, with the material of Emerson's insertion ("that . . . loaves.") incorporated at the point indicated.

[156] Philip Hone (1780–1851), mayor of New York in 1825, and Sir Charles

[93] A respectable old lady ⟨lived next⟩ had the misfortune to live ⟨next⟩ opposite the jail, in a county town and some old felons took special pleasure in insulting her with ribaldry whenever they saw her come to the window. The jail was pulled down, & removed; ⟨to⟩ and one of her friends congratulated her on the great relief she must experience in the loss of her bad neighbors. "O no," she replied, "She kind o' missed 'em." [157]

Works on art are like the ⟨collection⟩ Museums themselves, each of which has a few gems & the rest is rubbish. I want a manual which has all the works of the first style engraved & described; & then of the second style.

All the gems are fossil wine.[158]

The soldier cannot fold away his arms; nor the scholar his; *impediunt foris.*[159]

[94] When nature adds a little brain, she adds a little difficulty, or provides work for the brain to do. Were brains to be sinecures? A weevil, a mite, is born in the plum or the bark on which he is to feed; but she has not thought it necessary ⟨to⟩ when a man is born, to insert him in a mountain of bread & cheese.[160]

———

Joshua Bates said to me in London, that he had been here thirty years, & nobody had ever attempted to cheat him.

———

⟨At the opera only is enthusiasm permitted.⟩[161]

———

Robert Leslie (1794–1859), the painter; the exchange is not recorded in Hone's published diary.

[157] The reference is to Mrs. Kneeland of Cambridge. See *JMN*, VI, 251, VIII, 90–91.

[158] See Notebook England and Paris, p. [60] below.

[159] Cicero, *Pro Archia Poeta*, VII.16, of reading: "in the world it hampers not." See *JMN*, VI, 146; Notebook England and Paris, p. [62] below.

[160] Cf. p. [67] above.

[161] This canceled sentence, written in ink over the same words in pencil and

Miss H↑ennall↓. said at Edward street to C[arlyle]. "Do you think, if we should stand on our heads, we should understand better?" [162]

I reply to all the urgencies that refer me to this & that object indispensably to be seen, — 'Yes, to see all England well, needs 300 years; for what they told me was the merit of Sir John Soane's Museum, that it was well packed, — is the merit of England; it is tucked full in all corners & crevices with towns, castles, churches, villas, & galleries.' [163]

[95] [164]   At sea, 23 July, 1848.
Dragged day & night continually through the water by this steam engine, at the rate of near twelve knots, or fourteen statute miles, the hour, — the sea one long disgust, the nearing America my inviting port, England loses its recent overweight, America resumes its commanding claims ⟨on me⟩.
One long disgust is the sea. No personal bribe would lure one who loves the present moment. Who am I to be treated in this ignominious manner tipped up, shoved against the side of the house, rolled over, suffocated with bilge, mephitis, & stewing oil.

These lacklustre days go whistling over us & are those intercalaries I have often asked for & am cursed now with the worthless granting of my prayer. [165]

T.G.A[ppleton]. makes now his fourteenth passage. "Shakspeare will do." [166]

---

struck through in ink with a vertical use mark, appears also in Journal London, p. [94] above; Notebook ED, p. [67] below; "Manners," *W*, V, 112.

[162] "At one of the philosophical lectures in the Portman Square course" (*J*, VII, 478, n. 1).

[163] This paragraph, struck through in ink with two vertical use marks, is used in "Land," *W*, V, 38.

[164] A common pin is stuck through the manuscript leaf from p. [96] to p. [95].

[165] For "cursed now . . . prayer.", see Alexander Pope, *Moral Essays*, "Epistle II: To a Lady," l. 147 ("Atossa, curs'd with ev'ry granted prayer"), and "Fate," *W*, VI, 46–47. "One long . . . prayer.", transcribed from Notebook England and Paris, p. [59] below, is struck through in ink with a diagonal use mark and in pencil with a diagonal use mark. "Who am I . . . oil." is used in "Voyage to England," *W*, V, 29.

[166] Concerning Appleton, see Notebook England and Paris, p. [60] below, Journal London, p. [176] above.

He said, Kenyon was greatly amused with the story that Webster's mother was once pursued by an Indian, — and that he overtook her.

[96] I talked with Forster, Dickens, & Carlyle, on the prostitution in the great towns, & said, that, when I came to Liverpool, I inquired whether it was always as gross in that city as it then appeared to me? for it looked to me as if such manners betokened a fatal rottenness in the state, & especially no boy could grow up safe: but that I had been told, that it was not worse nor better than it had been for years. C & D replied, that chastity in the male sex was as good as gone in our times; and in England was ↑so↓ very rare, that they could name all the exceptions. Carlyle evidently believed that the same thing was true in America. I assured them that it was not so with us: that, for the most part, ⟨good⟩ young men of good standing & good education with us go virgins to their nuptial bed⟨s⟩, as truly as their brides. Dickens replied, that ⟨if⟩ incontinence is so much the rule with them that if his own son were particularly chaste, he should be alarmed on his [97] account, as if he could not be in good health.[167]

──────

↑None any work can frame   Y 230↓ [168]

People eat the same dinner at every house in England. 1. soup, ↑2.↓ fish; 3. beef, mutton, or hare, 4 birds, 5 pudding & pastry & jellies. 6 cheese, 7. grapes, nuts, & wine. ⟨At⟩During dinner, hock & champagne are offered you by the servant, & sherry stands at the corners of the table. Healths are not much drunk in fashionable houses. After the cloth is removed, three bottles, namely, port, sherry, ⟨&⟩ claret invariably circulate. What ⟨b⟩rivers of wine are drunk in ↑all↓ England daily! One would say, every guest drinks six glasses[.]

The habit of a dress dinner daily, generates a sort of talent of

[167] This paragraph, struck through in pencil with a vertical use mark on p. [96] and another on p. [97], appears also in Journal London, p. [116] above, and Notebook ED, pp. [222]–[223] below. There is a curved ink line running from "Dickens" in the first sentence through "towns" to "inquired".

[168] See *JMN*, IX, 343; cf. *JMN*, IX, 262, and "Poetry and Imagination," *W*, VIII, 43.

table-talk which reaches great perfection. The⟨y⟩ stories here told are so good, & the manner so excellent, that one is sure they must have been often told before, to have got such happy turns. Here come all manner of clever projects, of popular science, of [169]

[98] "Conductor, if it goes on snowing, when we come to St James's street, I will get down there." The man touched his hat, & replied, gravely, "Served it right, ma'am; I'll mention it." [170]

Turner resembles the portraits of Punch. [171]

At Stonehenge, it was impossible to forget Turner's pictures. In the English landscape the combed fields have the softest look, & seem touched with a pencil & not with a plough. [172]

Landseer the only genius of the Academy exhibition. Leslie very sensible & pleasing. There are many English portraits[,] the true national type. The Hως of Gibson, like the admirably finished pictures of Scheffer, show want of all object with great powers of execution, so that we get noble vases empty. [173]

At Cambridge they mow the grass every day.

At Cambridge King Henry's crown was full of birdsnests. [174]

[99] C[arlyle]. had all the kleinstadtlich traits of an islander & a Scotsman, and reprimanded with severity the rebellious instincts

---

[169] This uncompleted paragraph, struck through in ink with a vertical use mark, is used in "Manners," W, V, 114.

[170] The anecdote is expanded from an entry in Notebook England and Paris, p. [44] below.

[171] See Notebook Xenien, p. [5] below; Notebook ED, p. [130] below; "Character," W, V, 135.

[172] "In the . . . plough.", taken from Notebook England and Paris, p. [46₂] below, is struck through in ink with a vertical use mark and used in "Land," W, V, 34.

[173] "Landseer . . . empty." is transcribed from Notebook England and Paris, p. [46₁] below. Emerson is referring to the painters Edwin Henry Landseer (1802–1873), Charles Robert Leslie (see p. [92] above), and Ary Scheffer (1795–1858), and to the sculptor John Gibson (1790–1866), creator of the 'Hώς ("Dawn"), whose studio in Rome he had visited in 1833.

[174] This sentence is transcribed from Notebook England and Paris, p. [40] below.

of the native of a vast continent which made light of the British islands.[175]

Geologic History.   ↑*Melioration*↓

They combed his mane, they pared ⟨off⟩ his nails, they cut off his tail, set him on end, sent him to school, & made him pay taxes.[176]

I have no longer any taste for these refinements you call life, but shall dive again into brute matter.

"God's bairns are eath to lere." [177]

The English youth has a narrow road to travel. Besides his horse & gun, all he knows is the door to the House of Commons.[178]

Kenyon said, he had the two qualifications for a giver of dinners, good digestion & no heart.

Pillory of the second class.[179]

[100] I told Carlyle on the way to Stonehenge that, though I was in the habit of conceding everything in honor of England which Englishmen demanded, though I was dazzled by the wealth & power & success everywhere apparent, — yet I knew very well that the moment I returned to America, I should ⟨r⟩lapse again into the habitual feeling which the vast physical influences of that continent inevitably inspire of confidence that there & there only is the right home & seat of the English race; & this great England will dwindle

[175] This paragraph is expanded in Notebook ED, p. [227] below.

[176] This sentence is used in "Inspiration," *W*, VIII, 270.

[177] This "Scotch proverb" is transcribed from Notebook England and Paris, p. [52₁] below.

[178] This paragraph is transcribed from Notebook England and Paris, p. [50₂] below. It appears also in the "notes on English politics" (used in Emerson's lectures) that are printed in *W*, V, 364–365.

[179] This phrase is transcribed from Notebook England and Paris, p. [50₂] below.

again to an island which has done well, but ⟨is⟩ has reached its utmost expansion.[180]

[101] I bring home from England 1. the Heimskringla, or seakings of Norway, translated by Laing.

2. Wood's Athenae Oxonienses

3 Bede

4 the Meghaduta

5 Lowth's Life of William of Wykeham

6 Wordsworth's Scenery of the Lakes.

7 Jacobson's Translation of Æschylus

8 John Carlyle's Translation of Dante.

9 John Mill's Political Economy.[181]

[102] I thought how great men build substructures & like Cologne Cathedral these are never finished. Lord Bacon begins,

[180] "I told . . . America," is struck through in ink with a diagonal use mark; the entire paragraph, struck through in ink with an additional diagonal use mark, is used in "Stonehenge," W, V, 275–276.

[181] Including (1) *The Heimskringla*, already cited, six of the works listed are among the surviving books of Emerson's library: (3) Beda Venerabilis, *Ecclesiastical History of England. Also the Anglo-Saxon Chronicle*, ed. J. A. Giles (London, 1847); (4) Kalidassa, *The Méga Dúta; or, Cloud Messenger*, trans. Horace Hayman Wilson (Calcutta and London, 1814); (6) *A Complete Guide to the Lakes, Comprising . . . Mr. [William] Wordsworth's Description of the Scenery of the Country, &c.*, ed. John Hudson, 3rd ed. (Kendal and London, 1846) — see Notebook England and Paris, p. [19] below; (7) *The Seven Tragedies of Aeschylus, Literally Translated into English Prose, with Notes Critical and Expository* [no translator's name; probably by William Jacobson], 3rd ed. (Oxford, 1843); and (9) John Stuart Mill, *Principles of Political Economy, with Some of Their Application to Social Philosophy*, 2 vols. (London, 1848). One other specific edition has been identified from Emerson's page-reference on p. [102] below: (2) Anthony à Wood, *Athenæ Oxonienses. An Exact History of All the Writers and Bishops Who Have Had Their Education in the . . . University of Oxford . . .*, 2nd ed., 2 vols. in one (London, 1721). Emerson bought an unspecified edition of (5) Robert Lowth, *The Life of William of Wykeham, Bishop of Winchester*, first published in 1758; on November 8, 1848, he borrowed a 1759 edition from the Harvard College Library. Emerson also carried with him unbound sheets of (8) *Dante's Divine Comedy: The Inferno. A Literal Translation*, by J. A. Carlyle (London, 1849), from which the first American edition (New York, 1849) was set following Emerson's negotiations on Carlyle's behalf with Harper & Brothers: see *L*, IV, 124–125 and *passim*.

Behmen begins, Goethe, Fourier, they all begin; we credulous believe, of course, they can finish as they begun. If you press them, they fly to a new topic, & here again open a magnificent promise which serves the turn of interesting you, & silencing your reproaches.[182]

↑Fate↓ [183]

As soon as the children are good, the mothers are scared, & think they are going to die.[184]

In Wood's Athenae Oxon. Vol II p 31⟨8⟩7. is the Judge's speech to the Jury in the trial of Thomas Weaver, recommending him to mercy because he is a man of parts & learning[.] [185]

[103] Dr Kraitsir & all Harro Harrings, Mazzinis, Rufinis, Major Tochmans, & Chopins, should be made to translate, spell, construe, parse, & render into all languages, the old lines,

> "How small of all that human hearts endure
> The part that laws or kings can cause or cure." [186]
>
> > [Samuel Johnson, "Lines Added to
> > Goldsmith's 'Traveller,' " ll. 1–2]

Religion in England. Sterling, Vol. I, cx[,] lii[,] ccxxx [187]

---

[182] This paragraph is used in "Instinct and Inspiration," *W*, XII, 70.

[183] "Fate" is in pencil.

[184] This sentence, struck through in ink with a vertical use mark, is used in "Considerations by the Way," *W*, VI, 259.

[185] Anthony à Wood, *Athenæ Oxoniensis*, 1721. Thomas Weaver (1616–1662) published *Songs and Poems of Love and Drollery* in 1654. Cf. "Greatness," *W*, VIII, 315.

[186] For " 'How small . . . cure.' ", see p. [3] above. In addition to Kraitsir, Harring, and Chopin, all previously mentioned, Emerson is referring to the Italian patriot Giuseppe Mazzini (1805–1872); his associate Giovanni Ruffini (1807–1881), who spent much of his life in England and wrote novels in English; and Major Gaspard Tochman (1795?–1880), a New York lawyer who championed the cause of Poland.

[187] John Sterling, *Essays and Tales*, ed. Julius Charles Hare, 2 vols. (London, 1848). Hare's "Sketch of the Author's Life" quotes Sterling's comments on the low state of religion in England (I, cxliii ff.) and offers Hare's own analysis (I, ccxxx ff.). On Emerson's receipt of this work while in Manchester, see *L*, IV, 53; a copy is in his library.

I find C[arlyle]. always cunning: he denies the books he reads; denies the friends he has just visited; denies his own acts & purposes; — By God, I do not know them — and immediately the cock crows.[188]

↑Of Dante
        F[oreign] Q[uarterly] Review Apr 1844↓ [189]

Preach not.
Prends garde à l'emphase, qui n'est que le langage de la vanité satisfaite; says Cardonnet in George Sand[.] [190]

[104]   Mass. Q. Review —

            A. B. Alcott
            H. D. Thoreau
            W. E. Channing
            J. E. Cabot
            T. D. Parker —
            C. K. Newcomb
            S. G. Ward.
            G. P. Bradford.   "The Suppliants"
            Edward Bangs.
            Leonard Woods
            Horace Bushnell
            T. T. Stone
            J. R. Lowell
            B. P. Hunt.

[105] Mass. Quarterly Review.
        Write to Dr Samuel Brown
            Dr Bushnell, Hartford [191]

---

[188] See Luke 22:60; John 18:27.
[189] A survey of recent Dante scholarship, untitled, in the *Foreign Quarterly Review*, XXXIII (April 1844), 1–17. The insertion is in pencil.
[190] See George Sand, *Le Péché de Monsieur Antoine* (Paris, 1857), Ch. 13, p. 157.
[191] Writing to request an article for the *Massachusetts Quarterly Review*, Emer-

[106]   Mass. Quarterly Review —

It is to be considered that we do not wish to have lees of wine after
we have drawn years ago the best.

But after much experience, we find literature the best thing; and
men of thought, if still thinking, the best company. I went to England, &, after allowing myself freely to be dazzled by the various
brilliancy of men of talent, — ⟨I⟩ in calm hours I found myself no
way helped; my sequins were all yellow leaves, I said I have
valued days (& must still) by the number of /aperçus/ [192] clear
insights/ I get, and I must estimate my company so. Then I found
I had scarcely had a good conversation, a solid dealing, man with
man, in England. Only in such passages is a reason for human life
given, and every such meeting puts a [107] mortal affront on Kings
& Governments by ⟨m⟩showing them to be ⟨contemptible.⟩ ↑of no
account.↓
Of course, these people, these & no others, interest us; these dear
& beautiful beings who are absorbed in their own dream. Let us then
have that told; let us have a record of friendship among six, or four,
or two, if there be only two of those who delight in each other, only
because both delight in the Eternal laws; who forgive nothing to
each other, who by their joy & homage to these, are made incapable
of conceit which destroys almost all the fine wits.[193] Any other affection between men than this geometric one of relation to the same
thing, is a mere mush of materialism.

      [108] ⟨It is⟩

[109] [blank]

---

son began a letter to Brown on shipboard and completed it at Concord early in
August, 1848 (*L*, IV, 102). Among the other possible contributors listed on pp.
[104]-[105] and not previously mentioned are Leonard Woods (1807–1878),
president of Bowdoin College, and Horace Bushnell (1802–1876), the Hartford
clergyman. On Emerson's reservations about continuing the *Review*, see his letters
written in August and September, 1848, to Theodore Parker and others (*L*, IV,
106–107, 108–109, 111–114).

[192] Cf. Notebook England and Paris, p. [52₂] below.

[193] Between "wits" and "Any" are two vertical lines, in ink.

[110] Dear Doctor, is there any resurrection? What do you think? Did Doctor Channing believe we should know each other? What questions are these! Go read Æschylus, or any other truly ideal poetry. Read Plato, or any seer of the interior realities. Talk with any Lycurgus, who can codify the moral laws. Simply recite to the recognising ⟨exp⟩ear of thoughtful men the substantial laws of the intellect & in the presence of the laws themselves they will never ask you such schooldame questions as these[.] [194]

[111]–[112] [leaf torn out] [195]
[113] The Indians live by the leg & not by the arm, and the muscles of the leg are strong as horses, those of the arm fat & flabby. A little wickedness seems good to make muscle. Poor decaying civilizees full of sloth & torpor can not run like wild goats & conies. Conscience is not good for legs. [196]
The gods deal very strictly with us, make out quarter-bills, & exact specie payment, allow no partnerships, no stock companies, no arrangements, but hold us personally liable to the last cent. Ah, say I, I cannot do this & that, my cranberry field, my burned woodlot, the rubbish lumber about the summerhouse, my grass, my crop, my trees. — [n] Can I not have some partner; can't we organize our new society of poets & lovers, & have somebody with talent for business to look after these things, some deacons of trees & grass & cranberries, & leave ⟨you⟩ ↑me↓ to letters & philosophy[?] * [197]

[114] But the nettled gods say, No, go to the devil with your arrangements. You, you, you personally, you alone, are to answer body & soul for your things. Leases & covenants are to be punctually signed

---

[194] "Dear Doctor . . . these" is used in "Immortality," *W*, VIII, 346–347.
[195] Emerson indexed p. [111] under Poor and p. [112] under Concord, Economy, Help, and Housekeeping.
[196] "A little . . . legs.", struck through in ink with a vertical use mark, is used in "Power," *W*, VI, 66.
[197] The asterisk presumably referred to an added note on the facing page, [112], which is now lacking. On Emerson's "burned woodlot", see *L*, IV, 109–110, for his letter of August 31, 1848, presenting a claim to the Fitchburg Railroad for damages resulting from a fire on April 10, 1848. The summerhouse had been built by Alcott and Thoreau during his absence in Europe.

& sealed."[198] ⟨and not flourished & mystified.⟩ Arithmetic & ⟨p⟩the practical study of cause & effect in the laws of indian corn & rye meal is as useful as betting is in England to teach accuracy of statement, or duelling in France or Ireland to make men speak the truth.

In Oxford no duel ever occurs, a document of the mildness & good nature of the Englishman.[199]

[115] Lord Melbourne sent his steward to his tenants in Nottingham & told them that they were to vote for whom they pleased. The tenants asked ⟨how⟩ ↑which candidate↓ his Lordship would prefer. The steward would not tell them. They asked the steward, which he should like? He refused to tell them. Then they put their heads together, & said, they thought my lord's body valet would be sure to know his mind, & so they asked to see him, that they might know how he would vote.[200]

As I reflect on the English, I perceive that they are eminently prosaic or unpoetic; that all the poetic persons whom I saw there, were deviations from the national type[.]

> Dear friend, where thy shadow falls
> Beauty sits & Music calls,
> Where thy form & favour come
> All good creatures have their home.
>   Hafiz.[201]

[116] ↑Heimskringla↓
    Why not choose a professor as the dog was chosen. Heimskringla 1. p. 400, or the husband by Queen Gyda[.] [202]

---

[198] "But the . . . sealed" is struck through in ink with a curved vertical use mark.

[199] This sentence from Journal London, p. [92] above, struck through in ink with a diagonal use mark, is used in "Universities," *W*, V, 200.

[200] This paragraph is struck through in pencil with a vertical use mark.

[201] The quatrain is struck through in ink with a vertical use mark. See "Translations," *W*, IX, 301.

[202] *The Heimskringla*, trans. Samuel Laing, 1844, I, 400–401, 399–400. "Why . . . Gyda" is in pencil.

King Olaf's mode of converting Eyvind to Christianity was to put a pan of glowing coals ⟨to⟩ ↑on↓ his belly, which burst asunder. Wilt thou now, Eyvind, believe in Christ? asks Olaf in excellent faith? Heimskringla Vol 1 p 445
↑another expedient of the adder in the mouth [*Heimskringla*, I,] p 448↓ [203]
These Norse go for Sigurd or Harald, but they never say, like the 1848 people, "I go for a principle."

Thorer Hiort was quicker on foot than any man, — but there Thorer left his life. ↑⟨1.450⟩ I. 446↓ Trial of strength in swimming between Kiartan & Olaf. I. [450-]451
Olaf's feats [I, p]p 454–5
These men never leave the ground; the corn, the kail & the herrings are always in sight[.] [204]

[117] [blank]
    [118] The Communities hitherto are only possible by installing the Devil as Steward; the rest of the offices may be well filled with saints. So in the Shaker society, they always send the devil to market. And in painting God, poetry & religion have always drawn the energy from hell. [205]
                    ↑See above, p. 113, concerning Conscience↓

E.C. said of N., that, if a man stays under water too long, he is sure to be drowned. [206]

[119] George Stephenson died the other day in England, the man who made the locomotive, the father of railroads, — and not an engineer on all our tracks heeded the fact, or perhaps knew his name.

---

[203] "King Olaf's . . . p 448", struck through in ink with two diagonal use marks, is used in "Worship," *W*, VI, 205.
    [204] This sentence, struck through in ink with a vertical use mark, is used in "Literature," *W*, V, 232.
    [205] This paragraph, struck through in ink with a diagonal use mark, is used in "Power," *W*, VI, 66.
    [206] Emerson is probably referring to Ellery Channing and Charles King Newcomb.

⟨The whistles of⟩ There should have been a concert of locomotives, and a dirge performed by the whistles of a thousand engines.

It is a sort of proverb with us that an Englishman who comes into America, must first be ruined before he can rise.

[120] Carlyle said, th⟨e⟩at "what was intolerable to him in A.H. was the twist that was in every thing he said,"[207] ⟨there must always⟩ and that he had now heard from him more reasonable words than ever before; for here he would leave in talking with me, his London out of the conversation.

———

It is a curious working of the English state that Carlyle should in all his lifetime have never had an opportunity to cast a vote.[208]

———

I spoke of friendship, but my friends & I are fishes in their habit. ⟨I⟩As for taking T.'s arm, I should as soon take the arm of an elm tree[.][209]

[121] In England old men are as red as roses[.]

To see contemporaries —
The merits of America were not presentable — the tristesse of the landscape, the quiet stealing in of nature like a religion, how could that be told?[n]
conscience not good for legs
Let them have virtue not separate but as they have hair. —
Journal should be a record of friendship[.]
I was to write of the superiority of wit that grows of superior stomach —[210]

———

[207] "A.H." is probably Arthur Helps, whom Emerson and Carlyle visited at Bishops Waltham after their excursion to Stonehenge. Within the quotation, the "t" in "to" is crossed in pencil.
[208] Cf. Notebook ED, p. [289] below: "Is Carlyle a voter?"
[209] This sentence is used in "Thoreau," W, X, 456.
[210] "In England . . . stomach —" is in pencil. For "conscience . . . legs", see p. [113] above.

When we read the primitive histories as the Pentateuch, the Edda, the Heimskringla, Vishnu Purana &c we think there were very few men when the actions of each had such importance & are circumstantially told. But when we look wisely & genially at our own life, we find the same eminences[,] the same sparseness & greatness.

[122] Henry Thoreau is like the woodgod who solicits the wandering poet & draws him into antres vast & desarts idle,[211] & bereaves him of his ⟨wits⟩memory, & leaves him naked, plaiting vines & with twigs in his hand. Very seductive are the first steps from the town to the woods, but the End is ⟨indigence⟩ ↑want↓ & madness. —

We have many platforms of work[:] thus I have the Review & Lectures[;] glad should I be to be free of these & left to my studies[.] Yes, but I have heard the callings of a higher muse & would leave all for that. In the lower ⟨ones⟩works, we have no lack of prompters. In the highest where we most need admonition each has himself only to friend.

↑⟨Thor's house 540 platforms⟩↓ [212]
In Kew Gardens you should ask for Moly & Haemony.

[123] In the winter of 1832–3 I sailed in a brigantine from ⟨Syracu⟩Malta to Syracuse, and the master & whole crew on learning where we (Holbrook, Kettell, & I,) came from, got up out of their chest an old soiled Italian gazetteer, & read the account of *Boston* with eagerness & its 25 000 population, curious to know ⟨from⟩ what far Siam or Pegu their passengers had dropped from[.] [213]

---

[211] For "antres . . . idle", see Shakespeare, *Othello*, I, iii, 140.
[212] See Journal CD, p. [134] above. These four words are struck through in ink with five diagonal lines, apparently to indicate cancellation rather than use.
[213] This paragraph is transcribed from Notebook England and Paris, p. [54] below; the commas after "Syracuse", "I", and "from" are added in pencil. For another version of the incident, see *JMN*, IV, 121.

In my woodlot, the pokeweed & mullein grow up rankly in the ruins of the shanties of the Irish who built the railroad.[214]

I am struck with the unimportance of our American politics. We prosper with such vigour that like thrifty ⟨pl⟩ trees which grow in spite of lice, borers, & mice, so we do not suffer from the profligate gang who fatten on us. — Same energy in Greek Demos.[215]

The bears in the Jardin des Plantes fight & I /thought/wanted/ to call the keeper thinking the bigger would hurt the young one but I found they were tough & did not hurt each other. So I remembered them when I saw bigger boys bullying less ones in London[.]

[124] Eddy declares that his horse does not wag his tail, because his tail is a tin tail.

What was that which broke with so loud a noise? said Olaf.
Norway from thy hands, O King! replied Einar[.] [216]

The English dislike the American style of civilization, yet are doing all they can to bring it in. America exceptional in all Mill's paragraphs, & ⟨one⟩the reader expects applause, but finds insult.[217]

When the fog rolled suddenly up in Halifax harbour, & showed the shore & town, the whole ship's company involuntarily clapped their hands.[218]

Revolution. In a wild universal discontent & insurrection one wonders how a castle is taken, how combination is effected. But the compression of the streets makes a rude discipline & organization[.] [219]

---

[214] This sentence and the remainder of p. [123] are in pencil.

[215] "I am . . . Demos." is struck through in pencil with a vertical use mark.

[216] Cf. *The Heimskringla*, trans. Samuel Laing, 1844, I, 479.

[217] These two sentences, transcribed from Notebook England and Paris, p. [54] below, and struck through in ink with two vertical use marks, are used in "Cockayne," *W*, V, 150–151.

[218] This sentence is transcribed from Notebook England and Paris, p. [54] below. The *Europa*, on which Emerson returned from Liverpool to Boston, was detained nine hours by fog off Halifax harbor on Tuesday, July 25, 1848 (*L*, IV, 101).

[219] These two sentences are expanded from a notation in Notebook England and Paris, p. [62] below.

[125]   "Ici on fait son courrier"

Shall we not maintain our poets? Shall we suffer those to die of whom the horizon & the landscape speak to us, day by day? They never mention their owner or their diggers, Irishmen or negroes, ↑any more than ants & worms,↓ but superciliously forget these, & fill me with allusions to men & women who owned no acre, & had no practical faculty, as we say.
Our action is sub-action. 'Tis not in the harmony of things.

To say otherwise is skepticism[.]

He cannot bring us in October a poor bushel of beans; but is not an accomplished & cultivated man worth something? ⁿ
The soldier cannot fold away his arms, nor can the scholar. impediunt foris.²²⁰

[126] I observe among the best women the same putting of life into their deed that we admire in the Seton (was it) who put her arm into the bolt ⟨fo⟩ to defend Queen Mary ²²¹ or in the women in the old sieges who cut off their hair to make ropes & ladders for the men.

W.E.C[hanning]. remarks in Alcott the obstruction of his egoism. Cultivated men ⟨‖ ... ‖⟩ always must be had; every body sends for them as for peaches. But what to do with this man, when you have first to kick away the man in order to get at what he knows.

In England I found wine enough; as Dr Johnson said, "for once in his life he had as much wall fruit as he pleased." In France I had the privilege of leaving my papers all lying wide in my room; for nobody could read English.²²²

———

[127] The Simony of Dumas; and of Mother Jordan.

²²⁰ See Notebook England and Paris, p. [62] below; p. [93] above.
²²¹ This "heroic deed," as Edward Emerson noted, "was not done by Mary Seton to save her Queen, but by Katherine Douglas on the night when James I of Scotland was murdered" (J, VII, 498, n. 1).
²²² See Hester Lynch Piozzi, *Anecdotes of the Late Samuel Johnson*, LL.D., as

↑— That each should in his house abide↓
Therefore was the world so wide,[223] that every man might live in
his own house, & not in a hotel, oh Fourier!

↑— That each should in his house abide↓
The farther from the root the sweeter are the grapes.

H.D.T[horeau]. working with A B A[lcott]. on the summerhouse,
said, he was nowhere, doing nothing.

A man who can make hard things easy, is an Educator.

Alcott declares that a teacher is one who ⟨|| ... ||⟩can assist the child in
obeying his own mind, and who can remove all unfavorable circumstances. He believes that from a circle of twenty wellselected children
he could draw ↑in their conversation↓ everything that is in Plato, &
as much better ⟨said⟩in form than it is in Plato, as the passages I read
him from the Heimskringla, are than Bancroft.

[128] He measures ages by teachers, & reckons history by
Pythagoras, Plato, Jesus, & Pestalozzi.   In his own school in
Boston, when he had made the school-room beautiful, he looked on
the work as half-done.
He said, that every great man of antiquity had an eminent philosopher
as his teacher.
And this is true for Pericles, Alexander, Alcibiades,

The soul is older than the body.

[129] We are very careful of young peartrees & defend them
from their enemies, from fireblight, suckers, grass, slugs, pearworm[,]

reprinted in *Johnsonian Miscellanies*, arranged and edited by George Birbeck Hill,
2 vols. (London, 1897), I, 217. For the second sentence, see Journal London, p.
[135] above.
  [223] See "Fragments on Nature and Life," XXI, *W*, IX, 354:
          "That each should in his house abide,
          Therefore was the world so wide."

but we let our young men, ⟨who⟩ in whose youth & flower all inferior kinds have their flowering & completion, grow up ⟨the p⟩ in heaps & by chance, take the rough & tumble, as we say, (which is the skepticism of education) exposed to their borers, caterpillars, cankerworms, bugs, moping, sloth, seduction, wine, fear, hatred,

[130] 6 August. Lucrezia Floriani of George Sand is a great step from the novels of one termination which we all read 20 years ago. It is a great step towards real life & manners & motives, and yet how far off the novel still is! This life lies about us dumb, the day, as we know it, has not yet found a tongue.[224] E[lizabeth].H[oar]. complains of this romance that the tendency is not high. I say, there are always two things to be done by the novelist; first, the ⟨laws⟩ aspirations of the mind are to be revered, that is, Faith; &, secondly, the way things actually fall out, that is, Fate. Fate & Faith, these two; and it seems as if justice were done, if the Faith is vindicated in the sentiments of the heroes of the tale, & Fate in the course & issue of the events.[225] ↑George Sand is quite conversant with all the ideas which occupy us here in America.↓

[131] Why did not the last generation of farmers plant the pears & plums & apples & grapes of whose growth time is the chief element & not leave it all to be done by us? ⟨Plainly it⟩ Ask in the market: a good pear will sell for a shilling. ⟨Ye⟩That price tells as plain as the human race can speak, that there are great & all but insuperable difficulties in raising these fine fruits in this climate, borer, mouse, curculio, & bug, & caterpillar have settled a democratic majority against these whig fruits and they have become a party of despair & only ⟨have⟩ ↑maintain a↓ local existence in some few protected Bostons & Vermonts.

That reply of the shilling is a quite impersonal parliamentary reply[;] it is a voice of things, of fates, of the general order of the world.[226] It is the ⟨quotation⟩ broker's quotation of stocks[.]

---

[224] "Lucrezia . . . tongue." is used in "Books," *W*, VII, 214.

[225] Between "events." and "George" is a vertical line in ink.

[226] "Why did . . . world." is struck through in ink with two diagonal use marks. Cf. "Wealth," *W*, VI, 108.

It is as a practical answer[,] however[,] subject to this question. Was it not a reply for the last generation, & [132] are there no new elements now which will make a new reply? ⁿ A broad slattern farming, it has been said, was the true policy of our New England men, & not the trim garden farming of ↑the↓ English. Neither were there many buyers of fruit. Now there are more people, the land is more easily manured, and rich fruits can be raised, fed, protected, & ripened. Now there are fences, also.

To me one good pear tree bearing Bartletts, is a verdict. Why should not my trees know the way towards the sky as well as yours? L did not believe in the new land that he could ever be domesticated until the old fruits of his former home, pears & plums, were once ripened on the new farm.

⟨I⟩When I go into a good garden & nursery, I think if ⟨I lived⟩it were mine, I should never go out of it.

[133] For copyright, it is to expect almost too much magnanimity to believe that our people having had the best English ↑new↓ books so long at 25 cents a volume, should now consent to deprive themselves of the privilege & pay dollars for them. It is like expecting us Concord people, ⟨n⟩after riding on the railroad now for two years, at 40 cents, & in one hour to Boston, ⟨should⟩ ↑on↓ now ↑⟨to⟩↓ discover↑ing↓ that we have violated some vested right of the old stagecoach company, ⟨& should now⟩ⁿ ↑to↓ consent ↑henceforward↓ to go back & pay them 75 cents & ride 3 hours.

[136] ²²⁷ I observe that all the bookish men have a tendency to believe that they are unpopular. Parker gravely informs me by word & by letter that he is precisely the most unpopular of all men in New England.²²⁸ Alcott believes the same thing of himself, and I, no

---

²²⁷ Emerson omitted both "134" and "135" in numbering the pages; no leaf has been removed.

²²⁸ "I . . . unpopular." is struck through in ink with a vertical use mark. The entry was evidently written before Emerson's similar observation in a letter of September 21, 1848, to his brother William that Parker "fancies himself unpopular" (*L*, IV, 114).

doubt, if they had not anticipated me in claiming this distinction, should have claimed it for myself.

Was it ⟨M M E⟩ who said she would borrow S's mantle, "for you know she is sick & wo'nt be likely to want it again, and so, if you have no objection, I'll keep it."

[137] We are all enriched here in Concord by the railroad results mentioned above. And 'tis a quite unlooked for result of these inventions that the geographical extent of the Union should now not be an objection to the ⟨Rep⟩Federal Government. Oregon is near to Washington & every day nearing. We do not now hear the threat of removing the Federal Capital across the Alleganies.
Who is not glad to hear of the fruit-cars, which bring 1600 bushels of peaches into Boston from New York every morning; of the milk--cars which carry $20 000 worth of milk from Concord to Boston ⟨every⟩ ↑in a↓ ⟨d⟩year.

[138] The old writers, such as Montaigne, Milton, Browne, when they had put down their thoughts, jumped into their book bodily themselves, so that we have all that is left of them in our shelves; there is not a pinch of dust beside. ↑The Norsemen wrote with a crowbar, & we with Gillott pens.↓ [229]
If housekeeping ↑& grocery↓ gets into the people so does yellow paper into the writer[.]
Constitution, pluck, makes wit, you say; then he will hear the most, who offers a minus instead of a plus face to the stranger[.]

A pedant cannot have an apple tree[;] he only has apple trees who knows them, & treats them as apple trees. Else the apple trees have him[.] [230]

The university clings to us[.]

[229] Joseph Gillott (1799–1873), English inventor, helped perfect the manufacture of steel pens.
[230] "If housekeeping . . . him" is in pencil.

[139] September 10. D'Israeli ↑the chiffonier↓ wastes all his talent in the House of Commons, for the want of ⟨a little⟩ character.[231] He makes a smart cutting speech, really ⟨adds⟩ introduces new & important distinctions, as ⟨the⟩ what he says in this new speech concerning "the sentimental principle of Nationality," which the Government have adopted; & what he says of "using forced occasions & invented opportunities;" instead of availing of events. But he makes at last no impression, because the hearer asks Who are you? What is dear to you? What do you stand for? And the speech & the speaker are silent, & silence is confession. A man who has been a man, has foreground & background. His speech, be it never so good, is subordinate & the least part of him and as this man has no planet under him but only his shoes, the hearer infers that the ground of the present argument may be no wider.[232]

[140] [233] You must put your melons in the sun[.]
None ever heard of a good marriage from Mesopotamia to Missouri and yet ↑right↓ marriage is as possible tomorrow as sunshine. Sunshine is a very mixed & costly thing as we have it, & quite impossible, yet we get the right article every day. And ⟨though⟩ we are not very much to blame for our bad marriages. We live amid hallucinations & illusions, & this especial trap is laid for us to trip up our feet with & all are tripped up, first or last. But the Mighty Mother who had been so sly with us, feels that she owes us some indemnity, & insinuates into the Pandora-box of marriage, amidst dyspepsia, nervousness, screams, Christianity, "help," poverty, & all kinds of music, some deep & serious benefits & some great joys. We find sometimes a delight in the beauty & the happiness of our children that makes the heart too big for the body. And in these ill assorted connections there is ever [141] some mixture of true marriage. The poorest ⟨brutalest⟩ Paddy & his jade, if well-meaning & welltempered, get some just & agreeable relations of mutual respect & kindly observa-

---

[231] The insertion is in pencil.
[232] Emerson's reference is to a speech by Disraeli on August 16, 1848, attacking the Government's conduct of British foreign relations; see the *Times* for August 17, p. 2, cols. 4–6, and p. 3, cols. 1–3.
[233] Pp. [140] and [141] are in pencil.

tion & fostering each of other. & they learn something, & would carry themselves wiselier if they were to begin life anew in another sphere.[234] But 'tis strange to see how little society there is, — none. Who attaches himself to his partner's greatness & holds him to his greatness? None. Yet it is as possible to help a man to be himself, as to help him pull ⟨an⟩a rope or load a hay cart. We are dragons & not angels[.]

Swedenborg & Behmen are great men because they saw that a spiritual force was greater than any material force. They knew, Swedenborg did, that a text of scripture would make men black in the face, drive them out of the house, pull down houses, towns,

[142][235] Montaigne right, & his critics Scaliger & Pascal wrong.

Net purses are in vogue & all the young people buy beads; then transfer tables & all make workboxes; then tissue paper; & just now, Journals, & every young woman wishes to edit a Journal.

The Arrowhead. Talent or almost genius seems to be the power of isolating by illumination an object[.]

It is a good mould that the cunningest statuary wants[.]

Tennyson↑'s poetry↓ is as legitimate a fruit of the veneering or cabinetmaker style of English culture, as the Dinnertable[.]

Conduct of Life   ☞ [236]
Alcott needs the devotion of his friend to him & deserves it, ⟨but⟩ and if I had nine lives, I would dedicate one to him; but they must be nine lives abreast. For now ⟨w⟩each man has the misfortune to have nine friends, & [143][237] when he is exhausted by one & that one d[e]parts behold the second is coming in at the door.

[234] "And ⟨though⟩ [p. [140]] . . . sphere." is used in "Illusions," *W*, VI, 316.
[235] This page is in pencil.
[236] The hand points to another entry concerning Alcott on the facing page, [143].
[237] Except for "The doctor . . . curing.", this page is in pencil.

The doctor can do the fast riding excellently, but not the curing.[238]

Intellect

There go to the conduct of the Understanding 7 volumes of latent heat, to one of patent; seven silences to one word[.]

I was accustomed to characterize Alcott in England, by saying that he was the one man I had met who could read Plato without surprise.

[144] The trilobium, which is the eldest of fossil animals, reappears now in the embryonic changes of crab & lobster. It seems there is a state of melioration, pending which, the development towards man can go on; which ⟨at⟩usually is arrested.

Modern Times

The immense amount of valuable knowledge now afloat in society enriches the newspapers, ⟨t⟩so that one cannot snatch an old newspaper to wrap his shoes in, without his eye being caught by some paragraph of pre⟨g⟩cious science out of London or Paris which he hesitates to lose forever. My wife grows nervous [145] when I give her ⟨a⟩waste paper lest she is burning holy writ, & wishes to read it before she puts it under her pies.

George Sand is a great genius, & yet owes to her birth in France her entire freedom from the cant & snuffle of our dead Christianity[.]

The Railroad is the only sure topic for conversation in these days. — That is the only one which interests farmers, merchants, boys, women, saints, philosophers, & fools.
And now we have one more rival topic, California gold.

The Railroad is that work of art which agitates & drives mad the whole people; as music, sculpture, & picture have done on their great days respectively[.]

[146] James Baker does not imagine that he is a rich man, yet he

[238] This sentence is rewritten in ink over substantially the same matter in pencil.

keeps from year to year that lordly park of his by Fairhaven Pond,[239] lying idly & nobly open to all comers, without crop or rent, like some Duke of Sutherland or Lord Breadalbane. With its hedges of Arcady, its sumptuous lawns & slopes, ↑the apple on its trees↓, the mirror at its foot, and the ⟨ridges⟩ ↑terraces↓ of Holloway Farm on the ⟨other⟩ ↑opposite↓ bank.

As we walked thither, Ellery proposed that we should have a water colour Exhibition in Boston. I say, Yes, but I should like better to have water-colour tried in the art of writing. Let our troubadours have one of these Spanish slopes of the dry ⟨basins or⟩ ponds or basins which run from Walden to the river at Fairhaven, in this September dress of colour, under this [147] glowering sky, — the Walden Sierras in September, given as a theme, & they required to ⟨pencil⟩-daguerrotype that in good words.

↑Individual↓
If our wishes were undertakers & sextons, we should soon bury half the population.

A Mr Randall, M.C. who appeared before the Committee of H. of Commons on the subject of the American mode of closing a debate, said, that "the *one-hour* rule worked well, made the debate short & graphic." [240] Nothing worse can be said of a debate than that it is *graphic*. The only place in which I know *graphic* to be well used, is Ben Jonson's "Minerva's graphic thread." [241]

[148] The *London twist*, it is a simple but potent secret in literature & consists in inverting the common sense & experience of mankind

----

[239] " 'Fairhaven Bay,' as it is usually called, is a widening of the South Branch of the Concord River, partly in Lincoln, partly in Concord" (*J*, VII, 504, n. 1). The "park" is Thoreau's "Baker Farm."

[240] Emerson may mean Alexander Randall of Maryland (1803–1881), who served in the House of Representatives in 1841–1843, or Benjamin Randall of Maine (1789–1859), who served in 1839–1843.

[241] "Upon Sejanus," in *The Works of Ben Jonson in Six Volumes* (London, 1716), I, 9, misquoted; see *JMN*, IV, 438n. The three sentences of the present entry are used in "Art and Criticism," *W*, XII, 292.

on any subject whatever, and affirming the reverse. Thus Mr Rae teaches that the ↑N[orth]. A[merican].↓ Indian agriculture was greatly more careful & painstaking than the English. My friend L. perceived no change in our party ⟨‖ . . . ‖⟩ after they met in Paris except that they had lost ground in ↑speaking↓ French; T. C[arlyle] thinks the only great /brave/heroic/ & suffering man in Europe is Nicholas; ⟨A.H⟩ the D. of Buckingham wished the dog who bit him a young wife & an estate in the country. Lamartine was an ass & a rogue when I was in London; & here at home, Henry always[n] ⟨maintained⟩ ↑complains↓ that the woods in [149] winter are sultry. "It was so dry that you might call it wet;" was the old verse. ↑Tennyson is a screech owl, and Saint Paul a slyboots.↓ [242]
↑Yes we are all made of the sun.↓ [243]

W.   Ah you should have gathered the tomatos yesterday, when I sent you.
B.   O but I don't know all the places in your garden where ⟨they grow.⟩ ↑to find them.↓
W.   The frost does.

[150] God is a substance & his method is illusion.[244]
Who is to save the present moment?
The Intellect is the head of the Understanding but is the feet of the Moral Power[.] [245]
God is reality & his method is illusion[.]
I know what I shall find if A[lcott]. brings me Mss. I shall have a

[242] John Rae (1813–1893) was a doctor to the Hudson's Bay Company and an Arctic explorer. "L." is possibly Dionysius Lardner (1793–1859), known for his *Cabinet Cyclopaedia*, who may have accompanied Emerson on his first visit to Blanqui's Club in Paris (*Life*, p. 348); for earlier comments on speaking French that may have been made by the same person, see pp. [56] and [71½] above. Concerning Carlyle and Czar Nicholas, see Journal London, pp. [58]–[59] above, and Notebook ED, pp. [201]–[202] below; on the Duke of Buckingham, see Notebook Xenien, p. [3] below, and Journal London, p. [173] above. "⟨A.H⟩" is Arthur Helps, on the evidence of Emerson's index. For the "old verse", see p. [12] above and "Thoreau," *W*, X, 479.
[243] This added sentence is in pencil.
[244] This sentence, struck through in pencil with three diagonal use marks, is used in "Montaigne," *W*, IV, 178.
[245] This sentence is in pencil.

Salisbury Plain full of bases of pyramids to each of which I am to build an apex[.] [246]

Life

What the deuce has the lapidary to concern himself with the quarry, or the washing whence his stone comes? Must he too be geologist, & prate of strata?

Memory

It is quite essential to the locomotive, that it should be able to reverse its movement, & ⟨go⟩ ↑run↓ backwards & forwards with equal celerity. Is it less needful to the mind that it should have this retroaction, & command its past act & deed? [247]

[151] [248] Every thing must walk   Every theory be bipedized

Every man takes care that his neighbor does not cheat him but a day comes when he begins to care that he do not cheat his neighbor. Then all goes well; he has changed his cart into the chariot of the sun.[249]

The Universities give a disparate[?] mechanical integrity & make it impossible to make a mistake[.] [250]

Cider is our national drink.
A[mos] B[ronson] A[lcott] is very dependent on his companion ⟨He⟩& clothes himself with *his* culture[.]

I ask him, are you sure you have a boy? Then I will help at his birth.

---

[246] "I know . . . apex" is in pencil.
[247] "It is . . . deed?" is used in "Memory," *W*, XII, 90–91.
[248] All the original writing on this page is in pencil.
[249] "Every man . . . sun.", rewritten in ink over the original pencil entry and struck through in ink with a vertical use mark, is used in "Worship," *W*, VI, 215.
[250] "The Universities . . . mistake" is struck through in pencil with a diagonal mark and partly erased.

It is better to hold the negro race an inch under water than an inch over[.]

Better races should perish if a new principle be taught; all the world may well be bankrupt, if they are driven so into a ⟨safe⟩ right Socialism[.]

[152] Races

You cannot preserve races beyond their term. St Michael pears have died out, and see what geology says to the old strata. Trilobium is no more except in the embryonic forms of crab & lobster[.] [251]

'Tis important that the eye should be achromatic, but *Swedenborg* sees all amiss with this dull prismatic blur of misplaced gaudiness.

Why do his images give no pleasure? [252]

I go twice a week over Concord with Ellery, &, as we sit on the steep park at ⟨N⟩Conantum, we still have the same regret as oft before.[253] Is all this beauty to perish? Shall none remake this sun & wind, the skyblue river, the riverblue sky, the yellow meadow spotted with sacks & sheets of cranberry pickers, the red bushes, the irongray house ↑with↓ just the colour of the granite rock, [153] the paths of the thicket, in which the only engineer↑s↓ ⟨is the cow⟩ ↑are the cattle grazing on yonder hill;↓ the wide straggling wild orchard in which nature has deposited every possible flavour in the apples of different trees. Whole zones & climates she has concentrated into apples. We think of the old benefactors who have conquered these fields; of the old man ↑Moore↓ who is just dying in these days,[254] who has absorbed such volumes of sunshine like a huge melon or pumpkin in the sun, — who has owned in every part of Concord a woodlot, ⟨& can now⟩

---

[251] See p. [144] above.

[252] "Tis important . . . pleasure?" is in pencil.

[253] "To the old Holloway farm . . . , because long owned by the Conant family, the name 'Conantum' was given, probably by Mr. Thoreau" (*J*, VII, 504, n. 1).

[254] Captain Abel Moore, Emerson's neighbor, died on September 30, 1848.

↑until he could↓ not find the boundaries of these, and never saw their interiors. But we say, where is he who is to save the present moment, & cause that this beauty be not lost? Shakspeare saw no better heaven or earth, but had the power & need to sing, & seized the dull ugly England, ugly to this, & made [255]

[154] fancy fan fancy fancy
     commandment   Mr   Concord
      commandment   RW Emerson

Fancy is the secondary act, as the imagination the primary. The fancy plays[;] the imagination works.[256]

---

it amiable & enviable to all reading men, and now we are fooled into likening this to that; whilst, if one of us had the chanting constitution, that land would no more be heard of.

The journal of one of our walks would be literature enough for a cockney, ↑—↓ or for us, if we should be shut up in our houses, ↑—↓ and we make no record of them. The cranberry ⟨f⟩meadow yonder is that where Darius Hubbard picked one hundred bushels in one [155] season worth 200 dollars, and no labor whatever is bestowed on the crop, not so much as to mow the grass or cut down the bushes. Much more interesting is the woodlot which yields its gentle rent of six per cent without any care or thought when the owner sleeps or travels, & /[is subject to]/fears/ no enemy but fire.[257] But E. declares that the Railroad has proved too strong for all our farmers & has corrupted them like a war, or the incursion of another race; ↑—↓ has made them all amateurs, given the young men an air their fathers never had; they look as if they might be railroad agents any day. We shall never see Cyrus Hubbard or Ephraim Wheeler or grass & oats or Oats & grass[,] Old Barrett or Hosmer, in the next generation. These old Saxons ⟨are⟩ have the look of pine trees & [156] apple trees, & might be the sons got between the two; con-

---

[255] The entry is continued on p. [154] following "fancy fan . . . imagination works."

[256] "fancy fan . . . works." is struck through in ink with a diagonal use mark.

[257] "Much more . . . fire." is used in "Country Life," *W*, XII, 147.

scientious labourers with a science born with them from out the sap vessels of these savage sires.

This savagery is natural to man, & polished England cannot do without it. That makes the charm of grousehunting and deerstalking to these Lord Breadalbanes[n] walking out their doors one hundred miles on their property, or Dukes of Sutherland getting off at last their town coat & donning their hunting gear, exasperated by saloons & dress boots.

But let us have space enough, let us have wild grapes and rock maple with tubs of sugar, let us have huge straggling orchards, let us have the Ebba Hubbard pear, hemlock, savin, spruce, ⟨alder⟩walnut and oak, cidermills with [157] tons of pumice, peat, cows, horses, paddies, carts & sleds.

We came to a fence which a well directed fan would lay flat. I had much discourse concerning the birth, death, & fate of man. E thought he should make a prayer to the Chance that brought him into the world. I, that when the child had escaped out of the womb, he cries:[n] I thank the bridge that brought me safe over. I would not for ten worlds take the next one's chance.[n]

Will they, one of these days, at Fourierville, make ⟨new⟩boys & girls to order & pattern? I want, Mr Christmas office, a boy, between No 17 & No 134, half & half of both; or you might add a trace of 113. I want another girl like the one I took yesterday only you can put in a leetle more of the devil.

[158] ⟨You must have detachment if you have⟩ Intellect[n] ↑detaches,↓ yet the way men of talent make fools of themselves is, by too much detachment.

A man knocks at my door & says, "I am, now for six years, devoted to the sun. I study the sun that I may thence deduce the laws of the universe." I say, ⟨yes but beware of the sun⟩ I will not dispute against the sun, but beware of taking any one thing out of its connexions, for that way folly lies.[258]

[258] See p. [9] above. Following this entry is a penciled note by Edward Emerson: " 'Mr Lazarus that worshipped the Sun' see BO. 87[.] I think Louisa Alcott tells of him in her books[.] See also what I heard of him in 'E[merson] in Concord' " — (Boston, 1890), p. 208: "There was a certain wandering prophet . . . who believed in the Sun. This saint would have gone attired in a sheet only, a

[159] A little too much ↑in ↑the↓ French novel↓ about this *superbe chevelure*. The less is said of that meteor the better. It is of quite unspeakable character, seat of illusion, & comes as near to witchcraft & humbugging, as anything in nature.

[160] [October 1, 1848.] Yesterday, the last day of September, Ellery & I went to Carlisle by the old road passing Daniel Clark's house into the region of the limekiln & the Estabrook farm & a country made up of vast orchards where the apple grows with a profusion that mocks the pains taken by careful cockneys who come out into the country & plant young trees & watch them dwindle. Here no hedges were wanted; the wide distance from any population ⟨protects⟩ is fence enough. Here were varieties of apple not found in Downing, the Tartar⟨ean⟩ic, & the Cow-apple, as E. said. — The ground was strewn with them in ↑red & yellow↓ heaps. They grew for their own pleasure[;] they almost lost price. Barberries flourished at the roadside, & grapes along the walls. The apples were of the kind which I remember in boyhood each containing a barrel of wine & half a barrel of cider. — ↑Touch-me-if-you-dare↓ [259]

[161] Books are ↑like↓ rainbows to be thankfully received in their first impression & not examined & surveyed by theodolite & chain, as if they were part of the railroad. Perhaps it would be good in the tuition of an emperor that he should never read the same book twice. I owed, — my friend & I, — owed a magnificent day to the Bhagavat Geeta. — It was the first of books; it was as if an empire spake to us[,] nothing small or unworthy but large, serene, consistent[,] the voice of an old intelligence which in another age & climate had pondered & thus disposed of the same questions which exercise us. Let us not now go back & apply a minute criticism to it, but cherish the venerable oracle.

---

garment readily unfolded or completely shed when he would receive benign influences shot down to him from the Sun-god, but that the mistress of the house, in the Community which he would have joined and converted, told him with decision that he must wear proper clothes or depart promptly. Under these restrictions he pined, soon took the road, and . . . was last seen going up a mountain, to come nearer to his deity. It is thought that he was absorbed into the Sun. Henceforth he was not seen among men."

[259] This paragraph is used in "Country Life," *W*, XII, 146–147.

[162] I still feel a little uneasiness about these novels. Why should these sorceries have a monopoly of our delicious emotions?ⁿ — The novel still weakly uses the cheap resource of property married away instead of earned, and that is the chief conjuring-stick it has; for the instincts of man always attach to property, as he knows what accumulations of spiritual force go to the creation of that, and sobs & heart beats & sudden selfsacrifice very easily result from the dealing with it. But the novel will find the way to our interiors, ⟨yet⟩one day, & will not always be novel of costume merely.²⁶⁰ These stories are to stories of real life what the figures which represent the fashions of ⟨each⟩ ↑the↓ month in the front page of the Magazine are to portraits & inspired pictures. We say, Give us earls & marquises, give || [163]–[164] || ²⁶¹

[165] hint of these things been shown. A sudden rise in the road shows us the system of mountains, and all the summits which have been just as near us all the year, but quite out of mind.²⁶² The inexorable Laws, the Ideas, the private Fate, the Instinct, the Intellect. Memory, Imagination, Fancy, Number, Inspiration, Nature, Duty,

Are you fond of drama? say the gods, said you so, my fine fellow? Verily? Speak the truth a little, & truth on truth, to every man ⟨you meet, & in houses, at tea boards, and to all persons⟩ ↑& woman↓; try that a few hours, & you shall have dramatic situations, ↑assaults↓ & batteries, & heroic alternatives ⟨fast enough⟩ to your heart's content.²⁶³

[166]²⁶⁴ I saw Alison, Thackeray, Cobden, Tennyson, Bailey, Marston, Macaulay, Hallam, D'Israeli, Milnes, Wilson, Jeffrey, Wordsworth, Carlyle, Dickens, Lockhart, Procter, Montgomery, Collyer, Kenyon, Stephenson, Buckland, Sedgwick, Lyell, ↑Edw.↓

---

²⁶⁰ This sentence is used in "Books," *W*, VII, 214.
²⁶¹ The leaf bearing these pages is torn out. Emerson indexed both under Alcott and Conduct of Life and p. [163] under Illusion.
²⁶² "hint of . . . mind.", struck through in pencil with three vertical use marks (one apparently over a line in ink), is used in "Illusions," *W*, VI, 322.
²⁶³ "you meet . . . persons" is canceled in pencil; "& woman" and "assaults" are inserted in pencil.
²⁶⁴ This page is in pencil.

Forbes, ⟨Delabeche,⟩ ↑Sam↓ Brown, ↑Rd.↓ Owen, Robt Owen, Cruikshank, Jenny Lind, Grisi, William Allingham, David Scott, William B Scott, Kinglake, Dickens,

De Tocqueville, Lamartine, Leverrier, Rachel, Barbés, Eastlake, Spence, Wilkinson, Duke of Wellington, Brougham, Joanna Baillie, De Quincey, Sir C Fellows, Sir Henry Delabeche, ⟨Marston,⟩ John Forster,[265]

and formerly, Coleridge, Landor,

[167] ↑*Spent words*↓

Every age soon gazettes a great quantity of words & phrases which for a time it has used with heat & exaggeration. Thus we are now disgusted with

standpoint, myth, subjective, the Good, the True,[266]

[168]–[169] [blank]
[170] [Index material omitted]
[inside back cover] [Index material omitted] [267]

---

[265] "I saw . . . Forster," is used in "Personal," *W*, V, 292–293. Of those listed who have not been previously identified or are not easily recognizable, the historian Sir Archibald Alison presided at the Manchester soirée at which Emerson spoke; Thackeray was present at several social gatherings in London that Emerson attended. John Westland Marston, a dramatic poet and editor of *Psyche*, called on Emerson in London; the poet James Montgomery received Emerson in Manchester. John Payne Collier, the Shakespearean critic, was present at a meeting of the Society of Antiquaries that Emerson attended in London; the geologists Adam Sedgwick and Edward Forbes spoke at meetings of the Geological Society when Emerson was a guest. The illustrator George Cruikshank was present at the Manchester soirée. Emerson heard Giulia Grisi sing at Covent Garden but there is no record of his hearing Jenny Lind in London (see *L*, IV, 70, 71). He dined with Alexander Kinglake at Procter's and presumably met Charles L. Eastlake at the National Gallery, of which Eastlake was Keeper. William Spence, the entomologist, attended Emerson's London lectures and later dined with him. Emerson's letters do not mention a meeting with the poet Joanna Baillie, who lived in Hampstead while Emerson was in England.

[266] This unfinished paragraph is used in "Art and Criticism," *W*, XII, 293.

[267] In pencil in the lower left corner, upside down, is written the price of the book: "2/6". The index material on the inside back cover, in ink, is an alphabetical reordering of the preliminary penciled index on p. [170].

PART TWO

Miscellaneous Notebooks

JK

1843? - 1847

Notebook JK, an assemblage of miscellaneous notes, most of them transcribed from Emerson's journal entries of 1838–1847, may have been begun during the winter of 1843–1844, which he devoted to preparation of *Essays, Second Series* (1844). On four pages ([31], [43], [73], [107]) are the notations "For 2d vol Essay" or "For Vol II of Essay"; another entry (page [103]) is marked "New Essay". Most of the topical headings run in alphabetical order: "Aristocracy", "Athenaeum", "Book", "Character", "Community", "Day", "Friendship", "Individualism", "Longevity", "Practical", "Nonresistance", "Quotation", "Reality", "Riches", "Ascension of State", "Woman", and "Wonder"; two sequences of pages on "Eloquence" that interrupt the alphabetical pattern bring together what Emerson had written in the mid-1840's concerning Daniel Webster (pages [123]–[139]) and Edward Taylor (pages [141]–[149]). The gathering and organization of this material may well represent a significant stage in Emerson's method of composition, a stage apparently in between what he called "Collections" (one-line references by particular topics to various journal entries) and material organized into longer paragraphs and sections of his lectures and essays. The previously loose leaves making up the notebook were later bound in hard covers, probably in 1847 after Emerson had titled Journal GH; "1847" appears on the front flyleaf, and there are subsequent cross-references to entries in Journals AB and CD made earlier in that year. Ten pages of additional notes written in the 1850's and 1860's are laid in between the front cover and page [i].

Notebook JK, like Emerson's Index II (dated "Sept 1847"), was written on unbound leaves of various stocks of paper that were later assembled in a volume bound with brown marbled boards. The two volumes have matching black leather spines, each ornamented with five pairs of horizontal gold lines; their similarity suggests that the binding was done by the same person or firm, perhaps at the same time. The cover of JK is 20.5 x 26.5 cm, inscribed "JK" in ink. Measurements of the component leaves, especially along the horizontal axes, are necessarily approximate. Nine types of paper can be distinguished. Most of the leaves are variants of type A, a blue paper 19.8 x 25 cm ruled on either one or both sides:

A_1, ruled on both sides (pages 17–18, 21–22, 27–28, 33–38, 43–44, 47–48, 51–

52, 55-56, 59-60, 63-64, 67-68, 71-72, 75-76, 79-80, 83-86, 89-90, 93-94, 99-100, 103-104, 111-112, 115-120), and

A₂, ruled on one side only (pages 19-20, 23-26, 29-30, 39-42, 45-46, 49-50, 53-54, 57-58, 61-62, 65-66, 69-70, 73-74, 77-78, 81-82, 87-88, 91-92, 95-98, 101-102, 105-106, 109-110, 113-114, 121-122).

The eight other types, designated B through I in the order of their first occurrence in the volume, are these:

B. Plain blue paper, 20.2 x 24.9 cm (pages i-ii, 1-2);

C. Waxed blue paper, 19.9 x 25.6 cm (pages 3-4, 5-6);

D. Plain blue paper, 20.2 x 25.9 cm (pages 7-8);

E. Waxed white paper, 19.9 x 25.9 cm (pages 9-16);

F. White paper, ruled on one side only, one leaf 19.9 x 25.2 cm (pages 31-32) and another 19.2 x 24.9 cm (pages 107-108);

G. Plain blue paper, 20.4 x 25.7 cm (pages 123-136, mostly on Daniel Webster, and 141-150, mostly on Edward Taylor);

H. Plain blue paper, 20.2 x 25 cm (pages 137-140, a canceled draft of a letter dated October 26, 1846, on one page plus three pages on Webster);

I. Plain blue paper, 19.9 x 24.9 cm (pages 151-154).

Part of one leaf, pages 127-128, has been cut away. Including flyleaves (pages i-ii, 153-154), there are 156 pages, of which 73 are blank (pages ii, 1-4, 6, 10-12, 13-15, 19-20, 22-24, 26, 28, 30, 34-35, 38-40, 44, 46, 49, 50, 52-54, 56-58, 61-62, 65-66, 68-70, 76-78, 80-82, 84, 87-88, 90-92, 97, 101-102, 104-105, 108, 110, 112-115, 118, 120-122, 128, 136, 151, 154). All pages are numbered in ink except 62 which are unnumbered (pages i-ii, 2, 4-6, 10, 12, 14, 16, 18, 20, 22, 24, 26, 30, 38, 40, 42, 44, 46, 50, 52-54, 58, 60, 62, 64, 66, 68, 70, 74, 76, 78, 80, 82, 84, 86, 88, 90, 92, 94, 96, 104, 108, 110, 112, 114, 116, 118, 120, 122, 124, 126, 127-128 (msm), 134, 136, 148, 150, 154). Printed matter is mounted on the inside front cover and on pages 34, 105, 152, and 153; a number of unbound leaves are laid in. Between the inside front cover and page i are three loose sheets. One, 18 x 22.9 cm, has been folded once to make the four pages here designated fcv_a, _b, _c, and _d. The second, 14 x 22.9 cm, creased but now unfolded, is designated fcv_e and _f. The third, 24.8 x 39.5 cm, has been folded once to make the four pages designated fcv_g, _h, _i, and _j. Laid in between pages 16 and 17 are two loose leaves, each printed on the recto only. One, 14.5 x 22.2 cm, torn along the right and left margins, may have been removed from a book; it carries seven four-line stanzas of Latin verse, unsigned, captioned "Savagius Landor Lamartino." The other, part of a broadside 25 cm in width and torn irregularly along the bottom margin between 14.7 and 15.5 cm from the top, is captioned "On the Present Position of English Unitarians in Reference to the American Slavery Question." and is addressed "*To the Rev. Edward Tagart, Secretary to the British and Foreign Unitarian Association.*" Between page 154 and the inside back cover is another broadside, or perhaps a printer's proof, irregularly torn along the right margin, 11.2 x 26.2 cm on its widest and longest axes, on the recto of which are comic verses entitled "Subject: A Collusion between a Aleygaiter and a Water-Snaik." (cf. *JMN*, VII, 262).

Emerson supplied numbers for only 94 of the 156 component pages of JK, usually but not always omitting those for left-hand pages. Addition of the leaf bearing pages 31-32 (see type F in the analysis above) evidently obliged him to alter the original number of the next page from "31" to "33" and to make similar changes in succeeding pages through 133 wherever a number had previously been written; these changes have not been individually recorded in the printed text. There are no changes in the numbering of pages 135–153.

[front cover]   JK

[front cover verso] [1]   [blank]
        [front cover verso$_a$] [2] The party of virility rules the hour, the party of ideas, the age. *KL* 136

———

        The Library gains as much by weeding as by filling. *O* 270 [3]

———

What is bravely done is of one age; what is written for the ⟨world⟩ ↑world's↓ good, of all ages. Vegetius   E 74 [4]

———

        There are nations subsisting on one book. *NO* 272, E 192, [5]

Painting & Sculpture decay; poetry, eloquence, science, & history are perenial through books[.]

———

Books written for one reader. BL 115

———

[1] Two clippings from unidentified newspapers concerning public speaking are mounted on the front cover verso. One, from a German-language paper published in New York City, quotes an article from the *Karlsruher Zeitung*; the other, from an English paper evidently printed early in 1846, as dated notices overleaf indicate, reports a passage of debate in the House of Commons.

[2] For a physical description of pp. [fcv$_a$]–[fcv$_j$], see the bibliographical head-note to Notebook JK. Pp. [fcv$_a$]–[fcv$_d$], comprising a single folded sheet, were evidently written in the autumn of 1864 in preparation for a lecture on "Books" delivered in December of that year. The first citation which follows, to Journal KL, p. [136], refers to an entry dated October 19, 1864; other citations are to Journal NO and Notebook BL, written in 1859. These and other later journals and notebooks referred to on pp. [fcv$_a$]–[fcv$_j$], except for Index Major, are planned for publication in later volumes. Footnotes locate items in earlier journals which have already been published in *JMN*.

[3] See *JMN*, IX, 428.

[4] Journal E, p. [74], printed in *JMN*, VII, 311, gives the Latin version; the translation appears also in Index Major, p. [27].

[5] For Journal E, p. [192], see *JMN*, VII, 387.

NOTEBOOKS OF RALPH WALDO EMERSON

Best value of books that they suggest more thoughts than they record, that the reader thinks faster & better than the author.

[front cover verso$_b$] 'Tis with thought as with the thunderbolt which strikes but an inch of ground, but the light of it fills the horizon.[6] *RL* [i.e., KL] 173

———

It makes a ⟨|| ... ||⟩ tie between men to have read the same book[.]

———

What a signal convenience is fame. Do we read all authors to grope our way to the best? No, but the world selects for us the best, & we select from these our best[.] *W* 67 [7]

[front cover verso$_c$] La Grange thought Newton fortunate that the law of gravitation could be discovered but once. ↑&c.↓ See *AZ* 166

"One thought fills immensity." *Blake* [8]

↑Intellect. *Index Major* 169,↓ [9]

[front cover verso$_d$] [blank]
[front cover verso$_e$] ↑*Races 322 Index*↓ [10]

Aptness of races to special work   *DO* 21

Small armour in the Museum at Copenhagen   *VS* 9

⟨Indian⟩ ↑Hindoo↓ soil reacts on all comers, *IO* 40

Aptness of races to special work. DO ⟨188⟩ ↑21↓

---

[6] Cf. "Fragments on the Poet and the Poetic Gift," XXXII, *W*, IX, 334.

[7] See *JMN*, IX, 212, and "Books," *W*, VII, 195.

[8] See "The Marriage of Heaven and Hell," Plate 8, line 16, in *The Complete Writings of William Blake*, ed. Geoffrey Keynes (London and New York, 1957), p. 151.

[9] "Intellect . . . 169," is added in pencil; "*Index* . . . 169," is set off by a curved pencil line to the left and above.

[10] Pp. [fcv$_e$]–[fcv$_f$], comprising a single leaf, cite passages listed in Emerson's Index Major, compiled in 1847 and added to later.

The Indian is said to be unable to stand the gaze of the white   *W* 95 [11]

Races that have been from earliest time articles of luxury as the Negro. *D* 82 [12]

Nature now & then drops a link   *DO* 188
Aptness of races to special work. *DO* 21 [13]
Smelting pot of Europe in the dark Ages. *Y* 119 [14]

———

There are races that have been from the earliest time articles of luxury, — as the negro. *D* 82.[15]

———

The negro makes the greatest amount of happiness out of the smallest capital.

———

A man's capital Must be in him[.]
All capital is of recent creation[.]

———

Rich by agenc[i]es that wrought before we were born. *CD* ⟨138⟩ 138

[front cover verso$_f$] [blank]
[front cover verso$_g$] [16] The 5 or 6 great men when they look at each other, find themselves near & intimate[.] *TU* 241

———

"So that the State only exists, I shall never want anything," said Condé, & paid the army himself. *AZ* 156

———

The secret of fine society is that every man comes to it from still higher ground. *Y* 133 [17]

———

[11] See *JMN*, IX, 227; cf. "Civilization," *W*, VII, 20.
[12] See *JMN*, VII, 58.
[13] See above.
[14] See *JMN*, IX, 300.
[15] See *JMN*, VII, 58, and above.
[16] Pp. [fcv$_g$]–[fcv$_j$], comprising a single sheet, also cite passages in Emerson's Index Major, all of them appearing on pp. [124]–[125].
[17] See JMN, IX, 304.

"When I count puddings, I shall d⟨y⟩ie," said Luther.[18]

———

See Vasari's account of Leonardo da Vinc⟨h⟩i. Bohn Vol II. p. 390 [19]

———

If a man's centrality is incomprehensible to us, we may as well snub the sun[.] *TU* 253

———

"An infinitude of tenderness is the chief gift and inheritance of all the truely great men." Ruskin.
                "Two Paths." p. 37 [20]

———

All greatness is in degree, & there is more above than below. *XO* 169

———

"The way from Rome is the way to Rome." [21]

———

The comet coming to fetch Bolingbroke.
                Spen⟨s⟩ce's Anecdotes
                        of Pope.[22]

———

Very fine relations are established between every clear spirit, and all bystanders. *XO* 169

———

His recognition by others is not necessary to him.

———

Whenever Heaven sends a great man into the world, it whispers the secret to one or two confidants.[23]

———

[18] See *JMN*, VI, 349; Journal CD, p. [86] above.
[19] Giorgio Vasari, *The Lives of the Most Eminent Painters, Sculptors, and Architects*, trans. Jonathan Foster, 5 vols. (London, 1850–1852), in Emerson's library.
[20] John Ruskin, *The Two Paths: Being Lectures on Art, and Its Application to Decoration and Manufacture* (New York, 1859), in Emerson's library.
[21] See *JMN*, IX, 274.
[22] Joseph Spence, *Anecdotes, Observations, and Characters of Books and Men* (London, 1820), p. 316. For the anecdote, see front cover verso[n] below.
[23] See *JMN*, IX, 105, and "Uses of Great Men," *W*, IV, 32.

Roger Cotes of whom ↑Sir↓ Isaac Newton said, "If he had lived we had knowen something." [24]

[front cover verso_h] Sometimes, but rarely, we have found ↑a man↓ superior to his talent, — who had money in his pocket, & did not use it. [25]

Pope & Spence adored Lord Bolingbroke & ⟨thought⟩ ↑agreed↓ that something in him looks as if he was placed in this world by mistake. Pope said there is so, & when the comet appeared to us a month or two ago, I had sometimes an imagination that it might possibly be come to our world to carry him home as a coach comes to one's door for other visiters. [26]

[front cover verso_i] [blank]
[front cover verso_j] [blank]
[i]   R.W. Emerson
                                            1847

JK

[ii]–[4] [blank]
[5] Aristocracy
Is the ideal society always to be only a dream, a song, a luxury of thought, & never a step taken to realize the vision for living & indigent men, without misgiving within, & wildest ridicule abroad? Between poetry & prose must the great gulf yawn ever, & they who try to bridge it over be lunatics or hypocrites? And yet the too dark ground of history is starred over with solitary heroes who dared to believe better of their brothers & who prevailed by actually executing in some part the law, (the high ideal) in their own life, &, tho' a hissing & an offence to their contemporaries, yet they became a

[24] See *JMN*, III, 13.
[25] See Journal LM, p. [66] above.
[26] See front cover verso_g, above.

celestial sign to all succeeding souls, as they journeyed through nature. How shine the names of Abraham, Diogenes, Pythagoras, & the transcendant Jesus in antiquity[!][27]

[6] [blank]

[7] In our best moments society seems not to claim equality, but requires to be treated like a child, to whom we administer camomile & magnesia, on our own judgment, without consultation. What we can do is law enough for the other. And we glance for sanction at the historical position of scholars in all ages, whom we commend in proportion to their selfreliance. But when our own light ⟨beams less steadily &⟩ flickers in the socket, suddenly the pupil seems riper, & more froward, & even assumes the mien of a patron whom we must court.

———

Do you say that all the good retreat from men, & do not work strongly & lovingly with them? Well, it is fit & necessary that they should treat men as ghosts & phantoms, here for our behoof, here to teach us [8] dramatically, as long as they have not attained to a real existence, existence in their own right, that is to say, until the uprise of the soul in them. Then we shall, without tedious degrees, treat them as ourselves: they will be ourselves. Now they are not ourselves: why should we say they are?[28]

[9]   ↑Aristocracy↓
Heroic dreams taught us that the Golden Table never lacks members: all its seats are kept full; but with this strange provision, that the members are carefully withdrawn into deep niches with curtains; so that no one of them can see any other of them. And each believes himself alone. In the presence of the ⟨Round Table⟩ ↑Chapter↓, which assembles visibly once in five, or once in twenty five years, it is easy for each member to carry himself regally & well. But in the absence of his colleagues, & in the presence of mean people, he is tempted to conform to the low customs of towns. The honor of a

[27] This paragraph is transcribed from a letter to Mary Moody Emerson, October 21, 1838; see L, II, 170, and JMN, VII, 114.
[28] For the entries on pp. [7]–[8], see JMN, VII, 256–257.

Member consists in an indifference to the persons & interests about him & the pursuing undisturbed the career of a Brother, as if always in their presence, & as if no other existed.[29]

[10]–[12] [blank]
    [13] *Athenaeum*

One in every town to be owner & residuary legatee of all works of art, picture, engraving, statue, and to make that town selfrespecting & respected of others.* But chiefly to work upon its own young. Mrs Jameson's Rotterdam professor. Give depth to a town. Let the residence of your body be a residence for your soul & for all souls. Use of noble families. Willingness of the people to provide one permanent owner in every community as a sort of treasurer for the community. Democrats must find some succedaneum for that permanency of aristocracy[.]
Daedalus
Gallery of Sculpture for every family. N 41 [30]
atrium
Every man's house should be approached through a wood[.] [31]

[14]–[16] [blank]
[17] [32] Things said for conversation are chalk eggs[.] [33]

↑*See O 42, 43,↓ [34]

[29] "Aristocracy" is added in pencil. "the Golden Table . . . existed." is used in "Aristocracy," *W*, X, 60–61.

[30] "Daedalus" is probably a reference to John Sterling's poem of that title, as in *JMN*, IX, 24, where "Sculpture" is also mentioned; the poem is quoted in "Uses of Great Men," *W*, IV, 21. For "N 41", see *JMN*, VIII, 263.

[31] Cf. *JMN*, IX, 105.

[32] As described in the bibliographical headnote to Notebook JK, there are two loose leaves laid in between pp. [16] and [17]: one carries seven four-line stanzas of unsigned Latin verse captioned "Savagius Landor Lamartino."; the other, captioned "On the Present Position of English Unitarians, In Reference to the American Slavery Question.", is addressed "*To the Rev. Edward Tagart, Secretary to the British and Foreign Unitarian Association.*"

[33] This sentence is struck through in ink with four diagonal use marks. See *JMN*, IX, 15, and "Social Aims," *W*, VIII, 96.

[34] *JMN*, IX, 372.

God will have life to be real; we will be damned but it shall be theatrical.[35]

Let others grumble that they see no faeries nor muses; I rejoice that my eyes see the erect eternal world, always the same & erect, without blur or halo.[36]

We live as we must, & call it by the best names we can.[37]

A gun is a liberalizer.[38]

The condition of participation in any man's thought is entering the gate of that life. No man can be intellectually apprehended. As long as you see only with your eyes, you do not see him. You must be committed, before you shall be entrusted with the secrets of any party.[39]

[18] Let the river roll which way it will, cities will rise on its banks.[40]

Rail-roads make the country transparent[.]

The perfect unit can alone make a perfect member.[41]

[19]–[20] [blank]
[21]   ↑Book↓

The book only characterizes the reader. Is Shakspeare the delight

---

[35] See *JMN*, IX, 23.

[36] See *JMN*, IX, 24; Journal AB, p. [77] above; "The Superlative," *W*, X, 166.

[37] This sentence is struck through in ink with a vertical use mark and in pencil with a vertical use mark. See *JMN*, VIII, 412, and "Experience," *W*, III, 57; cf. *JMN*, IV, 315, and Notebook Man, p. [48]: "We do what we can, & then make a theory to prove our performance the best." Notebook Man will be published in a later volume.

[38] See *JMN*, IX, 48, 281; cf. Journal AB, p. [112] above, and "Culture," *W*, VI, 142.

[39] For these four sentences, see *JMN*, IX, 50.

[40] Cf. *JMN*, IX, 223.

[41] For "Rail-roads . . . member.", see *JMN*, IX, 78.

of the nineteenth century? That fact shows where we are in the ecliptic of the soul.

Fame characterizes those who give it.[42]

[22]–[24] [blank]
[25] ↑Book↓
There has been much selection before it comes to you. All the books of the world, the newspapers, journals, reports, laws, are written by the successful class, & so have the tone of affirmation & of advance.[43]   ↑printed in *"Books"*(?)↓

[26] [blank]
[27]   ↑Book
                                           Translation↓

The Italians have a fling at translators, *i traduttori traditori;* but I thank them. I never read any Latin, Greek, German, Italian, scarcely any French book in the original, which I can procure in an English translation. I like to be beholden to the great metropolitan English speech, the sea which receives tributaries from every region under heaven, the Rome of nations; & I should as soon think of swimming across Charles River when I wish to go to Boston, as of reading all my books in originals, when I have them rendered for me in my mother's speech.[44]

---

[42] "Book" is in pencil. For "The book . . . the soul.", see *JMN*, VII, 488, and "Quotation and Originality," *W*, VIII, 194. With "Fame . . . it.", cf. "Milton," *W*, XII, 248: "a man's fame . . . characterizes those who give it, as much as him who receives it.", and "Worship," *W*, VI, 224: "The fame of Shakspeare . . . characterizes those who give it."

[43] "Book" is in pencil. This paragraph, struck through in ink with a vertical use mark, is used in "Books," *W*, VII, 195. See *JMN*, VIII, 152; Journal AB, p. [2] above.

[44] See *JMN*, VIII, 357, IX, 55. "Book" and "Translation" are in pencil. This paragraph, struck through in ink with a diagonal use mark, is used in "Books," *W*, VII, 204. In the left margin of p. [27] is the penciled notation "printed"; the hand may be Emerson's but is more likely that of his son, who throughout the manuscript has noted titles of essays in which passages of Notebook JK are used. Similar penciled notations and queries ("printed", "printed?") occur also on pp. [41], [48], [55],

[28] [blank]
[29] ↑Character↓

The things of a man for which I visit him were done in the dark &
in the cold.[45]

The man, it is his attitude.[46]

Say not, you are sufficient to yourself, but have nothing to impart: —
I know and am assured, that, whoever is sufficient to himself, will, if
only by existing, succour me also.[47]

Freedom is frivolous beside the tyranny of genius.[48]

[30] [blank]
[31] For 2d vol Essay

Community

The worst of community is that it must inevitably transform into
charlatans the leaders by the endeavor continually to meet the expectation & admiration of this eager crowd of men & women seeking
they know not what who flock to them. Unless he have a Cossack
roughness of clearing himself of that which does not belong to him
⟨Cossack⟩charlatan he must be.[49]

People cannot live together in any but necessary ways.[50]

---

and [59] below; on p. [83] below, where "printed", in ink, occurs within the text
itself, the hand is clearly Emerson's own.

[45] This sentence is struck through in pencil with a vertical use mark. See Journal
TU (to be published in a later volume), p. [34], and "Behavior," W, VI, 189.

[46] Possibly a reference to Daniel Webster: see L, III, 88 (October 5, 1842);
JMN, VIII, 277 (October 8, 1842).

[47] See JMN, IX, 24.

[48] See JMN, VIII, 394.

[49] This paragraph is used in "Life and Letters in New England," W, X, 354.
Another version of the passage, in JMN, VIII, 218, refers specifically to George and
Sophia Ripley.

[50] See JMN, VIII, 222. This sentence is used in "Life and Letters in New
England," W, X, 368.

One would say that agricultural association would certainly follow manufacturing assoc[iatio]ns & fix the price of bread. See *K* 90 [51]

[32] I think no persons whom I know could afford to live together *on their merits.* Some of them could much better than others, but not through their power to command respect, but because of their easy genial ways. That is, could live together by aid of their weakness & inferiority. [52]

———

The perfect unit can alone make a perfect member. [53]

The propagandists of Fourierism whom I have seen are military minds, & their conversation is always insulting, for they have no other end than to make a tool of their companion. [54]

[33] Plaindealing is the best defence of manners & morals between the sexes. The reason why there is purity in marriage, is that the parties are universally near & helpful. If their wisdoms also come near & meet, there is no danger of passion. Therefore, the remedy of impurity is to come nearer. [55]

A great deal of money was wasted in ⟨large⟩providing large cities with a nocturnal police. At last, it is found, that, gas light, & now the new electric light, which destroy night, supersede the police. [56]

[34]–[35] [57] [blank]

---

[51] *JMN,* VIII, 232.

[52] This paragraph is used in "Life and Letters in New England," *W,* X, 368.

[53] See p. [18] above.

[54] Cf. *JMN,* IX, 100.

[55] See *JMN,* VIII, 391–392, where "plain dealing . . . sexes." is attributed to George P. Bradford, speaking of Brook Farm. "Plaindealing . . . sexes." is used in "Life and Letters in New England," *W,* X, 368.

[56] See Journal RS (to be published in a later volume), p. [233]: "A good lamp is the best police"; "Worship," *W,* VI, 224: "gaslight is found to be the best nocturnal police."

[57] Mounted on p. [34] with sealing wax is a printed notice, 14.5 x 11 cm,

[36] The young people think it the vice of the age to exaggerate individualism, and they adopt the word *humanity* & go for "the race". Hence the Phalanx, Owenism, Simonism, the Communities. In theology, the same spirit has produced Puseyism, which endeavours to rear the Church as a balance & overpoise to the conscience. Clubhouse.

But though it is ⟨foolish⟩ ↑absurd↓ to leave out either of these elements, yet the poetry, the sublime, are still on the solitary side. The *a priori* convictions are there. The plans of Owen & Fourier are enforced only by counting & arithmetic. All the fine aperçus are for individualism. The Spartan broth, the hermit's cell, the lonely farmer's life are poetic; the phalanstery, the selfsupporting village, are culinary & mean[.] [58]

[37] Credit, it seems, is to be abolished. Can you not abolish faces & character, of which credit is the shadow? As long as men are born babes, ⟨so long⟩ they will live on credit for the first twelve or fourteen years of their life.

Every man has in his countenance a promise to pay, & hence credit. Less credit will there be? You are mistaken. There will be always more & more[.] [59]

↑Stealing dividends   U 81
Farmer's dollar heavy   U↓ [pp. 63–64] [60]

[38]–[40] [blank]
    [41] The hint of the dialectic is more valuable than the dialectic.

---

headed "PRACTICAL RULES, FOR CONDUCTING A CONVERSATIONAL MEETING." and concluding "*the subject for consideration this Evening is*" — with a space to be filled in; the verso is blank. The form may have been used to announce Bronson Alcott's "Conversations."

[58] For "The young people . . . Clubhouse.", see *JMN*, VIII, 249; for "The *a priori* . . . & mean", see *JMN*, IX, 334.

[59] "so long" is canceled in pencil. For "Credit . . . & more", see *JMN*, VIII, 158; the present passage, struck through in ink with a diagonal use mark, is used in "Social Aims," *W*, VIII, 84.

[60] The insertion is in pencil. See *JMN*, IX, 50–51, 41, and "Wealth," *W*, VI, 101–102.

One who has seen one proof ever so slight of the terrific powers of this organ will remember it all the days of his life. The most venerable proser will be surprised with silence. It is like the first hint that the earth moves, or that iron is a conductor of fluids, or that granite is a gas. The solids, the centres, rest itself, fly & skip. Rest is a relation, & not rest any longer. Ah! these solid houses, real estates, have wings, like so many nimble musquitoes, & do exceedingly hop & ⟨‖ ... ‖ly⟩avoid me.[61]

[42] ↑Day.↓

Gertrude said, that the days at Mull were all different, & only joined by a beautiful love of the same object. ↑R 140↓ [62]
Here your astronomy is an espionage. I dare not go out of doors & see the moon or stars, but they seem to ask me how many lines or pages are finished, since I saw them last. Not so, as I told you, was it at Mull. Life is not there a college examination.
The days come & go like muffled & veiled figures sent from a distant friendly party, but they say nothing, &, if we do not use the gifts they bring, they carry them as silently away. ↑CD 4↓ [63]

[43] For Vol II of Essay

↑Day

Days at Mull	R 140
Muffled figures	CD 4
Gr[?] of today	E 102, 219, 214, 258↓ [64]

The ascetic of every day is how to keep me at the top of my condition,

---

[61] This paragraph is struck through in pencil with a vertical use mark. See *JMN*, IX, 214; Notebook Platoniana, p. [22] below.
[62] See *JMN*, VIII, 422. "R 140" is in pencil.
[63] "CD 4" is in pencil. For "Here your . . . at Mull.", see Journal AB, p. [74] above; for "Life . . . examination.", see Journal GH, p. [66] above. "Gertrude . . . away.", struck through in ink with a vertical use mark, is used in "Works and Days," *W*, VII, 181, 168.
[64] "Day . . . 258" is added in pencil; "Day . . . today" has been partly erased. For the references to Journals R and E, see *JMN*, VIII, 422, VII, 330, 399, 397, 417–418.

because a good day of work is too important a possession to be risked for any chance of good days to come.[65]

Days that are days.

You must treat the days respectfully. You must be a day yourself, and not interrogate life like a college professor. Every thing in the Universe goes by indirection. There are no straight lines.
Life is only good when it is magical & musical; a perfect timing & consent, & we know nothing about it.[66]

↑Every day was a new snarl of perplexities for him to unwind.↓ [67]

[44] [blank]
[45] Wisdom flies from us at our unintelligent question.[68]

"The more angels, the more room." [69]

The plenty of the poorest place is too great, the harvest cannot be gathered.

[46] [blank]
   [47] ↑Friendship↓ [70]

It is the grace of new friends to be frank, & of old friends to be reticent.[71]

---

[65] See *JMN*, VIII, 176.
[66] With "There are no straight lines", cf. *JMN*, VIII, 339, 397, IX, 361, and "Uriel," ll. 21-22, *W*, IX, 14. "You must . . . it.", struck through in ink with a vertical use mark, is used in "Works and Days," *W*, VII, 180, 181.
[67] The addition is in pencil. Emerson included this sentence in Index Major, p. [150], under the heading "Human Life"; no journal source is given.
[68] See *JMN*, VIII, 177.
[69] Cf. Emanuel Swedenborg, *A Treatise Concerning Heaven and Its Wonders, and also concerning Hell*, Section 71. (The London, 1723 edition is in Emerson's library.) This sentence is struck through in pencil with a vertical use mark. See *JMN*, VIII, 320, 337; "Address to the Temperance Society at Harvard, Mass."; "Swedenborg," *W*, IV, 126.
[70] The insertion is in pencil.
[71] See *JMN*, VIII, 396.

[48] Whoso sees Law, does not despond, but is inflamed with great desires & endeavours based on his perfect trust. Whoso desponds therefore, ⟨‖ ... ‖⟩betrays his blindness.[72]

[49]–[50] [blank]
[51] ↑Individualism↓ [73]

National characteristics stand no chance beside individual. Physicians say every constitution makes a new fever. So is it with persons. Our national traits may appear so long as we are drowsy, but put us in good spirits, — search us with thought, — & all nations are men together. ⟨The⟩I remember the first Englishman I met in travelling was a frank affectionate fellow, & the first Frenchman was a mystic.[74]

[52]–[54] [blank]
[55] Knowledge is the straight line. Wisdom is the power of the straight line, or the square. Virtue is the power of the square, or the solid. Thus my friend reads in the Cultivator concerning the method of planting & hoeing potatoes, or follows a farmer hoeing along the row of potato hills; that is knowledge. At last he seizes the hoe, and, at first with care & heed pulls up every root of piper-grass. As the day grows hot, & the row is long, he says to himself, This is wisdom, but one hill is like another; I have mastered the art: it is trifling to do many times over the same thing; and he desists. But the last lesson was still unlearned: the moral power lay in the continuance, in fortitude, in working against pleasure to the excellent end, & con-quering all opposition. He has knowledge, he has wisdom, but he has missed virtue, which he only acquires who endures[n] routine, & sweat, & postponement of ⟨fancy⟩ ↑ease↓ to the achievment of a worthy end.[75]

---

[72] "Whoso sees . . . blindness." is struck through in ink with a vertical use mark. See *JMN*, VII, 333, and "Considerations by the Way," *W*, VI, 264.
[73] The insertion is in pencil. Below it is a question mark (Edward Emerson's?), also in pencil.
[74] For this paragraph, see *JMN*, VIII, 339–340. The dashes on p. [51] have been added in pencil.
[75] For "Knowledge is . . . worthy end.", see *JMN*, IX, 298–299.

[56]–[58] [blank]
[59] Longevity

For any grandeur of circumstance length of time seems an in-dispensable element. Who can attach anything majestic to creatures so shortlived as men?[n] The time that is proper to spend in mere musing is too large a fraction of the threescore ⟨years⟩ & ten years to be indulged to that greatness of behaviour.

The brevity of human life gives a melancholy aspect to the profession of the architect[.] [76]

What a pity that a farmer should not live three hundred years.[77]

We must infer our destiny from the preparation. We are driven by instincts to hive innumerable experiences which are of no visible value, & which we may revolve thro' many lives in the eternal whirl of generation, before we shall assimilate or exhaust[.] [78]
[60] And yet though I have often lamented the brevity of life it is easy to see that the stability of human beings depends on that consideration. Who would stay in Concord who had heard of Valencia, but that there is not time to establish himself there without too great a hazard of his happiness in the few years that remain. Therefore we stick where we are.[79] But if we had a lease of a thousand years we should try Madeira, the Marquesas, Valparaiso, Virginia, Wales & Switzerland and Sicily.

[61]–[62] [blank]
[63] Nature asked whether troop & baggage be two things; whether the world is all troop or all baggage, or whether there be any troop that shall not one day be baggage? Easy she thinks it to show you the Universal Soul; we have all sucked that orange but would you please to mention what is an Individual. She apologized

---

[76] For "For any . . . architect", see *JMN*, VIII, 320.
[77] See *JMN*, VII, 476, IX, 75.
[78] For "We must . . . or exhaust", see *JMN*, IX, 116.
[79] For the paragraph to this point, see *JMN*, IX, 443–444.

for trifling with you in your non-age & adding a little sugar to your milk that you might draw the teat, & a little glory afterward to important lessons,—but declared that she would never tell you another fib, if you had quite settled it that Buddhism was better than hands & feet, & would keep ⟨your⟩that conviction in the presence of two persons. As for *far* & *too far*, she wondered what it meant. She admires people who read, & people who ⟨write⟩look at pictures, but if they read until they write, or look at pictures until they draw them, she curses them up & down. She has the oddest [64] tastes & behaviour. An onion which is all coat, she dotes on, & among birds, she admires the god-wit; but when I hinted that a blue weed grew about my house called *self-heal*, she said a coxcomb named it; but she teaches cobwebs to resist the tempest, & when a babe's cries drove away a lion, she almost devoured the darling with kisses. She says her office of dragoman is vacant; though she has been much pestered with applications, and if you have a talent for asking questions, she will play with you all your life, but if you can answer questions, she will propose one, which, if you answer, she will die first. She hates authors, but likes Montaigne.[80]

Surprise & casualty are the apples of her eyes.[81]

[65]–[66] [blank]
    [67] In Nature the doubt recurs whether Man is the cause or the effect. Are beasts & plants degradations of man or are these the prophecies & preparations of nature practising for her masterpiece in man?ⁿ Culminate we do not: but that point of imperfection which we occupy is it ↑on the way↓ up or down? [82]

    ↑The two histories   U↓[83]

[68]–[70] [blank]

[80] For this paragraph, see *JMN*, VIII, 322–323: an entry dated February 7, 1843.
[81] This sentence is struck through in ink with five vertical use marks. See "Nature, I," ll. 7–8, *W*, IX, 225.
[82] See *JMN*, VIII, 362.
[83] The insertion is in pencil. See *JMN*, IX, 77; cf. also *JMN*, IX, 241–242.

[71] The same depth which dew gives to the morning meadow, the fireflies give to the evening meadow. Fire, though a spark on the chimney-back, is always a deep.[84]

Paint costs nothing, say the Dutch: Sunshine costs less, yet is finer pigment.[85]

[72] Practical
The most abstract truth is the most practical. How quickly the whole community is touched by an academical discourse on theism. At an imagined assault of a cardinal truth the very mud boils. But wit, *old* poetry, *old* philosophy, & mathematics are favorite amusements with men of letters, for these have no claws, no dangers.[86]

[73] For 2d vol Essay
Our bodies often do not fit us, but caricature & satirize us.[n] Thus short legs which constrain a man to short mincing steps, are a perpetual insult & contumely to him.[87]

In the morning a man walks with his whole body; in the evening only with his legs; the trunk is carried along almost motionless[.][88]

⟨On⟩Only the face is well alive, amongst our people: the trunk & limbs have an inferior & subsidiary life, as if only supporters of the head. The head is finished, the body only blocked. In Kentucky, in Carolina, we ↑often↓ see a body which is also alive.[89]

People say, when you shudder, some one is walking over your grave;

[84] For the paragraph, see *JMN*, VIII, 178. "The same . . . evening meadow." is struck through in ink with two diagonal use marks.
[85] "Paint . . . pigment." is struck through in ink with two diagonal use marks. See *JMN*, VIII, 16, 264, and "Considerations by the Way," *W*, VI, 264.
[86] This entry headed "Practical", obviously recalling the controversy generated by Emerson's Divinity School Address of 1838, also reflects his thinking of the 1830's: for the first sentence, see *JMN*, V, 175, and *Nature*, *W*, I, 4; for the complete entry, see *JMN*, VII, 95.
[87] "Our bodies . . . him." is struck through in pencil with a vertical use mark. See *JMN*, VIII, 216, and "Beauty," *W*, VI, 298.
[88] See *JMN*, VII, 168.
[89] For "Only the face . . . alive.", see *JMN*, VIII, 42–43.

they describe a murder & insults offered to a murdered body, as a successful revenge; & to pluck out the quivering heart, is thought to consummate the harm. They do not see that a man is as much a stranger in his own body as another man would be.[90]

[74] "I go a beggar to the sunset but in the morning I am equal to nature[.]"   E[lizabeth] H[oar] [91]

[75] ↑Nonresistance↓ [92]

I wish people would not be ⟨af⟩so afraid as they are of Anarchy. We have had an interregnum once in Massachusetts & woke up with our heads on our shoulders, & not a pane of glass broken. When somebody adduced a ⟨certain⟩ family of ↑good↓ children as examples of the value of a careful education ⟨Aunt Mary⟩ ↑a wise woman↓ replied "My good friend, they were born to be educated". It stands just so with this superstition good whigs have concerning our debt to the laws. I always wish to answer, Good friend, we are a lawful people. The laws ⟨is⟩ ↑are↓ a fruit of this people, like their obedience to the laws. Men, — these men are lawful, & make & obey laws.[93]

   ↑Lovers safe as the sun   R 161↓ [94]

When 30 000 000 of people are all striving to keep their feet ⟨i⟩on the ground & their heads in the air it is not strange that they should not be sprawling & rolling over each other, but erect & balanced.

[76]-[78] [blank]
   [79] Quarrels are not composed on their own grounds, but only by the growth of the character which subverts their place & memory. In the life of a new idea we form new relations to all persons: we have become new persons, & do not inherit the wars or the friendships

---

[90] For "People . . . would be.", see *JMN*, VII, 79.
[91] See *JMN*, VIII, 246.
[92] The insertion is in pencil.
[93] For "When somebody . . . obey laws.", see *JMN*, IX, 239.
[94] The addition is in pencil. See *JMN*, VIII, 433.

of that person we were. — If the misunderstanding could be healed it would not ↑have↓ existed.⁹⁵

When we quarrel, O then we wish we had always kept our appetites in rein that we might speak so coolly & majestically from unquestionable heights of character.

——

↑Never quarrel with vulgar people; they are sure to have the advantage of you.↓⁹⁶

——

[80]–[82] [blank]
    [83] Quotation

Whoever can write something good himself is thence forward by law of the muse⟨'⟩s' parliament entitled to steal at discretion.⁹⁷

Quotation is good only when the writer goes my way & better mounted than I & gives me a cast, as we say.ⁿ But if I like the gay equipage so well as to go out of my road, I had better have gone a-foot.⁹⁸

——

↑printed↓

——

All reading is a kind of quotation.⁹⁹

[84] [blank]
[85]   ↑Reality↓

It is ever well with him who finishes his work for its own sake; & the state & the world is happy, that has the most of such finishers.

⁹⁵ For this paragraph, see *JMN*, VIII, 29.
⁹⁶ See *JMN*, VII, 463.
⁹⁷ See *JMN*, IX, 113, and "Shakspeare," *W*, IV, 198.
⁹⁸ "Quotation . . . a-foot.", struck through in ink with a vertical use mark, is used in "Quotation and Originality," *W*, VIII, 189. See *JMN*, IX, 82.
⁹⁹ This sentence is struck through in ink with a vertical use mark. Cf. *JMN*, IX, 112; "Plato; or, the Philosopher," *W*, IV, 42: "Every book is a quotation. . . ."

The world will do justice to such; it cannot otherwise: but never on the day when the work is done & presented. But it is forever true that every man settles his own rate.[100]

⟨[That the thing done, that]⟩ ↑Forever & ever↓ the quality avails, & not the opinion entertained of it.ⁿ ⟨[is a lesson which all things teach, & no man can sufficiently learn.]⟩ When I come to a self-relying man, in a play or a novel, who breasts the change of Fortune with stoutness, I pause & read it over again. Landor is attacked savagely in Blackwood; yet nothing in the attack is memorable⟨;⟩ and ⟨in⟩ ↑to↓ Landor we have still to go back & refresh ourselves with ⟨that⟩ ↑some↓ wise remark or ⟨that⟩ elegant illustration.[101]

↑Much of the time every man must [86] be his own friend↓[.] [102]

[87]–[88] [blank]
[89] Riches

A man should not be rich by having what is superfluous, but by having what is essential to him like a manufacturer or engineer or astronomer, who has a great capital invested in his costly apparatus. How to animate all his possessions.[103] If he have any not animated by his quality & energy, let him sell & convert them into things nearer to his nature. Such a rich man excites no envy. He has no more than he needs & uses. I wish to be near Boston, because I use Boston.[104]

The heart of mankind would affirm that he is the rich man ⟨‖ ... ‖⟩-

---

[100] "Reality" is inserted in pencil. This paragraph, struck through in pencil and in ink with two vertical use marks, is used in "Worship," W, VI, 225–226. See also *JMN*, IX, 349.

[101] See *JMN*, IX, 251–252; the attack was Edward Quillinan's parody entitled "Imaginary Conversation, Between Mr Walter Savage Landor and the Editor of Blackwood's Magazine," *Blackwood's Edinburgh Magazine*, LIII (April 1843), 518–536. "Landor is . . . illustration." is struck through in ink with a vertical use mark; the entire paragraph is used in "First Visit to England," W, V, 9–10.

[102] See *JMN*, IX, 209.

[103] Cf. "Wealth," W, VI, 97: "Some men are born to own, and can animate all their possessions."

[104] For "A man . . . Boston.", see *JMN*, IX, 301.

only in whom the people are rich & he is the poor man in whom the people are poor.[105]

↑Saadi's Rich man   AB 15
See what money will buy, O.41
Riches   AB 82↓ [106]

[90]–[92] [blank]
        [93] *Rich & poor.* Alas the poor are the poor of these rich. The rich also are no better; they are the ⟨p⟩rich of these poor.[107]

All stealing is comparative. If you come to absolutes, pray who does not steal? The rich man steals his own dividends.   ↑See U 81↓ [108]

I do not observe that many men can aid others in the direct way. Commonly every man occupies every inch of his ground. The poor, or the middle class can better help than the richer.[109]

        ↑Farmer's dollar heavy   U↓ [110]

        [94] I think the best argument of the Conservative is this bad one that he is convinced that the angry democrat who wishes him to divide his park & chateau with him will on entering into the possession instantly become conservative, & hold the property & spend it as selfishly as himself. For a better man, I might dare to renounce my estate; for a worse man, or for as bad a man as I, why should I? All the history of man, with unbroken sequence of examples, establishes this inference. Yet is it very low & degrading ground to stand upon.

---

[105] "The heart . . . are poor.", struck through in ink with a vertical use mark, is used in "Wealth," *W*, VI, 97.
        [106] The insertion is in pencil. For O. 41, see *JMN*, IX, 372.
        [107] See *JMN*, VIII, 264.
        [108] The insertion is in pencil. "The rich man . . . dividends." is struck through in ink with five vertical use marks. See *JMN*, VIII, 267, IX, 51 (U 81); p. [37] above.
        [109] For "I do . . . richer.", see *JMN*, VIII, 333.
        [110] The insertion is in pencil. Cf. *JMN*, IX, 41; p. [37] above.

We must never reason from history, but plant ourselves on the ideal.[111]

[95] Gold represents labor, & rightly opens all doors; but labor is higher, & opens secreter doors; opens man, & finds new place in the kingdom of intelligence. ↑See also CD 77↓ [112]

[96] The rich take up something more of the world into man's life. They include the country as well as the town, oceanside, Niagara, the far West, & the old European homesteads of man in their notion of available material. And there do well.[113]

[97] [blank]
[98] Producer & consumer. Luckily in the contingency of glutted markets every man who is a producer, is also able to throw himself on his reserved rights as a consumer. An iron bar is not only a bolt but also a conductor.[114]

[99] We do not easily conceive that the Greek mythology was believed at Athens so fast the key to such possibilities is lost[;] the key to the faith of men perishes with the faith. A thousand years hence it will be more conceivable that the acute Greeks beleived[n] the fables of Mercury & Pan, than that these learned & practical nations of modern Europe & America, these physicians, metaphysicians, mathematicians, critics, & merchants, believed this Jewish apologue of the poor Jewish boy & how they contrived to attach that accidental history to the religious idea, & this famous dogma of the Triune God, &c. Nothing more facile, so long as the detachment is not made. Nothing so wild & incredible the moment when that shall happen.[115]

When a considerable work has been produced, as the Shakspear-

---

[111] For this paragraph, see *JMN*, IX, 113.

[112] The insertion is in pencil. See *JMN*, VIII, 194.

[113] "The rich . . . well.", struck through in ink with two vertical use marks, is used in "Wealth," *W*, VI, 95. See *JMN*, IX, 233.

[114] For this paragraph, see *JMN*, IX, 151.

[115] For this paragraph, see *JMN*, VIII, 196. "We do not . . . possibilities is lost" is struck through in ink with a vertical use mark.

ian Drama, the Gothic Cathedral, the Egyptian Cyclopean architecture[,] [100] the ladder is drawn up & the methods are ⟨no longer⟩
lost. The history can only be understood by the idea that produced it.
& we cannot by any learning come into that. Shakspeare & the rest
are lost arts, & we must do something else, that undone something
which is now hinting & working here in & around us.[116]

[101]–[102] [blank]
[103] New Essay

Those who live for the future, must always seem selfish to those who
live for the present.[117]

Faith in ecstasy consists with total inexperience of it.[118]

Every man has his own courage, & is betrayed because he seeks in
himself the courage of other persons.[119]

"When we grow old," said Alcott, "the beauty steals inward." [120]

The ground of Hope is in the infinity of the world, which infinity
reappears in every particle. I know, against all appearances, that there
is a remedy to every wrong, & that every wall is a gate.[121]

[104]–[105] [122] [blank]
    [106] Ascension of State

   Lo how fast the great Critic instructs, discerns, separates the
dead from the living, the flesh from the spirit! See the living veins

---

[116] "When a . . . us." is struck through in pencil with a vertical use mark. See
JMN, VIII, 354–355.
[117] See *JMN*, VIII, 432, and "Character," *W*, III, 103.
[118] This sentence, struck through in ink with three vertical use marks, is used in
"Worship," *W*, VI, 213; see *JMN*, VIII, 218.
[119] See *JMN*, IX, 112; Journal AB, p. [103] above; "Courage," *W*, VII, 270.
[120] See *JMN*, IX, 180.
[121] For these two sentences, see *JMN*, IX, 137.
[122] Pasted to this page is an unidentified newspaper clipping, headed "*Martin
Luther*", concerning Luther's comments on marriage.

of strata run, detaching as bark & burr, what we thought was stock & pith. See laws to be no laws, & religions to become impieties, & great sciences mistakes, & ⟨m⟩great men perverters.[123]

[107] For 2d vol Essay

Truth is our only armor in all passages of life & death! ⟨O⟩Your companion will forget the words that you spoke, but the part which you took remains in his memory. I will speak the truth also in my secret heart or *think the truth* against what is called God.[124]

Liars also are true. Truth is the moral gravitation, & let a man begin where he will, & work in whatever false direction, he is sure to be found instantly afterwards arriving at a true result.[125]

Do not give up your thought because you cannot answer an objection to it. Consider only whether it remains in your life the same which it was[.][126]

[108] [blank]
[109] Form is the mixture of matter & spirit, it is the visibility of spirit.[127]

[110] [blank]
[111] Take the peaches from under the tree, & carry them out of sight of the tree, and their value is indefinitely enhanced. That is the main secret of commercial value to put the tree out of sight. Drop your penknife or pencil on the ground. What a costliness it wears in that unaccustomed place! Housekeepers say, that tea &

---

[123] For this paragraph, see *JMN*, VII, 323.

[124] "Truth is . . . God." is extracted from a journal entry of February 4, 1842, referring to the recent death of Emerson's son Waldo; see *JMN*, VIII, 199–200, and "Worship," *W*, VI, 230. "Truth is . . . his memory." is struck through in ink with a vertical use mark and in pencil with a curved diagonal use mark.

[125] For these two sentences, see *JMN*, IX, 213.

[126] "Do not . . . was", struck through in pencil with a curved vertical use mark and in ink with a vertical use mark, is used in "Worship," *W*, VI, 230; see *JMN*, IX, 282.

[127] See *JMN*, IX, 117.

toast always relish better away from home. "Another's wine is best," said Diogenes.[128]

[112]–[114] [blank]

[115] There are three wants which can never be satisfied; that of the traveller who says *Anywhere but here*; that of the rich, who wants *something more*, and that of the sick, who wants *something different*.[129]

[116] [blank]
[117] Woman

Our greatest debt to woman is of a musical character, & not describable.

It is the worst of her condition that its advantages are permissive. Society lives on the system of money & woman comes at money & money's worth through compliment. I should not dare to be woman. Plainly they are created for that better system which supersedes money. But today, ————————. On our civilization her position is often pathetic. What is she not expected to do & suffer for some invitation to strawberries & cream. Mercifully their eyes are holden that they cannot see.[130]

[118] [blank]
[119] A highly endowed man with good intellect & good conscience is a Man-Woman, & does not so much need the complement of Woman to his being as another. Hence his relations to the sex are somewhat dislocated & unsatisfactory. He asks in woman sometimes the Woman, sometimes the Man.[131]

---

[128] For " 'Another's . . . Diogenes.", see *JMN*, V, 254; for "Take . . . Diogenes.", see *JMN*, IX, 309–310; for "Take . . . enhanced.", see *JMN*, IX, 375. "Take . . . sight.", struck through in ink with a vertical use mark, is used in "Wealth," *W*, VI, 87.

[129] See *JMN*, VIII, 142. This sentence, struck through in ink with three vertical use marks, is used in "Considerations by the Way," *W*, VI, 266.

[130] Cf. Luke 24:16. For "Our greatest . . . see.", see *JMN*, IX, 108.

[131] For this paragraph, see *JMN*, VIII, 175.

[120]–[122] [blank]
[123] Eloquence

Mr Webster loses nothing by comparison with brilliant men in the legal profession: he is as much before them as before the ordinary lawyer. At least I thought he appeared among these best lawyers of the Suffolk bar, like a schoolmaster among his boys. His wonderful organization, the perfection of his elocution, & all that ↑thereto↓ belongs [—] voice, accent, intonation, attitude, manner [—] are such as one cannot hope to meet again in a century.

Then he is so thoroughly simple & wise in his rhetoric. Understanding language & the use of the positive degree, all his words tell, & his rhetoric is perfect [—] so homely, so fit, so strong. Then he manages his matter, hugs his fact so close & will not let it go, & never indulges in a weak flourish though he knows perfectly well how to make such exordiums & episodes & perorations as may give perspective to his harangue without in the least embarrassing his plan, or confounding [124] his transitions. What is small, he shows as small & makes the great great. In speech he sometimes roars & then every word is like the blow of an axe. His force of personal attack is terrible[;] he lays out his strength so directly in honest strokes & all his powers of voice, arm, eye, & whole man are heartily united & bestowed on the adversary that he cannot fail to be felt. His splendid wrath when his eyes become lamps, is good to see, so intellectual it is, & the wrath of the fact & cause he espouses, & not at all personal to himself.

His Christian religion is always weak[,] being merely popular & so most of his religion. ↑When↓ he [n] spoke of the value of character it was simply mercantile; it was to defend a man in criminal prosecutions & the like & bear him up against the inspection of all *but* the Almighty and in describing his client Wyman's character [125] he said he wanted that sternness of Christian principle which teaches to "avoid even the appearance of evil!"[132] And one feels every moment that he goes for the actual world, & never a moment for the ideal.

[132] William Wyman, president of the Phoenix Bank of Charlestown, had been charged with embezzlement; his first trial in Concord began in August of 1843, with Webster as one of the defense attorneys. Here Emerson has assembled comments he had written at the time on Webster's performance.

He is the triumph of the Understanding & is undermined & supplanted by the Reason for which yet he is so good a witness being every moment fed therefrom & his whole nature & faculty presupposing that, that I felt as if the children of Reason might gladly see his success as a homage to their law & regard him as a poor rude soldier hired for six pence a day to fight their battles. I looked at him with the same feeling with which I see one of those strong paddies toiling on the railroad.[133]

[126] Webster's power like that of all great masters is not in some excellent details but is total. He has a great & everywhere equal propriety. He has the propriety, the power of countenance, & the gravity of a Sachem. But he is so much a piece of Nature & to be admired like an oak or an elephant that I have set his Concord visit in the same line of events with the Herr Dreisbach & his caravan which came hither the foregoing week. Then was shown the power of cats. The tiger & the leopard whose body is like a wave in its perpetual flexility[.]

I cannot consent to compare him with his pretended competitors. But when the Clay men & Van Buren men & Calhoun men have had all their way & all their political objections have been conceded & they have perched their little man whichever it be on the top of the martinbox of state, then & not before, will we begin to state the claims of this world's man, this strong ⟨paddy⟩ ↑athlete↓ of the times, & laws, & state, to his place in history.[134]

[127] Garrison is a virile speaker; he lacks the feminine element which we find in men of genius. He has great body to his discourse, so that he can well afford occasional flourishes & eloquence[.]

He is a man in his place: he brings his whole history with him

---

[133] For the comments on pp. [123]–[125], see *JMN*, VIII, 357–358 ("Mr Webster loses . . . to be felt."), 359 ("His splendid . . . to himself."), 358 ("His Christian . . . railroad."). "His wonderful . . . transitions." (p. [123]) is used in "The Fugitive Slave Law," *W*, XI, 221–222.

[134] For these two paragraphs, see *JMN*, VIII, 362–363. "Webster's power . . . propriety." is used in "The Fugitive Slave Law," *W*, XI, 222.

wherever he goes: there is no falsehood or patchwork, but sincerity and unity[.] [135]

Lord Coventry, says Clarendon, had in the plain way of speaking & delivery without much ornament of elocution a strange way of making himself believed, the only justifiable design of eloquence.[136]

[128] [remainder blank]
[129]   ↑Printed in "Eloquence."↓
I was in the courthouse a little while to see the sad game. But as often happens the judge & jury[,] the government & the counsel for the prisoner were on trial as much as he. The prisoner's counsel were the strongest & cunningest lawyers in the commonwealth, they drove the attorney for the state from corner to corner taking his reasons from under him, & reducing him to silence, but not to submission. When hard pushed, he revenged himself in his turn on the Judge, by requiring the Court to define what a Trust was. The Court thus hard-pushed, tried words, & said every thing it could think of to fill the time; supposed cases & described duties of cashiers, presidents, & miscellaneous officers that are or might be; but all this flood not serving the cuttle fish to get away in, the horrible shark of district attorney being still there grimly awaiting [130] with his "The Court must define", the poor Court pleaded its inferiority; the superior Court must establish the law for this; — and it read away piteously the decisions of the Supreme Court, but to those who had no pity. The Judge was forced at last to rule something, & the lawyers saved their rogue under the fog of a definition. The parts were so well cast & discriminated that it was an interesting game to watch.
The Government was well enough represented. It was stupid, but it had a strong will & possession, & stood on that to the last. The Judge

[135] See *JMN*, IX, 267. The top half of the manuscript leaf (pp. [127]–[128]) has been cut away. "Garrison . . . unity" is from Edward Emerson's transcription, in ink, of the original passage, as his note explains: "[The upper half of page 127 in JK, of which this is a copy, was presented by me at Christmas, 1911, to Francis J. Garrison[.] E. W. Emerson". The leaf bearing his note and inscription is pasted to the remaining segment of p. [127], preceding "Lord Coventry . . . eloquence."
[136] Edward Hyde, 1st Earl of Clarendon, *The History of the Rebellion and Civil Wars in England* . . . , 6 vols. (Boston, 1827), I, 108. See *JMN*, VI, 134.

was no man, & had no counsel in his breast; yet his position remained real, & he was there merely as a child might ⟨be⟩have been to represent a great Reality, the justice of states which we could well enough see there beetling over his head, & which his trifling talking no wise affected [131] & did not impede, since he was innocent & well meaning. There are judges on all platforms, & this of child-judge, where the position is all, is something.

Three or four stubborn necessary words are the pith & fate of the business; all the rest is expatiating & qualifying. Three or four real choices, acts of will of somebody, the rest is circumstance, satellite & flourish.[137]

There was Webster, the great cannon, loaded to the lips. He told Cheney, that if he should close by addressing the jury, he should blow the roof off. As it was, he did nothing but pound. Choate put in the nail & drove it; Webster came after & pounded. The natural grandeur of his face & manners always satisfies; easily great, there is no strut in his voice or behaviour as in the others. Yet he is all wasted. He seems like a great actor who [132] is not supported on the boards and Webster, like the actor, ought to go to London. Ah if God had given to this Democrat a heart to lead New England, what a life & death & glory for him. Now he is a fine mantel-ornament, costly enough to those who must keep it; for the great head aches, & the great trunk must be curiously fed & comforted.

↑↑G[eorge].B[radford]. said,↓ The Judge looked like a schoolmaster puzzled by a hard sum who reads the context with emphasis↓[.] [138]

[133] Webster
1844 17 August at Bunker Hill [139]

---

[137] "I was in [p. [129]] . . . flourish.", struck through in ink with intersecting diagonal marks on p. [129] and vertical use marks on pp. [130] and [131], is used in "Eloquence," *W*, VII, 86–88. See *JMN*, IX, 249–250.

[138] For "There was Webster . . . emphasis", see *JMN*, IX, 250–251.

[139] For the material which follows on pp. [133]–[134] ("A prodigious . . . landscape." and "On the top . . . white tiers."), see *JMN*, VIII, 425–426, where Emerson dates his successive entries "18 June" and "22 June" 1843, not "1844 17

A prodigious concourse of people, but a village green could not be more peaceful, orderly, sober, & even affectionate. The ground within the ⟨M⟩Square at the Monument was arranged to hold 80 000 persons. Boston & Charlestown were ⟨all⟩ ↑filled up with↓ one vast throng, but friendly & intelligent as cousins.

Webster gave us his plain statement like good bread: yet the oration was feeble compared with his other efforts, & even seemed Polonius--like with its indigent conservatisms. When there is no antagonism as in these holiday speeches & no religion[,] things sound not heroically. 'Tis a poor oration ⁿ that finds ↑G.↓ Washington for its highest mark. The audience give one much to observe, — they are so lightheaded & light timbered, every man thinking more of his inconveniences than of the objects of the occasion, & the hurrahs are so slight & easily procured.

Webster is very good America himself[.]

[134] It was evident that there was the monument, & here was Webster, & he knew well that a little more or less of rhetoric signified nothing; he was only to say plain & equal things, grand things, if he had them, & if he had them not, only to abstain from saying unfit things, & the whole occasion was answered by his presence. It was a place for behavior much more than speech, & Mr Webster behaved well, or walked through his part with entire success. He was there as the representative of the American Continent; there in his Adamitic capacity; & that is the basis of the satisfaction the people have in hearing him, that he alone of all men does not disappoint the eye & ear, but is a fit figure in the landscape.

↑On the top of a house I saw a company protecting themselves from the sun by an old map of the U. States. A charitable lumber-merchant near the Bridge, had chalked over his counting room door, "500 seats for ladies: free." And there the five hundred sat in white tiers.↓

[135] Webster

August". "It was evident . . . landscape." is used in "The Fugitive Slave Law," *W*, XI, 221.

"A man like me," said ⟨Talley⟩Mirabeau, "might accept a hundred thousand crowns, but I am not to be bought for that sum."[140]

[136] [blank]
[137] Webster
⟨W⟩⟨Lord⟩Lord Brougham, it is said, called Webster "a steamengine in breeches."[141]
When he comes into the house astronomy & geology are suggested, the force of atoms; here is the working nature; a spark also he has of the benignant fire, & that enables him to make an economy of his coals for the laboratory & for the altar, which had been otherwise only a kitchen fire.[142]

It seems the quixotism of criticism to quarrel with him, because he has not this or that fine evangelical property. He is no saint, but the wild olive wood, ungrafted⟨,⟩ yet by grace; but, according to his lights, a very true & admirable man. His expensiveness seems to be necessary to him. Were he too prudent a Yankee, it would be a sad deduction from his magnificence. I only wish he would not truckle. I do not care how much he spends. His force is a part of nature, & the world, like any [138] given amount of azote or electricity[.]

He works with that closeness of adhesion to the matter in hand, which a joiner or a blacksmith uses. & the same quiet but sure feeling of right to his place, that the oak or the rock have to theirs. Other men are dilettanti but he is a piece of the world[.]

After all his talents have been described there remains that perfect propriety which belongs to every world genius which animates all the details of action & speech with the character of the whole so that his beauties of detail are endless. Great is life.[143]

[140] See *JMN*, IX, 138, quoting Etienne Dumont, *Recollections of Mirabeau, and of the Two First Legislative Assemblies of France*; see the London, 1832 edition, p. 231.
[141] Cf. *JMN*, IX, 29: "A newspaper lately called Daniel Webster 'a steam engine in breeches'. . . ."
[142] For "When he . . . fire.", see *JMN*, IX, 389.
[143] For "It seems . . . life.", see *JMN*, VIII, 361–362.

⟨great⟩ ↑His↓ natural ascendency of aspect & carriage —

E.H. said she talked with him as one likes to go behind Niagara Falls; so she tried to look into these famed caverns of eyes & guage their depth. In his case modesty ceased to be a virtue. Glad of one man who carried himself erect & grand, it was sufficient for the rest of mortals to duck & be ashamed of themselves.[144]

[139] This natural Emperor has also the kingly talent of remembering persons & knowing to whom he has been introduced in the million. Knows all his sheep's faces. Every day he adjourned the court by taking up his hat & looking ⟨steadily⟩ ↑coolly↓ at the judge who then bade the crier adjourn court.[145]

———

Webster. See O 51, 102,
     R 26 [146]

[140]   ⟨Concord, 22 October, 1846.

Rev. Danl. Austin, Chairman.
          Dear Sir,
                    ⟨My dear⟩ You shall, if you please leave my name out, this season, from your list of lecturers, & oblige your obedient servant.
                    R. W. Emerson⟩ [147]

[141] ↑Eloquence: E T. Taylor:↓

It was a pleasure yesterday to hear Father Taylor preach in our country church. Men are always interested in a man, & the whole various extremes of our little village society were for once brought together. Black & white, grocer, contractor, lumberman, methodist, & preacher, joined with the regular congregation in rare union.*

*Nobody but Webster assembles the same extremes[.]

---

[144] For Elizabeth Hoar's comments, see *JMN*, VIII, 361.

[145] For this sentence, see *JMN*, VIII, 359.

[146] *JMN*, IX, 374, 389, VIII, 362ff.

[147] This letter is not printed in *L*. The canceled draft, struck through in ink with a diagonal line, appears upside down on p. [140] as it now stands in the manuscript; pp. [137]–[140] comprise a single sheet, once folded.

The speaker instantly shows the reason in the breadth of his truly social nature. He is mighty nature's child, another Robert Burns trusting heartily to her power, as he has never been deceived by it, & arriving unexpectedly every moment at new & happiest deliverances. How joyfully & manly he spreads himself abroad! It is a ⟨P⟩true Punch & Judy affair, his preaching. The preaching quite accidental, & ludicrously copied & caricatured from the old style, as he found it in some Connecticutt tubs; as well as he can, he mimics & exaggerates the parade of method & logic of text & argument but after much threatening to exterminate [142] all gainsayers by his syllogisms, he seldom remembers any of the divisions of his plan after the first; & the slips & gulfs of his logic would involve him in irreparable ridicule, if it were not for the inexhaustible wit by which he dazzles & conciliates & carries ⟨away⟩ captive the dullest & the keenest ⟨hunter⟩ ↑hearer↓[.] [148]

He is perfectly ⟨fr⟩sure in his generous humanity. He rolls the world into a ball & tosses it from hand to hand.[149] He says touching things, plain things, cogent things, grand things, which all men must perforce hear. He says them with hand & head & body & voice: the accompaniment is total & ever varied. "I am half a hundred years old, & I ↑have↓ never seen an unfortunate day. — There are none." — "I have been in all the four quarters of the world, & I never saw any men I could not love." "We have sweet conferences & prayer meetings: we meet every day. There are not days enough in the year for us."

[143] Everything is accidental to him[:] his place, his education, his church, his seamen, his whole system of religion a mere confused rigmarole of refuse & leavings of former generations. All has a grinning absurdity, *except* the sentiment of the man. He is incapable of thought; he cannot analyze or discriminate; he is a singing dancing drunkard of his wit. Only he is sure of his sentiment. That is his

[148] The cancellation and insertion are in pencil.

[149] This sentence is struck through in ink with two diagonal use marks. Cf. "Eloquence," *W*, VII, 90: "Put the argument into a concrete shape, into an image, — some hard phrase, round and solid as a ball, which they can see and handle and carry home with them, — and the cause is half won."

mother's milk that he feels in his bones, ↑that↓ heaves in his lungs, throbs in his heart, walks in his feet. & gladly he yields ⟨himself⟩ to the sweet magnetism & sheds it abroad on the people ⟨rejoicing in his power⟩." Hence he is an example, I at this moment say, the single example /(we have)/I can ⟨now⟩ think of/ of an inspiration; for a wisdom not his own, not to be appropriated by him, which he cannot recall or even apply, [144] sails to him on the gale of this sympathetic communication with his auditory. There is his closet, his college, his confessional. He discloses secrets there, & receives informations there, which his conversation with thousands of men (& he knows every body↑)↓ ⟨in the world almost)⟩ & his voyages to Egypt & journeys in Germany & in Syria never taught him. Indeed I think all his talk with men & all his much visiting & planning for the practical, in his Mariner's House, &c &c is all fantastic, all stuff. I think his guardians & overseers & treasurers will find it so. Not the smallest dependence is to be put on his statement of facts. Arithmetic is only one of the nimble troop of dancers he keeps. No, this free happy expression of himself & of the deeps of human nature, of the happier sunny facts of life, of things connected & lying amassed & grouped in healthy nature, — that is his power [145] [150] & his teacher. ⟨He is so confident that⟩ ⟨this⟩His security breathes in ⟨all⟩ his manners & gestures, in his tones & the expressions of his face, & he lies ↑all↓ open to men, a man, & disarms criticism & malignity by perfect frankness. We open our arms too & with half closed eyes enjoy this rare sunshine. A wondrous beauty swims ⟨all the time⟩ over the picture gallery, & touches points with an ineffable lustre[.]
[Obviously he is of the class of superior men, & every one associates him necessarily with Webster, & if Fox & Burke were alive, with Fox & Burke.]

What affluence! There never was such activity of fancy. How wilful & despotic is his rhetoric. "*No, not the blaze of Diogenes' lamp* added to the noonday sun would suffice to find it," he said. Every thing dances & disappears, changes, becomes its contrary in his sculpturing [146] hands. How he played with the word *Lost* yesterday! the parent

[150] "Eloquence & Taylor" is written in ink as an index heading at the top of this page.

who had lost his child. *Lost* became *found* in the twinkling of an eye. So will it always be.

His whole work is a sort of day's sailing out upon the sea not to any voyage but to take an observation of the sun, & come back again. Again & again & again we have the whole wide horizon [—] how rare & great a pleasure! That is the Iliad, that is picture, that is art, that is music. His whole genius is in minstrelsy. He calls it religion, methodism, Christianity, & other names; it is minstrelsy, he is a minstrel, all the rest is costume.

For himself it is easy to see that tho' apparently of a moderate temperament he would like the old cocks of the bar-room a thousand times better than their temperate monitors[.] [151]

[147] What an eloquence he suggests. Ah could he guide those grand seahorses of his, with which he rides & caracoles on the waves of the sunny ocean. But no; he sits & is drawn up & down the ocean currents by the strong sea-monsters; — only on that condition that he shall not guide. ⟨*How many*⟩ One[n] orator makes many. How many orators sit mute there below. They come to get ⟨str⟩justice done to that ear & intuition which no Chatham & no Demosthenes has begun to satisfy.[152]

He is valuable as a psychologic curiosity: a man with no proprium or peculium, but all social. Leave him alone & there is no man: There is no substance, but a relation.[153] His power is a certain mania or low inspiration that repeats for us the tripod & possession of the ancients. I think every hearer feels that something like it were possible to himself, if he could consent. [148] He has sold his mind for his soul (soul in the ⟨low⟩ semianimal sense, soul including animal spirits).[n] Art could not compass this fluency & felicity. His sovereign security results from a certain renunciation & abandonment. He runs

---

[151] For the entries on Edward T. Taylor on pp. [141]–[146], see *JMN*, IX, 233–235.

[152] For "What an . . . satisfy.", see *JMN*, IX, 236–237. "*How many*" is canceled in pencil. "⟨*How many*⟩ . . . satisfy.", struck through in ink with a vertical use mark, is used in "Eloquence," *W*, VII, 63.

[153] The period is added in pencil.

for luck, & by readiness to say every thing, good & bad, ↑now & then↓ [154] says the best things. Then a new will & understanding organize themselves in this new sphere of no-will & no-understanding; &, as fishermen use a certain discretion within their luck; to find a good fishing ground, or the berry women to gather quantities of whortle berries, so he knows his topics & his unwritten briefs, & where the profusion of words & images will likeliest recur. With all his volleys of epithets & imagery, he will ever & anon hit the white. He called God in a profusion of other things "a charming spirit." He spoke of "men who sin with ingenuity, sin with genius, sin with all the power they can draw." But you feel this inspiration, it clothes him like an atmosphere, & he marches into the untried depths with the security of a grenadier.

[149] ↑E T. Taylor & Eloquence↓
H⟨is⟩e will weep, & grieve, & pray, & chide, in a tempest of passionate speech, & never break the perfect propriety with a single false note, & when all is done, you still ask, or I do, "What's Hecuba to him?" [155]

↑This country has been saved from the curse of good land. Where you find good land you have rank grass, bad cattle, & weak men. Where there is bad land ↑& plenty of grasshoppers↓ you have calm wellguaged industry, good buildings, great crops, strong men.↓ [156]

[150] Wonder
————

I went to the circus, & saw a man ride standing on the back of two galloping horses, a third being interposed between the two. As he rode, the sinews of his limbs played like those of his beasts. One horse brought a basket in his teeth, picked up a cap, & selected a card out of four. All wonder comes of showing an effect at two or three removes from the cause. Show us the two or three steps by which

---

[154] The insertion is in pencil.
[155] The quotation marks are in pencil. Cf. *Hamlet*, II, ii, 559. For "He is valuable" [p. [147]] . . . to him?' ", see *JMN*, IX, 259.
[156] "This country . . . men." is struck through in ink with a curved diagonal use mark.

the horse was brought to fetch the basket, & the wonder would cease.[157]

[151]–[152] [158] [blank]

[153] [159] The St Michael's pear of the present day is a vast forest scattered throughout the gardens of N. America & England yet subject in all the quarters of its dispersion to the diseases incident to the parent stock, &, like a disease, or an animal race, or any one natural state, it wears out, & will have an end. Each race of man resembles an apple or a pear[:] the Nubian, the Negro, the Tartar, the Greek, he vegetates, thrives & multiplies, usurps all the soil & nutriment, & so kills the weaker races & receives all the benefit of culture under many zones & experiments, but his doom was in nature as well as his thrift, & overtakes him at last with the certainty of gravitation.[160]

[154] [blank]
[inside back cover] [161] [Index material omitted] [162]

---

[157] For this paragraph, see *JMN*, VII, 358.

[158] Pasted to p. [152] is a clipping of two paragraphs from an unidentified German-language newspaper, headed "Londoner Bücherauktionen." In the margin Emerson has written in pencil "£2260." — a rendering in figures of a phrase in the text.

[159] Pasted to the left margin of this page so that both recto and verso can be read is a clipping of 38 paragraphs in French from an unidentified newspaper, captioned "FEUILLETON DE LA DEMOCRATIE PACIFIQUE. / HORTICULTURE." and signed "A. YSABEAU."

[160] For this paragraph, see *JMN*, VII, 90.

[161] Laid in between p. [154] and the inside back cover is a printing of "A Collusion between a Aleygaiter and a Water-Snaik" by G. H. Derby ("John Phoenix"), a bit of comic verse much enjoyed by Emerson: see *JMN*, VII, 262, n. 740. For a physical description of the leaf bearing the poem, see the bibliographical headnote to Notebook JK.

[162] The index, headed "CONTENTS.", is written in ink; there is no preliminary draft in pencil.

Pocket Diary I

1820–1847

Entries in this pocket diary belonging to earlier years (1826, 1829, 1830, 1831) are printed in *JMN*, III, 338–348; two entries from 1847, on pages [1] and [7], are reproduced here. For a bibliographical description of the notebook, see *JMN*, III, 338.

[1] [...]¹

1847, Dec 20	£
	35
	30
	10
	═══
	75
	15
	17

[2]–[6] [...]
[7] [...]²

---

[7] 1847 Oct
    pd Gilbert in full
    pd E. Codman in full
    pd C. G. Ripley Esq in full   5.00
    pd my passage to Liverpool   80.
    pd Colombe in full

¹ See *JMN*, III, 339, n. 4. The entry for December 20, 1847, is in pencil over erased pencil writing, following an entry for July 2, 1831, in ink.
² The line across the page, in pencil, follows an earlier entry of c. 1829–1831; see *JMN*, III, 342. The entry for October 1847 is in pencil.

Bought 5 sovereigns   24.20
pd H D Thoreau in full   16.
5 Cash to Mrs R E on a/c   20.00 [3]

[3] "Gilbert" and "E. Codman" have not been identified; Emerson had paid an earlier debt to "Gilbert & Sons" in 1843 and was acquainted with John Gilbert, a West India merchant, and Timothy Gilbert, a manufacturer of pianos, both of Boston (*L*, III, 141; IV, 176, 216). For another memorandum concerning Christopher Gore Ripley, see Journal GH, front cover verso above. The payment for Emerson's passage to Liverpool is also recorded in *JMN*, VIII, 575. Both Anthony Colombe and Henry Thoreau helped with the maintenance of Emerson's property before and during his absence in Europe.

England and Paris

1847–1848

This notebook, according to Emerson's own notation on page [2], was bought for six pence in Liverpool on October 30, 1847. To it he transferred earlier records, perhaps beginning with a notation of funds received in Boston on September 3 and 16, 1847, for his English friend Charles Lane (page [71]) and continuing (starting on page [1]) with his own expenses since reaching Liverpool. Most of the entries consist of records of expenses (pages [1]–[27]); miscellaneous memoranda, some of which were subsequently transferred to or expanded in Journal London, Journal LM, or Notebook ED (pages [30]–[69], page [71]); a schedule of lecture engagements in England and Scotland (pages [72]–[77]); and lists of names and addresses of British acquaintances (page [70], pages [78]–[inside back cover]). The latest dated entry, on page [49_2], was made at Amesbury on July 7, 1848, during Emerson's expedition to Stonehenge with Thomas Carlyle.

Notebook England and Paris is written in a pocket notebook with stiff paper covers marbled in red, blue, and buff, 10 x 16.2 cm. The front cover bears an octagonal paper label inscribed in ink: "Note Book / England / Paris / 1847-8"; the back cover is blank. Twenty leaves of white paper have been folded and sewn to make 80 ruled pages, unnumbered, for which pagination has been supplied here. Emerson's records of expenses are entered in ink, as are most of the lecture engagements and the names and addresses listed at the back; some of the names and most of the other notes and memoranda are in pencil. Inscription on the front cover verso is upside down with reference to the pages immediately following; inscription on pages 46_2–53_2 is upside down with reference to the pages immediately preceding, being written from back to front beginning on page 53_2. Fifteen pages are blank (28–29, 32–39, 54–55, 66–68).

[front cover]   Note Book
                                 England

                                 ———

                                  Paris

                                 ———

                                 1847–8

[front cover verso] [1] 20 shillings Rothing
                    30 shillings
                            Rockinghorse

⟨Width⟩Length of step 1 ft 5
width   7½ inch

[1] 1847
Liverpool   £   s.   d.[2]
Oct   22 Steward   1   "   0   "   0
         23 Duties on 20 lb. books at the
            Custom House inclusive of   "   11   "
            books of James Brown charged
            " 4 s " 9d
            Carman for Carrying luggage
            to Waterloo Hotel   " ⟨18⟩ "   9
            12 Stamps for postage   "   1   "
         25 hat   1   "   0   "   0
            bill at Waterloo H.   1   "   6   "
            cab to RailRoad   "   1   "
            porter   "   "   6
            ticket to Manchester   0   "   6   "   0
      ↑Manchester↓
            Cab to Office   0   "   1   "
            Cab to Railway   "   1   "   6

───

[1] This page is in pencil, written upside down in relation to the writing on
p. [1] below. "30 . . . Rockinghorse" is set off with a wavy curved line at the
left. Between "Rockinghorse" and "Length" is a pencil sketch of a set of four steps.
    [2] In the entries which follow, each figure is usually accompanied by a ditto mark
to indicate either pounds or shillings (e.g., 1 " 3 "). In the present text these marks
have been silently normalized if made imperfectly, though they have not been supplied if lacking.

		£		s		d
	Ticket to London	1	"	10	"	
	↑⟨London⟩Birmingham↓					
	Dinner		"	2	"	6
	"Bradshaw's Guide" [3]		"		"	9

[2] 1847 London

		£		s		d
Oct	25 Cab from Euston Square to Chelsea	0	"	4	"	6
	26 Visiting cards	0	"	1	"	0
	27 pd Charles Lane	92	"	17	"	9
	29 Chambermaid at Chelsea	0	"	6	"	0
	Ticket to Liverpool	2	"	5	"	0
	Cab to Railway	0	"	4	"	
	At Birmingham, tea	0	"	1	"	6
↑Liverpool↓	Cab.	0	"	1	"	0
	30. Pears	0	"	0	"	7
	envelopes & paper			1	"	7
	This Acc. Book	0	"	0	"	6
	24 postage stamps	0	"	2	"	0
	To Capt. E Caldwell by the hands of Mrs Blodgett	4	"	0	"	0
	Sundries		"		"	6
	Umbrella	0	"	16	"	0
	cap	0	"	4	"	0
Nov	2 Expense at Waterloo Hotel	2	"	1	"	6

[3] 1847 Liverpool

		£	s	d
Nov	2 Chop	0	0	10
	Cab		1	
	ticket to Manchester		6	
	cab to Mrs Massey's] [4]		1	6

[3] *Bradshaw's Monthly Railway and Steam Navigation Guide, for Great Britain and Ireland.*

[4] Emerson lodged with Mrs. Massey in Fenny Street while in Manchester; see *L*, III, 437, for his account of the landlady's services. In Liverpool he lodged with Mrs. Hill (pp. [5], [8] below).

	pears						6
	beggars						3
"	3. pantaloons	I	"	15	"	0 [5]
	ticket to Liverpool		"	6		
	cab		"	I	"	
	4 Expense at Waterloo	0	"	8	"	6
	porter					6
	ticket to Man[cheste]r		"	5	"	6
	refreshments	0	"	I	"	0
↑Manchester↓						
	Cab to Fenny Place			I	"	6
	5 paseterie	0	"	I	"	5
	wafers	0		0		I
	pears	0	"	0	"	4
	6 cab to cars			I		
	ticket to Liverpool			6		

[4] [Received

1847 Liverpool

Oct	24 Received of Captain E. Cald-					
	well a loan of	4	"	0	"	0
↑London↓						
	27 Recd of Baring & Brothers &					
	Co[6] on a/c	102	"	17	"	9
Nov	3 Liverpool					
	Recd of Baring & Brothers; on					
	a/c	10	"	0	"	0
	17 Recd of Baring & Brothers on					
	a/c	10	"	0	"	0
	20 Recd of T. Hogg for Liver-					
	pool M[echanics]. I[nstitute].	32	"	0	"	0

[5] The entries on p. [3] to this point were first written in pencil, then rewritten in ink except for the two zeros after "Chop".

[6] The banking house of London. Its sole American agency, in Boston, was in charge first of Thomas W. Ward and then of his sons, Emerson's particular friend Samuel G. Ward and his brother T. C. Ward. Among Emerson's acquaintances in London, Joshua Bates, American born, was for a time the acting head of the firm, and Alexander Baring, Lord Ashburton, was a member of the family.

24	Recd of Mr Penny for Man-ch[ester] Athenaeum	44	"	2	"	0
29	Recd of Manchester Mechan-ics' Institution	29	"	8	"	
30	Of Roscoe Club	5	"	5	"	0
Dec 9	Of Derby Soc[iet]y.	14	"	14		
	Nottingham	28				
	Preston	10	"	0	"	0
	Huddersfield	6	"	0	"	0
21	Leicester.	14				
	Chesterfield,	5		5		
	Birmingham	15	"			
	Worcester	10				

[5] Paid
1847
Nov. 6, ↑Liverpool↓ To steward for

	porterage	0	"	1	"	0
	Dinner	0	"	2	"	6
	Show	0	"	0	"	1
	Newspaper					5
	inkstand		"	1	"	8
	ink				"	6
	paper ↑8d↓ & envelopes ↑4d↓	0	"	1	"	0
7	⟨sh⟩ticket to Manchester	0	"	6	"	1
	↑Manchester↓					
	cab		"	1	"	
8	brogans	0	"	10	"	0
	cab		"	1	"	0
	map of Manch[este]r					6
	map of Liverp.					6
9	cab to Greenheys	0	"	3	"	0
10	cab to railroad			1		
	ticket to Liverpool	0	"	6	"	
	cab to Mrs Hill's		"	1		
	tweed pants	1	"	10	"	0
	handkerchief	0	"	8	"	6

[6] Paid
1847 ⟨Man⟩Liverpool

Nov	10	stiffener	0	"	0	"	6
		dinner	0	"	2	"	3
		beggar					·3
	11	ticket to Manchester	0	"	6	"	0
		↑Manchester↓					
		Cab	0	"	1	"	
		tolls—	0		1		0
		Mrs Massey's bill	0	"	16	"	3½
		washing	0	"	2	"	0½
		cab	0	"	1	"	
	12	cab	0	"	1		6
	13	cab	0	"	1	"	
		ticket to Liverpool	0	"	6	"	0
		cab to Stafferd st		"	1		
	⟨14⟩	⟨ti⟩dinner	0	"	2	"	2
	14	⟨cab⟩ticket to Man[cheste]r	0	"	6	"	0
		cab	0	"	1	"	0
	16	cab			1		
	17	cab	0	"	1	"	0

[7] Paid
1847

Nov	17	Ticket to Liverpool	0	"	6	"	0
		cab	0	"	1	"	0
		Stamps postage	0	"	2	"	0
	1⟨8⟩7	⟨ticket⟩ dinner	0	"	2	"	6
	18	ticket to ⟨L⟩Manchester			6		
		cab			1		
		blk. hkf 1/2	0	"	4	"	10½
		kid gloves	0	"	2	"	9.
		socks	0	"	1	"	4
		Shoes	0	"	9	"	6
	⟨20⟩	cab			2	"	6
	20	cab	0	"	1	"	0
		ticket to Liverpool			6		

	dinner					3		
17	Mrs Massey's bill	0	"	19	"	0
22	ticket to Manch[este]r			6		
23	paper	0	"	1	"	6
24	Mrs Massey's bill for lodgings					
	3 weeks at 1 " 4,	3	"	12	"	0
	for sundries			6		3
25	To Baring & Brothers for					
	A[bel] Adams	70	"	0	"	0

[8] 1847 Paid

Nov	25	Cab	0	"	1	"	0
		Ticket to Liverpool	0	"	6	"	0
		Valise	0	"	18	"	0
		cab	0	"	1	"	0
	26	Cab	0	"	1	"	0.
		ticket to Manch[este]r	0	"	6	"	0
		cab	0	"	1	"	3
		To Mrs Hill for lodging tea					
		& washing	2	"	10	"	0
	27	hose			1	"	4
	28	cab	0	"	1	"	0
	29	postage stamps	0	"	1	"	0
	30	cab	0	"	1	"	0
		ticket to Liverpool	0	"	6	"	0
		cab	0	"	1	"	0
Dec	1	Waterloo Hotel	0	"	9.	"	0
		cab & ticket to Manch[este]r	0	"	7	"	0
		cab	0	"	1	"	0
		black silk hose			3	"	6
		paper		"	6	"	
		cab twice			2		
		porter			1		
		ticket to Preston & porter	0	"	6	"	6

[9] 1847 Paid

Dec	⟨3⟩2	Inn at Preston	0	"	6	"	0

		£		s		d
	ticket to Manch[este]r			6		
	cab	0	"	1	"	6
	Mrs Massey's a/c			10		6
	↑1 doz↓ ale	0	"	4	"	0
3	ticket to Rochdale			3		
5	cab	0	"	5	"	0
6	cab			2		
	fare to Nottingham	1	"	1	"	6
	soup		"	1	"	
7	To Derby fare	0	"	3	"	0
	cab			1		
⟨9⟩8	fare to Nottingham	0	"	3		
9	fare to Derby & cab	0		4		
10	fare to Nottingham	0	"	3		
11	cab	0	"	3		
12	fees at Wollaton Hall	0		3		0
13	paper &c			3		
	Evangel of Love [by Henry Sutton]	0	"	3	"	6
	fees			5		
	fees at Newstead			4		
	washing			1		2
	cab	0	"	3	"	0
	fees			1		
14	cab			1		
	Fare to Manchester	1	"	1	"	6
	⟨cost⟩ Sundries			1		

[10] 1847 Paid

↑Dec↓	14 A Ireland, Esq. for various expenses	1	"	8	"	0
	15 Mrs Massie board, lodging, & washing 3 weeks	3	"	17	"	0
	ticket to Preston & cab	0	"	8	"	0
	16 lodgings			2	"	6
	ticket & cab to Manch	0	"	7	"	6
	cab	0		2		0

	ticket to Birmingham	0	"	16	"	0
	cab	0	"	1	"	6
	fees			1	"	6
17	ticket to Manchr			15	"	
	cab			3		
	sundries			2		
17	ticket to Huddersfield	0	"	7	"	0
	cab	0	"	3	"	4
19	ticket to Manchr	0	"	7	"	0.
	cab	0	"	1	"	6.
20	cab ⟨to⟩			2	"	6
	ticket to Leicester	1	"	⟨2⟩		
	dinner	0	"	2	"	0
	cab	0	"	2	"	10
21	fees	0		5		
	cab	0		3		
22	cab & ticket to Derby	0		7		
	ticket to Chesterfield	0		7		
	fees	0		2		
23	ticket to Birm[in]g[ham]	0	"	9	"	
	cab	0	"	3	"	
	fees			1		
24	cab ⟨& ticket⟩[n]	0	"	2	"	6

[11] 1847 Paid

Dec							
24	ticket to Manchester	0	"	15	"	0
	Times Newspaper, 4 times	0	"	2	"	0
	cab	0	"	2	"	3
	brushes	0	"	1	"	6
27	Baring, Brothers, & Co. by an order for £100. on James Lester, Esq. Liverpool Union Bank,	100.		0	"	0
	Paid J. Sewell for changing money into order on Liverpool, £100.	0	"	3	"	6
28	Pd for newspapers			1		

	Mrs Massey's bill & washing							
	& sundries	2	"	10	"	5
	Postage stamps		"	5	"	
29	cab.		"	2	"	6
	ticket to Worcester	1	"	⟨15⟩⟨2⟩		0
	Fly			6		
	Star & Garter Inn	1	"	1	"	0
	fees at Cathedral & China Wks	0	"	5	"	

[12] 1847 Paid

Dec	31	fee to cabman	0	"	1	"	0
		fare to Manchester	1	"	2	"	0
		cab	0	"	2		0
		breakfast	⟨1⟩	"	1	"	6
		sundries	0		1		0
		Tennyson's Poem	0	"	4	"	6

1848

Jan	3	⟨T⟩Cab	0	"	2		
		ticket to Leeds	15	"	0		0
		cab	0	"	1		
	4.	fees & cab	0	"	2	"	8
	1	ticket to ⟨Bradford⟩ ↑Rawdon↓	0	"	1	"	6
		porter	0	"	1	"	0
		ticket to & from B[radford].	0	"	2	"	0
	5	fees & cab		"	2		
		ticket to Halifax	0	⟨7⟩8			0
		porter & maid	0	"	2		
	6	Halifax to Leeds	0	"	7		
		cab & fees	0	"	3		
	7	coach to Ripon	0	"	7	"	6
		Ripon Inn	0	"	8		
		Stamps	0	"	1		0
		Halifax Church	0		1		0

[13] 1848 Pd.

Jan	8	To York	0	"	2		6

416

	To Normanton	0	"	5			
	To Manchester	0	"	15			
	Breakfast	0	"	1		6	
	cab		"	1			
9	Paid A Ireland. Esq cash borrowed	3	"	0		0	
10.	⟨Piece⟩Mrs Massey's a/c for sundries	⟨17⟩0	"	17	"	2	
	cab			2			
	pencil	0	"	0	"	6	
	Leeds	⟨1⟩		12	"	0	
	cab			1		6	
11,	fees			2			
12	cab	0	"	4	"		
	Sheffield	0		10			
1⟨3⟩	fee			2			
	razors			9			
	knives			4			
	inkstand			2			
	Show fee			3			
	cab			2			
13	York			15			
	cab			1			
	fees			1			
	Guide &c			4			
	cab			1			

[14] Received

1848			£					
Jan	3	By loan for A. Ireland	3	"	0	"	0
	4	Of Bradford Institute	5	"	5	"	0
	13	Of York Institute	5	"			
	14	Of Leeds Institute	21	"	0	"	0
		Of Sheffield	21	"			
		Of Beverley, Bridlington & Driffield	15				
		Of Halifax	10	"	10	"	

			ENG		PAR		
	Of Glasgow	10	"	10	"	
	Of Edinb.	21	"		
	Of Barnard Castle	5	"	5	"	
	Of Newcastle	14	"	14	"	
	Of Dundee	10	"	10		
	Of Perth	10	"	10		
	Of A. Ireland, Esq. on a/c	35	"		

May	Of G. W. Nickisson on a/c of					
	First "Essays" [7]	16	"	10	"	0
	1. Of Baring, Brothers, & Co.					
	cash	10	"	0	"	0
	Of Hottinguer & Co					
	Of Hottinguer & Co					
	Of A Clough on loan					
	Of J Chapman on a/c	2	"	0	"	0

[15] 1848 Paid

Jan	14	York ⟨fees⟩to Leeds	0	"	5	"	
		Inn	0	"	2		6
		fees			1		
		cab			2		
		newspapers			2		
	15	Manchester			10		
	17	cab	0	"	2	"	
		to Sheffield			7		
		cab			1	"	6
	1⟨8⟩7	cab			1	"	6
		fees			2	"	6
		fare to Beverley			18		
	21	visit to Flanberry	0	"	10	"	3
		expense at hotel at Beverley			6		
	20	Expense at Bridlington			7		
		cars to B			6	"	6
	21	cars to Driffield			2		6

[7] Nickisson had published the authorized English edition of Emerson's *Essays* (1841).

		£		s		d
22	Expense at inn, Driffield	0	"	7	"	
	ticket to Manchester	1	"	3	"	6
[16] 1848	Newspapers	0	"	2	"	
Jan 22	toothbrush			1		
	fees			1		
	cab	0	"	1	"	⟨3⟩6
17	5 tickets to Mr Cameron's lectures,	2	"	0	"	0
24	Mrs Massie's bill for lodgings, expenses, & washing	7	"	4	"	4
⟨Feb 1⟩ 27	2 Handkerchiefs					
	ticket to Free Trade Banquet					
	& cab	0	"	5	"	6
Feb 7	cab			2		
	Ticket to Halifax					
8	cab					
	ticket to ⟨B. Castle⟩					
	Expense ⟨at⟩ inn					
	Carriage to B. Castle	0	"	17	"	0
	boy guide & show			2		
9	Inn at B.C.			6		
	coach		"	4	"	6
	ticket to Newcastle					
[17] 1848						
Feb 10	cab					
11	Telegraph message [8]			14	"	6
	cab					
	ticket to Edinb					
	fee to servant —	0	"	2	"	6
12	fee at Royal Acad.			2		
	cab			⟨2⟩4		
13	cab					

[8] See Journal London, p. [30] above.

	£		s		d
14 cab			1		
ticket to Glasgow	0	"	8	"	0
expense at inn	0	"	15	"	
1⟨6⟩5 ticket to Edin			8		
cab			1	"	6
16 cab			2		
17 cab & ticket to Glasg[ow]			9	"	6
18 cab from Observatory	0	"	3	"	
ticket & cab to Edin			9	"	6
19 tolls			2		
envelopes 1/6. & Standish for					
S[amuel] B[rown] 1.	1	"	1	"	6
20 cab	0	"	1	"	6
21 cab	0	"	1	"	
[18] 1848 Feb. 21 Ticket to Dundee	0	"	8	"	6
ferry					6
porter	0	"	1	"	0
22 umbrella	0	"	15	"	0
cab			1		
ticket to Perth	0	"	3	"	0
23 expenses at P[erth]	0	"	7	"	6
ticket to Dundee	0		3	"	2
porter					6
24 Washing, &c	0	"	3	"	0
cab			1		
ticket to P	0	"	3	"	6
⟨B⟩Coach Earn Bridge			2		
25 Expense at P			4		
Coach &c to Glasgow			15		
ticket to Paisley			1		
sundries			1		
26 ticket to Glasgow	0	"	1	"	
cab & fees &c			2	"	6
ticket to Kendal	1	"	11	"	0
ticket to Berthwaite			1	"	6
tea			1		

		£		s		d
[19] 1848. Feb. 2⟨6⟩7	Ticket to Ambleside	0	"	2		0
	Expense at Berthwaite	0	"	4	"	0
29	"Wordsworth's Guide"⁹	0	"	5	"	0
	paper	0	"	⟨8⟩0	"	8
1 March 1	fees			5		
	ticket to Kendal			3		
	coachman					6
	ticket to Manchester	0	"	14	"	0
26 Feb	Dinner at Carlisle	0	"	3	"	0
↑March↓						
1	cab to Mrs Massey			2		
2	paper &c			6		
⟨3⟩2	Mrs Massey's bill inclusive of washing, & all sundries,	9	"	7	"	10
	Ticket to London by Express Train—	2	"	2	"	6
	cab in Manchester					
3.	Expense at Euston Hotel		"	6	"	6
	cab to Strand		"	2	"	
4.	Deposited with Baring, Brothers & Co, London	36	"	0	"	0
4	—do with do	35	"	0	"	0

		£		s		d
[20] 1848.						
March	cab. 2					
	cab. 1					
	cab. 2					
	cab 1	0	"	6		0
	French theatre	0	"	4	"	6
	pantaloons & waistcoat	3	"	0	"	0.
	map	0	"	1	"	0
	almanac			1		
	hkf 1	0	"	9	"	6
	gloves			2	"	6

⁹ Cf. Journal LM, p. [101] above: "I bring home from England . . . Wordsworth's Scenery of the Lakes."

gloves		3	"	6
12 letters to America	0 "	6	"	6
washing	0 "	3	"	0
cab & bus at sundry times	0 "	5	"	0 [10]
Montaigne, gift to Mr Phillips [11]				
Laing's Heimskringla				
Visit to Hampton Court	0 "	6	"	6
Frock coat	3 "	16	"	0
cabs	0 "	10	"	0
Princess's Theatre	0	6		0

[21] 1848
London

March	20	To Ralph & Co for [12]			
		postages	0 "	4	" 0
		cabs	0 "	10	" 0
March	30	To Oxford	0 "	12	" 0
		to guide	0 "	2	" 0
		to servants	0 "	2	" 6
Apr	1	to London		13	" 6
		hat	0 "	12	" 0
		shoes	0 "	13	" 0
		washing	"	4	" 6
		washing	"	4	"
		washing	0 "	3	" 6
		cab	0 "	2	" 0
		Bus,es.	0 "	8	" 0
		washing, 4 weeks,	0 "	13	" 6
		opera		5	6
		Ralph & Son for dress coat	3 "	15	
		Postages			

[10] This entry is in pencil.

[11] George Searle Phillips ("January Searle"), who had arranged Emerson's lectures at Huddersfield; in 1855 Phillips published Emerson, His Life and Writings.

[12] "To . . . for" has been smudged, probably as an intended cancellation: see the entry for "Ralph & Son" on April 1.

for sundry books to Mr Chapman

[22]¹³ 1848

Polytechnic, 1 s compass 1.6	0	"	2	"	6
cabs 3 buses 3			6		

May   1   £1 " 7 " 6

Francs   39. 10
            148. 5
            103.
            90
            55
            69
          —
           504   francs seems to be about the amount
I spent in Paris to which add 10. pounds taken thither in gold from
Baring & Co & 33 francs borrowed of Clough in Paris & repaid in
London[.]

[23] 1848
May   1 Pd for carrier of passport   0 " 2 " 0.
       6. cab to London Bridge   0 " 2 "
         fare to Folkeston[e] 2d Class   0 " 13 "
         steamer to Boulogne   0 " 8
         steward, 6. porter 6   0 " 1 " 0
         Bradshaw   ⟨6⟩ 6
         porter at Boulogne   1

                           ———
                    ⟨francs⟩Francs

       7 Lodging & breakfast
         custom house   1
         gloves   3
         porter

---

¹³ On this page the writing beginning with "May 1" is in pencil.

fare to Paris	28		
cab	1	"	10
map	1		
theatre	3		
dinner	2		
Hotel Montmorency			

⟨2⟩17 Defraillir for frock coat 110
　　　 francs; waistcoat 25   135.
　　22 Pd concierge for breakfasts; &
　　　 for washing   13.5

[24] 1848   Paris   *Francs.*
May   28 Paid Concierge for all sundries
　　　　 to date   16.1.0
　　　　 Pd for steel purse   7.
　　　　　　 pin   4.
　　　　 ticket to stalle d'orchestre The-
　　　　 atre Italien   6
　　　　 Concierge for rent of rooms &
　　　　 service for one month ——   90
　　　　 washing ⎫
　　　　 breakfasts ⎬   13
　　　　 errands ⎭
　　　　 pd for 2 heads of St Simon for
　　　　 E. P. Clark [14]   ⟨4⟩3.5.0
Pd for *Guide de Paris*   2.
　　　　 cab   1.5.0
　　　　 concierge   5.
　　　　 ticket to Theatre Francais   7.
　　　　 Ticket again   6.
　　　　 Racine's Phedre   1

[25] 1848   Paris   Francs centimes
May

　　　　 Racine's Mithridate   1.

---

[14] Clark was cashier of the New England Bank, in Boston.

	Ticket to Theatre Italien	6.
	Loan of the Play, *Lucrece*	1.
	[Dinner daily at the Palais Royal⟨e⟩ may be reckoned at 2.20 centimes say for 25 days	⟨3⟩55.
	coffee at night 25 times at 50 centimes	12.50
	Breakfast is included in the ⟨prices⟩ sums paid to the concierge & at the rate of 19 sous per day]	
	cab	2
	cab	2
	cab	1
	cab	3
	cab	1
	ticket to Club des femmes	1
	Ticket to Blanqui's Club	1

[26] 1848	Paris	*Francs*
May	Paid ticket to ⟨Blanqui's⟩Barbe's Club	1.
	Paid to Salon de Lecture for 1 month	6.
	Newspapers	3.
	Wine 3 bottles	3.
	Jardin d'Hiver	1.
	Bal Mabille	3.
June	1 Pd Concierge gift	5.
	Commissionaire &c	3.
	2 Ticket to Boulogne in 2d Class	21
	At Amiens paid for visit to the Cathedral	2.
	At Boulogne porter	1
	Dinner & servants	5
	Porter	1

425

Commissionaire	I
Steamboat to Folk[e]stone	8.
Steward	I
Needlebox bought at Boulogne	3.50

[27] 1848		£.		s.		d.
June 3 At Folk[e]stone expense						
at Royal George		0	"	5		3
Customs House &c						
porter		0	"	3	"	
Ticket in Express train to London		I	"	6	"	0
Cab to Strand		0	"	I	"	9

[J. Chapman paid Clough for
me price of "Friesdichens" 18
francs, & a loan to me of 15
francs in Paris.] [15]

$$\begin{array}{ll} 18 & \\ 31 \quad 160 \; \big) \; 264 & \quad (1 \\ \underline{18} \qquad\quad \underline{160} & \\ 54 \qquad\quad 104 & \\ 1\langle6\rangle7\,\big)558 \quad \big(\;33 \\ \underline{\;\;\big)51} \qquad\quad \underline{8} \\ 48 \qquad\quad 264 \end{array}$$

[28]–[29] [blank]

    [30] [16] Steamboat condenses 200 gallons of fresh water from the steam of salt water per hour.[17]

Memorandum

1848

---

[15] The computations which follow on p. [27] are in pencil, written upside down in relation to the previous entries.

[16] Pp. [30] and [31] are in pencil.

[17] This sentence, struck through in pencil with a vertical use mark, is used in "Civilization," *W*, VII, 24–25.

Sept   N. Barrett — cider.

———

    M Fuller; W[iley?]. & P[utnam?].

———

———

[31] *Work*

———

Spread the sand by brook[.]

———

Remove apple tree[.]

———

[32]–[39] [blank]
[40][18] 3 000 Clarke
   2 500 Smith
     Orr
     Fraser[19]

At ⟨Oxford⟩ K[ing] Henry's crown was full of birdsnests.[20]

[Sir Thomas] Lucy ha⟨d⟩s ⟨1⟩7000 acres and £14 000 a year. When his second son was born he was much at a loss how to provide for him. He took F[lower]'s grandfather to counsel, & bred him for the church & gave him the living of the parish[.][21]

---

[18] This page is in pencil.

[19] The first three entries on p. [40] are presumably concerned with unauthorized English publishers of Emerson's works: Henry G. Clarke & Co. of London had published *Nature, An Essay; And Lectures on the Times* in 1844; William Smith of London published *Nature: An Essay. And Orations* in 1843 (dated 1844); William S. Orr and Co. of London published *Essays, Lectures & Orations* in 1848. The reference to "Fraser" is unexplained.

[20] This sentence, struck through in pencil with a diagonal use mark, is transcribed in Journal LM, p. [98] above.

[21] "Lucy . . . parish", struck through in pencil with a vertical use mark, is transcribed in Journal London, p. [103] above; see also Journal LM, p. [75] above. Emerson evidently heard this story from Edward Fordham Flower, whom he saw at Coventry and at Flower's home in Stratford on July 12, 1848. Flower had spent some boyhood years in Illinois; in 1849 he and his wife visited Emerson in Concord.

[41] [22] Times
   35 000 ⟨s⟩ copies of the Times
8 000 since february increase
10 to 12 000 copies per hour since 1814
   1788 or 9 [23]

Mrs N[orton]. said two failures were D[israeli] & M[ilnes.]
   letter to Lord Brougham [24]
Milnes
   Oxford education indurates like Styx Achilles[.] [25]

Englishman a lump of red dough out of which gradually emerges wit, learning, fine culture[.] [26]

[42] Topics of ⟨C⟩conversation in England. Irish affairs, General suffrage, pauperism, public education, right & duty of govts to interfere with increase of population, taxes,[27]

[43] Ventilation, Dead Question, Music, Early Closing,[28]

[44] [29] Served it right ma'ame. I'll mention it.
gems
Gray's hints to the D[uke] of Grafton
To find pain I cannot go wrong[;] I plant cypresses wherever I go[.] [30]

[22] This page is in pencil. See Plate II.
[23] "35 000 . . . or 9", struck through in pencil with a vertical use mark, is transcribed in Journal London, p. [49] above.
[24] "Mrs . . . Brougham", struck through in pencil with a vertical use mark, and "letter . . . Brougham", struck through in pencil with an additional vertical use mark, are expanded in Journal London, p. [173] above.
[25] This sentence, struck through in pencil with a vertical use mark, is amplified as a remark of Carlyle's in Journal London, p. [57] above; see also Notebook ED, p. [206] below.
[26] Cf. "Culture," W, VI, 152.
[27] This uncompleted entry, in pencil and struck through in pencil with a vertical use mark, is transcribed in Journal London, p. [174] above.
[28] This uncompleted entry, in pencil, is expanded in Journal LM, p. [9] above.
[29] This page is in pencil.
[30] "Served . . . go", struck through in pencil with a vertical use mark, is ex-

Brummel was a sort of inverse St Peter who could tread the waters of humbug without sinking[.] [31]
The lark who was hatched last year & the wind that was hatched many thousand of years ago [32]

[45] [33] G. H. Smallbone. George Inn, Amesbury [34]

$$
\begin{array}{r}
24 \\
170 \\
153 \\
24 \\
30 \\
\hline
398
\end{array}
$$
[35]

[46₁] Landseer the only genius of the Academy exhibition. Leslie very sensible & pleasing[.] There are many English portraits[,] the true national type. The ΗΩΣ of Gibson like the admirably finished pictures of Scheffer show want of all object with great powers of execution. So that we get noble vases empty[.] [36]

[47₁]–[51₁] [blank in front-to-back sequence] [37]

---

panded in Journal LM, p. [98] above. On "Gray's hints", see Journal London, p. [169] above, and Notebook ED, pp. [132]–[133] below. In "Stonehenge," W, V, 279, Emerson quotes Carlyle as saying, "I plant cypresses wherever I go, and if I am in search of pain, I cannot go wrong."

[31] This sentence, struck through in pencil with a vertical use mark, is transcribed in Journal London, p. [58] above; see also Notebook ED, p. [208] below.

[32] "The lark . . . ago", struck through in pencil with a vertical use mark, is used in "Stonehenge," W, V, 277, where the words are attributed to Carlyle.

[33] This page is in pencil.

[34] Here Emerson and Carlyle stayed on July 7, 1848 ("Stonehenge," W, V, 276).

[35] The correct sum is 401.

[36] "Landseer . . . empty", in pencil and struck through in pencil with a vertical use mark, is transcribed in Journal LM, p. [98] above.

[37] Printed below is a sequence of seven pages written in pencil, appearing upside down with reference to the writing on the preceding pages, that begins on p. [53₂] and ends on p. [46₂], using the subscript numbers to denote the back-to-front writing. The entries on these pages were occasioned by the visit of Emerson and Carlyle to Amesbury, Stonehenge, Wilton, and Salisbury on July 7 and 8, 1848.

[53₂] Greater men lived & died in those ages than any since. In fact ⟨at⟩ ↑about↓ the time these writers appeared the last of these were already gone[.] [38]

[52₂]   John Wood
          Robert Napier
          George Burns [39]

At Coventry spire 300 ft church 300 ft [40]
     days valued by the apercus [41]

[51₂] ↑grass↓ thyme daisy meadowsweet nettle thistle buttercup goldenrod [42]

The smaller stones are granite[;] the bigger sarsens or hard sandstone. [43]

no trees

I who had just come from Sedgwick's megatheria & mastodons at Cambridge believed absurdly that men or elephants of a bigger bone had laid up these rocks on one another, [44]

     [50₂] Besides his horse & gun all he knows is the door to the H[ouse] of C[ommons]. [45]

     moral engineer [46]

---

[38] "Greater . . . gone" is used in "Stonehenge," *W*, V, 280.

[39] Probably John George Wood (1827–1889), a popular English writer and lecturer on natural history. Robert Napier (1791–1876) was a Scottish marine engineer associated with the Cunard Company, which the Scottish shipowners George and James Burns (1795–1890, 1789–1871) helped to found in 1839 — see p. [62] below.

[40] Cf. "Stonehenge," *W*, V, 285.

[41] This entry is expanded in Journal LM, p. [106] above.

[42] "grass . . . goldenrod" is used in "Stonehenge," *W*, V, 277.

[43] Cf. "Stonehenge," *W*, V, 278.

[44] The geologist Adam Sedgwick (1785–1873), whom Emerson had heard at a meeting of the Geological Club in London, held a professorship at Cambridge University, which Emerson visited on July 6, 1848. "I who . . . another," is used in "Stonehenge," *W*, V, 278.

[45] This sentence is transcribed in Journal LM, p. [99] above.

[46] This phrase is used in Journal LM, p. [24] above.

The trilithons of Stonehenge are the simplest & surest structures. Like Achilles' tomb⟨s⟩ on plain of Troy they keep the vaunt of Homer through all ages.[47]

showery England
delicious sward
pillory of 2 class [48]

[49₂] Amesbury 7 July
Stonehenge[:] Brown dwarves on a vast Wiltshire down
Gray stones on a gray evening[,] here were they[,] nettles & butter cups at their feet within the enclosure[,] larks singing over them & the wind old as they ringing among the conscious stones[.] [49]

↑C[arlyle] talked of↓ happiness.ⁿ ⟨paid[?] in[?] life⟩ I fancied the stones had no philosophy of that kind. It is a quiet temple of Destiny [50] & so   constructed with infinite judgment in a place where it must ever be conspicuous from far to tens of thousands of eyes[.]

[48₂] They understood the English language these British stones of the two talkers one from America one from Scotland who came up to this old ark of the race.[51]

These at least spoke a language which all men understand and in a long solitude of millenniums still keep these undisturbed uninclosed downs. High green barrows lifted themselves all around on the plain[,] the old contemporaries & compatriots of the circle[.] [52] And a shepherd of Sal[i]sbury Plain kept his flock within sight & a

---

[47] These two sentences are used in "Stonehenge," *W*, V, 277.

[48] This phrase is transcribed in Journal LM, p. [99] above.

[49] In "Stonehenge," Emerson describes Stonehenge as looking "like a group of brown dwarfs in the wide expanse" and refers to its buttercups, larks, and wind; on the morning after he and Carlyle arrived at Amesbury he "engaged the local antiquary, Mr. Brown, to go with us to Stonehenge . . . and show us what he knew of the 'astronomical' and 'sacrificial' stones" (*W*, V, 276, 277, 280).

[50] Cf. "Stonehenge," *W*, V, 279.

[51] This sentence is used in "Stonehenge," *W*, V, 279.

[52] This sentence is used in "Stonehenge," *W*, V, 276.

shower drove the sad haymakers to protect [47₂] even now on the fall of night their spread windrows[.]
In the showery England the grass grows long & dark[.] [53]

Evidently it were possible to some C[harles] Fellowes to arrive stone by stone at the whole history of this structure. It is yet new & recent. Here are we in its early times. A thousand years hence they will thank us for ⟨what w⟩ the history we shall now save if we begin it. No tree in sight[,] no house. Hayricks only & a bagman passed[.] The geologist had pecked at every stone.[54]

[46₂] The combed fields have the softest appearance & seem ⟨not⟩ touched with a pencil & not with a plough.[55]

[52₁] "God's bairns are eath to lear." Scotch proverb [56]

[53₁] [blank in front-to-back sequence]
[54] [57] Eng[lish] men dislike Am[erican]. style of civilization yet are doing all they can to bring it in.[58]

Every man is somebody like Hugh or Grove Blanchard or Seth Blanchard or Edmund Hosmer[.] [59]

We clapped our hands in Halifax harbour, when the fog rolled suddenly up & showed the town.[60]

---

[53] The shepherd and haymakers appear in "Stonehenge," W, V, 276; the shower, the haymakers, and "showery England" (see p. [50₂]) in "Stonehenge," W, V, 280.

[54] "Evidently . . . begin it." is used in "Stonehenge," W, V, 278–279; the hayricks, the bagman, and the geologists' marks appear in "Stonehenge," W, V, 276, 278.

[55] "The combed . . . plough.", struck through in pencil with a curved vertical use mark, is transcribed in Journal LM, p. [98] above; see "Land," W, V, 34.

[56] This entry is in pencil; the quotation is transcribed in Journal LM, p. [99] above.

[57] This page is in pencil.

[58] This sentence is transcribed in Journal LM, p. [124] above; see "Cockayne," W, V, 150.

[59] Cf. Journal GH, p. [140] above, and Journal London, p. [14] above.

[60] This sentence is transcribed in Journal LM, p. [124] above.

In the brigantine at Syracuse the whole crew & capitano got hold of a soiled Gazetteer & read *Boston* with curiosity to know from what Siam or Pegu we mariners had dropped.[61]

[55] [...] [62]
    [56] [63] On the conduct of life
Luck. farmer looking on vines

Rothschild. Buxton's Life
Voting. How small of all [64]

A.S. played poor

The other was, ⟨A W⟩ If a man has no sphere, there's a reason for it. Observe whether his platform be a planet or only his own shoes, & do not suppose that the cause he urges now will have any longer support than his former abodes.[65]

    [57] [66] Once more on the conduct of life. Always to be at home carry bibles in your pocket[.]

[58] Wm. Lane
            6.15
            2.00

[59] [July 23, 1848.] One long disgust is the sea[:] no personal bribe would lure one who loves the present moment. Who am I to be treated in this ignominious manner, tipped up, shoved against the

---

[61] "In the . . . dropped.", struck through in pencil with a vertical use mark, is transcribed in Journal LM, p. [123] above.
[62] On this page is a pencil sketch of a chair.
[63] This page is in pencil.
[64] The entries on p. [56] to this point are incorporated in the lecture outline on p. [3] of Journal LM above, headed "On the Conduct of life." For Rothschild . . . Life", see Journal LM, p. [37] above; for "How small of all", see Journal LM, p. [103] above.
[65] Between "planet" and "cause" are two intersecting lines in pencil resembling a half circle and a large V, possibly made by accident.
[66] Pp. [57] and [58] are in pencil.

side of the house, rolled over, suffocated with bilge, mephites, & stewing oil? [n] Shakspeare will do. These lacklustre days go whistling over us, and are the intercalaries I have often asked for & am cursed now with the worthless granting of my prayer[.] [67]

[60] [68] Kings are made for honor not for long life   Heimsk[ringla,] Vol 3 p 147

Bravery is half victory   [*Heimskringla*, III,] p 101 [69]

"Upon the stem
I'll sail with them"   [*Ibid.*, III, 81]

All the gems are fossil wine[.] [70]

A[ppleton]. crosses the 14th time.
Pope was in S. America & met a Yankee who gave him notions. [71]

[61] [72] I have seen AB, CD, EF, &c.

America exceptional & one would expect eulogy, but finds insult. Yet they are Americanizing England as fast as they can.
The Eng[lish]men said, Are there any Americans, Is there any one with an American idea?
The artists found in my face the Indian type. [73]

Advantage of betting. Accurate knowledge. Is Missisppi or Missouri longest? About the same length. About! that won't do. I've a bet upon it. Capt. L[ott]. says, The boat is yet to be built that will go 19

[67] See the entry headed "At sea, 23 July, 1848" in Journal LM, p. [95] above; "Shakspeare will do" is evidently an observation made by Thomas Gold Appleton during the voyage.
[68] This page is in pencil.
[69] *The Heimskringla*, trans. Samuel Laing, 1844.
[70] This sentence, struck through in pencil with a vertical use mark, is transcribed in Journal LM, p. [93] above.
[71] "A. crosses . . . time." is transcribed in Journal LM, p. [95] above. "Pope . . . notions.", struck through in pencil with a vertical use mark, is expanded in Journal London, p. [176] above.
[72] This page is in pencil.
[73] Cf. Journal London, p. [177] above.

miles thro' the water. Denies our distances. They are loose. In Eng[lan]d., they would be all measured to a half a foot.[74]

[62] [75] compression of the streets & of the cause [76]

Soldier cannot fold away his arms nor scholar.
impediunt foris [77]

———

George & James Burns. Glasgow
Saml Cunard   Halifax
S. S. Lewis   Boston
Edw. Cunard Jr   New York
D & C MacIvor   Liverpool
J B Ford   London [78]

———

[63] [79] sign of Revolution
impossible to live sans immense fortune
12 newspapers a day to keep au courant [80]

nature prix fixe

ici on fait son courrier

Sea between Dover & Boulogne the standing army [81]

[74] "Advantage . . . foot.", struck through in pencil with a vertical use mark, is transcribed in Journal London, p. [175] above.
[75] This page is in pencil.
[76] This entry is expanded in Journal LM, p. [124] above.
[77] Cf. Journal LM, pp. [93], [125] above.
[78] "George . . . London" is set off by marginal lines, in pencil. All of the persons listed may have been associated with the Cunard Company: Samuel Cunard (1787–1865), born in Halifax, Nova Scotia, joined with the Burns brothers (see p. [522] above) and David M'Iver of Liverpool in its founding; Samuel S. Lewis was its Boston agent.
[79] This page is in pencil.
[80] The observation is expanded in Journal London, p. [162] above, with reference to the 200 newspapers of Paris.
[81] The observation is expanded in Journal London, p. [163] above. With "ici . . . courrier", cf. Journal LM, p. [125] above.

[64] William Mathews, Esq.   Edgbaston Birmingham

[65] B. Dockray. Dalton Square. Lancaster [82]
    B.

Mr E F Flower   Stratford upon Avon

[66]–[68] [blank]
    [69] [83] every hand in the street outstretched for a penny & every
hand in the house

[70] J. O. Murray, 17 Rue de Beaux Arts. Paris.
    Memoirs of Geol. Survey. Vol. 1. Ed⟨d⟩w. Forbes [84]

John Davison   2 Bush Hill Hatton Garden ⎫
Robert Henderson   4 Skinner St, Snow Hill ⎬ Rockinghorse [85]
Paul Leach   11 Union Court Holborn ⎭

[71] [86] 1847 Sept 3 Recd of Boston Savings Bk
                on a/c Charles Lane his deposit
                with interest   131.33

            16 Recd of Joseph Palmer on ⎫
                a/c C. Lane (being the balance ⎬ 323.36 [87]
                of a note on demand for ⎪
                $400. with interest ⎭

[82] Emerson wrote to Benjamin Dockray on July 11, 1848, alluding to Dockray's
praise of his poems; Dockray had given him a marked copy of the London edition
of 1847 on the day of Emerson's first London lecture (L, IV, 98).

[83] This page is in pencil.

[84] "Memoirs . . Forbes" is in pencil. The reference, evidently added in 1856
or later, is to a posthumous monograph by Forbes: "On the Tertiary Fluvio-Marine
Formation of the Isle of Wight," *Memoirs of the Geological Survey of Great Britain,
and of the Museum of Practical Geology* (London, 1856).

[85] "Rockinghorse" is written vertically in the right margin. Davison, Henderson, and Leach of Rockinghorse (see front cover verso above) have not been identified.

[86] The entries on this page are written vertically.

[87] The figure appears as "323.96" in an entry in Notebook Books Small [Se-
quence II]: see *JMN*, VIII, 575 and n. 122. Emerson evidently acted as a collector
for Lane, who had sold Fruitlands to Palmer.

[72]⁸⁸ 1847

Nov	2 Tue.	Manchester Athenaeum I ["Uses of Great Men"]⁸⁹
	3. Wed.	Liverpool Mechanics I ["Uses of Great Men"]
	4 Thurs.	Manchester Ath. II ["Swedenborg: the Mystic"]
	5 Fri	
	6 Sat	Liverpool Mech II ["Swedenborg: the Mystic"]
	7 Sun	
	8 Mon	Manchester Mechanics I ["Eloquence"]
	9 Tuesd	⟨L⟩Manchester Ath III ["Montaigne: the Skeptic"]
	10 Wed	Liverpool Mech. III ["Montaigne: the Skeptic"]
	11 Thurs	Manchester ⟨Mech⟩Ath. IV ["Shakespeare: the Poet"]
	12 Fri	
	13 Sat	Liverpool Mech IV ["Shakespeare: the Poet"]
	14 Sun	
	15 Mon.	Manchester Mechan. II ["Domestic Life"]
	16 Tuesd.	Manchester Athen. V ["Napoleon: the Man of Action"]
	17 Wed	Liverpool Mech. V ["Napoleon: the Man of Action"]
	18 Thurs.	*Manchester Soirée* ↑VI↓ ⁹⁰

⁸⁸ On this page "Manchester" (Nov. 11) and "Manchester Athen." (Nov. 16) are written in ink over the same words in pencil; "VI" (Nov. 18) is written and circled in pencil.

⁸⁹ Where titles of Emerson's lectures are supplied, the information is based on Townsend Scudder III, "Chronological List of Emerson's Lectures on His British Lecture Tour of 1847–1848," *PMLA*, LI (March 1936), 243–248, which was compiled from reports in British newspapers mentioning his individual lecture engagements.

⁹⁰ Scudder, p. 245, n. 4, points out that Emerson's lecture on "Goethe," originally scheduled for this date, was rescheduled for November 23 because of the Annual Soirée. For Emerson's speech at the Soirée, see Notebook ED, pp. [25]–[39] below.

19	Fri	
20	Sat.	Liverpool Mech. VI ["Goethe: the Man of Letters"]
21	Sun [91]	
[73] Nov 22	Mon	Manchester Mechan III ["Reading"] [92]
Nov 23	Tues	Manchester Ath VI ["Goethe: the Man of Letters"]
24	Wed	⟨Liverpool Mech⟩
25	Thurs	Mr Rathbone's
26	Fri	
27	Sat	
28	Sun	
29	Mon.	Manchester Mechanics IV ["The Superlative in Manners and Literature"]
30	Tues	Liverpool [Essay and Discussion Society of the] Roscoe Club ["Reading"]
Dec. 1,	Wed.	Preston ["Napoleon"]
2	Thurs	Dr Hodgson
3	Friday	Rochdale.[93]
4	Sat	
5	Sun	
6	Mon	Nottingham ↑Napoleon↓
7	Tuesd	Derby ["Napoleon"]
8	Wed	Nottingham ↑Domestic Life↓
9	Thurs	Derby ["Shakespeare"]
10	Fri	Nottingham ↑Shakspere↓ [94]
11	Sat	
12	Sund	

[91] The entries from November 2 through November 21 are struck through in ink with a vertical line.

[92] Also called "Books," as in the entry for December 13, 1847, on p. [74] below.

[93] Probably not a lecture engagement. Scudder, p. 245, though reporting that the local press of Rochdale makes no mention of Emerson's visit, assumed that this appointment was for a lecture, but Emerson's record of cash payments during November, 1847, p. [4] above, includes no entry for an honorarium at Rochdale.

[94] On p. [73], "Napoleon", "Domestic Life", and "Shakspere" are added in pencil.

[74]⁹⁵ 1847

Dec	13	Monday	Nottingham ↑Books↓ ↑*At Newstead*↓
	14	Tuesday	⟨Huddersfield⟩Chesterfield
	15	Wed	Preston ["Domestic Life"]
	16	Thursd	Birmingham ↑Napoleon↓
	17	Friday	Huddersfield ["Napoleon"]
	18	Sat	Huddersfield ["Domestic Life"]
	19	Sun	
	20	Mond	Leicester ["Shakespeare"]
	21	Tuesd	Leicester ["Domestic Life"]
	22	Wednes.	Chesterfield ["Domestic Life"]
	23	Thurs.	Birmingham ↑Dom Life↓
	24	Fri	
	25	Sat	
	26	Sun	
	27	Mon	
	28	Tues	
	29	Wed	Worcester ["Eloquence"]
	30	Thurs	Worcester ["Domestic Life"]
	31	Fri.	
1848			
Jan	1	Sat⁹⁶	
	2		
	3	Mon	Leeds ["Shakespeare"]
	4	Tu	Bradford
	5	Wed	Halifax ["Napoleon"]
	6	Thurs	Leeds ["Uses of Great Men"]
	7	Fri	Ripon ["Domestic Life"]
	8	Sat	
	9	Sun	
	10	M.	Leeds ["Domestic Life"]
	11.	Tu.	Sheffield Domestic Life

⁹⁵ On this page, the following names are written in ink over the same words in pencil: "Leicester" (twice), "Chesterfield", "Leeds", "Bradford", "Halifax", "Leeds", "Ripon", "Leeds", "Sheffield" (twice), "York", "Leeds". "Books", "Napoleon", and "Dom Life" are added in pencil.

⁹⁶ The entries for December 13 through January 1 are struck through in ink with a vertical line.

	12	Wed	Sheffield Humanity of Science[97]
	13	Th.	York ["Domestic Life"]
	14	Fri	Leeds ["Reading"]
[75][98]	1848		
Jan	15	Sat	
	16	Sun	
	17	Mon	Sheffield Napoleon[99]
	18	Tues	Sheffield Shakspere
	19	Wed	Beverley ↑Napoleon↓
	20	Thurs	Bridlington ↑Dom Life↓
	21	Fri	Driffield ↑Napoleon↓
	22	Sat	
	23	Sun	
	24	Mon	
	25	Tues	
	26	Wed	
	27	Thurs	
	28	Fri	
	29	Sat	
	30	Sun	
	31	Mon	
Feb	1	⟨Sun⟩ Tues.	
	2	⟨Mon⟩ Wed.	
	3	⟨Tues⟩ Thurs.	
	4	⟨Wed⟩Friday	
	5	⟨Thu⟩Saturday	
	6	⟨Fri⟩Sunday	
	7	Mon	Halifax ["Domestic Life"]
	8	Tues	Barnard Castle ["The National Characteristics of the Six Northern States of America"]

[97] Scudder, p. 246, cites local newspapers to show that Emerson lectured instead on "Napoleon."

[98] On this page, "Sheffield" is twice written in ink over the same word in pencil. In the entries for January 19–21, the added titles are in pencil. There is a vertical line in pencil to the right of the entries for January 22–February 5.

[99] Scudder, p. 246, shows that on this date Emerson gave "The Humanity of Science," which he had originally intended to deliver at Sheffield on January 12.

9	Wed	Newcastle ["Shakespeare"]
10	Thurs	Newcastle ["The National Characteristics of the Six Northern States of America"]
11	Friday	Edinburgh ["Natural Aristocracy"]
12	Saturday	
13	Sunday	
14	Monday	⟨Edinburgh⟩ Glasg[ow: "Napoleon"]
15	Tuesd	⟨Glasgow⟩ Edin[burgh: "The Genius of the Present Age"]

[76] 1848 Feb

16	Wed	⟨Edinburgh⟩ [Paisley: "Napoleon"]
17	Thurs	Glasgow ["Domestic Life"]
18	Fri	Edinburgh ["Shakespeare"]
19	Sat	Edinburgh ["Eloquence"]
20	Sun	
21	Mon.	Dundee ["The Spirit of the Times"]
22	Tues	Perth ["Eloquence"]
23	Wed	Dundee ["Eloquence"]
24	Thurs	Perth ["Napoleon"]
25	Fri	⟨Newcastle⟩ Paisley ↑Robt Stewart↓ [100]
26	Sat	
27	Sun	

[77][101] Wed

[June] 21 Wednes.

22	Thurs	
23	Fri	Exeter [Hall: "Napoleon"]. Mrs Montagu [102]
24	Sat.	J.L.
25	Sun.	Mr Field
26	Mon.	Marylebone ["The Superlative in Manners and Literature"]

[100] "Robt Stewart" is in pencil. Stewart has not been identified.

[101] All entries on this page are in pencil except (1) portions of the entries for June 29 and 30: "Carlyle" and "Hall", and (2) portions of the entries for July 2–4: "Sun Mr Procter", "Mon Mr Rolt at 7. 52 Harley St", and "Tuesd".

[102] Possibly Anne D. B. Montagu, who wrote to Emerson on June 30, 1848 (L, VI, 524).

27	Tues.	Exeter Hall ["Domestic Life"]
28	Wed.	Lord Morpeth ↑Lord Lovelace↓
29	Thurs.	↑Carlyle↓
30	Fri	Exeter ↑Hall↓ ["Shakespeare"]
[July] 1	Sat	Chapman
2	Sun	Mr Procter 6¾
3	Mon	Mr Rolt at 7. 52 Harley St
4	Tuesd	Mr Kenyon
5	Wednesday.	4 Mr Bubier [103]
6	Thursday.	Cambridge
7		

[78] C K Patmore   19 Randolph st, Camdentown
Mr H. Crabb Robinson   30 Russell Square

Mr W. A. Case   20 Upper Gower st

Mr Macready. 5 Clarence Terrace — Regents Park [104]
Mrs Jameson, 30 Eastbourne Terrace Hyde Pk
Geo O'Gorman   39 Dorset st Portman Sq
W. Stirling   38 Clarges street
Miss Stirling   44 ⟨Wigmore street⟩ ↑Welbeek↓

Dr Ashburner, 65 Grosvenor st.
Dr Forbes   12 Old Burlington st
Mr Yates   49 Upper Bedford Place
Mr Jay. Fenton's Hotel
Mrs Crowe   22 Suffolk st Pall Mall
Miss Ellen Rendall. Adelphi [105]

---

[103] George B. Bubier had written Emerson on November 9, 1847, and again in June or July of 1848 (L, VI, 381).

[104] "Regents Park" is written on the facing page, [79], within a circular line to indicate that it is part of Macready's address. The English tragedian William Charles Macready (1799–1873) had brought letters to Emerson in Boston from Carlyle and Harriet Martineau in 1843; in London, Emerson saw him in *King Lear* in March of 1848 and visited him on June 29 (L, III, 223; IV, 44, 95).

[105] O'Gorman and Yates have not been identified. Stirling wrote to Emerson in June and July of 1848 (L, VI, 595). Jane Stirling entertained Emerson at dinner

[79] Mrs. S. C. Hall. Rosery, Old Brompton

⟨M⟩Dr Carpenter   6 Regents Terrace Gloster Gate
       Morell
Mr Gillies   23 Northumberland St. New Road, York Gate,
     Regents Park
Lady Byron   ⟨47? Upper Brook st⟩ ↑115 Park Lane↓

C. Patmore   5 Brecknock Crescent Camdentown
⟨R. P. Gillies   20 Allsop Terrace, Regents Park⟩
Miss Stirling   55 Welbeck Street
D W Bartlett
Mrs Ashurst [106]

[80] [107] In a/c with A[bel].A[dams].

By cash 342.75	To pd Atlantic Bk	81. 16
328	Metcalf	233. 77
2.⟨6⟩17[?]	Fitchburg	100.
	H.D.T	30.[108]

with Frédéric Chopin on June 15, 1848, and sent him a ticket to Chopin's *matinée musicale* on June 23 (*L*, IV, 84; Journal London, p. [210] above). Mrs. Crowe of Edinburgh was in London in June of 1848 and went with Emerson to the Carlyles' on June 22 (*CEC*, pp. 440, 441). Emerson evidently became acquainted with Ellen Rendall through Mr. and Mrs. W. Fisher, Jr., of Sheffield (*L*, IV, 16, 46, 144–145).

[106] Mrs. Hall, Mr. Gillies, and D. W. Bartlett have not been identified. On June 8, 1848, Bancroft introduced Emerson to Lady Byron, who invited him to call (*L*, IV, 81). "Mrs Ashurst" may be Mrs. William Henry Ashurst, the mother of Mrs. Joseph Biggs of Knighton, near Leicester, where Emerson visited in December of 1847; Ashurst, a solicitor, called on Emerson at Concord in 1853 (*L*, IV, 379).

[107] The following items on this page are in pencil: "328", "100", "Dr Spurgen . . . Piccadilly", and "Mrs Atkinson 37 Gordon Square".

[108] The accounting is partly explained by Emerson's correspondence from abroad. A letter of December 31, 1847, to his wife mentions his having remitted money to Adams in two letters through the Barings and includes an order on Adams to cover a check protested by the Atlantic Bank, as a letter from Henry Thoreau had reported (*L*, III, 461). A letter of March 9, 1848, to his brother William observes that the money he had sent home had gone to pay a printer's bill—presumably from "Metcalf," the Cambridge publishing house, "& to pay a note at the Atlantic Bk, & tailors, & to pay new assessments on two shares of Fitchburg [Rail Road] stock" (*L*, IV, 36).

Dr Spurgen \ French Holborn 56
Miss Rendall Fench 163
Mr Bates & Mr Amory ↑69 Pall Mall↓ Weigall
Mrs Wedgewood
Mrs Jameson
Morgan 12 Stratton st Piccadilly
Espinasse 7 Harper st Bloomsbury

———

Mrs Atkinson 37 Gordon Square

———

Mr Forster 58 Lincolns Inn Fields
W Mathews 13 Upper Seymour St, Portman Sq
Edwin Field; 41 Bedford Row.
Mrs Drummond 18 H Park Garden
Miss Taylor 55 Guilford
Amory & Campbell 69 Pall Mall
H Hallam 24 Wilton Crescent
Conyngham. 7 Clifford st Bond st.[109]

[inside back cover] [110] Dr Carlyle 19 Hemus Terrace, Chelsea
    Halifax ⟨Mr Carter[?]⟩
    Huddersfield Mr Brodhead
    Greenwich Mr Wilkinson

[109] The entries on p. [80] apparently date from March and April of 1848. Dr. Spurgen (or "Spurgin"—see inside back cover below), W. Mathews, French, Fench, and Campbell have not been identified. Jonathan Amory was a fellow passenger on Emerson's return voyage (L, IV, 101). Weigall is probably the Henry Weigall listed on the inside back cover below. Emerson dined on April 13 with Mr. and Mrs. Hensleigh Wedgewood (Pocket Diary 3, p. [66] below; L, IV, 55); Wedgewood was a mathematician and philologist, married to a daughter of Sir James Mackintosh. In April and May Emerson had a number of engagements with John Minter Morgan. Espinasse may be his Manchester friend Francis Espinasse. Emerson called on Mrs. Atkinson in March and had breakfast and dinner engagements with John Forster in April. Mrs. Drummond entertained Emerson on March 15 (Pocket Diary 3, p. [58] below; L, IV, 41). Emily Taylor wrote to Emerson at some time in 1848 (L, VI, 600). "Conyngham" may be the "friend of John Sterling's" whom Emerson met on April 20—possibly Sterling's cousin William Coningham or Conyngham (L, IV, 48, n. 176).

[110] The remaining entries are in pencil except for "Dr Hutton . . . Hyde Park"; "Halifax . . . Spurgin" is struck through in pencil with a diagonal line.

                    Martin 24 James st Buckingham Gate
Marylebone   ⟨M⟩Dr Mackay
Reading   Tagart
⟨Sheffield⟩   Dr Spurgin
Mr Henry Weigall   27 Somerset st Portman Sq

Mr Procter   13 Upper Harley St Cavendish Sq
Mr Hensleigh Wedgewood, 42 Chester Terrace, Regents Park
Mr Bates   46 Portland Place

D Jefferson   5 Kingsgate st Holborn
Dr Spurgin   38 Guildford st Russell Sq
1 Adam st. Adelphi. Miss Rendall
Mr Lyell, 11 Harley st
Dr Hutton   5 Hamilton Place Kings Cross
Heraud   28 Burton st
↑Mr↓ Gibson, 31 Westbourne Terrace
↑Mr↓ Martineau   17 Westbourn st. Hyde Park [111]

---

[111] Carter[?], Brodhead, and Tagart have not been identified. Martin may be
the writer Theodore Martin, mentioned earlier. In 1857 Emerson wrote a letter
of introduction for Dr. Charles Mackay of London (*L*, V, 89)—possibly the
journalist and poet (1814–1889). Hutton may be Robert Hutton, whom Harriet
Martineau introduced to Emerson, as Rusk conjectures (*L*, IV, 65, n. 232), or more
probably Richard Holt Hutton (1826–1897), an English editor, theologian, and
man of letters who later wrote about Emerson. John A. Heraud, formerly editor of
the *Monthly Magazine* and later on the staff of the *Athenaeum*, had been in correspondence with Emerson before the latter's voyage to England. Richard[?] Martineau
wrote to Emerson on April 11, 1848 (*L*, VI, 514).

Pocket Diary 3

1848–1849

Pocket Diary 3 is a notebook devoted primarily to recording Emerson's social engagements in London between March 14 and May 7, 1848. Other notations concern his subsequent lecture engagements in New England between November 21, 1848, and March 31, 1849, along with miscellaneous expenditures, computations, and memoranda.

Pocket Diary 3 is written in a commercially published book entitled "The / Gentleman's / Pocket Book / Almanack / 1848. / Penny & Sons London / Price 2/6"; the volume is bound in dark red leather with blind plain filled borders. The covers proper measure 7.5 x 12.2 cm; the front cover extends an additional 9 cm into a tongue which, when the book is closed, fits into a leather holder fastened to the back cover. A paper label pasted to the spine is inscribed "1848." in ink. The pages measure 7.5 x 12 cm. The book includes a frontispiece and title page; 32 pages of useful information (parliamentary acts, postal regulations, railways, office-holders, currency, etc.); 112 unnumbered pages for "Memorandums and Engagements, for 1848." (pages 33–144); an almanac for 1848 (pages 145–157); listings of bankers (pages 158–199), royalty (pages 200–201), peers (pages 202–218), members and officers of the House of Commons (pages 219–233), and other miscellaneous information (pages 234–240). Emerson's notes, some in ink and some in pencil, occur on fcv, i, 34, 44–45, 58, 60, 62, 64–65, 66–67, 68–69, 70, 72, 74, 80, 111, 130, 132, 134, 136, 138–145, and 240–241. Inside the front cover is an expandable pocket containing a scrap of paper of approximately 14.5 x 1.5 cm inscribed in pencil:

   Thro Livingston Wells & Co
   To Maquay Pakenham & Co Florence
   &[?]. Pakenham Hooker & Co. Rome
—evidently agents through whom mail could be addressed to Margaret Fuller, then in Italy (see *L*, III, 446; *CEC*, p. 435).

  Headings and dates within the section for "Memorandums and Engagements" are printed from type. Printed matter of this nature in Pocket Diary 3 has been reproduced here only where it is directly relevant to Emerson's own handwritten entries. The pages designated as "blank" are those without inscription by Emerson; the presence or absence of printed matter is not specified.

446

[front cover verso] [1] Atlantic Bk
31 March [1849]   178
                        61
                       ─────
                       117
                        25
                       ─────
                        92.
                       12.29
                      ─────
                     ⟨8⟩79.7⟨0⟩1

[i]   8)550
                          68⟨2⟩7
                           ─────
                              8
       5 50   ─────
        68   5.4⟨5⟩96
       ─────
       6.18

[ii]–[33] [blank]
[34] Lodige's   Hackney
─────

John Francis
     Leatherseller's Buildings
     London Wall
─────

[35]–[43] [blank]
[44] [2]   pd Kendall   .10
            ticket to Groton   .40
                  to Worc   .80
                  porter   .10
                  dinner   50

[1] The computations on the front cover verso and p. [i], written upside down in pencil, correspond to entries in Emerson's record of accounts for 1849 in Account Book 4. On March 30 he wrote checks on the Atlantic Bank for $61, $25, and $12.29; on March 31 he deposited $25 in the Middlesex Institution for Savings to the accounts of his three children and also paid a balance of $12.29 due on John Brown's "bill of January".

[2] This page is in pencil.

```
              cab                    25
       ticket to Albany            4.25
              coffee                 6
   Expense at Springfd.            2.06
                                  ───────
                                  8.⟨4⟩52
```

[45]³   8.52
             .50 cab at Albany
           ───────
             9.02
             2.50 at Del. House
              12
              50
              12
              12
             4.25
             .50
              80
              40
           ───────
           18 33
              12
              25
           ───────
           18.70

[46]–[57] [blank]
[58]⁴ [MARCH 1848]

T.	14.	Mr Bancroft 7
W.	15.	Mr Procter ⟨Miss⟩Mrs Drummond
TH.	16.	Mr Chapman
F.	17.	Mrs Bancroft at 11
		Miss Swanwick⁵ at 8½
S.	18.	Mr Milman at 10 AM

---

³ This page is in pencil.
⁴ The dates on this and the following pages through p. [138] are printed from type. On p. [58] the engagements are in pencil.
⁵ Probably Anna Swanwick (1813–1899), translator of Aeschylus, Schiller, and Goethe.

[59] [blank]
[60]⁶ Su.   19.   Hampton Court
                        Mr Bancroft's
                        Sir W. Molesworth's

       Th.   23.   Mr Baring at 7.30 ⁷
       F.   24.   Lord Ashburton's 7.15
       S.   25.   Mr Hutton's at 6

[61] [blank]
[62]⁸ [April]
       S.   1.   Lord Northampton at 9 o'clk

[63] [blank]
[64]⁹ M.   3.   Mr Lyell 7 o'clock
       T.   4.   Dr Carpenter 8½   6 Regents Park
                        Terrace.   Gloucester Gate
       W.   5.   Geologic Club. Clunns Hotel; Piazza;
                        Covent Gard[en] 6 o'clock
       Th.   6.   Dr Carpenter 3
                        Mr Crawshay 4
       F.   7.   Mr Enfield¹⁰ Windmill Hill Hamp-
                        stead at 6
                        Mr Tagart   33 Porchester Terrace
                        Bayswater

[65] [...]
[66]¹¹ Su.   9.   Mr Wilkinson   4 to 5 PM

⁶ On this page the engagements are in pencil.
⁷ William Bingham Baring, the eldest son of Lord Ashburton, later 2nd Baron Ashburton. See L, IV, 43, for Emerson's account of the occasion.
⁸ On this page the engagement is in pencil.
⁹ On this page the engagements are in pencil. "6 Regents . . . Gate" and "Hotel; Piazza . . . o'clock" run over onto p. [65].
¹⁰ Crawshay and Enfield, apparently London residents, may be related respectively to George Crawshay of Newcastle upon Tyne and William Enfield of Nottingham, who had previously entertained Emerson.
¹¹ On this page the engagements are in pencil. "42 Chester . . . Park", "Terrace New . . . Baker St", and "beck St . . . Square" run over onto p. [67].

T.   11.   Sir Charles Fellows 11½
                  Carlyle at 7

Tʜ.   13.   Mr Wedgewood at 6½ PM
                      42 Chester Terrace Regents Park
F.   14.   Dr Forbes at 6
S.   15.   Mrs Gillies[12] 20 Allsop Terrace New
                      Road nearest Baker St
                  ⟨Mr Field⟩
                  Miss Sterling   44 Welbeck St Caven-
                      dish Square

[67] […]
[68][13] Sᴜ. 16.   Mr Field
       M.   17.   Mr Morgan at 6
                      ⟨Mr Gaskell   27 Curzon st⟩[14]
       T.   18.   ⟨Mr Foster   58 Lincoln's Inn Fields at
                          5 o'clock⟩
       W.   19.   Mr Gibson 6 o'clock   Breakfast with
                          Mr Forster 31 Westbourne Terrace
                          Hyde Park
       Tʜ.   20.   Mr Teschemacher
                          5 o'clk
       F.   21.   C. K. Patmore 7 o'c 5 Brecknock Cres-
                          cent Camdentown
       S.   22.   Mr Field at 2

[69] […]
[70][15] T.   25.   J Forster Esq 58 Lincolns Inn Fields at
                          5 [16]

---

[12] Eliza Maria Gillies wrote to Emerson on May 1, 1848, alluding to two visits
he had made her and acknowledging his influence on her writing (*L*, IV, 70).

[13] On this page the engagements are in pencil. "Fields at 5 o'clock", "Breakfast
. . . Forster", and "Hyde Park" run over onto p. [69].

[14] The Gaskell entry, as Rusk notes, is "canceled by a faint line"; Mrs. Gaskell
had died shortly after writing Emerson to extend a dinner invitation (*L*, IV, 58).

[15] On this page the engagements are in pencil.

[16] At this dinner Emerson met Charles Dickens; Carlyle was also present (*L*,

W. 26.   Mr Morgan
Th. 27.   Mr Bailey   271 Holborn at 6 o'cl

S.   29.   Mr Knight's [17]

[71] [blank]
[72] [18] Su. 30.   Mr Appleton
     [May]
     Tu. 2.   Antiquarian Society
     W.   3.   Mr Ames & Warren
     Th. 4.   Mr Morgan
     F.   5.   Mr Patmore [19]
     S.   6.   Mr Hutton

[73] [blank]
[74] [20] Su. 7.   Mr Field

[75]–[79] [blank]
[80] [21]   X51
                         4
                       ———
3'50 Atl[antic].   204.
170   Mas[sachusetts]. 16.
            City.   28.
                        33

IV, 66). See Journal London, p. [116] above, and Notebook ED, pp. [221]–[223] below.

[17] Emerson dined "with Miss Martineau at Mr Knight's" (L, IV, 64); Harriet Martineau and Charles Knight were literary collaborators.

[18] On this page the engagements are in pencil.

[19] At this dinner Emerson met Alfred Tennyson; see Journal London, p. [130] above, and Notebook ED, pp. [178], [181] below. Concerning Thomas Gold Appleton and Pelham M. Warren, both of Boston, and Seth Ames of Lowell, all recent arrivals on the *Caledonia*, see Emerson's letter of May 4 and 5, 1848, to his wife (L, IV, 66–67), which also mentions dinner at the Society of Antiquaries and the engagement at Patmore's.

[20] On this page the engagement is in pencil.

[21] This page is in pencil. The calculations begin with dividends anticipated from the Atlantic, Massachusetts, and City Banks.

$$\begin{array}{r} 170 \\ 451 \\ 176 \\ \hline 627 \end{array}$$

[81]–[110] [blank]

[111]²²	5		50 Sent	
	126		40 pd	40
	25		50 bought	25
	10		5 pd R[uth?] E[merson?]	25
	—		8 cash	2 00
	166		—	12
			153	1.50
			8.	2 00
			—	12
			161	25
			1.25	70
			50	40
			1.00	—
			.25	7.99
			—	
			164.00	

[112]–[129] [blank]
[130] [NOVEMBER]

T.	21.	⟨Lowell⟩
W.	22.	⟨Lowell⟩ ↑Lowell↓ Institute

[131] [blank]
[132]

T.	28.	Lowell Institute
W.	29.	⟨Lowell Institute⟩

[133] [blank]
[134]²³ [DECEMBER]

M.	4.	J[ames] F[reeman] C[larke]? ²⁴

---

²² This page is in pencil.

²³ On this page "J F C ?" is in pencil; the first three letters of "Newburyport" are written in pencil and rewritten in ink.

²⁴ Emerson wrote Clarke on November 3, 1848, agreeing to lecture at the Freeman Place Chapel in Boston on either December 4 or December 11 (L, IV, 120–121). He lectured there on "Plato" on December 4.

        W.   6.   Providence
        Th.   7.   Newport[, R.I. "England"] [25]
        F.   8.   Newburyport

[135] [blank]
[136] [26] M.   11.   J F C ?
        T.   12.   Concord
        W.   13.   Lowell

[137] [blank]
[138]   W.   20.   Lowell

        S.   23.   Waltham

[139] [1849]
    April   1 Sun
            2 Mon
            3 Tu
            4 Wed
            5 Th   Fitchburg
            6 Fri   Worc[ester]
            7 Sat
            8 Sun
            9 Mon
           10 Tu   Alcott's
           11 Wed
           12 Th
           13 Fri
           14 Sat
           15 Sun
           16 Mon
           17 Tu
           18 Wed
           19 Th

[25] The titles of this and other lectures following Emerson's return from abroad
are given in William Charvat, *Emerson's American Lecture Engagements: A Chronological List* (New York Public Library, 1961), pp. 23ff.
[26] On this page "J F C ?" is in pencil.

20 Fri
21 Sat
22 Sunday
23 Mon
24 Tues
25 Wed
26 Th
27 Fri
28 Sat
29 Sun
30 Mon

[140]²⁷ [DECEMBER 1848]

| M. | 25. | New Bedford |
| W. | 27. | Boston M[ercantile]. L[ibrary]. Assoc[iation]. ["England"] |

[141] Jan

| 3 [1849] | Boston ["London"] |
| 26 Friday | Albany |

[142] Monday Jan 1

	2	
Wed	3	Boston ["London"]
	4	
	5	
	6	
	7	
	8	
	9	
Wed	10	Concord
	11	Woburn
	12	
	13	
	14	
Mon	15	Boston
	16	W. Newton

²⁷ The dates on this page are printed from type.

Wed	17	Salem ["England and the English"?]
	18	
	19	
	20	
	21	
Mon	22	Boston
	23	Roxbury
Wed	24	
Thurs	25	
Fri.	26	Albany
	27	
	28	
	29	Boston
	30	
	31	⟨Concord N H⟩ ↑Portland Me↓

[143] [28]	Thurs Feb	1	Chelmsford
		2	⟨Worcester⟩
		3	
		4	
	Mon	5	Boston
		6	Charlestown
	Wed	7	Concord ["London"]
		8	Chelmsford
		9	⟨Worcester⟩
		10	
		11	
		12	Boston
		13	⟨Taunton⟩ W Newton
	Wed	14	Gloucester
		15	Chelmsford
		16	Worcester
		17	
	Sund	18	
		19	Charlestown

[28] On this page the following cancellations are in pencil: "Worcester" (Feb. 2), "Worcester" (Feb. 9), and "Taunton" (Feb. 13).

	20	Framingham ["England"]
Wed	21	Worc
Thurs	22	Northampton
Fri	23	Cabotville
	24	
	25	
	26	⟨Charlest⟩Providence
	27	Framingham ["London"]
Wed	28	E. Lexington

[144] ²⁹ Mar.

1	Thurs Chelmsford
2	Fri Worcester
3	Sat
4	Sun
5	M
6	Tu Manchester
7	Wed Cambridge ["England"]
8	Th Chelmsford
9	Fri Worcester
10	Sat
11	Sun
12	Mon
13	Tu Social Circle
14	Wed ⟨Manchester⟩
15	Th Chelmsford
16	Fri Wor
17	Sat
18	Sun
19	Mon
20	Tu Alcott ⟨Woonsocket⟩
21	Wed ⟨Wor⟩ Cambridge
22	Th ⟨Andover⟩ ↑Milton↓
23	Fri Worcester
24	Sat
25	Sun
26	Mon ⟨Westford⟩ Milton

²⁹ On this page "Manchester" is in ink over pencil.

27	Tu
28	Wed Portland
29	Th Westford
30	Fri Worcester
31	Sat 5 A M Fitchburg[30]

[145]

Apr.	1	Sun
	2	Mon
	3	Tues
	4	Wed
	5	Thurs
	6	Fri

[146]–[239] [blank]
[240][31] Atl[antic]. B[ank]

$$82$$
$$10$$
$$\overline{}$$
$$72 + 75 = 147$$

[241] Monday, Wed, Fri,
[On the] Science of those proportions by which the human head & countenance as represented in [Works of] ancient Greek art are distinguished from those of ordinary nature   By D[avid]. R[amsay]. Hay. [(Edinburgh, 1849).] Royal 4to. 25 plates

[30] The figures for "14" through "31" have been written over; for "18" through "31", Emerson has added a second column of dates to the left, for clarity (omitted here).
[31] Pp. [240] and [241] are in pencil.

457

Xenien

1848, 1852

The title of Notebook Xenien is supplied by the editors from Emerson's notation on its inside front cover: "I have copied some sentences from this little book in *NO* under the title of *Xenien*"; the word appears not in the text of Journal NO, which he began in February, 1855, but in index references to four of its pages ([142]–[145]) where material from the notebook is transcribed. Although a few of the entries in Xenien refer to earlier years (1834, 1839, 1840), much of the material concerns Emerson's European trip of 1847–1848, when he carried the notebook for recording memoranda. There are also references to later events, such as the death of Margaret Fuller Ossoli in 1850, and notes for Emerson's "Address to Kossuth at Concord, May 11, 1852."

Notebook Xenien is written in a homemade pocket notebook with stiff red-orange paper covers that lack inscription. Both covers and leaves are roughly rectangular in shape, the edges measuring from 7.8 to 8.1 cm along the horizontal axis and from 10 to 10.5 cm along the vertical axis. The notebook was originally sewn together through three irregularly spaced holes; now only a segment of heavy thread remains, running through one leaf and the stub of another. The covers are heavily worn, and a number of the pages written in pencil are smudged. The 34 leaves are cut from heavy laid watermarked gray paper, unruled, with chain lines running vertically, separated by intervals of 2.5 cm. There are 68 unnumbered pages, for which pagination has been supplied. Inscription is preponderantly in pencil. Except for small stubs, the leaves bearing pages 1–2 and 15–16 have been torn out; some inscription is visible on the fragment of page 1 but not on pages 2, 15, and 16. Pages 7, 10, 19, 21–22, 27–32, and 34–55 are blank. One edge of page 32, otherwise blank, has been cut through a calligraphic border inscribed in ink. The inside front cover is inscribed in both ink and pencil; the inside back cover is blank. Page 33 is written upside down in relation to its immediate context, and there are two later sequences of inscription from back to front, on pages 68–67 and pages 65–56.

[front cover] [blank]
[front cover verso] *Books*
    Thorpe
Hope Architecture
Curzon's Travels in Levant [1]
↑Layard *Vol* 2 70 188↓ [2]

I have copied some sentences from this little book in *NO* under the
title of *Xenien.* [3]

[1] [4]

        ||msm|| it was observable
        ||msm|| to the whole
        ||msm|| red

[2] [blank?]
    [3] D[uke]. of B[uckingham]. when the dog bit him, wished him
a young wife & an estate in the country. King of Naples said of his
troops, No matter how you dressed them, they would all run away. [5]

[1] (1) Benjamin Thorpe, *Northern Mythology, Comprising the Principal Popular
Traditions and Superstitions of Scandinavia, North Germany, and the Netherlands,*
3 vols. (London, 1851–1852); vols. II and III are in Emerson's library. (2)
Thomas Hope, *An Historical Essay on Architecture,* 2 vols. (London, 1835). (3)
Robert Curzon, *Visits to Monasteries of the Levant* (London, 1851), which Emerson
borrowed from the Boston Athenaeum September 11–October 7, 1852. See the list
of books in *JMN,* VIII, 551, 552.
  [2] The insertion is in pencil. Emerson's reference is to Austen Henry Layard,
*Nineveh and Its Remains: with an Account of a Visit to the Chaldæan Christians of
Kurdistan, and the Yezidis, or Devil-Worshippers; and an Inquiry into the Manners
and Arts of the Ancient Assyrians,* 2 vols. (London and New York, 1849). In II, 70,
Layard describes an exhibition of Arabian horsemanship that involved no little
personal danger to himself; II, 188, deals with the language and race of the ancient
Assyrians and of the Chaldaeans of Kurdistan, whom Layard considered their modern
descendants.
  [3] Edward Emerson observes in a note to "Goethe," *W,* IV, 288, that the term
"was used by Goethe and Schiller to denote epigrams."
  [4] The leaf bearing pp. [1] and [2] has been partly torn out, leaving a stub
varying from 1.1 to 3 cm in length. There is writing, in pencil, on the fragment of
p. [1] only.
  [5] "D. of B. . . . away.", struck through in pencil with a vertical use mark, is
transcribed in Journal London, p. [173] above; see also Journal LM, p. [148]
above.

Mr Kenyon's opinion about gem-like character of stained glass windows at St George's Chapel, Windsor: Lady Morgan would have carpets spread & tread the jewels in.[6]

5.	32.5
32.50	15.
14.20	20.
2.50	——
2.25	67
25	
1.60	

[4] The French have this wonderful street courage. The least dislike[,] the smallest unpopularity is intolerable to them, but they will take your fire with indifference. And is this a world to hide virtues in? [n] There must be revolutions to bring them out[.][7]

   [5] O at the opera in wait for L. for dissection. E. was asked to write the notice of C. in the Times.

Turner resembles the portraits of Punch[.]

——

At Stonehenge 'twas impossible to forget Turner[.]

——

Owen's Marsupial Carnivora [8]

[6] 94 stones now at S[tonehenge.]
160 might compose the temple within a circle of 3 miles diameter,
160 barrows —
Saw one Druid's barrow[.]
astron[omical]. stone [9]

   [6] "Mr Kenyon's . . . jewels in.", in pencil and struck through in pencil with a vertical use mark, is transcribed in Journal London, p. [170] above; see also Notebook ED, p. [135] below. The figures which follow are written vertically along the bottom margin of p. [3].
   [7] On French street courage, see Journal GH, p. [69] above. "The French . . . out", in pencil and struck through in pencil with a vertical use mark, is transcribed in Journal London, p. [166] above.
   [8] "Turner resembles . . . Carnivora" is in pencil. With "Turner . . . Punch",

[7] [blank]

[8]   Certain things

The present race are wanted for 50 years — the idealist for always. You are to stand for the last[.]

There is never a fine aspiration but was on its way to ⟨an institu⟩ ↑its body↓ or institution[.] ¹⁰

[9] Look up Kant on History[.]

To deal with your intellections as hardly & vigorously as carpenter with his chisel & board & set him aside ¹¹

[10] [blank]

[11] A man bears beliefs as a tree bears apples[.] ¹²

[12] Apple country most ornamental heaps ¹³

[13] In Maine they spill the liquor. It is not property. But it is but one step to say to the man You are a barrel of poison & cannot be allowed to infect the state with your virus. You shall ⟨|| ... ||⟩ Go into the street. ⟨|| ·.. ||⟩

School ⟨gets into⟩ ↑taps↓ the pocket[.] ¹⁴

---

cf. Journal LM, p. [98] above; Notebook ED, p. [130] below; "Character," W, V, 135.

⁹ "94 stones . . . stone", in pencil, is used in "Stonehenge," W, V, 277.

¹⁰ "The present . . . institution", in smudged or partly erased pencil and struck through in pencil with a vertical use mark, is transcribed in Journal NO, p. [143] (to be published in a later volume).

¹¹ "Look up . . . aside", in smudged or partly erased pencil, is transcribed in Journal NO, p. [143]; "To deal . . . aside" is struck through in pencil with a diagonal use mark.

¹² This sentence, in smudged or partly erased pencil and struck through in pencil with a vertical use mark, is transcribed in Journal NO, p. [143].

¹³ "Apple . . . heaps", in smudged or partly erased pencil, is struck through in pencil with a diagonal use mark.

¹⁴ "In Maine . . . pocket", in smudged or partly erased pencil, is struck through in pencil with a diagonal use mark.

[14] Margaret was heroic, humane, courteous, made society where she came. She had lived in civility & that element is lost in her to our city[.] [15]

[15]–[16] ||msm|| [16]

[17] Beauty [has] rightful privilege[:] may do what none else can, & it shall be blameless. Indeed all privilege is that of Beauty; 1. of face, 2. of form, 3. of manner, 4. of brain or Method.

Of the[?] Despair [17]

[18] I believe in society, in grace, courtesy[.] [18]

[19] [blank]
     [20] The sun burning his beams so flamboyant
idealism
Circumst[ance] of circumst is timing & placing. Wretch would be Pericles in Olympus. Europe of Europe comes out here. Atlantic seive
Yesterday is the professor[.] [19]

[21]–[22] [blank]
[23] [20] Hour follows hour & eternity eternity without doubt for the believer[.] [21]

---

[15] "Margaret . . . city" is in pencil. If the reference is to Margaret Fuller Ossoli, the entry must have been written after Emerson received news of the shipwreck off Fire Island, July 19, 1850, which took her life and the lives of her husband and infant son.
     [16] Part of this leaf has been torn out, leaving a blank stub of between 1.6 and 2.1 cm in length.
     [17] "Beauty . . . Despair" is in smudged or partly erased pencil. "Beauty . . . Method", struck through in pencil with a vertical use mark, is transcribed in Journal NO, p. [143].
     [18] "I . . . courtesy", in pencil, is struck through in pencil with a vertical use mark.
     [19] "The sun . . . professor" is in pencil. "The sun . . . here" is struck through in pencil with a vertical use mark. "Circumst . . . seive" is transcribed, with some alteration, in Journal NO, p. [143].
     [20] This page is in pencil.
     [21] This sentence is transcribed in Journal NO, p. [142].

The great fortune is a controlling call like chemistry. But [does] not suffice[;] must have adaptation also or else sufficiency Napoleonic[.]

——

Manners the growth of broad lands alike in London & Canton[.] [22]

[24] [23] in a bad fix
chaotic age
pot belly
ticket paying
phrenology
Life expensive but probably was always[,] only we forget the shillings as we do the vermin[.] [24]

——

the black drop

——

[25] [25] Age
Nature phil.

⟨a⟩ fought in the air [26]

——

culture of calamity

——

Culture
        the few great points

——

There is in crustacea a thick skull [—] to be beleived charity & protection [—] & out of meanness the preparation [26] [27] of magnificence[.]

——

[22] "The great . . . Canton" is transcribed, with some alteration — e.g., "New York" for "Canton" — in Journal NO, p. [144].
[23] This page is in pencil; "pot belly" and "phrenology" are struck through in pencil with vertical use marks.
[24] "Life . . . vermin" is transcribed in Journal NO, p. [142].
[25] This page is in pencil.
[26] "Age . . . air" is struck through in pencil with a vertical use mark. Cf. "Wealth," W, V, 161, and "Works and Days," W, VII, 163: "the next war will be fought in the air."
[27] This page is in pencil.

Naturalist can carry us no farther than the vesicle which has the capacity of change into oak, ape, man, & god.[28]

———

[27]–[32] [blank]
[33] [29] Mrs Crowe's House
Miss Cushman
Tavistock Hotel[?]
Tavistock Square

[34]–[55] [blank]
[56]–[65] [30] [...]
[66] Kennett's History of England 25 s.

———

Lowth, Life of Wm of Wykeham

———

Camden's Brittannia translated by Holland 7 or 8 s.

———

Britton's Beauties of Eng[lan]d. Wales

———

Hainault — Abrégé Chronologique de l'histoire de France

———

Bede. — Bohn. 4 s.

———

Collins' Peerage 1745 ↑or any time before Egerton Brydges↓
———   12/6 [31]

[28] The entries on pp. [25] and [26] may be Emerson's notes on one of Richard Owen's lectures: see Journal London, p. 257 above and n. 215. "There is . . . magnificence" and "Naturalist . . . god." are struck through in pencil on pp. [25] and [26] with discontinuous vertical use marks.

[29] This page is in smudged or partly erased pencil, upside down in relation to the previous entries. The first notation may be associated with Emerson's dinner at Mrs. Crowe's in Edinburgh on February 13, 1848 (L, IV, 19; Journal London, pp. [31]–[32] above). He had previously called on Charlotte Cushman in Manchester (L, IV, 5).

[30] The entries on pp. [56]–[65] and [67]–[68], in pencil and written from back to front, are printed in sequence following p. [66] below.

[31] These seven items, written here in pencil, are transcribed as "Carlyle's List" in Journal London, p. 283 above; see n. 304 to that passage for the full titles. The same list also appears in Notebook ED, p. [110] below, and Notebook Books Small

[68] ⟨Nothing⟩
No part of the population interests except the children & the young women[.]
unspoilable

———

God the pivotal centre

———

Necessity & Selfishness the two traps which young sophomores learn to play

———

Paris efflorescence of France [32]

[67]   Series & Degree
Hybernation is long sleep[;] sleep is short hybernation[.]

———

Metamorphosis is intelligible only on this doctrine that world repeats ⟨w⟩World.

In swimming world, it swims; in creeping world it creeps; in flying world, it flies. Come up to higher plane still, act passes into thought & flies with finer wing[.] [33]

[65] natura simillima sibi [34]

[64] What said Ole Bull?
Who is Mrs Ellet?

↑22↓ October 1840 ⟨22⟩
    and *a Day in Groton*

———

[Sequence II], *JMN*, VIII, 564. (In *JMN*, VIII, 564, n. 80, the cross-reference to Notebook Xenien should read "p. [66].")

[32] See Journal London, p. [137] above.

[33] "Hybernation is . . . wing" appears to be occasioned by one or more lectures by Richard Owen that Emerson heard at the Royal College of Surgeons in London. For similar phrasing concerning "hybernation", see Journal London, p. [119] above, and Notebook ED, p. [123] below.

[34] "A character very like his own" (Ed.).

465

1839 July 11 Jamaica P[lains]
1849 8 March Rome
    What sacrifices[35]

[63] ⟨S. G. W[ard] Oct 1834⟩[36]

Our sympathy is more valuable that it is antagonistic. It has been argued & its basis explored[;] it will last & will draw all to itself[.]
Opposition is our belt & tonic. ⟨o⟩No opinion will pass but must stand the tug of war.[37]

[62] We do not thank you but we see you as the angel of freedom crossing sea & land, crossing parties, nationalities, & conceits, the servant of a truth which you worthily teach[,] [61] dividing populations & taking to your share only the good[.]
a kind of kardiometer

Everything excellent is in minorities[.] [38]

[60] The people of this town wish to signify their regard & faith. They do not believe in cheers & huzzas but they think that the graves of our heroes around us throb to a step that sounds like their own[:]

---

[35] Some or all of the entries on p. [64] appear to involve Margaret Fuller. In a letter of June 3, 1844, Emerson told her of hearing Ole Bull (1810–1880), the Norwegian violinist (L, III, 252). In 1845–1846 Mrs. Elizabeth Fries Lummis Ellet (1818–1877), a prolific minor writer of New York, engaged in scandalmongering concerning Edgar Allan Poe and Mrs. Frances Locke Osgood; Anne C. Lynch and Margaret Fuller called on Poe to request return of Mrs. Osgood's letters. Mrs. Ellet published "Female Poets of America" in the *North American Review*, LXVIII (April 1849), 413–436. During September and October of 1840 Emerson and Miss Fuller had exchanged a series of letters on their friendship; October 22, 1840, may be the date of one of her "frank & noble & affecting" letters (L, II, 352).
[36] "S. G. W" is set off by rectangular lines, below and to the right. There may have been still earlier pencil writing underlying the "S."
[37] "Our sympathy . . . war.", struck through in pencil with a vertical use mark, is used in "Address to Kossuth," *W*, XI, 398; "Opposition . . . war." is transcribed in Journal NO, p. [145].
[38] "We do not . . . kardiometer" is struck through in pencil with vertical use marks on pp. [62] and [61]; "We do not . . . minorities" is used in "Address to Kossuth," *W*, XI, 399.

The mighty tread
brings from the dust the sound of liberty [39]

[59] They wish [to] pay homage to courage & to perseverance[,] to a man whose steps have no choice but are planted[.]

[58] We know the austere law of liberty, that it must be reconquered day by day, that it subsists in a state of war, that it is always slipping away from those who boast it & to those who fight for it[.]

[57] You have achieved the right to interpret Washington. It is not those who live basely in the city called by his name but those who think like him all over the world that can understand him[.] [40]

[56] Few men know where they are going[.]

Property always sympathizes with possession[.] [41]

[inside back cover] [blank]

[39] Cf. John Wilson (Christopher North), "On Reading Mr. Clarkson's History of the Abolition of the Slave Trade," ll. 48–49; see *JMN*, IV, 46–47. "The people . . . liberty", struck through in pencil with a vertical use mark, is used in "Address to Kossuth," *W*, XI, 397–398.

[40] "They wish . . . understand him", struck through in pencil with single vertical use marks on pp. [59]–[57], is used in "Address to Kossuth," *W*, XI, 397, 399, 400; "They wish . . . fight for it" is transcribed in Journal NO, p. [145].

[41] This sentence is used in "Address to Kossuth," *W*, XI, 400.

Platoniana

1845–1848

Platoniana, though physically not a notebook, is so designated for convenience of reference (like The Universe in *JMN*, I) in accordance with the policy of the edition. It comprises a loose set of related notes concerning Plato and his writings that Emerson assembled in the folder bearing the title "Platoniana". On the basis of internal evidence these notes can be dated circa 1845–1848. Much of the material corresponds closely to passages in Journals W and Y (1845; see *JMN*, IX) written when Emerson was composing his lecture on Plato. Other entries, however, date from 1847 and 1848: there is an extract from Plato's *Gorgias* that appears also in Journal CD (1847); another passage in Platoniana is common to both Journal W (1845) and Notebook JK (assembled in 1847); a linking of Plato with Goethe is made both in Platoniana and in Journal LM (1848); and there are quotations from three books about Plato, those by Sewell, Schleiermacher, and Ast, that Emerson borrowed on November 8, 1848, probably while at work revising the lecture on Plato in anticipation of *Representative Men* (1850).

Notebook Platoniana is a collection of loose and unpaged leaves of various sizes and stocks, some of them folded, that are assembled within a larger sheet of white paper which has been folded once to make a cover measuring 19 x 24.5 cm, worn along the bottom edges; the front of the cover is inscribed "Platoniana" in ink. Exclusive of the cover there are 44 pages, for which pagination has been supplied, comprised of six types of paper, here designated A through F in the order of their first occurrence as the manuscript now stands:

  A. Unruled white paper folded once to make four pages, each approximately 19.2 x 24.8 cm (pages 1–4, 7–10);

  B. Unruled white laid paper, unfolded, 12.7 x 20.2 cm, with chain lines running horizontally at intervals of 3.1 cm (pages 5–6);

  C. Unruled blue paper, unfolded, 20.2 x 25 cm, embossed in the upper left corner with an oval design in which "CRANE" is centered (pages 11–12, 23–34, 37–38, 41–42);

  D. Unruled blue-green paper folded once to make four pages, each approximately 20 x 25.2 cm (pages 13–22, 39–40);

  E. Unruled cream paper, unfolded, 20.2 x 26 cm, torn along the right margin (pages 35–36);

F. Faintly ruled white paper, unfolded, 19.4 x 24.7 cm, torn along the left margin and embossed with a circular design in the upper left corner (pages 43–44).

The front cover and 36 of the pages are inscribed in ink, with page 38 carrying only the word "Platoniana" written upside down in relation to the matter on preceding pages; there is additional writing in pencil on pages 16 and 27; pages 6, 8, 10, 24, 32, 34, 36, and 44 are blank. Page 30, which carries the number "83" in the upper right corner, was evidently part of another manuscript at some time.

Also laid in the folder are (1) a picture-card, 8.6 x 12.6 cm, advertising English Parian busts of Wendell Phillips, Charles Sumner, Robert Collyer, and John A. Andrew, for sale by Jones, McDuffee, & Stratton of Boston; and (2) a blank check on the New England Trust Co. of Boston for "Dividend No. 38, of Pullman's Palace Car Co., of Chicago, Ill., payable February 15th, 1877." The entire folder is in turn laid into Emerson's Index II, dated "Sept. 1847".

[front cover]

———

Platoniana

———

[front cover verso] [blank]
[1] *Plato*[1]   Sewell

"By common consent, the series of the dialogues must open with the *Phaedrus*."

"Internally, this contains the germ of all the others."

"From this, all the other dialogues run out through a series of skeptical unconclusive[n] disputations to four great works of an entirely different character, — grave, massive, dogmatic, & final, — the *Republic*, the *Laws*, the *Timaeus*, & the unfinished fragment of the *Critias*."

"These four form one grand group openly connected together."

p 36[2]

[2] One of the chief intellectual faculties which Plato, like other ancient philosophers, proposed to exercise & develop, was ⟨the⟩ Memory. μνημονικὴν αὐτὴν ζητωμεν δεὶν εἶναι

---

[1] "*Plato*" is followed by a vertical line, in ink.
[2] All four sentences are quoted, somewhat inaccurately, from a single paragraph in William Sewell, *An Introduction to the Dialogues of Plato* (London, 1841). Emerson borrowed this book from the Harvard College Library on November 8, 1848.

[See *Clouds*, 465 & passim   Repub. lib. VI.]

Sewell p 215 [3]

[3]   Schlei[e]rmacher p 77 [4]

The *Lysis*. What in the Phaedrus is bro't forward in the mythical form, that, love has its source in the identity of the ideal between two persons, — is here proved dialectically. —

The manner in which the doubts raised against the earlier position, that resemblance is the source of friendship, are applied to this also, — is to be looked upon as the key to the whole —

Like is only then unprofitable to Like, ⟨when⟩ when a man confines himself to his own external personality & to an interest in his own sensuous being

[4] *Schleiermacher*   *Republic*

In *Symposium*
"he whom Socrates once gets into conversation must hold out the whole night, & even to the morning dawn, tho' others have all made off or surrendered themselves to sleep; & that he is as little wearied by repeating his own or other persons' arguments, as of investigating & developing the truth from the first in common with others." — [5]

as little wearied as a broker in making money.   /U/ [6]

[5] *Powers*
    Imagination

[3] Sewell, *An Introduction to the Dialogues of Plato*, 1841. Emerson has bracketed Sewell's footnote, translating the title *Nubes* as "Clouds". In *JMN*, IX, 281, noting Plato's esteem for memory, he cites a comparable passage from *Phaedrus* in *Oeuvres de Platon, traduites par Victor Cousin*, 13 vols. (Paris, 1822–1840), VI, 122.

[4] The three sentences which follow are quoted, inaccurately, from Friedrich Schleiermacher, *Introductions to the Dialogues of Plato*, trans. William Dobson (Cambridge and London, 1836), which Emerson borrowed from the Harvard College Library on November 8, 1848.

[5] Schleiermacher, *Introductions to the Dialogues of Plato*, 1836, p. 350. "In *Symposium* . . . others.' — " is struck through in ink with a wavy vertical use mark.

[6] Emerson's intended reference is obscure; the phrasing given does not appear in Journal U or the other journals of the mid-1840's, V, W, Y, and O.

Memory
Understanding
Sense
These are the gods[.] [7]

As these rule so is the color of the day[.]
They rank themselves one to reign & one to serve[.]
And life consists in the disclosing of essence or character[.]
Thoughts create things & the laws of thought interest[.]
Pace[.] [8]

[6] [blank]
[7] "A statue stands firm on its base; a virtuous man on firm resolutions"; said Socrates. And I esteem ↑it↓ the distinction of good men
that they are obligable.

It is the badge & indispensable condition of ⟨my⟩ the members of my
Round Table that they are of that excellent clay that their word
binds them. "Good men," said Socrates, "must let the world see that
their manners are more firm than an oath."

[8] [blank]
[9] Morals

You are you & I am I.

[10] [blank]
[11] *Plato*
    Socrates
never forgetful of the cardinal virtue of a teacher to protect the pupil
from his own influence.

———

"For I well know that if ever any one discoursing with another wished to
know that about which he discoursed this is my case." Soc. in Gorgias [9]

———

[7] On "the powers of the mind", see also pp. [23] and [43] below.
[8] "In peace" (Ed.).
[9] Taylor, *The Works of Plato* . . . , 1804, IV, 360.

mares, soup pans, shoemaker, sycamore, spoon, cock, & quail [10]

———

Landor thinks he should have known that a kitten would become a cat. (when marrying)

———

Humour of the Hippias   T.P. Vol III p 419 [11]

———

Xantippe said the state suffered a thousand miseries & every thing was changed [—] everything except Socrates who always wore the same look coming in & going out of the house. Ælian [*Variae Historiae,* IX.vii]

[12] For I know how to pr⟨es⟩ocure one witness of what I say, namely, him with whom I discourse but I bid farewell to the multitude [*Gorgias,*] Taylor Vol 4 p ⟨366 or 364⟩386 [12]

Definition of a Philistine in Theaetetus [13]

———

⟨leads⟩ is led by a scroll of paper as beasts by dry leaves   RS 125

————————

↑Soc↓ "Like those who make a hungry animal follow them, by holding up to him a green bough or some fruit, so you, whilst you hold in your hand that roll of paper, could draw me without difficulty to the end of Attica, & farther, if you would." [14]

[13] Plato
    In First Alcibiades [15]
    Socrates. Come then. By what means might it be found what is the

---

[10] "mares . . . quail", struck through in ink with two vertical use marks, is used in "Plato; or, the Philosopher," *W,* IV, 72. Cf. *JMN,* IX, 328.

[11] Taylor, *The Works of Plato . . . ,* 1804. Taylor's note 2, p. 419, calls particular attention to the humor of the *Hippias.*

[12] Taylor, *The Works of Plato . . . ,* 1804. See Journal CD, p. [59] above.

[13] Emerson quotes the passage on p. [15] below.

[14] *Phaedrus,* in Cousin, *Oeuvres de Platon,* 1822–1840, VI, 11. This same passage is also quoted in Journal RS (to be published in a later volume), p. [125], as Emerson notes above.

[15] The extracts from this dialogue which follow are taken from Taylor, *The Works of Plato . . . ,* 1804.

very self of every thing? for so we might perhaps find what we ourselves are. [I, 81]

Soc. If the eye would see itself, it must look in an eye,[16] & in that place of
the eye too where the virtue of the eye is naturally seated, & the
virtue of the eye is sight. ———— And the soul, if she would know
herself, must look at soul, & especially at that place in the soul, in
which wisdom the virtue of the soul is ingenerated, & also at whatever
else this virtue of the soul resembles.

Do we know of any place in the soul more divine than that which is
the seat of knowledge & intelligence? [I, 89–90, abridged]

[14] *Soc.* Do you know by what means you are to escape[?]
Alc. Through you.
Soc. You ought to say; *If God pleases.* [I, 95]

———

Soc. I wish you may persevere. But I am terribly afraid for you not that I
in the least distrust the goodness of your disposition; but perceiving
the torrent of the times, I fear you may be borne away with it in
spite of your own resistance & ⟨m⟩of my endeavors in your aid. [I, 96]

[15] Republic
"He is a fool who deems anything ridiculous but what is bad
X X or who attempts to be serious in any other pursuit but that of the
good." [17]

[Wheeler is earnest but for peat meadow[.] [18]

For the *Daemon of Socrates*, & the life of a philosopher, see
Republic Book VI
    Taylor [*The Works of Plato* . . . , 1804,] vol 1 p 333

"A boy is the most difficult to manage of all wild beasts" [19]   *Laws*
    [Taylor, *The Works of Plato* . . . , 1804, II,] p 203

---

[16] "The eye," Emerson had written in April of 1842, "cannot see itself"; see
JMN, VIII, 220.
    [17] *Republic*, Book V, in Taylor, *The Works of Plato* . . . , 1804, I, 291–292,
slightly misquoted.
    [18] Presumably Ephraim Wheeler of Concord, as in Journal LM, p. [155] above.
    [19] This sentence, struck through in ink with a vertical use mark, is used in
"Culture," *W*, VI, 139. See also Journal RS, p. [12], and Journal TU, p. [91];
both journals will be published in a later volume.

Plato's definition of Philistine in Theaetetus

Soc. Looking round, therefore, now see that no profane person hears us. But those are profane who think there is nothing else than that which they are able to grasp with their hands; but do not admit that actions & generation & every thing which is invisible, are to be considered as belonging to a part of essence.[20]

[16] As the Giant was cut up every night in Valhalla to be whole again for combat next morning so Plato remains inevitably wise & good though all that is objected to him is true[.] [21]

"We know all things as in a dream, & are again ignorant of them according to vigilant perception." In Sophista [22]

In Timaeus he describes the world's soul as blended of two principles, one the principle of the same; the other the principle of difference.[23]

[17] Plato
        Republic

Swedenborg's law of series appears (Cousin IX p 226) e.g. bad state made up of bad men: soliform eyes: [24]

Books are worth reading that settle a principle as lectures are: All

---

[20] Taylor, *The Works of Plato* . . . , 1804, IV, 24; see p. [12] above.

[21] "As the . . . true" is in pencil.

[22] Taylor, "General Introduction . . . ," *The Works of Plato* . . . , 1804, I, lxvii; see *JMN*, IX, 213.

[23] See Taylor, *The Works of Plato* . . . , 1804, I, 515ff; *The Cratylus* . . . , trans. Thomas Taylor, 1793, pp. 463ff.

[24] Cousin, *Oeuvres de Platon*, 1822–1840; Emerson is citing a passage in Book IV of the *Republic*. The same phrasing also occurs in *JMN*, IX, 215; cf. *JMN*, IX, 214: "Swedenborg's law of series appears p 226 — The characters & manners of a state are in each of the individuals who compose it." The phrase "soliform eyes" is used in "Plato; New Readings," *W*, IV, 83; a note to the passage attributes the adjective "soliform" to Cudworth (*W*, IV, 320).

others are tickings of clocks & we have so much less to live, the robbers! [25]

Objections made to Repub[lic] are shallow. He keeps a cob[b]ler a cobbler: but that is only illustration to show that each action & passion ↑should↓ keep ⁿ its orbit. There is no cobbler to the *Civitas Dei*, which alone he would build.
Caution for the sake of emphasis with which he broaches his doctrine that kings should be philosophers.[26]

Alfieri's plant [—] man; bad: T.P. i. p 328 [27]

Beauties of the majority Vol X p 22 [28]
S[amuel] H[oar']s & Judge A[llen']s jury & Judge S[tory]'s [29]

———

The fine laid on the just ↑refusing↓ to govern is the punishment of being governed by base persons[.] [30]

[18] B[ook]. III[:] he declares his Guardians shall not handle gold or silver but shall be instructed that there is gold & silver in their souls which will make men willing at all times to give them without money that they want.
A coinage not corruptible for here with this organic gold we can buy

---

[25] "Books . . . robbers!", struck through in ink with two diagonal use marks, also appears in Journal W (1845): see *JMN*, IX, 214.

[26] For "Objections . . . philosophers.", see *JMN*, IX, 214.

[27] Emerson was reading *The Autobiography of Vittorio Alfieri* in January of 1847: see *JMN*, IX, 464–465. On "Alfieri's plant [—] man", see *Lectures*, I, 242, and *JMN*, IX, 215. Emerson's page reference to Taylor, *The Works of Plato . . .* , 1804, concerns a passage in *Republic*, Book VI: "And shall we not, Adimantus, said I, in the same manner, say that souls naturally the best, when they meet with bad education, become remarkably depraved?"

[28] Cousin, *Oeuvres de Platon*, 1822–1840; see *JMN*, IX, 216.

[29] See *JMN*, VIII, 360 and 445, on the subject of jury trials: Judge Charles Allen told Emerson at Concord that "9 out of 10" trials are "right"; Samuel Hoar said "5 out of 6". Cf. *JMN*, IX, 216; in Journal RS, p. [5], to be published in a later volume, is another version of the note on juries, dated October, 1848.

[30] *Republic*, Book I, in Taylor, *The Works of Plato . . .* , 1804, I, 125. This sentence is struck through in ink with a diagonal use mark. See *JMN*, IX, 184, 266; "Plato; New Readings," *W*, IV, 84; "Eloquence," *W*, VII, 62.

bread & garments & tools but cannot make an ill use of it to buy comfits & brandy.[31]

B[ook] VIII at the end. Of Women   See W 21 [32]

"The whole of life Socrates, (said Glauco) is with the wise the measure of hearing such discourses as these" (no counting of the clock is here)
　　[*Republic*, Book V,] T[aylor]. [The Works of] P[lato]. [. . .
　　　　　　　　　　　　　1804,] vol I, p 289 [misquoted]

"There is not never was and never will be a moral education which can avail against that of which the People disposes. I mean my friend a human education, & of course except, according to the proverb, that which is divine. ⟨But⟩ Be assured that if in such gov[ernmen]ts. there be found any soul which escapes the common shipwreck & is what it ought to be it is a divine protection which has saved it." [33]
　　[*Republic*, Book VI,] Cousin [*Oeuvres de Platon*, 1822–1840,]
　　　　　　　　　　　　　　　　　Vol X p[p.] 20[–21]

[19] Plato.
In all America there is not leisure to read The Republic & The Laws, Timaeus, & Theaetetus[.]

　　Plato & Swedenborg ↑i.e. a superior mind↓ anticipate by implication all the later discoveries e.g.[:]

"The heart which is ↑both↓ the fountain of the veins & of the blood which is vehemently impelled thro' all the members of the body in a circular progression."　　　　　　　　　　　　　　　Timaeus
　　Taylor [The Works of Plato . . . , 1804,] Vol II p 545

Necessity of Deity rushing into distribution　V 59

---

[31] See *JMN*, IX, 184. The first sentence, from *Republic*, Book III, in Taylor, *The Works of Plato* . . . , 1804, I, 258, is used in "Plato; New Readings," *W*, IV, 84.
　　[32] In Journal W, *JMN*, IX, 190, Emerson quotes the passage from *Republic*, Book VII, and another passage on women from *The Laws*, Book VI, taken from Taylor, *The Works of Plato* . . . , 1804, I, 385, II, 174.
　　[33] " 'The whole . . . saved it." is struck through in ink with a diagonal use mark. " 'The whole . . . these' " is used in "Plato; or, the Philosopher," *W*, IV, 64, and "Works and Days," *W*, VII, 179.

Nature will outwit the wisest writer   V 108 [34]

———

Swedenborg's law of series appears, *Cousin:* [*Oeuvres de Platon,*
1822–1840,] *Vol* IX p 226 [35]

———

In his 7th letter, To the friends of Dion[,] Plato declares that
he has never written & will never write the things which belong to
his most serious meditations.[36]

[20] Body cannot teach wisdom, in Phedo[:] i.e. after all our
accumulation of facts, just as poor in thought. Z 3 [37]

Boston or Unitarian immortality compared with the Platonic, Scaldic,
Indian

"For we should dare to affirm the truth especially when speaking concerning the truth." [38]
    Phaedrus T[aylor]. [The Works of] P[lato]. [. . . , 1804,] III
                                                           p 323

Every discourse should resemble an organized animal[.]
    [*Phaedrus,*] Taylor's [The Works of] P[lato]. [. . . , 1804,]
                                                    Vol III p 352

Protagoras. Socrates' just objection to being ridden by poetic quotation   Cousin Vol III p 93 [39]   just as we to Scriptures

sensible people put away such childishness as conversing through the
wisdom of flutes — & use their own[.]
Also the criticism on the speech of Pittacus[:] It is difficult to continue to be good [*Ibid.,* III, 84ff,] [21] equivalent to Wordsworth's

[34] For Journal V, p. [59], see *JMN,* IX, 123; the passage quoted is transcribed
on p. [25] below. For Journal V, p. [108], see *JMN,* IX, 149.
[35] See p. [17] above.
[36] Cf. Epistle VII, in Taylor, *The Works of Plato* . . . , 1804, V, 619.
[37] See *JMN,* VI, 288–289; Journal GH, p. [9] above. "Body . . . wisdom" is
used in "Plato; or, the Philosopher," *W,* IV, 70.
[38] " 'For . . . truth.' " is struck through in ink with two vertical use marks.
See *JMN,* IX, 275.
[39] *Oeuvres de Platon,* 1822–1840.

> "And the most difficult of all to keep
> Heights which the soul is competent to gain" [40]
> [Cf. Wordsworth, *The Excursion*, IV, 138–139]

Plato anticipates us, Pereant qui ante nos[.] Every brisk young man who says fine things in succession to each reluctant generation, as, Rabelais, Erasmus, Rousseau, Alfieri, Goethe, Carlyle is some reader of Plato translating into the vernacular wittily his good things[.] [41]

Modern Europe is all Plato[.] [42]

Measure of merit this perpetual modernness since the author has not been misled by the shortlived local accidental but abode by real & abiding traits.[43]

↑Great havoc among originalities to read P. We have reached the mountain from which all these drift-boulders were detached. Bible of the learned for 2⟨0⟩200 years, & when Swedenborg or Augustin or Locke or Bacon say the same thing we fairly infer he read it. Yet how easy to say *My thunder*. Poor little fellows[.]
All our propositions are related[.]
The broadest generalizer of course anticipates all the particulars comprised in his thesis.↓ [44]

[22] [45] Understanding lame & laughable   J 124 [46]

---

[40] See *JMN*, IV, 87, VIII, 242, IX, 123, and "Inspiration," *W*, VIII, 296.

[41] For "Plato anticipates . . . things", see *JMN*, IX, 215. "Pereant qui ante nos" — "May those who have said our ideas before us perish" (Ed.) — also occurs in *JMN*, VII, 194; cf. *JMN*, V, 385, and "Books," *W*, VII, 198.

[42] See *JMN*, IX, 215, and "Books," *W*, VII, 198.

[43] See *JMN*, IX, 215–216.

[44] "Great havoc . . . thesis.", struck through in ink with three discontinuous use marks, is transcribed in Journal W (1845), where Emerson introduces the passage with the phrase "As I have elsewhere written": see *JMN*, IX, 216. "Plato anticipates . . . thesis.", struck through in ink with an additional vertical use mark, is used in "Plato; or, the Philosopher," *W*, IV, 39–40, 45.

[45] Worked out in ink along the right margin of this page, opposite "As for the . . . p 108", is a computation: 5½ x 40 = 220, x 8 = [17]60.

[46] See *JMN*, VIII, 188. The reference is to a passage in *The Commentaries of*

Propriety. He has prescribed the manners of philosophy. What dignity, what reverence[.]

As for the Phædo; the spirit never gossips   K 78 [47]

Pericles, in Phaedrus, Cousin Vol 6 p 108 [48]

Plato died writing at the age of 81[.] [49]

What is Plato but Moses speaking Greek? said Numenius.[50]

The hint of the Dialectic is more valuable than the dialectic. One who has seen one proof, ever so slight, of the terrific powers of this organ, will remember it all the days of his life. The most venerable proser will be surprised into silence. It is like the first hint that the earth moves or that iron is a conductor of fluids, or that granite is a gas. The solids, the centers, rest itself, fly & skip. Rest is a relation, & not rest any longer. Ah these solid houses[,] real estates have wings like so many nimble musquitoes & do exceedingly hop & avoid me.[51]

[23] *Plato*
In Theaetetus he defines a Philistine[.] [52]

Proclus on the Timaeus of Plato, trans. Thomas Taylor, 2 vols. (London, 1820), I, 469: "The God who is the Demiurgus of the corporeal nature, is lame in both feet"; "the Gods laugh at him."

[47] See *JMN*, VIII, 228.

[48] Socrates is discussing the influence of Anaxagoras on Pericles. An English version of the passage cited occurs in "Literature," *W*, V, 241.

[49] See Cicero, "De Senectute," V.13: Plato "died, pen in hand, in his eighty-first year."

[50] Emerson's source has not been located. Cf. "Numenius" in *Suidae Lexicon*, ed. Ada Adler, 2 vols. (Stuttgart, 1967), II, 481: "τί γάρ Πλάτων ἢ Μυσῆσ Ἀττικίζων."

[51] "The hint . . . avoid me.", struck through in ink with a wavy diagonal use mark, is transcribed both in Journal W (1845), *JMN*, IX, 214, and in Notebook JK, p. [41] above.

[52] See pp. [12], [15] above.

Coincidence with Goethe's remark about the seriousness of nature[,] in Phaedrus [53]

T[aylor, The Works of] P[lato . . . , 1804,] vol III p 336

———

But the charioteer from a vision of this kind recovers the memory of the Nature of Beauty, &c.   *See it.*[54]

↑He called the powers of the mind gods, a beautiful personification↓[.] [55]

[24] [blank]
[25] Plato
Timaeus
One must look long before he finds the Timaeus weather. But at last the high cold silent serene morning comes at early dawn with a few lights conspicuous in the heaven as of a world just created & still becoming & in these wide leisures we open that book[.]   ↑Printed↓

A little opium in it; tête exaltée: the figures wear the buskin, & the grandiose tragic mask: it is all spoken from the tripod, tho' in admirable keeping[.] [56]

———

'Tis the most difficult of tasks to keep
Heights which the soul is competent to gain [57]

Granted sadly granted. But the necessity by which Deity rushes into distribution[,] into variety & particles, is not less divine than the unity from which all begins. Forever Demiurgus speaks to the junior gods as in the old tradition of the Tim⟨.,⟩aeus, "Gods of gods that mortal natures may subsist & that the Universe may be truly all.

[53] See Journal LM, p. [29] above, where Emerson's reference is to Goethe's "The Collector and His Friends."
[54] *Phaedrus*, in Taylor, *The Works of Plato* . . . , 1804, III, 336.
[55] See p. [5] above: "*Powers*".
[56] For "One must . . . keeping", see *JMN*, IX, 236; cf. Journal GH, p. [82] above. "One must . . . book", struck through in ink with a vertical use mark, is used in "Works and Days," *W*, VII, 169–170.
[57] See p. [21] above.

Convert or distribute yourselves acc[ording]. to your nature to the fabrication of animals[."] [58]

[26] In the doctrine of the organic character & disposition is the origin of *caste*[:] "Such as were fit to govern into their composition the informing deity mingled gold; military, silver[;] iron & brass for husbandmen & artificers." ↑Tim⟨.⟩aeus↓ [59]

[27] Movement of the earth   Cousin XII p[p.] 135[-136.] See note to same [*Ibid.*, XII, 343-344] [60]
Of the Circulation of the blood   p. 519 [61]
Of Beauty in works of art[:]

"When therefore an artificer in the fabrication of any work looks to that which always subsists according to *the same*, &, employing a /paradigm/ model/ of this kind, expresses ⟨the⟩ ↑its↓ idea & power in his work, it is then necessary that the whole of his production should be beautiful. But when he beholds that which is in generation, ——————————————— far from beautiful." [*Timaeus*,] p 455 [62]

———————   ↑parallel translation in Cousin XII, 116↓ [63]

"That which Being is to generation, the same is truth to opinion." [*Timaeus*. Cf. *ibid.*, XII,] 456

—————

[58] Either Taylor, *The Works of Plato* . . . , 1804, II, 511-512, or *The Cratylus* . . . , trans. Thomas Taylor, 1793, pp. 472-473; the quotation has been slightly condensed. On "Deity rushes into distribution", see p. [19] above. In *JMN*, VIII, 401, Emerson cites the "High speech of the Demiurgus to his gods in Timaeus"; in *JMN*, IX, 123, this same entry occurs, beginning with the quotation from "The Excursion."

[59] See *JMN*, IX, 287, quoting *The Akhlāk-I-Jalāly* . . . , 1839, p. 37. The *Timaeus* is incorrectly cited; see *Republic*, Book III, in Taylor, *The Works of Plato* . . . , 1804, I, 258, and p. [18] above. "In the doctrine . . . artificers.' ", struck through in ink with a vertical use mark, is used in "Plato; or, the Philosopher," *W*, IV, 66.

[60] *Timaeus*, in Cousin, *Oeuvres de Platon*, 1822-1840.

[61] Taylor, *The Cratylus* . . . , 1793. Cf. p. [19] above, where Emerson quotes the same passage, citing Taylor, *The Works of Plato* . . . , II, 545.

[62] Taylor, *The Cratylus* . . . , 1793. " 'When . . . beautiful.' ", struck through in ink with a vertical use mark, is used in "Plato; or, the Philosopher," *W*, IV, 69-70.

[63] Cousin, *Oeuvres de Platon*, 1822-1840. The insertion is in pencil.

Divination &c. [*Timaeus*, p.] 521 [64]

⟨D⟩Our guilt involuntary   [*Timaeus*, p.] 545 [65]
Fault of birth fault of education   [*Timaeus*, p.] 546 [66]
Appeasing & ⟨remedial⟩ medicinal power of astronomy   [*Timaeus*, pp.] 482 and 551

[28] Transcendental & divine has the dominion of the world on the sole condition of not having it. He only is sought who does not wish to be sought. Fruitur fama [67] is a solecism. Poet least a poet when he sits crowned. Muses mourn & turn away.[68]

[29] Plato
Socrates
He was what our Yankees call "an old one."
Being demanded what things were in the other world, he answered, "Neither was I ever there nor ever did I speak with any that came from thence."

A Franklin ish wisdom[:] he showed one who was afraid to go on foot to Olympia that it was no more than his daily walk within doors if extended at length would easily reach[.] [69]

———

very cool;

———

It was not much that the players should personate him on the stage for the potters frequently did on their stone jugs — as it is not

———

[64] The passage is quoted in Journal GH, p. [72] above. This and the following citations on p. [27] are from Taylor, *The Cratylus* . . . , 1793.

[65] "For no one is voluntarily bad: but he who is depraved becomes so through a certain ill habit of body, and an unskilful education."

[66] ". . . all such as are vicious are so through two involuntary causes; the existence of which we should always rather ascribe to the planters than to the things planted, and to the educators rather than to the educated."

[67] "He delights in fame" (Ed.).

[68] For other versions of the matter in this paragraph, see *JMN*, VIII, 528, IX, 420.

[69] Cf. Xenophon, *Memorabilia*, III.xiii.5.

long since we had from England Lord Brougham on the andirons[.] [70]
He thought Lysias's oration ingenious & eloquent but not stout &
manly[.] [71]

[30] [72] When they had done he went up into the chair & with
an angry smile began his unpremeditated answer not as a suppliant
or guilty person but as if master of the Judges themselves with a free
contumacy proceeding from the greatness of his mind.

———

Socrates entered the prison & took away all ignominy from the place,
which could not be a prison whilst he was there.

Crito bribed the jailor, but Socrates would not go out by treachery.
Whatever inconvenience ensue, nothing is to be preferred before
Justice. These things I hear like pipes & drums whose sound makes
me deaf to everything you say.[73]

"The death of this sole person, saith Eunapius, bro't a general calamity
upon the city, for it may easily be collected by the computation of times,
that, from thenceforward the Athenians did nothing considerable, but the
city by degrees decayed, & with it all Greece." *Eunapius* [74]

[31] "He shall be as a god to me who can rightly divide & define" [75]

[70] "He was . . . old one.' ", "A Franklin ish . . . cool;", and "It was . . .
andirons", struck through in ink with vertical use marks, are used in "Plato; or, the
Philosopher," *W*, IV, 71, 72.
[71] In *Phaedrus*, 234E ff, Socrates comments unfavorably on an oration of Lysias
read to him by Phaedrus. Lysias, according to Diogenes Laertius, wrote a defense for
Socrates that the latter thought unsuitable for use at his trial; see *Lives of Eminent
Philosophers*, II.40–41, and Thomas Taylor, *The Works of Plato* . . . , 1804, IV,
198.
[72] This page bears the number "83" in pencil in the upper right corner.
[73] "Socrates entered . . . say." is used in "Plato; or, the Philosopher," *W*, IV,
74–75.
[74] "Lives of the Philosophers and Sophists," 462. Cf. Philosotratus and Eunapius,
The Lives of the Sophists, trans. Wilmer Cave Wright, in the Loeb Classical Library
(1922), p. 383.
[75] Plato, *Phaedrus*, 266, quoted in Francis Bacon, *Novum Organum*, trans. Peter
Shaw, 2 vols. (London, 1802), II, 21; see *JMN*, V, 79, VI, 209, and "Plato; or, the
Philosopher," *W*, IV, 47.

"And when I think I perceive in any one an intelligence which can embrace at once the whole & the details of an object, I tread with respect in his steps as on those of a god." (Phaedrus   Cousin
[*Oeuvres de Platon*, 1822–1840,] VI p 98)

Inscription over Plato's door[:]

'Who knows not geometry, enter not here.'

Plato adduces the real strength of the negative side. In Gorgias see Callicles' part.
Taylor [*The Works of Plato* . . . , 1804,] Vol 4 p 402
[*Ibid.*, IV,] 409

Callicles anticipates Fourier & says, "Gratify." [*Gorgias, ibid.*, IV,]
p. 409 [76]

↑Same↓ absence [n] of energetic national faith as we now deplore — Jupiter & the rest have a most mythologic air.[77]

[32] [blank]
[33] Plato
Thomas Taylor   died 1835, 1 Nov. aet. 77

See V 4 [78]

Euphuism

(Gen Introd to P[lato]. p lxxxiv) calls Bacon's Novum Organ[u]m the baseless fabric of a vision[.] [79]

---

[76] Callicles holds that "he who intends to live properly, should suffer his desires to be as great as possible, and should not restrain them . . . "; on Fourier's position as Emerson understood it, see *JMN*, IX, 115: "Fourier said, Man exists to gratify his twelve passions . . ."; 189: "Fourier is of the opinion . . . that, 'abstinence from pleasure . . . appeared to him a great sin.'"
[77] See *JMN*, IX, 301.
[78] The page in Journal V includes a brief sketch of Taylor's career. See *JMN*, IX, 96–97.
[79] See *JMN*, IX, 194.

In the translation of Cratylus (note to p 30) T[homas]. T[aylor].
says Christianity is a certain most irrational & gigantic impiety
αλοχιστος και γιγαντικη ανοσιουζγια [80]

[34] [blank]
   [35] All philosophers believe in some remote place where the
dream is realized. Plato in some far East (Repub[lic,] B[ook] vi p.
228). Swedenborg in Africa. Fourier in harmonic planets. But Plato
wiselier, "which tho' it be not our earth must have a pattern of it
laid up in heaven for him who wishes to behold it, & beholding,
resolves to dwell there." (Repub[lic,] B[ook] IX p 349) [81]

Plato
Men are not moved except rightly ⟨as⟩no more than stones fall with-
out gravity[.]
Plato is sound & sincere[.]
It needed a catholic mind able to honour the ⟨law⟩ ideal or laws of the
mind and at the same time Fate or the order of Nature[.]

[36] [blank]
   [37] This is the view we take of Plato[,] that with a wonderful
balance of faculties of the contemplative & of the administrative he
saw the Eternal
      and the Superficial
or had an equal strength of Contemplation and of Understanding,
so as to make a just synthesis, or *putting together* of these two.

But a synthesis implies a hand;
   these two faculties imply a certain nature which gave them their
direction;
In him that hand was Intellect;

   [80] Taylor, *The Cratylus* . . . , 1793. Emerson is quoting Taylor's note, which
continues: "as Proclus elegantly calls the established religion of his time. . . ." See
JMN, IX, 49.
   [81] Both this reference and the reference immediately preceding it cite an unidentified edition of Plato's *Republic*. The citations Emerson gives are not to the translation of either Cousin or Taylor that he had been using, or to the new Bohn edition
of Plato that began appearing in 1848.

As other men, as Jesus, saw the world & man & God thro' the moral sentiment; so Plato saw them thro' the Intellect; and always under that condition.

And by strict necessity, therefore, the Science to which he holds all beings amenable is Dialectics.

This is the virtue & this the defect of his genius.[82]

[38] [...] [83]
[39] Plato

↑"And when I think I perceive in any one an intelligence which can embrace at once the whole & the details of an object, I tread with respect in his steps ⟨&⟩as in those of a god."

Phaedrus Cousin p 98 [*Oeuvres de Platon,* 1828–1840,] Vol VI↓ [84]

Definitions

Law is a distribution of intellect[.]
νου διανομη [85]

Of Courage, *Cousin: Vol* 9 p 214
    Justice   [*Ibid.,* IX,] p 221
    Temperance   [*Ibid.,* IX,] p 218 [86]
    Time
    Eternity [87]

---

[82] On Plato's power of synthesis and the mingled virtue and defect of his genius, see "Plato; or, the Philosopher," *W*, IV, 75.

[83] "Platoniana" is written on this page, appearing upside down in relation to the matter on p. [37].

[84] See p. [31] above.

[85] See *JMN*, VIII, 365, " 'Law is the distribution of intellect.' Proclus", from *The Six Books of Proclus . . . on the Theology of Plato*, trans. Thomas Taylor, 2 vols. (London, 1816), I, 331, in Emerson's library.

[86] As in *JMN*, IX, 214, Emerson is here referring to three definitions set forth in *Republic*, Book IV, and citing the Cousin translation: *Oeuvres de Platon*, 1822–1840, IX.

[87] Among other passages, Emerson may have been thinking of the reference in the *Timaeus* to time as a "moving image of eternity": see Taylor, *The Cratylus . . .*, 1793, p. 466.

Soul (Taylor) Vol III p 320 selfmotive nature[88]
Man ib[id.] ib[id.,] p 326[89]
    Cousin VI p 55 [*Phaedrus*, in *Oeuvres de Platon*,
                                      1822–1840:]

le propre de l'homme est de comprendre le géneral, c'est à
dire ce qui dans la diversité des sensations peut être compris
sous une unité rationnelle[90]

Meno's definition of Virtue, is,

> "To feel a joy from what is fair
> And o'er it to have power."[91]

Analogy is identity of ratio, the most beautiful of all bonds —
in *Timaeus*[.]

[40] P. says of the Good that "all things are for its sake & it is
the cause of every thing beautiful."[92]

[41] Plato   Parmenides
                              Ast. p 250
"Important also is the conference of Parmenides with Socrates
on Ideas, & their relation to actual things, in which Socrates really
leads,[93] & Parmenides only points out to him the difficulties which
attend the reception of Ideas. Perhaps the conclusion of the "Par-

---

[88] *Phaedrus*, in Taylor, *The Works of Plato* . . . , 1804: "Since then it appears
that a self-motive nature is immortal, he who asserts that this is the very essence and
definition of soul, will have no occasion to blush."

[89] The passage, also in *Phaedrus*, deals with successive incarnations of souls in
both human and animal forms.

[90] "le propre de . . . rationnelle" is struck through in ink with a vertical use
mark.

[91] In Journal Y (1845) Emerson quotes both the passage in Greek, from *Meno*
77B, and Cousin's French translation, in *Oeuvres de Platon*, 1822–1840, VI, 159:
see *JMN*, IX, 267.

[92] *The Six Books of Proclus . . . on the Theology of Plato*, trans. Thomas
Taylor, 1816, I, 125. See *JMN*, VIII, 219, 364; *JMN*, IX, 280; "Plato; or, the
Philosopher," *W*, IV, 57; "The Scholar," *W*, X, 271.

[93] " 'Important . . . leads," is struck through in ink with a curved diagonal
line, possibly a use mark.

menides" contained precisely the most essential point, namely, the solution of the contradiction which arises out of the admission of pure Unity & of pure Al⟨e⟩tereity, through the Doctrine of Ideas: Since Ideas are as the higher & certainly vital (not mere abstract) conceptions, the d⟨ea⟩aemoniacal band which hoops in and reconciles the contradiction of Unity & Altereity (consequently Eleaticism & the Heraclitic Dualism). Through these are the two worlds the Intelligible & the Sensuous (which Eleaticism knew not how to join) set in strictest union, whilst the aggregate Actual is an image of the Ideal life, & only in relation to this can be conceived as subsistent & true; [n] so that the Ideal [42] (the Universal or Unity) stands so related to the Real (the Individual Life, ⟨A⟩Multiplicity), as the centre to the periphery: the One is necessarily connected with the other, ⟨the⟩ Life also ↑is↓ neither the one nor the other, but the Unity of both. Since what is the Centre else than the periphery in itself folded, in its origin inclosed? What the periphery but the extended & unfolded centre? Thus interpenetrate Rest & Motion, Being & Not Being ↑(Difference & Alterability)↓ or Unity & Variety in the life of things."   Friedrich Ast [94]

[43] Plato
Plato called the powers of the mind⟨s⟩ gods, a beautiful personification[.] [95]

[44] [blank]

[94] Friedrich Ast, *Platon's Leben und Schriften* (Leipzig, 1816), p. 250. Emerson borrowed this book from the Harvard College Library on November 8, 1848.
[95] See pp. [5] and [23] above.

488

Warren Lot

1849

Warren Lot, a title supplied by the editors, applies to two sets of Emerson's memoranda written in a notebook dated "April 1849": (1) 13 manuscript pages headed "Planting & Rearing Hedge" and (2) 5 manuscript pages recording trees set out in 1847 and after in two tracts of land, the "Heater Piece" across the road from Emerson's house, and the "Warren Lot".

The Warren Lot notes run back to front in a pocket account book that Emerson had used for financial records since the late 1820's. The notebook is comprised of 42 leaves folded and sewn to make 84 unnumbered pages within a leather cover, 10.4 x 16.1 cm. Each page has faint horizontal rules and bolder vertical rules, the latter forming columns for dates, items, and amounts in dollars and cents. For the earlier sequence of entries, dated 1828–1840, Emerson inscribed one cover, in ink: "*Emerson* . . . Chardon Street Boston"; for the Warren Lot entries he reversed the book and inscribed the other cover, also in ink: "Hedge Fence . . . April 1849". Nearly all inscription, in both sequences, is in ink. Pagination has been supplied in terms of the later sequence of entries. Thirty pages are torn out except for stubs (1–12, 29–38, 47–48, 79–84); there is one blank page (26).

[front cover]

———————

Hedge
Fence.

———————

April 1849 [1]

[1] Written upside down, in ink, between "April 1849" and the line below "Hedge Fence." is (1) a column of dates, all canceled: "1828", "1829", "1830", "1831", "1832"; and (2) the figures "60", triply underlined, and "20". Emerson used this notebook for keeping his accounts during the five years listed.

[front cover verso]
Warren lot front 293¾ ft.
House lot front ↑231

$$\begin{array}{r} 524 \\ 2 \\ \hline 1048↓\,^2 \end{array}$$

[1]–[12] [six leaves torn out] ³

---

[13]   Planting & Rearing Hedge

Mark a strip of ground 3 or 4 ft. wide along the line where the hedge
is to grow. Thoroughly trench it with a spade 18 inches deep. A
good dressing of any manure that is not so coarse as to be unmanage-
able in planting, must be ⟨tu⟩put on the soil, & turned under, whilst
the trenching is going on. [14] The soil must be thoroughly pulverized, & freed from stones, lumps, & rubbish, before planting.

Now for the plants.
Assort them in two parcels[,] those of large, & those of small size; the
smaller, for the riche⟨r⟩st part of the ground; larger on the poorest.

[15] Then trim the plants. Cut down the top or stem to within about
an inch of what was the ground line, (so that it will, when planted
again, have but an inch of stem above the soil,) and by shortening all
the larger roots about one third.

[16] The hedge should be planted in a double row, with the
plants placed not opposite, but alternate, thus;

X   X   X   X   X
X   X   X   X

The rows should be six inches apart, and the plants one foot apart in

---

² The figures from "231" through "1048" are added in pencil. See Notebook
Trees[A] [Sequence II], *JMN*, VIII, 545, for additional measurements.
³ There are isolated figures, written in ink, on the stubs of pp. [9]–[12], in-
dicating that these pages had been used for Emerson's accounts.

the rows. This will [17] require 32 plants to a rod, or 2000 plants to 1000 feet.

Having pulverized the soil, set down the line firmly for the first row, and, with a spade, throw out a trench about 8 or 10 inches deep, [18] keeping its upright or firm bank next to the line. Drop the plants along the line, about the distance they will be needed, & then plant them, 12 inches apart, keeping them as nearly as possible in a straight line. [19] Press the earth moderately round the stem of the plant with the foot, when the filling in of the pulverized soil is nearly completed.

Having finished this row, take up the line & fix it again six inches distant. Open [20] the trench in the opposite direction, & set the plants in the same manner.

The whole of the prepared strip of ground must be kept loose with the hoe, & free from weeds. Then light [21] dressings will be required for the two or three first summers to effect this.

Next spring, let the whole of the new growth be cut down to within six inches of the ground.

The following spring, cut back the last season's shoots, leaving only one foot of the current season's [22] growth. This will leave our hedge altogether 18 inches high.

The third year, shorten back the tops so as to leave again one foot of the year's growth. The hedge will now be 2½ feet high.

[23] This course must be pursued every spring, until the hedge is of the desired height & form, which will take place in 5 or 6 years.

Buckthorn will make a pretty good hedge in 5 years.

The hedge arrived at its 6th year, should be about 6 feet high, tapering ⟨in form,⟩to the top, & three [24] feet wide at base. This is high enough for common purposes.

When the hedge has attained the size & shape which is finally desired, it is not allowed to grow any larger. Two shearings or clippings are necessary every season, to keep it in order, [25] one in June, & the other, at the end of September.

[26] [blank]
[27]

Heater Piece
East line, six standard apples set out 1847 [4]
123 (⟨next⟩s.e. corner) Roxbury Russet
124 (next north) Hubbardston
12⟨6⟩5 Hubbardston
126 Hubbardston
127 Hubbardston
128 Baldwin

[28] [...] [5]
[29]–[38] [five leaves torn out] [6]
      [39] *Urbaniste* (by ⟨kitchen⟩back door)
      Napoleon. (next Bartlett pear)
      Dunmore (by east barn-door)
      Hacon (by Arbour)

(Heater ⟨p⟩Piece Oct 1848)

Southmost standard
      1   Roxbury Russet
      2   Fall Harvey
      3   Holmes Apple
      4   ⟨Hubbardston⟩ Brown House

---

[4] See *JMN*, VIII, 545: "1847, April 26 J. Hosmer set out for me 24 appletrees in the Warren lot 6 apple trees in the east side of the heater piece, and 40 pears in Warren lot". Emerson had previously numbered 122 trees: see *JMN*, VIII, 541.

[5] Omitted are records of payments made in January, 1840, written upside down in relation to the Warren Lot sequence.

[6] Figures on the surviving stubs indicate that these pages contained records of payments made during the months prior to January, 1840 (p. [28]).

⟨St Ghislain⟩   ?
Hubbardston
⟨Catillac⟩
⟨Charles of Austria⟩
⟨Hacon⟩
⟨Charles of Austria.⟩

[40] Warren Lot (beginning at the N.E. corner) [...]⁷
[41]–[49] [...]⁸
[50] [...]⁹
[51]–[inside back cover] [...]¹⁰

⁷ On pp [40]–[41] are listed Rows I–V of the Warren Lot trees: numbers 1–43,
with a few additions (33½, 34½, 35½, 42½). The list is substantially identical
to that in Notebook Trees[A] [Sequence II], printed in *JMN*, VIII, 546–548.

⁸ On p. [42] are records of payments made in December, 1833-July, 1835. Part
of the leaf bearing pp. [43]–[44] has been torn out: there is no writing on the stub
of p. [43]; that on the stub of p. [44] records payments made during December,
1832. Pp. [45] and [46] record payments made during May–November, 1832. Part
of the leaf bearing pp. [47] and [48] has been torn out; writing on the stubs shows
that these pages recorded payments made in January–May, 1832. P. [49] records
payments made in February–December, 1831. All of these entries are written upside
down in relation to the Warren Lot sequence.

⁹ On p. [50] Emerson listed Rows VI–VIII of the Warren Lot trees plus trees
"S[outh]. of h[e]ater" and n[orth]. of path": numbers 44–64 with one addition:
48½. The list, substantially identical to that in Notebook Trees[A] [Sequence II],
printed in *JMN*, VIII, 548–549, is here omitted.

¹⁰ Pp. [51]–[78] record payments made in June, 1828-January, 1831. Part
of the leaves bearing pp. [79]–[84] has been torn out; writing on the stubs shows
that these pages recorded payments made before June 10, 1828 (p. [78]). Writing on
the inside back cover pertains to the years 1829–1830, as a notation in the upper left
corner indicates. All of these entries are written upside down in relation to the Warren Lot sequence.

ED

1 8 5 2 – 1 8 5 3

Notebook ED ("England") is a retrospective reordering of materials concerning Emerson's first and second visits to England. Most of its entries, arranged topically rather than chronologically, are transcriptions from his earlier journals and correspondence of 1832–1833 and 1847–1848. From internal evidence the compilation of the notebook can be dated 1852–1853: on page [i], Emerson notes the population of Great Britain and Ireland as of 1851; on pages [40]–[48] he transcribes his speech of April 23, 1852, at Montreal; on page [68] he cites the *Courrier des Etats-Unis* for June 24, 1852; on page [289] he refers to a communication of April, 1853; and in addition there are cross-references, *passim*, to such journals of the 1850's as BO, CO, and GO. It may have been Notebook ED that Emerson had specifically in mind when writing to his brother William from Cincinnati on December 17, 1852, in the midst of a lecture tour, of his wish "to be at home, where I have now accumulated tasks. For my English notes have now assumed the size of a pretty book, which I am eager to complete; and some other papers have got nearly ready for printing" (*L*, IV, 332).

Notebook ED is written in a copybook bound in green marbled boards with brown leather corners and spine. The cover measures 17.5 x 21.8 cm. The spine, which is badly worn, is inscribed "ED"; there may have been additional inscription where depressions in the leather surface are now visible. The front cover is inscribed "ED" in ink; on the two leather corners and on the lower left spinal strip "England" or "ENGLAND" is written in ink; the back cover is also inscribed "ED" in ink at the upper left, lower left, and lower right. The pages, unruled, are 17.4 x 21 cm. Including flyleaves (i–ii, 289–290), there are 292 pages, of which 63 are unnumbered (i, ii, 1, 21, 31, 42–45, 77, 79, 81–82, 88, 92₁, 93₁, 92₂, 93₂, 102–105, 123, 134, 139, 143, 153, 156–157, 161–165, 195, 197, 202–203, 212–213, 216–219, 241–243, 248–249, 256–259, 261, 263–267, 271, 284–285, 270), 42 are numbered in pencil only (20, 24–25, 30, 48, 50, 56–57, 60, 64–68, 70, 74, 78, 80, 98–101, 109 — erroneously numbered "111", 138, 152, 158–160, 170, 180, 186–187, 190–194, 196, 198–200), 18 are numbered in pencil and renumbered in ink (16–17, 58, 88, 90, 108, 110, 118–120, 128, 130, 148–150, 168, 178, 188–189), and the remaining 169 are numbered in ink. Perhaps to compensate for an error within the unnumbered pages (paginated 92₁, 93₁, 92₂, 93₂ by the editor), Emerson did not use numbers 96 and 97. There are 43 blank pages (71, 73–74, 77–84, 91, 92₁, 93₁, 98–102, 104–105, 138–139, 151, 153–154, 156–165, 220, 268, 271, 275–276, 283, 285) and two others are blank except for mounted clippings (72, 103). Other clippings are mounted on the front cover verso, pages 118–119, and 220. The following items are laid in between the pages indicated: (1) 56–57, a printed leaf, 10.1 x 18 cm, from an address by Edward Everett delivered in 1838, with a note concerning unequal distribution of property in England; (2) 86–87, a sheet of laid paper, 10.8 x 17 cm, twice folded to make six pages to which the numbers 86ₐ–86f have been assigned, with Emerson's inscription in ink on 86ₐ and in pencil on 86b; (3) 110–111, a loose leaf, 12.9 x 20 cm, to which the page numbers 110ₐ–110b have been assigned, with Emerson's inscription in ink under the canceled heading "Books"; (4) 122–123, a paragraph clipped from an unidentified newspaper, 6 x 9.8 cm, concerning the *Times* of London; (5) 266–267, a printed announcement, 12.8 x 20.4 cm, of a dinner meeting of the Boston Latin School Association to be held on December 17, 1879. There are also two irregularly cut slips of paper evidently intended as bookmarks, one of approximately 3.5 x 18.6 cm pinned to page 166 opposite the beginning of Emerson's notes on Thomas De Quincey, the other of approximately 3.4 x 18.8 cm pinned to page 276 opposite the beginning of Emerson's second group of notes concerning Alfred Tennyson.

○

[front cover]   ENGLAND

ED

England   England

[front cover verso] [1] Et penitus toto divisos orbe Britannos.

[Virgil,] *Æn*[*eid*]. I. 67,[2]

Caesar [3]

Territa quaesitis ostendit terga Britannis.[4]

Lucan. [*The Civil War*, II, 572]

---

[1] Pasted to the upper left corner is a clipping from an unidentified newspaper summarizing votes in the British House of Lords "on the motion to pass the Catholic relief bill to a second reading"; the voting had taken place on April 4, 1829.

[2] Properly, Virgil, *Eclogues*, I, 66; see Journal London, front cover verso. (All cross-references in Notebook ED to other journals or notebooks in this volume are, of course, to materials printed above.)

[3] This word is written and circled in pencil.

[4] "[He] turned his back in panic to the Britons whom he went out of his way to attack."

Article on "Leet, Shire, & Parliament,"

Ed. Rev. Vol 36
1821–2 [5]

↑See Many texts for England & America
in *GO* 126, 127, 128, 187↓ [6]

[i] Area of Great Britain, square miles.   83 828

In England, square miles   5⟨7,812⟩1,205
  Wales   7,263

                                                   58,⟨6⟩4⟨4⟩68
According to Macculloch [7]   57,812
  Scotland   26,016
Population of Great Britain & Ireland, 1851
                    27,400 000
              of G. Britain Colonies & India
                    140 000 000
              1/6 of the earth's population
Property of the soil rests in 12 000 estates holden by clergy & corpora-
tions   12,000
and private landholders   20,000

in 1822;   32,000

In 1786, were 250 000 landholders.
  ↑House of Lords (M'C[ulloch].) 450
  House of Commons   658
There are 500 British islands↓[.] [8]

---

[5] An untitled review of three recent books on English law and lawcourts, in the issue of February, 1822, pp. 287–341; "Courts of the Ancient English Common Law—the Leet—the Shire—Parliament." appears as a running head throughout.

[6] The ink line above "See Many . . . 187" curves down at the right, partly encircling "America". Journal GO will be published in a later volume.

[7] See John Ramsay McCulloch, *M'Culloch's Universal Gazetteer* . . . , 2 vols. (New York, 1851), I, 454. Emerson's source for the other figures given has not been identified.

[8] See Journal London, p. [i].

[ii] *France* 200 000 square miles
Population 32,000 000

[1]   To M[argaret].F[uller]. at Rome.
Old cities.   4 June 1847 [9]
Rome is keeping its old promise to your eyes & mind; Rome, which
always keeps its promise, & which, like Nature, has that elasticity of
application to all measures of spirit. These millennial cities, in their
immense accumulations of human works, find it easy to impress the
imagination, by gradually dropping one piece after another of whim,
blunder, & absurdity, [2] — hay, stubble, & bladders, — until nothing
but necessity & geometry remains.

"Henry VIII. adorned his landscapes with the ruins of abbeys;
Cromwell, with those of castles," says Gilpin, (Cumberland Vol II.
122,), of "these two masters" [10]

London   ⟨2,250000⟩ souls,
                    2,362 236
extends over an area of 78 029 acres or 122 square miles

[3] Alfieri said, "that Italy & England are the only countries in
which it is desireable to live; the former, because there nature
vindicates her rights, & rises triumphant over the evils inflicted by
the governments; the latter, because art conquers nature, & transforms a rude ungenial land into a paradise of comfort & laughing
abundance." [11]

[4] A manly ability, a general sufficiency, is the genius of the
English. They have not, I think, the special & acute fitness to their
employment that Americans have, — but a man is a man here, — a
quite costly & respectable production, in his own, & in all other eyes.

---

[9] For the full text of Emerson's letter, see *L*, III, 400–401.

[10] William Gilpin, *Observations on Several Parts of England, Particularly the
Mountains and Lakes of Cumberland and Westmoreland, Relative Chiefly to Pictur-
esque Beauty, Made in the Year 1772*, 3rd edition, 2 vols. (London, 1808).

[11] Cf. *JMN*, V, 413; Journal London, p. [182]. This paragraph, struck through
in pencil with a vertical use mark, is used in "Land," *W*, V, 34.

And I hesitate to read here many a ↑disparaging↓ p⟨a⟩hrase which I have been accustomed to throw into my writings, about poor, thin, unable, unsatisfying bipeds.[12]

[5]   *National traits.*
The Englishman is cheerful, & his voice is.

Englishman has hard eyes; he is great by the back of the head.[13]

He has great security of manner. Every man in the first class carriages is a possible lord. Yet ⟨they⟩ all look alike. And every man I meet in London, I think I know.[14]
"The English, in the street, always walk straight before them, like mad dogs;" says the French editor of La Patrie.[15]

"Ils s'amusaient tristement, selon la coutume de leur pays;" says Froissart.[16]

[6]   ↑National traits.↓
          W. E. Forster of Rawdon told me, he had repeatedly ridden all the way from London to Leeds, in the first class carriage, with the same persons, & no word exchanged. The clubhouses were established to cultivate social habits, & it is rare that more than two eat together, &, oftenest, you eat alone.

"Ils s'amusaient tristement, selon la coutume de leur pays."

Melancholy cleaves to the Saxon mind close as to the tones of an Aeolian harp.[17]

---

[12] "I hestitate . . . bipeds." is used in "Manners," *W*, V, 106.

[13] For these two sentences, see Journal London, pp. [62], [9], and Journal LM, p. [15]. "Englishman has . . . head." is struck through in pencil with a vertical use mark. With "The Englishman . . . voice is.", cf. "Character," *W*, V, 128.

[14] For "Every man . . . know.", see Journal London, p. [44]; with "Every man . . . lord.", cf. "Ability," *W*, V, 101.

[15] " 'The English . . . La Patrie.", struck through in pencil with two vertical use marks, is used in "Race," *W*, V, 70; see Journal London, p. [9].

[16] This sentence, struck through in pencil with a vertical use mark, is used in "Character," *W*, V, 128; see Journal London, pp. [9], [51].

[17] For "W. E. Forster . . . alone.", see Journal London, p. [16], and "Char-

[7]   ↑National traits.↓

Their ruddy & bluff appearance was well enough marked by T[horeau]. who said, that, ↑what↓ we reckon a good Englishman, is, in this country, a stage-proprietor.[18]

Their nationality is intense[.]

Englishman is clean, methodical, veracious, proud, obstinate, comfort--loving, industrious, accumulative, nautical[.] [19]

I suppose, all the Saxon race at this day, Germans, English, Americans, — all, to a man, regard it as an unspeakable misfortune to be born a Frenchman.[20]

[8] Englishman must have foothold. Security is in his face & manners, because he has solidity in his foundations, & ⟨proceeds⟩ method in his proceedure. The English secure the essentials, according to their light, & it falls, at present, on bodily good, — health & wealth. The Cyclops operative cannot subsist on food less solid than beef, and the masters cannot understand that there is any way to success but on ⟨real⟩ capital & ⟨systematic⟩ economy.[21]

[9] Everywhere I observe an exact economy & nothing of that uncalculated headlong expenditure which families use in America. If they cannot pay, they do not buy. An Englishman says, I cannot

---

acter," *W*, V, 129; for " 'Ils . . . pays.' ", see p. [5] above and note; for "Melancholy . . . harp.", see *JMN*, V, 107. Page [6] is struck through in pencil with a vertical use mark.

[18] "Their ruddy . . . stage-proprietor." is struck through in pencil with a vertical use mark. Cf. Journal London, p. [60].

[19] "Their nationality . . . nautical" is in pencil. "Englishman is . . . nautical" is struck through in pencil with a vertical use mark; cf. "Manners," *W*, V, 106–107.

[20] For "I suppose . . . Frenchman.", see *JMN*, VI, 354, and Journal TU, p. [84], to be published in a later volume. The sentence here, struck through in pencil with a vertical use mark, is used in "Cockayne," *W*, V, 146.

[21] For "The English secure . . . wealth.", see *JMN*, IX, 419; for "The Cyclops . . . beef," see *JMN*, IX, 420. This paragraph is struck through in pencil with a vertical use mark; "The English secure . . . wealth." is used in "Ability," *W*, V, 84.

afford it. For they have no presumption of better fortunes, next year, as our people have.[22]

They have, in the highest degree of any existing nation, practical ability. They can do, and they do. The nation sits in the immense costly city which it has built, — a London extended into every man's house, [10] though he lives in Van Diemen's Land, or Capetown. Real faithful performance of what is undertaken to be performed, they honor in themselves, & exact in others, as a certificate of equality with themselves. The modern world is theirs.[n]

The commercial relations of the world are so intimately drawn to London, that, it seems, as if every dollar in the world contributed to strengthen the English government.[23] They[n] have made it: they make it, day by day; and, if all the wealth on earth should perish ⟨‖ . . . ‖⟩today, by war, or deluge, they ⟨feel⟩ know themselves competent to replace it.[24]

[11]   "In close intrigues, their faculty's but weak,
                 For, generally, whate'er they know, they speak;
                 And often their own councils undermine
                 By mere infirmity, without design;
                 From whence, the learned say, it doth proceed,
                 That English treasons never can succeed;
                 For they're so openhearted, you may know
                 Their own most secret thoughts, & others too."
                                          Defoe
                 "The meanest English plowman studies law,
                 And keeps thereby the magistrates in awe."
                                          Defoe [25]

---

[22] "Everywhere . . . people have.", struck through in pencil with a vertical use mark, is used in "Wealth," *W*, V, 156. See Journal London, p. [62].

[23] This sentence, from Journal London, p. [15], is written at the bottom of p. [11]; Emerson marked it for insertion after "theirs" with a hand sign and the symbol "B" on p. [10] and a second "B" on p. [11].

[24] "They have, in . . . replace it.", including the sentence inserted from p. [11], is struck through in pencil with single vertical use marks on pp. [9], [10], and [11] and used in "Ability," *W*, V, 92.

[25] Daniel Defoe, "The True-born Englishman," Part II, ll. 15–22 and 196–197. Both passages are struck through in pencil with vertical use marks; the first is used in "Truth," *W*, V, 126.

[12] A man deposited in Dublin Bank, £100, in a sealed box; & then advertised to all somnambulists, mesmerisers, & others, that, whoever could tell him the number of his ⟨cheque⟩ note, should have the money. He let it lie there six months, — the newspapers now & then stimulating the attention of the adepts, ⟨n⟩but none could tell him: and he said, Now let me never be bothered more with this proven lie.[26]

[13] They are factitious people. Though they have their full share of genius. Thus their whole position & prosperity are factitious or *tours de force*. Subsisting by a colonial system, by manufactures, by navigation laws, &c &c. Their University-system which makes Greek & Latin alive, galvanizes Greek & Latin & unnec[e]ssary mathematics into the creation of a university-aristocracy. So much of their literature & journalism is antiquarian & manufactured. Lockhart, Macaulay, Hood, Moore, Scott himself, Southey, Gifford, Croker, Hallam, ↑Whewell,↓ were all men ↑⟨Whewell,⟩↓ whose natural [14] determination could hardly be now ascertained, but who were forced by the tastes & gimcracks they found uppermost, into the particular provinces they entered;[n] so members of Parliament are made, & Churchmen. And so, at this moment, every ambitious young man in England studies geology. Birmingham, birminghamizes all.[27]

[15]   *Traits*

Melancholy cleaves to the Saxon mind as closely as to the tones of an Aeolian harp.[28]

Lord Chief Justice Fortescue, in the reign of Henry VI, says, that "the inhabitants of England are rich in gold & silver, & in all the necessaries & conveniences of life. They drink no water unless at certain times upon a religious ⟨pena⟩score, & by way of doing penance.

---

[26] Emerson heard this anecdote from Carlyle; see Journal London, p. [56], and Journal LM, p. [27]. The paragraph, struck through in pencil with a vertical use mark, is used in "Truth," *W*, V, 124–125.

[27] This paragraph is struck through in pencil with a vertical use mark.

[28] "Melancholy cleaves . . . harp." is struck through in ink with three diagonal use marks. See p. [6] above.

They are fed in great abundance with all sorts of flesh & fish, of which they have plenty everywhere: they are clothed throughout in good woollens," &c. &c. ap. Johnston, I. 72.[29]

[16] "He that is afraid of anything," said Dr Johnson, "is a scoundrel." [30]

———

Patience an eminent English virtue.

———

"I bequeath my patience to Mr R. Peel;"—and Peel, the sublime of mediocrity, has come to be the model man of England.
English like a fair stand-up fight[.] [31]

[17]   To *M[argaret]. F[uller]. Dec*ember [5], 1847 [32]
    Yet I hear nothing lately of our friends S. & W. & E. & A.[33] The goods of that country ↑(America)↓ are original & incommunicable to this (England); I see that well. It would give me no pleasure to bring valued persons thence, & show them to valued persons here; but lively pleasure to show to these last, those friends at home, in their own place.
    Shall we not yet,— you also— as we used to talk,[34]— build up

[29] William Johnston, *England As It Is, Political, Social, and Industrial, in the Middle of the Nineteenth Century,* 2 vols. (London, 1851), borrowed from the Boston Athenaeum, August 13–23, 1852. This paragraph, struck through in pencil with a vertical use mark, is used in "Race," *W*, V, 69.
[30] Cf. *The Works of Samuel Johnson, LL.D. Together with His Life, and Notes on His Lives of the Poets,* by Sir John Hawkins, 11 vols. (London, 1787), XI, 199, as cited in James Boswell, *The Life of Samuel Johnson,* ed. George Birbeck Hill and L. F. Powell, 1934–1950, III, 1, n. 2. Emerson may have encountered the remark in William Johnston, *England As It Is,* 1851, II, 88. It is also quoted in Journal GO, p. [83], written circa July 1852. Journal GO will be published in a later volume.
[31] This sentence, struck through in pencil with a vertical use mark, is used in "Race," *W*, V, 63.
[32] See *L*, III, 446–448; the extracts on pp. [17]–[19] below are printed in *J*, VII, 368–369.
[33] "S. & W. & E." are identified in the full text of the letter, which reads "Caroline [Sturgis Tappan], or Elizabeth H[oar]., or Sam Ward"; "A." is presumably Bronson Alcott.
[34] "The goods . . . talk," is struck through in pencil with a vertical use mark.

a reasonable society in that naked unatmospheric land, & effectually serve one another?

[18] I observe that many young men here look wishfully to America: I never dare say to them, Go; though I might go in their position. I observe that the idea of owning woodlands, &c. is very attractive to the English imagination. Yet our young men find it all but impossible to live in the great continent.

[19]   ↑*Traits*↓

——

toughness.

——

Among the men made for work, *dura ilia*,[35] seemingly not of flesh & blood but of brass & iron[,] Coke, Mansfield, Gibbon, Johnson [36]

——

strong body, vast memory.

——

Dequincey says, he wishes "the morals of the middle classes of England, combined with the manners of the highest, — or — the morals of the gentry with the manners of the nobility." "No morality which is built less on the mere amiableness of quick sensibilities, or more entirely on massy substructions of principle & conscience, than the morality of the British middle classes."

[20]   ↑*Traits*↓

In England the Understanding rules & materialistic truth[.]

the becoming, the fit, the discreet, the brave, the advantageous

But they could not produce such a book as the Bhagavat Geeta[.]

Dr Johnson is liked for his courage[:] "A man who is afraid of any thing is a scoundrel." [37]

[21] [blank]

[35] "Tough stomachs" (Ed.). See *JMN*, IX, 339.

[36] "Among . . . Johnson", struck through in pencil with a vertical use mark, is used in "Universities," *W*, V, 207.

[37] See p. [16] above. "In England . . . scoundrel.' " is in pencil.

[22]   England.
See in *GH* 143–145, Notes on England in the year 1500, translated
from the Italian, & printed for the Camden Society, 1847.

[23]–[24] [blank]
[25]   *Mr Emerson's Speech*
                    At the Annual Soiree of the
                    Athenaeum, Manchester.
        18 November, 1847.[38]

It is pleasant to meet this great & brilliant company, & doubly
pleasant to see the faces of so many distinguished persons. But,
gentlemen, I have known all these persons before. When I was at
home, they were as near to me as they[n] are to you. The arguments
of the "League" & its leader, are known to all [26] the friends of
free trade. The gaieties & genius, the political, ↑the↓ social, the parietal
wit of "Punch," goes duly, every fortnight, to all the bookclubs, & to
every boy & girl in Boston, New York, & Philadelphia.
Sir, when I came to sea, I found the "History of Europe" ⟨i⟩on the
cabin↑-table↓ of the ship that brought me here, the property of the
captain of the ship, — as a sort of programme or playbill, [27][n] to
tell the seafaring New-Englander what he shall find on his landing
here. And, as for Dombey, Sir, there is no land where the sun shines,
that Dombey does not; no land where paper exists to print on, that
it is not found. No man who can read, that does not read it, &, if he
cannot, he finds some charitable ⟨person⟩son or daughter of Adam
who can, & hears it.
    But these things are not for me; these compliments, though
[28] true[,] would better come from one who felt & understood

[38] Substantially the same as in "Speech at Manchester," *W*, V, 309–314. At the
time Emerson was preparing his speech he expected to see "Alison, Cobden, Dickens,
Jerrold, & other English notorieties" at the meeting (*L*, III, 436); his opening
paragraph alludes accordingly to Richard Cobden, a leader of the Anti-Corn Law
League; Douglas Jerrold, a well-known contributor to *Punch*; Sir Archibald Alison,
author of *History of Europe During the French Revolution* (1833–1842), who
presided at the soirée; and Charles Dickens, whose *Dombey and Son* was currently
appearing (1847–1848). Dickens and Jerrold did not attend, however, as Emerson
notes in *English Traits* (*W*, V, 309).

these merits more. I am not here to exchange civilities with you, but rather to speak of that which, I am sure, interests these gentlemen much more than their own praises. That which is good in holidays & working days, the same in one century & in another century. That which lures a solitary American in the woods with the wish to [29] see England, is not these, but the moral peculiarity of the Saxon race, — its commanding sense of right & wrong, — the love & devotion to that; — which is the imperial trait, which arms them with the sceptre of the globe. It is this, which is at the foundation of that aristocra⟨cy⟩t-ic character, which certainly wanders into strange vagaries, so that its origin is apt to be lost sight of, but which, [30] if it should lose this, would find itself paralysed, & a cipher.

And, in trade, & in the mechanics' shop⟨s⟩, gives that honesty in performance, that thoroughness & solidity of work, which is a national characteristic.

This ⟨is one:⟩ ↑conscience is one element,↓ and the other is, that fidelity of fellowship, that habit of friendship, the homage of man to man, running [31] through all classes, — the electing of worthy persons to a certain fraternity, to acts of kindness, & warm & staunch support, from year to year, from youth to age, — which is alike lovely & honorable to those who render, & those who receive it; — which stands in strong contrast enough, with the superficial attachments of other races of men, their excessive courtesy, & short lived connexion.

[32] You will think me very pedantic, gentlemen, but holiday though it be, I have not the smallest interest in any holiday, except as it celebrates real & not pretended joys. And I think it just, that, in this time of gloom & commercial disaster, of affliction & beggary in these districts, that, on these very accounts, ⟨that⟩ ↑which↓ I speak of, you should not [33] fail to keep your literary anniversary, as a day of congratulation. I seem to hear you say, that, for all that is come & gone yet, we will not reduce by one chaplet, or one oakleaf, the braveries of our annual feast.

For, I must tell you, that I was given to understand, in my childhood, that the British ⟨I⟩island, from which my forefathers came, was no [34] lotus-garden, no paradise of serene sky, & roses, & music, & merriment, all the year round, — no, but a cold, foggy, mournful country, where nothing grew well in the open air, but robust men & ⟨women⟩virtuous women, and these of a wonderful fibre & endurance; that their best parts were slowly revealed, — their virtues did not come out, until they quarreled; — they did [35] not strike twelve the first time; [39] — good lovers, good haters, — and you could know little about them, till you had seen them long, & little good of them, till you had seen them in action: that, in prosperity, they were moody & dumpish, but in adversity, they were grand. Is it not true, sir, that the wise ancients did not esteem the ship parting with flying colours from the port, [36] but only that brave sailer which came back with torn sheets & battered sides, stript of her banners, but having ridden out the storm.

And so, gentlemen[,] I feel in regard to this aged England, with the possessions, & honours, & trophies, & also with the infirmities, of a thousand years, gathering around her, irretrievably committed, as she now is, to many [37] old customs, which cannot be suddenly changed, — now pressed upon by the transitions of trade, & new & all incalculable modes, & fabrics, & arts, & machines, & competing populations, — I see her not dispirited, not weak, but well-remembering that she has seen dark days before, ⟨inst⟩indeed with a kind of instinct that she sees a little better in a cloudy day, &, that, in storm & battle, & calamity, she has a secret vigour, & a pulse [38] like a cannon. — I see her, in her old age, not decrepit, but young, — & still daring to believe in her power of endurance & expansion. Seeing that, — I say, All hail! Mother of nations, — Mother of heroes, — with strength still equal to the time; still wise to entertain, & swift to execute the policy which the mind & heart of mankind requires in the present hour, & thus only hospitable to the foreigner, & truly a home to the thoughtful [39] & generous, who are born in the soil.

So be it! so let it be! But, if it be not so, if the courage of England goes with the chances of a commercial crisis, I will go back to the capes of Massachusetts, & my own Indian stream, & say to my countrymen, The old race are all gone, & the elasticity & hope of mankind must henceforth remain on the Allegany ranges, or nowhere.

[39] See *JMN*, VIII, 450.

[40]

*Mr Emerson's Speech
at the Dinner of the St George's
Society, Montreal, 23 April, 1852.*[40]

Mr President,

I am flattered by the invitation to respond to the sentiment of the Chair, though I am quite uncertain of being able to show this company how cordially I do it. But you are to know, that we Americans feel our relation to England to be so strict, — we have kept our pedigree so pure, — that we praise very willingly England, as [41] a son praises his mother. I hope you will not recall M. Talleyrand's speech to the youth who vaunted his mother's beauty[:] "Mais, donc, c'était M. votre pere qui n'était pas si bien." [n] — So I hope you will not be provoked to criticize the American element in us, that differences us from the English.

I have taken up so much ↑of the↓ time of my friends in Montreal, that I must cut short what I have to say.

But it strikes me, [42] that England owes her splendid career ⟨in history,⟩ to the rare coincidence of a good race & good place. It was a lucky fit. We say, in a yacht-race, that, if the boats are anywhere nearly matched, it is the man that wins. Put the best sailing master into either boat, & he will win.

England is like a ship anchored in the sea, at the side of Europe, & right in the heart of the modern world.[41] As soon as this [43] ship got a hardy crew into it, they could not help becoming the sailors & factors of the globe. It was like a man living in a lighthouse, — his boys ⟨must⟩ learn to swim like fishes, & their playthings are boats, and, as, in ⟨the craft of⟩ sailing ⟨over⟩ ↑round↓ the ⟨warlike⟩ world, ⟨when "there was no peace beyond the Line,"⟩ [42] there were plenty of hard knocks going, they were good at that game too. So, these

[40] Emerson was in Montreal for a course of six lectures under the auspices of the Mercantile Library Association, April 19–24, 1852.

[41] See Journal London, p. [i]. This sentence is used in "Land," *W*, V, 41.

[42] A maxim of the Buccaneers, quoted in *JMN*, IV, 101, and "War," *W*, XI, 158, from *Lives and Voyages of Drake, Cavendish, and Dampier; including an introductory view of the Earlier Discoveries in the South Sea, and the History of the Bucaniers* (Edinburgh, 1831), p. 228.

507

stout fellows went up & down the world, & were more abroad than they were at home, [44] & took early lessons in the game of annexation, until they have got a good part of the world in their hands. Well, the more they went abroad, the more they found to do at home, for, having, as shopmen say, the very best ↑business-↓*stand* in the ⟨world⟩ ↑whole planet↓, — they were sure of a sale of all the goods they can possibly manufacture.[43]

With this prosperity, the virtues of the race shone [45] out. 'Tis said, there are not as great individuals now, as once, on earth. Some countries only furnish officers; & others, men. Old Russia, men; & Sparta, officers. France, England, America, furnish officers & engineers to Russia & Turkey.[44] But England has good rank & file: and there is not a ⟨town⟩ county or a town in England, but has yielded its contingent of worthy men, in old or in new times, to the country & the race. The first name for intellect in the human race is [46] Shakspeare; — the first for capacity in exact science, is ⟨n⟩Newton; and where, out of his country has Milton his superior in epic or in lyric song? What lawgiver in learning & reason has excelled Bacon? These four: Yet this is the country of Chaucer, Spenser, Hooker, Taylor, Dryden, & Locke. And the race is not yet extinct: witness Scott, Byron, ⟨Engl⟩Coleridge, Wordsworth,

[47] These heroes of peace have been flanked by the heroes of action, by the Drakes, Blakes, Cavendishes, Cooks, Marlboro's, Nelsons, Wellingtons.

And, one would say, th⟨at⟩e island has so long been the abode of a civil & free race, that the very dust ⟨&⟩is the remains of good & brave men, & the air retains the virtue their souls have shed into it, & they who inhale it, feel its quality. But I do not say these things to feed your pride & mine, but because we ⟨are⟩ are [48] to hear the appeal of the ancestors to the children.

We must feel as the Romans who put the statues of their fathers in the Atrium, that every time the man entered his door, he might pass through the line of his forefathers.

---

[43] See Journal London, p. [15]. This sentence is used in "Land," *W*, V, 41.

[44] There is a vertical pencil mark in the left margin extending from "Some countries" to "Turkey."

"We must be free or die, who speak the tongue
That Shakspeare spake; the faith & manners hold
Which Milton held; in everything, we are sprung
From earth's first blood, — titles manifold." [45]
[Wordsworth, "It is Not to be Thought of," ll. 11–14]

----

[49]

The commercial relations of the world are so intimately drawn to London, that it seems as if every dollar in the world contributed to strengthen the English ⟨g⟩Government.[46]

[50] "But, in a Protestant nation, that should have thrown off these tattered rudiments long ago, after the many strivings of God's Spirit, & our fourscore years vexation of him in this our wilderness, since reformation began, — to urge these rotten principles, & twit us with the present age, which is to us an age of ages, [51] wherein God is manifestly come down among us to do some remarkable good to our Church or State, is, as if a man should tax the renovating & reingendering spirit of God with innovation, & that new creature for an upstart novelty."

John Milton
Animadversions [Sec. V]
Jenks Vol. 1. 200,[47]

[52] Aristocracy

"The house of chivalry decayed
Those obelisks & columns broke & down
That strook the stars, & raised the British crown
To be a constellation
Once to the structure went more noble names
Than to the Ephesian temple lost in flames
When every stone was laid by virtuous hands" [48]

---

[45] "We . . . who speak . . . held;" is also used in "Poetry and Imagination," *W*, VIII, 69.

[46] This sentence is struck through in ink with three diagonal use marks. See *Journal London*, p. [15]; pp. [10] and [11] above; "Wealth," *W*, V, 162–163.

[47] *A Selection from the English Prose Works of John Milton*, ed. Francis Jenks, 2 vols. (Boston, 1826), in Emerson's library.

[48] Cf. Ben Jonson, *Prince Henry's Barriers*, ll. 31, 33, 37–39, 49–51; for ll. 49–51, see *JMN*, I, 343.

[53] These sea-kings may take to their floating castles once again, & swear anew never to sleep under a smoky roof, nor to own a yard of land.[49]

———

See too Gibbon's famous sentence to the like effect.

———

Here is the passage as Knox quotes it[:]

"Should it ever happen, that, in Europe brutal military despots should succeed in extinguishing the liberties of men threatening with the same unhappy fate the inhabitants of this island [54][50] they, mindful of their Saxon origin, would doubtless escape across the ocean, carrying to a new world their institutions, religion, & laws."[51]

Here is the passage as Gibbon writes it, *Decline & Fall* Vol. [VI,] *p 406* [:]

"Should the victorious barbarians (from the desarts of Tartary,) carry slavery & desolation as far as the Atlantic ocean, ten thousand vessels would transport beyond their pursuit the remains of civilized society; [55][52] and Europe would revive & flourish in the American world, which is already filled with her colonies & institutions."[53]

"A scoffing spirit inevitably prevails" (in a party consisting entirely of English)   *Warburton ap Johnston*[54]

———

men of business.

———

See account of the Saxons from *Sidonius apud* Camden, transcribed in T 124[55]

---

[49] See Journal London, p. [2], and "Character," *W*, V, 141.

[50] "*Traits.*" is written in ink as an index heading at the top of this page.

[51] Robert Knox, *The Races of Men: A Philosophical Enquiry into the Influence of Race over the Destinies of Nations* (London, 1850), p. 63.

[52] "*Traits.*" is written in ink as an index heading at the top of this page.

[53] Edward Gibbon, "General Observations on the Fall of the Roman Empire in the West," *The History of the Decline and Fall of the Roman Empire*, 12 vols. (London, 1821), in Emerson's library. The phrase in parentheses is Emerson's.

[54] William Johnston, *England As It Is*, 1851, I, 126, quoting Eliot Warburton, *The Crescent and the Cross.*

[55] See *JMN*, VI, 368–369.

[56]   ↑*Open-dealing.*↓

The English is aboveboard & direct, he disdains in fighting, to strike a foul blow, he disdains secret ballot. It is "out of his nature to assassinate even property"[.]

"Considering the abject respect ⟨for truth⟩ which Truth meets with in England, from persons of all politics," — &c

Sir Francis Head.

[57] [56]   Limitation

I find a prose in certain Englishmen which exceeds in wooden dead-ness all rivalry with other countrymen, & seems today, like the gates of Hell, "Leave all hope behind."

↑See BO 164↓ [57]

It is a nation where mediocrity is entrenched & consolidated, & funded & decorated in an adamantine manner.[58]

The people have wide range, but ascending scale in their specula-tion. An American, like a German, has many platforms of thought. [58] But an Englishman must be humoured or treated with tender-ness as an invalid, if you wish him to climb.[59]

He is finished like a seashell. After the spines & volutes are all formed, or, with the formation the hard enamel varnishes every part, — Pope, Swift, Johnson, Gibbon, Goldsmith, Gray. It seems an in-demnity to the Briton for his precocious maturity. He has no generous daring in this age. The Platonism died in the Elizabethan. He is [59] shut up in French limits.

[56] Laid in between pp. [56] and [57] is a leaf bearing pp. 37 and 38 of *An Address Delivered Before the Mercantile Library Association at the Odeon in Boston September 13, 1838* by Edward Everett (Boston: Wm. D. Ticknor, 1838); "Edward Everett" is inscribed in ink by Emerson at the top of p. 37, which is headed "Note to Page 13." Everett's note deals with unequal distribution of property in England, from Anglo-Saxon times to the nineteenth century.

[57] The insertion is in pencil; Journal BO will be published in a later volume. The allusion is to Dante, *Inferno*, III, 9.

[58] For "I find . . . manner.", see Journal London, p. [73]. The present entry, struck through in pencil with a vertical use mark, is used in "Manners," *W*, V, 111–112.

[59] For this paragraph, see Journal London, p. [63].

But Birmingham comes in, & says, "Never mind; I have some patent lustre that defies criticism. Moore made his whole fabric of the lustre, as we cover houses with a shell of inconsumable paint[.]" [60]

"What a fuss," says M[argaret].F[uller]., "these English make about presenting *thoughts* to an audience. What tedious prelude of apology for taking liberty to utter anything beyond the poorest truisms." &c ↑Red↑-book↓ 184 ([Journal] "London")↓ [61]

Plato is only read as a Greek book. Mr Hallam asked me, at Lord Ashburton's, whether Swedenborg were all mad, or partly knave? He [60] knew nothing of Thomas Taylor, nor did Milman, nor any Englishman. [62]

[61]   *Public Schools*

"In their playgrounds & in their rooms courage is universally admired cowardice or meanness universally despised manly feelings noble sentiments & generous conduct are fostered & encouraged; the spoiled child of rank whose face had been most obsequious↑ly↓ smoothed *down*wards, by the rough hand of the school, is rubbed upwards, until his admiration of himself, of his family, & of the extraordinary talents of his maiden aunt, are exchanged for a correcter estimate [62] which eventually makes him a better ↑a↓ wiser & a happier man. In short, the unwritten code of honour which, like a halo, shines around the playgrounds of our public schools ever has done & ever will do all that can be performed to make those who have the good fortune to exist⟨s⟩ under it, *gentlemen*."

Sir F. Head. [63]

[63] "I believe the parallelogram between Oxford street, Piccadilly, Regent Street, & Hyde Park, incloses more intelligence & human ability,

----

[60] For "He is finished . . . paint", see Journal London, p. [127]; for "He is finished . . . the lustre," see Journal AZ, pp. [26]-[27], to be published in a later volume. In the present entry, "He is finished . . . every part," struck through in pencil with a vertical use mark, is used in "Manners," *W*, V, 111.

[61] "Red . . . ('London')" is in pencil.

[62] For "Plato . . . book.", see Journal London, p. [60]; for "Mr Hallam . . . Englishman.", see Journal London, p. [129], and cf. Journal LM, p. [35].

[63] In this entry the following are added in pencil: the "ly" of "obsequiously"; the commas after "school", "upwards", and "aunt". The two sentences are used in "Universities," *W*, V, 208.

to say nothing of wealth & beauty, than the world ↑has↓ ever collected in such a space before."

Sydney Smith.

[64] *India* ↑*Revue des Deux Mondes*↓
British India extends from 7th to 34th degree of N. latitude
from 69° to 92° E. longitude
covers 1,400 000 squ. miles. (or ten or twelve times the size of France) & contains 150 to 180 millions of souls.[64]

[65] ↑Society↓
Dined at Lord Ashburton's, at Lady Harriet Baring's, attended Lady Palmerston's Soirée; saw fine people at Lady Morgan's, & at Lady Molesworth's, Lord Lovelace's, & other houses. But a very little⟨e⟩ is enough for me, & I find that all the old deoxygenation & asphyxia that have in town or in village existed for me in that word a "party", exist unchanged in London palaces. Of course the fault is wholly mine, but I shall at least know how to save a great deal of time & temper henceforward.[65]

[66] Again[:]

You will wish to know what Mr Bull really says to me, & is to me. I confess, I am, much of the time, in that unhappy state which evening parties throw me into, — the parlour Erebus; — and that solitary infirmity of mine Mr Bull is the last person to forgive.[66]

Sir H. Wotton said of ↑Sr.↓ Philip Sidney, that "his wit was the measure of congruity."[67]

[64] See Francis Edwards, "Les Civiliens. Moeurs administratives de l'Inde anglaise," *Revue des Deux Mondes*, II (1848), 201–229.
[65] This paragraph is transcribed from Emerson's letter to Margaret Fuller, London, April 25, 1848 (*L*, IV, 62–63).
[66] These two sentences are transcribed from Emerson's letter to his wife, Manchester, December 1, 1847 (*L*, III, 444).
[67] As in *JMN*, V, 47, and *Lectures*, I, 354, Emerson is quoting from Izaak Walton, "The Life of Sir Henry Wotton," in *Reliquiae Wottonianae or a Collection of Lives, Letters, Poems*, 4th ed. (London, 1685), p. 37. The sentence is used in "Manners," *W*, V, 112.

[67]   ↑*Decorum.*↓

They are trained to the highest inoffensiveness.[68]

Taste is tyrannical in England.[69] The censure before which parliaments turn pale, is, — that, such a thing is not in good taste. At the opera, only, is any enthusiasm permitted.[70]
"The upper classes have only birth," say people here, "& not thoughts." Yes, but they have manners, & 'tis wonderful how much talent runs into manners. Nowhere & never so much as in England.[71]

[68] An Englishman discovers a dissenter by his manners.[72]

On one occasion, Thalberg played on the piano, at Windsor, & the Queen accompanied him with her voice. On the news of this getting abroad, all England shuddered from sea to sea. It was never repeated.[73]

"When Mario (M[archese]. di Candia) and Julia Grisi sing at the house of Lord Wellington & other great persons, a cord is stretched between them & the invited guests."[74]

Courrier des Etats Unis 24 Juin
1852 [XXIX, No. 197, p. 1]

[69] A Frenchman may possibly be clean; an^n Englishman is conscientiously so.[75]

An Englishman of fashion is like one of those souvenirs, bound

---

[68] "They . . . inoffensiveness." is struck through in pencil with a vertical use mark. See Journal London, p. [44].

[69] Cf. *JMN*, V, 119, and VI, 350, and "Manners," *Lectures*, II, 139.

[70] For this sentence, see Journal London, p. [23]; Journal LM, p. [94]; "Manners," *W*, V, 112. It is struck through in.pencil with a vertical use mark.

[71] " 'The upper . . . England.", struck through in pencil with a vertical use mark, is used in "Aristocracy," *W*, V, 186.

[72] See Journal London, p. [29].

[73] "On one . . . repeated." is struck through in pencil with a vertical use mark. See Journal London, p. [68], and "Manners," *W*, V, 112.

[74] This sentence is used in "Aristocracy," *W*, V, 194. See also Journal London, p. [62].

[75] This sentence, struck through in pencil with a vertical use mark, is used in "Manners," *W*, V, 107.

in gold & vellum, enriched with delicate engravings, on thick h⟨e⟩ot-
-pressed vellum paper, fit for the hands of ladies & princes, but with
nothing in it worth reading or remembering.[76]

These young men walk in a very narrow path. After they have
left the University, all they know, is, their club, & the way to the
door of the House of Commons.[77]

[70] "It is in bad taste," is the most formidable word an Englishman can pronounce.[78]

↑See on skill to pack an evening party   *CO* 254↓ [79]

[71]–[74] [blank] [80]
[75]   Brag
Was never such arrogancy on the face of the earth as the tone
of this paper. Every slip of an Oxonian or Cantabrigian who writes
his first *leader*, assumes that *we* subdued the world, before we sat
down to write this particular Times. But the habit of brag runs
through all classes, from the Premier & Lord Palmerston & the
Times, ⟨down⟩Wordsworth, Carlyle, Macaulay, down to the boys of
Eton.[81]

They delight to tell at dinner-tables a story that came from
Rogers, I believe, of a Frenchman & Englishman who quarreled.
Both were [76] averse to fight, but their friends put them up to it, &
there was at last no getting off. It was agreed, at last, that they should

[76] For this paragraph, see Journal London, p. [128]; it also occurs in Journal
AZ, p. [70], to be published in a later volume. Struck through in pencil here with
a vertical use mark, it is used in "Manners," *W*, V, 112.

[77] See Notebook England and Paris, p. [50₁], and Journal LM, p. [99].

[78] See *JMN*, VII, 178, and Journal TU, p. [141], to be published in a later
volume. This sentence, struck through in pencil with a vertical use mark, is used
in "Manners," *W*, V, 111.

[79] The insertion is in pencil. Journal CO will be published in a later volume.

[80] Pp. [71]–[74] are without inscription. Pasted to p. [72] is a clipping from
the *British Medical Journal*, March 24, 1877, p. 366: a letter to the editor from
E. F. Flower headed "Bearing-Reins for Horses."

[81] For this paragraph, see Journal London, p. [51]; cf. "The Times," *W*, V,
269, and "Cockayne," *W*, V, 150.

be left alone in the room, with pistols, & the lights put out. The Englishman, to be perfectly sure of hurting nobody, fired up chimney, & brought down the Frenchman.[82]

[77]–[84] [blank]
[85]   ↑Culture↓
Gilpin's Forest Scenery is a good example of the sincerity of British culture.[83]

↑The Universities, and↓ Wood's Athena⟨e⟩e Oxonienses, ⟨is⟩ ↑are↓ another national monument.

The Greenwich Observatory & Ephemeris; the British Museum; the Lycian Marbles; the excavations & monuments from Nineveh; the Crystal Palace; the Arctic Voyages; Herschel's Catalogue of Southern stars; are other national monuments of the genius of this singular people. Gibbon's Decline & Fall; the translations of the Greek Drama;

[86] Wood's Athenae[n] Oxonienses is a proper ornament for this England: it is a pasture oak and Hakluyt & Purchas & Fuller.[84]

William of Wykeham

[86a][85] Collingwood was offered a medal for 14 February ↑1797↓ at St Vincent. He refused it until he received a medal for 1 June 1794[.][86]

---

[82] See Journal London, p. [198]; Journal LM, p. [27]; "Cockayne," W, V, 149.
[83] This sentence is transcribed from Journal London, p. [183].
[84] This sentence is used in "Universities," W, V, 201.
[85] Pp. [86a]–[86f] comprise a twice-folded sheet laid in between pp. [86] and [87]: see the bibliographical headnote to Notebook ED.
[86] "Collingwood . . . 1794" is used in "Truth," W, V, 122–123. Emerson's reference is to two naval battles: the British victory over the Spanish fleet off Cape St. Vincent and the earlier triumph over a French fleet off the British coast, when Collingwood was unmentioned in the dispatches of its commander, Lord Howe.

[86ᵦ] 1 to 22 Up[land?]
23 to 96 Border
34 to 49 Glade
91 to 97 Ridge
61 to 69 Knoll [87]

[86ᵧ]–[86ᵩ] [blank]

[87]   *Worthies.*

Sir Henry Wotton is a good model Englishman, equal to business or to study, able in both, yet had been as good in any other of
twenty ways. Ask him for a counsel, he can give one. He pourtrays a
man, as if he had seen many, & as good as Homer had. Earl of Essex
⟨ye⟩ Duke of Buckingham were men, & equal to their high fortunes.
They were no *Presidents of the United States.* Sir Kenelm Digby
↑(see p 287 of this book)↓
    ↑Nelson
    Wellington
    Saml Johnson↓

[88]   *Worthies.*

Never country had so many good citizens. The Worthies of
England[.]
Never had country so many good fellows going about the world &
each one bringing home something useful. Sr H. Wotten brought
home melon-seeds; Raleigh, tobacco & potatoes[.] [88]
Hargraves invented the spinning jenny & died in Nottingham Workhouse[.] [89]

[89]   *Worthies*

    Earl Grey (of the Reform Bill)

————

Richard Beauchamp Earl of Warwick (1381–1439)

[87] "1 to . . . Knoll" is written in pencil on p. [86ᵦ] (between the folds of the
inserted sheet), at a right angle to "Collingwood . . . 1794" on p. [86ₐ].
[88] The comma after "Raleigh" is added in pencil.
[89] This sentence is used in "Wealth," *W*, V, 158.

Sigismond Emperor told King Henry V. that no Christian king had such another knight, for wisdom, nurture, & manhood; & caused him to be named the *"Father of Courtesie."*

At a joust in France, fighting with Sir Collard Fines, he so bore himself, the French thought he was tied to the saddle; & to confute their jealousies, he alighted & remounted. At the Council of Constance, his retinue amounted to 800 horse. "Our success in France lived & died with him." Crossing into Normandy, the ship was tossed with such a tempest, that Warwick caused himself & lady & infant son to be bound to the mainmast with his armour & coat of arms upon him, that he might be known & buried aright. Yet he died in his bed.
——   ↑See *Fuller.* II. 472↓ [90]

[90]   *Worthies*
Camden (p 266) quotes this Tetrastich made on commendation of Queen Maud (of Henry I.) [:]

"Prospera non laetam fecere nec aspera tristem
    Aspera risus ei, prospera terror erant
Non decor effecit fragilem non sceptra superbam,
    Sola potens humilis, sola pudica decens." [91]

and of Sir Francis Drake one (Cowley?) wrote[:]

---

[90] Thomas Fuller, *The History of the Worthies of England*, ed. John Nichols, 2 vols. (London, 1811); Emerson borrowed vol. II from the Boston Athenaeum, September 11–October 27, 1852. "Sigismond . . . *Courtesie.*' " is used in "Aristocracy," *W,* V, 175.

[91] William Camden, *Britain, or A Chorographicall Description of the Most Flourishing Kingdomes, England, Scotland and Ireland,* trans. Philemon Holland (London, 1637), borrowed from the Boston Athenaeum by Emerson, September 27–December 23, 1852. Holland renders the lines as follows:

"No prosp'rous state did make her glad,
Nor adverse chances made her sad:
If fortune frown'd, she then did smile;
If fortune frown'd, she feard the while.
If beauty tempted, she yet said nay,
No pride she took in scepters sway:
Shee onely high, her selfe debas'd,
A lady onely faire and chast."

Drake, pererrati novit quem terminus orbis
    Quemque semel mundi vidit uterque polus,
Si taceant homines, facient te sidera notum,
    Sol nescit comitis immemor esse sui.[92]

———

Of Empress Maud daughter of Henry I wife of Henry IV Emperor of Germany & mother of Henry II of England[:]

Magna ortu, majorque viro, sed maxima partu
Hic jacet Henrici filia sponsa parens.

Wellborn, still better wedded, ⟨but⟩ childed best
The bones of Henry's daughter wife & mother rest [93]

———

Camden cites "an old verse of K. Henry II's death" [:]

"Mira caro, sol occubuit, nox nulla secuta est." [94]

[91]–[93₁] [95] [blank]
    [92₂] "I can never think that place my country, where I cannot call a foot of paternal earth my own."
                                    Pope.
                                    Letter to Lady Montagu [96]

[93₂]   Wealth

hommage instinctif, continuel, féroce, au dieu de tous; l'or; la nation

---

[92] William Camden, *Britain*, trans. Holland, 1637, I, 200–201, where the lines are rendered as follows:
    "Sir Drake, whom well the worlds end knows, which thou did'st compasse round:
    And whom both poles of heaven once saw, which North and South doe bound:
    The Starres above will make thee knowne, if men here silent were,
    The Sunne himselfe cannot forget his fellow-travailler."
    [93] William Camden, *Britain*, trans. Holland, 1637, I, 284; the English rendering here is Emerson's.
    [94] William Camden, *Britain*, trans. Holland, 1637, I, 285, which reads ". . . sequuta est", rendering the line as: "A wonder great, the Sunne was set, and night there followed none." Cf. *JMN*, IX, 381.
    [95] Emerson erred in numbering the pages following [91]. What should have been designated pp. [92] and [93] (both blank) he left unnumbered; what should be p. [94] he numbered [92].
    [96] Cf. Letter XXI in *The Works of Alexander Pope*, 9 vols. (London, 1753), VII, 145.

animée de ↑la↓ fureur de paraître Paraître quoi? Riche, au dessus du rang qu'on occupe réellement. *Jules Lecomte.*[97]

"to be thought more opulent & tasteful, & on a footing of intimacy with a larger number of distinguished persons than they really are, is the great & laborious pursuit of four families out of five, the members of which are exempted from the necessity of daily industry."

Lord Jeffrey.[98]

[94] — "in this country, where poverty is infamous." *Sidney Smith.*[99]

Russel Family ⟨owns four miles⟩ square in the heart ⟨of the city⟩ of London[.] [100]

[95]–[105] [101] [blank]
[106]   *Universities*

"21 July 1683 the Convocation at Oxford caused the Leviathan of Thomas Hobbes to be publicly burnt in their School-Court or Quadrangle" [102]   Wood. [*Athenæ Oxonienses,* 1721]
                                              II. 664 [i.e., 644]

Qu. When, how, & by what authority, was the "Nemesis of Faith" burned? [103]

At Cambridge was ⟨B⟩Nicholas Bacon, Burleigh, Walsingham.

Francis Bacon
John Milton
John Dryden

---

[97] This same passage occurs in Journal CO, p. [84], where it is attributed to the *Courrier des Etats-Unis.* Journal CO is to be published in a later volume.

[98] Quoted in William Johnston, *England As It Is,* 1851, I, 128–129.

[99] Cf. William Johnston, *England As It Is,* 1851, I, 224. The remark is used in "Wealth," *W,* V, 153–154.

[100] This sentence, in pencil, is used in "Aristocracy," *W,* V, 181.

[101] Following what Emerson designated p. [94] is p. [95], both numbered in ink; then come "⟨100⟩98", "⟨101⟩99", and "101", all numbered in pencil; then four unnumbered pages; then "106", numbered in ink. By omitting [96] and [97] he corrected the error made in not numbering pp. [92]–[93].

[102] This sentence is used in "Universities," *W,* V, 202.

[103] Emerson is referring to James Anthony Froude's *The Nemesis of Faith* (London, 1849), which provoked organized clerical opposition to its author.

John Locke
Isaac Newton

[107] [blank]
[108] [104]   *Carlyle*   Criticism
                               Ruskin

Here is the English reputation of Carlyle. Is it founded on wit?
No, but on his revolutionary character, or his setting himself against
the mountainous nonsense of the age; & purer & higher had it been,
if it had not weaved into it brag & conceit[.]

Ruskin, again, & a great School of Protestants have [109] perceived the natural beauty over the conventional & that which is
⟨‖ ... ‖⟩forever[.]

Ten thousand ⟨Scotts &⟩ [105] Southeys & Macaulays are not equal to
one Wordsworth.[106]

————————

Carlyle again
Like all men of wit and great rhetorical power, he is by no
means to be held to the paradox ⟨of⟩ ↑the utters↓ today: he states it
well, & overstates it, because he is himself trying how far it will bear
him. But the novelty & lustre of his language makes [110] the hearers
remember his opinion, & ↑would↓ [n] [107] hold him to it long after he has
forgotten it.
Carlyle gave me a list of books which he advised me to buy. As
follows↑, See my red MS. called *London*
                          p 207↓ [108]
Kennett's History of England.   25 shillings.

————————

[104] Emerson first numbered pp. [108]–[109] in pencil as "110" and "111"; he
corrected "110" in pencil and then in ink to "108" but left [109] as "111".
[105] "Scotts" is canceled in ink and also circled in pencil; the penciling has been
extended to designate that "&" should also be canceled.
[106] This sentence is struck through in ink with six diagonal use marks.
[107] The insertion is written and corrected in pencil.
[108] The insertion is in pencil, partly erased. In addition to Journal London, p.
[207] (where the titles are fully identified), see also Notebook Xenien, p. [64];
JMN, VIII, 564; and, with variations, Journal AZ, p. [133], to be published in a
later volume.

Lowth's Life of William of Wykeham
Camden's Brittannia, translated by Holland. 7 or 8 shillings
Britton's Beauties of England & Wales.
Hainault. Abrégé Chronologique de l'Histoire de France.
Bede's Chronicle.
Collins' Peerage. 1745. (or any time before Egerton Brydges)
£12.6.

Memo. In 1833, I met Gustave D'Eichthal at an evening party at
Mr Horace Gray's, in Rome. He was what was then called a Saint
Simonian. He was well acquainted with Carlyle, & offered to give me
a letter of introduction to him. The next day he called on me & gave
me a letter to John Stuart Mill in London, requesting him to introduce me to Carlyle. In London, I found Mr Mill at the India
House, & he wrote to Carlyle, & advised my visit.

[110ₐ] [109] ⟨Books⟩

Not only Xy[Christianity] is as old as the Creation[,] not only
every sentiment & precept of Xy can be paralleled in other religious
writings, but a man of religious suscept[ibilit].y &, at the same time
conversant with men, say a ↑much↓ travelled man, can find the same
height in numberless conversations. The religious find religion where-
ever they associate.
When I find in people narrow religion, I find narrow [110ᵦ] reading[.]
Nothing is so ⟨divulgatory⟩ ↑expansive↓ as thought.[110] It cannot be
confined or hid. 'Tis easily carried. It takes no room[.]

[111]   *Rogers.*
Mrs Bancroft presented me to Samuel Rogers, Esq. Mr Rogers in-

---

[109] As shown by pinholes, the inserted leaf bearing pp. [110ₐ]–[110ᵦ] was at
one time attached to p. [110] so that p. [110ₐ] faced p. [111]. See the bibiographi-
cal headnote to Notebook ED.

[110] The comma after "narrow religion" is in pencil. "divulgatory" is canceled in
pencil; "expansive" is written in pencil and rewritten in ink.

vited ⟨me⟩ ↑us↓ to ⟨Br⟩breakfast, ⟨with Mrs B, at his house⟩ ↑with him↓ on Friday. ⟨Accordingly⟩ ⟨Just ⁿ before ten o'clock, on Friday morning, I attended Mrs B., in company with her son,¹¹¹ & young Butler of N.Y., to Rogers's⟩.¹¹² I suppose no distinguished person has been in England during the last fifty years, who has not been at this house; so that it has the *prestige* of a modern Pantheon. Mr R. received us with cold, quiet, indiscriminate politeness, & entertained us [112] with a store of anecdote, which Mrs B. ⟨very skilfully⟩ ↑knew how to↓ draw forth, about such people as ⟨she knew⟩ we cared most to hear of. Scott, Wordsworth, Byron, Wellington, Talleyrand, Madame de Stael, Lafayette, Fox, Burke, & crowds of high men & women had talked & feasted in these rooms, which are decorated ⟨also⟩ with every precious work. The mantel-piece was carved by Flaxman. An antique marble head Canova had brought with his own hands & set down in the place which it now occupies. Sir Francis Chantrey, [113]ⁿ dining one day with our host, asked him if he remembered the workman who made a cabinet for him (which was now in the apartment). "I was that man," ⟨sa⟩continued the sculptor. Here are vases from old Rome; & some of the best pictures in England; ⟨&⟩ casts of the Elgin marbles are⟨, in an ⟨‖ ... ‖⟩excellent way,⟩ ↑judiciously↓ let into the walls, ⟨[⟩ with⟨in⟩ ↑⟨with⟩↓ ⟨which]⟩ a flying staircase ⟨[⟩ mounts ↑⟨in the room⟩↓ ⟨]⟩ ↑near↓, so as to be examinable at every angle.¹¹³

Mr Rogers showed ⟨me⟩ ↑us↓ Milton's autograph, Pope's original bust, autograph letters of Washington, Franklin, Mozart, Fox, Burke, Dr Johnson, &c. [114] He read letters of Byron to himself, & I saw original manuscript of pages of Waverley, & so on, to any extent. This man's collection is the chief private show of London.¹¹⁴

---

¹¹¹ Alexander Bliss.

¹¹² The enclosing parentheses are added in pencil.

¹¹³ The changes after "walls" are in pencil. Emerson first marked phrases for revision by using square brackets; then changed "with⟨in⟩ ⟨which⟩" to "with" and tentatively changed "mounts" to "in the room"; next he substituted "near" for "in the room", cancelling "in the room" but still without cancelling "mounts"; finally, he erased the square brackets. The intended reading appears to be "with a flying staircase near, so . . . angle."

¹¹⁴ "Mrs Bancroft presented . . . London." is adapted from a letter Emerson had written to his wife from London, October 21 and 22, 1847: see *L*, III, 425–426.

Rogers's sentences are quoted almost as much as Sydney Smith's, for their ↑satirical↓ point↑.↓ ⟨& satire.⟩ It was he who said ⟨lately⟩ of Croker's article on Macaulay, in the Edinburgh, "that he had attempted murder, & committed suicide." [115] Sumner told me, that, one day, ⟨Rogers &⟩ [115] ⟨his⟩ he dined with Rogers, &, after dinner, they were saying plenty of hard things of ——————, author of a new novel. In the midst of it all, —————— himself was suddenly announced, ⟨M⟩and ⁿ walked in. "Ah!" said Mr Rogers, greeting him with great ↑apparent↓ cordiality, — "Ah! how kind! We were just this moment speaking of you!"

When Miss Cushman asked him whether he should not go to America?, he repli[e]d, "It was always my intention to visit America, before I died; but now that I have seen *you*, I have no longer any [116] desire to do so." ⟨On hearing⟩ ↑On hearing↓ of the marriage of Miss ↑Susan↓ [116] Cushman to Mr Musprat, he said, "that, he always understood, that, at the end of the Season, Miss ⟨Charlotte⟩ Cushman was to marry her sister." [117]

Rogers told us of Talleyrand's visit to him with the Duchess of Orleans blazing with beauty, & Pamela, ↑(↓afterwards Lady Fitzgerald,↑)↓ who was more attractive by the sweet seriousness of sixteen. Talleyrand's answer to Mme de Stael (he repeated) who asked him, "which he should [117] save, on a plank, in a shipwreck, Mme Recamier, or herself?" "Why, you can swim." When this Princess of Orleans was ⟨coming⟩ on ⟨the⟩ ↑her↓ way to England, and the question rose, if you could only know one English word, — one said, 'you could get along with "*Yes*."' But the princess said, "If I knew but one, it should be *No*; because *No* sometimes means *Yes*, but *Yes* never means *No*."

To a lady who wished to witness a great victory, Lord Wellington

---

[115] Emerson is in error; John Wilson Croker's unsigned review of Thomas Babington Macaulay, *The History of England from the Accession of James II*, 2 vols. (London, 1849), appeared not in the *Edinburgh Review* but in the *Quarterly Review*, LXXXIV (March 1849), 549–630.

[116] Emerson first left the name blank, then supplied it in pencil, and finally rewrote it in ink.

[117] For "When Miss . . . sister.' ", see Journal London, p. [84].

said, "Ah, Madam, a great victory is the greatest of tragedies, except one, a defeat."

[118] To an Englishman who said to the Persian Ambassador, "They worship the sun in your country," ⟨t⟩he replied, "So would you, if you ever saw him." [118]

[119] [119] [blank]
[120]   *Richard Owen.* [120]

Mr Richard Owen was kind enough to give me a card to his course of Lectures before the Royal College of Surgeons⟨, and I heard as many of the lectures as I could.⟩. [121] He is an excellent lecturer. His vinous face is a powerful weapon. He has a surgical smile, — and an air of virility, that penetrates his audience. A perfect selfcommand & temperance, master of his wide nomenclature, & stepping securely from stone to stone. But there was no need that he who thinks lightly of the [121] accumulation of facts, should run counter to his own genius, & attack the "transmutationists"; for it is they who obey the idea which makes him great. [122]

Mr. O. explained the process by which the bird roosts without falling in sleep; & that, by which the ostrich outspeeds the racer, the forepart of the body flying, the hind part running.

When the wings of a bird are outspaced, all the air-cells are distended[.]

[118] For "Rogers told [p. [116]] . . . saw him.' ", see Journal GH, [114]–[115]. Enclosing "When this . . . saw him.' " are parentheses added in pencil; a marginal notation reads "Turn to page 167" (where the anecdotes concerning the Cushman sisters are repeated). "To a Lady [p. [117]] . . . defeat.' " is used in "Quotation and Originality," *W*, VIII, 184, where the anecdote is attributed to Rogers.

[119] Laid in between pp. [118] and [119] is a clipping from an unidentified newspaper reprinting an article of four paragraphs headed "The Troubles of Riches." and credited at its conclusion: "—*London Times.*"

[120] Before the following entry is a parenthesis, added in pencil.

[121] "and I . . . could." is canceled in ink, with the period replacing a comma after "Surgeons".

[122] For this paragraph, see Journal London, pp. [19], [119]; Journal LM, p. [72½].

Spallanzani thought, birds swallowed pebbles from stupidity.[123]

[122] Mr O. told the story of Dean Buckland's objection to the gigantic Rat which pulled down the trees of the elder world, namely, that he would get killed by their fall: and, when the ⟨s⟩fossil skull of one was examined, it was found ↑to be double, and↓ of an immoderate thickness, and also with great fractures healed over.

The Jerboa rat & other animals of that kind are in enormous numbers, and prolific; have their function to destroy corrupt animal matter and are like the infusoria in that office.

The Bat analogous to the Cetacea[:] [123][124] one is a mammal adapted to swim & one a mammal adapted to fly. Then again analogous to the mole & the Shrew[,] one moving by displacing air & the other displacing earth. Spallanzani blinded & deafened a bat & strung threads across the room & the bat flew without touching them.
Sleep is the hybernation of the day. Hybernation is the sleep of the year. Light is not the exciting cause always, for some animals wake in the dark, & sleep in the day. Light was thought the exciting cause in reference to sleep, & Heat in reference to hybernation. And yet there are animals who sleep [124] during the hottest & dryest part of the equatorial year. The hybernation is determined by the season of food. The bat living on insects would die, when the insects died; but now, he sleeps thro' this long fast, without respiration.[125]

Mr Owen invited Hillard & myself to inspect the Hunterian ↑(John Hunter)↓ Museum, of which he is the Curator.[126] Afterwards, he would carry us to Turner the artist, who is his friend.

---

[123] For "Mr. O. . . . stupidity.", see Journal London, p. [86].

[124] Laid in between pp. [122] and [123] is a clipping from an unidentified newspaper concerning the *Times* of London (recto) and a day's proceedings in the House of Representatives (verso). At one time the clipping was pinned to p. [122].

[125] For "Mr. O. told [p. [122]] . . . respiration.", see Journal London, pp. [118]–[119].

[126] This sentence is used in "Personal," *W*, V, 293, where Emerson names his visit to the museum among "two or three signal days" of his stay in London. The date was June 29, 1848 (*L*, IV, 93; Journal London, p. [210]).

⟨He⟩ We met accordingly at his chambers & he showed us over the Museum with communicating a great deal of [125] valuable information ↑of↓ which I deeply regret that I omitted to make immediate record. He gave a sad history of the misuse & voluntary destruction of Hunter's MSS by Sir Everard Home who had built his own ↑scientific↓ reputation on the private use he had made of these MSS., & then destroyed them to hide his debt. He was displaced, & Owen himself appointed to the care of the Museum, & he does not like to sleep one night away from it. One of these days when the Museum shall be confided to other & sufficient hands, ⟨of⟩he said [126] he shall feel at liberty to come to America, & read lectures to the Lowell Institute, Boston, as Mr Lowell has pressed him to do. He thought Faraday would also come ⟨thither⟩ to Boston. Owen seemed to me an Englishman who had made a prodigious stride in scientific liberalism for an Englishman, & indemnified himself in the good opinion of his countrymen, by fixing a certain fierce limitation to his progress, & abusing [127] without mercy all such as ventured a little farther; these poor transmutationists, for example.

He carried us to Turner's Studio but Turner though he had written him a note to announce his visit was gone. So he showed us the pictures. In his earlier pictures, he said, Turner painted conventionally, painted what he knew was there, finished the coat & buttons: in the later he paints only what the eye ⟨sees⟩ really sees, & gives the genius of the city or landscape. He was engaged [128] to paint a whaleship, & he came, one day, to see Mr Owen, & asked to see a mullet (?) & begged him to explain to him, from the beginning, the natural history of the creature; which he did; & Turner followed him with great accuracy. In process of time, the picture was painted, & Owen went there to see his mullet.[n] "I could not find it," he said, "in the picture, but I doubt not it is all there." [127]

[129] He told us, that, one day, ⟨dining⟩ being present at the annual

----

[127] For "He carried . . . there.' ", see Journal London, pp. [178]–[179]. Written in pencil above "whaleship" is "Query, 'Slave Ship'? EWE[merson]"; above "mullet" in square brackets is "Agassiz said, a Clio". The commas after "earlier pictures", "said", "conventionally", "there", and "sees" are added in pencil.

dinner of the Royal Academy, which takes place in the Gallery itself, as ↑the↓ shades of evening darkened around, all the pictures became opake, — all but Turner's, & these still glittered like gems, as if having light in themselves.

I was much struck with the elevated manner in which Mr Owen spoke of the few men of science he named; of Agassiz, & others. He said, "Each had a manner, & a certain strength, & his own foible too, & he thought [130] he could well discern that in all they did, and I think, he added, I can see the same in myself, too."

Turner's[n] face, I was told, resembles much the heads of Punch. He has never permitted any head of himself to be painted; for, Mr Windus told me, he said, "People would never believe that all these handsome pictures were painted by so ugly a fellow." [128]
It was Miss   of New Haven who on reading Ruskin's book said, "Nature was Mrs Turner."

[131] [blank]
[132] With Mr Kenyon, & Hillard I joined the Jays in a visit to *Stokes Regis* [Stoke Poges], where is Gray's churchyard; then to Eton, where we found 6, or 700⟨0⟩ boys, the flower of English youth, some of them at cricket, on the green; others strolling in groups & pairs; some rowing in the river; & recalled Lamb's remark, "What pity that these fine boys should be changed into frivolous members of Parliament!"
Kenyon recalled verses of his own, of which I only remember, —

"O give us back our lofty youth!"

and the whole place remembered [133] Gray. Kenyon asked, if ever a dirty request was couched in more beautiful verses than in the hints touching livings & preferments, addressed to the Duke of Grafton, in the Cambridge Installation Ode.

"Thy liberal heart, thy judging eye,

[128] In Journal London, p. [165], Emerson states that Turner made his remark to Clarkson Stanfield. For "Turner's face . . . Punch.", see Notebook Xenien, p. [5]; Journal LM, p. [98]; "Character," *W*, V, 135.

The flower unheeded shall descry,
And bid it round heaven's altars shed
The fragrance of its blushing head;
Shall raise from earth the latent gem
To glitter on the diadem."
[Thomas Gray, "For Music" (1769), VI, ll. 7–12]

After seeing the Chapel, we went to Windsor, where the tickets of the Jays procured admittance for the [134] whole party to the private apartments of ⟨h⟩Her Majesty. We traversed the long corridors which form the gallery of sculpture & painting; then the chambers, dining-room, & reception rooms, of this palace. The green expanse of trim counties which these windows command, beginning with a mile of garden in front, is excellent. Then to the Royal Mews, where a hundred horses are kept[;] [135] listened reverentially to all that the grooms told us of the favorite horses; looked at the carriages, &c. If hard come to hard, the camel has a good deal of hump left to spend from.

In St George's Chapel, Mr Kenyon pointed out the true character of stained glass windows, which is, not in large figures or good drawings, but, in gem-like splendor & condensation. In like manner, he quoted Lady Morgan's notion on carpets, that they should be spread, not nailed; & there should not be great elaborate figures, but [136] such a disposition of forms & colors, that they should seem like jewels trodden in.

From Windsor, we went to Virginia Water, the toy-lake & toy fishing--house of George IV. Here is a made waterfall; & a made ruin, the "Persepolis of the woods," constructed of stones brought [137] from the ruins of Carthage. But the expense squandered on these grounds ⟨has⟩ ↑does↓ not ⟨helped to⟩ save them from the ⟨paltriness⟩ ↑⟨&⟩ ridicule↓ of a ↑tawdry↓ counterfeit⟨; & the spectator grudges his time).ⁿ Two red flags hanging from the little frigates afloat, were quite too important in the ↑raree-↓show. We suspected the two or three people in the boat were hired to sit there by the day; and ⟨one⟩ the eye ⟨questioned⟩ ↑mistrusted↓ the houses might be pasteboard, & the rocks ⟨were sugar⟩ ↑barley↓-candy.[129]

[129] For "With Mr Kenyon [p. [132]] . . . candy.", see Journal London, pp.

[138]–[139] [blank]

[140]   R. M. MILNES.

By the kind offices of Mr Milnes, Mr Milman, Lord Morpeth, & I
know not what other gentlemen, I found myself elected into the
"Athenaeum" Club, "during my temporary residence in England;"
—a privilege one must prize, not because only ten foreigners are
eligible, at any one time,—but because it gives all the rights of a
member in the library & reading-room, a home to sit in, & see the
best company, & a coffee room, if you [141] like it, where you eat
at cost.

Milnes, Milman, Crabbe Robinson & many good men are always to
be found there. Milnes is the most good natured man in England,
made of sugar: he is every where, & knows every thing; [n] has the
largest range of acquaintance, ⟨of anybody,⟩ from the Chartist to the
Lord Chancellor; fat, easy, affable, & obliging; a little careless &
sloven in his dress.

His speeches in ⟨the House⟩ ↑Parliament↓ are always unlucky, & a
signal for emptying the House,—a topic of great mirth to himself
& ↑all↓ his friends, who frankly twit him with it. He is so entirely at
home everywhere, & takes life [142] so quietly, that Sidney Smith
called him "the cool of the evening,"—and I remember, I was told
some anecdotes of exploits of well-bred effrontery.—They address
him now as *Citoyen* Milnes, since Punch's, that is, Thackeray's late
list of the Ministry: [130] but with some feeling between jest & earnest,
they speak of him, as really one who might play, one day, the part
of Lamartine, in England. [131]

Carlyle, at the first meeting of the London Library, proposed to
sacrifice Milnes, as a sort of acceptable Iphigenia. [143] When he

---

[169]–[171]; the quotation from Gray on p. [133] is not in the earlier version or
its antecedent in Notebook England and Paris, p. [44].

[130] See "A Dream of the Future," *Punch*, XIV, No. 349 (Jan.–June 1848), 107,
in which "Citizen Monckton Milnes" is listed as "Minister of Foreign Affairs, President of the Council, and Poet Laureate."

[131] For "By the kind [p. [140]] . . . England.", see the letter from Emerson
to his wife, London, March 23 and 24, 1848 (*L*, IV, 42).

breakfasted somewhere with the Archbishop of Canterbury, his friend said, "Now, Milnes, I beg you not to slap him on the back, & call him Canterbury, before breakfast is half over." His good humour is infinite; he makes bad speeches of exquisite infelicity, & joins in the laugh against himself. He is very liberal of his money, & sincerely kind & useful to young people of merit.[132] Coventry Patmore told me, that Milnes had procured him spontaneously the place he holds of sub-librarian in the British Museum; & that he had known many good ⟨things⟩ deeds of his. & Jane Carlyle testified to [144] his generosity, — rare, she said, among people of fashion, — with his money.

For my part, I found him uniformly kind & useful to me both in London & in Paris. He procured me cards to Lady Palmerston's soirée, introduced me, ⟨there,⟩ & took pains to show me all the remarkable persons there, the ↑Crown↓ Prince ⟨Royal⟩ of Prussia; the Prince of Syracuse; Rothschild[,] ↑a round young comfortable looking man↓; Mr Hope, reputed the richest commoner in England; the Turkish Ambassador; ⟨&⟩Lord Lincoln, head of the "Young England" party; and prince⟨s⟩ly ⟨&⟩ foreigners, whose [145] names I have forgotten.[133]

Milnes took pains to make me acquainted with Chevalier Bunsen & Lady B. whom I had already met at Mr Bancroft's; with young Mr Cowper, son of Lady Palmerston; with D'Israeli; and with Macaulay, whom I here met for the second time.[134] I had a few words with both Lord & Lady P. He is frank, (at least, in manner; — Bancroft says, far from frank in ⟨‖ . . . ‖⟩business,) affable, of a strong but cheerful & ringing speech.[135]

[132] For "Carlyle, at [p. [142]] . . . merit.", see Journal London, pp. [16]– [17].
[133] If the reference is indeed to Lord Lincoln (i.e., Henry Pelham Fiennes Pelham Clinton, 1811–1864, 5th Duke of Newcastle), Emerson was in error in associating him with the Young England movement of 1843 to 1847, which was led by Disraeli and Lord John Manners (i.e., John James Robert Manners, 1818–1906, 7th Duke of Rutland).
[134] The semicolon after "Bancrofts" and the commas after "Cowper" and "Macaulay" are added in pencil; commas after "Palmerston" and "D'Israeli" have been changed in pencil to semicolons.
[135] For "He procured [p. [144]] . . . speech.", see Emerson's letter to his wife, London, April 2, 1848 (L, IV, 47).

But I soon had enough of this fine spectacle & escaped. Milnes sent me again another card from Lady Palmerston, but I did not go.

[146] Milnes again befriended me at Sir William Molesworth's, where Bancroft carried me, one night, & made me acquainted with Dr Elliotson, & ⟨Lord || ... ||⟩ a very sensible young man, Member of Parliament whose name I have lost. At Paris, he carried me to De Tocqueville, and   and, at last, at my Exeter-Hall lectures in London, he took the chair, & made a ↑closing↓ speech full of praises, perfectly well meant, if not felicitous.

He is one of the most valuable companions in London too [147] for the multitude of anecdotes he tells about good people. And, at Paris, I found him equally acquainted with everybody & a privileged man with his pockets full of free cards, which admitted him everywhere.

He told of Landor, that he, one day, in a ⟨rage⟩towering passion, ⟨he⟩ threw his cook out of the window, & then presently exclaimed, "Good God! I never thought of those poor violets!" He said, he had talked with young Landor, lately, & told him, "he must be on his guard against his father's furious fits." "O no," he replied, "I just keep out of the way, when the fit comes; [148] and, besides, I am getting stronger, every day, & he is getting weaker." The last time he saw Landor, he found him expatiating on our custom of eating in company, which he esteems very barbarous. He eats alone, with half-closed windows, because the light interferes with the taste. He has lately heard of some tribe in Crim-Tartary, who have the practice of eating alone, & these he extols as much superior to the English, of course. Landor, walking in London, came [149] to the top of a street filled with people, & foamed at the mouth with indignation.[136]

Milnes said, in my presence, "that he desired nothing so much as to make a good speech in Parliament." The distinguished Mrs Nor-

[136] For "He told of Landor [p. [147]] . . . indignation.", see Journal London, pp. [82]–[83].

ton, (to whom I was carried one day by Carlyle,) said, that, "Milnes & Disraeli were the two remarkable political failures which she had known." [137]

At Lady Harriet Baring's[n] ↑dinner,↓ Carlyle & Milnes introduced me to Charles Buller, "reckoned" [150] they said ↑aloud,↓ "the cleverest man in England" — "until," added Milnes, "until he meddled with affairs:" — For Buller was now Poor-Laws Commissioner & had really postponed hitherto to make good the extraordinary expectation which his speeches in Parliament had created. [138]

[151] [blank]
[152]   ↑Religion
Dr Arnott's Story, *Red Book* p 111↓ [139]

A very evangelical young lady wanted the company to subscribe to send a missionary to India. "The people" she said, "believed in devils, & worshipped devils." Yes, said her Uncle, "I tell you, my dear, those are no jokes of devils, — those in India. They actually eat or cause to be destroyed one per cent of the population. But, niece, they worship devils too in Europe & news were just brought, that this is creeping into England, & instead of one per-cent, they say their devil sends to eternal damnation nineteen out of every twenty." The niece who had expected a contribution to her missionary purse shut her eyes & her mouth. [140]

[153]–[154] [blank]
    [155] Samuel Rogers on hearing of the marriage of Miss Susan Cushman with Mr Muspratt, said, "that he always understood that, at the end of the season, Miss Cushman was to marry her sister
    . When Miss Cushman asked him whether he should not go to America? he replied, "that it had always been his intention

---

[137] For this sentence, see Notebook England and Paris, p. [41]; Journal London, p. [173].

[138] Cf. *L*, IV, 43, for another account of the dinner and of Buller.

[139] "Religion . . . p 111" is in pencil; the reference is to Journal London.

[140] For this paragraph, see Journal London, pp. [111]–[112].

to visit America before he died, but now that I have seen *you*, I have no longer any desire to do so." [141]

[156]–[166] [142] [blank]

[167]   *Thomas De Quincey.*

At Edinburgh, ↑I↓ dined at Mrs Crowe's with De Quincey, David Scott, & Dr Brown. De Quincey is a small old man of 70 years, with a very handsome face, — a face marked by great refinement, — a very gentle old man, speaking with the utmost deliberation & softness. & so refined in speech & manners, as to make quite indifferent his extremely ⟨pr⟩plain & poor dress. For the old man summoned by message on Saturday by Mrs Crowe to this dinner, had walked on this rainy muddy Sunday ten miles from his house at Lass Wade [168] & was not yet dry, ⟨&⟩ &, though Mrs Crowe's hospitality is comprehensive & minute, yet she had no pantaloons in her house. He was so simply drest, that ten miles could not spoil him. It seemed, too, that he had lately *walked home*, at night, in the rain, from one of Mrs Crowe's dinners. "But, why did you not ride?" ⟨go in the coach⟩ said Mrs C., "you were in time for the coach." ⟨Mrs⟩ "Because, he could not find money to ride; he had met two street girls; one of them took his eight shillings out of his waist-coat pocket, & [169] the other, his umbrella." He told this sad story, with the utmost simplicity, as if he had been a child of seven, instead of seventy.

Here, De Quinc[e]y is serene & happy, among just these friends, with whom I found him: for, he has suffered in all ways, & lived the life of a wretch, for many years; & Samuel Brown, Mrs C., & one or two more, have saved him from himself, & from the bailiff, & from a fury of a Mrs MacBold, — his landlady, — & from opium; & he is now clean, clothed, & in his right mind. He might remind you of George P.B[radford].[,] of Ellery C[hanning].

[141] See both Journal London, p. [84], and p. [116] above.
[142] A strip of paper is pinned to this page, evidently as a bookmark for the entry on De Quincey beginning on p. [167].

[170] He talked of many things easily, — chiefly of social & literary matters, & did not venture into any voluminous music.

De Quincey has never seen Landor, but grieves over the loss of a finely-bound copy of "Hellenics," sent him by Landor. He has also lost *five*[143] manuscript books of Wordsworth's unpublished Poem. He loses everything. His simplicity is perfect. He takes Dr Brown into the middle of the street, to tell him where his lodgings are. Yet, on reckoning, it did not appear, that all his debts [171] exceeded a hundred pounds. He estimates *Paradise Regained*, very highly, thinks the author always knows which is his best book.

He said, Wordsworth appropriates whatever another says, so entirely, as to be angry if the originator claimed any part of it.

In conversing with Wordsworth, Dequincey had made some remark, which Wordsworth caught up, & amplified, & repeated, next day. De Quincey then observed, ⟨that he⟩ "I am glad you adopt that view of mine." "Yours"! said Wordsworth. "Yes, mine;" said De Q. — "No," cried Wordsworth, indignantly, "it is mine."[144]

[172] Festus was mentioned, — & I said, I did not esteem him a true poet. David Scott, in answer to my challenge for one good line, recited

↑"Friendship hath passed me like a ship at sea",↓

De Quincey said, that tautology of "ship" & "friendship" would ruin any verse.

De Quincey said, that Blackwood pays him 12 guineas the sheet; pays to others, 10; to Wilson, 20; the ⁿ Quarterlies pay 16, that is, a guinea a page. Blackwood once reached a circulation of 8000 copies.[145]

---

[143] The underlining is added in a different ink.

[144] For "at Edinburgh, I . . . house." (pp. [167]–[168]) and "Here, De Quincy . . . music." (pp. [169]–[170]), see Emerson's letter to his wife, Perth, February 21, 1848 (*L*, IV, 19). For "he had lately *walked* . . . umbrella.'" (pp. [168]–[169]) and "De Quincey has never . . . mine.'" (pp. [170]–[171]), see Journal London, p. [31]. De Quincey's anecdote of Wordsworth, expanded here, is given more briefly in "Quotation and Originality," *W*, VIII, 192.

[145] For earlier versions of the entries on p. [172], see Journal London, p. [33] (the discussion of Bailey's *Festus*) and p. [37] (the magazines).

[173] (When they first agreed, at my request, to invite DeQ. to dine, I could fancy that some figure like the organ of York Minster, would appear. —) In a tête à tête, I am told, he sometimes soars & indulges himself, but rarely in company. He invited me ⟨in the⟩ to dine with him on the following Saturday, at Lass Wade, where, since the death of his wife, (from whom he was separated for many years,) he lives with his three daughters.

Thither I went, with Mrs Crowe, & Dr Brown, in Mrs C.'s carriage. The second daughter, Florence, had a pleasing style of beauty. [174] His son Francis was also present, who is a medical student in the University. ⟨He⟩ ↑De Quincey↓ told us how his acquaintance with Wilson begun; for, though they were at Oxford together, they had never met, but De Quincey travelling in Wales had arrived at an inn, where he learned that a gentleman lay sick & sore with his wounds. For Wilson, in some of his mad pranks, had paid attentions to a country girl, at a theatre, and, after the play was over, ⟨t⟩her lover & his friends had [175] waylaid him & most ignominiously mauled him. And De Quincey, learning who it was ↑who was↓ in the house, ⟨had⟩ sent up his card, & made his acquaintance.[146]

Of Turnbull, (whom I had seen with Dr Brown,) it was told, that he had said, "he would go to hell for Sir William Hamilton." [147] Mrs Crowe insisted that Dequincey should go back to Edinburgh with us in the coach & should go to my lecture! a proposition to which he somewhat reluctantly assented, as, I think, he said, he had never attended a public Lecture, — or not for a great many years. — But the victorious lady put him [176] into the carriage. As we entered Edinboro, he grew very nervous, and Dr Brown saw the reason, & assured him that his old enemy (Mrs Macbold) had removed to another quarter of the city. "Ah," said De Quincey, "if one of the Furies should arrive in Edinburgh, it would make little difference at what hotel she put up." [148]

---

[146] For "(When they . . . daughters." and "The second . . . University." (pp. [173]–[174]), see Emerson's letter to his wife, Perth, February 22, 1848 (L, IV, 19–20, 22); cf. Journal London, p. [33]. On De Quincey and Wilson, cf. Journal London, p. [32].

[147] See Journal London, p. [32].

[148] With this and the preceding sentence, cf. Journal London, p. [36].

↑Dr Brown & Mrs Crowe told me in detail the story of his rescue from the hands of this Mrs MacBold, who was his evil genius, & had exercised a reign of terror over him, for years, — a very powerful & artful, largelimbed, redhaired beldame, from [177] whom flight to Glasgow, & concealment there, was the only help, whilst his friends, with Wilson, concocted the extrication of his valuable papers & literary MSS. from her custody. The woman followed him to Glasgow; met Dr Nichol's daughter in the street, (a child), & asked her pleasantly, if she knew where Mr De Quincey lived? the child said, Yes, &, at her request, conducted her to his retreat! He fled again. At Edinburgh, she sent a little girl to Prof. Wilson (with a napkin of his own by way of token,) ⟨asking⟩ "with Mr De Quincey's compliments," asking him to ⟨confide⟩ send him back, by the bearer, the bundle of papers he had left with him, — & he sent them!↓

[178]   *TENNYSON.*

I saw Tennyson, first, at the house of Coventry Patmore, where we dined together. His friend Brookfield was also of the party. I was contented with him, at once. He is tall, scholastic-looking, no dandy, — but a great deal of plain strength about him, &, though cultivated, quite unaffected. — Quiet sluggish sense & strength, refined, as all English are, — and good humoured. The print of his head in Horne's book is too rounded & handsome. There [179] is in him an air of general superiority, that is very satisfactory. He lives very much with his college set, Spedding, Brookfield, Hallam, Rice, & the rest⟨. To⟩ and has the air of one who is accustomed to be petted and indulged by those he lives with, like George Bradford. Take away Hawthorne's bashfulness, & let him talk easily & fast, & you would have a pretty good Tennyson.[149] He had just come home from Ireland, where he had seen much vapouring of the Irish youth against England, & described a scene in some tavern, I think, where a hot young man was flourishing a drawn sword, & swearing that he would [180] drive it to the hilt into the flesh & blood of Englishmen. Tennyson was disgusted, &, going up to the young

[149] "I saw Tennyson . . . rest" is expanded from a note in Journal London, p. [130]; for "Take away . . . Tennyson.", see Emerson's letter to his wife, Paris, May 17, 1848 (*L*, IV, 74).

man, took out his penknife, & offered it to him. "I am an English-man," he said, "and there is my penknife, and, you know, you will not so much as stick that into me." The youth was disconcerted, & said, "he knew he was not an Englishman." "Yes, but I am." Here-upon the companions of the youth interfered, & apologized for him, he had been in drink, & was excited, &c.

[181] Tennyson talked of Carlyle, & said If Carlyle thinks the Christian religion has lost all vitality, he is wholly mistaken. Tenny-son & all Carlyle's friends feel the caprice & incongruity of his opinions.[150] He talked of London as a place to take the nonsense out of a man. When "Festus" was spoken of, I said, that a poem must be made up of little poems, but that, in Festus, ↑were↓ no single ⟨line⟩ good lines; you could not quote one line. Tennyson quoted ⟨the line about putting his hand upon the sun & the five fingers made five nights.⟩

"there came a hand between the sun & us,
And its five fingers made five nights in air." [151]

[182][152] After dinner, Brookfield insisted that we should ⟨all⟩ go to his house. So we stopped an omnibus, &, not finding room inside for all three, Tennyson rode on the box, & B. & I within. Brookfield, knowing that I was going to France, told me, that, if I wanted him, Tennyson would go. "That is the way we do with him," he said: "We tell him, he must go, & he goes. But you will find him heavy to carry." At Brookfield's house we found young Hallam, with Mrs Brookfield, a very pleasing woman. I told Tennyson, that I heard [183] from his friends very good accounts of him, & I & they were persuaded that it was important to his health, an instant visit to Paris; & that I was to go on Monday, if he was ready. — He was very goodhumoured, and affected to think that I should never come

[150] For this and the preceding sentence, see Journal London, p. [130].

[151] See Philip James Bailey, *Festus* (Boston, 1849), p. 366. " 'there came . . . air.' " is in ink on top of "⟨the line . . . nights.⟩", which is in pencil. Emerson also quotes "And its . . . air.' " in Journal CO, p. [150]. Journal CO will be published in a later volume.

[152] "*TENNYSON.*" is written in ink as an index heading at the top of the page.

back alive from France,[153] it was death to go. But he had been looking for two years for somebody to go to Italy with, & was ready to to set out at once, if I would go there. I was tempted, of course, to pronounce for Italy; ⟨at once,⟩ but now I had agreed to give my course in London[.]

[184][154] He gave me a cordial invitation to his lodgings (in Buckingham Place,) where I promised to visit him before I went away.

On   I found him at home in his lodgings, but with him was a Church-clergyman, whose name I did not know, & there was no conversation. ⟨I told him⟩ He was sure, again, that he was taking a⟨n⟩ final farewell of me, as I was going among the French bullets, but promised to be in the same lodgings, if I should escape alive, [185] after my three weeks in Paris.[155] So we parted, I spent a month in Paris, &, when I returned, he had left London.

Carlyle describes him as staying in London through a course of eight o'clock dinners every night, ↑for months,↓ until he is thoroughly fevered: then, notice is given to one of his friends, as lately to Aubrey de Vere, who has a fine estate in Ireland ↑30 miles from Limerick,↓ —to come ↑&↓ carry him off bodily. Tennyson had capitulated, ⟨& surrendered,⟩ on three conditions; first, that he should not hear anything about Irish distress; 2. that he should not come down stairs to breakfast; 3. that he might smoke in the house. I think these were the three. So poor Tennyson who had been in the worst way, but had not force enough to choose where to go, & so sat still, was now disposed of.[156]

↑For *Tennyson*, again, turn to p. 277.↓

[186]   *Alexander Ireland, Esq.*

Alexander [157] Ireland approves himself the king of all friends

[153] For the sentence to this point, see Emerson's letter to his wife, Paris, May 17, 1848 (*L*, IV, 74). Emerson dined with Tennyson and Brookfield at Patmore's on May 5, 1848 (Pocket Diary 3, p. [72]; Journal London, p. [130]).

[154] "*Tennyson.*" is written in ink as an index heading at the top of the page.

[155] Emerson's appointment with Tennyson was at 1:00 P.M. on Saturday, May 6, 1848—the day of his departure for France (*L*, IV, 71). For Tennyson's promise "to be in the same lodgings," see also *L*, IV, 74.

[156] For "Carlyle describes . . . disposed of.", see Journal London, pp. [54]–[55].

[157] There is a large parenthesis or bracket, in pencil, before "Alexander".

& helpful agents, the most active unweariable & imperturbable, his sweetness & bonhommie in an editor of a polemic & rather ⟨powerful⟩ ↑influential↓ newspaper, is surpassing. I think there is a pool of honey about his heart which lubricates all the parts of his system, all his speech & expression with fine jets of mead. His good humour is absolutely comic.[158]

[187] Cameron & all the rest of this company are too deeply indebted to Carlyle, & would be better, like wine, for a voyage to India or to Nootka Sound.[159] Espinasse, who is really a man of wit & capacity, writes unmitigated Carlylese. And when I told Carlyle, that he ought to interfere, & defend that young man from him, Carlyle, he appeared piqued, & said, "he must write as he could, & be thankful."

[188] [blank]

[189]   *Carlyle.*

I found at Liverpool, after a couple of days, a letter which had been seeking me, from Carlyle, addressed to "R.W.E — on the instant⟨,⟩ when he lands in England," conveying the heartiest welcome & urgent invitation to house & hearth. And finding that I should not be wanted for a week in the Lecture-rooms[n] I came down to London, on Monday, &, at 10 at night, the door was opened to me by Jane Carlyle, and the man himself was behind her with a lamp in the hall. They [190] were very little changed from ⟨the fourteen years ago⟩ their old selves of fourteen years ago (in August) when I left them at Craigenputtock. "Well," said Carlyle, "here we are shovelled together again!" The floodgates of his talk are quickly opened, & the river is a plentiful stream. We had a wide talk that night, until nearly 1 o'clock, & at breakfast next morning, again. At noon or later we [191] walked forth to Hyde Park, & the palaces,

---

[158] For this paragraph, see the postscript to Emerson's letter to his wife, Birmingham, December 16, 1847 (*L*, IV, 452); the first two sentences are used in "Personal," *W*, V, 292. Ireland's newspaper was the Manchester *Examiner*.

[159] For this sentence, see Emerson's letter to Margaret Fuller, Manchester, December 5, 1847 (*L*, III, 447).

about two miles from here to the National Gallery, & to the Strand, Carlyle melting all Westminster & London into his talk & laughter, as he goes. Here, in his house, we breakfast about 9, & Carlyle is very prone, his wife says to sleep till 10 or 11, if he has no company. An immense talker, and, altogether as extraordinary in that, as in his writing; I think, even more so. You will never discover his real vigor & range, or how much more he might ⟨s⟩do, than he has [192] ever done, without seeing him. My few hours' discourse with him, long ago, in Scotland, gave ⟨him⟩me not enough knowledge of him; & I have now, at last, been taken by surprise, ⟨with⟩by him. He is not mainly a scholar, like the most of my acquaintances, but a very practical Scotchman, such as you would find in any saddler's or iron-dealer's shop, — & then only accidentally, & by a surprising addition, the admirable scholar & writer. If you would know precisely how he talks, just suppose [193] that our burly gardener, Hugh Whelan, had leisure enough, on the top of his day labor, to read Plato, Shakspeare, & Calvin, &, remaining Hugh Whelan all the time, should talk scornfully of all this nonsense of books he had been bothered with, & you shall have the tone & talk & laughter of Carlyle. I called him *a trip-hammer, with an Aeolian attachment.* ↑(See. *GH* p. 114)↓ [160] He has, too, the strong religious tinge, in the way you find it in people of that burly temperament. That, & all his qualities have a certain virulence, coupled, tho' it be, in his case, [194] with the utmost impatience of Christendom & Jewdom, & all existing presentments of the good old story. He talks like a very unhappy man, profoundly solitary, displeased & hindered by all men & things about him, & plainly biding his time & meditating how to undermine & explode the whole world of nonsense that torments him. He is respected here by all sorts of people, — understands his own value quite as well as Webster, — (of whom, his behavior sometimes reminds me, especially when [195] he is with fine people,) & can see society on his own terms.

C. & his wife live on beautiful terms. Their ways are very en-

---

[160] The insertion is in pencil; "*a trip-hammer . . . attachment.*" is underlined in pencil.

gaging, and, in her bookcase, all his books are inscribed to her, as they came from year to year, each with some significant lines.

His brother, Dr John C. has ended his travels, as a physician to the families of Duke of Buccleuch, & Countess Clare, — has retired on some sort of pension, & lives near them, in ⟨his⟩ lodgings, a bachelor, & is a good scholar on his own account.[161]

[196] ↑I see that I shall not readily find better or wiser men than my old friends at home:↓ — and,[n] though no mortal in America could pretend to talk with Carlyle⟨.⟩, — yet[n] he is as unique⟨,⟩ here, as the Tower of London; and neither would he, in any manner, satisfy them, or begin to answer the questions which they ask. He is a very national figure, & would by no means bear transplantation. Give my love to my gossips, great & dear, & say so much to them. They keep him here ↑like↓ a kind of portable cathedral bell, which they like to produce in companies, [197][n] where he is unknown, & set a-swinging to the consternation of all beholders, bishops, courtiers, scholars, writers, and, as no man is named or introduced here, great is the effect, & great the inquiry.[162]

————

I had a good talk with C. last night. He says over & over, for months, for years, the same thing. Yet his guiding genius is his moral sense, his perception of the sole importance of truth & justice; and he, too, says that there is properly no religion in England. He is quite [198] contemptuous about *"Kunst,"* also, in Germans, or English, or Americans. And has a huge respect for Duke Wellington, as the

[161] For "I found [p. [189]] . . . account.", see Emerson's letter to his wife written from Carlyle's house, London, October 27, 1847 (*L*, III, 422–424); there are minor variations, such as the interpolation on p. [193] from Journal GH. "He is not . . . *attachment.*" is struck through in pencil on pp. [192]–[193] with single diagonal use marks; "He talks . . . torments him." is struck through in pencil on p. [194] with a vertical use mark. "An immense talker [p. [191]] . . . his own terms." (p. [195]) is used in "Carlyle," *W*, X, 489–490.
[162] For this paragraph, see Emerson's letter to his wife, Liverpool, November 13, and Manchester, November 16 and 18, 1847 (*L*, III, 438). "Yet he . . . ask." and "so much . . . inquiry." are struck through in pencil with single vertical use marks on pp. [196] and [197]. "And, though . . . inquiry." is used in "Carlyle," *W*, X, 490.

only Englishman, or the only one in the Aristocracy, who will have nothing to do with any manner of lie.[163]

[199] Carlyle's realism is thorough. He is impatient of a literary trifler, &, if Guizot is to make essays, after being a tool, he thinks it nothing. Actors & actresses all mad monkeys. He saw Rachel in an impossible attitude, & learned that she could stand so, because her dress was loaded with lead. & he despises her ever since. [The English parliament with its babble he denounces. They gather up six millions of money every year, to give to the poor, & yet the people starve. He thinks, if they would give it to him to provide the poor with labor, & with authority to make them work, or shoot [200] them, & he to be hanged, if he did not do it, he could find them in plenty of Indian meal. These idle nobles at Tattersall's, there is no work or word of serious purpose in them, & they have this great lying church, and life is a humbug.

Of course, this new French Revolution is the best thing he has seen, and the teaching this great swindler, Louis Philippe, that there is a God's justice in the Universe, after all, is a great satisfaction.[164]

[201] Czar Nicholas is one of his few living heroes. For, in the ignominy of Europe, when all thrones fell like card houses, & no man was found with conscience enough to fire a gun for his crown, but every one ran away "in a cou-cou, ⟨through⟩ with his head shaved, through the Barrière de Passy," one man remained who believed he was put there by God Almighty to govern his empire, and, by the help of God, had resolved to stand there.

↑Edwin↓ Chadwick is another hero. Chadwick who proposes to [202] provide every house in London with pure water, — sixty

---

[163] For "I had a . . . lie.", see Emerson's letter to his wife dated by Rusk *c.* March 15, 1848 (*L*, IV, 39–40). "Yet his . . . England." is used in "Carlyle," *W*, X, 495; "He is . . . Americans." is used in "Stonehenge," *W*, V. 274.
[164] For "Carlyle's realism . . . satisfaction.", see Journal London, pp. [52]–[53]. "Carlyle's realism . . . nothing." is used in "Carlyle," *W*, X, 494. "The English" is set off with a large bracket, in pencil; "The English . . . meal.", struck through in pencil on both p. [199] and p. [200] with single vertical use marks, is used in "Carlyle," *W*, X, 492. "These idle . . . humbug." and "Of course . . . satisfaction." are used in "Carlyle," *W*, X, 495–496, 496.

gallons to every head, at a penny a week; — & Carlyle thinks that the only religious act which a man now a days can ⟨perf⟩securely perform is, to wash himself well.[165]

He values Peel, as having shown more valor as a statesman than any other of these men. Wellington he esteems real & honest, & as having made up his mind, once for all, that he will not have to do with any kind of a lie.[166]

[203] He reads Louis Blanc. He can't get any true light on Cobden's Free Trade. He does not believe with Cobden. Every laborer is a monopolist. The navigation-laws of this country made its commerce. St John was insulted by the Dutch, & came home, & got the law passed that foreign vessels should pay high fees, & it cut the throat of the Dutch, & made the English trade.[167]

If he should go into Parliament, the thing he should do, would be, to get those reporters thrust out, & so put an end at once to all manner of mischievous [204] speaking "to Bunkum," and wind-bags. In the Long Parliament, the only great Parliament, they sat secret & silent, grave as an Oecumenical council, & I know not what they would have done to any body that had got in there, & attempted to tell out of doors what they did.[168]

If such a person as Oliver Cromwell should come now, it would be of no use; — he could not get the ear of the House of Commons. You might as well go into Chelsea graveyard [205] yonder, & say, "Shoulder Arms!" & expect the old dead church-wardens to arise.[169]

---

[165] For "Czar Nicholas . . . well.", see Journal London, p. [59]. "Czar Nicholas . . . there." and "Edwin Chadwick . . . well." are used in "Carlyle," W, X, 496–497, 496.

[166] For "He values . . . lie.", see Journal London, p. [53]; cf. p. [198] above. The second sentence is used in "Carlyle," W, X, 496.

[167] For "He reads . . . English trade.", see Journal London, p. [56]. "He can't . . . English trade." is used in "Carlyle," W, X, 491, 492.

[168] For "If he . . . did.", see Journal London, p. [55]. The entry is used in "Carlyle," W, X, 491–492.

[169] For this paragraph, see Journal London, p. [57].

In architecture, he thought, it would be right now for an architect to consult only what was necessary, & to attempt no kind of ornament; and say; I can build you a coffin for such dead persons as you are, and for such dead purposes as you have, but no ornament.[170]

Chalmers, he valued, as a naïf, honest, eloquent man, who, in these very days, believed in Christianity; & though he himself long ago when he was in the habit of hearing him, had ⟨long⟩ ↑already↓ discovered, that it would not hold water, [206] yet he liked to hear him.[171]

He prefers Cambridge to Oxford. But Oxford & Cambridge education indurates the young men, as the Styx hardened Achilles, so that, when they come forth of them, they say; 'Now we are proof, we have gone through all the degrees, & are case-hardened against all the veracities of the Universe, nor man nor God can penetrate us!'[172]

His sneers & scoffs are thrown in every direction. He breaks every sentence with a scoffing laugh, 'windbag,' 'monkey,' 'donkey,' 'bladder,' and, let him describe whom he will, it is always "poor fellow!" [207] I said, What a fine fellow are you, to bespatter the whole world with ⟨these⟩ this oil of vitriol! ⟨I see you surrendered too with⟩ "No man," he replied, "speaks truth to me." — I said, "see what a crowd of friends listen to & admire you." He said, "Yes they come to hear me, and they read what I write, but not one of them has the smallest intention of doing these things."[173]

I said, on one occasion, ⟨W⟩How can you undervalue such worthy

---

[170] For this paragraph, see Journal London, p. [57]; it is used in "Stonehenge," W, V, 274.

[171] For this sentence, see Journal London, p. [54].

[172] For "He prefers . . . us!' ", see Notebook England and Paris, p. [41], Journal London, p. [57], and Plates II, III, and IV. The entry is used in "Carlyle," W, X, 496.

[173] For " 'No man . . . things.' ", see Journal London, p. [53]. Following "things.' " are the words "*Stop here*", written in pencil (by Edward Emerson?); there are also curved pencil lines before "I" in the succeeding line.

people, as I find you surrounded with, — M↑ilnes↓, & S↑pedding↓, & V↑enables↓, & D↑arwin, Lucas,↓ — & so forth. He replied, "May the benēficent gods defend me from ever sympathising with the like of them!" [174]

[208] "The idea of a pig-headed soldier who will obey orders, & fire on his own father, at the command of his officer, — is a great comfort to the aristocratic mind;" said Carlyle.

C↑arlyle↓ called ⟨l⟩Lady ⟨G⟩ ↑Duff Gordon,↓ — whom I met at Cambridge, a female Brummel, & said, Brummel was a sort of inverse St. Peter, who could tread the waters of humbug without sinking. [175]
T.C. thought the clubs remarkable signs of the times; that union was no longer sought, but only the association of men who would not offend one another. There was nothing to do, but they [209] could eat better.
He was very serious about the bad times.* He had seen this evil coming, but thought it would not come in his time. But now it is coming, & the only good he sees in it, is, the visible appearance of the gods. He thinks it "the only question for wise men, ⟨&⟩ instead of art & fine fancies, & poetry, & such things as Tennyson plays with, — to address themselves to the problem of Society. This confusion is the inevitable end of such falsehood & nonsense as they have been ⟨embroil⟩ embroiled with." [176]

↑* The Chartists were then preparing to go in a procession of 200 000 to carry their petition, embodying the six points of Chartism, to the House of Commons, on the 10 April 1848.↓

[174] Emerson's references, in addition to Milnes, are to Thomas Spedding (d. 1870), George Stovin Venables (1810–1888), Dr. Erasmus Alvey Darwin (1804–1881), and Frederick Lucas (1812–1855).
[175] For "Brummel was . . . sinking.", see Notebook England and Paris, p. [44]; for "'The idea . . . sinking.", see Journal London, p. [58]. "'The idea . . . said Carlyle." is used in "Carlyle," W, X, 493.
[176] For "T.C. thought . . . with.'", see Journal London, p. [99]; the footnote, lacking in the earlier version, is an addition here. "He was very . . . with.'" is used, exclusive of the footnote, in "Carlyle," W, X, 497.

[210] —————————

And here I may transcribe, from the worn out little pocket book, my first notes of Carlyle⟨.⟩↑, fifteen years ago.↓[177]

—————————

Carlisle, in Cumberland, 26 August 1833

Just arrived here from Dumfries. A white day in my years. I found the youth I sought in Scotland, & good & wise & pleasant he seems to me. Thomas Carlyle lives in the parish of Dunscore, 16 miles from Dumfries, amid wild & desolate heathery hills, & without a single companion in this region out of his own house. ⟨There he has h⟩His wife ↑is↓ a most accomplished & agreeable woman. Truth & peace & faith dwell with them. I have not seen more amiableness than is in his countenance. He speaks broad Scotch with evident relish. [211] "in London yonder," — "I liked well," — "aboot it," — "Ay, Ay," — &c &c[.]

Nothing can be better than his stories; — the philosophic phrase, — "The Duchess of Queensboro was appointed to possess this estate" — "by God Almighty," added the lady. He told the story of Wordsworth & the Earl of Lonsdale, — ↑a sort of Giles Overreach↓ who had set out to undermine the town of Whitehaven, — Liverpool duellist, — talked of Coleridge, Allan Cunningham, Hazlitt, ⟨Gigman⟩ Walter Scott, Sheriff of Selkirk. When Wordsworth went to his door he sent up this message,[178] "William Wordsworth wishes to see Walter Scott." Fraser's, he called *Mud Magazine*; Blackwood's *Sand Magazine*. Story of "grave of the last Sixpence," — a spot in the neighborhood so called. He described [212][n] his own seeing from the steps of a church in London the coronation-pageant of King William. — ⟨‖ ... ‖⟩His wife is Jane Baillie Welsh. John Welsh was son in law of John Knox. To his wife (John Knox's) King Jamie said, "Canna I mak him a bishop?" "I had rather toss his head here" she said, holding up her apron.

Criffel. Criffel's cap. We went out to walk over long high hills,

[177] The entries which follow, through "meat for his labor." on p. [218], are copied with minor changes from Journal Scotland and England (1833); see *JMN*, IV, 219–222. They are used in "First Visit to England," *W*, V, 14–19.
[178] The comma is added in pencil.

& looked at Criffel, & down into Wordsworth's country. There we sat down & talked of the immortality of the soul, of which he knew little. But he was honest & true. "Every event affects all the future: Christ died on the tree; that built Dunscore Kirk yonder: [213] That brought you & me together." Time has a merely relative existence, & hence his faith in his immortality[.]

Carlyle was born in Annandale. Multifarious reading. Tristram Shandy one of his first books. Robinson Crusoe. Robertson's America. Rousseau's Confessions discovered to him that he was not such an ass as he had imagined. Ten years ago he had learned German by the advice of a man he knew.

London is the heart of the world; wonderful only from the mass of human beings. Each lives in his own round. The baker's boy brings muffins, & that is all the Londoner knows about it.

Books. Puffing. I will tell you what you can hardly believe. Coulburn & Bentley paid £10,000. in one year for puffing. [214] Hence it came to be, that no newspaper is trusted now, — no books are bought, & the booksellers are on the eve of bankruptcy.

Pauperism, — crowded country — government should direct poor men what to do. Poor Irishmen come wandering over these moors. My dame makes it a rule to give to every son of Adam bread to eat, & to supply his wants to the next house, — but here are thousands of acres which might give them all meat, & nobody to bid these poor Irish go to the moor, & till it. They burned the stacks, & so found a way to force [215] the rich people to attend to them. Liverpool man that fought a duel. — Gibbon, splendid bridge from the new world to the old, built by him. Domestic animals. Wonderful ingenuity of Carlyle's pig. He had spent much time & contrivance in shutting him up in one part of his pen: but the pig learned how to let the board down, & foiled him.

Man the most plastic little fellow in the planet. He liked Nero's death, "*Qualis artifex pereo*."[179] He had made up his mind to pay his taxes to William & Adelaide Guelf, with great cheerfulness, as long as William is able to compel the payment, [216][180] — not a moment longer. Landor's principle is mere rebellion, and, he fears, that is the American principle. He himself worships the man that will manifest any truth to him.

Mrs Carlyle told of the disappointment when they had ↑on the invitation from Goethe,↓[181] determined to go to Weimar, & had packed their trunks, and the letter arrived from the bookseller, to say, that the book,[182] ("Specimens of German Literature") did not sell, & they could not go.

[217][183] The first thing Goethe sent ↑her↓[184] was the chain she wore round her neck; and how she capered, when it came! But since that time, he had sent her many things.

When I mentioned the "Burns" article in the Edin[burgh] Rev[iew]., she ⁿ said, "it always had happened to him, upon those papers, to hear of each, two or three years afterwards."

T.C. prefers London, to any other place to live in. John S. Mill is the best mind he knows. More purity, more force.ⁿ He has worked himself clear of Benthamism.

[218][185] Talking of America, the best thing in Stewart's book, was, the story of the going across the way from the tavern to find the bootblack in his own house, dining on roast turkey, — that, in that country, a man can have meat for his labor.[186]

⟨He us⟩ His only companion to speak to, was the minister of Dunscore Kirk. And he used to go sometimes to the Kirk, & envy the

---

[179] "What an artist the world is losing!" Suetonius, *De Vita Caesarum*, VI, 49.

[180] "CARLYLE 1833" is written in ink as an index heading at the top of this page.

[181] "on the . . . Goethe," is in ink over a pencil version of the same material.

[182] The comma is added in pencil.

[183] "1833" is written in ink as an index heading at the top of this page.

[184] The insertion, first written in pencil, is rewritten in ink.

[185] "CARLYLE." is written in ink as an index heading at the top of this page.

[186] "Stewart's book" is James Stuart, *Three Years in North America*, 2 vols. (Edinburgh, 1833); for the anecdote, see Stuart, II, 27, and *JMN*, IV, 222.

poor parishioners their good faith. But he seldom went, & the minister had grown suspicious of them, & did not come to see him.

---

[219]   Carlyle.

Edward Irving & Thomas Carlyle kept schools at the same time at Kirkcaldy & Dysart, respectively, & were in the habit of walking together along the beach. Irving was the private tutor of Dr Welsh's daughter, & in visiting Irving at that house, Carlyle first saw her. She had the choice of these two remarkable men, & elected Carlyle. Her father did not give his consent, & the marriage was by a sort of elopement. They were afterwards obliged to go & live at Craigenputtock, ⟨t⟩an estate belonging to Dr Welsh.

[220] [blank] [187]
[221]   *CARLYLE.*

25 April, 1848. Dined with John Forster, Esq. Lincoln's Inn Fields, & found Carlyle, & Dickens, & young Pringle. Forster, who has an obstreperous cordiality, received Carlyle with loud salutation, "My Prophet!" Forster called Carlyle's passion, Musket-worship. There were only gentlemen present, & the conversation turned on the shameful lewdness of the London streets at night. ⟨Carlyle said, & the others agreed, that chastity for men was as good as given up in Europe.⟩ "I hear it," he said, "I hear whoredom in the House of Commons. Disraeli betrays ⟨it⟩whoredom, & the whole H. of Commons universal incontinence, in every [222] word they say." I said, that, when I came to Liverpool, I inquired whether the prostitution was always as gross in that city, as it then appeared? for, to me, it seemed to bet⟨ray⟩oken⟨ed⟩ a fatal rottenness in the state, & I saw not how any boy could grow up safe. But I had been told, it was not worse nor better, for years. C. & D. replied, that chastity in the male sex was as good as gone in our times; &, in England, was so rare, that they could name all the exceptions. Carlyle evidently

[187] On this page are pasted three unidentified newspaper clippings: (1) "Mr. Carlyle and the Londoners. To the Editor of the Examiner and Times.", a brief exchange of "letters" dated May 20 and 22, 1867; (2) "Mr. Carlyle, Mr. Ruskin, and the Londoners."; (3) "Making Fun of Carlyle.", quoting verses from *Punch*.

believed that the same things were true in America."— He had heard this & that, of New York, &c. I assured them that it was not so with us; that, for the most part, young men [223] of good standing & good education with us, go virgins to their nuptial bed, as truly as their brides. Dickens replied, "that incontinence is so much the rule in England, that if his own son were particularly chaste, he should be alarmed on his account, as if he could not be in good health. Leigh Hunt," he said, "thought it indifferent." ↑Dickens told me, that Miss Coutts had undertaken to establish an asylum for vicious girls taken out of the street. She had bed, clothed, schooled them, & had them taught to sew, & knit, & bake, that they might be wives for the Australians. Then she proposed to send them out, at her charge, & have them provided for until they married. They liked all this, very well, until it came to sailing for Australia. Then, they preferred going back to the Strand.↓ [188]

[224] Carlyle is no idealist in opinions, but a protectionist in political economy, aristocrat in politics, epicure in diet, goes for murder, money, punishment by death, ⟨& all the pretty⟩ slavery, & all the pretty abominations, tempering them with epigrams. ↑His seal holds a griffin with the word, *Humilitate*. He is a covenanter-philosophe & a sansculotte-aristocrat.↓

Mr Wicksteed told me of an American* who enlarged to Carlyle on free institutions, sure of his sympathy; and Carlyle replied, "that he, on the whole, preferred a tranquil, large-minded, white Russian, to any other kind of man." [189]

[225] He finds nothing so depressing to him as the sight of a great mob. He saw, once, "three or four miles of human beings, & fancied that the *airth* was some great cheese, & these were mites." [190]

↑* It was Mr Lord, the lecturer, as I have learned since.↓

[188] For "25 April [p. [221]] . . . indifferent.' ", see Journal London, p. [116], and Journal LM, pp. [96]–[97]; for "Dickens told me . . . Strand.", see Journal London, p. [107].

[189] See Journal London, p. [59]. "Mr Lord," mentioned in Emerson's footnote, may be Nathan Lord (1792–1870), then president of Dartmouth College, or his nephew John Lord (1810–1894).

[190] For this and the preceding sentence, see Journal London, pp. [55]–[56]. They are used in "Carlyle," *W*, X, 493.

It is droll to hear this talker talking against talkers, & this writer writing against writing.

He has such vigor of constitution that he can dispose of poison very well. He is a bacchanal in the strong waters of vituperation. His talk will often remind you of what was said of Dr Johnson, "If his pistol misses fire, he will knock you down with the butt-end." [191]

[226] Carlyle complained of the Americans, that they dislike the coldness & exclusiveness of the English, & run away to France, & herd with their countrymen, & are amused, — instead of manfully staying in London, & confronting Englishmen, who really have much to teach them, & acquiring their culture. He observed ⟨a⟩this timidity, & constant sense of being disliked, in Coolidge. But everything provincial bores the Englishman. [192]

[227] Yet it must be said of Carlyle that he has the *kleinstadtlich* traits of an islander & a Scotchman, and believes more deeply in London than if he had been born under Bow-bells, and is pretty sure to reprimand with severity the rebellious instincts of the native of a vast continent which makes light of the British islands. [193]

He is an inspired cockney.

↑When I saw him, in 1848, he was reading Wright's Translation of some of Plato's Dialogues, with displeasure. [194] I was told by Clough, in 1852, that he has since changed his mind, & professes vast respect for Plato.↓

---

[191] For "It is droll . . . writing.", see Journal London, p. [57]. " 'If his . . . butt-end.' " was applied to Johnson by Goldsmith "in the witty words of one of Cibber's comedies," according to Boswell; see James Boswell, *The Life of Samuel Johnson, LL.D.*, ed. George Birbeck Hill and L. F. Powell, 1934–1950, II, 100; IV, 274; V, 292. "He is a . . . butt-end.' " is used in "Carlyle," *W*, X, 493–494.

[192] For "Carlyle complained . . . Englishman.", see Journal LM, p. [23]. "Carlyle complained . . . culture." is used in "Stonehenge," *W*, V, 275.

[193] This paragraph is expanded from Journal LM, p. [99].

[194] The reference is to *The Phaedrus, Lysis and Protagoras . . . A New and Literal Translation . . .* , by Josiah Wright (n.p., 1848).

[228] Carlyle is *malleus mediocritatis*.[195] He detects weakness on the instant in his companion, & touches it. The young men are eager to see him; but it strikes me like being hot to see the Mathematical or the Greek Professor, before they have got their lesson. It needs something more than a clean shirt & reading German, to visit him. Carlyle is a vivacious aggressive temperament, & unimpressionable. The literary, the fashionable, & the political man, each fresh from triumphs in his own sphere, comes eagerly to see this man, whose fun they have so heartily enjoyed, — sure of a welcome, — [229] and are struck with despair at the first onset. His firm, victorious, cutting, scoffing, vituperative declamation strikes them with chill & hesitation.[196]

I fancy, too, that he does not care to see anybody whom he cannot eat & reproduce tomorrow, in his pamphlet or pillory. Alcott was meat that he could not eat, & Margaret F. likewise, & he rejected them, at once.

He is the voice of London, — a true Londoner with no sweet country breath in him, & the instigation of these new Pamphlets is the indignation of the nightwalking in London streets. And 'tis curious, the [230][197] magnificence of his genius & the poverty of his aims. He draws his weapons from the skies, to fight for some wretched English property, or monopoly, or prejudice. A transcendental John Bull, delighting in the music of Bow-bells, — who cannot see across the Channel, but has ⟨the⟩ skill to make divine Oratorios in praise of the Strand, Kensington, & Kew.[198]

He looks for such an one as himself. He would willingly give way to you & listen, if you would declaim to him, as he declaims to you. But he will not find such a mate. And a short plain dealing & com-

[195] "A hammer against moderateness" (Ed.).

[196] For "The young . . . visit him.", see Journal London, p. [126]. "The young . . . visit him." is used in "Carlyle," *W*, X, 491; "He detects . . . touches it." and "Carlyle is . . . hesitation." are used in "Carlyle," *W*, X, 493.

[197] "*Carlyle*" is written in ink as an index heading at the top of this page.

[198] For "And 'tis . . . Kew.", see Journal AZ, p. [139] (to be published in a later volume).

munication of results, as when Dalton & Dana met, &, without speaking, scratched down on scraps of paper chemical formulas, surprising each other with authentic proof of a chemist, — that he does not care for.[199]

––––––––––

[231]   *Wordsworth.*
    I transcribe from my old pocket book rude notes of my first visit to Wordsworth.[200]

Ambleside, 28 August, 1833. This morning I went to Rydal Mount, & called upon Mr Wordsworth. His daughters called in their father[,] a plain-looking elderly man wearing goggles. He sat down & talked with great simplicity. ↑He had↓ much[n] to say of America; the more, that it gave occasion for his favorite topic, that society is being enlightened by a superficial tuition, out of all proportion to its being restrained by moral culture. Schools do no good. Tuition is not education: — ↑he↓ thinks more of the education of circumstances, than of tuition. 'Tis not whether there are offences of which the law takes cognizance [232][201] but whether there are offences of which the law does not take cognizance. Sin, sin, is what he fears. And how Society is to escape without greatest mischiefs from this source, he cannot see. [He has even said, what seemed a paradox, that they needed a civil war in America, to teach them the necessity of knitting the social ties stronger.

"There may be," he said, "in America, some vulgarity of manner; but that's not important. That comes out of the pioneer state of things. But, I fear, they [233] are too much given to the making of

[199] Emerson is referring to the chemists John Dalton (1766–1844) and Samuel Luther Dana (1795–1868), English and American, respectively.
    [200] The entries which follow, through "Dr C. had sat.)" on p. [244], are copied with minor changes from Journal Scotland and England (1833); see *JMN*, IV, 222–225. They are used in "First Visit to England," *W*, V, 19–24. The square brackets within the entries are in pencil.
    [201] *WORDSWORTH.*" is written in ink as an index heading at the top of this page. Pinholes in the middle of the page, above "even", indicate that at one time some item was fastened to it.

money, and, secondly, to politics; that they make political distinction the end, & not the means. And, I fear, they lack a class of men of leisure, — in short, — of gentlemen, — to give a ⟨‖ ... ‖⟩ ↑tone↓ of honor to the community. I am told, that things are boasted of, in the second class of society, there, that, in England, (⟨are⟩ God knows, are done in England, every day,) but would never be spoken of. My friend Col. Hamilton at the foot of the hill ↑who was a year in America↓ assures me, that the newspapers are ⟨base⟩ ↑atrocious↓, & accuse members of Congress of stealing spoons."]

[234] [202] In America, he wished to know, not how many churches or schools, but what newspapers? He had been told ↑&c. &c.↓ He was against taking off the tax on newspapers in England, which the reformers represented as a tax upon knowledge, — for this reason, that they would be inundated with base prints.

Carlyle, he thinks⟨,⟩ insane sometimes; Goethe's Wilhelm Meister, he abused heartily. ["All manner of fornication. It was like the crossing of flies in the air. He had never got further than the first book, so disgusted was he. He threw the book [235] across the room." I spoke for the better parts of the book, & he promised to look at it again.]
Carlyle, he said, wrote most obscurely; allowed that he was clever & deep, but that he defied the sympathies of everybody. Even Mr Coleridge wrote more clearly, though he always wished Coleridge would write more to be understood. He led me out into his garden, & showed me the walk in which thousands of his lines were composed. His eyes are inflamed. No loss, except for reading, because he never writes prose; and poetry, he carries [236] [203] even hundreds of lines in his memory, before writing it. !!

He said, he had just been to visit Staffa, &, within three days, had made three sonnets on Fingal's Cave, & was composing a fourth,

---

[202] "*WORDSWORTH.*" is written in ink as an index heading at the top of this page.

[203] "WORDSWORTH" is written in ink as an index heading at the top of this page.

when he was called in to see me! He said, "if you are interested in my verses, perhaps you will like to hear these lines." I assented gladly; & he recollected himself for a few moments, & then stood forth, & repeated in succession the three entire [237] [204] sonnets, with great spirit. I thought the second, & third, more *beautiful*, than any of his printed poems. The third is addressed to the flowers, which, he said, especially the *ox-eye daisy*, are very abundant above it. The second alludes to the name of the cave, which is, *Cave of Music*: the first, to the circumstance of its being visited by the promiscuous company of the steamboat.

"Calm as the universe," &c

——

"Which the supreme Geometer ordained" [205]

[238] [206] This reciting was so unexpected & extraordinary, — he, the old Wordsworth, standing forth & reciting to me in a garden walk, like a schoolboy "speaking his piece," — that I at first had nearly laughed; but, recollecting myself, that I had come thus far to see a poet, & he was chaunting poems to me, I saw, that he was right, & I was wrong, & gladly gave myself up to hear.

[239] [207] I told him, I hoped he would publish his promised poems. He said, he never was in haste to publish, partly, because he altered his poetry a good deal, & every alteration is ungraciously received, after printing: but what he wrote would be printed, whether he lived or died. I said, Tintern Abbey was the favorite poem with the public, but, that, more contemplative readers preferred the *Excursion*, & the ⟨s⟩*Sonnets*. He said, "Yes, they are better to me." He preferred those of his poems which touched the affections, to any others; for, what was [240] more didactic, what was theories of

---

[204] "*Wordsworth*" is written in ink as an index heading at the top of this page.

[205] The quotation marks enclosing these two lines, the comma after "universe", and "&c" are in pencil. Emerson quotes, inaccurately, ll. 9 and 14 of "Flowers on the top of the Pillars at the Entrance of the Cave," Sonnet XXX of Wordsworth's Itinerary Poems of 1833; he also heard XXVII and either XXVIII or XXIX.

[206] "*WORDSWORTH.*" is written in ink as an index heading at the top of this page.

[207] *Wordsworth.*" is written in ink as an index heading at the top of this page.

society, & so on, might perish quickly; but these others were κτημα ες αει, what was good today was good forever.[208] He preferred the sonnet on the feelings of a highminded Spaniard to any other! (So I understood him) and "⟨t⟩The two Voices." & quoted with great pleasure the verses addressed "⟨t⟩To the Skylark." — It was in this connexion, that he spoke of the Newtonian Theory, as if it [241] might be superseded⟨,⟩ & forgotten; & of Dalton's atomic theory.

"The object of his talking on political aspects, was, to impress it on me, & all good Americans, to cultivate the moral, the conservative, &c. &c. & never to call into action the physical strength of the people; as lately had been done in the Reform Bill, &c. ↑in England, — ↓ ⟨a thing⟩ ↑an effect↓ prophesied by De Lolme."

He had broken a tooth, lately, by a fall, when walking with two lawyers, & said, "he was glad it did [242] not happen forty years ago," whereupon they praised his philosophy.ⁿ
He likes Lucretius's poem far better than any other poem in Latin. ⟨&⟩ Farⁿ more a poet than Virgil. His system is nothing, but his illustrations. — Faith, he said, is necessary ⟨&⟩to explain anything, ⟨&⟩to reconcile the foreknowledge of God with human evil.
Cousin he knew nothing of, but the name.

[243] Then, to show me what a common person in England could do, he carried me into the inclosure of his clerk, a young man to whom he had given this slip of ground, which was laid out, or its natural capabilities shown, with much taste.
He then walked near↑ly↓ a mile with me, talking, & ever & anon stopping short to impress the word or the verse, & finally parted from me with great kindness, & returned across the fields. His hair is ↑white, but there is nothing very striking about his↓ [244] [209] ↑appearance.↓ He alluded ↑with much satisfaction↓ to his conversation with Dr Channing, who had recently visited him, ⟨with much satisfaction,⟩ (laying his hand on a particular chair, in which Dr C. had sat.)

---

[208] "what . . . forever." is Emerson's rendering of κτημα ες αει, as in *JMN*, IV, 224 (where the Greek phrase is misprinted).
[209] "*Wordsworth*" is written in ink as an index heading at the top of this page.

Dr Bowring told me, that Wilson & Hogg went to see Wordsworth. The morning was fine, there was a rainbow, and every thing was genial. Hogg said to Wordsworth, "This is a fit spot for poets to meet in." Wordsworth drew himself up with disdain, saying, "Poets indeed!" [210]

[245]   *Second Visit to Wordsworth.* [211]
                                          1848

At Ambleside, I was the guest, for two days, of Harriet Martineau. On Sunday ⟨evening⟩ ↑afternoon↓, I think, we called on Wordsworth, & found him asleep on the sofa. [212] He seemed a little short & surly as an old man suddenly waked before he had ended his nap, but soon became full of talk on French news,—bitter old Englishman that he is—bitter on Scotchmen too. "No Scotchman can write English." He detailed [246] "the two models, on one or the other of which all the sentences of the historian Robertson are framed. Nor could Jeffrey, nor the Edinburgh reviewers write English; nor can Carlyle, who is a pest to the English tongue. Gibbon cannot write English."

The Edinburgh Review, he said, wrote what would tell, & what would sell. He thought the Edinburgh Review had changed its whole tone of literary criticism, from the time when a letter was written to the Editor by Coleridge. After that, it [247] had greatly more breadth. Mrs Wordsworth ↑once↓ had ⟨had⟩ the Editor's answer in her possession.

Tennyson, he thinks, a right poetic genius, though with some affectation. He had thought the elder Tennyson, (now Mr Turner, I believe,) at first, the best poet, but must now reckon Alfred the true

[210] This paragraph is copied with minor changes from Notebook France and England (1833); see *JMN*, IV, 412.
[211] The entries under this heading, through "remark." on p. [253], are used in "Personal," *W*, V, 294–297.
[212] Emerson arrived at Ambleside on Sunday, February 27, 1848, and departed on Wednesday, March 1, for Kendal and Manchester (Notebook England and Paris, p. [19]). In his correspondence at the time, he reported a visit of an hour and a half to Wordsworth on Monday, February 28 (*L*, IV, 25; *CEC*, p. 439).

one. In speaking of I know not what style, he said, "To be sure, it was the manner,—but, then, the matter always comes out of the manner."

He thought Rio Janeiro ⟨the⟩ the best place for the capital[.] [213]

[248] We talked of English national character, &c. I told him, as I usually did all English scholars, that it was not creditable that no one in all the country knew anything of Thomas Taylor, the Platonist, whilst in every American library his books are found. I said, ⟨i⟩If Plato's Republic were published as a new book today in England, do you think it would find any readers? He confessed, it would not;—"And yet," added, after a pause, (with ⟨a true born Englishman's⟩ ↑that↓ conceit that never deserts a true born Englishman,) "And yet, we have embodied it all."
[249] His conversation is ⟨always simple, &⟩ ↑not↓ usually ⟨not⟩ distinguished by any thing forcible. His opinions of French, English, Irish & Scotch, &c. seemed ⟨mere⟩ rashly formulized from little anecdotes ⟨he had⟩ of what had befallen himself & Mrs Wordsworth in a diligence or a stagecoach. ⟨When their precious selves went a travelling.⟩ Occasionally his face lights up, ⟨& he says something good⟩ but ⟨I thought⟩ I could easily ⟨supply⟩ ↑find↓ such table talk as this without cost of journeys. He ⟨is a fine healthy old man⟩ ↑had a healthy look↓ [214] with weatherbeaten face, face [250] corrugated,— especially the large nose,—
And it is, perhaps, a high compliment to the cultivation of the English, generally, when we find him not distinguished.

H⟨.⟩↑arriet↓ M⟨.⟩↑artinow↓ said that Wordsworth in his early housekeeping at the cottage was accustomed to offer his friends bread & plainest fare. If they wanted anything more, they must pay him for their board. I ⟨heard the story with admiration, as evincing⟩

---

[213] For "The Edinburgh Review . . . capital", see Journal London, pp. [46]– [47]; on Tennyson Turner, see also Journal London, p. [130].
[214] From "When their" through "old man" the cancellations are both in pencil and in ink; "find" is inserted in ink; "had . . . look" is inserted in pencil and re-written in ink.

↑replied ⟨it⟩that it evinced↓ English pluck, more than any anecdote I knew.[215]

[251] I think it was Mr Greg told the story of Walter Scott's staying a week with Wordsworth, & slipping out every day under pretence of a walk to the Swan-Inn for a cold cut & porter. One day ⟨walking⟩ ↑passing↓ with Wordsworth ⟨past⟩ ↑near↓ [216] the inn, he was betrayed by the landlord's asking him if he had come for his porter. H[arriet].M[artineau]. represented the Wordsworths as having served the whole neighborhood, not at all by their cultivation, but by setting a good example of thrift, & a good careful decent household.

In London, Barry Cornwall ⟨said⟩ told me that he knew Wordsworth very well, early in life — & that Wordsworth [252] had no personal friend. He was not amiable, & he was stingy. He would receive anything, but he never gave. I replied by quoting these Westmoreland praises of his exemplary temperance & economy. But he replied, "Ah, he would spend well enough when Lord Lonsdale came to see him." It was Sir James Lowther who was the Sir Giles Overreach who ruined the elder Wordsworth, who was his steward. The last Lord Lonsdale had given to the Wordsworths [253] 10,000 pounds in consideration of the debts of his father to their father.[217]

Sir Charles Fellowes showed me at his house in London, a watch that once belonged to Milton, his ⟨name⟩ ↑initials↓ being engraved on the face. He told me that ⟨he on one occasion⟩ he showed this to Wordsworth, who took it in one hand, then drew out his own watch, & held it up, with the other, before the company, — but no one made the expected remark.[218]

---

[215] For this paragraph, see Journal London, p. [41]. "heard . . . admiration," is canceled both in pencil and in ink; "replied ⟨it⟩" is inserted in pencil; "replied" is rewritten in ink; "that . . . evinced" is in ink, with "that" on top of "⟨it⟩".

[216] "walking" and "past" are canceled both in pencil and in ink; "passing" and "near" are inserted in pencil and rewritten in ink.

[217] For this paragraph, see Journal London, p. [87].

[218] For this paragraph, see Journal London, p. [42]. "name" and "on one occasion" are canceled in pencil as well as in ink; "initials" is in ink over a pencil version of the same word.

[254] *From the old Journal of 1833, I transcribe the following notes of my visit to Coleridge.*[219]

London, 5 August, 1833. This morning I went to Highgate & called at Mr Gillman's, & sent up a note to Mr Coleridge requesting leave to see him. He sent down word that he was in bed, but if I would call after 1 o'clock, he would see me. I named 1 o'clock.

I returned at one, & he appeared:—a short thick old man, with bright blue eyes [255] in a black suit & a cane, and anything but what I imagined. A clear clean face, with fine complexion,—a great snuff-taker, which presently soiled his cravat, & neat black suit.— He asked, ⟨if⟩ ↑whether↓ I knew Allston; & launched into a discourse on his merits & doings, when he knew him, in Rome—how Titianesque, &c.

Then he spoke of Dr Channing, & what an unspeakable misfortune to him, that he should have turned out an Unitarian [256] after all. Then he burst into an indignant declamation on the folly & ignorance of Unitarianism, its high unreasonableness, & took up Bishop Waterland, which lay (put there for⟨e⟩ the occasion, I fancied,) on the table, & read me, with great vehemence, two or three pages of MSS. notes written by himself in the fly leaves,—passages, too, which, I believe, are in the "⟨a⟩Aids to Reflection." As soon as he stopped to take breath, I remarked to him, that, [257] though I was interested in his explanations, it would be cowardly not to inform him that I was an Unitarian.—"Yes," he said, "I supposed so," & continued as before.

He spoke of the wonder, that, after so many ages of unquestioning acquiescence in the doctrine of St Paul, the doctrine of the Trinity, which was, also, according to Philo-Judaeus, the doctrine of the Jews before Christ,—this handful of Priestlians should take on themselves [258] to deny it, &c. &c. He[n] was very sorry, that Dr Channing,—a man to whom he looked up,—No, to say he looked *up* to him, would be to speak falsely,—but a man whom he looked *at*, with so much interest, should embrace such views. But, when he saw Dr C.,

[219] The entries which follow, through "showed me the way." on p. [267], are copied from Notebook France and England (1833); see *JMN*, IV, 407–408, 409–412. They are used in "First Visit to England," *W*, V, 10–14.

he had hinted to him, that he was afraid he loved Christianity, for what was lovely & excellent,—he loved the [259] good in it, & not the true. "And I tell you, Sir, that I have known many persons who loved the good, for one person who loved the true. But, it is a far greater virtue to love the true for itself alone, than to love the good for itself alone." He knew all this about Unitarianism perfectly well, because he had once been an Unitarian, & knew what quackery it was. He had been called, "the rising Star of Unitarianism". He proceeded to expatiate on the Trinitarian doctrine of the Deity [260] as being Realism, &c[,] upon the idea of God not being essential but super-essential, upon *trinism* & *tetrakism,* upon the *will* being that by which a person is a person; because, if one should push me in the street, & so I should force the man next me into the kennel, I should at once exclaim "I did not do it, Sir," meaning it was not my *Will.*[n]

[261] I said, when there was a pause, that many Unitarians were good readers of his books, who did not subscribe to his theology. He said, "that if I should insist on my faith here in England, & he on his, his would be the hotter side of the fagot."

I asked about the extract from the Independant's pamphlet in the 3d volume of "the Friend."[n] He replied, that, it was really taken from a pamphlet in his possession, entitled the Protest [262] of one of the Independants, or something to that effect. I told him how excellent I thought it. "Yes," he said, "the man was a chaos of truths, but lacked the knowledge that God was a God of order. Yet the passage would no doubt strike me more in the quotation than in the original, for he had filtered it." — I was rising to depart, when he said, "I do not know whether you care about poetry, but I will recite some verses [263] I lately made upon my baptismal anniversary," and he recited with great emphasis, standing, ten or twelve lines, beginning, "Born unto God in Christ."

He asked me, where I had been travelling; &, on learning that I had been in Malta & Sicily, he compared one place with the other, repeating what he had said to the Bishop of London, when he returned from that country. "That Sicily was an excellent place to study political economy, [264] for in any town there it was only necessary to ask what the government enacted, & reverse that, to know what ought to be done. It was the most felicitously opposite course to everything good & wise. There were only three things, which the government brought on that garden of delights, namely, itch, pox, and famine. Whereas, in Malta, the force of law & mind was seen in making that barren rock of Semi-Saracen [265] inhabitants, the seat of population & plenty." Going out, he showed me in the parlour Allston's picture, and told me, "that, Montague, a picture dealer, once came to see him, & the moment he laid eyes on this, said, 'Well you have got a picture!' thinking it a Titian, or a Paul Veronese. Afterward, as he talked, with his back to the picture, Montague put up his hand, & touched it, & exclaimed, 'By Heaven! this picture is not ten years old,' — so ⟨intensely⟩ delicate & skilful was that man's touch."

[266] I asked him, if he had any correspondence with his American Editor, President Marsh, of Burlington College? He said, No, for he had received his book & letter, at a time when he was incapable of any effort, & should soon send him some new books. He asked,[220] if I had seen his "Church & State"? He begged me to call on Mr Allston from him, & present him his regards.

But I have put down the least part of the discourse of Mr Coleridge. I was in the room an hour, [267][221] & much of the discourse was like so many printed paragraphs in his book, — perhaps the same, — not to be easily followed.

Almost nobody at Highgate knew his name. I asked several persons, in vain. At last, a porter wished to know, "if I meant an elderly gentleman, with white hair?" Yes, the same. — "Why, he lives with Mr Gillman." "Ah yes, that is he." So he showed me the way.

[220] The commas after "said", "No", and "effort" are added in pencil; that after "asked" is in both pencil and ink.

[221] At one time pinned to p. [266] and now laid in between pp. [266] and [267] is a printed announcement of a dinner of the Boston Latin School Association to be held on December 17, 1879.

[268] [blank]

[269] The road from ⟨New York⟩ Liverpool to New York is long, crooked, rough, ⟨&⟩ rainy, & windy. Even good company will hardly make it agreeable. Four meals a day is the usual expedient[,] four & five, (& the ⟨poisonous⟩ ↑extreme↓ remedy shows the ex⟨tremity⟩asperation[n] of the case.) & much wine & porter are the amusements of wise men in this sad place.

Never was a ⟨di⟩ well-appointed dinner with all scientific belongings so philosophic a thing as at sea. ↑Even↓ the[n] ⟨rash⟩ restless American finds himself, at last, at leisure.

[270] The letter-bag is Captain Hoxie's best passenger. It neither eats nor drinks, & yet pays in Liverpool a passenger's fare. Captain H. tells me that he usually carries between 4 & 5000 letters each way. At the N. Y. Post Office, they count his letters, & pay him two cents for every one: At Liverpool, two pence. He received in Liverpool £39. the last time.[222]

[271] [blank]

[272] At Edinburgh, I was introduced to Professor Wilson, and, the next day, went up to the University to hear him lecture.[223] Before the lecture, we called on him in his private room, & sat ten or fifteen minutes with him. He was goodnatured & affable, but nothing important was said. I asked him how old De Quincey was? he said, he knew, but would not tell, for they were contemporaries at Oxford. His lecture was heavy, I thought of our dear fat S[tetson]., ⟨& then of broken⟩ but it was S without the wit[:] perfervidum ingenium [273] Scotorum [224] yes but heavy as a speaking ox. He foamed at the mouth with physical exertion & not a ray of wit or thought. It was in the[n] course on Moral Philosophy[.]

Two gentlemen shot two dogs of Wilson's, that had belonged to his wife. They came, & made their apology. But Wilson carried

[222] "The road from [p. [269]] . . . last time." is adapted from Journal Sea 1833: see *JMN*, IV, 238–239.

[223] According to Emerson's letters at the time, he met Wilson on February 12, 1848, and heard him lecture not on "the next day" but on February 15 (*L*, IV, 18–19).

[224] "The ardent temperament of the Scots" (Ed.).

it to the law. Their friend came to Wilson, & hoped he would have the magnanimity to forgive them. "Magnanimity, sir, — Was there ever any so enormous as mine? Those [274] two men stood where you now stand, & I did not pitch them out of the window." ↑See more details of Wilson in ↑my MS↓ *London*, p. 32.↓[225]

[275]–[276] [226] [blank]
[277]   ↑Alfred↓ *Tennyson, again.*
Tennyson was in plain black suit and wears glasses. Carlyle thinks him the best man in England to smoke a pipe with, & used to see him much; had a place in his little garden, on the wall, where Tennyson's pipe was laid up.

He has ⟨more⟩ ↑other↓ brothers, I believe, ⟨than⟩ ↑besides↓ Tennyson Turner, the elder; and, I remember, Carlyle told me ↑with glee,↓ some story of one of them, who looked like Alfred, & whom some friend coming in, found lying on the sofa, & addressed him, "Ah Alfred, I am glad to see you" — and he said, "I am not Alfred, I am Septimus; I am the most morbid of all the Tennysons." [227]

[278] I suppose he is selfindulgent, & a little spoiled & selfish, by the warm & universal favor he has found. Lady Duff Gordon told me,[228] that the first day she saw him, he lay his whole length on the carpet, & rolled himself to her feet, & said, "Will you please to put your feet on me for a stool."

Coventry Patmore described him as very capricious, & as ↑once↓ spending the evening with a dozen friends, "not to be sure his equals, but [279] as nearly his equals as any that could be collected," yet Tennyson would not say a word, but sat with his pipe, silent, &, at last, said, "I am going to Cheltenham; I have had a glut of men." When he himself proposed, one day, to read Tennyson a poem which he had just finished, that Tennyson might tell him of anything which his taste would exclude, Tennyson replied, "Mr Patmore, you can

---

[225] "See . . . 32." is in pencil. For "At Edinburgh [p. [272]] . . . window.' ", see Journal London, pp. [32] (on De Quincey's age) and [38].
[226] A strip of paper is pinned to this page, evidently as a bookmark for the entry on Tennyson beginning on p. [277].
[227] For "Carlyle told . . . Tennysons.' ", see Journal London, p. [46].
[228] At Cambridge on July 6, 1848: see p. [208] above.

have no idea how many applications of this sort are made to me." [229]

[280] Dr T. P. Shepherd of Providence,[230] who travelled in the East with W. Stirling, told me, that he met Tennyson at a hotel in Amsterdam, & lived there a fortnight with him, not knowing his name, but riding out with him to see the environs, & meeting at the *table d'hote*. He set his servant to ascertain from Tennyson's servant, his master's name; but the man was only a *valet de place*, & did not know; for Tennyson scrupulously concealed his name, & got into trouble with the [281] police, about his passport. ⟨On⟩ Dr S. thought he must be Carlyle, from the strength & brilliancy of his conversation, until he spoke of Carlyle.ⁿ ⟨&⟩One day, however, he recited the "Moated Grange, Mariana," & inquired of Dr S. if they liked such verses in America. ⟨&⟩Dr S. replied, "Yes, he knew the verses; they were by Tennyson; &, though he could not say, they were widely known, yet they had a very cordial troop of admirers in the United States." "Well," replied the other, "I am Tennyson." [231] And thereafter their acquaintance was intimate, & he made Dr S. promise to visit him in England. But when Dr S. [282] [232] was in England, & inquired for him, he found, he said, that he was in a kind of retreat for the sane, which they keep there, & so saw him not.

[283] [blank] [233]

[284] [234] Long ago in Boston, Mr George Bancroft invited me to his house & introduced me to Lord Morpeth.

In England, Lord Morpeth now changed to Lord Carli[s]le invited me to dine with him,[235] & introduced me to his sister the Duchess of Sutherland and

---

[229] For "Coventry Patmore [p. [278]] . . . to me.' ", see Journal London, p. [115].

[230] Thomas Perkins Shepherd (1827?–1877), a graduate of Brown University and Harvard Medical School, elected to the Common Council of Providence in 1848 and to the Rhode Island Senate in 1853.

[231] A penciled note at this point reads "Turn back to *page 189*"; a penciled bracket follows.

[232] *"TENNYSON"* is written in ink as an index heading at the top of this page.

[233] There is a diagonal mark in pencil on this page, possibly made to direct attention to the following page.

[234] This page is in pencil.

[235] On June 28, 1848; see Notebook England and Paris, p. [77]; Journal Lon-

[285] [blank]

[286] For a summary or verdict on the Universities, full of good sense, see Johnston's "England as it is" Vol. II. p. 122 [236]

———

John Lyon (in Qu. Eliz. time) founded Harrow School directing his bounty to "be bestowed on such as are most meet for towardness, poverty, & painfulness;" &c

———
                    Johnston [*England As It Is*, 1851,] I. 303.

[287] Sir Kenelme Digby (b. 1603)[:] "his person was handsome & gigantic, he had so graceful elocution & ⟨so⟩noble address, that, had he been dropt out of the clouds in any part of the world he would have made himself respected. Skilled in six tongues; he huffed his Holiness (at Rome) but, it is said, cringed to Oliver Cromwell.[237]
                    See [Wood,] Ath[enae]. Ox[onienses]. [1721,]
                    Vol. II. p. 351

[288]   *Chartism.*
        Chartism
⟨1. Universal suffrage
 2. Biennial Parliament ?   Annual?
 3. Paid Members
 4 Vote by ballot
    Electoral districts⟩

    1. Universal Suffrage   ⎫
    2. Vote by ballot   ⎪
    3. Paid legislation   ⎪
    4. Annual Parliament   ⎬   The six points of Chartism
    5. Equality of electoral   ⎪
       districts   ⎪
    6. No property qualification⎭

———

don, p. [210]; *L*, IV, 93–94. George William Frederick Howard, formerly Viscount Morpeth, became the 7th Earl of Carlisle on the death of his father in 1848.
    [236] William Johnston, *England As It Is*, 1851, II, 122–123, quotes an unnamed "gentleman who has seen much of European life, and . . . much of Oxford."
    [237] Cf. "Ability," *W*, V, 79, which is based on this same passage.

[289]   *Questions*
    What is the Latin Grace at Oxford?
        Benedicto benedicatur [238]
Is Carlyle a voter? Was Coleridge?
What are the ⟨5⟩6 points of Chartism? ↑See them ⟨stated in *LM*
18,⟩↓ ↑See opposite page↓

———

What is the law touching Jewish franchise[?]

———

What is the present state of E. India Company[?]

———

What was the ⟨a⟩Address of 4000 Brit. Merchants to the Emperor
of the French, Apr. 1853, which L[or]d. Campbell stigmatised, as,
not far short of high treason? [239]

———

To what King did the Londoners say, "Leave us the Thames".[240]

[290] [Index material omitted]
[inside back cover] [Index material omitted] [241]

---

[238] "What is . . . benedicatur" is in pencil. Cf. "Universities," *W*, V, 200:
"A youth . . . pronounced the ancient form of grace before meals . . . , *Bene-
dictus, benedicat; benedicitur, benedicatur*"—i.e., "Let the blessed bless; he is blessed,
let him be blessed" (note, *W*, V, 370); the speaker, according to Journal DO, p.
[104], was Emerson's host at Oxford, Arthur Hugh Clough. Journal DO will be
published in a later volume.
    [239] Speaking in Paris in behalf of a deputation of London merchants, Sir James
Duke had presented a declaration favoring "relations of peace and amity" between
France and Great Britain. John Campbell, 1st Baron Campbell (1779–1861), then
Chief Justice of the Queen's Bench, addressing the House of Lords on April 4, 1853,
objected not to the sentiments expressed but to an action taken without governmental
authorization.
    [240] James I: see "Land," *W*, V, 42.
    [241] A preliminary index is written in pencil on p. [290]; the alphabetical index
on the inside back cover is written in ink with additions in pencil.

Textual Notes

Index

Textual Notes

A B

11 Even **20** wine. **21** ⟨a⟩there **27** As **29** infor-[62]mation. | com[64]munity"
38 ⟨wi[?]⟩rich **40** ⟨to[?]⟩sent | Though **41** ‖said[?]‖ **52** ⟨ex[?]⟩proper **53**
⟨w[?]⟩hot **56** ⟨Philan[?]⟩Hari

C D

61 ["O" cancels quotation marks] **63** his the **69** he | the **70** of ↑for↓ **71** It
76 ↑he↓ **78** superiors. **79** wheel. **81** Every | Publicly **82** scoop | In | bring |
beauty, **89** Doctor"↓ ... Buonaventura ... 1274 ... Aquinas ... 1274 ... Bacon ...
1294 ... ones. **96** tall **101** With **105** it; **110** comes | Gardening **112** And
116 it![?] **117** true **121** Moth | Publicly

G H

125 ⟨C[?]⟩hapman **133** Small | Especially **135** I ↑From these↓ **136** & **137**
flagellate | indeed ... dialects.₂ all dialects ... Sanscrit₁ | J⟨e⟩↑a↓m↑ie↓ **141** Acad-
emy," **149** it ↑to **150** ⟨fu[?]⟩ **154** And | Such **156** requires.) **162** religion. |
What **165** Such | h novels **168** Manchester. **175** de-[105]mons | hag⟨dons⟩
↑lets↓ **176** Liver[106]pool | Yet **177** negro; **182** weeks.↓: **195** their

Sea-Notes

204 ⟨squalls⟩ & | Great

London

220 continued.) **230** Was **241** H⟨‖ ... ‖⟩e said **243** ↑⟨with⟩↓ **244** patriotism.
246 matter. **254** decent **257** miles." **259** 'slept | fol-[125]lowing **265** de, | a

L M

292 times. **296** no **305** It **310** scholar. **313** Tomorrow | defence. **314** aim, |
works, **316** law. | spand⟨al⟩ril. (?) **320** voyage. **321** avail. **330** loaves.↓ **340**
trees; — **341** sealed, **343** told. **346** something. **349** reply. | & ⟨should now⟩
355 has always **359** Breadalbane's | cries | I would ... chance.₂ I thank ... over.₁ |
intellect **361** emotions.

J K

381 wh⟨ich [he only ?]⟩o endures **382** man. **383** man. **384** us, **386** say,
387 it, **389** ⟨r⟩be⟨c⟩leived **393** He **397** oration. **401** his⟩ power. **402** one |
spirits.)

England and Paris

415 cab & ⟨ticket⟩   **431** Happiness   **434** oil.

Xenien

460 in.

Platoniana

469 unconulusive   **175** keeps   **484** Abo̶o̶nce   **488** true$_2$ & subsistent$_1$

ED

500 theirs ↑☞ B↓; | they   **501** entered,   **504** thay | play-[27]bill,   **507** bien,”
514 An   **516** Athenaee   **521** ↑wo⟨o⟩↑ul↓d↓   **523** just | Chan[113]trey,   **524**
⟨M⟩And   **527** mullet,   **528** Turner ⟨I⟩’s   **529** But . . . time. [p. [136]]$_2$ Here . . .
Carthage. [pp. [136]-[137]]$_1$ **530** thing.   **533** Baring’s,   **535** The   **540** Lec-
ture↑:↓rooms   **542** And | Yet | com-[197]panies,   **547** de-[212]scribed   **549** She
| force,   **551** America,   **554** Much   **557** philosophy.” | far   **561** “He   **562** *Will.*”
| Friend,”   **564** ex⟨tremity⟩ ↑asperation↓ | The | the a   **566** Carlyle,

Index

This Index includes Emerson's own index material omitted from the text. (Index material of Journal London in a hand other than Emerson's is also included here.) His index topics, including long phrases, are listed under "Emerson, Ralph Waldo, INDEX HEADINGS AND TOPICS"; the reader should consult both the general Index and Emerson's. If Emerson did not specify a manuscript page or a date to which his index topic referred, the editor has chosen the most probable passage(s) and added "(?)" to the printed page number(s). If Emerson's own manuscript page number is an obvious error, it has been silently corrected.

References to materials included or to be included in *Lectures* are grouped under "Emerson, Ralph Waldo, LECTURES." References to Emerson's letters, whether quoted in the text or cited in notes, are grouped under "Emerson, Ralph Waldo, LETTERS"; this listing has been provided for volume X primarily because passages from Emerson's letters written in England comprise a significant part of the retrospective Notebook ED. References to drafts of unpublished poems are under "Emerson, Ralph Waldo, POEMS." Under "Emerson, Ralph Waldo, WORKS" are references to published versions of poems, to lectures and addresses included in *W* but not in *Lectures*, and to Emerson's essays and miscellaneous publications. Kinds of topics included under "Emerson, Ralph Waldo, DISCUSSIONS" in earlier volumes are now listed only in the general Index.

A., 38, 95, 154, 265
Abbott, Mr., 259
Abelard, Peter, 169
Aberdeen, Lord, 309
Abolition, 28, 32, 110
Abraham, 372
Academy, 30, 52, 141, 320, 334, 419, 429, 528
Achilles, 117, 233, 428, 431, 545
Acroyd, Mr., 210, 280
Adam, 81, 119, 121, 209, 504, 548
Adams, Abel, 102, 413, 443
Adams, Rev. H. W., 60, 61n, 62
Adams, John, 37
Adams, John Couch, 7, 141
Adams, John Quincy, 37
Adelaide, Queen of England, 549
Adimantus, 475n
Advertising, 192
Advocates' Library, Edinburgh, 240
Ælian, *Variae Historiae*, 472
Aeolian harp, 99, 498, 501

Aeschylus, 43, 336, 340, 448n; *The Seven Tragedies*, 336n; *The Suppliants*, 338
Aëtius, *De Placitus Philosophorum*, 188n
Affinity, 103–104
Affirmative, 10, 99, 110, 326
Afrasiyab, 74
Africa, 95, 242, 485
Agassiz, Jean Louis Rodolphe, 37, 112, 139, 164, 306, 527n, 528
Age, the, 99, 143–144, 169, 300, 314, 329, 353, 362, 367, 389–390, 463
Agoult, Marie de Flavigny, Comtesse d', 277
Agrippa, Cornelius, 5, 165
Akhlāk-I-Jalāly, 322n, 481n
Albany, N.Y., 448, 454, 455
Albertus Magnus, Saint, 89
Alboni, Marietta, 260
Alborz, 75
Alchemy, 311
Alcibiades, 347, 473
Alcott, Miss, 142n
Alcott, Amos Bronson, 16, 20, 22, 32, 47,

54, 97, 110, 111, 113, 116, 117n, 125n,
129n, 142, 147, 153, 154(?), 156, 173,
175, 244, 258, 326, 338, 340n, 346, 347,
349, 352, 353, 355, 356, 361n, 377–378n,
390, 453, 456, 502, 553
Alcott, Louisa May, 94n, 142n(?), 359n
Alexander the Great, 117, 118, 347
Alexandria, Va., 172
Alfieri, Vittorio, 50, 278, 475, 478, 497;
Autobiography, 475n
Alfred the Great, 168, 258
Algerines, 36
Ali, Caliph, 106, 159
Ali, Mohammed, 267n
Alison, Sir Archibald, 361, 362n; *History
of Europe*, 504
Allegheny Mountains, 350, 506
Allen, Judge Charles, 475
Allen, William, 128, 129n, 285
Allfadir, 107, 115
Allingham, William, 129, 130n, 362
All Saints Church, Derby, England, 185
Allston, Washington, 561, 563
Alsager, Thomas M., 188, 189n, 190
Alternation, 45
Amazons, 83
Ambleside, England, 421, 554, 558
Amelioration, 156
America, 24, 36, 37, 73, 77, 79, 80, 111,
112, 146, 148, 151, 154, 156, 185, 193,
197, 221, 224, 226, 235, 236, 243, 244,
250, 255, 270, 276, 295, 297, 303, 314,
329, 332, 333, 335, 343, 345, 348, 389,
397, 422, 431, 434, 476, 496, 499, 502,
503, 508, 510, 524, 527, 533, 534, 542,
549, 551, 554, 555, 566
American(s), 5, 30, 31, 46, 50, 61, 73, 77,
95, 102, 171, 172, 178, 190, 195, 197,
206, 215, 216, 218, 222, 226, 233, 235,
243, 249, 277, 299, 303, 320, 432, 434,
497, 499, 505, 507, 511, 542, 549, 551,
552, 557, 559, 563, 564
American Academy of Arts and Sciences, 52
American government, 29, 350
American history, 35
American language, 179, 185, 298
American politics, 345
Americanism, 297
Americanize, 161, 434
American Revolution, 37, 148, 297
Ames, Seth, 451
Amesbury, England, 429, 431
Amiens, France, 272, 425

Amory, Jonathan, 444
Amsterdam, Holland, 566
Analogy, 307, 487
Anarchy, 385
Anatomy, 32, 306
Anaxagoras, 479n
Anaximenes, 188n
Ancients, 8, 33
Andover, Mass., 456
Angelo, Michael, *see* Michelangelo
Angle of vision, 76, 133, 173
Anglesey, Marquis of (Sir Henry William
Paget), 192
Angleterre, 209, 309
Anka, 73
Annandale, Scotland, 548
Annual Register, The, 45
Antaeus, 330
Antarctic Zone, 301
Anthropomorphism, 73, 80, 87–88, 110–111
Anti-Corn Law League, 191, 504
Antigonus, King, 294
Aplomb, 234, 261, 289
Apollinaris Sidonius, Gaius Sollius, 510
Appleby, George, 128, 129n
Appleby, W., 281
Appleton, Thomas Gold, 276, 303, 305, 332,
434, 451
Aquinas, Thomas, Saint, 89
Arabia, 73, 307
Arabian(s), 71, 72, 142
Arabic language, 90
Arago, François, 294
Arbor, 97, 116
Arboretum, 12–13, 18, 105
Archimedes, 310
Architecture, 15, 110, 165, 173, 204, 233,
265, 268, 279, 306, 316, 545
Arctic voyages, 516
Ardebil, Iran, 93
Ardmore, Scotland, 207
Aretin, Marguerite, 166
Arian, 168, 219, 298
Aristides the Just, 30
Aristocracy, 38, 52, 65, 75, 97, 102–103,
118–119, 134–135, 138, 140, 149, 153,
156, 161, 167, 170–171, 176, 193, 198,
233, 235, 249, 277, 291–292, 300, 325,
328–329, 371–373, 373, 501, 505, 509,
514
Aristophanes, 35, 48, 167n; *The Clouds*, 470
Aristotle, 28, 110
Arkwright, Sir Richard, 260n, 290

Armagh, Bishop of, 186
Arndt, Ernst Moritz, 177n
Arnim, Elisabeth ("Bettina") Brentano von, 6, 38
Arnold, Matthew, 281
Arnold, Thomas, 282(?); *History of the Later Roman Commonwealth*, 283n
Arnott, Dr. Neil, 254, 313, 533
Arnoult, Dr. Emile, 126, 135, 157n, 158
Arrington, Alfred W., 54
Art, 4, 9, 96, 115, 165, 331, 334, 481, 497
Arthur, King, 117, 209
Arthur, Prince, 192
Artist, 133, 149, 319–320
As, Asa, 70, 100, 108, 109, 116
Asaph, 65
Ascension of state, 390–391
Ascetic, 290, 379–380
Asgard, 70n, 74, 131
Ashburner, Dr., 258, 442
Ashburton, *see* Baring, Alexander
Ashurst, William Henry, 443n
Ashurst, Mrs. William Henry (?), 443
Asia, 301, 307, 330
Asiatics, 30, 50, 62, 131
Assemblée Nationale, 265, 308, 309
Ast, Georg Anton Friedrich, 487, 488; *Platon's Leben und Schriften*, 488n
Astor, John Jacob, 290
Astronomy, 9, 28, 64, 114, 135, 482
Athenæum (London), 179, 249, 275, 445n
Athenaeum, 373
Athenaeum Club, London, 242, 303, 530
Athenians, 483
Athens, 60, 389
Atkinson, Mrs., of London, 284, 444
Atlantic Bank, Boston, 443, 447, 451, 457
Atlantic Ocean, 11, 12, 43, 62, 462, 510
Atossa, 332n
Atrium, 508
Attenburrow, H. C., 129, 189
Attenburrow, Miss M., 129n
Attica, 60, 472
Aubrey, John, 166
Augustine, Saint, 478
Austin, Charles, 242, 304(?)
Austin, Rev. Daniel, 399
Australia, 228, 252, 551
Autobiography, 16–17, 25, 48, 49, 50, 79, 94, 107, 120, 144, 147, 157, 171, 296, 319, 322, 328, 331–332, 344
Autograph Cottage, 180
Aytoun, William Edmondstoune, 223, 275;

The Bon Gaultier Ballads, 223, 275
Ayvaz, 71, 92, 93, 106
Azrail, 72

B., Miss (of Plymouth?), 136
B., Mr., 265, 355
B., Mr., of Boston, 38
B., Mr., of Derby, England, 258
B., Mrs., 265
B., R., Mr., 202
Babylon, 306
Bacon, Francis, 1st Baron Verulam, 28, 45, 48, 134, 146, 166, 336, 478, 508, 520; *Essays*, 166; *Novum Organum*, 483n, 484
Bacon, Francis (d. 1839), 229
Bacon, Roger, 89, 110
Bacon, Sir Nicholas, 520
Badges, 13, 151, 292
Bailey, Mr. (writer for *The Times*), 211–212, 228, 280(?), 361(?), 451(?)
Bailey, Mr. and Mrs., 212n, 281n, 284, 451
Bailey, Philip James, 75, 130, 189, 280(?), 361(?), 451(?); *Festus*, 75, 130n, 221, 281n, 535, 538
Baillie, Joanna, 362
Baker, James, 353
Baker Farm, 353–354
Balder, 74, 109, 115, 132
Ballads, 120
Baltimore Caucus, 55
Balzac, Honoré de, 203n
Bana, 9, 89
Banachie, 172n
Bancroft, George, 300(?), 347, 443n, 448, 449, 531, 532, 566
Bancroft, Mrs. George, 179n, 230(?), 448, 522, 523
Bancroft family, 240n, 242n, 252, 260–261n, 284n
Bandinel, Bulkeley, 245
Bangor, Me., 102
Bangs, Edward, 126, 338
Bannockburn, Scotland, 282
Barbès, Armand, 262, 263, 265, 323, 362
Barbès' Club, 262, 263, 318(?), 323, 425
Barga, Italy, 118
Baring, Alexander, 1st Baron Ashburton, 235(?), 249, 260, 304, 410n, 449, 512, 513
Baring, Lady Harriet, 513, 533
Baring, William Bingham, 449
Baring Brothers & Co., 130n, 410, 413, 415, 418, 421, 423, 443n

Barnard, Rev. Charles F., 21n
Barnard Castle, England, 225, 284, 418, 419, 440
Barnard family, 177
Barnes, Thomas, 188, 189n, 227, 229
Barr, Mrs., 282
Barrere, Odillon, 265
Barrett, Mr., of Concord, 358
Barrett, Nathan, Jr., 427
Barrière de Passy, 234, 543
Barrot, Camille Hyacinthe Odilon, 265n, 296
Barry, Sir Charles, 212
Barstow, Captain, 175
Bartlett, D. W., 443
Bartram, William, *Travels through North and South Carolina, Florida, the Cherokee Country,* 166
Bat, 256–257, 526
Bates, Joshua, 130, 236, 237(?), 331, 410n, 444, 445
Bavieca, 117
Beaton, David, 221
Beattie, James, 115; "The Minstrel," 115n
Beauchamp, Richard de, Earl of Warwick, 517–518
Beaufort, 184
Beaumont, Francis, 69, 154, 166; Beaumont and John Fletcher, *Laws of Candy,* 65
Beauty, 167–168, 291, 358, 390, 462, 480, 481
Bede, Saint, *Ecclesiastical History of England. Also the Anglo-Saxon Chronicle,* 283, 336, 464, 522
Beggar's Bush, 135
Behmen, Jakob, 337, 352
Behmenism, 148
Being, 481
Bela, 55
Belfast, Ireland, 129
Belgium, 85
Beli, 257
Beliefs, 461
Believer, 462
Belisarius, 117
Bennachie (Banachie?), 172
Benthamism, 549
Bentley, Richard, 548
Béranger, Pierre Jean de, *Chansons: Nouvelles et dernières,* 77n; "Le Ménétrier de Meudon," 77n, 101
Berlin, Germany, 228
Berserkir, 184
Berthwaite, 420, 421

Berwick-upon-Tweed, England, 218
Bethune, David, 221
Betting, 276, 434
Beverley, England, 194, 279, 417, 418, 440
Bhăgvăt-Gēētă, 6, 360, 503
Bible, 5, 46, 245, 279, 433, 478; *OT:* Exodus, 4; Genesis, 4, 35, 196, 255; Proverbs, 8n; Psalms, 11n; *NT:* 47; James, 147n; John, 137n, 338n; Luke, 338n, 392n; 2 Peter, 136n; Romans, 147n
Bibliothèque Nationale (formerly Bibliothèque du Roi), Paris, 240
Bifrost, 108
Bigelow, Mr., 102
Biggs, Caroline Ashurst, 191
Biggs, Elizabeth Ashurst, 191
Biggs, Joseph, 128, 129n, 191n
Biggs, Mrs. Joseph, 443n
Bilskirnir, 108
Biography, 25, 171
Birch, R. W., 128, 129n, 185
Birmingham, England, 128, 190, 191, 192, 260, 284, 409, 411, 415, 436, 439, 501, 512
Bixby, Daniel, 128
Black, Rebecca, 125, 128, 171, 172
Blackburne, T. B., 129, 130n, 284
Blackwood's Edinburgh Magazine, 223, 275, 387, 535, 547
Blake, Robert, 508
Blake, William, 368; *The Complete Writings,* 368n; "The Marriage of Heaven and Hell," 368n
Blanc, Jean Joseph Charles Louis, 232, 544
Blanchard, Grove, 432
Blanchard, Hugh, 432
Blanchard, Seth, 432
Blanqui, Louis Auguste, 262, 263, 267, 273, 319, 323, 355n
Blanqui's Club, 262n, 263, 273, 318(?), 319, 323, 355n, 425
Blecker, Mr., 107
Bliss, Alexander, 523n
Blodgett, Mrs., 409
Blois, Henry of, 257
Blood, 27, 481
Blood, Perez, 315
Blouse, 314
Blythe, Alfred Turner, 129, 130n
Böckh, August, 59, 60, 86; *The Public Economy of Athens,* 8, 59–60, 86–87
Bodleian Library, Oxford, 240, 245
Body, 384, 477

Böhme, Jakob, 337, 352

Bolingbroke, Henry St. John, 1st Viscount, 232, 370, 371, 544

Bonaparte, Napoleon, 69–70, 71–72, 75, 110, 112, 118, 159, 216, 254n, 269, 289, 297, 309, 463

Bonaventura, Saint, 89

Book(s), 5, 6, 13, 17, 89, 99, 116, 156, 165–167, 314, 336, 360, 367–368, 374–375

Boonton, N.J., 171

Boston, Mass., 14, 21, 22, 32, 37, 38, 52, 72, 80, 97, 100, 102, 118, 141, 157, 176, 205, 206, 220, 276, 306, 344, 347, 348, 349, 350, 354, 375, 387, 397, 433, 435, 454, 455, 477, 504, 527, 566

Boston Asylum and Farm School for Indigent Boys, 40

Boston *Daily Advertiser*, 157

Boston *Daily Chronotype*, 46, 289n

Bostonian, 139

Boston Latin School, 326

Boston Latin School Association, 563n

Boston Mercantile Library Association, 454

Boston *Post*, 154, 157

Boston Savings Bank, 436

Boston Society of Natural History, 52

Boswell, James, 189; *The Life of Samuel Johnson*, 42n, 502n, 552n

Botany, 153

Boulogne, France, 262, 272, 423, 425, 426, 435

Bourbon, Louis Joseph de, Prince de Condé, 369

Bourbon-Orléans, *see* Orléans, Duchess of

Boutwell, George Sewell, 52

Boy, 473

Bradford, George Partridge, 46, 54, 126, 338, 377n, 396, 534, 537

Bradford, Sophia, 310

Bradford, England, 193, 211, 416, 417, 439

Bradshaw's Monthly Railway and Steam Navigation Guide, 409, 423

Brag, 238, 515

Bragg, Dr., 132

Bragi (Brage), 132

Brain, 40–41

Bray, Charles, 281

Brayton, Captain (David? Isaac?), of Nantucket, 63

Brayton, Isaac, of Ravenna, O., 46

Breadalbane, Earl of, 186, 354, 359

Bridlington, England, 189, 196, 197, 417, 418, 440

Briedablik, 132

Bright, John, 194n

Bright family, of Rochdale, England, 216n

Brighton, Mass., 102, 207

Brindley, James, 119, 120n

Brisbane, Albert, 37

Bristed, Charles Astor, 229, 250, 275; *Five Years in an English University*, 229, 250, 275

Britain, 218, 252, 279, 297, 505

British, Briton(s), 41, 209, 241, 251, 259–260, 296, 308, 431, 495, 503, 509, 511, 516

British India, 513

British Islands, 209, 335, 496, 552

British Medical Journal, 515n

British merchants, 568

British Museum, 195, 239, 240, 244, 247, 250, 252–253, 295, 309, 317, 516, 531

Britton, Captain, 204

Britton, John, and Edward Brayley, *The Beauties of England and Wales*, 283, 464, 522

Brockhaus' Konversations-Lexikon, 48, 201

Brodhead, Mr., of Huddersfield, England, 444, 445n

Brook Farm, 64

Brookfield, Rev. William Henry, 261, 537, 538, 539n

Brookfield, Mrs. William Henry, 538

Brookline, Mass., 207

Brooks, Mr., of Medford, Mass., 81

Brooks, Charles Timothy, 128

Brooks, Captain William, Jr., 64

Brougham, Henry Peter, Baron Brougham and Vaux, 24, 214n, 248, 276, 362, 398, 428, 483

Brown, Mr., of Amesbury, England, 431

Brown, Frank, 19

Brown, James, 128, 408

Brown, John, 447n

Brown, Dr. Samuel, 180, 181, 220, 221, 222, 223, 227, 281, 282, 338, 362, 420, 534, 535, 536, 537

Brown, Shipley & Co., Liverpool, 200

Brown, William, 275n

Browne, Sir Thomas, 350

Bowring, Sir John, 558

Brummell, George Bryan, 233, 429, 546

Brumoy, Pierre, 35

Brunel, Sir Marc Isambard, 98, 129n

Bruno, Giordano, 28
Brut, 209
Bubier, George B., 442
Buccaneers, 507n
Buccleuch, Walter Francis Scott, 5th Duke of, 542
Bucephalus, 117
Buckland, William, 256, 361, 526
Buddha, 9, 89
Buddhism, 383
Buddhists, 323
Bulkeley, Rev. Edward, 186, 188(?)
Bulkeley family, 177, 188
Bull, John, 513, 553
Bull, Ole Bornemann, 465, 466n
Buller, Charles, 533
Bunker Hill, 396–397
Bunkum, 232, 544
Bunsen, Lady, 531
Bunsen, Baron Christian Karl Josias von, 531
Buonarroti, Michelangelo, see Michelangelo
Burdett-Coutts, Baroness Angela Georgina, 252, 551
Burke, Edmund, 44, 401, 523; On the Sublime and Beautiful, 45
Burleigh, William Cecil, 1st Baron of, 520
Burlington College, Vt., 563
Burns, Sir George, 430, 435
Burns, James, 430n, 435
Burns, Robert, 400
Burritt, Elihu, 267
Burton, Robert, 5, 166
Bushnell, Horace, 338
Butler, Mr., of New York, 523
Butter, Mr., 259
Buxton, Sir Thomas Fowell, Memoirs, 290, 305, 433
Byron, Anne Isabella Milbanke, Lady, 443
Byron, George Gordon Noël Byron, 6th Baron, 48, 78, 91, 189n, 329, 508, 523; Childe Harold's Pilgrimage, 329; Don Juan, 27n

C., Mr., 460
C., Mr., of Boston, 38
Cabot, James Elliot, 46–47n, 54, 283n, 338; A Memoir of Ralph Waldo Emerson, 289n
Cabotville, Mass., 456
Caesar, Gaius Julius, 29, 40, 257, 495
Caesars, 139
Cain, 219

Caldwell, Captain E., 176, 204, 205, 206, 207, 409, 410
Caledonia (ship), 451n
Calhoun, John C., 394
California, 353
Callicles, 113, 484
Calvin, John, 541
Calvinism, Calvinists, 94, 148, 303
Cambridge, England, 278
Cambridge, Mass., 72, 133, 320, 456
Cambridge Library, 220
Cambridge Telescope, 114, 135
Cambridge University, England, 153, 212, 233, 240, 250, 278, 286, 334, 430, 442, 520, 545, 546
Camden, William, 510, 518–519; Britain, 283, 464, 518–519n, 522
Camden Society, 199, 504
Cameron, John, 168, 419, 540
Camidge, Dr. John, 195
Campbell, Mr., 444
Campbell, John, 1st Baron Campbell, 568
Campbell, John, 4th Earl of Breadalbane, 186, 354, 359
Campbell, Thomas (?), 259
Canada, 29, 293
Canning, George, 183
Canova, Antonio, 523
Canterbury, Archbishop of, 215, 242, 531
Canterbury, England, 279
Canton, China, 463
Cape Clear, 206
Cape Cod, 157, 303
Cape Sable, 175
Cape St. Vincent, 516
Capetown, South Africa, 500
Capital punishment, 36
Cappadocia, Turkey, 168, 219
Carbutt, Mayor, of Leeds, England, 189, 211
Carbutt, Mrs., 211
Cardonnet, 338
Carlisle, England, 421, 547
Carlisle, Mass., 73, 360
Carlyle, Jane Baillie Welsh, 129n, 227, 235, 531, 540, 541–542, 547, 549, 550
Carlyle, Dr. John Aitken, 128, 129n, 336, 444, 542
Carlyle, Thomas, 73n, 78, 120n, 126–127n, 129n, 130n, 145, 168n, 179, 180, 188n, 189n, 214, 216, 227, 230–234, 240n, 243, 249, 255, 256n, 259, 261, 265n, 281n, 283, 286n, 294, 299, 301n, 311, 321(?), 330, 332, 333, 334, 335, 338, 343, 355,

361, 428–429n, 431, 442, 450, 478, 501n,
515, 521, 522, 530, 531n, 533, 538, 539,
540, 541, 542, 543, 544, 546, 547, 548,
549, 550, 551, 552, 553, 555, 558, 565,
566, 568; "The Life of Robert Burns,"
549; *Oliver Cromwell's Letters and
Speeches*, 179, 302; *Specimens of German
Literature*, 549
Carlylese, 540
Carolina, 384
Carpenter, William Benjamin, 257, 284, 443,
449
Carter (?), Mr., 444, 445n
Carthage, Africa, 274, 529
Case, W. A., 287n, 442
Case, Mrs. W. A., 287
Casella, Alfredo, 70
Cassiopeia, 64
Cassivellaunus, 257
Caste, 481
Catherine, Queen, 274
Catholicism, 143, 177–178, 303
Catholic Relief Bill (1829), 495
Cavendish, William, Duke of Newcastle, 508
Cecil, William, 1st Baron Burleigh, 520
Cellini, Benvenuto, 61, 69, 142
Centrality, 15, 34, 370
Chadwick, Sir Edwin, 119, 120n, 234, 243,
257, 543, 544n
Chalmers, Rev. Thomas, 224, 231, 545
Chambers, Robert, 130, 221; *Vestiges of the
Natural History of Creation*, 130n
Chambers, William, 221n, 222–223
Chamly Bill, 92
Champs-Elysées, Paris, 327
Chance, 359
Chandler, Daniel, 40
Channing, William Ellery (1780–1842),
313, 340, 557, 561
Channing, William Ellery (1818–1901),
32, 83, 105, 116, 167, 168, 193, 293,
304(?), 318, 338, 342, 346, 354, 357,
358, 359, 360, 534; *Conversations at
Rome*, 105–106
Channing, William Henry, 54
Chantrey, Sir Francis Legatt, 523
Chapman, John, 125, 126–127n, 221n,
239n, 278n, 286, 418, 423, 426, 442, 448
Character, 12, 307, 308, 376
Charlecote, England, 251
Charles XII, King of Sweden, 13
Charles River, 375
Charlestown, Mass., 397, 455–456

Charlotte, Princess, 180
Charlotte, Queen, 248
Charron, Pierre, 118
Chartism, 239, 280, 316, 546, 567, 568
Chartist(s), 211, 214, 217, 239, 242, 251,
298, 300, 310, 311n, 325, 530, 546
Chartres, France, 98
Chastity, 83, 255, 333, 550–551
Chatham, Earl of, 75, 402
Chatsworth House, Edensor, England, 18
Chaucer, Geoffrey, 98, 113, 165, 508; *Roman
de la Rose*, 98
Chauncy, Charles, 44
Chauncy family, 177
Cheating, 356
Chelmsford, England, 186
Chelmsford, Mass., 455, 456
Cheltenham, England, 255, 565
Chemistry, 28, 104, 112, 137, 252, 291, 317
Cheney, John Milton, 19, 20n, 396(?)
Chesterfield, England, 129, 190, 411, 415,
439
Chevalier, Michel, 265
"Chevy Chase" (ballad), 172
Child, children, 294, 337, 465
China, 270
Chinese Classical Work . . ., The (tr. D.
Collie), 6n
Chiser, 73
Choate, Rufus, 33, 396
Chodzko, Alexander, *Specimens of the Popu-
lar Poetry of Persia*, 71, 72, 85, 86, 92–
93, 106
Chopin, Frédéric François, 285, 337, 442–
443n
Christendom, 307, 541
Christianity, 50, 177–178, 231, 242, 261,
342, 351, 353, 393, 402, 485, 522, 538,
545, 562
Christian Remembrancer, 302
Christmas, Mr., 359
Church, 119–120, 259, 307, 378, 543
Churchill, John, 1st Duke of Marlborough,
508
Churchill, Sarah, *née* Jennings, Duchess of
Marlborough, 332n
Cibber, Colley, 552n
Cicero, Marcus Tullius, *De Oratore*, 4n; *De
Senectute*, 479n; *Letters to Atticus*, 209n;
Pro Archia Poeta, 331n
Cid, The, 42, 75, 104, 117, 118, 172
Circumstance, 117–118, 139, 142–143, 462
Cities, 150, 497

City Bank, Boston, 451
Civilization, 82
Clackmannanshire, Scotland, 282
Clare, Countess of, 542
Clarendon, Edward Hyde, 1st Earl of, 166, 183, 395; *History of the Rebellion*, 245, 395n
Clark, Daniel, 360
Clark, E. P., 245(?), 424
Clarke, Edward Daniel, 245; *Travels*, 245n
Clarke, Henry G., & Co., 427
Clarke, James Freeman, 54, 452, 453
Clay, Henry, 394
Cleopatra, 69, 78
Clergy, 219, 224, 254
Cleveland, Duke of, 225–226
Cleveland, John, "On Scotland" or "The Rebel Scot," 219n
Cleverness, 138, 148
Climate, 77, 96, 102, 193, 195, 196, 315
Clinton, Henry Pelham Fiennes Pelham, 5th Duke of Newcastle ("Lord Lincoln"), 531
Clissold, Augustus, 26
Clough, Arthur Hugh, 129, 280, 281n, 317, 321(?), 418, 423, 426, 552, 568n; *The Letters and Remains*, 262
Club(s), 22, 32, 54, 109, 214, 249, 314, 321, 323, 546
Club de la Révolution, 262, 263, 318(?), 323, 425
Club des Clubs, 268
Club des conspirateurs, 267
Club des Droits de l'homme, 262n, 263, 273, 318(?), 319, 323, 355n, 425
Club des Femmes, 268, 425
"Club of Notables," 20, 22, 54(?)
Cobbett, William, 213
Cobden, Richard, 191n, 194n, 221, 225, 227, 232, 295, 361, 504n, 544
Cochituate, Lake, 90
Cockburn, Henry Thomas, 222
Cockney(s), 50, 92, 107, 150, 167, 358, 360, 552
Codman, E., 405, 406n
Coeur de Lion (Richard I of England), 183
Coffin, Owen, 64
Coke, Sir Edward, 503
Colada, 117
Colburn and Bentley, publishers, 548
Coleridge, Samuel Taylor, 66, 134, 146, 167, 227, 362, 508, 547, 555, 558, 561–563, 568; *Aids to Reflection*, 561; *On the Constitution of Church and State*, 563

Collier, John Payne, 361, 362n
Collingwood, Cuthbert, Baron Collingwood, 516
Collins, Arthur, *The Peerage of England*, 283, 464, 522
Colman, Henry (?), 240, 257
Colman family, 177
Cologne, Germany, 336
Colombe, Anthony, 19, 111, 405, 406n
Commitment, 374
Commune de Paris, 265
Communication, 553–554
Communism, 154, 308
Communities, 342, 376, 378
Compensation, 36–37, 115
Compound interest, 67
Conant family, of Concord, 357n
Conantum (i.e., Holloway Farm), 357
Concealment, 20, 38, 41, 110, 307, 322
Concord, Mass., 16, 21, 156, 169, 170, 186, 304, 307, 349, 350, 357, 358, 382, 394, 399, 453, 454, 455
Concord, N.H., 60, 455
Concord River, 133
Conduct of life, 120, 290–291, 352, 433
Confucius, 6, 110, 311; "Memoirs of Confucius," 6n
Congress, 29, 304, 320, 555
Coningham (Conyngham?), William, 444(?)
Connecticut, 69, 400
Conscience, 34, 39, 505
Conservative, the, 388–389
Conspiration, 267
Constantinople, Turkey, 302
Consumer, 389
Contemplation, 485
Conversation, 9–10, 14–15, 28–29, 109–110, 147–148, 201, 206, 276, 314, 315, 320, 333–334, 339, 373, 379
Conversations-Lexicon (*Brockhaus' Konversations-Lexikon*), 48, 201
Cook, Captain James, 508
Coolidge, Joseph, 299, 552
Coombs, Mr., 162
Cooper, Thomas, 286
Cooperation, 154–155
Copenhagen, Denmark, 368
Copernican, 306
Copernicise, 35–36, 133, 317
Copyright, 222–223, 349
Corinne, 69, 70
"Corinne" (i.e., Margaret Fuller), 94
Corinth, Greece, 69

Cork, Ireland, 206, 207
Corn Laws, 191n, 239, 301
Cornwall, Barry, *see* Procter, Bryan Waller
Coronach, 172n
Cosmogonies, 35–36
Cossack, 376
Cotes, Roger, 371
Cotton, 15, 100, 175
Country life, 120
Courage, 28, 35, 42–43, 48, 79, 158, 165, 273, 310, 390, 434, 460, 486, 502, 503, 512
Courrier des Etats-Unis, 157n, 278–279, 514, 520n
Cousin, Victor, 167, 267, 557. *See also* Plato, *Oeuvres* (tr. Cousin)
Coutts, Thomas, 252n
Coventry, Lord, 395
Coventry, England, 430
Cowley, Abraham, 518
Cowper, William Francis, 531
Craig, H., 222
Craigenputtock, near Dunscore, Scotland, 540, 550
Crawshay, Mr., of London (?), 449
Crawshay, George, 128, 129n, 219, 220n, 449n
Credit, 378
Criffel (mountain), Scotland, 547, 548
Crimea, 241, 532
Critic (London), 212, 228
Critic, the, 390–391
Criticism, 88, 147–148, 521
Crito, 483
Crocker, Alvah, 100
Croesus, 66n, 105
Croisement(s), 44–45
Croker, John Wilson, 501; review of Macaulay's *History of England*, 524
Cromlechs, 254
Cromwell, Oliver, 179, 232, 497, 544, 567
Crossley, Mr., of Halifax, England, 210
Crowe, Catherine Stevens, 220, 282, 442, 464, 534, 536, 537
Croyland, England, 278
Cruikshank, George, 362
Crusaders, 192
Crusades, 279
Crusoe, Robinson, 144
Crystal Palace, London, 279, 516
Cudworth, Ralph, 166, 474n
Cultivator, 381
Culture, 156, 168, 463, 516

Cumberland (county), England, 547
Cunard, Edward, Jr., 435
Cunard, Sir Samuel, 435
Cunningham, Mr., of London, 239
Cunningham, Allan, 547
Curculio(s), 18, 95, 318, 348
Curzon, Robert, *Visits to the Monasteries of the Levant*, 459
Cushman, Charlotte, 242, 464, 524
Cushman, Susan, 242n, 243, 524, 533
Cuvier, Baron Georges Léopold Chrétien Frédéric Dagobert, 164
Cyclops, 499

Dabistán, or School of Manners, The, 90
Dabrado, Antonio, 118
Daedalus, 373
Daguerre, Louis Jacques Mandé, 167
Daguerreotype, 174
Dalton, John, 554, 557
Dana, Samuel Luther, 554
Dante Alighieri, 46–47n, 48, 89, 91, 336, 338; *Inferno*, 238n, 336n, 511n; *Vita Nuova*, 47, 166
Danton, George Jacques, 42
Dark Ages, 82, 122, 369
Darlington, England, 225
Darwin, Erasmus Alvey, 546
Daubeny, Charles G., 246
Davis, Maurice, 129, 130n
Davison, John, 436
Day(s), 49, 61, 104, 379–380
Dead-reckoning, 201
Decorum, 514
Defoe, Daniel, 500; "The True-Born Englishman," 500; *Robinson Crusoe*, 548
Defraillir (tailor, Paris), 424
Deity, 163
De la Beche, Sir Henry Thomas, 255, 362
Delamarre, Theodore-Casimir, 212n, 498
Delane, John Thadeus, 228
Delf, Thomas, 46, 125, 126n, 239
Delolme, Jean Louis, 557
Delusions, 21
Demand and supply, 254, 322
Demetrius, 310
Demiurgus, 479n, 480, 481n
Democrat(s), 34, 388, 396
Demoniacal, the, 47
Demosthenes, 13, 30, 402
De Quincey, Emily, 221
De Quincey, Florence, 221, 536
De Quincey, Francis, 536

De Quincey, Margaret, 221
De Quincey, Thomas, 145, 220, 221, 223, 227, 282, 362, 503, 534, 535, 536, 537, 564, 565n; *Suspiria de Profundis*, 50; *Works*, 248
Derby, George Horatio ("John Phoenix"), "A Collusion between a Aleygaiter and a Water-Snaik," 404n
Derby, England, 128, 185, 217, 411, 414, 415, 438
Derbyshire, England, 194
Desâtir, The, or Sacred Writings of the Ancient Persian Prophets . . . , 6
Descartes, René, 35
Despair, 216, 238, 257, 313, 462
Detachment, 143, 159, 359, 389
de Vere, Aubrey Thomas, 231, 539
Devil(s), 30, 254, 533
Devonshire, Dukes of, 18, 105
Dews, the, 65
Dial, The, 46, 125n, 278n
Dialectic, 132, 378–379, 479, 486
Dibdin, Thomas Frognall, 6, 98
Dickens, Charles, 130, 193, 203, 252, 255, 286n, 333, 361, 362, 450–451n, 550, 551; *Dombey and Son*, 504
Dictionary, 9, 89
Diderot, Denis, 166
Difference, 474
Digby, Sir Kenelm, 517, 567
Dinah, 177
Dinner, 333, 335
Dinornis, the, 252
Diogène, 157n
Diogenes, 372, 392, 401
Diogenes Laertius, *Lives of Eminent Philosophers*, 483n
Dion, 477
Discontinuity, 40
Discourse, 477
Distinterestedness, 308
Disraeli, Benjamin, 1st Earl of Beaconsfield, 24, 48, 119, 255, 275, 351, 361, 428, 531, 533, 550
Divination, 159, 482
Division of labor, 152
Dockray, Benjamin, 436
Doherty, Hugh, 262, 321, 326
Donegal, Ireland, 129
Dorchester (ship), 204
Doric architecture, 316
Douce, Francis, 245
Douglas, Katherine, 346n

Dover, England, 435
Downing, Andrew Jackson, *The Fruits and Fruit Trees of America*, 85n, 360
Drake, Sir Francis, 508, 518–519
Drama, 361
Dream(s), 96, 201, 294, 320
Dreisbach, Herr, 394
Driffield, England, 417, 418–419, 440
Druids, 460
Drummond, Mrs., of London, 444, 448
Dryden, John, 508, 520
Dublin, Ireland, 222, 232, 501
Dublin University, 240
Dudevant, Aurore, *see* Sand, George
Dueling, 246, 341
Duff-Gordon, Lady Lucie, 233, 546, 565
Duke, Sir James, 568n
Dumas, Alexandre (1802–1870), 105, 120, 203, 265, 346(?)
Dumfries, Scotland, 547
Dumont, Etienne, *Recollections of Mirabeau* . . . , 398n
Dundee, Scotland, 223, 279, 284, 418, 420, 441
Dunlap, John, 221
Dunscore, Scotland, 547, 548, 549
Dunsford Station, England, 185
Dupin, Amandine Aurore Lucie, *see* Sand, George
Dutch, the, 232, 384, 544
Duties, 115
Dwight, John Sullivan, 54
Dysart, Scotland, 181, 550
Dyspathy, 54

E|| . . . ||, 144n
E., Mr., 171, 202, 304
E., Mr., of London (?), 460
E., Mrs. R., 406
Earth, 9, 481
East India Company, 568
Eastlake, Sir Charles Lock, 362
East Lexington, Mass., 456
Eblis, 155
Economist, 275
Economy, 235, 499
Ecstasy, 390
Edda, 6, 88, 90, 108, 131, 132, 344. *See also* Snorri Sturluson
Edinburgh, Scotland, 130, 219, 220, 222, 223, 240, 277, 284, 418, 419–420, 441, 534, 536, 537, 564
Edinburgh, University of, 536, 564

Edinburgh Review, 46, 152n, 227, 228n, 256, 275, 496, 524, 549, 558, 559n

Education, 15, 49, 51, 146, 233, 276, 294, 310, 428, 471, 475–476, 482, 512, 545, 554

Educator, 347

Edwards, Francis, "Les Civiliens. Moeurs administratives de l'Inde anglaise," 513n

Egg, 139, 142–143

Eglinton *or* Eglintoun, Archibald William Montgomerie, Earl of, 183

Eglinton Castle, Ayrshire, 183n

Egypt, 245, 401

Egyptian architecture, 316, 390

Egyptians, 82

Eichthal, Gustave d', 265, 522

Einar, 345

Eldon, John Scott, 1st Earl of, 247

Eleaticism, 488

Elgie, F. T., 129, 130n, 198

Elgin Marbles, 523

Elindnor, 108

Eliot, George (Mary Ann *or* Marian Evans), 281n

Elizabeth I, Queen of England, 185, 567

Elizabethan age, 260, 511

Ellet, Elizabeth Fries Lummis, 465, 466n; "Female Poets of America," 466n

Elliotson, Dr. John, 532

Elocution, 178–179

Eloquence, 23–25, 77, 78, 320, 393–397, 399–403

Emerson, Bulkeley (son of Joseph Emerson of Malden), 186, 188(?)

Emerson, Edith (daughter), 24, 125n, 181, 327

Emerson, Edward Waldo (son), 345

Emerson, Elizabeth Bulkeley (grandmother of Joseph Emerson of Malden), 186

Emerson, Ellen Tucker (first wife), 125n, 188, 306n

Emerson, George Barrell, 125n

Emerson, George Samuel, 125

Emerson, Hannah (daughter of Joseph Emerson of Malden), 186

Emerson, Rev. Joseph (of Malden; great-grandfather), 177, 186–187, 188

Emerson, Joseph (son of Joseph Emerson of Malden), 186

Emerson, Lidian (Lydia) Jackson (second wife), 135n, 353; recipient of letters from Emerson, 179n, 180n, 181n, 185n, 189n, 190n, 203n, 204n, 207n, 215n, 220n, 224n, 226n, 231n, 231–232n, 237n, 239n, 240n, 242n, 243n, 244n, 258n, 267n, 269n, 284n, 305n, 311n, 323n, 327n, 328n, 443n, 513n, 523n, 530n, 531n, 535n, 536n, 537n, 539n, 540n, 542n, 543n

Emerson, Mary Moody (aunt), 65, 126, 168, 350, 372, 385

Emerson, Mary Moody (wife of Joseph Emerson of Malden), 186–187

Emerson, Ralph Waldo, Account Book 4, 169n, 447n; Index II, 133, 135, 290; Index Major, 318n, 367n, 368, 369n, 380n; Index Minor[A], 33n; Journal AZ, 28n, 149, 368, 369, 512n, 515n, 521n, 553n; Journal BO, 238, 259, 293n, 359n, 511; Journal CO, 86n, 215–216n, 515, 520n, 538n; Journal D, 43, 90, 113, 369; Journal DO, 368, 369, 568n; Journal E, 133, 172, 367, 379; Journal EO, 55; Journal G, 44, 133, 329; Journal GO, 496, 502n; Journal IO, 368; Journal J, 5, 6, 24, 25, 31, 44, 53, 164, 165, 478; Journal K, 43, 46, 132, 133, 163, 377, 479; Journal KL, 367, 368; Journal N, 5, 42, 324, 373; Journal NO, 367, 459, 461n, 462n, 463n, 466n, 467n; Journal O, 4, 6, 11, 14, 24, 29, 30, 33n, 34, 37, 40, 42, 45, 73, 76, 78, 91, 94, 133, 134, 135, 155, 160, 163, 290, 291n, 312, 329, 367, 373, 388, 399, 470n; Journal R, 5, 6, 14, 31, 46, 54, 96, 134, 379, 385, 399; Journal RS, 103, 213, 250, 251, 290, 291, 293, 312, 377n, 472, 473n, 475n; Journal RT, 90; Journal Scotland and England, 547n, 554n; Journal TU, 107, 157, 318, 369, 370, 376n, 473n, 499n, 515n; Journal U, 31, 166, 291, 312, 378, 383, 388, 470; Journal V, 6, 30, 43, 133, 134, 163, 297, 470n, 476, 477, 484; Journal VS, 368; Journal W, 24, 31, 36, 42, 90, 94, 134, 291, 368, 369, 470n, 475n, 476, 478n, 479n; Journal XO, 370; Journal Y, 49, 133, 135, 163, 290, 322, 333, 369, 470n, 487n; Journal Z, 6, 134, 477; Notebook Autobiography, 167; Notebook BL, 367; Notebook Books Small, 436n, 464–465n; Notebook France and England, 558n, 561n; Notebook LI, 6; Notebook Man, 374n; Notebook Morals, 59n; Notebook PY, 91, 315; Notebook Sea 1833, 564n; Notebook Σ,

41, 79, 114; Notebook T, 117n, 510; Notebook Trees[A], 19n, 20n, 94n, 118n, 490n, 493n. *See also* "Chronology," xxvi-xxvii, and "Self" in the General Index

INDEX HEADINGS AND TOPICS: "Acroyd," 280; "Affirmative," 10, 22–23; "Affirmative in Trees," 99; "Agassiz, [Jean Louis Rodolphe]," 306; "Age" or "The Age," 99, 143–144, 169, 289, 291(?), 293(?), 314, 353, 362, 389–390, 463; "Alboni, [Marietta]," 260; "Alcott, [Amos Bronson]," 15(?), 32, 113, 142, 153, 173, 175, 244, 326, 346–347, 352, 355–356, 361; "Alfieri," 278; "All biography auto-biography," 171; "America," 8–9(?), 29, 30, 73, 77, 79, 95–96, 102, 111, 139, 151(?), 161, 297, 320, 335, 343, 345; "American" or "Americans," 320, 502; "Anarchy," 385; "Anatomy," 32; "Ancients," 8, 33; "Ancients & Moderns," 33; "Animals," 16; "Animal spirits," 33; "Anthropomorphism," 73, 80, 87–88; "Apple," 350, 357, 360; "Appleton, Tho[ma]s. [Gold]," 276, 303; "Arabian Superlative," 72; "Arboretum," 12–13, 18; "Architecture," 306, 316; "Area," 497; "Aristocracy," 38, 52, 65, 69, 73, 75, 97, 115, 117, 118–119, 135, 138, 140, 149, 150, 153, 156, 163, 170, 176, 193, 300, 341, 371–372, 372–373, 509; "Arnott, Dr. [Neil]," 533; "Art," 9, 16, 29, 96, 331, 334; "Artist," 156, 178, 319–320; "Ascension of State," 390–391; "Ashburner, Lord [i.e., Dr.]," 258; "Ashburton dinner," 513; "Assessors," 307; "Association," 145; "Astronomy," 114; "Anthenaeum," 373, 530; "Athenaeum Speech Manch[ester].," 504; "Atmosphere," 135; "Attic measures," 59, 87; "Australia," 252; "Autobiography," 16–17, 25, 48, 49, 50, 79, 94, 144, 147, 157, 171, 296, 319, 322, 328, 331–332, 334; "Mr. 'B' at theatre," 258; "Badge," 13, 55; "Bailey, [Mr. (reporter)]," 211–212; "Bailey (Festus) [i.e., Philip James]," 75, 130(?), 189(?); "Ballads," 13, 22; "Bandinel, [Bulkeley]," 245; "Base men," 110–111; "Bat," 256–257; "Bates, Joshua," 236; "Battery," 289; "Beattie, [James]," 115; "Beauchamp, [Richard de, Earl of Warwick]," 517; "Beaumont & Fletcher," 154–155; "Beauty," 94; "Beginnings," 336–337; "Bhagavat [Gēētă]," 360; "Bias," 77; "Bible," 245, 255, 279; "Biography," 25, 171; "Blackwood['s Magazine]," 223; "Blouse," 314; "Bodleian Library," 240, 245; "Body," 40–41, 384; "Bonaparte, [Napoleon]," 69; "Book" or "Books," 5, 7–8, 17, 83, 91, 99, 116, 282, 336, 360, 374–375, 459, 522; "Book auction," 404n; "Books, list of," 17, 521–522; "Bore," 322; "Boston," 14, 38, 52, 157, 344; "Boulders," 10, 50, 162; "Bradford & Leeds," 211; "Brag," 515; "Bristed, [Charles]," 213(?), 275; "Britain," 279; "British Islands," 209; "British Museum," 239, 252; "Brown, Dr. S[amuel].," 222; "Buckland, [William]," 256; "Burke, [Edmund]," 44; "Burritt, [Elihu]," 267; "Byron, [George Gordon, 6th Baron]," 78, 91, 329; "Cafe Procope," 32; "Cambridge [England]," 250, 278, 520; "Cambridge [Mass.]," 133; "Cambridge Telescope," 114; "Camden, [William]," 518; "Capable of immense resolution," 510; "Carbutt, [Mayor, of Leeds]," 211; "Caricatures (Eng[lish])," 248; "Carlyle, [Thomas]," 78, 179, 230–234, 249, 255, 259, 299, 333, 334–335, 335, 343, 521, 540–554; "Carlyle — list of books," 283; "Cathedrals (Eng[lish])," 279; "Catholics," 177–178; "Certain things," 461; "Chadwick, [Sir Edwin]," 234, 242–243, 257; "Chalmers, Dr. [Thomas]," 224–231; "Chambers, Bros. [William and Robert]," 221–223; "Channing, [William Ellery (1818–1901)]," 167–168, 318, 338, 346, 357, 360; "Character," 12, 308, 351, 376; "Chartism" or "Chartists," 217, 239, 251, 280, 300, 314, 316, 325–326, 567; "Chastity," 83, 255, 333; "Chatsworth," 18; "Children," 337; "Chimney," 280; "Churches (French)," 271, 279; "Cid," 117; "Circumstance" or "Circumstances," 117–118, 142–143; "Cities," 140, 150; "Cities old," 497; "Civilization," 82; "Cleaveland, Duke of," 225; "Clergy," 219, 224, 254; "Cleverness," 60–61, 61–62, 62, 63, 138, 145–146, 148, 171–172; "Climate," 77, 96; "Clough, A[rthur] H[ugh]," 317; "Club" or "Clubs," 20, 22, 32, 54, 214, 249, 263,

267, 268–273; "Coals to a market," 176; "Cobbett, [William]," 213; "Cobden, [Richard]," 221, 225; "Coleridge, [Samuel Taylor]," 561–563; "Commerce," 391–392; "Communication," 145, 154; "Communism," 308, 310, 312, 314, 342, 347; "Community," 64–65, 347, 376, 378; "Compensation," 20, 36–37, 93, 115, 147; "Concealment, On the Beauties of," 20; "Concentration," 61; "Concord," 21, 32–33, 133, 167–168, 169, 304, 340n, 353–354, 358; "Concord walks," 21, 27, 95, 103, 304, 340, 353, 354, 357, 360; "Conduct of life," 290–291, 352, 361, 433; "Connection," 14–15, 26, 29; "Conservative," 388–389; "Contagion," 103; "Conversation," 9, 14–15; "Copyright," 349; "Cornwall, [Barry (Bryan Waller Procter)]," 210(?), 244; "Cosmogonies," 35–36; "Cotton," 15; "Cotton-Age," 100; "Country to live in," 497; "Courage," 13, 27, 28, 35, 42–43; "Court," 395; "Coutts, (Miss [Angela Georgina Burdett])," 252; "Credit," 378; "Criticism," 88, 94, 521; "Croisement," 44–45; "Crossley, [Mr., of Halifax]," 210; "Crowe, (Mrs. [Catherine Stevens])," 220; "Croyland (monks)," 278; "Crystal Palace," 187; "Culture," 346, 516; "The Culture of the Intellect," 132; "Currency," 49; "Custom," 151; "[John] Dalton & [Samuel Luther] Dana, the Chemists," 554; "Dante [Alighieri]," 338; "Day," 32, 49, 379–380; "Death," 31, 50; "Decorum," 514; "Delabeche [Sir Henry Thomas De la Beche]," 255; "Demosthenes," 13 or 30; "De Quincey, [Thomas]," 220, 282, 534, 537; "Of the[?] Despair," 462; "Destiny," 31, 382; "Detachment," 143, 326, 352, 359; "Devil," 342; "Devils (India)," 254; Dialectic," 378–379; "Dickens, [Charles]," 252, 255, 550; "Dictionary," 9, 89; "Disraeli, [Benjamin]," 533; "The Divine Man," 118; "Division of Labor," 152; "Dollar," 83; "Drake, Sir Fra[ncis]," 518–519; "Dreams," 294, 320; "Dress," 61, 296, 298; "Dulness," 300; "Dyspathy," 54; "Economy," 340n; "Edda," 88, 107–109, 131, 132, 138; "Edinburgh Review," 256; "Editors," 275; "Education," 49, 51, 147,

156, 294, 347, 348, 356; "Egg," 142–143; "Eichthal, [Gustave d']," 522; "Eldon (Lord) [John Scott, 1st Earl]," 246–247; "Elgin Marbles," 239–240; "Eloquence," 23–25, 49–50, 77, 320, 393–397; "Eloquence: E[dward] T. Taylor," 399–403; "[Emerson,] Edith," 24, 181; "[Emerson,] Edward," 345; "[Emerson,] Ellen Tucker," 188; "Emerson, Jos[eph]," 186–187; "Emerson, M[ary]. M[oody].," 168, 350; "Energy," 342, 345; "England," 138, 145–146, 168, 178, 180–181, 183–185, 196, 198–199, 214, 234, 238–239, 244, 247, 255–256, 295, 329–330, 504; "England — it is the Times Newspaper," 191–192; "English," 212, 215, 226, 230, 235, 259–260, 260; "English Aristocracy," 193; "English betting," 276; "English Conversations," 276; "English distances," 276; "English Estates," 225–226; "English idioms, phrases, &c," 193–194; "English manufacturers," 210, 211, 216; "Englishmen," 214, 219, 226–227, 238, 280, 295, 301, 303, 343; "English names," 240–241, 251, 280–281; "English peculiarities," 297–298; "Eng[lish]. Vigour," 304–305; "Enthusiasm," 150, 159; "Equation," 148; "Ether," 116; "Eton," 222, 273–274, 275, 280; "Europe," 337–338; "European politics," 337–338; "Evangelical lady," 254; "Executive talent," 148; "Expense," 147, 298; "Expression," 68, 70, 78, 91, 115; "Fable," 131, 132, 138, 155; "Faces," 255, 295; "Fairie [John Farey]," 260; "False instinct," 103; "Fame," 68; "Faraday, [Michael]," 289n; "Farmer," 353–354; "Fashion," 78; "Fate," 30–31, 55, 337; "Fellows, Sir C[harles]," 252–253, 560; "Festus," 75; "Fiorentino, [Pier Angelo]," 278; "Fitz Stephen," 279; "Flower, [Edward Fordham]," 282, 515; "Folkestone," 272; "Form," 80, 94(?), 391; "Forster, [John]," 255, 550; "Fourier, [François Marie Charles]," 28 or 37 or 43 or 47 [one unlocated item in Journal B, indexed without page reference], 377; "Frames for prints," 242; "France," 296–297, 314, 318–319, 327, 329–330; "Francis (J[ohn])," 258; "Freedom," 25, 52, 55, 90, 112, 117–118; "French," 261–262,

268–273; "French language," 141, 157–158; "Frenchman," 158; "The French Student," 157–158; "French Superlative," 141; "Frey," 55; "Friend," 68; "Friendship," 156, 327, 339, 341, 343, 380; "Fuller (Margaret)," 278; "Garden," 16, 80, 91–92, 93, 95, 95–96, 101, 103, 105, 110–112, 118, 137, 350, 404; "Garrison, [William Lloyd]," 94, 394–395; "Genius," 25, 30, 51, 54, 73, 80, 91, 92, 138, 164, 170, 325; "Gentlemen," 512; "Geologic History," 335; "Gibbet Lane," 210–211; "[William] Gilpin's 'Forest Scenery,'" 278; "Glasgow," 218, 222; "God," 342, 355–356; "Goethe, [Johann Wolfgang von]," 143, 336–337; "Gordon, Lady Duff," 546; "Gorse," 253; "Grasshopper," 119; "Great men," 12, 14, 40, 52, 318, 336–337; "Greeks," 35; "Green (J[ohn]. H)," 278; "Greenhouse," 18; "Hafiz, [Shams ud-din Mohammed]," 65–66, 67–68, 68, 88–89, 165; "Hair," 360; "Halifax Mills," 210; "Hallam, [Henry]," 260; "Hampstead," 272; "Head," 32; "Health," 174; "Heater Piece," 492–493; "Hedge Fence," 489–490; "Heimskringla," 341–342, 344, 345, 350; "Help," 309, 340n; "Helps, A[rthur].," 343, 355; "Hilarity," 132, 381, 384; "Hill, Sir R[owland].," 272; "Hillard, [George Stillman]," 273–274; "History," 82, 100, 144, 169, 289, 322, 325–326, 390; "Hobby," 293, 315; "Hooker, [Sir William Jackson]," 247; "Hope," 390; "Horoscope," 34, 170–171; "Horse," 86, 92; "Hospitality," 259; "Housekeeping," 340n; "House of Commons," 213, 242; "Hunt, Leigh," 255; "Idea," 306; "Idealist" or "Idealism," 155, 162, 223; "Idĕrsäy," 215; "Idioms," 195; "Illusion," 309, 351, 355–356, 361; "Imagination," 15–16, 41, 48, 50; "Immortality," 50–51, 147, 294, 308, 312, 340; "India," 513; "Indirection" [one unlocated item in Journal AB, indexed without page reference], 148; "Individual," 302, 310, 312, 347, 354; "Individualism," 139–140, 154, 156, 378, 381; "Inferiors," 78; "Insanities," 21; "Inscriptions," 253; "Inspiration," 60, 61–62, 69, 78, 279; "Instinct," 16; "Insufficient Forces," 110; "Intellect," 60–62, 97, 120, 131, 132, 145, 151–152, 159, 173, 182–183, 294, 306, 308, 310, 313, 326, 329, 352, 353, 355; "Intellect detaches," 159–160; "Interference," 103–104; "Ireland," 235; "Ireland, Alex[ander] Esq.," 539–540; "Irving, Rev. Edw[ard].," 180–181; "Jackson, C[harles] T.," 14; "Joking," 321–322; "Journal," 45–46, 54; "Journeyman," 105; "Judgment Day," 62, 94; "Kehl, [Mr., of Huddersfield]," 216; "Kenyon, [John]," 273–274, 332–333, 528; "Kew," 247; "Knowledge," 381; "Kraitsir, [Charles]," 337; "Kurroglou," 71, 85, 86, 106; "Labor," 152, 162; "Lamartine, [Alphonse Marie Louis de Prat de]," 269–270; "Land," 19; "Landor, [Walter Savage]," 241, 532; "Landowning," 93; "Language," 354; "The Latin 'Yes,'" 326; "Lawrence (Sir Thomas)," 241–242, 246–247; "Laws," 20, 54; "Laws of the World," 131, 132–133, 148, 152, 154, 305, 325, 329, 356; "Lazarus," 356, 359; "Lazarus the sun," 293; "Lecture on Reading," 5; "Lectures," 5, 18; "Legare, [Hugh Swinton]," and "Legare's Writings," 7–8; "Lehmann, [Charles Ernest Rodolphe Henri]," 277; "Life," 16–17, 25, 39, 41, 52, 53, 54, 54–55, 68, 76, 78, 80, 94, 103–104, 146, 162, 163, 356, 382(?); "Limitation," 511; "List of Books," 6, 17, 46–47; "Literature," 83(?), 341–342; "Lloyd (Jones)," 211–212; "Loci," 98; "London," 209, 236–238, 251, 255, 327, 497, 512–513; "London houses," 217; "Why London is London," 299; "Longevity," 31, 40–41, 50–51, 382; "Lords," 497; "Louis Philippe," 236; "Louvre," 267–268; "Love," 174; "Lowther (Sir James)," 244; "Loyalty," 385; "Luck," 305," "Lucy (Sir Tho[ma]s.)," 251; "Ludgate," 257; "Luther, [Martin]," 107; "L[y]cian (Art)," 252–253; "Macaulay, [Thomas Babington]," 242; "Manchester," 182, 217, 504; "Manners," 73, 79, 95, 195, 309; "Manufacturer," 40; "Man-Woman," 392; "Marriage," 351–352; "Marshall (James)," 211; "Martineau, [Harriet]," 225; "Mass[achusetts]. Q[uarterly]. Rev[iew].," 338–339, 352; "Maud, Queen," 518–519; "Mechanic Powers," 112; "Melbourne (Viscount) [William Lamb, 2d Viscount]," 275–276; "Melioration," 141, 335; "Memoranda," 125–126, 128; "Memoranda of Oxford," 250–251; "Memorandum," 19, 156, 274, 426–427, 522; "Memory," 356; "Men," 16–17, 22, 30, 34, 40–41, 50, 110–111, 156, 159, 170, 173, 175, 183, 376, 383, 392; "Mesmerism," 14, 37; "Metamorphosis," 41n, 76, 137, 147; "Michael Angelo's drawings," 246–247; "Microscopes," 257; "Milnes, [Richard Monckton]," 214–215, 242, 275–276, 530–533; "Milton, [John]," 509; "Miscellanies," 496–497(?); "Modern times," 173, 353; "Money," 174; "Monotone (bad)," 355–356; "Monotone (good)," 311; "Montaigne, [Michel Eyquem de]," 295, 350, 352; "Montreal Speech," 507; "Moods," 24, 53, 84; "Moral" or "Morals," 16, 20, 22, 41, 42, 54, 182–183, 320, 356–357, 471; "Morpeth, Lord [George William Frederick Howard, Viscount Morpeth]," 566; "Museum (British)," 239–240, 244, 252; "Music," 91, 101; "Musket Worship," 255–256; "Mythology," 24, 48, 65–66, 68, 73, 80, 83, 96, 100, 110, 289; "Nantucket," 62, 63; "Napier, [McVay]," 256; "Napoleon," 71–72; "Nasty," 191–192; "A National Man," 40–41; "National traits," 498–499, 510; "Nature," 26, 27, 62, 80, 96, 143, 163, 167, 168, 169, 302, 325, 331, 382–383, 383; "La Nature aime les Croisements," 44–45; "Necessity," 116; "Neglect," 91; "Nemesis," 93(?), 94(?); "Nesmith, [John]," 102; "Newcastle," 219–220; "Newcomb, C[harles] K[ing]," 143(?), 144(?), 151, 342; "New England," 177; "The New Religion," 306–307, 324; "Newspapers," 353; "Nicholas (Czar)," 233–234; "Nobility," 277–278; "Nonresistance," 385; "Norsemen," 341–342; "Norton (Mrs.) [Carolyn Elizabeth Sarah]," 275–276; "Novel" or "Novels," 15, 23–24, 48, 289, 361; "Obelisk," 267; "Old cities," 497; "One Idea," 119–120, 293, 315; "On the Beauties of Concealment," 20; "Open-dealing," 511; "Operatives," 216; "Opportunity," 25; "Orchard," 18–19, 50, 95, 99, 103; "Orientalist," 90–91; "Originality," 141–142, 155; "Osman," 33, 39, [one unlocated item in Journal

CD, indexed without page reference]; "Owen (Richard)," 215–216, 243, 253–254, 256–257, 277, 321, 525–528; "Oxford," 245, 248, 250–251, 520; "Paint," 30, 52, 302–303, 384; "Palais Royal," 270; "Pantheism," 175; "Pantheon," 253, 271; "Paris," 263–265, 266, 268–269, 271–272, 294, 322–323, 324; "Parliament," 182, 212–213, 253; "Partiality," 76–77; "Party," 373–374; "Pathology," 109, 113; "Patmore (Coventry)," 255; "Patriotism," 161; "Paul's, St.," 230(?), 241; "Pauperism," 299; "Pear" or "Pears," 19, 85, 95, 103, 118, 154; "Penny post," 236; "Persistency," 41–42; "Personalities," 282; "Personality," 308; "Piece Hall (Halifax)," 210; "Place," 391–392; "Plain dealing," 377; "Planting & Rearing Hedge," 490–491; "Platforms," 84, 110, 115; "Plato," 113–114, 245–249, 302, 469, 471–477, 479–480, 482–485, 486–488; "[Plato,] Parmenides," 487–488; [Plato,] Protagoras," 477–478; "[Plato,] Republic," 470, 473, 474–475; "Pluck," 174, 192; "Plural London," 236–237; "Poet" or "Poets," 68–69, 91, 109, 113, 115, 346; "Poetry," 48, 132, 144, 172; "Poetry & Criticism," 147; "Poison," 93, 105; "Police," 34; "Polidore Virgil," 279; "Politics," 29, 337(?); "Poor," 282, 340n; "Pope, A[lexander].," 519; "Poverty," 244–245, 257, 258–259; "Power," 117, 311–312; "Power & Circumstance," 117–118; "Powers," 470–471; "Practical," 114, 138, 146, 148, 155, 346, 384; "Preaching," 338; "Preach not," 338; "Present," 171, 173; "Present & Future," 171; "Public Schools," 512; "Quarrel," 385–386; "Quarterlies," 223; "Queries," 280; "Questions," 22–23, 31–32, 48, 109–110, 169, 568; "Quotation," 386; "Races," 353, 356–357; "Rachel [Elisa Félix]," 269; "Railroad," 99, 101–102, 342–343, 349, 350, 353, 358; "Raphael's Cartoons," 246–247; "Rats," 256; "Reaction," 147; "Reading," 5, 66–67, 95, 116, 147, 165, 172; "Realism" or "Reality," 55, 93, 94, 149, 153, 155, 156, 305, 307, 308, 315, 318, 322, 324–325, 329–330, 345, 351, 386; "Religion," 176, 177, 187(?), 306–307, 314, 324,

533; "Religion (Eng[lish].)," 279; "Revolution," 296–297, 312, 318, 345; "*Revue des Deux Mondes*," 513; "Rhetoric," 56; "Rhyme," 85, 86, 115; "Rich," 11, 12, 29, 36, 387, 388; "Rich & poor," 104–105, 118, 150, 151, 162, 173(?), 174, 188, 388; "Richard of Devizes," 279; "Riches," 305, 322, 354, 387; "Rocking Stones," 83, 145, 147–148, 152; "Rogers (Samuel)," 242, 522; "Rome," 497; "Ruskin, [John]," 521; "Russell (Lord John [1st Earl Russell of Kingston Russell])," 211(?), 244, 254; "Saadi [Muslih-ud-Din]," 11, 245; "Safford, [Truman Henry]," 60, 61, 62; "Sand, George [Amandine Aurore Lucie, *née* Dupin, Baronne Dudevant]," 92, 262, 338, 348, 353, 361; "Schleiermacher, [Friedrich Ernst Daniel]," 470; "Scholar," 6–7, 8–9, 28–29, 34, 35, 52–53, 78, 80, 94, 98, 109, 112, 113, 176, 296; "Science" or "Sciences," 28, 121, 164; "Scotch," 218; "Scotland," 534(?) or 547(?) or 550(?) or 564(?) [in Notebook ED]; "Scott (David)," 277, 282; "Scott, [Sir Walter]," 180; "Sea," 175, 293, 320, 332, 564; "Sea line," 293; "Second Visit to Wordsworth," 558; "Selfexistence & selfhelp," 39; "Selfhelp," 39, 132; "Selfpoise," 83, 145, 148, 152; "Selfreliance," 39; "Selkirk, [Lord]," 255; "Series & Degree," 465; "Servant," 140; "Sewell, [William]," 469; "Sewers (London)," 257; "Shakespeare, [William]," 10, 70, 86(?); "Shelley, [Percy Bysshe]," 75; "Shepherd, (Dr.) T[homas]. P[erkins].," 566; "Skeptic," 84, 97, 107, 151; "Skepticism," 346, 359, 360; "Sleep," 320; "Smith (Sidney)," 214, 249, 254; "Society," 5, 9–10, 28, 31–32, 97, 163 339, 372, 513; "Socrates," 86, 113–114, 471–472, 482–483; "Solidity & Security," 499; "Solomon," 66–67; "[Robert] Southey's Chronicle [of the Cid]," 117; "Spanish painters," 268; "Speculative," 114; "Speech is to conceal," 38; "Spent words," 362; "State of melioration," 141; "States," 390–391; "Stealing," 184; "Subjects," 120; "Success," 29–30, 52, 54, 55, 314, 329–330; "Superlative," 18, 21, 33, 71, 72, 120, 132, 138, 141, 142, 143, 167–168, 319; "Superlative in life," 142; "Superstition," 13, 83, 96, 143, 151, 389; "Sutton, [Henry]," 189; "Swedenborg, [Emanuel]," 16, 26–27, 82(?), 144(?), 150, 352, 357; "Symbol," 307, 390n; "Tailor (Eng[lish].)," 243; "Talent," 300, 306, 312, 318, 352; "Taylor, E[dward]. T.," 399–403; "Taylor, Thomas," 484; "Telegraphy in Eng[land].," 382; "Telescope," 114; "Temperament," 12, 33, 40; "Temperance," 13, 88, 98; "Tennyson, [Alfred]," 231, 255, 261, 537–539, 565–566; "Thalberg, [Sigismund]," 236; "Theatre des Varietés," 137; "Thom (Rev D[avid])," 259; Thoreau, H[enry]. D[avid].," 106–107, 151, 234, 293, 343, 344, 347; "Thought" [entries in index to Journal GH not recovered]; "Times," 311, 314, 318; "Times Newspaper," 158, 188, 190, 191–192, 211–212, 227–230, 251, 428; "De Tocqueville (Mme. [Alexis])," 266; "Tools, 9, 10, 12, 53–54, 99, 100, 105, 110–111, 112, 117–118, 137, 139, 140, 311–312, 353; "Topics," 30; "Trades of despair," 238; "Traits," 291, 501, 503, 510; "Transcendental" or "Transcendentalism," 149, 150–151; "Transit," 16, 44; "Transition," 76, 82, 99, 159–160; "Translation," 375; "Travelling," 11, 49, 136, 138, 300–301; "Trees," 12–13, 18–19, 82, 95, 99, 116–117; "Trope," 105, 147; "True aristocracy," 153; "Truth," 391; "Truth stranger than fiction," 27; "Tucker, Ellen," 188; "Turner, [Joseph Mallord William]," 273, 277, 527; "Twist," 314, 343, 354–355; "Umbrelville," 137; "Unitarianism," 115–116; "Universities," 245–246, 250–251, 270, 520–521; "Value of a Servant," 140; "Van Mons, [Jean-Baptiste]," 85, 103; Variétés," 137; "Vaughan, [C. J.]," 282; "Velasquez, [Diego Rodriguez de Silvay]," 267–268; "Verses," 16, 65, 121, 122; "De Vigny, [Comte Alfred Victor]," 209–210; "Virtue," 381; "Voyage," 175, 564; "Vulgarity," 315; "Walter (of the Times) [John Walter III]," 251; "Wants," 392; "War," 79; "Warren Lot," 493; "Warwick, [Richard Beauchamp, Earl of Warwick]," 517–518; "Wealth," 174, 519–520; "Webster, [Daniel]," 144, 393, 396–399; "Wellborn," 12; "Westminster Abbey," 259; "Wheatstone, [Sir Charles]," 282; "Whim," 119–120; "Whip," 28, 53, 137; "Whip for our top," 137; "Why London is London," 299; "Wickste[e]d, [Rev. Charles]," 211; "Wilkinson, [James John Garth]," 145–146; "Will," 25; "Wilson, [John]," 220–221, 223–224, 564; "Winchester Cathedral," 257; "Windsor," 274; "Windus (Mr. [B. G.])," 277; "Wine," 10, 116, 346; "Wisdom," 381; "Wishes," 354; "Woman," 41n, 78, 83, 108, 305, 346, 350, 352, 392; "Wonder," 391–392, 403; "Wood," 516, 567; "Woodlot," 116–117; "Words," 354, 362; "Wordsworth, [William]," 187–188, 225, 226–227, 244, 554–559; "Work," 193, 427; "Worship of the Dollar," 83; "Worthies," 517–519; "Wotton, Sir Henry," 517; "Writer," 98–99, 149, 154–155, 174, 315, 325, 354; "Writing," 8–9; "Yankeedom," 101–102, 111

LECTURES: "Address to the Temperance Society at Harvard, Mass." (July 4, 1843), 380n; "Books," 367n, 438n, 439; "Conduct of Life," 120, 290–291; "Country Life," 120; "Domestic Life," 286n, 437, 438, 439, 440, 441, 442; "Eloquence," 25, 437, 439, 441; "England," 453, 454, 456; "England and the English," 455(?); "The Genius of the Present Age," 441; "Goethe," 437n, 438; "The Humanity of Science," 440; "Intellect," 120–121, 131, 132–135; "London," 454, 455, 456; "Manners," 514n; "Michel Angelo Buonaroti," 6n; Middlebury (Vt.) Oration (July 22, 1845), 120; "Mind and Manners in the Nineteenth Century," 328; "Montaigne," 437; "Morals," 120; "Napoleon," 216, 285–286n, 437, 438, 439, 440, 441; "Natural Aristocracy," 286n, 291n, 328n, 441; "The Natural Characteristics of the Six Northern States of America," 440, 441; "Plato," 452n; "Poetry and Eloquence," 328n; "Politics and Socialism," 328n; "Powers and Laws of Thought," 328n; "Reading," 5, 438, 439, 440; "Relation of Intellect to Natural Science," 328n; "The Scholar," 120; "Shakspeare," 10, 286n, 437, 438, 439, 440, 441, 442; "The Skeptic," 112;

Speech at the Annual Soirée of the Athenaeum, Manchester (November 18, 1847), 437n, 504–506; Speech at the Dinner of the St. George's Society, Montreal (April 23, 1852), 507–509; "The Spirit of the Times," 441; "The Superlative," 120, 286n, 438, 441; "Swedenborg," 26n, 437; "Tendencies and Duties of Men of Thought," 328n; "Uses of Great Men," 437, 439

LETTERS: to Rev. Daniel Austin, 399; to Edward Bangs, 126n; to Elizabeth Biggs, 191n; to Dr. Samuel Brown, 338; to Horace Bushnell, 338; to James Elliot Cabot, 47n; to Thomas Carlyle, 73n, 127n; to James Freeman Clarke, 452n; to Benjamin Dockray, 436n; to Lidian Emerson, 179n, 180n, 181n, 185n, 189n, 190n, 203n, 204n, 207n, 207n, 215n, 220n, 224n, 226n, 231n, 231–232n, 237n, 239n, 240n, 242n, 243n, 244n, 258n, 267n, 269n, 284n, 305n, 311n, 323n, 327n, 328n, 443n, 513n, 523n, 530n, 531n, 535n, 536n, 537n, 539n, 540n, 542n, 543n; to Mary Moody Emerson, 372n; to William Emerson, 125–126n, 157n, 191n, 194n, 349n, 443n; to S. M. Felton, 340n; to Margaret Fuller, 117n, 466n, 497, 502–503, 513n, 540n; to Elizabeth Hoar, 216n; to Thomas Jevons, 131n; to Theodore Parker, 339n; to Bryan Waller Procter, 126n; to Samuel Gray Ward, 26n, 28n

POEMS: "As moths to the light" (from Hafiz), 68; "But God will keep his promise yet," 97–98; "Day! hast thou two faces," 49; "From the beginning," 122–123; "Go out into Nature and plant trees," 65; "O Ellen, may these happy hours," 306n; "One by one to every creature," 121–122; "Rags & curds," 302–303; "The place on which the sole" (from Hafiz), 68; "To every creature," 81–82, 119, 121–122; "Well away sing, it one thing shows me," 16; "Where is Skrymir," 82, 122; "Who gave thy check the mixed tint" (from Hafiz), 67–68

WORKS: "Ability," 138n, 247n, 498n, 499n, 500n, 567n; "Address to Kossuth," 466n, 467n; "Aristocracy" (W, V), 182n, 185n, 186n, 191n, 193n, 213n, 226n, 235n, 241n, 249n, 251n, 277n, 300n,

514n, 518n, 520n; "Aristocracy" (*W*, X), 39n, 40n, 41n, 51n, 52n, 53n, 76n, 79n, 115n, 119n, 136n, 140n, 149n, 156n, 167n, 171n, 291n, 292n, 306n, 318n, 326n, 373n; "Art and Criticism," 354n, 362n; "Beauty," 274n, 384n; "Behavior," 21n, 376n; "Books," 5n, 6n, 24n, 49n, 98n, 165–166n, 167n, 348n, 361n, 368n, 375, 478n; "Boston," 8n; "Brahma," 37n; "Carlyle," 542n, 543n, 544n, 545n, 546n, 551n, 552n, 553n; "Celebration of Intellect," 310n; "Character" (*W*, III), 390n; "Character" (*W*, V), 210n, 212n, 214n, 234n, 334n, 460–461n, 498–499n, 510n, 528n; "Character" (*W*, X), 94n, 301n; "The Chartist's Complaint," 49n; "Civilization," 369n, 426n; "Clubs," 10n, 32n, 110n, 165–166n; "Cockayne," 132n, 168n, 198n, 214n, 215n, 219n, 230n, 280n, 301n, 345n, 432n, 499n, 515n, 516n; "Compensation," 115; "Concord Walks," 18n; "Considerations by the Way," 14n, 50n, 154n, 327n, 337n, 381n, 384n, 392n; "Country Life," 95n, 101n, 103n, 153n, 358n, 360n; "Courage," 13n, 43n, 310n, 390n; "Culture," 43n, 49n, 107n, 108n, 136n, 150n, 161n, 293n, 294n, 301n, 325n, 374n, 428n, 473n; "Days," 61n; "Demonology," 27n; Divinity School Address, 384n; "Editors' Address," 139n, 161n; "Education," 315n; "Eloquence," 25n, 44n, 77n, 242n, 395, 396n, 400n, 402n, 475n; *English Traits*, 504n; *Essays*, 115n, 418; *Essays, Lectures, & Orations* (London, 1848), 427n; *Essays, Second Series*, 44, 376, 379, 384, 391; "Ethnical Scriptures," 322n; "Experience," 374n; "Ezra Ripley, D. D.," 187n; "Fate," 34n, 39n, 55n, 132n, 143n, 257n, 332n; "First Visit to England," 387n, 547n, 554n, 561n; "The Fortune of the Republic," 112n; "Fragments on Nature and Life," 122n, 347n; "Fragments on the Poet and the Poetic Gift," 368n; "The Fugitive Slave Law," 394n, 396–397n; "The Garden," 122n; "Goethe," 459n; "Greatness," 42n, 43n, 78n, 79n, 153n, 337n; "Guy," 38n; "Horoscope," 34n; "Illusions," 352n, 361n; "Immortality," 51n, 308n, 340n; "Inspiration," 44n, 150n, 315n, 335n, 478n; "Instinct and Inspiration," 85n,

99n, 150n, 312n, 322n, 337n; "Land," 182n, 193n, 196n, 209n, 214n, 223n, 254n, 278n, 314n, 332n, 334n, 432n, 497n, 507n, 508n, 568n; "Life and Letters in New England," 376n, 377n; "Literature," 146n, 295n, 342n, 479n; "Manners" (*W*, V), 169n, 178–179n, 183n, 184n, 190n, 192n, 198n, 217n, 226n, 227n, 234n, 236n, 238n, 254n, 296n, 331–332n, 334n, 498n, 499n, 511n, 512n, 513n, 514n, 515n; "The Man of Letters," 314n; "Mary Moody Emerson," 65n; *Memoirs of Margaret Fuller Ossoli*, 70n; "Memory," 356n; "Milton," 375n; "Montaigne," 9n, 84n, 107n, 246n, 295n, 355n; *Nature*, 384n; *Nature, An Essay; And Lectures on the Times* (London, 1844), 427n; *Nature: An Essay. And Orations* (London, [1843]), 427n; "Nature, I," 383n; "Nominalist and Realist," 84n; "Perpetual Forces," 54n; "Persian Poetry," 55n, 66n, 67n, 69n, 70n, 73–74n, 75n, 89n, 90n, 165n; "Personal," 247n, 252n, 362n, 526n, 540n, 558n; "Plato; New Readings," 474n, 475n, 476n; "Plato; or the Philosopher," 113n, 386n, 472n, 476n, 477n, 478n, 481n, 483n, 486n, 487n; *Poems* (London, 1847), 127, 436n; "The Poet," 44n; "Poetry and Imagination," 86n, 91n, 138n, 148n, 172n, 307n, 333n, 509n; "Power," 28n, 41n, 82, 105n, 300n, 302n, 340n, 342n; "Powers and Laws of Thought," 104n, 131n, 136n, 138n, 141n, 143n, 146n, 152n, 159n, 173n, 296n, 313n, 316n, 317n; "The Preacher," 46n; "Quatrains," 33n; "Quotation and Originality," 89, 221n, 375n, 386n, 525n, 535n; "Race," 178–179n, 181n, 192n, 195n, 218n, 498n, 502n; "Religion," 196n, 219n, 223n, 279n, 307n; "Resources," 211n; "Result," 209n; "The Scholar," 25n, 487n; "Shakspeare," 10n, 35n, 155n, 386n; "Social Aims," 156n, 289n, 322n, 373n, 378n; "Society and Solitude," 28n, 29n, 53n, 163n, 296n; "Speech at Manchester," 504n; "Stonehenge," 258n, 281n, 299n, 311n, 336n, 428–429n, 430n, 431n, 432n, 461n, 543n, 545n, 552n; "Success," 67n, 153n; "The Superlative," 21n, 33n, 141n, 142n, 374n; "Swedenborg," 27n, 32n, 380n;

"Theodore Parker," 171n; "Thoreau," 294n, 343n, 355n; "The Times," 188–189n, 191n, 192n, 212n, 215n, 229n, 230n, 251n, 264n, 515n; "Translations," 341n; "Truth," 70n, 138n, 141n, 182n, 183n, 198n, 258n, 303n, 324n, 500n, 501n, 516n; "Universities," 245n, 246n, 247n, 250–251n, 341n, 503n, 512n, 516n, 520n, 568n; "Uriel," 380n; "Uses of Great Men," 14n, 15n, 94–95n, 370n, 373n; "Veracity," 174n; "Voyage to England," 175n, 176n, 201n, 202n, 203n, 204n, 205n, 206n, 207n, 320n, 332n; "War," 507n; "Wealth" (*W*, V), 132n, 214n, 244n, 463n, 500n, 509n, 517n, 520n; "Wealth" (*W*, VI), 11n, 12n, 80n, 93n, 112n, 171n, 251n, 305n, 325n, 330n, 348n, 378n, 387n, 388n, 389n, 392n; "Woman," 108n; "Works and Days," 32n, 61n, 76n, 146n, 168n, 379n, 380n, 463n, 476n, 480n; "Worship," 17n, 31n, 34n, 42n, 144n, 148n, 163n, 294n, 305n, 306n, 307n, 314n, 324n, 325n, 342n, 356n, 375n, 377n, 387n, 390n, 391n

Emerson, Ruth Haskins (mother), 452(?)

Emerson, Waldo (son of Rev. Joseph Emerson of Malden), 186, 188(?)

Emerson, Waldo (son), 6n, 11n, 391n

Emerson, Rev. William (father), 188(?)

Emerson, William (brother), 188(?); recipient of letters from Emerson, 125–126n, 157n, 191n, 194n, 349n, 443n

Empson, William, 275

Energy, 43, 163, 342, 345

Enfield, Mr. (of Hampstead?), 449

Enfield, William, 128, 129n, 189, 449n

England, 7, 11, 29, 34, 36, 119–120, 128, 145–146, 151, 158, 178–184, 189, 191–193, 196, 197, 199, 210, 214, 215, 218, 221, 226, 234, 236, 239, 244, 245, 248, 253–256, 259, 266, 270–273, 276–280, 282, 292–293, 295, 297–299, 301, 304, 306, 314, 327, 328–330, 332–333, 335–337, 339, 341–343, 346, 353, 358–359, 404, 428, 431–432, 434–435, 483, 495–497, 501–508, 511, 514, 516–517, 519, 523–524, 530–531, 533, 537, 540, 542, 550–551, 555, 557, 559, 562, 565–566. *See also* Angleterre

English Channel, 254, 553

English church, 259, 307, 543

English government, 214, 247, 252, 351, 500, 509

English liturgy, 10, 35

Englishman, 84, 151, 158, 168, 169–178, 180–185, 189–191, 192–193, 194–195, 197–199, 205, 206, 212–218, 219–222, 225–227, 234–236, 238–240, 247, 251, 253, 259–260, 261, 266, 272, 278, 280, 295, 298, 299, 301, 303, 304–305, 306, 313, 321, 324, 329, 335–336, 341, 343, 345, 349, 381, 428, 432, 434, 497–499, 502, 507, 510–512, 514, 515–517, 525, 527, 532, 537–538, 542–543, 552, 558–559

English names, 185, 240–241

English speech, 179, 191, 193–194, 250, 297–298

Enthusiasm, 150, 217, 291, 514

Ephesian, 509

Equation, 148

Equator, 96, 205

Erasmus, Desiderius, 478

Erceldoune, Thomas of ("Thomas the Rhymer"), "True Thomas and the Queen of Elfland," 23n

Erebus, 513

Espinasse, Francis, 126, 284 444(?), 540

Essence, 474

Essex, Earl of, 517

Essex (ship), 63n, 64

Estabrook farm, 360

Eternity, 486

Ether, 14, 116, 141, 164

Eton College, 222, 230, 274, 275, 280, 313, 515, 528

Etzler, John Augustus, 62; *The Paradise within the Reach of all Men . . .* , 62n

Euclid, 91

Eunapius, 483; "Lives of the Philosophers and Sophists," 483n

Euphuism, 484

Euripides, *Thyestes*, 59n; *Tragoediae*, 59n

Europa (ship), 276n, 345n

Europe, 13, 29, 37, 119, 138, 161, 199, 206, 217, 218, 233, 254, 255, 256, 264, 279, 298, 322, 324, 330, 355, 369, 389, 462, 478, 507, 510, 533, 543, 550

Europeans, 62, 106, 201

Euston Hotel, London, 421

Evanescence, 357–358

Evans, Mary Ann *or* Marian (George Eliot), 281n

Evelyn, John, 166

Everett, Edward, 220; *An Address . . . Before the Mercantile Library Association . . .* , 511n
Evesham, England, 128
Evolution, 99–100
Examination, 320
Examiner, 275, 550
Excalibur, 117
Executive talent, 148
Exeter Hall, London, 285, 441, 442, 532
Expression, 68, 70, 78, 91, 94, 115, 121, 144
Eye(s), 115, 121, 226, 357, 473, 498
Eylfi, 131
Eyvind, 342

Fable, 120, 155, 165
Fabliaux, 166
Facts, 133, 315, 477
"Fair Annie," 172
Fairhaven Bay (*or* Pond), 21, 354
Faith, 16, 204, 348, 484
Falkirk, Scotland, 282
Fame, 368, 375
Fancy, 4, 9, 401
Faneuil Hall, Boston, 7
Faraday, Michael, 225, 237, 289n, 527
Farey, John, 260
Farming, 105, 349
Fashion, 243, 296
Fate, 31, 50, 55, 74, 84, 90, 337, 348, 485
Faust, 75, 115
Fear, 502, 503
Félix, Elisa (Rachel), 323
Fellows, Sir Charles, 225, 240n, 252, 315, 362, 432, 450, 560
Felton, John, 180
Feminine element, 392, 394
Fench, Mr. (?), 444
Fenris, 109, 115, 116n, 132
Ferhad, 67
Feridun, 139
Ferrier, James Frederick, 223, 275
Field, Edwin Wilkins, 273, 277, 285, 441, 444, 450, 451
Filmore, Lewis, 228
Fines, Sir Collard, 518
Fingal's Cave, 555
Fiorentino, Pier Angelo, 278; "Lettres sur l'Exposition," 279n
Firdausi, *The Sháh Námeh*, 66n, 74n, 75n, 155n
Fire, 41, 384
Fisher, Mr., 119

Fisher, W., Jr., 129, 130n, 442–443n
Fitchburg, Mass., 100, 453, 457
Fitchburg Railroad, 100n, 139, 328, 340n, 443
Fitzgerald, Lady Pamela, 179, 524
Fitz Stephen, 279
Flamborough Head, England, 196
Flanberry, England, 418
Flaxman, John, 523
Flemish language, 198
Fletcher, Mr., 281
Fletcher, John, 69, 154, 166; and Francis Beaumont, *Laws of Candy*, 65
Flod‖ . . . ‖, 203
Florio, John, 295
Flower, Edward Fordham, 251, 282, 427, 436, 515n
Folger, Walter, 64
Folkes, Martin, 27n
Folkestone, England, 238, 272, 423, 426
Foord, Sophia, 125
Forbes, Edward, 361–362, 436, 442, 450; "On the Tertiary Fluvio-Marine Formation of the Isle of Wight," 436n
Forbes family, 177
Force, 110, 309, 352, 398
Ford, J. B., 435
Ford, John, 166
Foreign Quarterly Review, 302, 338
Form, 391
Formality, 313
Forster, John, 130, 252n, 255, 275, 301(?), 333, 362, 444, 450, 550
Forster, William E., 129, 130n, 214, 281, 498
Fortescue, Sir John, 501
Fortune, 170–171
Fortune (ship), 206
Foster, Mr., 301
Foucault, Jean Bernard Léon, 265n
Foucher, Leon, 265
Fourier, François Marie Charles, 28, 37, 43, 47, 100, 136, 290, 337, 347, 378, 484, 485
Fourierism, 377
Fourierville, 359
Fox, Charles James, 75, 315(?), 401, 523
Fox, George, 195
Foxcroft family, 177
Foxton, Frederick J., 130, 282
Framingham, Mass., 456
France, 36, 101, 119, 253, 265–267, 270, 273, 294–295, 299, 306, 312, 314, 319,

327, 329–330, 341, 346, 353, 465, 497, 508, 513, 518, 538–539, 552
Francis, John, 258, 447
Franklin, Benjamin, 53, 298, 304, 482, 483n, 523; *The Autobiography*, 304n
Fraser, Hugh (?), 427
Fraser's Magazine for Town and Country, 427(?), 547
Freedom, 25, 55, 90, 91, 112, 117, 165, 175, 325, 376
Free Trade, 43, 191, 232, 504, 544
Free Trade Banquet, Manchester, 194, 254n, 419
Free will, 55
French, Mr., 444
French, the, 13, 141, 158–159, 198, 261–263, 266, 268, 270–272, 273, 280, 293, 297, 299, 301, 303, 306, 318–319, 321, 322–324, 326, 327, 381, 460, 499, 514, 515–516
French government, 272, 294
French language, 128, 141, 150, 266, 267, 270, 299, 314, 320, 355, 375
French literature, 119, 158, 166, 174, 266, 360, 375
French Republic, 239, 270, 298
French Revolution, *1789*, 323, 324; *1830*, 297n; *1848*, 231, 267, 296, 297, 314, 319, 321, 323, 324, 435, 543
Frey *or* Freyr, 55, 100
Freya, 74
Friend, The, 562
Friendship, 13, 321, 327, 339, 343, 380, 387, 470, 505, 542
"Friesdichens," 426
Frigg *or* Frigga, 108, 109, 115
Froissart, Jean, 165, 212, 230, 498
Frost, Barzillai, 20
Frothingham, Nathaniel Langdon, 167
Froude, James Anthony, 130, 280, 281n; *The Nemesis of Faith*, 520
Fuller, Margaret (Marchesa d'Ossoli), 46, 47n, 94n, 180n, 278, 379(?), 427 462(?), 466n, 497, 502–503, 512, 553; recipient of letters from Emerson, 117n, 466n, 497, 502–503, 513n, 540n; "Vita Nuovissima," 47
Fuller, Thomas, 516; *The History of the Worthies of England*, 518
Fulton, Robert, 167, 290
Furies, 223, 536
Furness, Mr., 81
Furo, Mr., 190

Future, the, 171

G., Mr., 95, 171, 235
Gabriel, Archangel, 84, 93
Gai Science, 166, 294
Galle, Johann Gottfried, 7n
Ganglati, 108
Ganglot, 108
Gardening, 91–92, 93, 95, 100, 105, 110–112, 120, 137, 148, 349
Gardner, Edward, 64
Garrison, Francis J., 395n
Garrison, John, 19
Garrison, William Lloyd, 94, 394–395
Garrulity, 5
Gascoigne, George, 294
Gaskell, Mr., 450
Gaskell, Mary, 450n
Genera, 159
Generation, 481
Genius, 30, 31, 44, 51, 54, 73, 80, 92, 118–119, 134, 138, 164, 174, 176, 317, 320, 325, 376
Geological Club, London, 255, 449
Geological Society, London, 308
Geology, 252, 255, 335
Geometry, 484
George IV, King of England, 274, 529
George, Saint, 168, 219
German language and literature, 128, 150, 198, 375, 548, 553
Germans, 205, 235, 237, 304, 307, 499, 511, 542
Germany, 201, 297, 401, 519
Gertrude (Margaret Fuller?), 379
Giants, 131
Gibbon, Edward, 166, 167, 168n, 259, 503, 510, 511, 548, 558; *The History of the Decline and Fall of the Roman Empire*, 510, 516
Gibson, John, "Hως" ("Dawn"), 334, 429
Gibson, Thomas F., 284, 445, 450
Gibson, Thomas Milner, 194n
Gifford, William, 501
Gifts, 149
Gilbert, John, 405(?), 406n
Gilbert, Timothy, 405(?), 406n
Gilbert & Sons, 405(?), 406n
Giles, Mr., 315
Gill, Thomas Hornblower, 128, 129n, 190, 281, 284
Gillies, Mr., 443
Gillies, Eliza Maria, 450

Gillies, R. P., 443

Gillman, James, 561, 563

Gillott, Joseph, 350n

Gilpin, William, *Observations on Several Parts of England, Particularly . . . Cumberland and Westmoreland*, 497; *Remarks on Forest Scenery*, 278, 279n, 516

Giöll, 107, 108

Girardin, Emile de, 265

Gladstone, William Ewart, 183

Glasgow, Scotland, 218, 222, 284, 286, 418, 420, 435, 441, 537

Glauco(n), 476

Gloucester, England, Bishop of, 186

Gloucester, Mass., 455

God, 20, 34, 41, 59, 65, 68, 71, 81, 97, 98, 101, 106, 117, 137, 148, 164, 168, 176, 180, 182, 209, 219, 231, 233, 234, 241, 294, 306, 314, 321, 323, 326, 335, 338, 342, 355, 374, 389, 391, 396, 403, 432, 465, 473, 476, 480, 481, 486, 509, 532, 543, 545, 547, 555, 557, 562

Gods, 35, 55, 96, 108, 109, 117, 131, 132, 138, 167, 175, 203, 240, 241, 249, 252, 290, 324, 325, 340, 361, 464, 471, 480, 483, 484, 486, 488, 546

Goethe, Johann Wolfgang von, 40, 43, 47, 75, 89, 98, 107, 143, 167, 337, 448n, 459n, 478, 480, 549; *The Auto-Biography*, 48, 107; "The Collector and His Friends," 302, 480n; *Essays on Art*, 302n; *Sämmtliche Werke*, 72n; *Sprüche in Reim und Prosa*, 72; *Werke*, 91; *Wilhelm Meister*, 555

Goisfred, Abbot, 278

Golden Table, 372

Goldsmith, Oliver, 259, 511, 552

Good, the, 372, 487

Goodness, 328

Gordon, George Hamilton, 4th Earl of Aberdeen, 309

Goth, 89

Gothic architecture, 15, 316, 390

Government, 8, 156

Graeme, Yarborough, 196

Grafton, Duke of, 274, 428, 528

Grandeur, 291

Graphic, 354

Gratification, 484

Gray, Horace, 522

Gray, J. McEwen, 286

Gray, Thomas, 45, 259, 274, 428, 511, 528; "For Music," 274–275n, 528–529

Great Britain, 496. *See also* Britain

Greatness, 14, 52, 296, 318, 369–370

Greece, 74, 156, 483

Greek architecture, 15, 252, 316

Greek language and literature, 137, 168, 234, 259, 315, 375, 479, 501, 512, 516, 553

Greek mythology, 68, 83, 389

Greeks, 9, 35, 42, 45, 131, 345, 389, 404

Green, John H., 278; *Vital Dynamics*, 278

Green, William, 171–172

Green family, 177

Greenhouse, 18

Greenleaf family, 177

Greenwich Royal Observatory, 7, 516

Greg, William Rathbone, 219, 275, 281, 560

Grenville, Richard, 2d Duke of Buckingham and Chandos, 184, 198, 276(?), 355(?), 459(?)

Grey, Charles, 2d Earl Grey, 517

Grisi, Giulia, 237, 362, 514

Grote, George, 9

Grotius, Hugo, 10

Groton, Mass., 447, 465

Grove, James, 194

Guelph, William and Adelaide, 549

Guide de Paris, 424

Guilt, 482

Giuzot, François Pierre Guillaume, 230, 238, 296–297, 303, 314, 543

Gun, 374

Gustavus II, King of Sweden, 53, 176

Guy, 38, 322

Guy of Warwick, 117

Gyda, Queen of Norway, 341

Gyges, 38, 159, 174

Gypsies, 189

H., Dr., 141

H., Mrs., 136

Hafiz, Shams ud-din Mohammed, 34, 35, 47, 55, 67, 68, 88, 89, 120, 126, 128, 165, 341; *Divan*, 17n, 55, 67n, 73–74n, 89n, 90

Hagar, Mr., of Concord, 18

Hakluyt, Richard, 516

Hale, Mr., of Rutland, Vt., 125

Halifax, England, 210, 280, 284, 416, 417, 419, 439, 440, 444

Halifax, Nova Scotia, 345, 432, 435

Hall, Judge, 102

Hall, Basil, 203n
Hall, Mrs. S. C., 443
Hallam, Mr., 538
Hallam, Arthur, 261, 537
Hallam, Henry, 260, 304, 361, 444, 501, 512; *Introduction to the Literature of Europe,* 173
Hamilton, Col. Thomas, 555
Hamilton, Sir William, 220, 536
Hamlet, 149, 154
Hammer-Purgstall, Joseph von, 17, 89, 90; *Geschichte der schönen redekünste Persiens . . .* , 17n, 73–74n, 90; trans., *Baki's . . . Divan,* 90; trans., *Der Diwan von Mohammed Schemsed-din Hafis,* 17n, 55n, 67, 73–74n, 89n, 90; trans., *Montenebbi der grösste Arabische Dichter,* 90
Hampton Court, England, 195, 422, 449
Hancock family, 177
Handel, George Frederick, 195
Hanna, William, 220, 223, 275
Hanwell, England, 313
Harald, 342
Harding, Charles, 128, 129n
"Hardyknute," 172
Hare, Julius Charles, "Sketch of the Author's [John Sterling's] Life," 337n
Hargreaves, James, 517
Hari, 56, 74
Harring, Harro, 125, 337
Harris, Thaddeus William, 172
Harrison, W., 129, 130n
Harrow School, 282, 567
Hartford, Ct., 338
Harvard University, 47, 62. *See also* Cambridge, Mass.
Haven, Mrs. M. F., 32
Hawthorne, Nathaniel, 537
Hay, David Ramsay, *On the Science of Those Proportions by which the Human Head and Countenance . . . are Distinguished,* 457
Hazlitt, William, 547; *Conversations of James Northcote,* 17, 66; "Merry England," 212n; *Sketches and Essays,* 212n
Head, Sir Francis Bond, 511, 512
Health, 13, 174
Heart, 476
Heater Piece, 19, 492–493
Hector, 117
Hecuba, 403
Hedge, 19, 490–492

Hedge, Frederic Henry, 73
Hĕĕtōpădēs of Vĕĕshnŏo-Sărmā, The, 12n, 161n
Heimdal, 108
Heimskringla, see Snorri Sturluson
Hel, 108
Helena, 60
Hell, 238, 511
Héloïse, 169
Helps, Sir Arthur, 281, 343, 355
Hemans, Felicia Dorothea, 172
Hénault, Charles Jean François, *Abrégé Chronologique de l'Histoire de France,* 283, 464, 522
Henderson, Robert, 436
Hennall, Miss, 332
Henry I, King of England, 257, 518–519
Henry II, King of England, 279, 519
Henry V, King of England, 518
Henry V, King of Germany and Holy Roman Emperor, 519
Henry VI, King of England, 501
Henry VII, King of England, 192, 279
Henry VIII, King of England, 497; statue of, at Trinity College, Cambridge, 334, 427
Henry of Blois, 257
Heraclitic dualism, 488
Heraclitus, 159n
Heraud, John A., 445
Hercules, 75, 95
Hermann, Mr., 171–172
Hermann, Karl Friedrich, *Manual of the Political Antiquities of Greece Historically Considered,* 7
Herodotus, 253
Herschel, Sir John Frederick William (?), 150, 516
Herschel, Sir William (?), 150, 516
Hertfordshire, England, 324
Hervey, Thomas Kibble, 275
Hesperides, 95
Hibernation, 256, 465, 526
High Force, England, 225
Hill, Mrs., 409n, 411, 413
Hill, John Boynton, 46
Hill, Sir Rowland, 272, 273n
Hillard, George Stillman, 273, 274n, 526, 528
Hillogres, 108
Hindoo (Hindu) language, 90
Hindoo mythology, 68
Hindoo soil, 368

History, 100, 172, 185, 190, 252, 289, 322, 329, 344, 390

Hoar, Elizabeth, 216n, 348, 385, 399, 502

Hoar, Samuel, 475

Hobbes, Thomas, *Leviathan*, 520

Hobby, 315

Hodgson, W. B., 438

Hoffmann, Ernst Theodor Amadeus, 177n

Hogg, James, 180

Hogg, Thomas, 126, 410, 558

Holbrook, Silas P., 344

Holloway Farm, 354, 357n

Holyhead, Wales, 207

Home, Sir Everard, 527

Homer, 5, 6, 168, 172, 253, 431, 517; *Iliad*, 12, 402

Hone, Philip, 330

Honor, 512

Hood, Thomas, 501

Hooker, Richard, 508

Hooker, Sir William Jackson, 247

Hope, 390

Hope, Lady, 189

Hope, James Robert, 189n, 531

Hope, Thomas, *An Historical Essay on Architecture*, 459

Horne, Richard Henry, *A New Spirit of the Age*, 261, 537

Horoscope, 34, 170–171

Hosmer, Edmund, 432

Hosmer, John, 19, 358, 492n

Hospital of St. Cross, Winchester, England, 257

Hotel de Cluny, Paris, 271

Hotel de Ville, Paris, 265, 268

Hottinguer & Company, 418

House of Commons, 44, 45, 195, 213, 232–233, 236, 242, 244, 250, 253, 255, 295, 304–305, 321, 335, 351, 354, 430, 496, 515, 544, 546, 550

House of Lords, 182, 212–213, 496

Houses of Parliament, 212–213, 253, 530

How, T., "State Reports," 125

Howard, George William Frederick, Viscount Morpeth, 7th Earl of Carlisle, 285, 442, 530, 566

Howe, Richard, Lord Howe, 516n

Howe, Samuel Gridley, 45n

Hoxie, Captain, 564

Hrimthursar, 107

Hubbard, Cyrus, 358

Hubbard, Darius, 358

Huber, Victor Aimé, *The English Universities*, 246, 277, 278

Huddersfield, England, 216, 411, 415, 439, 444

Hudson, George, 98, 295

Hudson, James William, 125, 126n, 222

Hudson, John, ed., *A Complete Guide to the Lakes*, 336n

Hull, England, 130, 189

Hull, Mass., 73

Human life, 120

Humboldt, Baron Alexander von, 38, 43, 98

Humbug, 233, 299, 305, 314, 321, 429

Hume, David, 146, 151

Humor, 472

Hunt, Benjamin Peter, 46, 338

Hunt, Leigh, 255, 285, 551

Hunter, John, 526–527

Hunting, 317

Hussein Khan, 106

Hussey, Captain Isaac B., 63, 64

Hutton, Richard Holt (?), 445, 449, 451

Hutton, Robert (?), 445, 449, 451

Hyde, Mr., 162

Hyde, Edward, 1st Earl of Clarendon, 166, 183, 395; *History of the Rebellion*, 245, 395n

Hyde, George, 189, 211

Hyde Park Corner, London, 250

Iamblichus, 241; *Life of Pythagoras*, 49n, 322n; *On the Mysteries of the Egyptians, Chaldeans, and Assyrians*, 241n

Icelander, 88

Ideal, the, 470

Idealism, 155

Idealist, 162, 461

Ideas, 487

"Idĕrsāy," 194, 215

Idolatry, 24, 96

Illinois, 175

Imagination, 15, 23, 50, 91, 165, 358, 470

Immermann, Karl, 177n

Immortality, 171, 279, 294, 308, 312, 340, 477

Indexes, 105

India, 13, 18, 74, 254, 496, 513, 533, 540

India House, London, 522

Indian(s), North American, 11, 220, 277, 333, 340, 359, 369(?), 434

Indian meal, 151, 230, 341, 543

Indian mythology and religion, 83, 323, 477

Indirection, 148
Individual, the, 8, 118, 154, 187, 310, 312, 317, 325, 354, 378, 381, 488
Infinity, 390
Inspiration, 131, 132
Instincts, 382
Institut de France, Paris, 271
Intellect, 31, 97, 120, 131, 132, 136, 145, 146, 159, 190, 313, 326, 353, 355, 359, 368, 485–486, 508
Intellectuals, 22
Invalides, Church of the, Paris, 269
Iopas, 134
Ioways, 155
Iphigenia, 214, 530
Ireland, Alexander, 414, 417, 418, 539
Ireland, 207, 235, 280, 341, 496, 537, 539
Irish, the, 102, 114, 175, 215, 231, 276, 310, 345, 346, 428, 537, 539, 548, 559
Irving, Rev. Edward, 180, 550
Isaac, 196
Isaiah, 148
Ishmaelite, 162
Israelites, 96
Italy, 269, 270, 278, 497, 539
Italian(s), 80, 118, 238, 375
Italian language and literature, 199, 326, 375, 504
Ivo (Yves), Bishop of Chartres, 98

Jackson, Dr. Charles Thomas, 14n, 37, 46, 98, 141, 158, 167
Jackson, Dr. James, 51
Jackson, William M., 135
Jacobi, Friedrich Heinrich, 177n
Jacobson, William, 247n; trans., *The Seven Tragedies of Aeschylus . . .* , 336
Jamaica Plains, Mass., 466
Jamblichus, *see* Iamblichus
James I, King of England, 547, 568n
James I, King of Scotland, 346n
James, Henry, 46
Jameson, Anna Brownell Murphy, 287, 373, 442, 444
"Jamie," 11–12, 137
Jamieson, Robert, ed., *Popular Ballads and Songs*, 13, 23n, 172n
Jamshid ("Jamschid"), 73, 139
Janus, Temple of, Leicester, England, 191
Jardin des Plantes, Paris, 271, 345
Jardin d'Hiver, Paris, 425
Jay, William (?), and Mrs., 273–274, 442, 528, 529

Jefferson, Daniel, 128, 129n, 445
Jefferson, Thomas, *Works*, 8
Jeffrey, Francis, Lord, 220, 361, 520, 558
Jenks, Francis, ed., *A Selection from the English Prose Works of John Milton*, 509
Jerboa rat, 256, 526
Jeremiah, 148
Jerrold, Douglas William, 504n
Jesus Christ, 191, 255, 326, 342, 347, 372, 389 486, 548, 561
Jevons, Thomas, 130
Jew(s), 162, 181, 183, 328, 389, 541, 561, 568
Jewish Mythology, 68, 83, 389
Jewsbury, Geraldine Endsor, 129, 328
"Jock," 137
Jockey, 141
John, 250
John Gilpin (ship), 206
John of Gaunt, Duke of Lancaster, 191
John ("John Lackland"), King of England, 192
Johnson, Samuel, 40, 42, 78, 166, 259, 313, 346, 502, 503, 511, 517, 523, 552; *The Idler*, 313n; "Lines Added to Goldsmith's 'Traveller,' " 290, 337; *Works*, 502n, 503
Johnston, William, 510; *England As It Is*, 502, 510, 520n, 567
Joking, 321–322
Jones, Mr., 315
Jonson, Ben, 166, 295, 354; *Epicœne*, 201n; *Prince Henry's Barriers*, 509n; "Upon Sejanus," 354n; *Works*, 354n
Jordan, Mother, 346
Joseph of Exeter, *Antiocheis*, 209n
Journal des Débats, 265
Journals, 158, 352
Jove, 134
Judgment Day, 62, 94
Jupiter, 484
Jupiter Stator, Temple of, Rome, 306
Just, the, 475
Justice, 483, 486

Kaf, 65, 73, 74
Kai Kan, 139
Kalidasa, *The Méga Dúta*, 91, 336
Kant, Immanuel, 151, 307, 461
Karlsruher Zeitung, 367n
Karun, 66, 73, 105, 139
Kashan, Iran, 93
Kaus, 75

Keats, John, *Hyperion,* 70n
Kedleston Hall, Derby, England, 129n, 185
Kehl, Mr., 216
Kendal, England, 420, 421
Kendall, Mr., 447
Kendrick, Billy, 102
Kenelwalch, 258
Kennet, White, *A Complete History of England,* 283, 464, 521
Kenrick, Rev. John, 129, 130n
Kentuckian, 35
Kentucky, 96, 384
Kenyon, John, 273–274, 286, 333, 335, 361, 442, 460, 528, 529
Kepler, Johannes, 35, 110, 136
Ker, John, 3rd Duke of Roxburgh, 6n
Kercheval, Samuel, 8
Kettell, Samuel, 344
Kew Gardens, England, 195, 237, 244, 247, 249, 250, 344, 553
Keyes, John, 141
Keyes, John Shepherd, 20
Khoja Yakub, 71
Kiartan, 342
Killarney, Lake, Ireland, 182
King, 189
King, William, 1st Earl of Lovelace, 285, 442, 513
Kinglake, Alexander William, 362
"King Regner Lodbrog's Ode," 138
Kings, 434, 475
Kinsale, Ireland, 207
Kirkcaldy, Scotland, 181, 550
Kneeland, Mrs., of Cambridge, Mass., 331n
Knigge, Baron Adolf von, 177n
Knight, Charles, 192, 451
Knowledge, 135, 381
Knox, John, 547
Knox, Robert, 510; *The Races of Men: A Philosophical Enquiry . . . ,* 510n
Konversations-Lexikon, 48, 201
Koran, 41, 66n, 67, 89
Kossuth, Lajos, 466–467
Kraitsir, Charles, 37, 136, 337
"Kunst," 542
Kurroglou, 71, 72, 85, 86n, 92, 93, 98, 106, 117
Kvasir, 70
Kyrat, 86, 92, 93, 117

L., Mr., 355, 460
L., J., Mr. (?), 441

Labor, 389
"Lady Jane," 13, 172
Lafayette, Marquis de, 41, 193, 523
Lagrange, Joseph Louis, 368
Lamartine, Alphonse Marie Louis de Prat de, 215, 269, 270, 296, 308, 309, 355, 362, 530
Lamb, Charles (?), 274, 528
Lamb, William, 2d Viscount Melbourne, 276, 341
Lambert, M., 262
Lancaster, England, 436
Land, 93, 148, 403
Landor, Arnold, 241, 532
Landor, Walter Savage, 145, 220, 241, 362, 387, 472, 532, 535, 549; *Hellenics,* 220, 535
Landreth, P., 223, 275
Landscape, 201, 334, 343
Landseer, Sir Edwin Henry, 334, 429
Lane, Charles, 244n, 349(?), 409, 436
Lane, William, 125, 433
Laplace, Marquis Pierre Simon de, 35, 43
Lardner, Dionysius (?), 355n
Larken, Rev. Edward R., 281, 285
Lascars, 245
Lasswade, Scotland, 221, 534, 536
Latin, 22, 167, 326, 375, 501, 557, 568
Latiners, 98
Law(s), 152, 154, 163, 324, 339, 340, 361, 381, 385, 486
Law of series, 474, 477
Lawrence, Abbott, 102
Lawrence, Samuel, 102
Lawrence, Sir Thomas, 242, 246–247
Lawrence, Mass., 102, 280
Layard, Sir Austen Henry, *Nineveh and Its Remains . . . ,* 459
Lazarus, 293, 359n
Leach, Paul, 436
Leathersellers' Buildings, London, 447
Lebas, J. B., 267
Lecomte, Jules, 520
Ledru-Rollin, Alexandre Auguste, 265
Leeds, England, 125, 129, 189, 193, 211, 214, 416, 417, 418, 439–440, 498
Leeds Institute, England, 417
Legaré, Hugh Swinton, 59n; "Constitutional History of Greece," 7n; *The Writings,* 7–8
Leghorn, Italy, 118
Lehmann, Charles Ernest Rodolphe Henri, 277

Leicester, England, 128, 191, 411, 415, 439
Leroux, Paul, "Dieu," 314
Leroux Pierre, 265
Leslie, Sir Charles Robert, 330, 334, 429
Lester, James, 415
Lever, Charles James, 203
Leverrier, Urbain Jean Joseph, 7n, 141, 323, 362
Lewdness, 550
Lewis, Samuel S., 435
Lexington, Mass., 120
Liberté, 265n
Liberty, 467
Library, 54, 145, 367
Liebig, Baron Justus von, 104; *Chemistry in Its Application to Agriculture and Physiology*, 104n
Life, 52, 84, 146, 160, 163, 164, 356, 380, 382, 463, 471
Light, Mr., 259
Lilliput, 30
Limerick, Ireland, 231, 539
Limitation, 511
Lincoln, Lord, 531
Lincoln, England, 285
Lincoln, Mass., 18, 72
Lind, Jenny (Johanna Maria), 362
Linnaeus, Carolus (Carl von Linné), 153
Literacy, 252
Literary men, 51, 53, 99
Literature, 22, 32, 50, 83, 148, 155, 162, 164, 174, 193, 339
Liturgy, 10, 35
Liverpool, England, 129, 130, 175, 176, 178, 190, 200, 207, 218, 222, 259, 285, 333, 405, 408, 409, 410, 411, 412, 413, 415, 435, 438, 540, 547, 548, 550, 564
Liverpool Mechanics' Institute, 410, 437, 438
Liverpool Union Bank, 415
Lives and Voyages of Drake, Cavendish, and Dampier . . ., 507n
Lloyd's of London, 188
Lobster, 89
Locke, John, 307, 478, 508, 521
Lockhart, John Gibson, 257, 361, 501
Lodige, 447
Loke, 138
Loki, 74
London (England), Bishop of, 562
London, England, 125, 126, 128, 130, 141, 181, 195, 199, 209, 214, 217, 222, 226, 228, 229, 236, 237, 239, 240, 241, 243, 244, 249, 252, 255, 257, 263, 265, 266, 270, 273, 278, 279, 284, 286, 287, 295, 296, 297, 299, 314, 324, 326, 327, 328, 331, 334, 343, 345, 353, 355, 396, 409, 410, 421, 422, 423, 426, 435, 442, 443, 444, 445, 449, 450, 451, 463, 497, 498, 500, 509, 512, 513, 520, 522, 523, 531, 532, 538, 539, 540, 541, 543, 544, 547, 548, 549, 550, 552, 553, 560, 561
London Critic, 212, 228
London *Daily News*, 211
Londoner(s), 273, 299, 548, 553, 568
London Library, 214, 530
London *Morning Chronicle*, 211, 212
London Phalanx, 262n
London *Times*, 46, 125n, 158, 188, 189n, 190, 191–192, 195, 196, 211–212, 215, 221, 227–230, 231, 239, 250, 251, 260, 264, 281n, 296, 297, 302, 351n, 415, 428, 460, 515, 525n, 526n, 550n
London twist, 314, 343, 354
London, University of, 286
London Wall, 447
Longevity, 50, 382
Long Parliament, 232, 544
Lord, John (?), 551
Lord, Nathan (?), 551
Lord || . . . ||, 532
Lord's Prayer, 10
Lott, Captain E. G., 276, 434
Louis IX, King of France ("St. Louis"), 268, 271
Louis, Dr. Pierre-Charles-Alexandre, 158
Louis Philippe, Citizen King of France, 215, 229, 231, 236, 267n, 297n, 543
Louvain, Belgium, 85
Louvre, Paris, 265, 267, 271, 319
Love, 145, 470
Lovelace, William King, 1st Earl of, 285, 442, 513
Lovers, 385
Lowe, Robert, 228
Lowell, James Russell, 46, 338, 527(?); "Saturday Club," 123n
Lowell, Mass., 102, 452, 453; companies, 34; corporations, 307; mills, 102
Lowell family, 177
Lowell Institute, Boston, 452, 527
Lowth, Robert, *The Life of William of Wykeham*, 18, 283, 336
Lowther, Sir James, 244, 547(?), 560
Lowther, William, 2d Earl of Lonsdale, 244, 547(?), 560

Loyd, Samuel Jones (later Baron Over-stone), 190, 212, 230
Lucan (Marcus Annaeus Lucanus), *The Civil War*, 495
Lucas, Frederick, 275, 546
Luck, 290, 305, 433
Lucretius (Titus Lucretius Carus), *De Rerum Natura*, 557
Lucy, Sir Thomas, 251, 322, 427
Lud, 257
Ludgate, London, 237, 257
Lupton, Joseph, 189, 211
Luther, Martin, 40, 77, 98, 107, 134, 370, 390n; *Colloquia Mensalia . . .* , 98n
Luxembourg, Palais du, Paris, 271
Luxor (ship), 267
Luxury, 155
Lycian art, 252–253, 516
Lycurgus, 12, 52, 340
Lyell, Sir Charles, 284, 361, 445, 449
Lynch, Anne C., 466n
Lynch law, 148
Lyon, John, 567
Lysias, 483
Lytton, Edward George Earle Lytton Bul-wer-, 1st Baron Lytton of Knebworth, 203n

M., Dr., 141
Macaulay, Thomas Babington, 1st Baron Macaulay, 180, 230, 237, 242, 305, 361, 501, 515, 521, 524, 531; *The History of England*, 524n
MacBold, Mrs., 223, 534, 536–537
MacCormac, Henry, 129, 130n
McCulloch, John Ramsay, 496; *M'Culloch's Universal Gazetteer*, 496n
MacDonald, Francis, 286
MacDonald, John Cameron, 228
Machiavelli, Niccolò, 8
Machinery, 145, 184
M'Iver, C., 435
M'Iver, David, 435
Mackay, Dr. Charles (?), 445
Mackintosh, Sir James, 444n
Macphail's Edinburgh Ecclesiastical Journal and Literary Review, 223, 275
Macready, William Charles, 442
Madeira Islands, 382
Madeleine, Church of the, Paris, 271
Madness, 159
Magrath, Edward, 242
Mahomet, 322

Maine, 77, 461
Maine Depot, Boston, 139
Mainz (Mentz), Germany, 245
Majority, 475
Malden, Mass., 177, 186
Malibran, María Felicia, 258
Mallet, Paul Henri, *Northern Antiquities . . .* , 131n, 132n, 138
Malta, 344, 562, 563
Malvern Hills, England, 192
Man, 32, 118, 136, 197, 383, 475, 487, 497
Manchester, England, 126, 129, 168, 182, 184, 185, 217, 259, 266, 284, 289, 408, 409–410, 411, 412, 413, 414, 415, 416, 417, 418–419, 421, 504
Manchester, Mass. (?), 456
Manchester (England) Athenaeum, 411, 437, 438, 504; annual Soirée, 437, 504
Manchester (England) *Examiner*, 540n
Manchester (England) Free Trade Hall, 194
Manchester (England) Mechanics' Institution, 411, 437, 438
Manners, 73, 79, 83, 178, 184, 195, 197, 197–199, 226, 234, 236, 238, 241, 258, 268, 305, 377, 463, 498, 503, 512, 514–515
Manners, John James Robert, 7th Duke of Rutland, 531n
Man-Woman, 392
Manzoni, Alessandro Francesco Tomaso Antonio, 167
Marcellus, Marcus Claudius, 310
Mariner's House, Boston, 401
Mario, Giuseppe, Marchese di Candia, 514
Marriage, 351–352, 377, 472
Marquesas Islands, 382
Marrast, Armand, 265
Marryat, Frederick ("Captain Marryat"), 203
"Marseillaise," 136, 239, 323
Marsh, James, 563
Marshall, Mrs., of Concord, 144
Marshall, James, 211
Marshall, James Garth, 211
Marston, John Westland, 361–362
Martin, Sir Theodore, 223, 275, 287, 445(?); and William Edmondstoune Aytoun, *The Bon Gaultier Ballads*, 223, 275
Martineau, Harriet, 189n, 219n, 225, 281n, 289n, 442n, 445n, 451n, 558, 559, 560

Martineau, Rev. James, 281(?)

Martineau, Richard (?), 281(?), 445

Mary, Queen of Scots (Mary Stuart), 180, 346

Massachusetts, 148, 251, 330, 385, 506

Massachusetts Bank, Boston, 451

Massachusetts Quarterly Review, 45, 46, 54, 139n, 338, 339, 344

Massey, Mrs., of Manchester, 289n, 409, 412, 413, 414, 416, 417, 419, 421

Master and tools, 54

Mathematics, 60–62

Mathews, W., of London, 444

Mathews, William, 128, 129n, 190, 284, 436

Matilda *or* Maud, Empress of Germany, 519

Matilda *or* Maud, Queen of England, 519

Maurice, John Frederick Denison, 282; *The Religions of the World* (?), 283n

Mazenderan, King of, 75

Mazzini, Giuseppe, 337

Mechanics, 112

Medford, Mass., 80

Mediocrity, 238, 511

Melancholy, 498, 501

Melbourne, William Lamb, 2d Viscount, 276, 341

Melioration, 141, 335, 353

Memoirs of the Geological Survey of Great Britain . . . , 436

Memory, 356, 469, 471

Ménétrier de Meudon, 77, 101

Menu, 110

Merchant(s), 200, 224, 296

Mercury, 389

Merriwether, Mr., 241

Mesmerism, 14, 37, 163, 232, 301, 311, 501

Mesopotamia, 351

Metamorphosis, 74, 137, 147, 465

Metaphysics, 73

Metcalf and Co., Cambridge, Mass., 443

Mexican(s), 29, 36

Mexico, 40, 114, 247

Michael, Mr., 313

Michael, Archangel, 84

Michelangelo, 61, 90, 106, 150, 167, 246

Michelet, Jules, 301, 323

Middleton, Willoughby Digby, Baron, 185

Mill, John Stuart, 265n, 345, 522, 549; *Principles of Political Economy*, 336

Mills, Mr., 281

Milman, Henry Hart, 260, 304, 448, 512, 530

Milnes, Richard Monckton, later 1st Baron Houghton, 130, 168n, 214, 215, 241, 242, 275, 361, 428, 530–533, 546

Milton, John, 45, 50, 75, 166, 168, 225, 330, 350, 508, 509, 520, 523, 560: *Animadversions*, 509; *Comus*, 134; *Paradise Lost*, 10n; *Paradise Regained*, 220, 535; *Prose Works*, 509n

Milton, Mass. 456

Mimir, 107, 115

Mind, 165, 316, 470, 480, 485, 488

Minerva, 354

Minority, 30, 52, 466

Minott, George, 84

Miöllner (Thor's hammer), 131

Mirabeau, Honoré Gabriel Victor Riqueti, Comte de, 40, 398

Missionaries, 254

Mississippi River, 276, 434

Missouri, 351

Missouri River, 276, 434

Mitchell, Donald Grant ("Ik Marvel"), 280n

Mitchell, Thomas, 167

Mitchell, William, 46(?), 64, 114

Mixtures, 45

Mob(s), 28, 232, 551

Moderns, 33

Modern times, 173, 353

Mohammed, 322

Moinn, 108

Moir, David Macbeth ("Δ"), 223, 275

Molesworth, Lady, 513

Molesworth, Sir William, 449, 532

Monadnock, Mount, 303

Money, 30, 54, 56, 174, 311, 392, 470

Monmouth Street, London, 181, 296

Montagnards, 325

Montagu, Anne D. B. (?), 441

Montagu, Lady Mary Wortley, 519

Montague, Mr., 563

Montaigne, Michel Eyquem de, 9, 69, 95, 106, 138, 165, 350, 352, 383; *Essais or Essays*, 282, 283n, 422; *Essays* (tr. John Florio), 295

Montesquieu, Baron de La Brède et de Charles de Secondat, 307

Montgomerie, Archibald William, 13th Earl of Eglinton and 1st Earl of Winton, 183

Montgomery, James, 361, 362n

Monthly Magazine, 445n

Montmorency Hotel, Paris, 424

Montreal, Canada, 507

Moody, Mary (married Joseph Emerson of Malden), 186
Moody, Samuel, 186, 188(?)
Moody family, 188
Moore, Mr., 260, 512
Moore, Mrs., 126
Moore, Captain Abel, 82n, 84, 95, 100, 101, 125, 357
Moore, John, 19, 20n
Moore, Thomas, 66, 501; *Lalla Rookh*, 66n; *Poetical Works*, 66n
Moral engineer, 300
Morality, 135, 503, 505
Moral power, 355
Morals, 16, 22, 120, 164, 377, 471, 503
Moral science, 306
Moral sentiment, 486
More, Henry, 118
Morell, J. D., 300
Morgan, John Minter, 254n, 313, 315(?), 444, 450, 451
Morgan, Sydney, Lady, 274, 460, 513, 529
Morpeth, Viscount, *see* Howard, George William Frederick
Morris, Mowbray, 228, 229n
Mortimer's Hole, Nottingham, England, 185
Morton, William Thomas Green, 141
Mosaic History (i.e., Genesis), 255
Moscow, Russia, 326
Moseley, Rev. Arthur, 229
Moses, 479
Mount Vernon, Va., 163
Movement party, 326
Mozart, Wolfgang Amadeus, 523
Mozley, Rev. Thomas, 190, 211, 212n, 228, 229n
Mull, 32, 379
Müller, Karl Otfried, *The History and Antiquities of the Doric Race*, 8
Munroe, James, 125
Munroe, William, 19, 20n
Murray, J. Oswald, 15, 267, 436
Murray, William, 1st Earl of Mansfield, 503
Music, 49, 62, 77, 101, 151, 173, 292, 293
Musketaquid River, 156
Muspratt, James Sheridan, 242, 524, 533
Mutanabbi, al-, *Divan*, 90n
Mythology, 24, 68, 73, 83, 96, 110, 115, 131, 289, 389

N., Mr.(?), 276
Nahant, Mass., 303
Names, 29, 185, 240–241

Nantucket (Mass.) Athenaeum, 63
Nantucket (Mass.) *Enquirer*, 114n
Nantucket Island, Mass., 62, 63, 64, 102, 120, 303
Napier, Macvey, 256
Napier, Robert, 430
Napier family, 256
Naples, King of, 276, 459
Napoleon I, *see* Bonaparte, Napoleon
Napoleon III (Louis Napoleon), Emperor of the French, 568
Nasmyth, James, 219
National, 265
National Assembly, French, 268, 269
National Gallery, London, 528, 541
National Hall, Holborn, London, 239
Nationality, 76
National man, 40
National traits, 498–499
Natura, 89
Natural history, 136
Nature, 26, 34, 39, 41, 44, 65, 96, 105, 143, 150, 160, 161, 162, 163, 164–165, 167, 168, 169, 201, 255, 293, 302, 325, 351–352, 382–383, 404, 435, 463, 465, 477, 480, 485, 497
Navigation Laws, 236
Necessity, 116, 465
Neglect, 91
Negro(es), 177, 346, 357, 369, 404
Nelson, Horatio, Viscount Nelson, 43, 508, 517
Nemesis, 271
Neptune (planet), 7n, 141
Nero, 548–549
Nesmith, John, 102
Neuberg, Joseph, 189, 297(?), 305
New, Herbert, 128, 129n
New Bedford, Mass., 64, 454
New England, 53, 62, 119–120, 140, 177, 197, 278, 330, 349, 396
New Englander, 140, 504
New Hampshire, 102
New Haven, Conn., 250, 528
New Holland, 95
New Jerusalem, Church of the, 162
New Jerusalem Magazine, 27
New Times, 227–228n, 251
New York, N.Y., 21, 100, 157, 175, 197, 241, 276, 435, 504, 523, 551, 564
New York *Courier*, 280n
New York Post Office, 564
New York (state), 141, 350

Newbury, England, 186
Newburyport, Mass., 453
Newcastle-upon-Tyne, England, 128, 129, 219, 284, 418, 419, 441
Newcomb, Charles King, 46, 151, 152n, 160, 293, 318n, 338, 342
Newfoundland Banks, 175
Newman, John Henry (*later* Cardinal), 300
Newport, R.I., 453
Newspapers, 272, 323, 353, 435
Newstead, England, 414, 439
Newstead Abbey, England, 189, 279
Newton, Sir Isaac, 35, 41, 43, 368, 371, 508, 521; Newtonian Theory, 557
Niagara Falls, 78, 389, 399
Nichol, Miss, 537
Nichol, John Pringle, 537
Nicholas I, Czar of Russia, 233, 256, 355, 543
Nickisson, G. W., 418
Niebuhr, Barthold Georg, *History of Rome*, 282, 283n
Nineveh, 516
Nithhavgg, 108
Nobscot hills, Mass., 21
Non-resistance, 385
Nootka Sound, 540
Normandy, 518
Normanton (Yorkshire?), England, 417
Norse, Norsemen, Northmen, 156, 342, 350
Norse mythology, 68, 70, 83
North, Christopher, *see* Wilson, John
North America, 153, 397, 404
North American Review, 466n
Northampton, Spencer Joshua Alwyne Compton, 2d Marquis of, 449
Northampton, Mass., 456
North British Review, 220, 223, 275
Northcote, James, 66n, 166
Northumberland, Sir Algernon Percy, 4th Duke of, 300
Northumberland House, London, 300
Norton, Caroline Elizabeth Sarah ("the Hon. Mrs. Norton"), 275, 428, 532–533
Norton, Charles Eliot, 123n
Norton Lees (England?), 190
Norway, 345
Norwich (?), England, 225
Notre Dame de Paris, Cathedral of, 268, 271
Nottingham, England, 128–129, 185, 189, 193–194, 305, 307, 341, 411, 414, 438, 439, 517

Nottingham Castle, England, 185
Nottingham (England) Mechanics' Institute, 129n, 189n
Novels, 6, 48, 165, 167, 289, 348, 360, 361
Nubian race, 404
Numenius, 479

O. (?), 256
O., Mr., 460
Oak Hall, Boston, 79
Obelisk, Paris, 267
O'Brien, James, 298
Occidentalism, 90
Ocean Monarch (ship), 204
O'Connell, Daniel, 24, 211
Odeon, Boston, 306
Odin, 75, 89, 107
Œdumla, 131
Ofnir, 108
Ogdensburg, N.Y.(?), 102
O'Gorman, George, 442
Olaf I, King of Norway, 342, 345
Olympia, Greece, 482
Olympus, Mount, 462
O'Meagher, J. B., 228
Omnipresence, 35, 50, 249
One Idea, 119–120
"On the Present Position of English Unitarians . . . ," 373n
Open-dealing, 511
Opera, 68, 73, 217, 258, 331, 460, 514
Operative(s), 216, 312
Opinion, 481
Opportunity, 25, 30
Opposition, 466
Optimism, 50
Orchard(s), 18–19, 50, 95, 359
Oregon, 270, 350
Orientalism, Orientalist, 90–91, 95, 142, 166
Originality, 135, 141–142
Orléans, Duchess of, 179, 524
Orr, William S., and Co., of London, 427
Osborne, Thomas, 42
Osgood, Mrs. Frances Locke, 466n
O'Shaughnessy, Mr., 173
Osman, 14, 33n, 38, 39, 47
Ossoli, Margaret Fuller, Marchesa d', *see* Fuller, Margaret
Overreach, Sir Giles, 244, 547, 560
Overstone, Baron, *see* Loyd, Samuel Jones
Owen, Sir Richard, 216, 237, 243, 253(?),

256, 257, 277, 281, 285, 315, 362, 460, 464n, 465n, 525–528
Owen, Robert, 100, 253(?), 281, 321, 362, 378
Owenism, 378
Oxenbridge family, 177
Oxenford, John, 228, 300
Oxford University, 129, 130, 195, 220, 233, 245, 246, 247, 248, 250–251, 309, 341, 422, 427, 428, 520, 536, 545, 564, 568
Oxonian, 230, 311, 515
Oyster, 89
Ozanam, Antoine Frédéric, 46; *Dante et la philosophie catholique*, 46–47n

P., Dr., 115–116
Paddy, Paddies, 351, 394
Paget, Lord William, 192
Paget, Sir Henry William, 1st Marquis of Anglesey, 192
Paint, 30, 52, 259, 302–303, 384
Painting, 127, 191, 277, 310, 321, 334, 429
Paisley, Scotland, 420, 441
Palais de Justice, Paris, 265, 268
Palais-Royal, Paris, 263, 266, 270, 322, 425
Palgrave, Francis Turner, 130
Palladio, Andrea, 117n
Palmer, Joseph, 125, 436
Palmerston, Emily Lamb Temple, Viscountess, 189n, 513, 531, 532
Palmerston, Henry John Temple, 3rd Viscount, 515, 531
Palo Alto pen, 169–170
Pan, 389
Pandora, 351
Panizzi, Sir Anthony, 240
Pantheism, 175
Panthéon, Paris, 106, 175, 268–269, 271, 523
Paracelsus, Philippus Aureolus, 5
Paradise, 40, 72, 133, 329
Paradise, tree of, 73
Parcae, 84, 94
Paris, 15, 82, 105, 125, 141, 228, 240, 262, 263, 265, 266, 268, 270, 271, 272, 273, 277, 294, 302, 305, 320, 321, 322, 323, 324, 326, 327, 328, 353, 355, 423, 424, 425, 426, 436, 465, 531, 532, 538, 539
Parker, Theodore, 45n, 54, 126, 338, 349
Parliament, 183, 191, 230, 232, 274, 496, 501, 514, 528, 530, 532, 533, 543, 544, 567

Parmenides, 487
Parnassus, 99
Parsons family, 177
Parthenon, Athens, 252, 253
Pascal, Blaise, 98, 352
Patagonians, 181
Pathology, 113
Patience, 502
Patmore, Coventry Kersey Dighton, 240, 255, 261n, 316, 442, 443, 450, 451, 531, 537, 539n, 565, 566n
Patrie, 212, 498
Patriotism, 149, 161, 244
Paul, Saint, 355, 561
Paulet, Mr., of Liverpool, England, 182, 323
Pauperism, 258, 276, 299
Paxton, Sir Joseph, 98
Pears, 15, 19, 70, 79, 85, 95, 103, 111, 112, 118, 154, 161, 347, 348–349, 404
Peck, Captain, of Lincoln, Mass., 18
Peel, Sir Robert, 183, 191, 231, 290, 502, 544
Pegu, Burma, 344, 433
Pelasgi, 82, 131
Peloponnesian War, 60
Penmaenmawr, 207
Pennsylvania, 304
Penny, Mr., of Manchester, England, 411
Pens, 169–170
Penshurst, Kent, England, 313
Pentateuch, 344
Percy, Sir Algernon, 4th Duke of Northumberland, 300
Pericles, 29, 40, 82, 86, 164, 347, 462, 479
Persia, 139
Persian Ambassador, 525
Persian mythology, 68, 83
Persians, 95, 138, 142
Persistency, 41–42
Perth, Scotland, 217, 284, 286, 418, 420, 441
Pestalozzi, Johann Heinrich, 347
Peter, Saint, 233, 429, 546
Peterborough, N.H., 101
Phaedrus, 483n
Phalanstery, 154, 327
Phalanx, 378
Phidias, 82, 144
Philadelphia, Pa., 504
Philips, Samuel, 228
Philistine, 472, 474, 479
Phillips, Mr., of London, 293n

Phillips, George Searle ("January Searle"), 422; *Emerson, His Life and Writings*, 422n

Phillips, Sir Richard, 66

Phillips, Wendell, 47

Philo Judaeus, 561

Philosopher(s), 32, 473, 475, 479, 485

Philostratus and Eunapius, *The Lives of the Sophists*, 483n

Phocion, 30

Phrenology, 170, 463

Piece-Hall, Halifax, England, 210

Pied Piper, 77

Pierce, John (?), 46

Pillsbury, Parker, 127

Pindar, 59n

Piozzi, Hester Lynch, *Anecdotes of the Late Samuel Johnson*, 346n

Pipée, 119

Pittacus, 477

Pitt, William, Earl of Chatham (1708–1778), 75, 402

Pitt, William (1759–1806), 183

Place de la Concorde, Paris, 267, 324

Planter (ship), 63

Platforms, 115, 235, 344, 511

Plato, 15n, 29, 43, 47, 48, 67, 110, 112, 113, 115, 144, 166, 168, 234, 245, 249, 307, 326, 340, 347, 353, 469, 471, 472, 474, 476–477, 478, 479, 480, 482, 484, 485, 486, 487, 488, 512, 541, 552; *Cratylus*, 485; *The Cratylus, Phaedo, Parmenides, and Timaeus . . .* (tr. Thomas Taylor), 159n, 474n, 481n, 482n, 485n, 486n; *Critias*, 469; Epistle VII, 477; *First Alcibiades*, 472–473; *Gorgias*, 86, 87, 113, 113–114, 471, 472, 484; *Hippias*, 472; *Laws*, 469, 473, 476; *Lysis*, 470; *Meno*, 487n; *Oeuvres* (tr. Victor Cousin), 470n, 472n, 474, 475n, 476, 477, 479, 481, 484, 485n, 486, 487; *Parmenides*, 487–488; *Phaedo*, 477, 479; *Phaedrus*, 114, 302, 469, 470, 472n, 477, 479, 480, 483n, 484, 486, 487; *The Phaedrus, Lysis and Protagoras . . .* (tr. Josiah Wright), 552; *Protagoras*, 477; *Republic*, 469, 470, 473, 474–475, 476, 481n, 485, 486n, 559; *Symposium*, 470; *Theaetetus*, 159n, 472, 474, 476, 479; *Timaeus*, 5, 159, 166, 469, 474, 476, 480, 481, 482, 486n, 487; *Works* (tr. Floyer Sydenham and Thomas Taylor), 86, 87, 113–114,

159n, 302, 471n, 472, 473, 474n, 475, 476, 477, 480, 481n, 483n, 484, 485n, 487

Platonic immortality, 477

Platonism, 260, 511

Platonist, 559

Pliny, 85

Plotinus, 110

Pluck, 192

Plutarch, 165–166n; *De Placitis Philosophorum* [attributed], 187–188; "Of Garrulity," 294n; Life of Pericles, 164n; *Morals . . .* (1718), 59n, 188n, 294n; "Of Those Sentiments Concerning Nature . . . ," 188n

Plymouth, Mass., 136

Poe, Edgar Allan, 466n

Poet(s), 109, 224, 346

Poetry, 98, 113, 137, 144, 147, 171, 172, 249, 546

Poland, 269, 270

Police, 34, 377

Politics, 25, 29, 345

Polk, James Knox, 149

Pollard, Capt. George, Jr., 63, 64

Pollock, George H., 200

Polonius, 397

Ponsard, François, *Lucrèce*, 269, 425

Poole, Paul Falconer (?), 190

Poor, the, 388

Poor Laws, 212, 533

Poor man (*or* men), 11, 104, 118, 120, 188, 295, 312

Pope, Alexander, 259, 370, 371, 511, 523; "Epistle II: To a Lady," 332n; letter to Lady Montagu, 519; *Moral Essays*, 332n; *Works* (1753), 519n

Pope, James, 128, 129n, 281(?)

Pope, the, 276, 315, 434, 567

Population control, 276

Porphyry, 325

Porpora, 92

Porpora, Nicolo, 92n

Porte St. Martin, Paris, 263

Portland, Me., 455, 457

Portman Square lectures, London, 285–286n

Postal service, 236, 272, 564

Potter, Mr., of Bridlington, England, 189, 196

Poverty, 150, 244

Power, 77, 117, 161, 204–205, 311–312, 316, 394

Poynting, Rev. T. E., 284, 285n

Practical, 148, 153–154, 384

Practical Philosophy of the Muhammadan People . . . , 332n, 481n
Pratt, Miss, 65
Preaching, 164, 338, 399–400
Precision, 91
Prescott, William Hickling, 301
Present, the, 171, 173
Presse, 265
Preston, England, 191, 411, 413, 414, 438, 439
Priam, 320
Prickett, Sir ———, 196
Priestlians, 561
Primogeniture, 254
Princess Theatre, London, 422
Pringle, Mr., 255, 550
Proclus, 5, 43, 110, 485n; *Commentaries . . . on the Timaeus of Plato* (tr. Thomas Taylor), 478–479n; *The Six Books . . . on the Theology of Plato* (tr. Thomas Taylor), 486n, 487n
Procter, Bryan Waller ("Barry Cornwall"), 126, 244, 286, 300, 361, 442, 445, 448, 560
Producer, 389
Professor, professorship, 9, 28, 153, 380
Progress, 42
Prometheus, 6, 9
Pronunciation, 217–218, 297–298
Property, 308, 312, 361, 388, 467
Prophecy, 159
Prostitution, 333, 550
Protestant(s), 177–178, 509, 521
Proverbs, 10, 84
Providence, 25, 152, 187, 205, 329
Providence, R.I., 453, 456, 566
Prussia, Crown Prince of, 531
Psyche, 362n
Public Schools, English, 512
Puffing, 313
Punch and Judy, 400
Punch, or the London Charivari, 62, 195, 215, 248, 250, 334, 460, 504, 528, 530, 550n
Purchas, Samuel, 516
Puritan(s), 177, 217, 276
Puritanism, 303
Purpose, 22
Puseyism, 378
Pythagoras, 47, 49, 110, 326, 347, 372
Pythagorean music, 49, 62

Quakers, 172

Quarrels, 385–386
Quarterly Review, 275, 524n
Queensberry, Duchess of, 547
Quillinan, Edward, "Imaginary Conversation . . . ," 387n
Quincy, Josiah, Jr., 90
Quinet, Edgar, 301
Quixote, 83
Quotation, 386, 477–478

Rabelais, François, 35, 48, 98, 166, 478
Raby Castle, Staindrop, England, 225
Race(s), 8, 205, 357, 368, 404, 507, 508
Rachel, Mlle (Elisa Félix), 230, 263, 269, 323, 362, 543
Racine, Jean Baptiste, *Mithridate*, 269, 424; *Phèdre*, 269, 323, 424
Radnorshire, Wales, 130, 282
Rae, John, 355
Railroad(s), 12, 99, 100, 101–102, 114, 174, 188, 190, 300, 322, 342–343, 350, 353, 358, 374
Rakush, 117
Raleigh, Sir Walter, 517
Ralph & Co. (*or* Son), 422
Randall, Alexander (?), 354
Randall, Benjamin (?), 354
Randolph Gallery, Oxford, England, 247
Randolph, Vt., 60
Raphael (Raffaello Santi *or* Sanzio), 61, 90, 106, 246
Rat, 256, 526
Rathbone, William, 284, 285n, 438
Ravaisson-Mollien, Jean Gaspard Félix Lacher, 156, 157n
Ravenna, O., 46
Rawdon, England, 129, 216, 416, 498
Rawlings, Charles E., Jr., 129, 182 285(?)
Reading, 5, 34, 67, 116, 120, 147, 165, 203, 236, 297, 386
Reading, England, 445
Realism, 149, 153, 155, 330
Reality, 55, 386
Reason, 193, 394
Rebekah, 195
Récamier, Jeanne Françoise Julie Adélaïde, 179, 524
Redding's shop, Boston, 139
Reed, Sampson, 37, 171, 172n
Rees, Abraham, *Cyclopædia; or An Universal Dictionary of Arts and Sciences*, 260
Reeve, Henry, 228
Reform, 307

Reform Bill, 316, 517, 557
Reform Club, London, 212, 237n
Réforme, 265
Reid, David Boswell, 120, 293; *Illustrations of the Theory and Practice of Ventilation*, 293n
Relation . . . of the Island of England . . ., A, 197–199, 504
Religion, 42, 162, 177, 306–307, 324, 337, 393, 533
Religious sentiment, 213, 279
Rendall, Ellen, 442, 444, 445
Reserve, 308
Responsibility, 340
Revenue Laws, British, 44–45
Revolution, 190, 311, 312, 318, 318–319, 323, 345, 435, 460
Revue des Deux Mondes, 513
Revue Indépendante, 265n
Reyhan Arab, 92
Reynolds, Sir Joshua, 54n, 315
Rhayader, Wales, 130, 282
Rhetoric, 161
Rhine River, 214
Ribera, José ("Lo Spagnoletto"), 267
Rice, Stephen Spring, 261, 537
Rich, the, 11, 73, 104–105, 118, 120, 188, 235, 387–388, 392
Richard I (Coeur de Lion), King of England, 183
Richard of Devizes, *Chronicon de rebus gestis Ricardi Primi*, 279
Richards, Mr., 66n
Richardson, John, 228; *Recollections*, 228n
Richardson, Sir John, 228n
Riches, 150, 387–389
Richmond, England, 195, 315
Richter, Jean Paul Friedrich, *Titan*, 128n
Rintoul, Robert Stephen, 275
Rio de Janeiro, Brazil, 227, 559
Ripley, Christopher Gore, 125, 405, 406n
Ripley, George, 376n
Ripley, Rev. Samuel, 19, 125n, 126
Ripley, Sophia, 376n
Ripon, England, 129, 416, 439
Ripon, England, Cathedral, 279
Ripon Inn, Ripon, England, 416
Ritter, Heinrich, *The History of Ancient Philosophy*, 114n
Robertson, William, 558; *History of America*, 548
Robin Hood, ballads of, 172
Robinson, Henry Crabb, 285, 442, 530

Robinson, John Paul, 46
Rochdale, England, 185, 414, 438
Rochester (ship), 204
Rochester, N.Y., *American*, 264
Rockinghorse, England, 408, 436
Rocking stones, 83, 152
Rodrigo Díaz de Bivar, *see* Cid, The
Roebuck, John Arthur, 304
Rogers, Nathaniel Peabody, 28; *A Collection from the Newspaper Writings . . .*, 28n
Rogers, Samuel, 179, 242, 301, 515, 522, 523, 524, 525n, 533
Rogvaldar, 138
Rolt, John, 285–286, 442
Roman(s), 85, 138, 191, 195, 326, 508
Roman Catholic Church, 307
Roman de la Rose, 98
Rome, Italy, 89, 95, 105, 106, 265, 302, 306, 370, 375, 466, 497, 522, 523, 561, 567
Ropes, William, 126
Roscoe, Thomas, 239
Roscoe Club, Liverpool, 411, 438
Rossini, Gioacchino Antonio, *La Cenerentola*, 260; *Stabat Mater*, 237n
Rotation, 76, 77
Rotch, Mary, 172
Rothing, 408
Rothschild, Lionel Nathan, 98, 188, 237, 290, 531
Rothschild, Nathan Meyer, 290, 305, 433
Rothschild family, 305
Rotterdam, Netherlands, 373
Round Table, 372, 471
Rousseau, Jean Jacques, 269, 478; *Confessions*, 144, 548
Roxburgh *or* Roxburghe, John Ker, 3rd Duke of, 6n
Roxburghe ("Roxborough") Club, 6
Roxbury, Mass., 455
Royal Academy of Arts, Edinburgh, 419
Royal Academy of Arts, London, 334, 429, 528
Royal College of Surgeons, London, 525
Royal George Inn, Folkestone, England, 426
Royalton, Vt., 60
Rudebeh, 74
Ruffini, Giovanni, 337
Rush, Richard, 269
Ruskin, John, 273, 277, 521, 550n; *Modern Painters*, 528; *The Two Paths*, 370

Russell, Lord John, 1st Earl Russell of Kingston Russell, 214n, 244, 254, 290
Russell family, 520
Russia, 304, 508
Russian, White, 233, 551
Rustem, 74–75, 117
Rutland, Vt., 125
Ruy Díaz de Bivar, *see* Cid, The

S., Miss *or* Mrs., 350
S., A., 433
Saadi (Muslih-ud-Din), 9, 11, 47, 89, 245, 388; *The Gûlistân*, 11n, 48, 245n
Sacs, 155
Sæmund ("Soemund") the Wise, 88
Safford, Truman Henry, 60, 61, 62
Sailors, 175, 204
Sainte-Chapelle, Paris, 268, 271
St. George's Chapel, Windsor Castle, England, 274, 460, 529
St. George Society, Montreal, 507
St. Jacques de la Boucherie, Paris, 265, 268
St. James's Street, London, 334
St. Michael's Cathedral, Coventry, England, 430
St. Paul's Cathedral, London, 241
Saint-Simon, Comte de, Claude Henri de Rouvroy, 424
Saint-Simonian, 522
Saint-Simonianism, 378
Saint-Sulpice, Paris, 271
Salamis, Greece, 60
Sale, George, 67n
Salem, Mass., 455
Salisbury, England, 286
Salisbury Plain, England, 356, 431
Sallot, Friedrich von, 177n
Salop, England, 128, 285
Sam, 74
Sameness, 474
Sampson, Mr., 190
Sanborn, Deacon, 18
Sand, George (Amandine Aurore Lucie, *née* Dupin, Baronne Dudevant), 48, 92, 159, 203n, 262, 265, 338, 348, 353; *Consuelo*, 92n; *La Comtesse de Rudolstadt*, 92n, 177n; *Lucrezia Floriani*, 348; *Le Péché de Monsieur Antoine*, 338n
Sanderson, John, 281
Sandfly (ship), 206
Sanskrit, 137
Sappho, 70

Sarcasm, 24
Sargent, Mr., of Medford, Mass., 81
Savagery, 359
"Savagius Landor Lamartino," 373n
Saxon(s), 45, 358, 498, 499, 501, 505, 510
Scaldic literature, 74, 477
Scaliger, Joseph Justus, 352
Scarsdale, Nathaniel Curzon, 3rd Baron, 185
Scheffer, Ary, 334, 429
Schelling, Friedrich Wilhelm Joseph von, 35
Schiller, Johann Christoph Friedrich von, 150, 448n, 459n
Schirin, 67
Schleiermacher, Friedrich Ernst Daniel, 470; *Introductions to the Dialogues of Plato* (tr. William Dobson), 470n
Scholar(s), 6–7, 9, 28–29, 32, 34–35, 42, 43, 78, 84, 98, 107, 109, 120, 137, 146, 150, 165, 176, 296, 310, 320, 325, 331, 346, 372, 435, 541
School, 461
Schwann family, 216
Science, 10, 28, 118, 121, 161, 164
Sciolism, 162
Scipio Africanus, Publius Cornelius, 118
Scot *or* Scott, Michael, 165
Scotland, 134, 189, 197, 218, 280, 431, 496, 541, 547
Scott, Mr. (?), 203
Scott, David, 130, 220n, 221, 277, 281, 282, 362, 534, 535
Scott, Sir Walter, 48, 180, 189n, 203(?), 221, 501, 508, 521, 523, 547, 560; *Minstrelsy of the Scottish Border*, 23n, 172n; *Waverley*, 180, 523
Scott, William Bell, 129, 130n, 281, 362
Scottish language, 179, 180, 218, 547
Scottish people, 215, 218–219, 334, 541, 552, 558, 559
Scottish proverb, 335, 432
Scribe, Augustin Eugène, *Le Mariage d'Argent*, 63; *Oeuvres choisies*, 63n
Scripture(s), 196, 352, 477
Sea, 203, 205, 302, 332, 433, 564
Seahorse (ship), 206
Seakings, 210, 510
Sea-line, 201, 293
Second Church, Boston, 120
Seddon & McBride, Sculptors, Liverpool, England, 130
Sedgwick, Adam, 361, 362n, 430
Self, 4, 7, 10, 14, 15, 18, 19, 21, 28–29, 31–32, 33, 34–35, 36, 37–39, 53(?), 54,

59, 62, 63–64, 73, 79, 80–81, 93, 94, 103, 109–110, 116–117, 136, 141–142, 151, 153–154, 156, 158, 161, 167, 170, 171, 172, 173, 175–176, 177, 185, 187, 188, 189, 190, 191, 192, 194–197, 198, 206–207, 209, 210–211, 216–217, 219–226, 227, 237–238, 239, 244–246, 247–248, 252, 255–256, 258, 259, 260, 261–263, 266–274, 276–277, 279, 282, 284, 285–286, 289, 295, 296(?), 300–301, 304, 306(?), 310, 317, 321–324, 326, 327, 328–329, 332–333, 335–336, 344, 345, 349–350, 351–352(?), 354, 357–359, 360–362, 371, 379–380(?), 395, 396–397, 399, 403, 405–406, 408–427, 431–434, 436–442, 443, 447–457, 492, 498, 504, 507, 513, 522, 522–529, 530, 531–533, 534–537, 537–539, 540, 540–541, 542, 545–546, 547–548, 550–551, 554–558, 558–561, 561–563, 564, 566

Self, the, 308, 473
Selfexistence, 39
Selfhelp, 39, 132
Selfishness, 465
Selfpoise, 145, 146, 148, 152
Selfreliance, 372, 387
Selkirk, Lord, 255
Sense(s), 113, 471
Serdar, 85
Servant, 139, 140
Seton, Mary, 346
Seume, Johann Gottfried, 177n
Severn River, England, 192
Sewall, William, 250(?)
Sewall family, 177
Sewell, J., 415
Sewell, James Edward, 250(?)
Sewell, William, 469, 470; *An Introduction to the Dialogues of Plato*, 469n, 470n
Shakers, 342
Shakespeare, William, 10, 29, 70, 75, 83, 91, 144n, 193, 295, 332, 358, 374–375n, 389–390, 434, 508, 509, 541; *As You Like It*, 116; *Hamlet*, 149, 173n, 403n; *II Henry IV*, 10, 227n; *King Lear*, 172, 442n; *Macbeth*, 172; *Othello*, 344n; *Troilus and Cressida*, 78; *Twelfth Night*, 273n
Shannon, Rev. Mr., of Hull, England, 130, 189
Shattuck, Col. Daniel, 83
Sheaf River, England, 185
Sheba, Queen of, 66

Sheffield, England, 129, 185, 193, 417, 418, 439, 440, 445
Shelly, Percy Bysshe, 6, 75, 172
Shepherd, Dr. Thomas Perkins, 566
Shifnal, England, 128, 285
Ship, 201–207
Shipbuilding, 173
Shropshire *or* Salop, England, 128, 285
Shuttleworth, Mr., 281
Siam, 344, 433
Sicily, 382, 562–563
Sick, the, 392
Sidney, Sir Philip, 513
Siècle Constitutionelle, 265
Sigismund, Holy Roman Emporer, 518
Sigurd, 342
Sikhs, 36
Simonides of Ceos, 70
Simonism (i.e., Saint-Simonianism?), 378
Simorg, 65, 73, 74
Simplicity, 145, 146
Sistine Chapel, Vatican, 150
Skidbladnir (ship), 100, 138
Skrymir, 82, 116, 122
Sleep, 313, 320, 526
Sloane, Sir Hans, 27
Smallbone, G. H., 429
Smith, Rev. C. N., 60
Smith, Sydney, 180, 214, 249, 254, 513, 520, 524, 530
Smith, William, 427
Smith, William Henry, 223, 275
Smyrna, Turkey, 296
Sneyd, Charlotte Augusta, tr., *A Relation . . . of the Island of England . . .*, 197–199, 504
Snorri Sturluson, 88, 131; "Gylfi's Mocking," 87–88; *The Heimskringla*, 17, 138, 282, 283n, 336, 341–342, 344, 345n, 347, 422, 434; *The Prose or Younger Edda*, 17, 55, 70n, 87–88, 100n, 107–109, 115n, 116n
Snowdon, Mount, Wales, 207
Soane, Sir John, 332
Soar River, Leicester, England, 191
Sobrier, M., 265
Social Circle, Concord, 456
Socialism, 32, 290, 297, 307, 310, 312, 327, 357
Society, 8, 11, 15, 38, 51, 52, 97, 109, 249, 290, 302, 304, 369, 371–372, 373, 392, 462, 513
Society Islands, 305

Society of Antiquaries, London, 451
Socrates, 86, 87, 110, 113, 114, 298, 470, 471, 472, 473, 474, 476, 477, 482, 483, 487
Solar system, 165
Soldier(s), 79, 233, 239, 331, 346, 435
Solitude, 97
Solomon, King of Israel, 65, 66, 73, 84, 105, 139
Somerset House, London, 311
Somnambulists, 232, 501
Sorbonne, Paris, 270, 271
Soul, 294, 347, 372, 402, 473, 474, 487
South America, 205, 276, 434
Southey, Robert, 167, 501, 521; *Chronicle of the Cid*, 104, 117
Soyer, Alexis Benoît, 237
Spagnoletto, Lo (José Ribera), 267
Spain, 101, 184
Spallanzani, Lazzaro, 243, 256, 526
Spaniards, 268, 557
Spanish painting, 267–268
Sparks, Jared, 300, 301
Sparta, Greece, 508
Spartans, 50, 378
Spectator, 275
Speculation, 102, 147, 235
Spedding, James, 261, 537
Spedding, Thomas, 546
Speech, 38, 195
Spence, Joseph, 371; *Anecdotes, Observations, and Characters of Books and Men*, 370
Spence, William, 362
Spencer, John Charles, 3rd Earl Spencer, Lord Althorp, 183
Spenser, Edmund, 508
Spinoza, Baruch, 110, 307
Spirit, 391, 479
Spiritualism, 84, 143, 162
Spitalfields, London, 237
Springfield, Mass., 448
Spurgen *or* Spurgin, Dr., of London, 444, 445
Spurzheim, Johann Kaspar, 112
Stabler, Edward, 172
Staël, Madame de (Anne Louise Germaine, Baronne de Staël-Holstein), 69, 166, 167, 179, 523, 524; *Dix Années d'Exil*, 69n; *Oeuvres complètes*, 69n
Staffa, 555
Staley, William, 126, 129, 217, 281, 284
Stanfield, Clarkson, 273, 277, 528n

Stanley, Arthur Penrhyn, 280, 281n
Stanley, Thomas, *The History of Philosophy* (?), 166
Stansfeld, James, 210n, 211
Stansfeld, T. W., 129, 130n
Star & Garter Inn, Worcester, England, 416
State Street, Boston, 29, 32
Stealing, 184, 388
Steam, 173
Steffens, Henrik *or* Heinrich, 177n
Stephen, Fitz, 279
Stephenson, George, 167, 190, 290, 300, 342, 361
Sterling, Edward, 188, 227, 229
Sterling, John, 188n, 444n; "Daedalus," 373; *Essays and Tales*, 337
Sterne, Laurence, *Tristram Shandy*, 548
Stetson, Rev. Caleb, 54, 224, 564
Stewart, Robert, 441
Stirling, Jane, 442, 443, 450
Stirling, W., 442, 566
Stirling, Scotland, 282
Stock Exchange, London, 308
Stoddart, Sir John, 227
Stoke Poges, England, 274, 528
Stone, Rev. Thomas Treadwell, 54, 338
Stonehenge, England, 334, 335, 431, 460
Stone of Scone, 259
Story, Joseph, 46(?), 77, 475
Story, William Wetmore, 46(?)
Stow, Cyrus, 111
Strand, the, London, 421, 426, 541, 551, 553
Stratford on Avon, England, 282, 436
Strath Spey, Scotland, 313
Strauss, David Friedrich, 224; *Life of Jesus*, 224n
Strutt, Jedediah, 260
Strutt family, 260n
Stuart, Sir James, *Three Years in North America*, 549
Styx, River, 112, 233, 428, 545
Success, 54, 164
Suetonius (Gaius Suetonius Tranquillus), *De Vita Caesarum*, 549n
Suffolk County, Mass., bar, 393
Suffrage, 276
Sully, Duc de, Maximilien de Béthune, 166
Sumner, Charles, 47, 54, 299n, 524
Superlative, 33, 71, 72, 120, 141, 142, 319
Superstition(s), 13, 96, 143, 148
Supreme Court of Massachusetts, 395
Surgery, 163

Sutherland, Harriet Howard Leveson-Gower, Duchess of, 285, 566
Sutherland, Dukes of, 354, 359
Sutton, Henry, 189, 281; *Evangel of Love*, 189n, 414
Svafnir, 108
Swan Inn, Ambleside, England, 560
Swanwick, Mr., of Chesterfield, England, 129, 190
Swanwick, Anna, 448
Sweden, 13
Swedenborg, Emanuel, 16, 26–27, 28, 35, 37, 43, 126, 144n, 150, 162, 260, 304, 326, 352, 357, 474, 476–477, 478, 485, 512; *Angelic Wisdom . . .* , 27; *The Animal Kingdom*, 26n; *Economy of the Animal Kingdom*, 13, 26–27, 36; *Moral Suites*, 26; *Principia*, 26; *A Treatise Concerning Heaven and . . . Hell*, 380n
Swedenborg Church (Church of the New Jerusalem), 162
Swift, Jonathan, 259, 511
Swire, John, & Son, Liverpool, England, 129
Switzerland, 382
"Sylvan" (i.e., Captain Abel Moore), 95
Sylvester, Charles, 258, 260, 281; *The Philosophy of Domestic Economy*, 258n, 260n
Symbols, 15, 96
Sympathy, 466
Synesius, 166
Syracuse, Leopold de Bourbon, Count of (?), 531
Syracuse, Sicily, 344, 433
Syria, 96, 263, 401

T., P., 225
Tablet, 275
Tagart, Mr., of Reading, England, 445
Tagart, Rev. Edward, 285, 373n, 449
Tagart, Sara, 130
Tait's Edinburgh Magazine, 220
Talbot, Mr., 46
Talent, 308, 318, 324, 352, 371
Talleyrand-Périgord, Charles Maurice de, Prince de Bénévent, 30, 179, 318n, 507, 523, 524
Tamworth, England, 128
Tappan, Caroline Sturgis, 502
Tappan family, 177
Tartar, 31, 404
Tartary, 510

Taste, 4, 514, 515
Tattersall's (London), 230, 543
Taunton, Mass., 455
Tavistock, Hotel (?), London, 464
Tavistock Square, London, 464
Taylor, Edward T., 399–403
Taylor, Emily, 444
Taylor, Jeremy, 508
Taylor, Thomas, 260, 304, 484–485, 512, 559; "General Introduction . . . ," *The Works of Plato . . .* , 474n, 484
Taylor, Tom, 130, 286n, 287
Taylor, William Cooke, 179
Taylor, Zachary, 52
Taxes, 276
Tea, 89
Teacher, 347, 471
Tees River, England, 225
Telegraph, 14, 174, 188, 282
Temperament, 40, 88
Temperance, 98, 486
Tendency, 22
Tenderness, 370
Tennyson, Alfred, Lord, 227, 231, 249, 255, 261, 281, 352, 355, 361, 451n, 537–539, 546, 558, 565–566; "Mariana," 566; "Poem," 416; "Song," 111n
Tennyson, Septimus, 227, 565
Terrapin, 89
Teschemacher, Mr. (of London?), 450
Texas, 29, 54, 114
Thacher family, 177
Thackeray, William Makepeace, 361, 362n, 530; "A Dream of the Future," 530n
Thalberg, Sigismund, 236, 514
Thames River, England, 568
Théâtre des Italiens, Paris, 424, 425
Théâtre des Variétés, Paris, 263(?)
Théâtre Français, Paris, 263, 424
Thebais, 307
Thebes, Egypt, 267
Theism, 175, 384
Theophrastus, 5
Theseus, 75
Thiers, Louis Adolphe, 296
Thirlwall, Connop, 9; *History of Greece*, 283
Tholuck, Friedrich August Gottreu, 224
Thom, Rev. David, 130, 259
Thompson, Thomas Peronnet, 194n, 254
Thor, 74, 108, 115, 116, 131, 138, 344
Thoreau, Henry David, 19, 48, 54, 106, 107n, 116, 117n, 151, 234, 293, 294n,

338, 340n, 343, 344, 347, 354n, 355, 357n, 406, 443, 449
Thorer Hiort, 342
Thornton, Thomas, 228
Thorpe, Benjamin, *Northern Mythology* . . . , 459
Thorvaldsen *or* Thorwaldsen, Bertel, 105
Thought, 140, 146, 151–152, 154–155, 162, 169, 314, 316–317, 391, 471, 522
Time, 42, 204, 486
Times, see London *Times*
Titian (Tiziano Vecelli *or* Vecellio), 561, 563
Tizona, 117
Tochman, Gaspard, 337
Tocqueville, Alexis Charles Henri Maurice Clérel de, 362, 532
Tocqueville, Mme Alexis de, 266
Tools, 53, 100, 111, 112, 118, 139, 145, 174
Tottenham, England, 277
Tour St. Jacques, Paris, 265, 268
Tower of London, 542
Trafalgar Square, London, 244
Tragedy, 5
Traits, 291
Transcendentalism, 53, 149
Transit, 30, 31, 44, 120, 146
Transition, 4, 73, 76, 159–160
Translation, 166–167, 375
Travel, 11, 49, 136, 166, 192, 300–301, 320, 392
Trees(s), 12–13, 18–19, 27, 65, 80, 82, 95, 99, 101, 104, 105, 116–117
Trenton Falls, 49
Trevelyan, Sir Walter Calverly, 295
Trifles, 327
Trilobium, 353, 357
Trinitarian, 562
Trinity, doctrine of the, 561
Trope, 147, 160
Troubadours, 294, 354
Troy, 431
Truesdale, Thomas, 171–172
"True Thomas" (i.e., Thomas of Erceldoune), 22–23, 77
Truth, 329, 384, 391, 477, 481, 511
Tuba, 73
Tucker, Ellen, *see* Emerson, Ellen Tucker
Tuckerman, Joseph, 21n, 315
Tuileries, Paris, 265, 268
Tullia, 269
Tunaley, Thomas S., 128, 129n, 185

Turk, 315
Turkey, 508
Turkish Ambassador, 531
Turkish language, 90
Turnbull, William Barclay David Donald, 220, 536
Turner, Catherine, 189
Turner, Charles Tennyson, 227, 261, 558, 559n, 565
Turner, Joseph Mallord William, 273, 277, 334, 460, 526, 527, 528
Turner, Sharon, *History of the Anglo-Saxons*, 209n
Tuskar Light, Wales, 207
Tuttle, Captain, 309
Tuttle, Augustus, 40, 309(?)
Twiss, Horace, 188, 230
Tyas, John, 228
Tyr, 109, 115

Umbrelbury, 137
Understanding, 353, 355, 394, 471, 478, 503
Unitarian, 303, 305, 477, 561, 562
Unitarianism, 20, 115, 561, 562
United States, 55, 252, 297, 350, 397, 517, 566
Universal, the, 312, 317, 488
Universe, 31, 162
University, universities, 213, 250, 277, 350, 356, 501, 515, 516, 520, 567
Upcott, Mr., 180
Upham, Thomas C.(?), 125
Upham family, 177
Upjohn, Richard, 105
Useful, the, 151
Utgard, 138

Valencia, Spain, 382
Valfadir (Odin), 107
Valhalla, 74, 474
Valparaiso, Chile, 382
Value, 391–392
Vanbrugh, Sir John, *The Journey to London* (completed by Colley Cibber as *The Provoked Husband*), 66
Van Buren, Martin, 394
Van de Weyer, Sylvain, 236
Van Diemen's Land, 500
Van Mons, Jean-Baptiste, 85, 98, 103, 156
Vasari, Giorgio, *The Lives of the Most Eminent Painters* . . . (tr. Jonathan Foster), 370
Vattemare, Alexandre, 126, 156, 157n

Vaughan, C. J., 282
Vegetius (Flavius Vegetius Renatus), 367
Vehm, 92
Velázquez, Diego Rodríquez de Silva y, 267
Venables, George Stovin, 546
Venice, Italy, 245
Ventilation, 292, 293
Vergil, Polydore, 279
Vermont, 102, 348
Veronese, Paolo (Paolo Cagliari *or* Caliari), 563
Versailles, Palace of, France, 271
Very, Jones, 33n
Victoria, Queen of Great Britain and Ireland, 210, 236, 274, 514, 529
Vienna, Austria, 296
Vigny, Comte Alfred Victor de, 210; *Stello,* 210n
Villemarest, Charles Maxime Catherinet de, *Life of Prince Talleyrand,* 38n
Villiers, George, 1st Duke of Buckingham, 517
Vincennes, France, 323
Vinci, Leonardo da, 370
Virgil, 245, 557; *The Aeneid,* 134n, 495; *Eclogues,* 209n, 495n
Virginia, 382
Virginia Water, Windsor Castle, England, 274, 529
Virtue, 31, 69, 381, 460, 471, 473, 487
Vishnu, 9, 89
Vishńu Puráńa, 6, 56n, 344; tr. H. H. Wilson, 37, 308n
Voice, 234
Voltaire (François Marie Arouet), 269
Voting, 290
Vraie République, 265

W., Mr. (English?), 294, 321
W., Mr. (of Concord?), 153, 355
Wachsmuth, William, *The Historical Antiquities of the Greeks,* 7n
Walbran, Mr., of Ripon, England, 129, 130n
Walden Pond, 19, 21–22n, 126n, 354
Walden wood-lot, 19, 116
Waldo, Giles, 6
Wales, Prince of, 209n
Wales, 190(?), 207, 220, 303, 382, 496, 536
Walkelin *or* Walchelin, Bishop of Winchester, 258
Walker, George Alfred, 119, 120n, 293;

Gatherings from Graveyards, 293; *Graveyards of London,* 293n
Walpole, Horace, 4th Earl of Orford, 166
Walpole, Sir Robert, 1st Earl of Orford, 75
Walsingham, Sir Francis, 520
Walter, John (1776–1847), 212, 227, 230, 251
Walter, John, III (1818–1894), 227–228n, 251
Walter family, 177
Walters (sailor), 204
Waltham, Mass., 39, 453
Walton, Izaak, 166; "The Life of Sir Henry Wotton," 513n; *Reliquiae Wottonianae,* 513n
Wandering Jew, 51, 328
Warburton, Eliot (Bartholomew Elliot George Warburton), 510; *The Crescent and the Cross,* 510n
Ward, Mr., of Medford, Mass., 80–81
Ward, Robert Plumer, 228(?)
Ward, Samuel Gray, 46, 126, 297(?), 338, 410n, 466, 502; recipient of letters from Emerson, 26n, 28n
Ward, T. C., 410n
Ward, Thomas W., 410n
Ward, William George, 228(?)
Wardlaw, Lady Elizabeth, "Hardyknute," 172
Warren, Cyrus, 19n, 126n
Warren, Pelham M., 451
Warren Club, Boston, 52
Warren field *or* lot, 19, 93, 126n, 490, 493
Warwick, Richard de Beauchamp, Earl of, 517–518
Washington, George, 30, 397, 467, 523
Washington, D.C., 29, 350
Washingtonians, 224
Washington Irving (ship), 73, 125n, 175n
Waterford, Ireland, 207
Waterland, Daniel, 561
Waterloo Hotel, Liverpool, England, 408, 409, 410, 413
Watt, James, 290
Watts, Messrs., Manchester, England, 217
Watts, Mr., 162
Watts, Isaac, *Works,* 86n
Watts, Thomas, 295
Wealth, 174, 244, 291, 322, 324, 325, 463, 519–520
Weaver, Thomas, 337; *Songs and Poems . . . ,* 337n
Webster, Daniel, 34, 40, 47, 75, 144, 149,

220, 333, 376(?), 393–394, 396–398, 398–399, 401, 541

Wedgwood, Hensleigh, 444n, 445, 450

Wedgwood, Mrs. Hensleigh, 444

Wehme *or* St. Wehme, 92n

Weigall, Henry, 444, 445

Weimar, Germany, 549

Weiss, John, 54

Wellington, Arthur Wellesley, 1st Duke of, 179, 182, 214n, 231, 235, 362, 508, 514, 517, 523, 524, 542, 544; equestrian statue of, 194

Welsh, Jane Baillie, *see* Carlyle, Jane Baillie Welsh

Welsh, John, 547, 550

West (American), 389

West Newton, Mass., 454, 455

Westford, Mass., 456, 457

Western Railroad, 100

Westminster (London), England, 114, 541

Westminster Abbey, London, 195, 212, 259, 279

Westminster Review, 130n

Westmoreland, England, 219, 560

Wetherbee, Sol., 111

Whately, Richard, 181

Wheatstone, Sir Charles, 282

Wheeler, Ephraim, 358, 473

Whelan, Hugh, 541

Whewell, William, 249, 501

Whig(s), 20, 348, 385

Whim, 119

Whip for the top, 28, 30, 53, 137, 163, 300

Whiskey, 314

White, Rev. Mr., 187

White, Gilbert, *Natural History and Antiquities of Selborne*, 166

Whitehaven, England, 547

White race, 77, 369

Wicksteed, Rev. Charles, 129, 130n, 189, 211, 233, 551

Wight, Isle of, 303

Wildman, Col. Thomas, 189

Wiley & Putnam (?), 427

Wilkinson, James John Garth, 26, 46, 146, 262n, 281, 285, 286n, 362, 444, 449

Will, 25, 90

William IV, King of Great Britain and Ireland, 547, 549

Williamson, Mr., 129, 130n

Willie, 16

Willoughby, Sir Francis, 185

Wilson, James, 275

Wilson, John ("Christopher North"), 220, 223, 224, 361, 535, 536, 537, 558, 564, 565; "On Reading Mr. Clarkson's History of the Abolition of the Slave Trade," 467n

Wiltshire, England, 431

Winchester, England, Cathedral, 257–258, 279

Windsor Castle, England, 256, 274, 460, 514, 529

Windsor Hotel, Paris, 125

Windus, B. G., 273, 277, 528

Wine, 10, 101, 198

Winnipesaukee, Lake, 102

Wisconsin, 148, 226

Wisdom, 188, 307, 380, 381, 477, 482

Wishart, George, 221n

Wit, 513

Woburn, Mass., 454

Wollaton Hall, near Nottingham, England, 185, 414

Woman, women, 41n, 78, 83, 104, 108, 181, 305, 346, 350, 352, 392, 465, 476

Wonder, 403

Wood, Anthony à, *Athenæ Oxonienses*, 336, 337, 516, 520, 567

Wood, John George, 430

Woodfall, Mr., 298

Woods, Leonard, 338

Woonsocket, R.I., 456

Worcester, England, 129, 192, 193, 198, 411, 416, 439

Worcester, England, Cathedral, 192, 416

Worcester, Mass., 447, 453, 455, 456, 457

Words, 362

Wordsworth, John, 244, 560

Wordsworth, Mary Hutchinson, 227, 558, 559

Wordsworth, William, 221, 225, 227, 230, 244, 261, 281, 361, 477, 508, 515, 521, 523, 535, 547, 548, 554–560; *A Description of the Scenery of the Lakes in the North of England*, 336, 421; *The Excursion*, 220, 478, 481n, 556; "Itinerary Poems," 556; "It is Not to be Thought of," 509; "Lines composed a few miles above Tintern Abbey," 556; "Ode: Intimations of Immortality . . . ," 187; "The Two Voices," 557; "To the Skylark," 557

Work, 94, 162, 230, 505

World, 187

Worthies of England, 517–519

Wotton, Sir Henry, 513, 517
Wright, Henry G., 244n
Wright, Josiah, 552
Writing, 315, 317, 325, 350, 477–478
Wyatt, Matthew Cotes, 194
Wykeham *or* Wickham, William of, 246, 258, 516
Wyman, Jeffries, 306
Wyman, William, 393

Xanthippe *or* Xantippe, 472
Xanthus, Lycia, 315
Xenophon, 87, 165–166n; *Memorabilia*, 482n

Yale University, 250
Yankee(s), 102, 111, 144, 171, 175, 276, 398, 434, 482
Yates, Mr., 442
Yggdrasil, 74, 103, 107, 108, 163
Ymir, 87, 131

Yokdhan, Hai Ebn, *The Improvement of Human Reason . . .* (tr. Simon Ockley), 275n
York, England, 129, 186, 195, 416–417, 418, 440
York, England, Archbishop of, 152n
York, England, Institute, 417
York, England, Minster, 195, 196, 250, 254, 279, 316, 536
Yorkshire, England, 194
"Young England" Party, 531
Ysabeau, A., 404n
Yves ("Ivo") de Chartres, Bishop, 98

Zal, 74
Zdenko, 92
Zeta Ursi, 64
Zodiac, 86
Zohak, 155
Zoroastrian, 46
Zurbarán, Francisco de, 268